A LITERARY HISTORY OF WOMEN'S WRITING IN BRITAIN, 1660–1789

Drawing on three decades of feminist scholarship bent on redis-covering lost and abandoned women writers, Susan Staves provides a comprehensive history of women's writing in Britain from the Restoration to the French Revolution. This major new work of criticism also offers fresh insights about women's writing in all literary forms, not only fiction, but also poetry, drama, memoir, autobiography, biography, history, essay, translation, and the famil-iar letter. Focusing on the texts women created, rather than the lives they led, Staves illuminates the central role women's diverse accom-plishments in the art of writing played in the literary history of the period. Authors celebrated in their own time and now neglected, and those more recently revalued and studied, are given equal attention. The book's organization by chronology and its attention to history challenge the way we periodize literary history and insist that we must understand the significance of women's texts in their historical context. Each chapter includes a list of key works written in the period covered, as well as a narrative and critical assessment of the works. This magisterial work includes a comprehensive bibliography and list of modern editions of the authors discussed.

SUSAN STAVES is Paul Prosswimmer Professor of Humanities Emerita at Brandeis University, Massachusetts. She is the author of *Players' Scepters: Fictions of Authority in the Restoration* (1979) and *Married Woman's Separate Property in England, 1660–1833* (1990). With John Brewer, she has edited and contributed to *Early Modern Conceptions of Property* (1995) and with Cynthia Ricciardi she has edited Elizabeth Griffith's *Delicate Distress* (1999).

GW00537870

A LITERARY HISTORY OF WOMEN'S WRITING IN BRITAIN, 1660–1789

SUSAN STAVES

CAMBRIDGE
UNIVERSITY PRESS

CAMBRIDGE UNIVERSITY PRESS
Cambridge, New York, Melbourne, Madrid, Cape Town, Singapore,
São Paulo, Delhi, Dubai, Tokyo

Cambridge University Press
The Edinburgh Building, Cambridge CB2 8RU, UK

Published in the United States of America by Cambridge University Press, New York

www.cambridge.org
Information on this title: www.cambridge.org/9780521130516

First published 2006
Paperback edition 2010

Printed in the United Kingdom at the University Press, Cambridge

A catalogue record for this publication is available from the British Library

ISBN 978-0-521-85865-6 Hardback
ISBN 978-0-521-13051-6 Paperback

To the students of Brandeis University, undergraduate and graduate, who read these books with me

Contents

Acknowledgments

This book is deeply indebted to the work of other feminist literary critics and scholars who have engaged with texts and authors long virtually ignored or, when noticed, condescended to. I have tried to offer novice readers some guides to this now large body of work, but, as readers more familiar with the subject will understand, given the broad scope of my literary history, my direct references to this secondary literature in my text and in the select bibliography can only mention some of the highlights most important or most relevant to my history. I am grateful for the critical insights and scholarship of those I cite, but also for the contributions to my understanding of the field of many others from whose work I have profited less directly.

Ellen Messer-Davidow and Anthony Winner first suggested that I should write a literary history of women's writing in this period. Their intriguing and elaborately theorized proposal for a collaborative new feminist literary history of British women's writing in all periods eventually proved to be a more complicated project than was practicable, but I appreciate their having engaged me in the challenges they outlined. When this large-scale project was abandoned, Gary Kelly encouraged me, nevertheless, to continue with my part of the history.

Narrative literary histories like this do not lend themselves to being presented in sections as the usual conference papers or journal articles, so I have not presented portions of this volume in the way I would have done for another kind of book. I am, therefore, all the more grateful to Dena Goodman, Simon Dickie, Lincoln Faller, and the Eighteenth-Century Group at the University of Michigan for inviting me to precirculate one chapter to them and for the lively and helpful responses of the members of that group. The Orlando Project's Women and Literary History Conference provided significant discussions of the problems of women's literary history in several countries and periods. I was glad to have been invited to participate and to give a talk entitled "Terminus a Quo, Terminus ad

Quem: Chronological Boundaries in a Literary History," subsequently published in *Women and Literary History: "For There She Was,"* edited by two of the conference organizers, Katherine Binhammer and Jeanne Wood. Some material from that essay appears in this introduction. I am grateful also to the American Society for Eighteenth Century Studies and to the British Society for Eighteenth Century Studies for invitations to give two plenary lectures. Both offered welcome occasions to consider the methodological issues confronting the feminist literary historian and to participate in useful discussions with colleagues.

Closer to home, as my dedication suggests, I am grateful to the students of Brandeis University who, beginning in 1978, were willing to enroll in my course on "The Woman of Letters, 1660–1800" and to read these texts by women writers with me. Early versions of this course necessarily used texts not then in print. Thus students were compelled to read reproductions of texts I had made on a typewriter and, on occasion, more heroically, to read whole novels on microfilm. Our early experiences of confronting what I came to think of as "naked texts" – that is, texts without any surrounding critical commentary or scholarly apparatus – challenged us to develop our own readings and vividly illustrated how different the experience of reading an uncanonical text could be from the experience of reading a text that has become canonical. While I rejoice that many of hitherto obscure texts of these women writers have now become more canonical, and while I recognize that this literary history is part of the process of their canonization, I hope that we can all also from time to time imagine how we might read our books as naked texts.

Like many teachers of rediscovered books by women writers, I have benefited from responses to them by undergraduates for whom these books by women were the only eighteenth-century books they had yet encountered. The students' readings and assumptions, especially when contrasted with those of eighteenth- and nineteenth-century critics and readers, again and again illuminated how contested the concept of literary "realism" can be. I have also benefited from opportunities to work with Brandeis graduate students who became interested in these women writers. In the 1980s Cynthia Lowenthal courageously ignored the advice of others that writing a dissertation on Lady Mary Wortley Montagu would be professional suicide. Despite the warnings, she wrote a dissertation which became the first literary critical book on Lady Mary Wortley Montagu and she has flourished in the profession. Most recently, the field has been so transformed that another Brandeis doctoral student, Elizabeth

Ellington, could write an excellent feminist dissertation about methodological issues in recent "life and works" books on individual Restoration and Eighteenth-Century women writers – books, of course, in my bibliography for this literary history. It has been a privilege to share the enthusiasms and insights of these graduate dissertation writers, including also Ann Russell Zimmerman, Deborah Kaplan, Edith Larson, Claudia Thomas, Kathleen Grathwol, Pamela Lloyd, Marla Harris, Bea Britton Loprete, Leslee Thorne-Murphy, Cynthia Ricciardi, and Lori Davis-Perry.

I did my graduate work at the University of Virginia, which Thomas Jefferson thought of as an "academical village," but, since 1967 I have had the good fortune to live near Boston/Cambridge, which is an "academical city." For many decades, we have enjoyed an Eighteenth-Century Club, in the more recent decades metamorphosed into the Harvard Humanities Eighteenth-Century Seminar. Bringing together faculty and graduate students – and the occasional non-academic – interested in eighteenth-century studies, the club has offered a friendly and stimulating venue for presenting work-in-progress. I am particularly grateful to Ruth Perry (a founder of the Club), to Charles Knight and Arthur Weitzman (among its most faithful and long-term participants), to Lennard Davis and Beth Kowaleski-Wallace (who served at different times as my co-chairs), and to Lynn Festa, who has co-chaired the seminar with me for the last four years. I am also indebted to a still less formal club, one we call the "Bluestockings," a reading group in which I have had the chance to discuss some of the primary texts included in this history and to present a draft chapter for comment. The current "Bluestockings" are Lynn Festa, Susan Lanser, Mandy Nash Kudarauskis, and Ruth Perry. We all mourn the death of a former member, Jan Thaddeus, whose literary intelligence and broad knowledge of eighteenth-century history and literature added so much to our earlier conversations.

Finally, I welcome this chance to acknowledge important contributions to my happiness and well-being during the writing of this book from a few important friends who – although learned – are not scholars of the eighteenth century: Mary Campbell, Arlan Fuller, Paul Morrison, and Marshall Shatz.

Introduction

David Perkins's *Is Literary History Possible?* has been a *vade mecum* for me as I have been writing this book. Perkins explores post-modern challenges to existing conceptions of literature and history that suggest literary history has become impossible. His focus is on the kind of literary history that I have written in this volume: the single author narrative literary history of a national literature like Hippolyte Taine's *History of English Literature* (1863) or Francesco de Sanctis's *History of Italian Literature* (1870–71). Perkins also attends to histories of a particular period within a national literature, devoting a chapter to books and articles that attempt to explain the causes of English Romanticism, to state its important characteristics, and to establish its canon. Examples Perkins does not consider of literary histories closer to my project would include Bonamay Dobrée's *English Literature in the Early Eighteenth Century* (1959) and John Butt's *English Literature: The Mid-Eighteenth Century, 1740–1789* (1979), both volumes in the Oxford History of English Literature series.

Paradoxically, Perkins concludes that such literary history is both impossible to write with intellectual conviction and necessary to read. Among the reasons Perkins and others offer for the impossibility of literary history are that we no longer know what literature is, that designations of literary types like "genres, periods, schools, and movements" now look "baseless and arbitrary," and that the past itself is not representable.[1] Yet, as he also argues, students still need introductions to bodies of literature and much of the literature of the past is neither adequately intelligible nor enjoyable without the mediation of literary history.

The category literature has seemed increasingly problematic as consensus about which works ought to be in our literary canon or whether there ought to be a literary canon has broken down. Literary history necessarily exists in a hermeneutic circle with literature. Thus, as canons have broken down, literary history increasingly has an amorphous and shifting subject. Perkins is concerned with general literary history rather than with the history of women's writing or feminist literary history. Over the past few decades, however, feminist critiques of existing canons and feminist scholarship recovering and arguing for the merits of previously uncanonical texts by women have been the most powerful forces transforming what I will call the operative canon, that is, the set of texts being published, commented upon by people trained in literary studies, and taught in departments of literature. Feminist criticism has been ambivalent about whether its goal should be to place works written by women in the literary canon or to extirpate the idea of literary canon. Given that literature has become such a moving target, it is no wonder that Perkins finds literary history impossible.

My position is that we can identify works of literature and that we can write histories of them. Admittedly, the sorts of works considered literary may be somewhat different in different historical periods, but I think a literary history can aim to recognize both the ideas of the literary in the period it treats and the ideas of the literary in the period in which it is written. My literary history in this book includes a wide range of genres with good claims to be considered literature: poetry, drama, essay, biography, memoir, translation, familiar letter, history, travel narrative, and novel. To some readers, some of these forms may seem not a part of literature. Yet Butt in *English Literature: The Mid-Eighteenth Century* quite properly paid attention to essay, biography, memoir, familiar letter, history, and travel narrative, recognizing that contemporaries considered them significant literary genres, indeed, that writers of the period were especially interested in cultivating these nonfictional prose forms. Twenty-first-century readers may notice that these forms are now also of great interest to nonspecialist general readers, as any recent issue of *The Times Literary Supplement* will demonstrate.

Because literary forms other than the novel were important in the Restoration and eighteenth century and because I think that much of women's best writing was in forms other than the novel, the reader may be surprised to find that the novel – apparently at the center of the modern feminist canon – is not at the center of my account. Much of women's most intellectually vigorous writing was in nonfiction prose, not in the novel. Indeed, too often what modern critics have supposed were omnipresent constraints on women writers in this period were merely the conventions of the domestic novel. I agree with Clare Brant's recent argument that feminist criticism has been too uncritical of "the orthodoxies of literary history" that direct attention too exclusively to poems, plays, and, especially, novels – although I have already noted that these "orthodoxies" did not constrain good literary historians of eighteenth-century writing like Butt.[2]

Feminists concerned with women writers often add additional feminist reasons for the impossibility of writing literary history to the reasons Perkins offers. Practically, they point to the ferment in the field and argue that, minimally, it is too early to attempt synthesis. Theoretically, many resist both the necessity of selection and the evaluative criticism required by a literary history. Sharon Harris, in a strenuous and substantial introduction to her anthology, *American Women Writers to 1800* (1996), thoughtfully articulates these skeptical positions. Deeply suspicious of the category literature, Harris includes not only doggerel magazine verse, but also business letters, dying declarations, and petitions (some of which I doubt were written by women). She declares: "I believe it is far too early – if ever necessary – to establish a canon of early American women writers; the discipline of early American studies in general is currently engaged in what might be called a critical flux (a very healthy condition, I would argue) and deserves much more research and development before such considerations come under debate."[3]

Like many feminists, Harris is legitimately suspicious of aesthetic standards developed in an hermeneutic circle with a predominantly male canon. She wants to be maximally open to the possibility of alternative aesthetics that might emerge from reflection on women's writing. Consequently, she is excited by the possibilities of examining nontraditional genres where aesthetic standards have not been established and thus do not as readily condition our responses. These, she points out, "can at times bring a reader to the quite exciting position of having to find an alternative discourse as a means of explaining – to herself and others – what she values in these texts." Unlike some who merely point to a future when such an alternative aesthetic might be articulated, Harris proposes that what previously had been devalued as "discontinuity" in early women's journals, seen as "nonliterary," ought rightly to be valued as "associativeness born of interruptibility." She redescribes this kind of writing substituting positive terms for negative ones like "discontinuous" and "semi-literate":

The best of these writers does not want to tie down her thoughts to a linear pattern . . . she allows her mind to rove through multiple associations and – importantly – when these texts are written to be shared with another, she assumes that her reader will be willing and able to engage in these same fast and fluent mental shifts, grasping the complexity and infiniteness of the ideas engaged and the contingencies of meaning which her style conveys.[4]

I agree with Harris and many other feminist critics that earlier constructions of the canon of Restoration and eighteenth-century literature have wrongly excluded significant and meritorious work by women, but I do not agree with those who think that feminists must jettison the idea of literature or the idea of literary merit. I agree that new aesthetic values can be found in some previously devalued women's writing, but I do not agree with those who contend that we cannot make aesthetic evaluations of literary works that have any use or objectivity. Aesthetic or literary merit is an important principle of selection in my literary history.

It cannot be a sin against feminism to say that some women wrote well and others wrote badly, that some were intelligent, reflective, and original, others dull, unreflective, and formulaic. It has been my experience that many who advance the skeptical position that judgment of literary merit is impossible with respect to works that are objects of their academic study, nevertheless feel able outside their area of scholarly expertise to pronounce on the aesthetic merits of plays or movies they see or books they read. Indeed, they are often satisfied consumers or even writers of evaluative criticism in modern reviews. I do not see why a person like me who has spent the better part of forty years immersed in Restoration and eighteenth-century British literature and history should not be capable of some useful discrimination between a good eighteenth-century poem and a bad one. Several essays in a recent issue of *New Literary History* helpfully defend what one writer describes as the "quasi-objectivity of aesthetic truth." This writer, Allen Wood, a Stanford philosopher, defends a proposition of Hume's with which I agree: "no sensible person can take seriously the thesis that all painting or poetry, for instance, is of equal aesthetic merit."[5]

One important claim some seventeenth- and eighteenth-century women writers made was that they were capable of making aesthetic judgments. In a fine essay in the new Cambridge *History of Women's Writing in France*, Faith Beasley observes that the neoclassical French women of the salons challenged existing academic standards of taste and advanced a more worldly sensibility, to be acquired in the hetereosocial salons, as a sufficient, even preferable standard of taste.[6] Many feminist theorists have complained that there was a suspicious coincidence between the discovery of women writers and the proclamation of the death of the author; they elected to keep the idea of the author alive. Similarly, it seems to me that it would be a shame to abandon the idea of aesthetic merit just at the moment when we have a real opportunity to demonstrate both women artists' capacity to produce it and women critics' capacity to discern it. We can debate degrees or kinds of aesthetic merit without abandoning the idea that aesthetic merit exists. Some feminist abjuration of evaluative criticism derives from the militant anti-elitism of some feminisms. It may also arise from a feminist "ethic of care" that values nurturance and support rather than criticism.[7] Yet, sadly, I wonder whether this abjuration of evaluative criticism is not also a product of a lingering womanly reluctance to claim any authority, no matter how useful, well-earned, or justified.

In my view, all writing by women can validly be studied by one scholarly discipline or another – by social history, for example – but it does not follow that all writing by women is the proper object of literary study. In this book, for example, I treat some women's letters. Often these letters were written by women who were self-consciously writing in what they understood to be the literary genre of the familiar letter; they explicitly reflect on the literary merits of earlier writers of familiar letters. Occasionally, the writers were less self-consciously engaged in what they understood to be literary performances, but display an unusual artfulness with language, character, scene, and the relational dynamics peculiar to the familiar letter that I consider makes them literary. The vast majority of women's letters, however, serving more purely instrumental purposes, do not seem to be appropriately part of the subject matter of literature. Thus, although the letters of Martha Daniell Logan to John Bartram that Sharon Harris prints in her anthology are fascinating from the perspective of horticultural history, I do not consider them in my literary history. Similarly, much of the occasional political writing usefully discussed by Paula McDowell in *The Women of Grub Street: Press, Politics, and Gender in the London Literary Marketplace, 1678–1730* (1998) also lies outside the scope of my history. Like male writers, women writers of this period often produced inept or clichéd poems, or insipid and badly written novels. While sometimes misogynistic, contemporary reviewers' complaints about bad writing were often enough legitimate. My aim in this book is not to consider everything written by women, but rather to emphasize those literary works that were most original, most intelligent, best written, and most significant.

Recent historians of national literatures have been more bothered by the question of what literature is than by the question of what the nation was.

Despite much current scholarly interest in the construction of national identities and national cultures, this work has not yet had much impact on national literary histories. Presumably because America and Britain became separate countries after the War of American Independence, colonial American literature has conventionally been treated as part of American literary history and not as part of British literary history. However, because I believe that a national literary history ought to reflect the actual historical composition of the nation in the period it describes, my literary history considers women writing everywhere in Britain and the British colonies, including North America, so long as those colonies were part of the British Empire. It makes no more sense to exclude American colonial writers from British literary history than it would to exclude Irish writers, who are conventionally included. Thus, the American writers are present in my first six chapters, treating 1660 to 1776, then disappear in the seventh chapter at the point of the War of American Independence. Some of the American writers were self-consciously British patriots; even an oppositional writer like Abigail Adams was very aware of occupying a place within the British imperial system. Including the American writers helps underline the fact that British literature of this period was an imperial literature. It also reminds us that strains of Puritanism, religious dissent, anti-monarchalism, and republicanism that seem in some accounts virtually to disappear from English culture after the Restoration continued to develop offshore. The political radicalism of Catharine Macaulay in England in the 1770s may seem less sudden and surprising when we find Macaulay and the Adamses forming a united front in the 1770s.

My literary history is Janus-faced, one face turned toward the Restoration and eighteenth century, the other toward the twenty-first century. From one perspective, I aim to offer a picture of the literary work of Restoration and eighteenth-century women writers in which they and their contemporaries might recognize themselves and their accomplishments. Therefore, I attend to writers and works celebrated in their own time, even if they have not been of great interest to more recent criticism and may not seem of obvious interest to most twenty-first century readers. Thus, Elizabeth Rowe, whose Christian piety has not appealed much to modern tastes, but who was a critically celebrated and popular writer in her own time, and an inspiration to other women writers, has an important place in my history. So does Elizabeth Carter, who is even easier than Rowe to overlook from a modern perspective, in part because her major work was a translation from the Greek, *All the Works of Epictetus*, translation being a very visible part of the eighteenth-century literary system, yet less so of ours. Margaret Ezell in *Writing Women's Literary History* was right to complain that many earlier narratives of feminist literary history too relentlessly insisted on a development from an early feminine writing to a later, better, feminist writing, and ignored or too harshly criticized early women writers who did not attack patriarchy, denying the real diversity of women's writing.[8]

Perkins rightly insists that one function of literary history is "to set the past at a distance, to make its otherness felt."[9] Literary history can serve a salutary function in resisting a common impulse of humanist criticism, including feminist humanist criticism, to read all texts of the past as heralding and supporting our modern convictions. Some feminist critics, demonstrating more hermeneutical brilliance than historical imagination, have found subversion of patriarchy lurking beneath the surface of texts of apparently staggering conservatism or even misogyny. Here I have tried to allow these past texts to retain their otherness, so that the reader may experience what Perkins calls "the shock to values, the effort of imagination, the crisis for understanding and sympathy" of an encounter with the past.[10] Because this history considers Restoration and eighteenth-century women's quarrels with one another, it also resists the idea that they spoke with one voice.

The other Janus face of my literary history necessarily looks to our present time, reflecting an emerging canon of women's texts that have spoken most compellingly to modern readers, especially modern feminist critics and readers. The modern canon has especially valued the transgressive writers like Aphra Behn and Delarivière Manley, whose willingness to treat female sexuality and to attack male oppression of women made them appear to be our most useable foremothers. The dominant genre of this modern canon has been the novel, and undergraduates now regularly read Behn's *Oroonoko*, Manley's *Rivella*, Charlotte Lennox's *Female Quixote*, Frances Sheridan's *Sidney Bidulph*, and Frances Burney's *Evelina*. Three important twentieth-century literary histories of women's writing in the Restoration and eighteenth century all made the novel their central focus: B. G. MacCarthy's pioneering and feisty *The Female Pen: Women Writers and Novelists, 1621–1818* (1946–47), Jane Spencer's fine *The Rise of the Woman Novelist: From Aphra Behn to Jane Austen* (1986), and Janet Todd's deservedly influential *The Sign of Angellica: Women, Writing and Fiction, 1660–1800* (1989).

There are real tensions between these two Janus faces of my history, and the reader will have to judge how well I have managed them. The face turned toward the Restoration and eighteenth century sees women's nonfiction prose, religious writing, and translation as having been more significant than they are in the twenty-first century operative canon (although there are signs that the canon is shifting). The face turned toward our modern canon shares the preoccupation of feminist criticism with constructions of heroism, with stories of how women came to write of their own experience, and with questions of how women's writing gained cultural authority. As a feminist who has elected to write a history of women's writing, I am drawn toward emphasizing texts that foreground women's experience and texts that seem to represent progressive kinds of gender consciousness. Practically, considering texts that foreground women's experience helps lend some coherence to my own narrative. More theoretically, William Warner was probably correct to say that the question that "motivates virtually all post-Enlightenment feminist inquiry" – including mine – is "how does the female subject who would be free ... resist or negotiate some compromise with the power of ... patriarchy ... in order to win authority, in view of some possible future liberation?"[11] Such presentist concerns in feminist and other "minority" literary histories convince some that they are too ideologically driven and too narrow to lay claim to historical objectivity or truthfulness. Perkins, indeed, associates "minority" literary history with Nietzsche's antiquarian history, a mode so driven by desire to support feelings of community identity that it lacks objectivity and insists on celebrating "even mediocre achievements" of its minority with inappropriate "enthusiasm."[12] I do think, as I have indicated, that modern feminist criticism sometimes errs by overpraising mediocre works, supporting praise with inventive but implausible readings.

There is an important tension between my desire to foreground progressive kinds of gender consciousness, on the one hand, and, on the other hand, my desire to represent the full range of women writers' accomplishments, including many that are not about gender. Like Rita Felski, I am wary of reinscribing an essentialism of which feminists have rightly complained.[13] Thus, with some risk to the coherence of my narrative, I have also emphasized achievements of these writers as diverse as Anne Finch's intervention in the pastoral tradition and Macaulay's advocacy of freedom of the press. Using my historical imagination and what Perkins calls the law of sympathy I have also tried to enter as well as I could into even the more alien concerns of these early texts – like the conundrums Calvinism and Neoplatonism posed for Rowe – to understand what they aimed to accomplish when they were written.

Without abandoning evaluative criticism, I have tried to articulate sympathetically the merits and claims to attention of individual texts. In particular, considering some women writers who championed "virtue" rather than sexual liberation, I argue that they made virtue a more philosophically serious and interesting concept than modern readers might suspect and that the women writers of what I call "the party of virtue" more powerfully rebutted certain misogynistic assumptions than the transgressive women writers did. In cases where I have less admiration for particular texts than other intelligent modern critics do, I have departed from the usual authoritative stance of literary history to indicate briefly what these other views are and to offer bibliographical citations that will enable the reader to pursue those alternative approaches.

METHOD OF ORGANIZATION

Typically, literary histories that treat multiple genres use genre as a key organizing principle. Butt in *English Literature: The Mid-Eighteenth Century* relies almost entirely on genre, offering separate chapters on drama; history; travel literature, memoirs, and biography; essays; and letters, dialogues, and speeches. Fiction gets two chapters, one for the "Four major novelists" and one for "Other prose fiction." Poetry gets three chapters: one for poetry 1740–60, one for poetry 1760–89, and one for Scottish poetry. Unlike most users of this conventional genre structure, Butt makes an intelligent effort to justify his choice, arguing, "this was the last age in which writers were seriously affected by the doctrines associated with the traditional literary 'kinds.'"[14] A central theme of his history is the way "new 'kinds' derive from old by different processes, imitative or parodic, to which the biological term 'mutation,' may be applied."[15]

I have departed from this usual preference for genre as an organizing principle, choosing instead to organize this book chronologically. I have divided 1660–1789 into seven shorter periods, and begun each chapter with a brief account of significant events of that period and some remarks on its general characteristics. Except for two very minor bits of fudging, I have strictly confined myself in each chapter to considering only works originating in the years covered by that chapter. This has the salutary effect of forcing me to advance only generalizations that such evidence can support. It also advances the argument that women writers were much more engaged with the nondomestic events and ideas of their time than one might suppose from the evidence of the domestic novel.

A. E. Housman, the great classical scholar and poet of *A Shropshire Lad*, in 1915 memorably reviewed the latest volume of the *Cambridge History of English Literature*, one covering *The Period of the French Revolution*. He complained that the volume was insufficiently historical:

> History need not adhere to chronology and such anachronisms as the inclusion of Peacock in this volume and the postponement of Scott till the next are shifts of expediency which have no historical importance. But the order of date should be kept when nothing is gained by inverting it. Nothing is gained, nay much is lost, by an inversion which places Wordsworth on p. 93, Crabbe on p. 140, and Blake and Burns on still later pages; for this is an inversion not simply of chronological but of historical sequence. Historically considered, Wordsworth is the pivot of the epoch . . . No poet later born . . . entirely escaped his influence . . . But Burns was dead when the *Lyrical Ballads* were published, and Crabbe might have been dead too for all the good or harm they did him.[16]

Housman's advice to adhere to the order of date has seemed to me useful. Not only does it help to place women writers in the historical moments from which their works originated and to emphasize women's engagement with contemporary events and ideas, it makes it easier to discern women writers taking sides on pressing contemporary issues and responding to one another. An enormous amount of the secondary literature on these women writers has been biographical, often finding purely personal causes for apparent shifts in the direction of a particular writer's work. Famously – or perhaps now infamously – Eliza Haywood was supposed to have been driven from the writing of scandal chronicles to the writing of inoffensive novels because she was humiliated by Alexander Pope's satire on her in *The Dunciad*.[17] In this book, I treat Haywood's early work and her later work in separate chapters, suggesting ways in which it was representative of more general trends. Moreover, certain events within the literary system have consequences that help explain phenomena that affect more than one writer. For example, George Colman's managing of the Haymarket Theatre from 1777 to 1788 as a serious rival to Covent Garden and Drury Lane, and the unusual willingness of both Colman and Thomas Harris, manager of Covent Garden, to produce new comedies (rather than tested repertory plays) contributed to the successes of both Hannah Cowley and Elizabeth Inchbald.

One question that has to be settled before an internal chronology can be periodized is the question of what kind of dates are to be primarily considered: dates of authors' births and deaths, dates of composition of works or dates when works were performed or published. In this book I emphasize texts rather than authors' lives, and consequently use dates of texts rather than biographical dates. Other kinds of dates may also be relevant – for instance, the date of the introduction of actresses or the dates of various Licensing Acts – but they are more sporadically, less systematically so.

The question remains of whether to use dates of composition or dates of publication. In some literary histories, this would be a minor issue, since the two dates would rarely differ by more than a few years. In dealing with Restoration and eighteenth-century women writers, however, it is a major issue. Memoirs, letters, and journals are important forms in this period, and much of women's best and least self-censored writing was in these forms. Frequently, this life writing was not published until long after the author's death, often not until the early nineteenth century, and in some cases, not until the twentieth. Lucy Hutchinson's *Life of Colonel Hutchinson*, for instance, could not have been published in the Restoration when she wrote it because she expressed the point of view of the parliamentary party that had lost the Civil War. It was not published until 1806. Lady Mary Wortley Montagu's *Embassy Letters*, written between 1716 and 1718, were not published until shortly after her death in 1763. The bluestocking correspondence of Elizabeth Montagu, Elizabeth Carter, and Catharine Talbot was not published until Carter's nephew, the Reverend Montagu Pennington, published some of Carter's letters in his *Memoirs* of her life in 1807, followed by four volumes of *A Series of Letters between Mrs. Elizabeth Carter and Miss Talbot* in 1809, then three volumes of Carter/Montagu letters in 1817. Abigail Adams's brilliant letters to her husband John while he was away at the Continental Congress between 1774 and 1776 could have been used in treason prosecutions against either of them; they were not published until 1840.

The problem of choosing between a chronology of dates of publication and one of dates of composition for this history of women's writing is, therefore, a difficult one. In general, in this period, writing that had impact and influence was published writing – or, in the case of drama, produced writing. In so far as literary history is significantly and legitimately concerned with contemporary impact and influence, to prefer dates of publication over dates of composition makes sense. Nevertheless, it is true that, even in the later eighteenth century, some writers were, at least in limited circles, known to be talented writers on the evidence of manuscript circulation.[18] The later historian, Catharine Macaulay, knew the manuscript of Hutchinson's *Life* and tried to have it published in the second half of the eighteenth century, but failed. The contemporary reputations of Lady Mary Wortley Montagu, Elizabeth Carter, and Elizabeth Montagu depended in part on a limited circulation of their manuscript poems and letters. Given that so much good writing was not published until so long after composition, I have preferred to make my chronology one of dates of composition. (Of course, particularly in the case of volumes of poems, we are unsure of precise dates of composition of individual poems and may be forced to rely on the date of publication as a rough indicator of latest possible date of composition.) This choice of a chronology of date of composition has the additional advantage of allowing me to treat in the same chapter texts published many years apart but produced under and responding to the same historical circumstances, for instance, in chapter one, on 1660–89, Margaret Cavendish's *Life of the Duke of Newcastle* (1667) and Hutchinson's *Life of Colonel Hutchinson* (1806).

TEXTS

Much important recent work on the literary history of this period has explored the history of the book trade, the forms of literary patronage, reception history, and the economic and cultural position of authors. For example, Cheryl Turner, in *Living by the Pen: Women Writers in the Eighteenth Century* (1992), offered a catalogue of women's fiction, explored how much income women novelists were able to make, considered their relationships with their publishers, and described modes of readers' access to women's fiction. Turner's work has now been supplemented by further data in the impressive bibliographies compiled by James Raven and his collaborators, most recently, *The English Novel, 1770–1829. A Bibliographical Survey of Prose Fiction Published in the British Isles* (2000). Robert Hume and Judith Milhous have compiled and analyzed data on "Playwrights' Remuneration in Eighteenth-Century London" (1999). Catherine Gallagher in *Nobody's Story: The Vanishing Acts of Women Writers in the Marketplace, 1670–1820* (1994) looked at the careers of five women novelists and their textual self-representations to argue that the "the apparent negativity in the rhetoric of these women writers – their emphasis on disembodiment, dispossession, and debt – points not to disabling self-doubts but to an important source of their creativity, a fertile emptiness at the heart of eighteenth-century authorship."[19] Dustin Griffin in *Literary Patronage in England, 1650–1800* (1996) showed that patronage, even in traditional forms, continued to have some importance in writers' careers well after the appearance of commercial booksellers and their apparent hegemony in the literary marketplace.

This work on literary history has been useful to me; however, in this book, I have chosen to use this sort of literary history as background and to foreground texts written by women. To focus attention on these texts, every chapter begins with a list of the principal texts to be considered. The kind of literary history I write here is a subspecies of the history of art, a history in which what ultimately matters is the achievement of works of art: songs and symphonies for music history, paintings and pagodas for art history, poems and plays for literary history. In a literary history of women's writing, it is not enough to chronicle and to sympathize with women's sufferings under patriarchy; women writers must be judged by what they accomplished in their writing. To a significant extent, histories of an art describe and characterize the works that are their subjects. In some such histories, readers can be assumed to be familiar with the works and sheer description is less important than I believe it to be in my history, where, in part because this canon is so mobile and emerging, a good number of the works I consider are likely to be unfamiliar, even to specialists in the field. Given the unfamiliarity of some of these works, I have also quoted from them more liberally than is usual in literary histories, in part so that the reader might have some direct experience of their styles.

Perkins observes that one of traditional literary history's problems with narrative is that passages of analysis of particular texts slow down and interrupt its narratives. Whereas in a social history documents have importance as sources and evidence, in an history of an art form, works have an independent value as aesthetic objects. Thus, "they must be described in and for themselves."[20] The literary historian wants to describe the work, to give it an appropriate explanatory context, to suggest why it deserves the reader's appreciation, and what significance it has in the history of literature. There is, as Perkins points out, an inevitable tension between, on the one hand, the need to consider the work for its own sake and to offer literary criticism of it, and, on the other hand, the need to advance the larger narrative lines of the literary history. To go too far in the first direction of treating individual works for their own sakes risks hopelessly fragmenting the narrative, even swamping any possible narrative line.

Yet to neglect to treat works for their own sakes, however much it might enable a narrative line to proceed uninterrupted, has, I think, worse perils. A literary history without appreciative literary criticism, especially one like this that considers many texts not established in the literary canon, will fail to answer the question of why its texts matter, why they deserve to be the subjects of a literary history. Both Spencer's *Rise of the Woman Novelist* and Todd's *Sign of Angellica* succeed in part because of the quality of the literary criticism they offer. Similarly, a literary history that moves very quickly from one text to another, barely pausing for consideration of any of them, risks becoming a deadening list. At best, it may only be intelligible to the few readers who already have most of the works with which it deals fully present in their minds. I have, therefore, chosen to risk erring on the side of injuring the narrative line by the interruption of passages considering particular texts.

I have generally used the form of the text that appeared in its first edition. That is not the convention of most literary history, which typically deals with more established canonical authors and uses modern scholarly editions. For Restoration and eighteenth-century women writers, there are often no scholarly editions, and when these are available, they have often been prepared according to widely divergent principles. A few offer non-modernized texts, many offer partially modernized texts, and some have been aggressively modernized. The alternatives, when available, are likely to include modern reprints of late or collected editions, modernized editions, or editions prepared for classroom use. One reason I have here preferred to use first editions is that the first edition best supports my intent to capture chronological periods. The first-edition text normally best displays the author's intention and meaning closest to the date of composition and it shows us what the text was at the moment of its initial reception. For example, in Hannah Cowley's comedy *Which is the Man?* (1782), produced shortly after the British loss of the War of American Independence, a character declares that "intrepid spirit, nice honour, generosity, and understanding" are the crucial characteristics of a soldier. He goes on to say, in the first edition, "It is these which will make the British soldier once again the first character in Europe – It is such soldiers who must make England once again invincible, and her glittering arms triumphant in every quarter of the globe." Later editions, including the one used for the modern reprint of Cowley's plays, drop the awareness of defeat, printing "It is these which make the British soldier the first character in Europe – It is such soldiers who make England invincible, and her glittering arms triumphant in every quarter of the globe." Paratextual material – including dedications, prefaces, commendatory verse, prologues and epilogues to plays – especially valuable to the literary historian, is often altered or dropped entirely from subsequent editions, including some scholarly editions.

Moreover, most authors in this period, certainly most women authors, expected their printers to make needed corrections in manuscript copy and to impose a correct contemporary style on the text. Conventions of grammar, style, and spelling change significantly between 1660 and 1789. To cite texts from a combination of modern scholarly editions when available, first editions when they were the only edition available, late corrected editions, and modernized editions would be to introduce adventitious elements that made the styles of writers contemporary with each other appear more different from one another than they were. Some writers, like Behn, who have become familiar to many readers in modernized editions might seem more accessible in this form, but that accessibility is an artifact of editing that, in the context of this literary history, makes a spurious difference between such writers and their immediate contemporaries. To cite from first-edition texts gives the highest available level of confidence that what I claim was in a printed text as of a particular date actually was in it. This has perhaps been of special importance in considering poetry and what was characteristic of the poets. Since we have often come to know poets through collected works or, still more often, anthologies, the dates of individual poems, the sequence of publication of poems, and the range of kinds of poems the poet attempted often escape us. In this book, I have usually considered the first editions of volumes of poems, devoting some attention to the poetic personae the volume offers. Not surprisingly, I have been struck by the skewing effects of modern principles of anthologizing. To read these collections in their entirety reminds one that poems of feminist protest, fond as we are of them now, are rare compared to translations, occasional poems of compliment, and religious poems.

There are, of course, some disadvantages to citing texts in their first editions. Many of these women were not well served by their original printers and some of the texts contain significant numbers of errors, obvious and otherwise. I have addressed this disadvantage by emending errors in passages quoted, as though I were making a modern scholarly, nonnormalized critical edition of the passage. Any such emendations are indicated in the note on the passage. As I noted in discussing my choice of a chronological method of organization, some of my texts were not published until long after they were written; some, like the letters of Carter, in early nineteenth-century editions were probably heavily edited and even probably expurgated. Many of these manuscripts have disappeared. Ideally, consistent with my general method here, I would like to have consulted surviving manuscripts for those texts that were not published until long after their composition. However, in a book ranging as widely as this one does, that seemed an impracticable counsel of perfection, so I have settled for the best available printed edition in these cases.

More practically, readers may find my citations from first editions less convenient than citations from more available modern editions. I have had the very considerable advantage and pleasure of being able to read most of these texts in the form of the physical book first editions, mainly at the Houghton Library, and am convinced that the evidence of the physical book is valuable for the literary historian. The splendid magnificence of the large quarto first edition of Carter's *All the Works of Epictetus* dramatically contrasts with the awkward typography and cheap paper of the first edition of Mary Rowlandson's *True History of the Captivity and Restoration of Mrs. Mary Rowlandson*, reminding us of the cultural centrality of the former and the provincial marginality of the latter. The elegant printing of the five volumes of Burney's *Cecilia* shows that more had been invested in this book that in the typical novel of the day. Readers with less direct access to first editions, happily, are likely to have access to Wing microfilm of works between 1660 and 1700 and to a variety of on-line resources, including those of the Brown Women Writers' Project and the Eighteenth Century Collections Online. Some may also be able to use the microfilm in the Eighteenth Century series, which now offers a staggering range of titles, including almost every first edition I have had occasion to seek for in it. Moreover, convenient as our modern printed editions often are, ever since printed editions of these women writers began to appear in the 1970s, feminist teachers and readers have constantly lamented the speed with which they have subsequently gone out of print. We do need more nonmodernized scholarly editions of these texts and I have profited from those that are available. The reader will find a list of recommended modern editions on pp. 491–95.

PLOT

What, though, is the narrative line of this book? Perkins wryly suggests that there are essentially only three standard plots for literary histories: "rise, decline, and rise and decline."[21] The rise plot has understandably been the most popular. In national literary histories, it often becomes the rise of a particular people to the full expression of their national essence. This was the original plot of nineteenth-century German literary history and it continues to be an obsession in American literary history. In eighteenth-century studies, Ian Watt gave the rise plot an exceptionally influential presentation in *The Rise of the English Novel* (1957). Jane

Spencer's *Rise of the Woman Novelist* uses a similar plot, albeit one with an important qualification.

Significantly for the purposes of my book, since I consider both the novel and drama, the usual plot of histories of the drama from 1660 to 1789 is a decline plot, the opposite of the standard rise plot for the novel. Beginning with the brilliance and wit of Restoration comedy, the eighteenth-century drama succumbs to turgid tragedy and maudlin sentiment. Not only is this a general plot for drama history in this period, it is also the plot of the most recent literary history of women dramatists in this period, Margarite Rubik's *Early Women Dramatists, 1500–1800* (1998).

Focusing not so much on texts as on cultural ideas about women writers and women writers' ideas about themselves as writers, Norma Clarke has most recently narrated what she sees as *The Rise and Fall of the Woman of Letters* (2004) between 1660 and 1800. Clarke finds the Restoration and early eighteenth century more hospitable to women writers than the late eighteenth and early nineteenth centuries. She argues that even though the number of women writers increased, "prescriptive models of femininity hardened" and the definition of "serious authorship rapidly narrowed to exclude all but the male of the species."[22]

In so far as a literary history selects a particular *terminus ad quem* as the climactic state of affairs to be explained – and, usually, also celebrated – it will organize the narrative teleologically to explain how that point got reached. Perkins finds such teleological narrative organization disturbing in part because it seems to him reductive and in part because emplotment "activates archetypal emotions," setting up partisan enthusiasm for one genre versus another or one literary generation versus another in a way Perkins thinks is "uncritical."[23] Certainly admirers of eighteenth-century literature have often objected to the ways in which partisans of romanticism have characterized eighteenth-century literature in their literary histories.

I agree with Perkins that narrative is the logical form for literary history and that the chronological boundaries selected will profoundly shape particular narratives. But I think he worries excessively about reductionism and partisanship. Narrative of rise, decline, or rise and decline need not be simplistic, either in general history or in literary history. Consider, for example, George Sherburn and Donald Bond's volume covering 1660–1789 in *A Literary History of England*, edited by Albert C. Baugh.[24] Sherburn and Bond elected a plot of rise and fall, the rise of classicism and its disintegration. They clearly prefer classicism to sentimentalism, so the volume has an elegiac rather than a celebratory tone. Yet their rise and fall plot affords a very useful organizing principle and a nicely dramatic sense of the significant, without, I think, being unduly constraining. It also works well with their continuous attention to literary criticism being written during their period, a relatively unusual but suitably historical feature of their work, and one that I have imitated.

Inevitably, a major line of my plot is a change from the Restoration, when a woman playwright or a woman poet seemed a striking anomaly, to the late eighteenth century, when writing had become a more available career for literate women and when women were fairly widely accepted as writers in certain genres. Significant events in this plot line include the performances in 1662/3 of Katherine Philips's *Pompey*, the first play by a woman performed on the British public stage, as well as Behn's subsequent and greater success in having fifteen of her plays produced on the London public stage. In 1660, the overwhelming majority of Englishmen and Englishwomen believed that women lacked the intellectual and artistic capacities to become writers. Because this belief inhibited literary ambition in women, the early feminist arguments of Mary Astell and Judith Drake about women's intellectual capacities – and their practical advice about how women might educate themselves – were crucial contributions helping to embolden later women writers. Astell's move making it a Protestant woman's religious duty to cultivate her mind, to think critically about her culture, and perhaps subsequently to publish her conclusions contributed to emboldening first some writers who immediately followed her and then the later bluestockings, all the way to Hannah More.

Chapter one, "Public women, 1660–1689," opens at the Restoration of Charles II to the English throne after the Civil War and interregnum and closes at the end of Stuart rule and the death of Behn, the most important and conspicuously public woman writer of the Restoration. Behn adapted a courtly, secular, libertine poetic and dramatic tradition to her own purposes, positioning herself in a predominantly male London literary culture. Because women writers were still so anomalous, we want to understand what prompted the few women who did emerge as writers to do so. One important motive that prompted both royalists like Cavendish and supporters of Parliament like Hutchinson to write was the desire to record what they believed to be crucial historical truths about the tumultuous revolution and counterrevolution through which they and their husbands had lived. As had been the case during the Interregnum, Protestant religious conviction led even more women to write prayers, devotions, meditations, religious poetry, and, sometimes, narratives of persecution or pamphlets of religious controversy. At the colonial margins of British culture, men were eager to promote the publication of the work of the American Anne Bradstreet, who ardently denounced cavalier debauchery and irreligion, as evidence of the high level of piety and civilization the Puritan colonists had achieved in New England. This desire on the part of competing cultural groups to produce a public woman representative of their position continued to be a significant dynamic encouraging the publication of women's work.

Chapter two, "Partisans of virtue and religion, 1689–1702," covers the reign of William and Mary, whose assertively Protestant court encouraged religious, philosophical, and social reform movements attacking libertinism. The most systematic of the new feminist philosophers, Astell, refuted the idea that women were by nature intellectually inferior to men, rejected the established misogynistic ideas that silence was a woman's rhetoric, and argued that an enlightened understanding was the best basis for virtuous conduct. As Astell, Damaris Cudworth Masham, and Catharine Trotter all appreciated, the rejection of scholasticism and the appeals to reason in the new philosophies of René Descartes, Ralph Cudworth, Henry More, and John Locke minimized the disadvantages from which women had suffered because of their lack of access to advanced formal education. Astell's model, yoking together women's demand for better education, women's duty to develop themselves spiritually and intellectually, and women's obligation to participate in the reform of society, had great ideological strength. It could reassure women of the legitimacy of their aspirations despite the scorn that continued to be directed at those aspirations and it established alliances between women and churches that allowed women to appropriate some institutional resources to their own causes. In the theatre, Trotter offered a reformed tragedy and Mary Pix contributed to a newly moral and sentimental comedy. In poetry, Rowe was an important part of a movement that challenged French neoclassical orthodoxy by arguing for the superiority of biblical poetry and increasing the aesthetic appreciation of biblical poetry.

Chapter three, "Politics, gallantry, and ladies in the reign of Queen Anne, 1702–1714," covers the reign of Queen Anne, a period when the rise of Whig and Tory political parties and their importance as new patrons of writing made it seem, briefly, as though women as well as men might become political writers. Delarivière Manley's scandal chronicles, written for the Tories, made an important intervention in the development of realist fiction by representing in recognizable ways unidealized contemporary characters and their actions. However, as the playwright Susanna

Centlivre, a Whig partisan, observed, it soon enough became clear that since the most valuable reward of political writing, political office, was not available to women, women might be better advised to shift their attention to other forms. Queen Anne's championing of the party of virtue further emboldened Astell and her admirer, Lady Mary Chudleigh, whose poetry and prose also embrace the study of the new science as a way to enhance humankind's appreciation of the creation and the Creator.

At a time when the sharp politicization of writing also prompted the development of a counter discourse of at least ostensibly nonpolitical belles lettres, polite male gallantry seemed to celebrate the accomplishments of women writers: *Miscellanies* typical of the period offered poems and letters of men and women in single volumes, including male compliments to women. However, as Anne Finch, Countess of Winchilsea, and other women poets noticed, the conventions of male gallantry made it impossible for women so complimented to have any real knowledge of what their male colleagues thought of their work. Gallantry itself, viewed by most women writers with suspicion, became an important subject.

In Chapter four, "Battle joined, 1715–1737," we come to the early Hanoverian years when the monarch and the court lose cultural centrality to the more raucous and democratic worlds of party politics and the commercial marketplace. The triumph of satire over panegyric in this period encouraged women writers like Lady Mary Wortley Montagu, Elizabeth Thomas, and Mary Davys to develop their own critiques of masculine authority and to ridicule forms of masculinity and prestigious individual men. Such satire made masculine authority less awe-inspiring, less terrifying, and prepared women to challenge it. More soberly, Rowe campaigned against libertinism in widely read and admired poetry and prose; in her epic *Joseph* she used biblical history to develop a narrative of heroic chastity. Rowe also further developed the seventeenth-century tradition of meditative poetry, adapting it in ways that made it valued by religious readers. The chapter ends in 1737, simultaneously the date of the death of Rowe and the date of the Licensing Act, in which the government recognized the power of satire by giving the Lord Chamberlain the power of preproduction censorship over plays.

As the burgeoning commercial market created new opportunities for women writers like Eliza Haywood, elite male writers worried about women's increasingly significant challenges to the male monopoly on literary representation and market share. Haywood's success in publishing a large number of novels and in following in the tradition of Behn and Manley that grounded the authority of the woman writer in her superior knowledge of love contributed both to normalizing the idea of the woman writer and to reinforcing a troubling association between the woman writer and transgressive sexuality. Because the new empirical philosophy valued individual experience as a source of knowledge and because the commercial market valued novelty, women claiming to represent their own experience and middling-class provincial writers representing developing cities and towns had new opportunities. Thus, Mary Chandler, a Bath milliner, succeeded with wry poems alluding to her spinsterhood and her life in trade and with a major loco-descriptive poem on Bath celebrating the contemporary town with journalistic detail and an enthusiasm that promoted tourism.

Chapter five, "Women as members of the literary family, 1737–1756," considers a time when developing sentimental culture was celebrating the properly hierarchical family as the source of highest human pleasure and the basis for right social order. A good number of women writers found acceptance by playing the roles of daughter, sister, or wife to literary men. So long as they confined themselves to less prestigious literary forms and to opinions considered appropriate for women, earlier male hostility modulated to ostensibly friendly correction and assistance and they could hope for a measure of acceptance. Sarah Fielding, assisted by her brother Henry and by Samuel Richardson, and Charlotte Lennox, playing the role of daughter to Samuel Johnson, were able to establish significant and respectable literary careers. Such relations with male mentors and patrons, however, often entailed tension and conflict, as Sarah Fielding's often bitter exploration of the horrors of dependence and the psychodynamics of relationships of domination and subordination reveals.

As the gendered division of literary labor became more pronounced, women increasingly claimed special authority on women, on children, and on matters domestic. Thus, we find Haywood turning to writing conduct books, *The Wife* and *The Husband*, Fielding writing *The Governess* for children, and Hannah Glasse becoming celebrated as the author of a cookbook. For the mid eighteenth century, servants were also part of the family. Mary Leapor claimed some cultural authority based on her occupational experience as a servant and her willingness to represent household labor in poetry that asserted its value.

Developing earlier ideas from classical Platonism and Cambridge Neo-platonism, the philosophers Anthony Ashley Cooper, Earl of Shaftesbury, Francis Hutcheson, and David Hume offered new, more secular, ideas about a "moral sense." A new philosophical insistence that feeling has a key role in morality and moral discourse was a foundation of the emphasis on feeling in the literature of sensibility. In *Felicia to Charlotte*, a novel of ideas announcing its indebtedness to Shaftesbury, Mary Collyer reimagines the amatory novel as the novel of sensibility. Collyer rejected the novel of intrigue for epistolary fiction valuing psychology over plot and offered dramatic demonstrations of filial piety and family feeling as crucial marks of human worth. Like Collyer, Lennox also constructed a new woman's fiction against the amatory novel, and, in *The Female Quixote*, also against the scandal chronicle, importantly intervening in the contemporary debate about what kinds of narratives deserve to be stigmatized as trifling and false and what kinds ought to be celebrated as true histories.

While domestic writers celebrated the possibilities of happiness in the family, Con Phillips, Lady Frances Vane, Laetitia Pilkington, and Charlotte Charke continued a more defiant tradition of women's writing. Fusing autobiography with the scandal chronicle Manley had made infamous, these memoirists, women who had lost their reputations for chastity and respectability, challenged the emerging ideology of the sentimental family as ensuring love and protection for women. Daughter of Colley Cibber, Charke tells a tale of a father's plans for his daughter's imitating his own theatrical success gone horribly wrong. Pilkington narrates the advantages she gained by becoming a surrogate daughter, first to Jonathan Swift and later to the elderly Cibber.

For groups subordinated by gender or class, the cultivation of sentiment potentially offered more democratic ideas of human worth against which the privileged might be judged and found wanting. Yet uncritical celebration of tenderness and "natural" feeling in the family threatened to become a disabling orthodoxy, replacing more strenuous older religious and ethical conceptions of duty with less thoughtful, more psychologically ensnaring reverence for pity and "natural" affection.

Chapter six, "Bluestockings and sentimental writers," takes us from the beginning of the Seven Years War in 1756 to the beginning of the War of American Independence in 1776. As the great historical events of the Civil War had prompted some women to record their experiences of them, so now English women at home showed their patriotic engagement in national struggles and debates; many found the model of imperial Rome an exciting and appealing paradigm for what Britain was becoming. In contrast, Abigail Adams, writing in colonial Massachusetts, was inspired by the model of republican Rome and determined to sacrifice her private comforts to what she understood to be the stringent demands of public good. History, revivified by enlightenment experiments in philosophical history, and energized by public debates over constitutional questions and comparisons of empires, became a dominant literary mode. Macaulay's ambitious *History of England*, concentrating on the seventeenth century, reflected her original research and linked the seventeenth-century conflicts over the constitution and civil liberties to her advocacy of freedom of speech and freedom of the press in the political contests of the 1760s and 1770s.

The bluestocking writers – including Elizabeth Montagu, Elizabeth Carter, Hester Chapone, Hannah More, and Sarah Scott – continued Astell's campaign to insist that women were capable of serious intellectual work. They encouraged women to read serious books, to engage in strenuous intellectual and moral reflection, and to give of their time and money to charity. Like Astell too they maintained that women's cultivation of their reason was the best guarantor of women's virtue. Elizabeth Montagu, the so-called "Queen of the Blues," established an important salon where men and women, English people and foreigners, aristocrats and talented people of the gentry and middling classes, all gathered for conversation that was designed to promote, even create, refined sociability and knowledge. Her salons, and similar ones presided over by Elizabeth Vesey and Hester Thrale, were quasi-public spaces that allowed the *salonnière* to display her own intelligence and literary acumen and to become the patroness of less economically privileged women writers. The letters between Montagu and Carter, one of the women writers she benefited, show the writers overcoming some barriers of wealth and class and using the familiar letter as a discursive space to create a mutually reinforcing female community. Montagu's *Essay on the Writing and Genius of Shakespear* demonstrated the impact of historicist thinking on literary criticism and represented Montagu's bid for female literary critical authority. Carter's translation from the Greek of *All the Works of Epictetus* made English people feel that they had finally produced a female scholar to rival the famous French Anne Dacier. Her success with a challenging classical philosophical text struck many as surprising evidence of female intellectual capacity.

The bluestockings were not much interested in novels, but by this time the total number of novels and the number produced by women writers were both increasing significantly. Between 1756 and 1776 identifiable women writers published about eighty-seven novels. Most of these were sentimental domestic novels, pledged to advance sentimental versions of the cause of virtue, often influenced by Richardson. Both in sentimental fiction and in sentimental comedy, writers attempted to edify their audiences with articulations of the moral maxims contemporaries described as "delicate sentiments" and to engage and to please them with spectacles of virtue in distress. In the optimistic and most characteristic versions of the sentimental plot, female virtue has a power to reform erring men. In bleaker versions of the plot, like Sheridan's *Sidney Bidulph*, often focusing on marriage rather than courtship, a virtuous woman demonstrates both her capacity for suffering and a remarkable capacity for complex moral reflection, yet her virtue has very limited power to affect the world. The conventions of these sentimental novels generally confine respectable women within narrow domestic spheres and strict conventions of conduct, but these conventions are to a significant extent an artifact of the novel rather than realistic representations of women's experience, as is evident from women's writing in other forms.

Chapter seven, "Romance and comedy, 1777–1789," begins with the imperial crisis of the War of American Independence and ends just before the beginning of the French Revolution, a common marker for the beginning of Romanticism. After 1776, American women writers are no longer part of British literary history. British defeat in the War of American Independence intensified concerns over the remaining parts of empire, including the West Indies and India. Women writers engaged in debates over slavery and over whether imported wealth from India was a sign of refined civilization or a sign of dangerous luxury and corruption marking imperial decline. Heightened interest in the representation of place, in part a result of exposure to abundant news of foreign wars and colonial issues, prompted elaborate representations of place across genres and repeated efforts to articulate what was distinctive about British places.

As modern historiography turned to investigate the Middle Ages, scholars and critics complicated the idea that romance was a mode of the ideal and the imaginary. Romance, it now appeared, contained important truths about the history of modern European nations, and romance as a mode was not so firmly tied to "early" civilizations as enlightenment proponents of stadial theories of progress had maintained. Paradoxically, in this period romance permits invocations of history against the emergent authority of literary realism, even in a utopian romance like Lady Mary Walker's *Munster Village*. Profiting from the new historical scholarship, Clara Reeve in *The Progress of Romance* intervened in the developing history of prose fiction to argue against the idea that romance is merely a superstitious or primitive mode that ought properly to be replaced by realism. Experiments with historical romance, including Reeve's *Champion of Virtue*, set in the time of the Crusades, were harbingers of Radcliffe's gothic romance and Sir Walter Scott's historical romance. Charlotte Smith's *Emmeline: The Orphan of the Castle* used romance to continue the project of redefining heroinism, transforming older versions of female heroinism from seventeenth-century French romance and the popular romance of Behn and Manley. Her Emmeline is a modern girl, chaste, sentimental, devoted to the aesthetics of rural landscape, and most remarkable for her charitableness. Smith's *Elegiac Sonnets* transforms something as apparently unexotic as the rural Suffolk landscape of her own childhood into an idealized pastoral romance, now seen by the melancholy adult poet as hopelessly distant. Smith's *Sonnets* helps explain how earlier romance and sensibility are transformed into what we now recognize as the "romantic."

While both the underlying philosophy of sentimentalism and its literary conventions continued to compel considerable allegiance, writers also attacked what they considered sentimentalism's fallacies and sentimentalism's clichés. Comic conventions, which sanction irreverence, provided welcome opportunities to puncture the more tired and deadening assumptions of sentiment, including its assumptions about female docility, modesty, and delicacy. Building on Centlivre's accomplishments, Hannah Cowley reveled in topicality and in energetic, colorful dialogue remote from the frequently dull abstractions of sentimentality. She used her dramatist's talent for creating sympathy for contradictory positions to reveal how contested and contradictory the new paradigms of femininity were. Elizabeth Inchbald mixed a reformist sentimental comedy, one that took advantage of late eighteenth-century expressive acting styles, with a lower kind of laughing, even satiric, comedy. Cowley and Inchbald were sufficiently unafraid of vulgarity that they were willing to write farce as well as main-piece comedy and to include farcical elements in their main pieces. In fiction, Frances Burney's comic genius provided readers with a Dickensian plenitude of comic characters. For all the timidity Burney recorded in her journals, her ambitious novel *Cecilia* offered an omniscient narrator whose shrewd analysis of the foibles of her society reminds us that comedy depends upon a writer's willingness to judge as well as to laugh. In a different way, Hester Thrale Piozzi's *Anecdotes of the Life of Samuel Johnson* demonstrated the importance of the anti-authoritarian stance of comedy for the woman writer. Thrale Piozzi made Johnson into a complex comic character who strikingly evinces the human capacity for irrationality and self-delusion.

By 1789 women writers had become a normal, albeit minority, part of literary production. Between 1777 and 1789, for example, thirty-two plays by women were produced on the public stages and about 224 novels by women were published. More women – including Burney, Cowley, Inchbald, and Smith – now had substantial and celebrated literary careers lasting decades. While some women writers continued to come from the aristocracy and the gentry, increasingly women from the middling ranks, especially those from families of knowledge workers like teachers and booksellers, established themselves as writers. More women also took on the literary authority entailed in editing, anthologizing, reviewing, and writing literary biography and literary criticism. At the same time, most women writers still experienced considerable anxiety that their literary ambitions might somehow unsex them and engaged in self-censorship that constricted or weakened their work. Some took on the task of policing other women to keep them within the narrowed constraints of proper contemporary feminine domesticity. Our story of the rise of the woman writer is, therefore, bittersweet.

CHAPTER I

Public women: the Restoration to the death of Aphra Behn, 1660–1689

TEXTS

(place of publication is London, unless otherwise indicated; dates and places of performance are given for plays).

1662 Katharine Evans. *This is the Short Relation of some of the Cruel Suffering (For Truth's Sake) of Katharine Evans and Sarah Cheevers, in the Inquisition in the Isle of Malta*

1662/3 Katherine Philips. *Pompey, a Tragœdy* (Dublin, performed; 1663 printed Dublin and London)

1666 Margaret Fell Fox. *Women's Speaking Justified, proved and allowed of by the Scripture*

1666 Margaret Cavendish, Duchess of Newcastle. *Observations upon Experimental Philosophy* + *The Description of a New Blazing World*

1667 Margaret Cavendish, Duchess of Newcastle. *The Life of the Thrice Noble, High and Puissant Prince William Cavendishe, Duke, Marquess, and Earl of Newcastle*

1664–71 (written) (published 1806). Lucy Hutchinson, *The Life of Colonel Hutchinson*

1667 Katherine Philips. *Poems. By the Most deservedly Admired Mrs. Katherine Philips, The Matchless Orinda . . .*

1677 Aphra Behn. *The Rover: or, the Banish't Cavaliers* (Dorset Garden)

1678 (Boston). [Anne Bradstreet], *Several Poems: Compiled with great Variety of Wit and Learning*

1682 (Boston) Mary Rowlandson. *The Soveraignty and Goodness of God, Together, With the faithfulness of his Promises Displayed; Being a Narrative of the Captivity and Restauration of Mrs. Mary Rowlandson; A True History of the Captivity and Restoration of Mrs. Mary Rowlandson, A Minister's Wife in New England* (London)

1684 Aphra Behn. *Poems upon Several Occasions: With a Voyage to the Island of Love*

1687 Aphra Behn. *The Emperor of the Moon. A Farce* (Dorset Garden)

1688 Aphra Behn. *The Fair Jilt: or, the History of Prince Tarquin and Miranda*

1688 Aphra Behn. *Oronooko, or, the Royal Slave. A True History*

INTRODUCTION

Englishwomen alive to witness the Restoration of King Charles II to the throne in 1660 knew that they lived in remarkable times. Charles's father, Charles I, had lost a civil war, suffered imprisonment, and then been tried and executed in 1649 by the interregnum Parliament for treason against the people. Men and women nevertheless loyal to the Crown found it difficult to live under the government of the parliamentary "usurpers." Some suffered punishment for engaging in conspiracy against the new government, some had their property confiscated and sequestered, some went into exile on the continent. Then, in 1660, when the revolution failed and a counterrevolution succeeded in restoring a king to the English throne, it was the turn of those who had supported Parliament to experience repression and – sometimes – imprisonment and exile.

Women who lived through these dramatic reversals found it much less possible than usual to rely on custom to order their conduct or to direct their obedience to authority. During the interregnum, those royalists loyal to the House of Stuart despite Parliament's revolution found themselves in some degree of opposition to government, no matter how conservative they were inclined to be. Some royalist women negotiated with parliamentary committees of sequestration in hopes of regaining part of their families' confiscated estates. One such royalist woman, Margaret Cavendish, in London during the interregnum to negotiate with a committee of sequestration, observed women preachers; she disapproved of them, yet the phenomena of women preaching and publishing during the interregnum helped to suggest possibilities even for royalist women like Cavendish. Ironically, the fact of dissenting women's public voices helped to legitimate royalist women's developing public voices to rebut and denounce parliamentary or dissenting women and to proclaim their own loyalty to monarchy.

A few royalist women joined the royalist underground during the interregnum, working as subversive spies. One, Lady Anne Halkett, wrote a memoir of her adventures. The highlight of her secret career was aiding in the 1648 royalist rescue of James, the Duke of York, from captivity. She procures a dress of "mixt mohaire" with scarlet "under petticoate" for him to wear as a disguise. Lady Anne gets the appropriate measurements, orders the garment from her own tailor (who is compliant but puzzled by the measurements since "hee had never seene any woman of so low a stature have so big a waist"), produces the garment, then waits at a safe house to dress the Duke before he sets sail at Gravesend.[1]

Women from families discontented with the monarchy were still more apt to live dislocated lives. Even before the Civil War broke out in 1642, some Puritan families had already immigrated to America. Women from these families, notably Anne Bradstreet and Mary Rowlandson, became significant British colonial writers whose works were read in America and in England. In England, after the Restoration of Charles II, some women who had been loyal to Parliament's rebellion against the King continued to defend the "good old cause"; some chose active opposition or subversion. Lucy Hutchinson's enduring narrative of her husband's support of Parliament and his imprisonment after the Restoration could not be published during her lifetime, although it survived and made its way into print in 1806 after the intense political passions of the late seventeenth century had finally cooled.

QUAKER WOMEN, RELIGIOUS WOMEN

Both during the interregnum and after the Restoration, Quaker women were especially eager to publish pamphlets proclaiming their versions of the gospel, their visions, their advice about the right ordering of the world, and the histories of their preaching and persecution. The Quakers were prominent among the several Protestant sects that had listened to women preachers and prophets during the Civil War.[2] Shortly after the Restoration, Margaret Fell, a Quaker leader, met personally with Charles II; she published her appeal to the King and Parliament, insisting on the Quakers' peaceableness, defending their refusal to take oaths or pay tithes, and asking for an end to legal penalties against members of the sect.[3] Almost 40 percent of all the first editions of books and pamphlets published by women between 1660 and 1690 were religious writings by Quaker women.[4] Some Quaker women published narratives of their missionary work not only in England, but also in America, the Caribbean, Europe, and beyond. In 1664, in prison, Fell published her pamphlet, *Women's Speaking Justified*, rebutting the conventional interpretations of biblical texts like 1 Corinthians 14: 34, "Let your women keep silence in the church." She argued that men and women inspired by Christ were equally entitled, indeed, equally obliged, to proclaim the truths of the spirit. After her marriage to George Fox in 1669, she continued to publish and to do important work in the movement. From 1671, Fell Fox organized separate women's meetings at which women worshipped and spoke, collected money, administered charity, disciplined members, and judged the suitability of marriages. This Quaker tradition of empowering women as speakers and activists for righteousness and justice explains the dramatic overrepresentation of Quaker women – including Lucretia Mott, Susan B. Anthony, and Sarah and Angelina Grimké – as leaders of the nineteenth-century abolitionist and women's suffrage campaigns.

Although many of the Quaker (or Anabaptist) women's pamphlets – like those of their male coreligionists – are not likely to appeal to the general reader today, some of Margaret Fell's arguments for women's entitlement to speak on religious matters are repeated by later Church of England women and become grounds of entitlement for women to speak and write within Protestant Christianity. Occasionally the narratives of the female Quakers descend sufficiently from abstract prophecy and hermeneutical casuistry to offer vivid glimpses of the inspired and extraordinarily adventurous lives they led.

Among the most remarkable of these Quaker narratives is *This is the Short Relation of some of the Cruel Sufferings (For Truth's Sake) of Katharine Evans and Sarah Cheevers, in the Inquisition in the Isle of Malta* (1662). Evans and Cheevers had set out to proclaim the gospel to the inhabitants of Alexandria, Egypt, when they were delayed, imprisoned, and threatened with death in the cells of the Catholic Inquisition in Malta. Evans recounts their suffering, fasting, and the visions that sustain her resistance. She also makes clear the grounds upon which she is able to ignore the authority of the learned clerics who try to persuade both women that they are too ignorant and too foolish to decide doctrinal matters for themselves. She rejects the inquisitors' construction of their bringing heretical books and papers with them as a crime by using a defense that resembles Milton's argument in *Areopagitica* (1644): "We said, if there were any thing in them that was not true, they might write against it."[5] The inquisitors in Malta, like other learned men of the day confronted with arguments from the unlettered, retort that "*they did scorn to write to fools and asses that did not know true Latine.*" Hearing the voice of the Lord say to her, "Lift up your Voice like the noise of a Trumpet, *and sound forth my Truth like the shout of a King,*" Evans is convinced that the Lord has authorized her speaking and writing and represents herself as continuing to debate with the inquisitors.[6] (These gentlemen seem to have little stomach for executing two foreign women, and eventually let them go.) One of the inquisitors attempts to rebuke Evans by asking her why she does not work. She retorts boldly, "I said unto him, What Work dost thou do? he said he did write. I told him, I will write too, if he would bring me a Pen, Ink, and Paper; and I would write truth."[7] Much of the writing of late seventeenth-century women was prompted, not by aesthetic ambition, but by this impulse to write what they believed to be truths, most urgently, to record the truths of their own experiences and what they believed to be truths that men in positions of authority would not put in their records of the times.

While most of the women who wrote on religious, philosophical, or moral subjects in the late seventeenth century did not describe the extreme experiences of Evans and Cheevers, they drew similar inspiration from scripture and religion. Even if they were not Quakers who had visions and "inner light," they had strong Protestant religious feelings and personal religious convictions that sustained them against skeptics and scoffers. The increased availability of printed books of Psalms, prayers, devotional manuals, biblical commentary, and sermons encouraged lay people to develop their own religious lives, more independent of clergy, and provided models for pious women's imitation. Lady Anne Halkett, for instance, composed thousands of manuscript pages of religious meditations and biblical commentary for her own use.[8]

After the Restoration, upper-class Anglican women also began to take more prominent roles in religion, a number of them becoming celebrated for their piety, learning, and charity. Lady Dorothy Packington was famous for her learning and for establishing her home as a center for learned royalist clergy, including Bishop John Fell, Bishop John Pearson, and Richard Allestree.[9] Susannah Hopton anonymously published her *Daily Devotions, Consisting of Thanksgivings, Confessions, and Prayers . . .* In 1682 the *Meditations and Prayers* the Countess of Northumberland used for her personal devotion and her household worship were also published. Such Anglican women typically had close relationships with learned clergymen, who encouraged and assisted their study, recommended their conduct as models for imitation, and, sometimes, arranged for publication of their works and published biographical accounts of them, as George Hickes, the famous non-juring Bishop and Anglo-Saxon scholar did of Hopton.

It is hard to overestimate the importance of earnest Protestant Christianity throughout the Restoration and the eighteenth century as a motive for women writers deciding that they were required to reflect on their thoughts and experiences, take individual responsibility for the state of their souls and the moral conduct of their lives, and, not infrequently, provide written accounts of their thoughts and deeds for audiences ranging from their own families to the entire world.

CIVIL WAR BIOGRAPHIES: CAVENDISH'S *LIFE OF WILLIAM CAVENDISHE*

Understanding how remarkable these revolutionary times were and wanting to record the events and deeds they had witnessed emboldened women to write in the years immediately following 1660. Royalists looked to the newly restored King with hope that he would do justice and bring about better, less troubled and divisive days. But if justice were to be done, either by the King or by posterity, the truth about people's conduct during the interregnum must be clearly put in the written record. Women who urgently wanted to record and to justify the conduct of their husbands, and, to a lesser extent, themselves, during the Civil War and in the confusing years that followed produced a remarkable group of biographies and memoirs: Lady Halkett, Alice Thornton, Lady Ann Fanshawe, Brilliana Harley, Margaret Cavendish, and Lucy Hutchinson.[10] None of these books has the magisterial sweep or the polished literary style of the Earl of Clarendon's royalist *History of the Rebellion* (1702–4), but each of them makes a unique contribution to reporting the experiences of individuals during a defining period of English history.

The only one of these books published during the Restoration was *The Life of the Thrice Noble, High and Puissant Prince, William Cavendishe, Duke, Marquess and Earl of Newcastle* (1667), by his wife, Margaret, the Duchess of Newcastle. The life of the Duke was a subject of considerable historical significance. Not only was he a great magnate of the north of England, but in 1642, as an Earl, he responded promptly to Charles I's request that he secure the town and port of Newcastle for the royalists; he then become general of the King's northern armies. He raised significant numbers of troops for the King, paying many of them himself, and contributed large sums of money to the royalist war effort. Almost as promptly as Newcastle responded to the King's commission, Parliament impeached him for treason. He had some military success in the north, for a time impeding the efforts of the Scots army to join with the English parliamentary forces against the King and preserving the city of York for the King. Catastrophe struck at the battle of Marston Moor in July 1644. Led by Prince Rupert and Newcastle, 18,000 royalist troops were defeated by 27,000 parliamentary and Scots troops; Prince Rupert's cavalry was for the first time defeated by Cromwell's "Ironsides" and Parliament gained control of the north. Newcastle fought valiantly, personally leading troops on the field. Then, however, acting in a way that made his virtues debatable, he notified Prince Rupert that he intended personally to escape by taking a ship to Hamburg and did so. He spent the next sixteen years in exile on the continent with his wife, returning to England in 1660 with Charles II.

During the interregnum, Cavendish had already established herself as the first Englishwoman to publish extensively. The Newcastles paid printers to produce large folio volumes: *Poems and Fancies* (1653); *Philosophical Fancies* (1653), revised and expanded as *Philosophical and Physical Opinions* (1655); *The World's Olio* (1655); and *Nature's Pictures Drawn by Fancy's Pencil to the Life* (1656). After the Restoration, Cavendish continued her brisk pace of publication, revising some of her earlier works, adding more speculations about natural philosophy, two collections of plays (1662, 1668), *Orations* (1662), and *Sociable Letters* (1666). Evidence suggests that the Duke adored his wife and encouraged her efforts at self-education and expression. Her volumes are prefaced by his commendatory poems praising her genius in extravagant terms. Indeed, not only was he her most ardent contemporary admirer, he may have been virtually her only sincere one.

Even the proud Duchess of Newcastle – who made hubris a virtue – had to recognize that she did not possess the ordinary qualifications of an historian who proposed to address a great period of national history. In all her works she is exquisitely self-conscious about the issue of her authority to write on the subjects she has proposed. One of her ways of dealing with this problem is to attack the kinds of knowledge and qualifications conventionally supposed relevant; this becomes an important tactic for many women writers whose qualifications, conventionally considered, appear dubious. In a preface to her biography of the Duke, she notes that she is "ignorant of the Rules of writing Histories" and reports that she had begged the Duke for "some Elegant and learned Historian to assist" her lest she produce a "defective" history. The Duke, however, refuses, implicitly authorizing her independent production of the book by replying, "That Truth could not be defective."[11] Attacking the kind of large-scale political history that she was not competent to write, she deprecates "tedious Moral Discourses, with long Observations upon the several sorts of Governement that have been," praises a more personal history, which she labels "Heroical," and proclaims *Caesar's Commentaries* her model.[12]

Cavendish makes a further argument about her entitlement to this subject matter that, with variations, might have been made by all the women writers of these Civil War memoirs: "Nor is it inconsistent with my being a Woman, to write of Wars, that was neither between the *Medes* and *Persians, Greeks* and *Trojans, Christians* and *Turks*; but among my own Countrymen, whose Customs and Inclinations, and most of the Persons that held any considerable Place in the Armies, was well known to me . . ." Moreover, she points out, her husband acted "a chief part in that fatal Tragedy," attempting to defend "his most Gracious Soveraign from the fury of his Rebellious Subjects."[13] None of the royalist women writers, including Cavendish, shows comprehension of the political issues that precipitated and sustained the war. For each of them, the side of their husband is the side of virtue, the opposition, frequently called the "Malignants," the embodiment of viciousness.

Cavendish's *Life* of her husband has, nevertheless, been valued by many generations of readers. C. H. Firth, in his Victorian edition, declared, "The special interest of the book lies . . . in the picture of the exiled royalist . . . never losing confidence in the ultimate triumph of the right . . . in the portrait drawn of a great English nobleman of the seventeenth century; his manners and his habits, his domestic policy . . . all are recorded and set down with the loving fidelity of a Boswell."[14] Cavendish offers a *Life* in four parts: first, the Duke's military service until his defeat at Marston Moor; second, a narrative of his time in exile; third, the post-Restoration struggle to repair his estate; fourth, the sayings of the Duke, most offered in the form of maxim-like utterances. In her account of the Duke's military exploits, Cavendish labors under two handicaps: womanly unfamiliarity with warfare and the fact that she was not even acquainted with the Duke until his later exile. To supply these deficiencies, she tells us, the Duke permitted her to use the assistance of John Rolleston, his secretary, an eye-witness of his master's deeds during the war. Despite Cavendish's frequent attacks on romance in other works, her narrative in this *Life* represents the Duke as the idealized hero of a romance, a great man of absolute virtue who may suffer misfortunes but who never commits a wrong or bad act. His military defeats she ascribes to bad underlings: "it is remarkable, that in all actions and undertakings where My Lord was in Person himself, he was always Victorious, and prospered in the execution of his designs; but whatsoever was lost or succeeded ill, happen'd in his absence, and was caused either by the Treachery, or Negligence and Carelessness of his Officers."[15] (It does not seem to occur to her that generals who have treacherous, negligent, and careless officers cannot be very good generals.)

Much of the charm of the *Life* is produced by realistically plausible details that make her picture of this seventeenth-century nobleman fuse with the image of the romance hero: brave, loyal, chivalric, and tender. When Newcastle's troops capture the wife of a parliamentary general and bring her to him, he treats her chivalrously "with all civility and respect," sending her to Kingston-upon-Hull in his own coach.[16] Cavendish stresses her husband's capacity to evoke devotion in lesser beings, human and animal. We are told how his special regiment of foot, the "White-coats," valiant, stout, and faithful, "ever ready to die at my Lord's feet," got their name: "My Lord being resolved to give them new Liveries, and there being not red Cloth enough to be had, took up so much of white as would serve to cloath them, desiring withal, their patience until he had got it dyed; but they impatient of stay, requested my Lord, that he would be pleased to let them have it un-dyed as it was, promising they themselves would dye it in the Enemies Blood; Which request my Lord granted them, and from that time they were called White-Coats."[17] In an age when noblemen fought on horseback, noblemen naturally enough took an interest in horses and riding, but this nobleman's relations with horses were exceptional. He made a special study of dressage and published a treatise on it that was translated into French. Describing her husband's relations with his favorite horses, Cavendish reports: "And certainly I have observed, and, do verily believe, that some of them also had a particular Love to my Lord; for they seemed to rejoice whensoever he came into the Stables, by their trampling action, and the noise they made . . . and when he rid them himself, they seemed to take much pleasure and pride in it."[18]

During his exile, Newcastle's aristocratic *sprezzatura* conjures credit and money from all sorts of people, even from the sober burgers of Antwerp. He has only £90 when he decamps for Hamburg and Parliament naturally sequesters his estates. Nevertheless, he and Margaret live for sixteen years in a style which seems to them degradation, but which permits him to collect expensive horses and to entertain visiting notables.

Cavendish defends the Duke's absconding after Marston Moor, aware that others had severely criticized this action. Clarendon, for instance, while crediting Newcastle with personal courage in many battles and a genuine love of monarchy, thought he attended insufficiently to the work of generalship and was shocked at his conduct after Marston Moor, especially since he still had "absolute commission over the northern counties and very many considerable places in them still remaining under his obedience." In Clarendon's view, the conduct of Prince Rupert and

Newcastle after Marston Moor contributed significantly to making that battle, unnecessarily, a "fatal blow" to royalist hopes.[19] Declining to engage such critiques directly, Cavendish defends her husband's choice: "and having nothing left in his power to do his Majesty any further service in that kind; for he had neither Ammunition, nor Money to raise more Forces, to keep either *York*, or any other Towns, that were yet in His Majesties Devotion, well knowing that those which were left could not hold out long, and being also loath to have aspersions cast upon him, that he did sell them to the Enemy, in Case he could not keep them; he took a Resolution, and that justly and honourably, to forsake the Kingdom . . ."[20]

CIVIL WAR BIOGRAPHIES: HUTCHINSON'S *LIFE OF COLONEL HUTCHINSON*

The Restoration of the King in 1660, greeted with joy by royalists like Cavendish, represented catastrophic defeat for loyal supporters of the interregnum Parliament's attack on courtly corruption in the name of the liberty of the people. Death warrants were issued against the fifty-nine men who had acted as Charles I's judges and signed his death warrant. Captured regicides were judged guilty of high treason, drawn and quartered, and their body parts were displayed in public places. As for the regicides who were already dead, including Oliver Cromwell and Henry Ireton, their bodies were disinterred and the heads were cut off to be exhibited at Westminster Hall, where they remained for at least twenty-four years.[21] John Bunyan, who had served humbly in the Parliamentary army as a young man, refused to cease his unlicensed preaching after the Restoration; like other recalcitrant dissenters, male and female, he was jailed under the provisions of the Clarendon code, in his case for twelve years. Milton, Latin Secretary of State to Cromwell, was lucky to escape with his life.

Because of its attack on traditional hierarchy and custom and because of its emphasis on the need for every believer to study scripture and take responsibility for the welfare of his or her own soul, Puritan and dissenting culture had special consequences for women. The Bible was the one great book women were encouraged to read and to study closely; it was a literary as well as a spiritual resource that helped to compensate for their exclusion from the formal study of Greek and Roman classics that constituted privileged men's literary education. Although beleaguered during the Restoration, Puritan and dissenting culture was not extinguished. Among the more radical dissenting sects, including the Quakers, women continued to preach and to prophesy. Margaret Fell was jailed twice, once from 1664 to 1668, and again from April 1670 to April 1671, for offences that included holding unlicensed religious meetings and speaking at those meetings. One bit of "evidence" frequently adduced to demonstrate the insanity of dissent was its willingness to listen to women preachers.

This dissenting culture is memorably evident in Lucy Hutchinson's *Life of Colonel Hutchinson*, her husband. Colonel John Hutchinson was an officer in Parliament's army, commander of the town and Castle of Nottingham, and one of the signers of Charles I's death warrant. Lucy Hutchinson's *Life* has consistently been valued for its detailed account of important events in the Civil War as well as for its striking portrait of a dedicated religious independent. James Sutherland remarked that her biography gives "memorable glimpses of what the war meant to the common man, who seldom appears in the pages of the histories."[22] Like the Duchess of Newcastle, Hutchinson is concerned to record the sacrifices her husband made for his country (if not for his King), but she does so less obsessively and clamorously. Unlike any of the royalist women, Hutchinson gives insight into the grievances that led to armed rebellion. She complains of Roman Catholic favorites at court, of "the treasure of the kingdom being wasted by court caterpillars," of the ship money tax, and of the King's proroguing his uncooperative Parliament.[23] She shares her husband's conviction of the righteousness of Parliament's cause and his grief at its defeat. For Hutchinson, the Restoration means the end of the reign of "that glorious Parliament . . . not so fatal to itself as to the three nations [England, Wales, Ireland], whose sunne of liberty then sett, and all their glorie gave place to the fowlest mists that ever overspread a miserable people."[24]

The Bible provides Hutchinson with models through which she attempts to make sense of seventeenth-century history, especially of the excruciating problem of God's apparently having allowed the revolution of his saints to be defeated. She is amazed and disgusted at the fickleness of so many people who, apparently loyal to Parliament, then in 1660 turn out into the streets to welcome back the King, "as eager for their owne destruction as the Izraelites of old were for their Quailes."[25] She thus tries to understand the apostasy of the English by recalling the dark days when Moses led the Israelites out of bondage in Egypt into the wilderness, only to hear them complain and become nostalgic for the food they ate in slavery. Although God has provided them with miraculous manna for their journey, they lust after flesh; God therefore promises them flesh "until it come out at your nostrils, and it be loathsome unto you: because that ye have despised the Lord . . . and have wept before him, saying, Why came we forth out of Egypt?" (Numbers 11: 20). God rains down quails, then, "while the flesh was yet between their teeth, a great plague."

The *Life* existed for so long as a manuscript because of political considerations, not because Hutchinson preferred manuscript to print. Given Hutchinson's opposition to the King and her husband's politics, as well as the extreme candor of her stringent evaluation of living people, she almost certainly did not write her *Life* for immediate publication. The revival of Licensing Acts in the Restoration inhibited the publication of anti-monarchical writing, and, in any case, the contents of this manuscript could have been prosecuted as seditious libel or possibly even used as evidence in a treason prosecution. The manuscript is addressed to her children to give them what she believes is a true picture of the deeds and virtues of their father (who died in prison in 1664) and to correct what she regards as the lies of received royalist historiography. The book seems to have been written between 1664 and 1671; it was not published until 1806. Yet her narrative shows the eagerness of this dissenting culture for a print record and its conviction that truth requires to be published and has power in the world. When Colonel Hutchinson is imprisoned in the Tower, apparently on suspicion of being privy to the Yorkshire plot, and harshly treated by the jailer, both he and his wife threaten to expose the jailor's cruelties and injustices by printing a narrative of them. The Colonel actually did print such a narrative.

The importance of print, of reading, and of study for Puritan men and women is illustrated by Hutchinson's account of how she developed doubts about the scriptural basis for infant baptism, or "pedobaptism." She notes that some papers on the subject, seized by the Presbyterians from an independent meeting, came into her husband's possession. Pregnant, she studies them urgently, finds the arguments against the custom convincing, and asks her husband to respond to her doubts. Conscientious and studious himself, despite the worries of his military responsibilities in the midst of a war, John reads upon the subject and develops his own doubts: "Then he bought and read all the eminent treatises on both sides, which came thick from the presses at that time . . ." Eager not unnecessarily to give offence, John then invites representative clergy to dinner, states his doubts, and asks for their rebuttals. When their statements do not convince him, husband and wife decide not to baptize their new infant; for their trouble, they are called "fanatick and anabaptists and often glanced at in the publick sermons."[26]

Hutchinson's narrative of her husband's life is more realistic and less influenced by romance than the narratives of royalist women, yet the Colonel emerges as the kind of male hero who later appears in women's novels. She recounts the domestic side of her hero's character, a side neglected in most biographies of political and military men. She does not allow this more importance than "the greater transactions of his life," but she attends to it carefully in the formal character she gives of him and in a set of small episodes that are uncannily proleptic of topoi in later women's fiction.[27] Among the Colonel's virtues are chastity and respect for women: "he despis'd nothing of the female sex but their follies and vanities: wise and vertuous weomen he lov'd, and delighted in all pure, holy, and unblamable conversation with them, but so as never to excite scandall or temptation."[28] She gives relatively short shrift to their early romance (courtships "are to be forgotten as the vanities of youth"), but does tell the reader that what first aroused John's interest in her were "a fewe Latine books . . . upon an odde by-shelfe" in a Richmond house where he was staying.[29] He is told that they belong to the absent Lucy and that she is "reserved and studious" – which the ladies "esteem'd no advantage" – but his heart is "enflamed" at the thought of the studious stranger. As a father, he gladly acts as tutor for his children and spares no expense "for the education of both his sons and daughters in languages, sciences, musick, dancing . . ."[30] Just as they are about to be married, Lucy gets smallpox, an event that caused crises in many actual romances of the period and in many later novels. Yet John "was nothing troubled at it," but married her as soon "as she was able to quit the chamber, when the priest and all that saw her were affrighted to look on her . . ."[31] Once they are married, "So liberall was he to her, and of so generous a temper, that he hated the mention of sever'd purses, his estate being so much at her dispose that he would never receive an account of anie thing she expended. So constant was he in his love that when she ceast to be young and lovely, he began to shew most fondnesse . . ."[32] N. H. Keeble has pointed out that Hutchinson represents her husband as having "precisely those accomplishments upon which the royalists prided themselves, which, indeed, they supposed distinguished their civility from the vulgarity of all rebels and such schismatics." He adds that Hutchinson herself appears "no more the ungovernably brash Puritan hussy of a royalist caricature than John Hutchinson the oafish artisan."[33]

Hutchinson's *Life* extends beyond the personal to consider public events of the war, including battles, administrative challenges to the interregnum government, and political struggles among the parliamentary factions. She shows what it was like to endure street-to-street fighting in a town and gives memorable images like that of a Cavalier winter retreat from Nottingham, leaving a trail of blood "which froze as it fell upon the snow."[34] Sometimes her account of the internecine bickering among the citizens of Nottingham and the machinations of her husband's local "enemies" while he is governing the Castle can be tedious, yet it demonstrates the pettiness and stiff-necked stubbornness that weakened the parliamentary side. Unlike Cavendish, who offers first-person narrative, Hutchinson uses third-person, referring to her husband as "the Collonell" or "the Governor" and to herself as "Mrs. Hutchinson" or "his wife"; she thus claims the objectivity of historical narrative. As the authoritative historian, writing from a republican perspective, she condemns the follies of Charles I, the ambitions of Cromwell, and the ludicrousness of Cromwell's Barebones Parliament. She combines a narrative based on her own experience with supplementary materials. For example, she acknowledges Thomas May's *History of the Parliament of England* (1647), an account sympathetic to the parliamentary side, although in some respects she criticizes May. Her faith in the ultimate righteousness of the cause does not flag, but she allows herself to be surprised by the complexity of historical events. For instance, describing a battle for Nottingham, she comments: "no one can believe but those that saw that day what a strange ebbe and flow of courage and cowardize there was in both parties that day."[35]

Hutchinson's accounts of Charles I's capture and execution and their consequences for the regicides are moving. After the King escaped from the army's custody and fled to the Isle of Wight, Colonel Hutchinson was part of a parliamentary commission sent to negotiate with him. Yet he could not agree with a proposed treaty, debated all night in Parliament, being convinced "that the King, after having been exasperated and vanquisht and captiv'd, would be restor'd to that power which was unconsistent with the liberty of the people, who for all their blood and treasure and misery would reape no fruite but a confirmation of bondage . . ."[36] The then-sitting members of Parliament nevertheless ratify the treaty, Hutchinson enters his protest in the House book, the army purges forty-one members, and then the treaty is rejected. Realizing the fragility of the revolution and the vulnerability of all the actors in this national crisis, the Colonel is reluctant to serve as one of the judges in Parliament's trial of the King for "leavying warre against the Parliament and people of England, for betreying the publick trust reposed in him, and for being an implacable enemie to the Commonwealth."[37] Yet, Hutchinson writes, her husband and the other appointed judges saw in the King "a disposition so bent to the ruine of all that had oppos'd him, and of all the righteous and just things they had contended for, that it was upon the conscience of many of them that if they did not execute justice upon him, God would require at their hands all the blood and desolation which should ensue by their suffering him to escape when God had brought him into their hands . . ." Praying intently over his decision, Colonel Hutchinson agrees to sign the King's death warrant.

Colonel Hutchinson's signing the death warrant made him a likely target of royalist revenge at the Restoration; his wife's effort to use her rhetorical skills to avert his fate constitutes one of the most complex episodes in her narrative. Usually, Hutchinson reports herself entirely in sympathy with her husband's politics and decisions, going at his command to conduct small negotiations; on several occasions, she adamantly resists overtures from royalist relatives of hers to cooperate with them. However, once he is expelled from Parliament shortly after the Restoration and ordered to turn himself in, she, dreading "that he was ambitious of being a publick sacrifice . . . herein only in her whole life, resolv'd to disobey him and to emproove all the affection he had to her for his safety, and prevail'd with him to retire; for she sayd she would not live to see him a prisoner."[38] Without his knowledge, she writes a petition to the Speaker of the House of Commons in his name, a petition acknowledging that he has been guilty of a horrid crime that deserves no indulgence, pleading that he had been "seduc'd" by the subtle arts of others, and throwing himself on the mercy of the King and the new Parliament.[39] Told by a friend that the House "was that day in a most excellent temper towards her husband," without consulting him, she signs his name to the petition and submits it.[40] To her relief, Parliament responds by voting only a light punishment for him, barring him from public office for the rest of his life. She does not record the Colonel's words to her about this forgery of his signature at one of the most fateful moments of his life, but it is clear from her subsequent account of his attitudes when he is imprisoned on suspicion of participation in a plot against Charles II that he felt guilty about avoiding punishment endured by his comrades.

Hutchinson's account of her husband's imprisonment at Sandown Castle in Kent vividly describes the miserable physical conditions of the room where she visited him and his spiritual euphoria at finally being firmly relegated to the ranks of the persecuted saints. With a housewife's attentiveness to the physical details of rooms, desperately trying to care for her ill husband under adverse conditions, she observes that one door of his room opens "upon a platforme that had nothing but the bleake ayre of the sea, which every tide washt the foote of the Castle walls; which ayre made the chamber so unwholsome and damp that even in the summer time the Colonel's hat-case and trunkes, and every thing of leather, would be every day all cover'd over with mould; wipe them as clean as you could one morning, by the next they would mouldie againe . . ."[41] He dies in prison as a Puritan martyr, calmly, piously, saying, "'Tis as I would have it. 'Tis where I would have it."[42]

A PURITAN POET IN NEW ENGLAND: ANNE BRADSTREET

Lucy Hutchinson's *Life of Colonel Hutchinson* powerfully represents the experiences and the mentalities of Puritans who remained in England during the interregnum, but many of the most serious and most religious dissenters had been among the 21,000 English people who had left England for New England in the 1630s.[43] Milton had lamented what he imagined as their forced exile in *Of Reformation Touching Church-Discipline in England* (1641): "what numbers of faithfull, and freeborn Englishmen, and good Christians have bin constrain'd to forsake their dearest home, their friends, and kindred, whom nothing but the wide Ocean, and the savage deserts of *America*, could hide and shelter from the fury of the Bishops."[44] Similarly, Hutchinson charged Charles I's government with so persecuting the Puritans "that many of them chose to abandon their native country and leave their dearest relations, to retire into any forraign soil or plantation where they might, admidst all outward inconveniences, enjoy the free exercise of God's worship."[45] Among these settlers was Anne Bradstreet, a poet of considerable originality and distinction, and even greater literary historical importance.

Bradstreet was seventeen when she sailed in 1630 from Southampton to Massachusetts in the company of her father, Thomas Dudley, and her husband, Simon Bradstreet, a graduate of Emmanuel College, Cambridge. Both her father and her husband were members of the Massachusetts Bay Company, beneficiaries of a royal charter giving the company title to Massachusetts land. Their company, like the Royal African Company or the East India Company, was a joint state/private enterprise designed to promote trade and development in colonial lands in ways that would advance the honor and revenues of the Crown and the fortunes of private investors. The Massachusetts Bay incorporators were, in addition, motivated by desires to get farther from what they, with Milton and Hutchinson, saw as "the fury of the Bishops," to plant the gospel in foreign lands, and to establish cities more remarkable for holiness than London. The Crown, for its part, was pleased to see educated men of substance like these incorporators take their subversive selves across an ocean. Anne Bradstreet's father had been steward to the Earl of Lincoln; the Earl had been incarcerated in the Tower in 1627 for refusing to subscribe to what he considered an illegitimate Crown demand for a loan. Anne and many of this circle were also admirers of the Reverend John Cotton, who preached a farewell sermon to them at Southampton, "God's Promise to his Plantation," taking as his text 2 Samuel 7: 10: "Moreover I will appoint a place for my people Israel, and will plant them, that they may dwell in a place of their own, and move no more; neither shall the children of wickedness aflict them any more, as beforetime." Concerned about the religious purity of their settlement, unlike the incorporators of other chartered companies, the Massachusetts men bound themselves to inhabit their colony, avoiding rule by London directors. Ultimately, they hoped, their colony would be much more than a temporary refuge for them and a good investment: it would be a "Beacon set upon a Hill," an agent of redemption for an England mired in sin and in grave danger of reversion to Roman Catholicism.

The motives prompting the publication of Bradstreet's volumes of poems and the reasons given for engaging in such a virtually unprecedented practice as the publication of an eclectic volume of poems by a woman are worth considering. They reveal ideas and practices that recur frequently in the publication of women's poetry later in this period. First, it should be understood that most poetry in the seventeenth century was written for private manuscript circulation. Thus, Barbara Keifer Lewalski can describe the Jacobean Countess of Bedford, Lucy Harrington Russell, as a poet of the court coterie, "an amateur talented enough to produce verses on appropriate occasions and exchange them with her circle."[46] Sometimes, indeed, poems were written for the eyes of no one other than the poet. Noblemen and noblewomen almost invariably considered publication unnecessary and vulgar. Educated religious men and women often wrote poems as part of their private devotional exercises. Bradstreet's poetic contemporary in Massachusetts, Edward Taylor, did not seek publication of his religious poems, which remained unknown until the discovery of a manuscript in the twentieth century.

According to contemporary testimony, Bradstreet did not make the decision to publish her poems; John Woodbridge, her brother-in-law, very likely in consultation with Bradstreet's father and husband, did. He presents himself in the preliminary matter to the volume as an admirer, a facilitator, and a sober gentlemen whose testimony about the woman author will be important. Woodbridge attempts to squelch whatever suspicions the reader might have about whether the text could have been written by a woman and testifies to Bradstreet's good character as a woman. Finally, in a variant on one of the most conventional excuses for printing poems offered by seventeenth-century writers, he confides: "I fear the displeasure of no person in the publishing of these Poems, but the Author, without whose knowledg . . . I have presumed to bring to publick view, what she resolved in such a manner should never see the Sun; but I found that diverse had gotten some scattered Papers, affected them well, were likely to have sent forth broken pieces, to the Authors prejudice, which I thought to prevent . . ."[47] Whether this excuse was substantially true or not, Bradstreet's male relatives almost certainly had additional motives for conspiring to have her poems published.

Like other forms of colonial advertising designed to attract settlers by reassuring them about the possibilities for decent lives in various barbaric wildernesses, the publication of Bradstreet's *The Tenth Muse, Lately Sprung up in America* (London, 1650) and *Several Poems: Compiled with a great Variety of Wit and Learning* (Boston, 1678) was designed to demonstrate to English and colonial reading publics that civilization had been established in New England. Bradstreet's male relatives who decided to publish the volumes were important representatives of the colony, active not only in its governance but as lobbyists on its behalf. Furthermore, there is an implicit suggestion that Bradstreet's poems are evidence that New England has created a spiritually and morally better society than that of Old England. We will see this use of a "woman of ours" by men to boast of their civilization's outdoing a rival frequently later in this period, although later the more typical antithesis is not New England versus Old England but England versus France. In explaining the printing of these volumes, weight may also be given to the unusual interest Puritans and other unhappy Protestants had in establishing a print record of their sufferings and accomplishments, an interest Bradstreet shared.

Bradstreet's poems show remarkable range and intellectual ambition. In a late Renaissance tradition, the poet offers four quaternions in iambic pentameter couplets: "The Four Ages of Man," "The Four Elements," "The Four Seasons," and "The Four Monarchies." Bookish poems that reveal her reading in the natural sciences and history as well as theology, they also show the poetic influence of Phinias Fletcher's *The Purple Island* (1633) and, most importantly, of the French Protestant poet, Guillaume Du Bartas (1544–90), whose work she knew in Joshua Sylvester's English translation, *Bartas: His Devine Weekes and Workes* (1605) and whose genius she celebrated in a poem, "In honour of *Du Bartas, 1641.*" Many of the same poems appear in both *The Tenth Muse* and *Several Poems.* The quaternions were in both volumes, but thirteen poems said to have been "found amongst her papers after her Death," appeared in the 1678 volume for the first time.

One of Bradstreet's longer and particularly original poems, appearing in different versions in the different volumes, "A Dialogue between Old *England* and New, concerning their present troubles. Anno 1642," demonstrates her involvement in the cultural and spiritual rivalry between the colony and the metropole. The poem takes the form of a dialogue between a confident and inquisitive New England and a despondent, sighing Old England, addressed by her "Daughter" as "dear Mother." Old England acknowledges that her "Saints," the Puritans, have been scorned and "jeer'd." Even what Bradstreet saw as their heroic exile, their "flying for the truth" from a land soiled by "Sabbath-breaking" and "drunkenness," has been turned into "a jest" by the citizens of the jaded metropole. Old England "mockt the Preachers," yet now, she is forced to confess:

> The Sermons yet upon Record do stand
> That cri'd destruction to my wicked land:
> I then believ'd not, now I feel and see,
> The plague of stubborn incredulity.[48]

Unlike royalist women writing biography or memoirs of this period, but like Hutchinson, Bradstreet demonstrates awareness of the political issues in the Civil War, including complaints about the slowness of justice, the abuses of the Star Chamber and the Court of High Commission, the debate over royal prerogative, and the clash between royalist insistence on the ultimate authority of the King in the state versus parliamentary claims for the sovereignty of law. In the dialogue, Old England's woes during the fratricidal fighting of the war reduce her to pleading for pity and help from her daughter.

New England concludes the poem with cheerful prophecies of Protestant triumph, first in England where the Popish vestments of the High Church party, "*Baals* vestments," will be tossed onto a raging bonfire and justice restored through the leadership of noblemen like the Earl of Essex. Then a united and militant English Protestantism will march forth to sack Rome, citadel of the beast, even to Turkey, to triumph over Islam so as to produce a universal reign of holiness and Protestantism. Bradstreet's vision of the Protestant sack of Rome seems equally indebted to Edmund

Spenser and to the Book of Revelations, both important influences on her work:

> Bring forth the Beast that rul'd the world with's beck,
> And tear his flesh, & set your feet on's neck,
> And make his filthy Den so desolate,
> To th' stonishment of all that knew his state . . .[49]

The new poems published in *Select Poems* of 1678 are more "womanly" than the quaternions of the 1650 volume; most are at once less intellectually ambitious and more technically successful. In different tonalities, from grave to light, they offer a speaker who is clearly a loving wife, mother, and grandmother engaging the events of a woman's life: the temporary absence of a husband, the anticipation of childbirth, and the early deaths of children. All of these become important subjects for women's poetry. Among the most effective and moving is "Before the Birth of one of her Children," in twenty-eight lines of iambic pentameter couplets. Addressed to her husband, the poem offers a fine combination of dignity and intimacy. While the modern reader might expect a poem on such an occasion to be full of joyful anticipation, a seventeenth-century reader living in a world of high maternal mortality in childbirth as well as of high infant mortality would be less startled by the gravity with which the woman speaker, addressing her beloved husband, confronts the prospect of her own death in childbirth:

> How soon, my Dear, death may my steps attend,
> How soon't may be thy Lot to lose thy friend,
> We are both ignorant, yet love bids me
> These farewell lines to recommend to thee . . .[50]

The euphoric religious hope of the speaker in "Before the Birth of one of her Children" for a better, more joyous life for herself in heaven mingles with, but does not annihilate, her sadness and tenderness at the thought of a beloved husband left behind alone or her worry over the fate of children she could leave behind in the world:

> And when thou feel'st no grief, as I no harms,
> Yet love thy dead, who long lay in thine arms:
> And when thy loss shall be repaid with gains
> Look to my little babes my dear remains.
> And if thou in thy self, or loved'st me
> These O protect from step Dames injury.[51]

Bradstreet is strongly conscious of possessing a spiritual self that, however happily bound to a husband or a community, nevertheless has its own independent, more durable existence. Some of the euphoria she attaches to the idea of a heavenly existence after death seems to result from the relief of being "unbound" from others and more able to experience that sole self. The euphoria attached to escaping into heaven is also motivated by the hardships of early New England life, hinted at elsewhere in her poems.

As late as 1661, when she wrote a poem "Upon my dear and loving husband his goeing into England" (as a representative of the colony to persuade Charles II to renew the Company's colonial charter), alert as she is to the perils her husband faces on the Atlantic, Bradstreet still sees Massachusetts as a "Wilderness" requiring prayer that the sacrifices of its inhabitants in a harsh land have not been in vain:

> Remember Lord thy folk whom thou
> To Wildernesse ha'st brought
> Let not thine own Inheritance
> Bee sold away for Nought.[52]

"Contemplations," appearing for the first time in the 1678 volume, shows more attachment to the "delectable" sights of a rocky, brightly colored autumnal New England landscape. This is an accomplished long poem in a modified Spenserian stanza. The speaker's consciousness moves back and forth between the landscape, the Old Testament story of Adam and Eve and the life their children lived after exile from Paradise, and the realm of immortality. The poet seems compelled to compare elements of the worldly landscape with one another, anxiously querying which is the most excellent, and to try to judge between elements of nature and human life. Despite humankind's putatively noble birth, the ageless rocks seem to surpass aging humankind. Yet, the poet reminds herself, trees and even rocks and earth "shall darken, perish, fade and dye":

> And when unmade, so ever shall they lye,
> But man was made for endless immortality.[53]

She moves quickly from enjoyment of the music made by grasshoppers and "black clad" crickets who seem "to glory in their little Art," to distress that such "abject" creatures seem to praise their maker more efficaciously than she. The river – probably the Merrimack, which runs to the Atlantic near her home north of Boston – channels many brooks into a straight rush to the ocean, becoming an emblem of righteous longing for eternity. "Contemplations" ultimately and formally insists on the superiority of the immortal to the mortal. Yet the poem does not entirely repress the poet's love of New England nature, here actually "merry," in sharp contrast to the "sad thoughts" and "cruciating cares" of Calvinist humanity. Bradstreet's poems show her immersion in Protestant English poetic and learned traditions, but they also lay a foundation for the articulation of a new, distinctive, American consciousness.

KATHERINE PHILIPS'S *POEMS*

Engagement in the tumultuous and significant events of the seventeenth century prompted Cavendish and Hutchinson to narrate those events and to defend their husbands' roles in them, yet the complexities and dangers of public events in this period also inspired withdrawals into literal exile like that of the Bradstreets and other, "internal exiles," withdrawals from public life into what people hoped would be principled and secure rural retirement. The classical tradition provided models for such disengagement in Stoicism and in the *beatus vir* tradition, of which a favorite *locus classicus* was Horace's second epode celebrating the "happy man" (*beatus vir*), not a soldier or a politician, who peacefully cultivates and feasts upon the produce of his ancestral acres.[54] After the Restoration, when it became clear there would be no high office or place at court for the Duke of Newcastle, the Cavendishes repaired to their country house in Northumberland, where the Duchess spent her time reading and writing. Although Cavendish defended her retirement and praised its "sweet Pleasures and harmless Delights," the humble pleasures of the countryside never satisfied her. She chaffed with a sense that she had talents fit for public service that the world refused to employ. Her reading of history prompted in her "an Envy, or rather an Emulation towards Men, for their Courage, Prudence, Wit and Eloquence, as not to Fear Death, to rule Commonwealths and to Speak in a Friends' behalf . . ."[55] Envying Julius Caesar, as she confessed she did, and reading and writing about Plutarch's *Noble Romans*, Cavendish used her published texts, especially the *Orations*, as spaces in which she could attempt to demonstrate at least some of the male capacities she admired.

Katherine Philips less ambivalently celebrated the advantages of rural retirement in her posthumously published *Poems by the Most Deservedly Admired Mrs. Katherine Philips, the Matchless Orinda* (1667). This volume was rightly praised by contemporaries and continued to inspire other women writers long after Philips's early death from smallpox at the age of thirty-three in 1664. The daughter of a London merchant who supported the parliamentary side in the Civil War, Philips at sixteen had married a Welshman, who, like Hutchinson's husband, was an officer in the parliamentary army and a member of the interregnum Parliament. Despite this family background, Philips's own sympathies were decidedly royalist. In her literary career she cultivated connections with royalist poets and dramatists, notably Henry Vaughan and Roger Boyle; the royalist composer Henry Lawes set four of her songs to music. Like Bradstreet's, Philips's volume contains elegies on the deaths of children. Unlike Bradstreet's, it includes royalist panegyric and a few public poems like "Arion on a Dolphin to his Majestie in his passadge into England," praising the peaceableness and mercy of the restored Charles II.

Philips adopted the romance pseudonym of Orinda in the *Poems* to create a persona principally concerned to celebrate female friendship, love, and the virtues of rural retirement. Several of her literary friends engaged themselves in translating French romances, which served to keep courtly ideals alive while the royalists were out of power.[56] She associates her rural retirement with purity and "innocence," a favorite word. Although Philips knew the mid-century Anglican poetry of Vaughan and Thomas Traherne in which classical *beatus vir* ideas had been conflated with Christian ideas of the Edenic *hortus conclusus* and Neoplatonic mysticism, her own poetry was more secular. She does not discern the presence of God in her rural settings or praise a solitary retirement; instead, she inaugurates a newer ideal of a less religious, more sociable country life that was to have a powerful appeal throughout the Restoration and the eighteenth century. Rejecting the corruption of courts and the destructive tempests of the political world, Orinda seeks an aloofness from worldly affairs like that of the Lucretian gods, finding contentment in the pleasures of her garden, and still more pleasure in carefully selected and cultivated friendships. Contemporaries admired Philips's poems for their vision of an "innocent" world untainted by ambition, faction, duplicity, and greed, qualities all too depressingly evident in the early years of the Restoration, despite royalists' hopes for their counterrevolution.

Contemporaries also admired the purity and dignity of Philips's language. Although Philips praised Abraham Cowley and was influenced by him, she generally avoided attempts at metaphysical wit, achieving a plainer, more modern style closer to Edmund Waller's. Like other Cavalier poets, she is particularly good with short lines, often favoring iambic tetrameter, sometimes alternating with iambic trimeter. The brevity of the lines and the straightforward simplicity of the diction mirror the simplicity she celebrates. "A Country-life," for example, opens:

> How Sacred and how Innocent
>   A Country-life appears,
> How free from Tumult, Discontent,
>   From Flatterye or Fears . . .

The quiet and safety of her country life are contrasted to the tumult and catastrophe (including war and the execution of Charles I) that characterize the public world:

> I have a better Fate then Kings,
>   Because I think it so.
> When all the stormy World doth roar
>   How unconcern'd am I?
> I cannot fear to tumble lower
>   Who never could be high.[57]

The retreat to which she invites her friend in "A Retir'd Friendship. To Ardelia" is characterized by absences:

> Here is no quarrelling for Crowns,
>   No fear of Changes in our Fate;
> No trembling at the great ones frowns,
>   Nor any slavery of State.
>
> Here's no disguise nor treachery,
>   Nor any deep conceal'd design;
> From Bloud and Plots this Place is free,
>   And calm as are those looks of thine.[58]

Whether a nobleman or a gentleman could legitimately enjoy such retreat from responsibility for public affairs was debated in the Restoration by writers like John Evelyn, who shared some of Philips's views. A woman, however, did not have responsibility for governance, and thus was nicely suited to develop a more guiltless ideal. This disdain for public life as corrupt and the celebration of private retirement as virtuous is developed by some later women writers into a contrast between masculine corruption and feminine virtue. Also, beginning about the time of Thomas Gray, the normative stance of the male poet ceases to be that of the man engaged in public affairs, including politics, and becomes something closer to Philips's alienation from them.

Philips was also celebrated as a poet of friendship, a major subject of Cavalier poetry, and, subsequently, a crucial subject for women writers. During the interregnum, Earl Miner argued, "the rites of Cavalier friendship preserved the Constitution until it was once again the friends' turn to occupy the posts of church and state."[59] Miner thought of Philips's poems on friendship as having a "Platonic" purity and as differing from the masculine line of Cavalier poetry "in her austerity" and in that, for her, "making Love" concerns the soul alone.[60]

Recent feminist criticism has been especially interested in Philips's poems on women's friendship. A number of these poems, especially those addressed to "Lucasia," are passionate declarations of love. One of Philips's principal motives for writing seems to have been to declare her love in poems which were, in the first instance, presented in manuscript to the addressee, and very likely, at least initially, intended for limited circulation within her circle of friends. One of the most deservedly famous, "To My Excellent Lucasia, on our Friendship," begins rapturously:

> I did not live until this time
>   Crown'd my felicity,
> When I could say without a crime,
>   I am not thine, but Thee.[61]

Unlike marriage, idealized female friendship offered the possibility of an egalitarian human relationship for women.[62] Moreover, since most contemporaries doubted that women had the capacity for disinterestedness required by friendship, to celebrate female friendship was to claim that a woman could display the noble disinterest traditionally ascribed only to male friends. Boldly, then, Philips in "A Friend" insists:

> If Soules no Sexes have, for Men t'exclude
>   Women from Friendship's vast capacity,
> Is a Design injurious or rude,
>   Onley maintain'd by partial tyranny.
> Love is allow'd to us, and Innocence,
>   And noblest Friendships doe proceed from thence.[63]

Contemporaries treated friendship as a challenging subject of moral philosophy and Philips participated in that discourse. Francis Finch addressed his treatise, *Friendship* (1653) to "O noble Lucasia-Orinda," and the important Anglican divine, Jeremy Taylor, also addressed his *Discourse of the Nature, Offices and Measures of Friendship, with Rules of Conducting it. Written in Answer to a Letter from the Most Ingenious and Vertuous M. K. P.* (1657) to her. "A Friend" inventories the range of virtues required for friendship, not only disinterest, but also love, honor, sympathy, trustworthiness, the capacity to keep secrets (a capacity women were dramatically supposed to lack), wisdom, candor, and generosity.

Poems explores a range of conundrums posed by friendship. The Neoplatonism of the poems, for instance, produces an intriguing tension in the volume, as the poet repeatedly addresses the question of whether it makes any difference whether or not friends are physically present to one another. "A Dialogue of Friendship Multiplied" explores the question of whether friendship is necessarily exclusive to two people or whether it can admit more sharers.

"To my Lucasia, in defence of declared Friendship" seems to respond to Lucasia's protestations that Orinda's declarations were not desirable, arguing, in a poem that gets more metaphysical than most:

> Although we know we love, yet while our Soul
>   Is thus imprison'd by the Flesh we wear,
> There's no way left that bondage to controul,
>   But to convey transactions through the Ear.
>
> Nay, though we read our passions in the Eye,
>   It will oblige and please to tell them too:
> Such joys as these by motion multiply,
>   Were't but to find that our Souls told us true.

Looks from the beloved refresh:

> But when that Look is dress'd in Words, 'tis like
>   The mystique pow'r of Musick's Union;
> When the finger doth one Viol strike,
>   The other's string heaves to reflection.[64]

As one would expect in this Neoplatonic tradition (two of the Neoplatonist Henry More's poems got mixed into the first edition of her *Poems*), Philips's emphasis is on the contact, and even the intermingling, of the lovers' souls.

Recently, critics have heatedly debated whether Philips's poems like those to Lucasia can accurately be called lesbian. Arlene Stiebel, for example, has complained that most readings deny Philips's "lesbian sexuality and feeling," turning them into "sterile intellectual bonding."[65] She rightly points out that more than half of the collected *Poems* deal with Orinda's love for other women and that Philips adapts courtly love stances of male speakers to their mistresses to her recognizably female speaker addressing women. Philips's spirituality and her invocation of the "innocence" of her love Stiebel regards as strategic rhetorical moves, justifications for "such language of excess." Recognizing that contemporaries were not shocked by Philips's poems and that she was widely celebrated as a virtuous woman, Stiebel argues that she was nevertheless a lesbian and that lesbian declarations could not be heard in "a phallocentric culture that defines sexual behavior according to penile instrumentality; [in such a culture] sex exclusive of men is not merely unthinkable, it is impossible."[66] In a more recent, more historically nuanced book, Elizabeth Susan Wahl argues that Renaissance romance idealized adolescent female homoerotic attachments, but then, using the marriage plot, redirected those desires to men. What was different in Philips's representations, Wahl says, was that Orinda persists in courting women after her own marriage and theirs.

A major source of drama in *Poems* is that rapturous celebrations of union between female friends are followed by other poems, like "Injuria amici" or "To the Queen of inconstancy, Regina, in Antwerp," bitterly reproaching a once-loved friend who has betrayed the speaker's love and grieving the loss of a friend once beloved. Throughout the volume, there is tension between Philips's philosophical celebrations of friendship as perfect equality and union and her courtly love rhetoric, with its figures of conquest and submission. Wahl is right to say that marriage figures as a threat to female friendship and that the variety of relationships figured in *Poems* offers a conception of female friendship that has great social and psychological complexity.

We do not know, nor are likely ever to know, what personal sexual relations Philips had. To deprecate intellectual and spiritual passions as "sterile" or somehow less "intense" than physical passions, as Stiebel does, also seems to me not only an historical but also a human mistake, one of those Freudian legacies of which feminists especially ought to be wary. Discussing related debates in Renaissance studies, Deborah Shugar has usefully cautioned that erotic desire and sexual desire are not necessarily identical and that "In any culture where erotic longing provides the central metaphor for spirituality, desire cannot be equivalent to sexuality."[67] But since the *Poems* are both passionate and beautiful declarations of a woman's love for other women, they will have special value for women readers whose most passionate attachments are to women.

PHILIPS'S *POMPEY* ON THE PUBLIC STAGE

Philips engages more public subject matter in her verse translation of Pierre Corneille's *Le Mort de Pompée* (1643) as *Pompey, A Tragœdy*, the first play by a woman to be performed on the British public stage. *Pompey* premiered at the Smock Alley Theatre Dublin in February 1662/3 and subsequently was probably also performed in London; it was published in both Dublin and London. It was the public success of *Pompey* that prompted Richard Marriott's unauthorized publication of the first edition of Philips's *Poems* in 1664.[68] *Le Mort de Pompée* is a very original, disturbing play focusing on a moment in Roman history in 48 BC. Republican Rome, weakened by civil war and the ambitions of military leaders for foreign conquest, was about to be overcome by Caesar's tyranny. Given the play's articulations of republican ideology and the extent to which it is an elegy for the virtues of republicanism, at a time in the early Restoration when republicanism and civil war were exquisitely sensitive subjects, it is surprising that the government permitted Philips's faithful translation to be performed. The politics of the play were perhaps obscured by its being a Roman history play that adhered reasonably closely to the story offered by classical historians, a work of the admired (and not republican) Corneille, and by the fact that its patrons were powerfully placed aristocrats.

Literary translation in the Restoration could be a competitive art. Philips boldly elected to translate Corneille's rhymed alexandrines in heroic couplets. She knew she was competing with a distinguished group of London wits – Sir Edward Filmer, Sir Sidney Godolphin, Charles Sackville, Sir Charles Sedley, and Edmund Waller – who were collaborating on their own translation of *Le Mort de Pompée*, one produced after hers in London in December 1663. Philips offered a generally accurate translation, surprisingly close to Corneille's language, creating a reasonable English equivalent of his style.[69] Her project was encouraged, while she was in Dublin, by James Bulter, Lord Ormonde, Lord Lieutenant of Ireland; Roger Boyle, Lord Orrery, whose own first heroic drama, *The General*, also premiered in Dublin in 1662; the Countess of Cork; and Wentworth Dillon, Lord Roscommen, later honored by Dryden's poem in praise of his verse "Essay on Translated Verse" (1684). These luminaries seem to have been interested in Corneille's verse, in heroic drama, and in demonstrating that Dublin could produce serious art.

Throughout *Pompey* Egyptian monarchical principles confront Roman republican values. Defeated by Julius Caesar at Pharsalia in Greece, Pompey seeks refuge in Egypt with the young King Ptolomy, whose throne he had earlier helped to secure against popular revolt. Heeding the counsel of Machiavellian advisors and his own timorousness, Ptolomy orders that Pompey be assassinated; he hopes that Caesar will be grateful. Corneille daringly pushes the decorums of neoclassical French drama to their limits: Pompey never appears on stage alive. His death is narrated in

a long *récit* and his widow Cornelia, the clearest advocate of the republican point of view, brings his ashes on stage in an urn. In a world of
treachery and complex dissimulation, Cornelia alone seems to possess
heroic virtue. Captive, she nevertheless boldly tells Caesar of her contempt
for his violations of Roman law and scorns the Egyptians for their
acceptance of Caesar as ruler. She vows to stir up her sons to avenge
Pompey's death and demands to leave Egypt:

> This fatal shoare nothing does me present,
> But th' Image of their horrible Attempt,
> And thy new Conquest, with the giddy noise
> Of People who in change of Kings rejoyce . . .[70]

   The other, more immediately powerful characters are more ambiguous
and make the possession of political power seem disturbing. Cleopatra,
Ptolomy's sister, hopes that Caesar will restore her to her share of the
Egyptian throne; she loves Caesar but knows that republican Rome scorns
queens, especially foreign queens. A monarchist, she tells Caesar:

> And I would hope, that such a Man as you,
> May justly *Rome's* Capriciousness subdue,
> And her unjust aversion for a Throne
> She might see cause, for your sake, to disown . . .[71]

Caesar, ambivalently drawn both to Roman ideals and to personal ag-
grandizement, replies that as soon as he completes his conquest of Africa:

> [*Rome*] will be forc'd to study Complaisance:
> And you shall see her with a solemn State,
> At your Feet sacrifice her Pride and Hate . . .[72]

Brought up in a Puritan household, Philips knew how strong the Puritan
hostility to Charles I's French Catholic queen had been and knew that
Charles II had in May 1661 proclaimed to Parliament his marriage to a
Portuguese Catholic, Catherine of Braganza.

   Philips attempted to follow her success with *Pompey* with another verse
translation of Corneille, *Horace*, although she died before she could
translate the fifth act or revise. Sir John Denham completed her *Horace*
and it was also performed and printed. Philips's translations having
opened the way, in 1669 Frances Boothby became the first woman to
have an original play produced on the British public stage: *Marcella, or the
Treacherous Friend*, a double-plotted tragicomedy. In the upper plot, the
heroine escapes from a lecherous king to marry her true love; in the comic
plot, a canny widow outwits a fop.

ROWLANDSON'S *CAPTIVITY*

The extent to which women's narratives of their own experience in this period could have value both for the individual woman and for the particular community – or faction – of which she was a part is dramatically evident in Mary White Rowlandson's *True History of the Captivity and Restoration of Mrs. Mary Rowlandson* (1682). Rowlandson, born in Somerset, England about 1636, was the wife of the Reverend Joseph Rowlandson, a clergyman serving in Lancaster, in central Massachusetts. In 1676, during the war between the Nipmucs, Narragansetts, and Wampanoag and the English settlers known as King Philip's (or Metacom's) War, the Native Americans attacked Lancaster, killing many of the inhabitants and taking captive others, including Mary Rowlandson and three of her children. (New England indigenous peoples regularly took captives, accepting ransom for some, adopting others into their own families, and using many to perform forced labor.) Rowlandson was with the Narragansetts for eleven weeks and five days, made to walk about 150 miles, west to the Connecticut River, north into New Hampshire, and then back to central Massachusetts, where she was ransomed by her husband, using £20 supplied by "some *Boston* gentlewomen and M. *Usher*."[73]

Rowlandson's exciting and anguished narrative of her adventure was published with the approbation of her male relatives and friends, indeed, apparently at their initiative. According to what seems a reliable "Preface" by a male writer signing himself "*Per Amicum*," Rowlandson originally conceived the narrative as "a *Memorandum* of God's dealing with her," that she might always remember his mercies, but her friends decided to get it published, judging that it was "worthy of publick view" and that it was "altogether unmeet that such works of God should be hid from present and future Generations."[74] In her own text, Rowlandson cites the Psalmist as justification, declaring her purpose to be the same as his: "To declare the works of the Lord, and his wonderful power in carrying us along, preserving us in the Wilderness, while under the Enemies hand, and returning of us in safety again . . ."[75]

Rowlandson's *Captivity and Restoration* was the first long Indian captivity narrative; it initiated an important genre for defining American identity. Nancy Armstrong and Leonard Tennenhouse argue that Rowlandson's narrative demonstrated how, independently of social rank, gender or wealth, an individual could "acquire value simply because she was a source of writing." Indeed, Armstrong and Tennenhouse have gone so far as to claim that Rowlandson's narrative "converts a form of literacy based on the print vernacular into a new basis for English identity" and that, in textualizing "qualities of mind that resist illegitimate forms of domination," she suggests a paradigm for later novels like Samuel Richardson's *Pamela* (1740, 1742).[76] *The Captivity and Restoration* became one of the most popular books of the period in both the colonies and England; in addition to abridged versions of the story, by the end of the eighteenth century almost thirty editions of the complete narrative had appeared.[77]

Rowlandson cast her lurid adventures in the form of Puritan spiritual autobiography. Her account of Native American savagery provided documentation of the "need" for English conquest and helped to justify the colonial project of subduing or exterminating the indigenous peoples of New England. The winter landscape of colonial Massachusetts through which she is forced to walk appears to her a vast and howling wilderness in which only Native Americans, figured as black devils, could be at home. She necessarily observes many of their survival skills and even imitates some of them in the interest of her own survival. Yet she sees their knowledge of the environment without admiration, instead wondering at her own capacity to descend to acts of apparent savagery, a capacity that reminds her anew of her own sinful nature. She tells how they kill with guns, spears, and hatchets, how they display English scalps, and how one of the "Praying Indians," supposedly converted to Christianity, nevertheless is "so wicked and cruel, as to wear a string about his neck strung with *Christian* fingers."[78] Their cruelties to her include laughing at her weakness, forcing her to leave behind one child who dies in her arms, and tormenting her with (lying) tales of how another child has been roasted and eaten. That the Native Americans were prepared to commit acts of war against women and children was offered by the Puritans as evidence of their barbarism, even of their demonism. That an English wife and mother, a mere woman, could survive despite their cruelties and, more importantly, use the experience to deepen her own Christian convictions, seemed evidence of the great superiority of English civilization. Rowlandson dreads that Native American men will assault her sexually; when none of them attempts any such thing, she constructs their behavior toward her as an exceptionalist intervention of providence on behalf of the righteous.

Rowlandson's ability to find coherent form and meaning for her almost unimaginably strange adventures is a triumph of biblical hermeneutics. She structures her narrative in nineteen "removes," each encampment the Native Americans make seeming yet another "remove" or distancing from

Christian civilization. Her knowledge of scripture and her habits of spiritual meditation enable her to see likenesses between her present sufferings – almost so extraordinary as to be culturally unimaginable – and the sufferings of biblical characters. The overwhelming majority of her scriptural references are to the Old Testament, unsurprisingly, since the Puritans often cast themselves as God's chosen Israel and their enemies as Philistines or Canaanites. The Old Testament often represents Israelites in captivity and understands captivity as a test of faith or as a punishment for having fallen away from the Lord; Rowlandson thinks of Samson amidst the Philistines, Joseph as a slave in Egypt, and Daniel in the lion's den during the Babylonian captivity as proleptic of her own captivity. A "Sqaw" she meets looks like a scornful caricature of something between Milton's Philistine Delilah and a Restoration court lady: "A severe and proud Dame she was, bestowing every day in dressing herself near as much time as any of the Gentry of the land: powdering her hair and painting her face, going with her Neck-laces, with Jewels in her ears, and bracelets upon her hands; When she had dressed herself, her Work was to make Girdles of Wampom and Beads."[79] As for Bradstreet, for Rowlandson the material sights and sounds of the new colonial world are made to function as types of things already known.

Under the harsh conditions of a forced march through the winter woods, the existence and significance of food naturally attracts much of Rowlandson's attention. In order not to starve, she has to eat many things she had not previously considered acceptable food, including ground nuts (*apios americana*, also known as the Indian potato), stale and moldy crumbs of Indian cake, half-cooked horse liver, and broth from horse hooves. One day, one of her captors gives her a piece of bear; she hides it in her "stinking pocket" for a day and a night until she can find a kettle to boil it in, and then is surprised to find it "pleasant" – "now that was savoury to me that one would think was enough to turn the stomach of a bruit-Creature."[80] So "Wolvish" is her appetite, that when offered food from the fire, she eats it so quickly that she burns her mouth painfully – "yet I should quickly do the same again."[81] She knows that some of the colonists thought that if they destroyed the Native Americans' cornfields, they would die of hunger. She comes to marvel at how the Native Americans can nevertheless survive on food "that a Hog or a Dog would hardly touch," on bark, acorns, lilly-roots, "and several other weeds and roots that I know not," on beavers, squirrels, skunks, and rattlesnakes, even on old bones filled with worms and maggots: "they would scald them over the fire to make the vermine come out; and then boyle them, and drink up the Liquor, and then beat the great ends of them [the bones] in a Morter, and so eat them."[82]

What some readers might experience as a challenging adventure and others as a series of horrors is for Rowlandson a summons to discern the will of a benevolent God toward his elect. Appalled at her hunger and her appetites, she is eager to denounce the heathen, yet scripture teaches her that God must be the ultimate author both of her sufferings and of the heathen's survival. She thinks of the words of the prophets, Amos and Michah: "Amos iii. 6, *Shall there be evil in the City and the Lord hath not done it? . . .* Mich. vi . . . 9 . . . *Hear ye the rod, and who hath appointed it.*"[83] To Rowlandson, what she witnesses is not the skill of the Native Americans, but the hand of God, who miraculously provides "for such a vast number of our Enemies in the Wilderness, where there was nothing to be seen but from hand to mouth," in order to chastise the waywardness and imperfections of his Puritan settlers.[84] She thinks of Psalm 81, which recalls the captivity of Israel in Egypt, and in which God laments that if his people had obeyed him, then he would have vanquished their enemies. But, Rowlandson writes, now God's people have so offended Him, that instead of vanquishing their enemies, perhaps miraculously, in the midst of this harsh wilderness, "the Lord feeds and nourishes them up to be a scourge to the whole land."[85] Often written in the first person and providing a narrative of captivity, suffering, and retribution, the Psalms help provide Rowlandson with "a public, liturgical language that centers her experience in the communal sphere of meaning."[86] At the same time, as Dawn Henwood observes, the Psalms and the Old Testament prophets' denunciations of Israel's enemies help Rowlandson find words for her anger that legitimate its expression, indeed, that allow her to use the prophet's privilege to voice the anger of a vengeful God. Rowlandson's interpreting her sufferings as God's chastisement and testing of his elect is like Milton's in *Samson Agonistes* or, to cite an example also in the form of a spiritual autobiography recounting persecution, like Bunyan's narrative of his imprisonment under the Clarendon Code in *Grace Abounding to the Chief of Sinners* (1666).

APHRA BEHN AND THE THEATRE

The debauched court and town culture of London, from which the Bradstreets and the Rowlandsons had fled to Massachusetts, is fittingly represented by Aphra Behn, now celebrated as the first professional woman of letters in British literature. Behn exceeded even Cavendish in literary productivity; unlike the rather isolated Cavendish, Behn was well-known in London literary circles and had at least fifteen of her plays produced on the London public stage before her death in 1689. Recent scholarship has complicated our view of non-commercial closet drama, like that of Elizabeth Cary, Viscountess Faulkland, the first English-woman known to have written a tragedy, the Senecan *Tragedy of Miriam* (1613) or of Cavendish, pointing out that such works, even in manuscript, may have circulated among numbers of readers and may have had private performances, yet these closet dramas differed in public impact from the commercially produced plays of Philips, and especially, Behn. Moreover, in the late seventeenth century, a really successful play was usually the best way for a writer to make money, and Behn's plays made her the first woman writer to make significant sums of money from her writing. Behn's social origins are unclear. About all that can be said with confidence is that she was not aristocratic and never rich. She claimed to have been in Surinam, in Central America, as a young girl, and there is good evidence that she served as an English spy in Antwerp in 1666 and later spent time in a debtors' prison.

Behn aimed to be a Tory poet and playwright and was consistent in her adherence to the Stuarts. Like other Tory writers, Behn frequently treated Restoration politics as merely a warmed-over version of the Civil War, identifying interregnum royalists with later Tories and interregnum parliamentarians with later Whigs. Late in Charles II's reign, his failure to produce a legitimate heir to the throne threatened to result in his Roman Catholic brother, James, succeeding to the throne. Parliamentary agitation for an altered succession that would exclude James and guarantee a Protestant successor – the Exclusion Crisis of 1679–80 – aroused fear that strife between Parliament and the Crown would again bring civil war. Instead, the first English political parties began to emerge. Parliamentary advocates of Exclusion became the Whigs and the defenders of hereditary succession became the Tories. Like many, Behn identified the new Whigs with the Parliamentary party of the Civil War and interregnum. She adapted John Tatham's *The Rump; or, The Mirrour of the Late Times* (1660) into a farcical comedy, *The Roundheads* (1681). Set in 1659–60, the play ridicules the Puritans as base-born, venial, anarchistic, hypocritical drunkards. Its clergyman, Ananias Gogle, is seditious and lascivious. Lady Lambert, supposed on no good evidence to have been Cromwell's mistress, is transformed by the love of a royalist. Again, in *The City-Heiress: or, Sir Timothy Treatall* (1682), Behn skewers a Puritanical City politician, the eponymous old Sir Timothy, punishing him by allowing his disinherited royalist nephew to find his treasonable papers and blackmail him into allowing the nephew to inherit. Wilding, the nephew, palms off his discarded mistress on Sir Timothy. Like Dryden in "Absalom and Achitophel" (1682), Behn contributed to developing the powerful and enduring political stereotypes of Whigs as venial, hypocritical, anarchic, repressed and repressive, and of Tories as generous, open, jolly, and loyal. Although Behn received money for writing Tory propaganda, it cannot be said that she was as enthusiastically accepted as a champion of her faction as Hutchinson, Bradstreet, or Rowlandson were by theirs.

Behn's success as a commercial playwright was unprecedented; it challenged the male hegemony over public performance and over writing for publication more radically than the work of any of the other women discussed so far. The reception of Philips's and Boothby's plays suggested that a woman's play might be favorably received, at least as a novelty, and Behn's first play, *The Forc'd Marriage, or The Jealous Bridegroom* (1670), appeared with a prologue clearly announcing it as a woman's play. Subsequently, however, perhaps because Behn moved from heroic drama and tragicomedy to intrigue and sex comedy and as it became clear that she intended to become a professional playwright rather than the author of one or two plays, she encountered resistance. Satirists claimed an equivalence between a woman who made herself public by having a play produced or published and a woman who was available to the public as a prostitute. Since Behn had no family protection, was unmarried and reputed to have had an affair, and wrote libertine sex comedy, she was an obvious target for such attacks. In one of the better poems on the subject, "To the *Sappho* of the Age, suppos'd to Ly-In of *Love-Distemper*, or a Play," William Wycherley addressed Behn and played with the meanings of "public":

> Once, to your Shame, your Parts to all were shown, ⎫
> But now, (tho' a more Public Woman grown,)   ⎪
> You gain more Reputation in the Town;   ⎬
> Grown Public, to your Honour, not your Shame, ⎪
> As more Men now you please, gain much more Fame . . .[87] ⎭

Wycherley follows this with puns on "parts," bodily and intellectual, and puns on "clapped," venereal and theatrical. Behn dealt with this resistance by having some plays produced anonymously, thus encouraging the normative assumption that they had been written by a man.

At other times, however, Behn asserted a woman's right to have plays produced. In both "An Epistle to the Reader" in the *Dutch Lover* (1673) and "To the Reader" in *Sir Patient Fancy* (1678) she complains of prejudice against her as a woman writer, insists on her capacity to produce plays and her entitlement to do so, and attacks the legitimacy of male authority to claim otherwise. She denigrates the university learning that can produce tedious writing and stakes out comedy as a genre in which women's lack of access to formal education is not a disadvantage: "Plays have no great room for that which is mens great advantage over women, that is Learning." Claiming that a fop came to see her play and told everyone around him that it would be "woeful . . . for it was a womans," Behn retorts: "if Comedy should be the Picture of ridiculous mankind, I wonder any one should think it such a sturdy task, whilst we are furnish'd with such precious Originals . . ."[88]

When Behn's plays succeed, they do so because she combines skill in plotting intrigue comedy with skeptical questioning of conventional views about sexuality and morality. On occasion, she offers original explorations of the position of women both within conventional marriage and within the supposedly more open economies of desire in libertinism. Behn was like Cavendish (and like Dryden) in her eagerness to explore the intellectual ferment of the late seventeenth century as it produced the new science and the new philosophy of Descartes, Pierre Gassendi, Thomas Hobbes, Robert Boyle, and Robert Hooke. Unlike Cavendish, however, Behn joined with the libertines in a skeptical interrogation of the legitimacy of traditional morality, including the legitimacy of chastity as a virtue. Beginning in France in the seventeenth century, libertinism was a modern revival of ancient Epicureanism and hedonism. Its appeal to the realities of sense experience matched the interests of the new science. For seventeenth-century intellectuals disillusioned by the apparent failure of traditional religious and political ideals during the interregnum libertinism was an appealing alternative.

Less narcissistic than Cavendish and more attuned to contemporary society, Behn more vigorously and more publicly used reason to challenge both the exclusion of women from certain fields normally restricted to men – like the writing of commercial plays – and the fairness of a sexual double standard according to which men were to be celebrated for amorous conquests while women who freely explored the pleasures of sensuality were to be stigmatized as whores. Some of her plays are hard to distinguish from those of mediocre male contemporaries like Edward Ravenscroft or Thomas D'Urfey and her verse in tragicomedy or tragedy is distinctly inferior to Dryden's or to Thomas Otway's. Yet several of her prose comedies are dramatically skillful and original in their interrogations of the fairness of women's condition. Among these, I would include *The Rover: or, the Banish't Cavaliers* (1677), *Sir Patient Fancy* (1678), *The Feign'd Curtizans; or A Night's Intrigue* (1679), *The Second Part of the Rover* (1681), and *The Luckey Chance; or, An Alderman's Bargain* (1687). Counting by number of years produced between 1660–1800, *The Rover* was the fourth most popular play written by a woman (behind three comedies by Centlivre), having been produced during each of 51 years; it has also been successfully revived in recent years in both Britain and the United States.[89]

The Rover: or, the Banish't Cavaliers takes the audience back to the interregnum, to the world of defeated royalists in exile on the continent, the world Cavendish described in her life of her husband. The English heroes, Colonel Belvile and his friend Willmore, defeated by parliamentary forces, have been surviving as soldiers of fortune in continental armies; they now find themselves in Naples in carnival time. Belvile is a sincere lover, inhabiting a romance world in which money is not necessary. As in Cavendish's royalist narratives, if virtuous people lack money, it will find them. Exchange exists, but only of grace and favor for grace and favor. Characters display superior virtue and win the admiration and love of other characters, who then display their own superior virtue. Belvile exhibits chivalry, bravery, fidelity, and scrupulosity, then is rewarded with the hand of Florinda.

Belvile's more modern friend Willmore, the eponymous Rover, is a libertine, like Dorimant in Sir George Etherege's *Man of Mode*, produced a few months earlier. He argues for the value of sensual pleasure, attacks marriage, and condemns the conventionally virtuous as hypocrites. Hellena, the heroine, enjoys Willmore's rakishness, finding it exciting, amusing, and erotic, rather than offensive. Determined to choose her own lover, she declares, "I don't intend every he that likes me shall have me, but he that I like."[90] Willmore first falls in love with her wit, not her face, initially meeting her when she in disguise and masked during the carnival. When she tells him she is destined to enter a convent, he replies wittily, flirting both with her and with blasphemy: "A Nun! Oh now I love thee for't! There's no sinner like a young Saint – nay now there's no denying me, the Old Law had no Curse (to a Woman) like dying a Maid; witness *Jeptha's Daughter*." Hellena teasingly replies, playing his game of talking about sex under the guise of talking about the Bible and religion: "A very good Text this, if well handled; and I perceive Father Captain, you wou'd impose no severe penance on her who were inclin'd to Console herself, before she took her Orders."[91] However, Hellena is too intelligent and too self-controlled to succumb to such extramarital blandishments. Willmore insists, "Marriage is as certain a bane to Love, as lending Money is to Friendship." She retorts that, for a woman, to enjoy premarital sex is to risk ending alone with a "cradle full of noise and mischief, with a pack of repentance . . ."[92]

In *The Rover*, as in some of her other comedies, Behn explores, with unusual sympathy and penetration, the characters of women who have lost their reputations for chastity. She uses such characters to raise funda-mental questions about the justice of the rules of society, even the rules of morality. Many Restoration comedies set up oppositions between witty chaste girls and passionate mistresses, the chaste girls getting the heroes in the end. In *The Man of Mode*, for example, we see Dorimant discarding his mistress, Mrs. Loveit, as he is captured by the superior wit and beauty of Harriet. Mrs. Loveit's pseudo-tragic ranting serves mainly to render her ridiculous. Behn takes the plight of her mistress characters with greater seriousness. Taking advantage of the fact that talented actresses instead of boys now played women's parts, Behn collaborated with them to add new dimensions to female roles. For example, as Elizabeth Howe has argued, Behn capitalized on Elizabeth Barry's gift for tragedy when she wrote the part of Lady Galliard, the cast mistress in her comedy, *The City-Heiress* (1682), for Barry, depending upon her to make the echoes of tragic language in her speeches not ridiculous but affecting.[93]

Having been mistress to many, Angellica Bianca in *The Rover* is suffi-ciently disillusioned that she concludes: "Inconstancy is the sin of all Mankind; therefore, I am resolv'd that nothing but Gold, shall charm my heart."[94] The play text requires a memorable prop: a large picture of Angellica hung outside her apartments to advertise that her sexual services can be rented for the very large sum of one thousand crowns per month. This public display of the image of a woman has exactly the two effects Puritans and other objectors to the theatre feared: first, it evokes desire in male spectators, and second, it provokes violent quarrels among men. Seeing the picture and hearing of her reputation, Willmore and other male characters promptly lust after Angellica. Willmore, Don Antonio, the Viceroy's son, and other male characters repeatedly draw their swords as rivals for Angellica.

Unable to afford Angellica's favors, Willmore attacks her offer to exchange love for money. Within the logic of libertinism, an exchange of sexual pleasure for sexual pleasure is a legitimate transaction, whereas selling sex for money or marrying for money is not. His exploration of the legitimacy of the exchange Angellica proposes becomes more original as he considers the implications of fractionating value, inquiring how much of her time he might buy for one pistole (a Spanish gold coin worth about sixteen shillings) and suggesting that he might recruit other Englishmen to buy shares in her or that he might auction shares. There is logic to the proposition that if a month's sexual enjoyment of a woman is available for purchase, then she ought to be willing to give a prorated price for ten minutes. At the same time, Willmore mocks Angellica by flirting with this *reductio ad absurdum* of her offer. Behn here reminds us that the status of a woman is related to the exclusivity of the terms upon which she can be purchased. A woman who is available to only one man for her entire life is supposed to be the most valuable, a woman who negotiates long-term arrangements (like the kept mistresses of the Restoration) is more valuable than a woman who can be bought by a limited clientele for a night, who is, in turn, more valuable than the woman on the street prepared to turn short tricks for all comers.

Moreover, as we often do in Behn's relatively realistic comedy, we also have the sense that her character's consciousness has been affected by living in the midst of the late seventeenth-century financial revolution. Willmore's thoughts reflect new forms of commodification, including the creation of strange novelties like shares in ships or joint-stock companies. A traditional economic regime of just price was being supplanted by the modern regime of market price. This regime of market price seemed sordid to many. Not only women writers but even male writers who sold their work for money were vulnerable to charges that good art did not belong in a public marketplace.

Despite her first intentions, Angellica succumbs to Willmore's charms and importunings, giving herself to him for free and proposing that it be an exchange of love for love. In the social world she inhabits, her expectation that he will remain constant to her is virtually delusional. Ironically, railing at Willmore for faithlessness to her in his pursuit of Hellena, she reveals the crucial information that Hellena has a portion of 300,000 crowns that seals his decision to marry Hellena. As Angellica metamorphoses into a scorned, violent woman, there is pathos in her despair, yet also stupidity. At the end, she recognizes that she has overestimated the power a beautiful woman possesses:

> In vain I have Consulted all my Charms,
> In vain this Beauty priz'd, in vain believ'd
> My Eyes coul'd kindle any lasting fires . . .[95]

When she resorts to drawing a pistol on Willmore and threatening to kill him, she truly, by contemporary standards, "unsexes" herself, crossing a line between female and male. Drawing guns or knives becomes a fairly common mistress gesture, but, as here, it typically is ineffectual. Angellica cannot frighten Willmore or fire the gun. Willmore has made Angellica relinquish her scheme for profit as an independent contractor, revealed her capacity for what she finally calls "a mean submissive Passion" and soft slavery, but since she has already lost her chastity, there appears to be no acceptable female role for her.[96]

Behn's *Rover* exposes contemporary anxieties about the threats posed by two sorts of contemporary "public women": the actresses who for the first time in the 1660s appeared on the public stage, replacing those boy actors who had played women's parts before the Civil War, and those women like Behn who made themselves public by publishing their works. Behn, unlike Philips, far from claiming to have had her works published against her will, insisted that she had her plays produced and published for reasons like those that prompted many men to publish: desire for fame and money. A public prepared to tolerate or even to celebrate modest volumes of poems like Philips's or Bradstreet's or to read eagerly the exciting adventures of a good Christian wife like Rowlandson – who revealed no ambition to compete for literary fame – was less prepared, as Behn complained, to praise commercial comedies, as bawdy as those of men, written by a woman.

For twentieth-century feminists, Behn became the first woman writer clearly to articulate women's sexual desire and to represent women's sexual desire as deserving gratification. This subject matter is still only explored in limited ways by woman writers. From another point of view in the history of women's writing, Behn becomes the first nightmare foremother, the women writer who helps to forge the threatening link between transgressive writing and transgressive sexuality, the link according to which any woman who makes herself public by publishing simultaneously gives evidence that she is willing to make her body a public property, that she is herself a whore.

BEHN'S POEMS

Behn established herself as an exceptionally prolific and successful dramatist, but she also wrote poetry remarkable for frank eroticism and for its exploration of whether the free sexual enjoyment of the male libertine could be matched by the sexual enjoyment of a female libertine. Like many Restoration poets, Behn used a variety of poetic forms and genres, including songs, pastoral, translation, panegyric and commendatory verse, Pindarics in the manner of Cowley, and prologues and epilogues to plays. Her poems were printed in a number of collections alongside the poems of fashionable male poets; some were printed in her friend the Earl of Rochester's *Poems on Several Occasions* (1680) and for a time attributed to him. She published her own *Poems upon Several Occasions: With a Voyage to the Island of Love*, a substantial collection, in 1684. Despite her similarities in point of view and sometimes in style to gentleman amateurs "who wrote with ease" like Sedley and Etherege, her publication of this volume distances her from them since they declined to publish such volumes and, apparently, wrote smaller bodies of verse. In a different way, the volume also distances her from Philips and Bradstreet, who disclaimed ambitions for literary fame and whose work appeared amidst protestations that they did not desire publication. Behn published her poems without apology or excuse; indeed, she probably worked to collect the large number of commendatory poems from others prefaced to the collection, none of them, alas, by very prominent poets, and, sadly, some unsigned or signed only with initials. Nevertheless, *Poems upon Several Occasions* presents a poet involved in collegial relations with other writers. She includes a commendatory poem for her fellow comic dramatist Edward Howard's *The Six Days Adventure, or the New Utopia* (1671); two poems addressed to the scholarly translator, Thomas Creech; and a jocular, even taunting "Letter to a Brother of the Pen in Tribulation," on the subject of his having to endure the sweating-tub cure for venereal disease.

Although Behn argued that learning was not necessary, or perhaps even desirable, for a writer of comedy, as a poet in the early Augustan period and as a writer associated with classically educated male poets, she could not help but be self-conscious about her lack of classical learning and about most women's lack of access to learning. In a commendatory Pindaric ode she originally published in the second edition of Creech's translation of Lucretius' *De Rerum Natura*, "To Mr Creech (Under the Name of Daphnis) on his Excellent Translation of Lucretius" (1682), and then included in *Poems upon Several Occasions*, Behn expresses pain at her exclusion from the knowledge of classical languages and literature and gratitude to Creech for having made the Latin philosophical poet accessible. Lucretius was of great interest to seventeenth-century intellectuals as a powerful poet of celestial and terrestrial phenomena and an expounder of a theory of atoms. Milton imitates *De Rerum Natura* in parts of *Paradise Lost*, Cavendish shows the effect of Gassendi's revival of Lucretian and Epicurean atomism in *Poems and Fancies* and *Philosophical*

Fancies (both 1653), and Hutchinson used her Latin to do a verse translation of the entire poem. But as a materialist philosopher who attacked religious fear and as an Epicurean, Lucretius was especially dear to skeptics and libertines. Behn celebrates the power of reason in Lucretius and his scorn of religious superstition:

> And Reason over all Unfetter'd plays,
> Wanton and undisturb'd as Summers Breeze;
>   That gliding murmurs o'er the Trees:
> And no hard Notion meets or stops its way.
>   It Pierces, Conquers and Compels,
> Beyond poor feeble Faith's dull Oracles.
>   Faith the despairing Soul's content,
> Faith the Last Shift of Routed Argument.[97]

As Behn appreciates, translations from the Greek and Latin like Creech's increasingly gave less educated women writers at least partial access to important literary models and ideas, including those that challenged received opinions.

Of the Latin poets besides Lucretius, Behn was especially interested in Ovid, as were other women after her. Ovid writes about love in private life rather than about epic battle; he writes with wit, teasing himself with the smallness of his subjects and his own powerlessness before desire. Ovid's *Heroides*, verse epistles from legendary women addressed to their lovers, offered a key model for writing from a female subject position. In the *Heroides*, absent male heroes become less heroic and the passions and words of the women who write claim significance.[98] Behn contributed "A Paraphrase on *Ovid's* Epistle of *Oenone* to *Paris*," the fifth of the *Heroides*, to Ovid's *Epistles Translated by Several Hands* (1680), a volume edited by Dryden. Oenone, a nymph and daughter of a river god in Ovid, though a more humble shepherdess in Behn, reproaches Paris for abandoning her for Helen. Alone and sad, day after day Oenone climbs up to a high rock to view the sea, hoping for Paris's return. One day she sees a richly appointed ship bearing Paris and Helen:

> And fondly you were on her Bosome lay'd,
> Whilst with your perjur'd Lips her Fingers play'd;
> Wantonly curl'd and dally'd with that hair,
> Of Which, as sacred Charms, I Bracelets wear.[99]

Oenone reproaches her lover for breaking his vows to her, as do many of the female speakers in Behn's verse. Love triangles also recur frequently in Behn's poetry. The female speaker is often the woman who has lost the man.

Like many male Restoration and early eighteenth-century poets, Behn found imitation of classical poetry a good way to get out from under the problem of Christianity. Pagan Greek and Roman culture had high prestige and could allow a writer at least temporarily to pretend that Christianity and Christian sexual morality had not been invented. Behn's "Disappointment," a comic poem about a male lover who disappoints his lady by prematurely ejaculating, is ultimately a version of Ovid's *Amores* 3: 7. Ovid begins:

> No, I must face facts:
> she was lovely – she was glamorous – I was mad about her.
>
> But there I lay, with this girl in my arms, and nothing happened.
> The position was absurd.
>
> I wanted it badly enough, and so did she –
> but could I rise to the occasion?[100]

Behn comes to this poem of Ovid circuitously, depending on a French version of 1661 that appeared in an English translation in 1682.[101] Her version differs from those of various male poets by omitting later sections in which the man recovers his potency and in more attentively representing the disappointment of her active and desiring Cloris. Behn plays with the question of whether phallic power is as real as it usually seems to be or whether culture has invented it. Cloris tries to help Lysander by laying her hand "Upon that fabulous *Priapas*, / That Potent God, as Poets feign."[102] Cloris's aid is ineffectual, but Behn's image of the detumescent penis, presumably wet with prematurely ejaculated semen, is affectionate, even pleasantly periphrastic and pretty:

> Than *Cloris* her fair Hand withdrew,
> Finding that God of her Desires
> Disarm'd of all his Awful Fires,
> And Cold as Flow'rs bath'd in the Morning Dew.[103]

The pain and rage Behn's female speakers so often express at having been seduced and abandoned by men who apparently have the power to love and change lovers without consequence seems to find some temporary surcease in thus dwelling on the image of male impotence.

After the Restoration, the French influence on court culture and on the culture of the court wits was strong. As we have seen, during the interregnum a number of royalists, like Charles II himself and like Cavendish, spent time in exile in France. French poems, French plays, and French philosophers frequently provided models, ideas, and inspiration for late seventeenth-century writers; they provided especially attractive models for anti-Puritanical royalists. Like the poems of Restoration court wits, some of Behn's poems either announce themselves as based on French models or imitate French poems without explicit acknowledgment. The "Voyage to the Isle of Love," a poem of over 2,000 lines, is translated and adapted from Abbé Paul Tallemant's "Voyage de l'isle d'amour" (1663).[104] In an allegorical journey, Tallemant's male lover overcomes obstacles like Jealousy, Modesty, and Honor until he finally enjoys his mistress. Behn's long opening poem in *Poems upon Several Occasions*, "The Golden Age. A Paraphrase on a Translation out of French," declares allegiance to a very unpuritanical, epicurean hedonism. Ultimately deriving from Torquato Tasso's pastoral play *Aminta* (1573), most likely by way of a still unidentified French version, Behn's vision of the Golden Age is that of a soft primitivism, a pastoral idyll in which work is not needed for survival, war unknown, and government and religion unnecessary. She places special emphasis on the possibilities for erotic pleasure in a world where desire is benign, shame absent, and opportunties for id gratification apparently infinite. Religious authorities and moralists who condemn sexual pleasure are guilty of a "fond mistake"; now the "freeborn" "by right of Nature" assert their claim to pleasure. Two strophes heatedly denounce "cursed Honour . . . who first dids't damn / A Woman to the Sin of shame."[105] Honor, "Foe to Pleasure," "base Debaucher of the generous heart," is summarily banished to a court figured as a place of ambition.[106] At the end, the poem commands a new Golden Age to begin in which love again will reign without hypocrisy; the only rule for the young and the beautiful will be *carpe diem*.

Translation, adaptation, and imitation were important modes for male and female poets of the Restoration, but a major problem for women poets was to figure out what to do with poetic forms in which the masculine speaking position had been naturalized. As Dorothy Mermin put it, "The task of the woman poet has been to redefine woman's position in poetry; to become the subject who desires and speaks."[107] One can see Behn explicitly addressing this task in a poem like "In Imitation of *Horace*," where she loosely imitates Horace's Ode 1: 5. Horace speaks to a beautiful woman who lets a credulous young man who makes love to her suppose that she is his prize for eternity, although the older speaker knows that she will be unfaithful. Behn makes her speaker a woman, addressing a young man with "Amorous Curles of Jet," "Coral Lips," and "Amber Breath."[108] She is his "Slave," but pleads with him to "forbear / Thy words of Melting Love," since his "tender force" is irresistible, and "To taste these Sweets lets in a Certain Death."[109]

Behn's song "The Willing Mistress" deftly reverses the conventional *carpe diem* lyric in which the speaker, assumed to be male, tries to persuade a woman to have intercourse with him, as, for example, in Andrew Marvell's "To his Coy Mistress" (posthumously published, 1681).[110] Behn's female speaker is neither reluctant, nor cold, nor passive. Her only reluctance seems witty reluctance to name the penis or intercourse, reluctance calculated to press the reader to acknowledge his or her shared sexual awareness in order to read the poem:

> A many Kisses he did give:
>   And I return'd the same
> Which made me willing to receive
>   That which I dare not name . . .
>
> He did but Kiss and Clasp me round,
>   Whilst those his thoughts Exprest:
> And lay'd me gently on the Ground;
>   Ah who can guess the rest?[111]

The claim to special knowledge and authority in speaking of love becomes a major ground of women's writing, although the frank eroticism of Behn and some other early writers like Delarivière Manley soon gives way to chaster, more sentimental versions of love.

All the better Restoration libertine poets complicate their paeans to the naturalness and joys of fulfilled sexual desire with glimpses of the darker side of libertinism. In the Earl of Rochester's poetry, the male libertine quest for pleasure is thwarted, variously, by jealousy, the superiority of anticipation to fulfillment, impotence, hangover, venereal disease, and even the rivalry of dildoes. Behn, trying to work out a female libertinism, confronts the woman's problems of out-of-wedlock pregnancy, lost reputation, and, most painfully, male lovers who, once sexually satisfied, rapidly grow indifferent. Lysander in "To Lysander, who made some Verses on a Discourse of Loves Fire," is typical:

> What Lover wou'd pursue a single Game,
> That cou'd amongst the Fair deal out his flame?[112]

To utopian idylls of eager desire satisfied, *Poems upon Several Occasions* counterposes fantasies of abandoned, injured women exacting revenge. Thus, the humbled speaker in "The Return" warns her "Pityless" Amyntas:

> But Shepherd beware,
> Though a Victor you are;
> A Tyrant was never secure in his Throne;
> Whilst proudly you aim
> New Conquests to gain,
> Some hard-hearted Nymph may return you your own.[113]

Behn imaginatively adapted seventeenth-century pastoral to her own purposes, often, as in "The Willing Mistress" or "The Return" using selected elements of pastoral nomenclature and setting in lyrics shorter than conventional pastoral. She usually abandoned normative pastoral's commitment to the representation of an idyllic world of pleasure and innocence in order to write libertine pastoral in which she uses pastoral setting to suggest the naturalness of adult sexuality. Her pastoral speakers tend to be more realistically contemporary than classically timeless; they include female speakers, who, if present at all in conventional pastoral, were usually present as silent listeners. Renato Poggioli in *The Oaten Flute* memorably commented that the pastoral is "a private, masculine world, where woman is not a person but a sexual archetype, the eternal Eve."[114] Bruce Smith, writing more recently about Renaissance English pastoral, remarks, "Arcadia is a society in which men do all the feeling and all the talking." He argues that in the golden world of Renaissance pastoral, "What we discover . . . is male bonding in its purest form, unadulterated by women, uncomplicated by social hierarchy, uncompromised by disguise."[115] While neoclassical pastoral in some ways seemed a virtually exhausted and vacuous form, because the male speaking position was so naturalized in pastoral, once women poets like Behn began imagining speaking shepherdesses they invented original variations.

In "Selinda and Cloris. Made in an Entertainment at Court" Behn builds her poem on the formal turn-taking dialogue of pastoral, but replaces the usual shepherds with two shepherdesses. Cloris has loved Alexis but he has abandoned her. She speaks to Selinda, who Alexis now adores, urging Selinda to disdain him:

> A Votary you deserve who ne'er knew how,
> To any Altars but your own to bow.[116]

Selinda's heart is "unconquer'd," yet she understandably wonders whether Cloris's advice is prompted by "Friendship" or by "Jealousie." Cloris warns of Alexis's dangerous power and suggests that she was deceived by his apparent submissiveness in courtship, as he performed many pastoral services for her, seeking her lost lambs, singing to her, gathering flowers. In pastoral poetry generally, as Frank Kermode put it, the poet allows "his complexities to colour his talk of the rustic shepherd"; he maintains a double consciousness in which his shepherds are at once a contemporary vision of the Golden Age and, simultaneously, "in a way contemptible in their simplicity and coarseness."[117] Behn's shepherdesses tend to have stronger doses of the urban complexities of their author than most; the delights of the natural world – except for those of sexuality itself – are also weaker than usual in her pastoral. Here Selinda's response to Cloris's invocation of the power of Alexis's humble services evokes a smile by demonstrating more sophistication than simplicity:

SELINDA:
  Cloris, such little Services would prove
    Too mean, to be repaid with Love;
    A Look, a Nod, a Smile would quit that score,
  And she deserves to be undone, that pays a Shepherd more.[118]

A conventional ending for a two-speaker pastoral celebrating harmony and equality is the mutual exchange of gifts, as in Virgil's fifth eclogue Menalcus gives Mopsus his reed and Mopsus gives Menalcus his shepherd's crook. At the end of "Selinda and Cloris," as Cloris hopes that an Alexis scorned by Selinda might return to her, Selinda says:

    Secure thy Fears, the Vows he makes to me
    I send a Present, back to thee . . .[119]

That Alexis's vows – synecdoche for Alexis himself – could be turned into a present, functioning like a bowl or a shepherd's crook, here seems to express Selinda's disdain for his inconsequentiality. Yet it also serves, like a more normal pastoral present, as the sign of a bond between the two women, who end by singing together, expressing "The heights of Love and Amity."[120] In Behn's poem, however, one does not feel perfect symmetry between the speakers, perfect equality, or perfected happiness. One might take Cloris's warning of Selinda as a kind of gift, but she does not speak explicitly of any "present" she can offer Selinda at the end. Nor does one have much confidence that Selinda's gift of Alexis to Cloris will lead to Cloris's securely enjoying her swain. The faithlessness of men in Behn's verse means that her pastoral landscapes are littered with ruined and abandoned shepherdesses.

Prologues and epilogues to plays were important forms of Restoration occasional verse; Behn, like other successful playwrights, wrote them for her own plays and for the plays of others. Notable literary personages helped publicize other playwrights' work by providing prologues or epilogues. Prologues often addressed the kind of play the audience was about to see and made claims about its merits and innovations; hence, they were one of several kinds of contemporary verse in which we find literary criticism. Epilogues were somewhat similar, although one of the special pleasures of Restoration epilogues was that writers enjoyed sending the audience out of the theatre with sharp reminders that what they had seen was a play and that the actors as people were different from the characters they had just played. Behn wrote an epilogue to her own *Sir Patient Fancy* to be spoken by Mrs. Gwin, who had acted Lady Knowell, the rich mother of the heroine. The play satirizes Lady Knowell as a learned woman who preens herself on reading Greek, Latin, and Italian classics in the original languages, and as a sexually predatory woman who tries, unsuccessfully, to steal her daughter's lover. In the epilogue, addressed to the men in the audience, Gwin appears as the cheeky, teasing actress to attack the foolishness of male coxcombs in the audience who rely on unthinking custom to damn a play simply because a woman wrote it. Behn and Gwin align themselves with worldly-wise wits, able to laugh at themselves as well as at the less intelligent "pit-buffoons." Behn acknowledges her ruined reputation for chastity and, apparently the actresses', turning sexual knowledge into a claim to authority and entitlement to write:

> That we [women] have Nobler Souls then you, we prove,
> By how much more we're sensible of Love;
> Quickest in finding all the subtlest waies
> To make your Joys: why not to make you Plays?[121]

The epilogue insists that Behn's unlearned farcical comedy that "artfully" copies the reality of contemporary life is more pleasing and relevant than learned comedy that follows the neoclassical rules of unity of "action, time, and place."

BEHN'S LATER CAREER

Late in her career, Behn turned increasingly to translation from the French, to court panegyric, and to fiction. In the 1670s, the rivalry between the two London theatre companies, the King's Company and the Duke's Company had whetted managers' appetites for new plays. Unfortunately for dramatists, however, in the early 1680s both companies were struggling and the two merged to form a single United Company. This company, now a monopoly, owned repertory plays from both earlier companies; hence its managers saw less need for new plays. This depressed market for plays contributed to motivating Behn to gather her poems for publication in *Poems upon Several Occasions*. Translation from French also proved an increasing resource. Noting that Behn in late 1683 said she had been to Paris "last Spring," her biographer finds that her early diffidence about her grasp of French is replaced by increasing confidence in her knowledge of French language and culture as she translates more French texts in the last years of her life.[122]

Clearly hoping for royal patronage, after 1682 Behn also published a series of panegyrics to various Stuart royal personages. Since, as later women writers were to see clearly, the most valuable form of royal patronage was appointment to public office, women writers could only hope for less valuable monetary or other presents (like jewels) as patronage rewards for themselves. (A married woman might hope for an office for her husband; Philips probably hoped for some leniency toward her husband, who had been a Colonel in Cromwell's army. But Behn was not married.) Behn's Stuart panegyrics appeared as reasonably handsome separate publications, but her expectations of fine rewards were disappointed and, in my opinion, the Pindaric mode of these public poems was not one in which she excelled. The relation of Behn and other women poets to the Greek poet Pindar was usually less fortunate than their relation to Ovid. Pindar, famed for rushing eloquence and originality in meter and diction, wrote victory odes to men who triumphed at the Olympic Games, odes celebrating the victories and weaving in mythic stories. Pindar's poems were difficult and highly structured, but by the time of Cowley, the Pindaric ode came to mean simply an enthusiastic irregular ode. Late seventeenth-century poets often used Pindaric odes to celebrate abstractions, as Behn does in "On Desire." The late seventeenth-century conception of the Pindaric ode produced much decadent, inflated panegyric, many abortive attempts to sound inspired. For untrained women poets especially the notion that Pindaric was an "irregular" form seemed to license bad versification, cobbling together prosaic lines of various lengths with often flat rhymes. Some of Behn's least successful poems are her decadent baroque public panegyrics in this Pindaric mode, for example, "A Pindarick Poem on the Happy Coronation of His most Sacred Majesty James II and his Illustrious Consort Queen Mary" (1685). There the effort to rise succumbs to bathos as admiring throngs await the Queen:

Big with *Prophetick Joy,* they lab'ring wait
To utter Blessings *wonderful* and *great . . .*[123]

While the Stuart Pindaricks look back to an exhausted poetic mode, Behn's fourteen or so fictions point forward to the more promising possibilities of the novel. Most of Behn's fictions are shorter, amorous novellas. They show the influence of several new strains in French fiction after the mid-seventeenth-century French civil wars, especially of a shift from the long romance to the shorter *nouvelle historique* and *nouvelle gallante.* Even Madeleine de Scudéry's ten volume romance, *Artamène ou le Grand Cyrus* (1649–53), translated into English as *Artamenes, or The Grand Cyrus. An Excellent New Romance* (1653–55), already showed some elements that were to become features of the novel, notably lengthy correspondence between principal characters. An early example of the *nouvelle historique,* Madame de La Fayette's *Le Princesse de Montpensier* (1662), translated into English as *The Princess of Montpensier* (1666), abandoned the Sidneyesque Arcadian and utopian settings of romance's Greek models for a more modern setting, in this case sixteenth-century France. Both the *nouvelle historique* and the *nouvelle galante* turned from the idealism and the distant settings of romance toward more realism and more contemporary settings, the *nouvelle historique* typically concerning itself with the psychology of love and the *nouvelle galante* being more interested in the plotting of love affairs. The ideal love of earlier romance was increasingly replaced by visions of the "rapacious and destructive power of sexual passion."[124]

Behn in her fiction, as in her poetry, is endlessly fascinated with the power or powerlessness of beauty, admiring beauty and deeply sympathetic to characters who are vulnerable to beauty's charms. Thus, in *The Fair Jilt; or, The History of Prince Tarquin and Miranda* (1688), set in seventeenth-century Antwerp, we read that Francisco discovers:

the most wond'rous Object of beauty he had ever seen, dress'd in all the Glory of a young Bride; her Hair and Stomacher full of Diamonds, that gave a Lustre all dazzling to her brighter Face and Eyes. He was surpriz'd at her amazing beauty, and question'd whether she was a Woman or an Angel at his Feet. Her Hands, which were elevated, as if in Prayer, seem'd to be form'd of polish'd Alabaster; and he confess'd, he had never seen anything in Nature so perfect, and so admirable.[125]

This blazon reproduces the superlatives of romance.

Miranda, however, behaves less like a heroine of romance than like a cross between a villainess of heroic drama and a sexually predatory woman of farce. She begins as a Beguine (a lay sister in an order of nuns) struck by a passion for Francisco, who is a priest. She pursues him first with passionate letters and presents of expensive jewels. When he does not respond, she pursues him into the confessional, where she sexually assaults him. Behn seems to revel in the opportunity to create an ambiguity as to whether this scene is shockingly blasphemous or an exposé of the depravity of continental nuns. Like Rochester and, later, the Marquis de Sade, Behn is alert to the erotic charge of the forbidden, the erotic thrill of the blasphemous. Other stories feature incestuous lovers. She also likes gender reversals, as here the woman becomes the sexual predator and the man has to try to resist.

The story alternatively describes Miranda as a heroine capable of extraordinary passion, as a victim of the irresistible power of love, and as a wicked woman deserving of moral condemnation. Initially, the narrator describes love as "the most noble and divine Passion of the Soul," and as "an illustrious Passion," albeit one that "in some unguarded and ungovern'd hearts . . . rages beyond the Inspirations of a *God all soft and gentle*, and reigns more like a *Fury from Hell*."[126] As in romance, superior people experience the most intense passions, although here we seem invited to consider that virtuous love is less great than love that inspires criminality. "*I love with a Violence* which cannot be contain'd within the Bounds of reason, Moderation, or Vertue," Miranda declares.[127] Her criminality is considerable. She tries to blackmail Father Francisco into having sex by threatening to accuse him of rape if he declines; when he refuses, she makes good her threat and has him sentenced to prison to await death by burning. When Prince Tarquin arrives in Antwerp, she determines to marry him, prompted more by vanity and a desire to share in his splendor than by love. Miranda embezzles her younger sister's marriage portion in order to maintain their lavish household expenditure. Attempting to avoid discovery of this crime, she seduces a teenage page-boy, who is enamored of her, to murder her sister. He fails, is apprehended, and sentenced to hang. Still glamorous and the cynosure of all eyes, Miranda is sentenced to stand under the gibbet while the page is hanged:

all the Windows were taken down, and fill'd with Spectators, and the Tops of Houses; when, at the Hour appointed, the fatal beauty appear'd. She was dress'd in a black Velvet Gown, with a rich Row of Diamonds all down the fore-part of the Breast, and a great Knot of Diamonds at the Peak behind; and a Petty-coat of flower'd Gold, very rich, and lac'd . . . the Prince led her, bare; follow'd by his Foot-men, Pages, and other Officers of his House . . .[128]

Still unrepentant, she seduces Tarquin, who continues to be enamored of her, to kill her sister, forging letters to divert suspicion to the page's relatives. Tarquin also fails, is apprehended, and sentenced to death. But when his execution is botched, both Tarquin, who continues to adore her, and Miranda are pardoned.

More clearly than in the poetry, one sees in fictions like *The Fair Jilt* that for Behn love entails conquest and domination. Up to a point, one can share the excitement of feminist critics who celebrate Behn's gender-bending reversals as giving agency to female characters and as destabilizing the received orthodoxies of gender. To my mind, though, there is a crazed absolutism in Behn's exaltation of a supposedly noble love, like Tarquin's, that will baulk at nothing to satisfy the demands of a criminal beloved. The duty and desire of a lover in romance to serve a virtuous beloved have become dissociated from the ideals instantiated by love objects in romance, surviving alone as pure abjection. Hutchinson's Puritan ideal of love which insists that true love must be ardent but not idolatrous and that it depends upon and enhances virtue contrasts sharply with Behn's. Some have found that the contradictions in Behn's fiction between an exaltation of lovers willing to lose all for love and the narrator's prudential or moral condemnation of criminality generate ironies, but for me they remain contradictions.[129]

Like many of Behn's narrators, the narrator of *The Fair Jilt* claims to have been an eyewitness of many of the events of her tale and to have confirmed the authenticity of others by interviews with Franciscan priests. In fact, the events of Behn's story generally correspond to a notorious case from the 1650s involving one Theresa Mechelen of Antwerp and the botched execution of her husband for attempting to murder her sister. As this sort of fiction moved away from romance to engage new material from journalism or contemporary scandal, plots could become chaotic and odd; Behn, however, uses her dramatist's sense of plot to mitigate these effects.

EXOTIC AND IMAGINED OTHER WORLDS IN BEHN AND CAVENDISH

While Behn contributed to the development of psychological and social realism in her poetry and comedy, like other late seventeenth-century British writers, Behn and Cavendish were also intrigued by the exotic. To Rowlandson's account of the strange inhabitants of North America, Behn in *Oroonoko; or, The Royal Slave* (1688) added an account of the exotic inhabitants of Africa and Surinam. Behn and Cavendish were also fascinated by the strange new worlds revealed by the telescope and the microscope. Among Behn's translations from the French was *Discovery of New Worlds* (1688), from Fontenelle's *Entretiens sur la pluralitié des mondes* (1686), a dialogue between a philosopher and a noblewoman about astronomy, intended for the education of ladies. In a much lighter vein, Behn engaged astronomy in her late farce, *The Emperor of the Moon* (1687). Cavendish, throughout her career, wrote about the new science and the new philosophy. Her ingenious fiction, *The Description of a New World, Called the Blazing World* (1666), is a pioneering example of what would now be called science fiction. In the historical world of Cavendish's *Life . . . of William Cavendishe* her husband is defeated in battle and her actions are virtually without consequence, but in the imaginary, phantasmagoric Blazing World the heroine commands absolute admiration and has complete power and intellectual authority. For Cavendish and for other women writers after her, when the realities of social life are profoundly unsatisfactory, utopian fiction could provide relief from its constraints and suggest alternative possibilities for a different future.

Subtitled "A True History," Behn's most famous fiction, *Oroonoko, or, the Royal Slave* (1688), combines the appeal of romance, of heroic tragedy, and of colonial travel and adventure narrative. Like Rowlandson's captivity narrative, it tells the story of a virtuous person who is captured, enslaved, and made to traverse regions of the globe profoundly unfamiliar to seventeenth-century English readers. Oroonoko is a young African prince captured by an English slave trader and sold into slavery in an English colony in Surinam, on the coast of Latin America. Although the narrator of his story insists that it is a true story to which she herself was an eye-witness, Oroonoko resembles the heroes of seventeenth-century romance, valiant in battle, possessed of "Greatness of soul" and "refin'd Notions of true Honour," "capable of the highest Passions of Love and Gallantry."[130] In Surinam, he re-encounters his true love, the beautiful and virtuous Imoinda, a "black Venus," also a captive slave. Conscious of his noble rank and disdainful of the ignominy of servitude, especially stung by the fact that he is about to become the father of a child who will be born a slave, Oroonoko leads a slave rebellion. He addresses about 150 male slaves on the misery and injustice of their fate, reminding them of how they "Toyl'd on all the tedious Week till black *Friday*, and then, whether they Work'd or not, whether they were Faulty or meriting, they promiscuously, the Innocent with the Guilty, suffer'd the infamous Whip, the sordid Stripes, from their Fellow *Slaves* till their Blood trickled from all Parts of their Body; Blood, whose every drop ought to be Reveng'd with a Life of some of those Tyrants, that impose it . . ."[131] The other slaves, except Imoinda and one other, lack Oroonoko's heroic courage, so in battle they yield to promises of pardon for their rebellion and desert him. Oroonoko is captured, bound, and horrifically tortured. Rather than permit Imoinda to survive and be raped by the colonists, with her consent, Oroonoko cuts her throat. Oroonoko is finally tied to a stake and endures with amazing stoicism as his white tormenters first castrate him, then cut off his ears and his nose, and finally his arms, until he is, at last, dead. (The savagery of Oronooko's punishment is akin to that of the sentences meted out to the rebellious regicides, whose sentences included castration, disemboweling, and having their body parts displayed in public places.)

Oroonoko is a puzzling mixture of several contradictory strains in seventeenth-century narratives of the new world: fascination with the exotic, play with the possibility that the new world contained utopias, disgust and fascination with barbaric cruelty, and interest in the possibilities of commercial and political exploitation. Behn's Surinam contains the wonders of strange flora and fauna like the electric eel, friendly dancing Indians who serve food on leaf plates, and tales of gold up the Amazon River, as well as the horrors of African slavery. Although later adaptations of Behn's *Oroonoko* were used in the eighteenth-century campaigns for the abolition of slavery, the original novel expresses horror at the spectacle of a nobleman and a prince enslaved, rather than a more general critique of the slave trade. A number of recent critics have also seen Oroonoko as in part a reflection of Charles I, for whose execution Oroonoko expresses abhorrence.

Behn's farce, *The Emperor of the Moon* (1687) makes lighthearted comedy out of Dr. Baliardo's conviction that there is another world in the moon, populated by demigods, and complete with its own government and religion. The plot comes from an Italian *commedia* acted in France, Nolant de Fatouville's *Arlecchino, imperatore nella luna*, but much of the dialogue is Behn's. The play demonstrates her familiarity with earlier seventeenth-century voyages to the moon, including Francis Godwin's *Man in the Moon* (1638) and Cyrano de Bergerac's *Histoire comique des états et empires de la lune* (1656). Some imaginary voyages principally aimed at satire, but Behn's genial *Emperor* is more about having fun with a rich mix of ideas and jargon and about the pleasures of theatricality. The ideas and vocabulary are drawn from a promiscuous mix of the new science, astrology, ancient kabala, and Rosicrucianism. Young lovers manipulate Dr. Baliardo's risible credulity, bringing a large telescope on stage to show him the inhabitants of the moon. (They accomplish this trick by putting a glass with the requisite pictures on it at the far end of the telescope.) The lovers exploit Dr. Baliardo's fatherly desire to have his daughter Elaria marry well by convincing him that the lunar Emperor has seen Elaria from afar and will descend to their house in Naples to make her his Empress. Her lover, of course, plans to disguise himself as the Emperor.

While we laugh at Dr. Baliardo's credulity, we are also entertained and delighted by a mélange of wonders associated with the lunar world, sometimes finding it difficult to disentangle arcane Renaissance elements from fragments of a more modern science aiming at economic practicality. Claiming to have traveled to the moon and to have a good map of it, Scaramouch talks to the Doctor using technical terms from alchemy, including *urinam vulcani*, the urine of Vulcan. A certain blacksmith, Scaramouch reveals, has grown rich from *urinam vulcani*, since he uses it to extract iron from his own feces – thus saving on materials costs – "and if at any time Nature be too infirm, or he prove Costive [i.e., constipated], he has no more to do, but to apply a Load-stone *ad Anum*."[132] As Swift was to do later in *Gulliver's Travels*, Behn here notices the dreams of the new science that knowledge of the secrets of nature will produce great wealth.

The farce ends with a dazzling spectacle more typical of opera. To welcome the visit of the lunar demigods, the Doctor's gallery is richly adorned with scenes and lights. The set shows the hill of Parnassus, an alley of trees, and eight or ten "*Negroes upon Pedestals*." Kepler and Galileo descend in chariots with "*Perspectives in their Hands*."[133] A large flying platform, decorated with signs of the zodiac, carries actors dressed as signs of the zodiac. The Doctor falls on his face in awe, then Kepler raises him to witness the lovers marrying in the midst of the pageantry. Scaramouch reveals the deception, and Don Charmante explains that it was devised to relieve him from imposture and scandal to his "Learned Name." The Doctor resolves to burn his books and to accept his daughter's marriage. The amazing spectacle seems more the point than the recantation. *The Emperor of the Moon* was Behn's second most-performed play after *The Rover*, and the fifth most popular play by a woman of this period; it was performed in each of 32 years between 1687 and 1748.[134]

When Behn died in 1688/89, her literary accomplishment was publicly recognized by her burial in Westminster Abbey. At the same time, the intensity of the criticism and misogynist satire directed at her, as well as her own complaints about misogynist prejudice against her work and the rather bleak picture of women's lot in contemporary society that emerges from her work, make it clear that neither women writers nor women generally had, by 1688/89 secured accepted places in the public world. Unlike most Quaker women writers who published only one title each, Margaret Fox continued to publish until her death in 1702, but she did not aim at literary excellence or fame and radical dissenting prose like hers was beneath the notice of the literary world. Bradstreet was supposed to be a poet prevailed upon by her male relations to allow what was essentially one volume of poems to be published. Philips was celebrated as a poet in part because she seemed to deprecate desires for worldly public power or fame and to celebrate private, retired friendship. Hutchinson's work remained unpublished. Rowlandson, having written one remarkable and influential book, slipped back into obscurity.

CAVENDISH'S *BLAZING WORLD*

Of the writers discussed in this chapter, Cavendish had the most acute desire to have public power and, like Behn, she articulated her desire for literary fame. One of Cavendish's most wonderfully imaginative works, *The Description of a New World, Called the Blazing World* (1666), addresses these desires by turning away from what Cavendish considered to be the unsatisfactory conditions of the actual world to invent a more pleasing utopian fantasy. Formally inventive, *The Blazing World* builds its narrative from generic elements including the philosophical essay, romance, utopian fiction, dialogue, travel narrative, and beast fable. It seems to be the first utopian fiction in English written by a woman, although perhaps the recent term, "speculative fiction," now used to refer to science fiction and fantasy, is a more apt one. Unlike other seventeenth-century imaginary voyages – Cyrano de Bergerac's, for instance – Cavendish's is not satiric. The heroine is quickly transported to a strange world inhabited by people brightly colored (in azure, purple, scarlet, and so on) and races of intelligent hybrids including bear-men, fish-men, and worm-men. This world is adorned with dazzling jewels; its abundant diamonds come in many colors and "are splendid so far beyond the Diamonds of this World, as Pebble-stones are to the best sort of this Worlds Diamonds."[135] (Behn and Cavendish share the courtier's delight in splendid jewels and sumptuous costumes.) Immediately, the emperor of this world adores the heroine, makes her his Empress, and gives her absolute power to govern his world. Some elements of the story come from romance, including this willingness of the Emperor and other inhabitants to admire, even revere the heroine. (Rowlandson, in her strange new world, more realistically found herself a captive slave.) When Cavendish imagines a world to please herself, she conjures up one in which a woman has great power and wealth, indeed, one in which a woman controls the public world.

Much of the fascination of *The Blazing World*, however, comes from Cavendish's curiosity about the new science, and the book is an early example of science fiction. On the continent during the interregnum, in salons maintained by William and his brother Charles, Cavendish heard discussions of the new science and philosophy, especially competing theories of atomism. Here she encountered the ideas of Gassendi and Descartes and made the acquaintance of English royalists who had scientific and philosophical interests, including Hobbes, Sir Kenelm Digby, and Walter Charleton.[136] In 1667, parlaying her status as a Duchess into an invitation, she became the first woman to make a visit to the new Royal Society, chartered by Charles II in 1662. Some members feared her perceived ridiculousness might rub off on them, but class and gender decorums persuaded them to accommodate her wish to see experiments performed. Large crowds gathered to witness the Duchess make her very public visit. Boyle used a vacuum pump to do an experiment showing that air had weight and a 60 lb loadstone to demonstrate magnetism on a compass held 7 feet away. He displayed chemical reactions, probably including one that mixed two colorless liquids, sulfuric acid and aniseed oil, to produce, "together with some Heat and Smoak, a Blood-Red Colour."[137]

In the Blazing World, the Empress organizes the various creatures into investigative schools and societies. The bear-men become her experimental philosophers, the bird-men astronomers, the ape-men chemists, and the parrot-men orators and logicians. Even before her arrival, they were already more "ingenious and witty in the invention of profitable and useful Art" than the people of her original world.[138] The Empress asks them the sorts of questions intriguing to contemporaries interested in the new science and philosophy – What kind of substance is air? How is snow made? – as well as the old questions that fascinated the alchemists, forerunners of chemists like Boyle, "Can gold be made by art?" Rather than present any method for resolving disagreement, dialogues array possible answers, emphasizing the pleasure these creatures, and Cavendish, take in disputation. Debate over the nature and causes of the plague pits some, who use microscopes, and who suggest that the plague is caused by "a body of little Flies like atoms, which go out of one body into another, through the sensitive passages," against others, the majority, who claim that it is caused "by the imitation of Parts; so that the motions of some parts which are sound, do imitate the motions of those that are infected and that by this means, the Plague becomes contagious, and spreading."[139] On occasion, Cavendish puts what she considers a naive question into the Empress's mouth, replying to it with what she considers a better-informed, wiser response from one of her animal philosophers. The Empress, for example, asks about color as "an immaterial thing," using an old term from scholastic philosophy. After laughing with un-characteristic rudeness, the worm-men explain that there are no immater-ial substances and proceed to elaborate on Cavendish's own favorite idea of Nature as a single, entirely material, self-moving body.

Despite her curiosity about the new science and her apparent acceptance of what was for the time a radical materialism, Cavendish is profoundly skeptical about empirical methods. She observes that her scientists, even aided by microscopes and telescopes, foment disputes instead of resolving them and she fears such disputes will create factions and political instabil-ity. To her mind, anything is possible and no method, scientific or logical, can rule out possibilities. Conveniently, perhaps, this leads her to the empowering conclusion that her own speculations might be as correct or more correct than anyone else's.[140]

In the second part of *The Blazing World*, the Empress appears as a more traditional hero, using her access to a creatively invented military technol-ogy to engineer the rescue of the King of her original country from his enemies. Here she has the assistance of the "Duchess of Newcastle" as a character first summoned to the Blazing World to be the Empress's scribe. Male luminaries like Galileo, Descartes, Hobbes, and Sir Thomas More (author of *Utopia*, 1516) are said to be too attached to their own opinions and too scornful of a woman's ideas to be willing to serve the Empress, whereas the Duchess is recommended as a "plain and rational writer." The Empress and the Duchess become collaborators and friends. The two women strategize and prepare a terrifying naval and air force of thousands from the Blazing World, to be led by the Empress. Fish-men underwater pull ships by golden chains and fish-men and bird-men are armed with firestones cut into tapers and candles. This firestone illuminates the night sky and, because it burns when wet, incinerates the enemies' ships. In a scene reminiscent of the warrior heroines Brademante in Ludovico Ariosto or Britomart in Spenser, the Empress appears armed with shield, buckler, spear, and cap. Unlike these heroines, she does not fight. Nevertheless, she appears at night, in glowing diamonds, transformed like an epic hero "in splendourous Light, surrounded with Fire." Like Christ – thanks to the fish-men, who allow her to walk on their backs – she appears to walk on the ocean water. In exchange for destroying all the enemies of the King and his people's enemies, she declares, she wants only their acknowledgment of her power and her loyalty to her native country. Such an amazing spectacle of a powerful, public woman causes the observers to wonder whether they are viewing a goddess or an angel or a sorceress or a devil. The one possibility that escapes them is that they are looking at a human woman.

However satisfying this fantasy of a woman with public power was to Cavendish, in *The Blazing World* the Empress, the "Dutchess," and Cavendish the author – with help from the Spirits of the World – argue themselves into believing that power and fame in the world are less desirable than imaginative power. They proclaim that any mortal can create a world populated with immaterial subjects, a world that can be controlled and enjoyed without opposition. In an "Epilogue to the Reader," Cavendish glories in the world she has authored, invites readers who will to become her subjects, and readers who dislike being subjects to create worlds of their own.

CONCLUSION

The women writers discussed in this chapter experienced the unsettling events of the Civil War, the interregnum, and the Restoration counter-revolution. Many of them were literally unsettled in that these events made their continuous residence in England unappealing or impossible. Thus, the royalist Cavendish lived on the continent with her husband after he ceased to fight in the King's army in 1644 until the Restoration in 1660 made return to England safe. Bradstreet and Rowlandson had immigrated with their families to Massachusetts, a colony imagined by its Puritan inhabitants as a place of exile for godly Englishmen and women. Behn probably ventured to the colony of Surinam on the coast of South America and certainly went to Holland in 1666 as an English spy directed to help foil schemes hatching between Dutch and English radicals for an invasion of England that would again bring down monarchy and restore a republic.

A major consequence of the dramatic political reversals of this period was that women could not rely on tradition and custom to order their behavior or beliefs. Authority itself was unsettled, forcing even the obedient to make fundamental decisions about whom to obey. Ironically, the avalanche of Puritan and radical Quaker women's preaching and writing provided a model and an excuse for royalist women's professions of loyalty.

Because women writers were still so anomalous, we want to understand what prompted the few women who did emerge as writers to do so. In this chapter, we have seen that an important motive for several women writers was to record what they believed to be the historical truths about the revolution and the counterrevolution through which they and their husbands had lived. Large-scale political and military history was left to male writers, but women, notably Cavendish and Hutchinson, found that their experience of these dramatic and significant events allowed them to write family memoirs of enduring interest. As had been the case during the interregnum, Protestant religious conviction led even more women, genteelly educated and barely educated alike, to write prayers, devotions, meditations, religious poetry, and, sometimes, narratives of persecution or pamphlets of religious controversy. The Quaker Margaret Fox argued that women ought to be allowed to speak in church and to preach the gospel. In the American colonies, Rowlandson, descendant of Puritan settlers who had fled what they thought religious persecution in England, wrote a riveting narrative of her own capture by Native Americans, a foundational text in the invention of a new kind of colonial narrative crucial to American culture's self-imagination. Using travel narrative, philosophical essay, and romance as partial bases for the imaginative fiction of her *Blazing World*, Cavendish invented a utopian fantasy that simultaneously projected the absolutist Royalist ideology to which she remained faithful and suggested that women, lacking power in the real world of politics and war, might create their own more satisfying textual worlds.

Behn articulated crucial issues surrounding the exclusion of women from elite literary education. Of the writers considered in this chapter, only Hutchinson seems to have commanded Latin and Greek language and literature, and thus to have acquired the equivalent of the literary education seventeenth-century universities aimed to provide. As Behn suggested in her poem to Creech on his translation of Lucretius, women's exclusion from elite literary education meant that they were excluded from knowledge of important ideas and subjects. Since women's knowledge of language and literature was inferior to men's, it also seemed to follow that women would be poorer writers. However, as we have seen, Behn harbored ambivalences about this exclusion. On the one hand, it saddened and pained her, as it did many women who struggled to learn.

On the other hand, she identified ways in which conventional and prestigious literary knowledge might be at best irrelevant and at worst an obstacle to literary achievement. Thus, she staked out comedy as a genre where direct observation of human behavior was better than knowledge of dramatic rules. In different ways, other women writers of this period aimed to make a virtue out of a necessity by suggesting that they had kinds of knowledge as valuable as or more valuable than the knowledge of educated men. Most obviously, they had knowledge of their own experience, which provided them with new literary subjects like female friendship and a mother's feelings in anticipation of the birth of a child. Cavendish engaged in what her admirers might call a strong refusal to credit the emerging authority of experimental science, trumpeting instead her own genius and her ability to create alternative imagined worlds. Most radically, Quakers like Fox thought their inner light trumped not only classical and worldly knowledge, but knowledge of Scripture as well.

For most Restoration women writers, the single book which most compensated for their exclusion from formal literary study was the Bible. Both Anglican and dissenting Protestantism encouraged women's serious study of the Bible and, as we have noted, the press in the second half of the seventeenth century published increased numbers of devotional manuals, sermons, and works of biblical hermeneutics for laypeople. The Bible provided not only passages for poetic paraphrase, but a fundamental set of narratives and an interpretive tradition that, as we have seen in Rowlandson's *Captivity*, a woman writer could use to structure her narrative.

Lyric poetry was throughout the seventeenth and eighteenth centuries an important genre for women writers. The three most important women poets of the Restoration all, in very different ways, revised existing poetic conventions, which represented women as objects of desire, to imagine women as speaking subjects. Philips's *Poems* offered impressive technical skill, an engaging description of rural retirement away from the corruptions of the court, and complex meditations on female friendship. Her elaboration of the ideal of rural retirement was influential on later writers, male and female, of verse and of prose, a harbinger of the later stance of the artist cut off from political power who claims superior virtue and truthfulness. Philips's treatment of female friendship and of women's love for one another introduced subjects of great importance to later women readers and writers. The *Several Poems* of the American Bradstreet reflected a range of English seventeenth-century Protestant poetic and learned traditions, but they also articulated a new, distinctively American consciousness. Movingly, also, they voiced the thoughts and feelings of a wife and mother, subsequently major subjects of women's poetry.

Behn's *Poems* came from a very different, secular, libertine seventeenth-century poetic tradition. She adapted libertine pastoral and song to her own purposes, sometimes, in idyllic modes, using them to claim the naturalness of sexual desire, at other times, painfully suggesting that the pleasures of male libertinism produce female suffering. Behn was important in claiming, both in her poetry and in her fiction, a special womanly expertise on the arts and truths of love. While this claim could serve to reinforce misogynist stereotypes of woman as the lustful sex, it also served as a ground upon which many subsequent women poets, fiction writers, and writers of scandal chronicles claimed special knowledge to authorize their own writing.

In *Pompey* Philips produced the first play written by a woman ever performed on the British public stage. Behn subsequently established herself as one of the most commercially successful playwrights of the Restoration, having at least fifteen plays produced before her death in 1689. Behn's poetry, translations, and fiction, but especially her plays, established her as the most conspicuously public woman writer of the Restoration. Her best comedies are original in their critical, if cynical, explorations of women's situations in marriage and in the relationships of libertine love. Seizing the opportunity offered by the introduction of talented actresses to the English stage, Behn found new ways to use the spectacle of the female body. Avoiding the stereotypical comic cast mistresses of male Restoration comedy, Behn, in collaboration with the talented actresses now playing women's parts, created more complex mistresses with greater ranges of feeling.

Even at this early point in our history, British culture was conflicted about the desirability of women writers. While there was certainly misogyny and mockery of women's writing, probably too much has been made of these as massively dominant responses. Philips, Bradstreet, and Behn all enjoyed considerable contemporary success and appreciation; Behn as the most productive enjoyed the most. Too much has been made of late-seventeenth-century women writers' not publishing or publishing anonymously as signs of women's diffidence and self-doubt, since many male writers also confined themselves to manuscript and since the overwhelming majority of books published between 1660 and 1689 were published anonymously.

An important countervailing force to misogynistic prejudice against women's writing was the desire of competing groups to produce women who publicly represented their positions. The political intensity and factionalism of this period made much writing by both men and women clearly partisan, but it also contributed to a literary state of affairs in which some men were motivated to encourage women to appear in print as advocates for their cause or as examples of the excellence of their faction. As we have seen, Bradstreet was ardent in her denunciations of English Cavalier debauchery and irreligion and the men around Bradstreet were eager to offer her poetry as evidence of the high level of piety and civilization the Puritan colonists had achieved in New England. Fox wrote to describe her experiences and to make her own arguments, but she also published political advice to the Restoration government attacking its intolerance of dissenters and a rebuttal of a Church of England clergyman's sermon on oath-taking. On the opposite side of the political spectrum, Behn celebrated Tory court culture and ridiculed the alleged hypocrisy of Puritans and Whigs. She profited from a theatre in which the government enforced conformity to royalist ideology and she wrote her share of court panegyrics and dedications to royalist noblemen, expecting and receiving some of the usual rewards.[141]

At the end of 1688, the Stuart court culture Behn had represented and celebrated came to an end when James II fled to France, leaving William and Mary to succeed to the throne. Behn survived only long enough to die on 16 April 1689, five days after their coronation. As we shall see in the next chapter, the libertine culture of the Stuart court and of Behn was to be put on the defensive by an earnest Protestantism increasingly supported by the new philosophy.

CHAPTER 2

Partisans of virtue and religion, 1689–1702

INTRODUCTION

During the reign of William and Mary (1689–1702) religious and pious people interested themselves in developing their own spiritual lives and in making common cause against skeptics about religion, libertines, and people they considered to be behaving immorally. As I noted in the previous chapter, women in the seventeenth century had composed devotional books that were occasionally published. In the reign of the Roman Catholic James II (1685–88), Catholic writers, freed from censorship, published devotional and apologetic literature. They claimed that

90

Catholic devotional literature, including that written by the Catholic female saints, abbesses, and laywomen, was far superior to what Protestants had produced. In the subsequent reign of Protestant William and Mary, Protestant women were eager to show that they could offer models of devotion as valuable as those of Catholics. For their part, Church of England clergy were eager to demonstrate that there were Anglican women who were models of piety and theological soundness.

Many devout and literate Protestants of this period wrote poetry as part of their practice of personal prayer, religious meditation, and spiritual self-development, with no intention of publishing their work. Of the published religious poetry, much is in the form of meditations on such subjects as the last judgment, heaven, hell, death, and Christ's sacrifice on the cross. The longest poem in the collection that Mary Astell, the important feminist philosopher, presented to the Archbishop of Canterbury in 1689 is a meditation, "Judgment," a vision of the day Jesus will come to take the righteous to heaven with him and to consign the faithless and the vicious to hell.[1]

Informal Bible study and prayer groups of lay members of the Church of England, apparently first organized in London in 1678, spread throughout the country. In 1698 the Society for Promoting Christian Knowledge (SPCK) was organized to encourage these groups and to urge them to add charitable outreach programs for the Christian education of poor children. Church of England clergy were active in many of these groups, and it was to the Bible study and prayer group in the parish of the Reverend Samuel Wesley that his wife Susanna began to preach and teach herself in 1712. (These groups were the origin of the later "Methodist classes" organized by Susanna's son John, groups which produced more women preachers.) Susannah Hopton's adaptation of *Devotions in the Ancient Way of Offices, With Psalms, Hymns, and Prayers for Every Day of the Week* (1700) was published with a preface by George Hickes, a learned Anglican clergyman; he recommended the book as especially suited to use by "the *Religious Societies*, of whose Rise and Progress the World hath Lately had an Account, by the Reverend Mr. Woodward."[2]

Societies for the Reformation of Manners were also organized to use the state police power in aid of reform. These societies pressed local magistrates to indict men and women guilty of prostitution, public drunkenness, cursing, gambling, and failure to attend church. Abstracts of the applicable laws and instructions for giving information to magistrates were published. In 1691, at the suggestion of Bishop Edward Stillingfleet, Queen Mary "earned for herself a special position as the patron of reform" by writing to the Middlesex justices of the peace urging them to be models of righteous conduct and to prosecute vigorously offenders against morality. Other publications instructed citizens dissatisfied with the performance of their local magistrates how to press charges against them.[3]

Many writers and publishers joined the movements for religious and moral reformation. Richard Steele, still an army Captain, offered a kind of Christian courtesy book praising St. Paul as a better model than Caesar in *The Christian Hero: An Argument Proving that no Principles but those of Religion are Sufficient to make a Great Man* (1701). The *Athenian Oracle*, which published the first poems of the most important woman poet of this period, Elizabeth Singer Rowe, was one of the periodicals committing itself to the causes of religious and moral reformation. In the theatre, the immorality of earlier Restoration drama like Behn's was most famously denounced by the Reverend Jeremy Collier in *A Short View of the Immorality, and Profaneness of the English Stage . . .* (1698). Collier attacked the Restoration drama's representation of successful libertinism; its language of blasphemy, swearing, sexual jokes, and double entendre; and its mockery of religion and the clergy. The theatre, he insisted, must "recommend Virtue, and discountenance Vice."[4] Among others, Catharine Trotter, playwright and philosopher, in the preface to her tragedy, *The Fatal Friendship* (1698), welcomed the project of making the theatre a force for discouraging vice and recommending "firm, unshaken Virtue." Trotter's friend, Lady Sarah Piers, celebrated what she took to be the difference between earlier Restoration writers and Trotter in a commendatory poem:

> The fam'd *Orinda*'s and *Astrea*'s Lays
> With never dying Wit bless'd *Charles*'s Days
> And we supposed Wit could no higher rise,
> Till you succeeding, tear from them the Prize,
> More Just Applause is yours who check the Rage
> Of Reigning Vice that has debauched the Stage.
> And dare shew Vertue in a vicious Age.[5]

As Behn's work had shown, whatever advantages libertinism might have had for men, in an age when there was a double standard of sexual morality for men and women and no effective contraception, from a woman's perspective, hedonism and libertinism usually led to female suffering.

While the legitimacy of women's reading and writing romances was debated, Protestant Christianity clearly required women to read and to think about Scripture, devotional literature, and theology. Dissenting women continued to publish the apocalyptic and prophetic writing and the narratives of conversion and persecution that had arisen during the Civil War. Quaker women still published at a high rate, producing thirty titles during the 1690s, including Abigail Fisher's epistles to young Quakers and the itinerant preacher Barbara Blaugdone's *Account of the Travels, Sufferings, and Persecutions* (1691). One of many dissenters enduring punishments provided by the Restoration Clarendon Code that aimed to re-establish the Church of England by criminalizing dissenting religious practices, Blaugdone writes of being frequently jailed and of being whipped "till the Blood ran down my Back."[6]

Jane Lead, a mystic and millenarian prophet, founder of the Philadelphian sect, published books of biblical commentary and revelation, including a massive three-volume spiritual autobiography, *A Fountain of Gardens, Watered by the Rivers of Divine Pleasure, and Springing up in all the Variety of Spiritual Plants* (1696–1701). Influenced by Jacob Böhme, Lead attacked reliance on reason. She taught that the Divine was both male and female and that God would restore the fallen world to its prelapsarian state. Increasingly, however, better educated and more intellectual Church of England women were moved to write and sometimes to publish serious work on religious and philosophical subjects.

WOMEN PHILOSOPHERS

The reign of William and Mary is remarkable for the emergence of women writers willing and able to engage in public controversy about the new philosophies articulated by René Descartes (*Discourse on Method*, 1637; *Principles of Philosophy*, 1644); the Cambridge Platonists, including Ralph Cudworth and Henry More; and John Locke (*Essay on Human Understanding*, 1689). The new philosophy's rejection of scholastic authority and its emphasis on the power of reason and sense experience as the sources of knowledge potentially minimized the intellectual disadvantage from which women suffered because of their lack of access to university education. It encouraged women to challenge patriarchal custom with arguments from reason and their own experience. That Descartes and Locke elected to publish their philosophical work in their native vernacular languages, instead of in Latin, also helped make the new philosophy more accessible to women than older philosophy had been. The power of Cartesian rationalism to encourage feminist ideas had been made evident in François Poullain de La Barre's *The Woman as Good as the Man: Or, the Equality of Both Sexes* (French, 1673; English 1677).[7]

Among the women who ventured to publish on philosophical and theological subjects in this period were Damaris Cudworth Masham, daughter of the Cambridge Platonist, Ralph Cudworth; Mary Astell, important as an early feminist philosopher and as a religious and political philosopher; Catharine Trotter, a literary child prodigy who went on to write in defense of Locke's philosophy; and Judith Drake, most probably the author of *An Essay in Defence of the Female Sex* (1696). Astell and Drake were part of what Moira Ferguson has called "the first sizable wave of British secular feminist protest in history," occurring from the mid 1680s until about 1713 – although, as we shall see, it is misleading to call Astell's feminism "secular."[8]

The women who emerged as philosophical controversialists in this period began with an access to learning that was unusual for women, but also asserted themselves to form intellectual relations with male philosophers and theologians. Philosophers to whom these women wrote letters on philosophical questions typically expressed initial surprise that a woman would be interested in such issues and amazement that a woman was capable of such understanding, but several distinguished male philosophers and theologians of the day entered into significant correspondences with women. In the 1680s Damaris Cudworth corresponded with Locke (who later became a permanent guest in her home) and in 1704–5 with Gottfried Leibniz. The Oxford Platonist and Church of England clergyman John Norris responded to Astell's request that they correspond about his theological ideas and her reservations about some of them by engaging in a ten-month correspondence that he then suggested should appear as *Letters Concerning the Love of God between the author of the Proposal to the Ladies and Mr. John Norris* (1695). In contrast to the single-voiced treatise, the letter, unpublished or published, becomes a favored form of enlightenment discourse, in part because it suited contingent inquiry and the exchange of ideas and experiences.

Philosophy, theology, and politics remained closely connected in the late seventeenth century; major political events, especially the specter of King James II's attempting to return England to Roman Catholicism, heightened interest in fundamental questions of the grounds of religious authority and religious truth. During his brief reign (1685–88), the Roman Catholic James II had made sincere efforts to return Protestant England to Roman Catholicism. Roman Catholic apologetical writing that would previously not have been permitted publication was encouraged during

James's reign. Some Protestants converted to Roman Catholicism, notably the poet laureate, John Dryden, who defended Roman Catholic theology in his longest poem, *The Hind and the Panther* (1687). James made efforts to prevent Church of England clergy from attacking Roman Catholicism, but these efforts were relatively unsuccessful; indeed, they strengthened the national resistance to his reign that forced his abdication in the Glorious Revolution of 1688–89. During the reign of William and Mary, defenders of Protestantism were encouraged to develop vigorous and learned defenses of Protestantism against both Roman Catholic critiques and new secular philosophies. The Toleration Act of 1689, part of the Glorious Revolution settlement, permitted open, licensed worship by Protestant dissenters from the Church of England; in some influential circles, hope revived for a more comprehensive Protestant Church of England, one that would certainly include both Anglicans and Presbyterians. Many English readers also followed with interest events and writings in the late-seventeenth-century counter-Reformation French Roman Catholic Church. In France, Jesuits, favored by Louis XIV, struggled with Jansenists, who were accused of adopting heresies recalling those of John Calvin. Madame Guyon, a quietist with a considerable following among French men and women, during the years 1688 to 1703 was frequently detained for alleged heresy in various convents and in the Bastille.

Among the pious, especially among laypeople who had no professional obligation to defend the special tenets of their own Church's doctrines – a category that included women writers – one sometimes sees signs of a religious eclecticism willing to look across sectarian divisions, even those between Roman Catholics and Protestants, for moral, spiritual, and devotional inspiration. Thus, Norris, a Church of England clergyman, and Astell, a faithful daughter of the Church who wrote *The Christian Religion as Profess'd by a Daughter of the Church* (1705), nevertheless both drew inspiration from the work of Nicolas Malebranche (1638–1715), a French Roman Catholic Oratorian. Susannah Hopton adapted *Devotions in the Ancient Way of Offices* for Anglican use from a book by the English Roman Catholic, John Austen. Hickes's introduction to Hopton's *Devotions* instructs Protestants that it is false to suppose that "no true Fruits of Piety" can come from Roman Catholics.[9] The poet Elizabeth Rowe was a dissenter also interested in religious and philosophical subjects; she first published her poems in a periodical, *The Athenian Mercury*, edited by John Dunton. The official religion of *The Athenian* was Church of England, but it avoided sectarianism and was hospitable to most dissenting Protestant sects. The gentlemen proprietors and contributors to *The Athenian* included Dunton, a dissenter; the Reverend Samuel Wesley, originally a dissenter but ordained in 1689 as a clergyman of the Church of England, and the Reverend John Norris, Mary Astell's friend.

MASHAM'S *DISCOURSE CONCERNING THE LOVE OF GOD*

A major issue for intellectuals in this period was how to understand the implications of the new philosophies, including that of Descartes, for religion. Most late-seventeenth-century philosophers sought to escape from scholasticism, to rely on rational argument, and to produce versions of the new philosophies that were compatible with Christianity and that supported ethical human conduct. The Cambridge Platonists had been concerned both to refute what they took to be the irreligion of Hobbes and to celebrate the power of reason. Malebranche was influenced by Descartes, but rejected Descartes's doctrine of innate ideas; he argued that the soul was linked directly to universal reason, that Christ as universal reason illuminated human minds, giving them, if they were properly attentive, an intellectual intuition of essences. Norris was attracted to Malebranche's vision "of an Ideal World, existing in the mind of God, of which the material world was only an imperfect copy" and to Malebranche's claim that "we see all things in seeing God, and that we perceive God immediately, by the union of our spirits with His, not by means of an Idea."[10] Norris dedicated his *The Theory and Regulation of Love* (1685) to Damaris Cudworth, Lady Masham, but she thought his admiration for Malebranche seriously mistaken and offered her own critique of Malebranche in *A Discourse Concerning the Love of God* (1690).[11]

Masham's *Discourse Concerning the Love of God* (1690), her first book, is a work of early enlightenment philosophy, using rational argument rather than argument from authority, and invoking principles and methods of argument generally consistent with those of Locke's *Reasonableness of Christianity* (1695) and with emerging Latitudinarianism.[12] Masham confutes the contention of Malebranche and Norris that people are obligated to love and desire God alone and that the love of inferior creatures is sinful. She saw that Malebranche's position entailed an extreme contempt of the world and of human relations, contempt that, however suited to a celibate Roman Catholic priest living in a religious community, devalued family and social life. According to Masham, God created man as a rational, sociable creature with natural desires conducive to a moral life and to happiness in society. Love of our family members and friends are natural affections, created by God, not, as Malebranche insists, sinful desires to be extinguished. "It is certain," she writes tartly, "that if we had no Desires but after God, the several Societies of Mankind could not long hold together, nor the very Species be continued."[13] To offer a supposed model of true religion that requires renunciation of natural desire and withdrawal from society, as Malebranche does, she argues, is to offer an impossible model that will increase skepticism toward religion and destroy the obligations of social life. For humans to aspire to this model is, at best, as useless as it would be for "the Fishes (if they were capable of it) to propose, or pray to God, that they might fly in the Air like Birds; or Ride Post-Horses as Men do."[14]

Recognizing the sincerity of Malebranche's piety and characterizing his writing as the "Rapture of a Devout Mind," not the product "of Philosophical Disquisition," Masham nevertheless warns that his position represents a kind of irrational enthusiasm and unsociable solipsism. Those who try to follow Malebranche's advice to love no creature in the world and try to devote themselves to solitary contemplation of God will not only neglect their moral duty to do good in the world, but will "be more likely to grow wild than to improve as Christians."[15] Masham does not offer much detail about the practices of monasteries and hermitages she condemns, but contemporary readers would have been familiar with some of the severe austerities – like the wearing of hair shirts or belts with metal spikes pointed at the flesh – adopted even by some counter-Reformation laymen, including Pascal.[16] In her judgment, Malebranche and Norris have failed to offer a philosophical theology that can serve as an adequate basis for human moral conduct.

Masham engages Malebranche's epistemological position. Malebranche had insisted that God was the only cause of our sensations of the world, that our minds had no access to the material world of objects, and that our ideas of that world are implanted in our minds by God when we have need of them. He thus departed from Descartes's theory of innate ideas. Masham replies that it reflects adversely on the wisdom of God to suppose that his creation of our eyes, ears, and other sense organs with such "wonderful exactness and curious Workmanship" was pointless.[17] As Patricia Springborg has observed, Masham offers "well-reasoned arguments," and "demonstrates considerable philosophical agility in her technical discussion."[18]

Masham's methods of contesting Malebranche's use of scriptural authority show the power of an emerging modern historicist hermeneutic. She accepts the authority of Scripture (and finds it in harmony with the moral law revealed by reason), but subjects Malebranche's proof-texts to an historical and contextual test: could the original hearers of the biblical words – of Moses or of Jesus, for example – possibly have understood them as having the meanings Malebranche suggests? This becomes an effective technique for mocking scholastic elements, including the nice distinctions between "efficient" and "occasional" causes, remaining in Malebranche's work.

ASTELL

Like Masham, Mary Astell wrote clearly and confidently about significant theological and philosophical issues, and like Masham, she explicitly engaged Malebranche and Norris, although Astell was less critical of Malebranche than Masham was. Astell was the most systematic of the feminist and philosophical women writers of the Restoration and early eighteenth century. Her first published work, *A Serious Proposal to the Ladies, for the Advancement of their True and Greatest Interest. By a Lover of her Sex* (1694), urged women to take themselves seriously as rational and moral beings. It was continued in *A Serious Proposal. Part II* (1697), offering detailed guidance to women readers about what and how to read and how to develop greater capacity for rational thinking. Astell was especially famous in her lifetime for the practical proposal she offered in *A Serious Proposal*: that a "*Religious Retirement*" be established where upper-class women could go to live by themselves, free from "the rude attempts of designing Men."[19] In this new institution, women were to study, to learn enough to teach other women, and to use the institution as a base from which to engage in "spiritual and corporal Works of Mercy, relieving the Poor, healing the Sick, mingling Charity to the soul with that they express to the Body, instructing the Ignorant, counseling the Doubtful, comforting the Afflicted, and correcting those that err and do amiss."[20] To many contemporaries, this proposed institution looked like a Roman Catholic convent; thus, it was sometimes called the "Protestant nunnery." It did aim to restore to women some of the benefits for cultivating women's learning, teaching, and experience of administering institutional charity that had been lost to Protestant women by the Reformation. But Astell's proposal would have given its women inhabitants more liberty than a Roman Catholic convent, not requiring – or even permitting – vows and allowing women to leave if they wished to marry or for any other reason.

Acknowledging that the empirically observable behavior of women made them appear inferior to men, Astell argues that this apparent inferiority was a consequence, not of women's natural inferiority, but of inferior education and what she calls "Tyrant Custom" or what we might call "socialization." She urges women not to behave like "those useless and impertinent Animals, which the ill conduct of too many, has caus'd them to be mistaken for."[21] Women, she thinks, were fooled by social practices, like male flattery that made women imagine they were admired, when, in truth, most men had contempt for them. Like the Dutch Anna Maria van Schurman, author of *The Learned Maid or, Whether a Maid be a Scholar* (Latin, 1641; English, 1659) and the English Bathshua Makin, the author of *An Essay to Revive the Antient Education of Gentlewomen, in Religion, Manners, Arts and Tongues . . .* (1673), Astell describes a rigorous program of education designed to develop women's minds so as to make what she is convinced are their natural abilities apparent. Her attack on the deformative power of custom and her confidence in the power of education to improve the condition of women anticipates the kind of enlightenment argument Mary Wollstonecraft made much later in her better known *Vindication of the Rights of Woman* (1792).

The curriculum Astell proposed reflected both the philosophical influences on her and her high estimate of women's intellectual capacity. She recommended that the women inhabitants, who were presumed to know French as a consequence of conventional ladies' education, study modern French philosophers, including Descartes and Malebranche. Astell also recommended study of the work of Anne Dacier (1654–1720), an important French classicist who had translated Sappho, Terrance, and other Greek and Latin authors into French, and the poetry of Katherine Philips, to "excite the Emulation of the English Ladies."[22]

The rhetorical effectiveness of the *Proposal* derives in part from Astell's skill and intelligence in analyzing the condition and mentalities of contemporary ladies. She directs many of her arguments to persuading them that they can become more virtuous, more dignified, more admired, happier creatures if they will heed her advice. Her persona is, as the subtitle indicates, that of a woman "Lover of her Sex," one who pities women for the abuses they endure and for the mental and spiritual infantilism and darkness to which custom has consigned them:

When a poor Young Lady is taught to value her self on nothing but her Cloaths, and to think she's very fine when well accoutred. When she hears say, that 'tis Wisdom enough for her to know how to dress her self, that she may become amiable in his eyes, to whom it appertains to be knowing and learned; who can blame her if she lay out her Industry and Money on such Accomplishments, and sometimes extends it farther than her misinformer desires she should?[23]

Astell assumes her typical female reader is neither vicious nor stupid, but, realistically enough, simply poorly informed and in need of instruction, cajoling, encouragement, and reassurance. The woman reader, seeking to remove herself from the category of women Astell reveals to be objects of pity and contempt, is instructed that she need not be dependent on access to formal education, since God has endowed every woman with natural reason and natural powers of expression: "And since Truth is so near at hand, since we are not oblig'd to tumble over many Authors . . . but may have it for enquiring after in our own Breasts, are we not inexcusable if we don't obtain it?"[24] *Part II* offers a method for a woman who wishes to improve her powers of reasoning, but who might be diffident about her capacity to do so and unsure how to proceed. Astell explains rules of logic and gives practical suggestions, for example, that women should read difficult books, try to state their arguments to themselves, and then discuss them with other people, perhaps better able to understand them.

Following the Cambridge Platonists, Astell insists that an enlightened understanding will lead to virtuous conduct, that virtue is more pleasurable than vice, and that enlightened reason will also lead to joyful contemplation of the Divine. Should the religious retirement be established, its inhabitants are also promised the delights of friendship, described rhapsodically. Alessa Johns has shown that Astell develops a theory of female friendship that sees a virtuous woman, herself an image of God, able to function as an object of desire and emulation for other women; within the utopian female community "all women can through loving imitation and union become direct resemblances of the divine Mind." The community itself Astell describes as "the 'Paradise' your mother Eve forfeited." Astell published her work in part to serve as an object of emulation for other women.[25]

It is difficult to overestimate the importance of Astell's model yoking together women's demand for better education and women's obligation to develop spiritually and to participate in the reform of society by organizing charitable institutions. The ideological strength of this position allowed faithful daughters of the state church like Astell to appropriate to their own causes some of the authority and resources of the state. Given the climate of moral reform and institution founding in the 1690s, it is conceivable that an institution like the one Astell proposed could have been founded in the 1690s. Madame de Maintenon had convinced Louis XIV to establish a girls' school, albeit one for younger girls with a less philosophical curriculum, at Saint Cyr in 1686.

The charitable outreach Astell proposes, especially the missions of "instructing the Ignorant, counselling the doubtful, comforting the Afflicted, and correcting those that err and do amiss," was very much in accord with the goals of the SPCK. Indeed, Astell's vision of reformation made her *Proposal* vulnerable to Masham's charge that this sort of religion represented "enthusiasm." Dismissing objections to the education of single women on the ground that they have no children to teach, Astell exclaims:

the whole World is a single Ladys Family, her opportunities of doing good are not lessen'd but encreas'd by her being unconfin'd. Particular Obligations do not contract her Mind, but her Beneficence moves in the largest Sphere. And perhaps the Glory of Reforming this Prophane and Profligate Age is reserv'd for you Ladies, and that the natural and unprejudic'd Sentiments of your Minds being handsomely express'd, may carry a more strong conviction than the Elaborate Arguments of the Learned.[26]

No English women's college was immediately established. In 1709, however, Astell did found a charity school of the kind promoted by the SPCK; hers was for the daughters of Chelsea Hospital veterans and continued until 1862.[27] Astell's activism in the charity-school movement was also characteristic of other notably pious Anglican women writers of the very late seventeenth and early eighteenth centuries, including Elizabeth Burnet (1661–1709), author of the posthumously published *Method of Devotion*. As the wealthy widow of Bishop Gilbert Burnet, Burnet established a large number of schools for the instruction and education of poor children.[28] Astell's ideas, although not Astell's name, were also widely disseminated in *The Ladies Library*, compiled by the Reverend George Berkeley (famous as an idealist philosopher, but also a clergyman of the Church of England). *The Ladies Library* reprinted without attribution almost 150 pages of *Part II* of the *Serious Proposal*, and was itself frequently reprinted.[29] Astell's activism foreshadows the later campaigns and writings of Sarah Trimmer and Hannah More in organizing the more widespread Sunday-school movement and, later still, the work of Victorian women writers and activists of the Church, notably Charlotte Yonge, and the militancy of members of the Women's Christian Temperance Union.

Like the Quaker Margaret Fox, Astell expressed the Protestant conviction that women had souls as worthy as men's souls and that each individual woman must take responsibility for her own soul. A devout member of the Church of England, Astell did not overtly challenge the authority of the established state Church; indeed, she defended it against its challengers in several published works. Yet she insisted that it was useless, even dangerous, for women simply to be taught "the Principles and Duties of Religion" without their also being required to exercise their reason "to inquire into the grounds and Motives of Religion": only a woman who has cultivated her religious understanding, a woman who "is able to give a Reason *why*" she is good, can be depended upon to be a good Christian – or a faithful wife.[30] Astell's Anglican piety did not depend on the "inner light" of the Quakers or the personal prophetic revelation of a Jane Lead and did not disdain human learning. Her religious convictions drove her to serious biblical, theological, and philosophical study and made her an inspiration to contemporary and later women intellectuals including Judith Drake, Elizabeth Thomas, Lady Mary Chudleigh, Elizabeth Elstob, and Lady Mary Wortley Montagu.

The works of Astell and other early women philosophers including Masham were also important because the works themselves exhibited women's potential for rational thought. Cavendish's work, in so far as it was known, suggested that a woman might be curious about questions in philosophy and natural science, but it did not impress contemporaries as a demonstration of a woman's capacity for rigorous analysis or the development of reasoned argument. Women in the seventeenth century were in a situation very roughly analogous to the situation of African slaves: in both cases, most white men (and women too, for that matter) did not believe that women or Africans possessed the rational capacities that white men did. Therefore, just as Anglo-African writers later made crucial and unique contributions to the cause of abolition by demonstrating their own capacity for rationality in their published work, so writers like Astell and Masham in their published work gave what was actually significant empirical evidence that a woman could think and argue at a high level. Moreover, when Astell argued that training women's minds in the arts of reasoning and discourse was the surest way to promote women's virtue, she rejected the established misogynist ideas that silence was a woman's rhetoric and that verbal facility in women was a mark of impurity.[31] How important Astell's display of women's capacity for rationality and expression was to women readers is evident in Elizabeth Thomas's panegyric, "To *Almystrea* [Mary Astell], on her Divine Works":

> Too Long! indeed, has been our Sex decry'd,
> And ridicul'd by Men's *malignant Pride* . . .

That *Women* had no *Souls* was their Pretence,
And *Women's* spelling passed for *Women's* Sense.
When you, most generous, Heroine! stood forth,
And show'd your Sex's *Aptitude* and *Worth* . . .
Redeem the coming Age! and set us free
From the false Brand of *Incapacity*.[32]

As a philosopher and theologian, Astell in *Some Reflections on Marriage* (1700) did not reject the sacramental character of marriage or the husband's right to his wife's love, honor, and obedience. However, she recognized that the ideology of marriage was linked to political ideology. According to the Lockian political theory of the Glorious Revolution, James II had forfeited his right to the people's obedience by behaving tyrannically; the people were, therefore, free to reconstitute a new government that would rule in the best interests of the people. The people or their representatives in Parliament were free to enter into a new "contract" by inviting William and Mary to become king and queen, as Parliament did. Because sovereignty in the state was traditionally analogized to sovereignty in the family, this renegotiation of the ground of political sovereignty led to speculation and debate about the grounds of husbands' sovereignty over wives.[33] Astell famously inquired: "if Absolute Sovereignty be not necessary in a State, how comes it to be so in a Family? or if in a Family why not in a State; since no Reason can be alledg'd for the one that will not hold more strongly for the other? If the Authority of the Husband so far as it extends, is sacred and inalienable, why not of the Prince?"[34]

Potentially, the new Whig ideology of the Glorious Revolution opened a way to claims for women's rights. In the 1690s, such claims typically appear tentatively and jocularly in comedies. Astell, however, was not sympathetic to Locke's political ideology; she believed that the social order was divinely ordained and hierarchical, not based on voluntary contract. Indeed, Patricia Springborg, a modern political theorist, considers Astell one of Locke's most important early critics and finds that she exposes "the absurdity of voluntarism on which social contract theory is predicated."[35] Given that contemporary Whigs were arguing for the rights of male subjects but not for the rights of women, Astell calls attention to the inconsistency of their position. She accepts both the authority of kings and the authority of husbands – for those women who have them. She herself never married.

Nevertheless, in *Some Reflections on Marriage*, Astell points out that, under contemporary social conditions, decent women's efforts to obey some actual husbands required heroism, indeed, sometimes virtual martyrdom. *Some Reflections* was occasioned in part by the notorious situation of Hortense Mancini, a niece and ward of the French Cardinal Mazarin, who had married her to the Duke of Meilleraye. The Duke ran through his wife's fortune and attempted to impose his extreme religious ideas on her (for example, he allegedly forbid her to nurse on fast days).[36] When she demanded a separation, he sent her to an abbey, from which she escaped, eventually to the court of Charles II. Astell did not countenance what she regarded as the frivolous and dissolute life the Countess lived in London, but she vividly evokes the miseries wives could suffer in unfortunate marriages:

> To be yok'd for Life to a disagreeable Person and Temper; to have Folly and Ignorance tyrannize over Wit and Sense; to be contradicted in every thing one does or says, and bore down not by Reason but Authority; to be denied ones most innocent desires, for no other cause but the Will and Pleasure of an absolute Lord and Master, whose Follies a Woman with all her Prudence cannot hide, and whose Commands she cannot but despise at the same time she obeys them; is a misery none can have a just Idea of, but those who have felt it.[37]

Because Astell insists that a wife owes an inalienable duty of obedience to her husband and because she describes a large array of unsatisfactory and deplorable kinds of husbandly behavior, her picture of marriage is grim.

Part of the problem, in Astell's analysis, was that men were taught to overvalue themselves and women to undervalue themselves; she uses a range of irony and sarcasm to drive these points home. Sardonically, she remarks:

> . . . alas! what poor Woman is ever taught that she should have a higher Design than to get her a husband? Heaven will fall in of course; and if she makes but an Obedient and Dutiful wife, she cannot miss of it. A Husband indeed is thought by both sexes so very valuable, that scarce a Man who can keep himself clean and make a Bow, but thinks he is good enough to pretend to any Woman . . .[38]

Here, as elsewhere in her work, Astell challenges the assumptions behind conventional language and names for things. Discussing courtship, she reverses love poetry's metaphors of conquest, "taking the position of the pursued rather than the pursuer," so that the result of a successful courtship becomes not a triumphant conquest but a sinister capture.[39] As in *A Serious Proposal*, Astell suggests that however necessary marriage might be for the continuation of the species, individual women might well form for themselves "higher Design[s]."[40]

ROWE'S *POEMS ON SEVERAL OCCASIONS*

Like Masham and Astell, the poet Elizabeth Singer Rowe declared herself firmly allied to the causes of religion and virtue. She was early understood to be a woman poet who continued the line of Katherine Philips and who departed from the libertinism of Behn. As contemporary philosophers did, Rowe concerned herself with questions about whether only God could be the proper object of love or whether other kinds of love for God's creatures or God's creation had legitimacy.

Like the work of many subsequent women (and men) poets, Rowe's poetry first appeared as individual poems in a periodical, in Rowe's case, in *The Athenian Mercury,* edited by John Dunton. The rise of the periodical – publications that went beyond newspapers to offer miscellaneous contents including essays, poems, and reviews – in this period offered amateur and professional writers an increasingly large number of hospitable forums for their literary work. The author of a monograph on the *Athenian* has described Rowe "as a kind of female poet laureate" for the gentlemen proprietors and contributors to the *Athenian.*[41] These gentlemen, as I mentioned previously, included the Reverend Samuel Wesley and the Reverend John Norris, Mary Astell's friend and correspondent. Dunton and Rowe were both dissenters.

As a religious poet, Rowe has some of Anne Bradstreet's militant Christianity and also some of the Anglican spirituality of George Herbert, the latter a poet the *Athenian* explicitly recommended for study.[42] Rowe read Norris and developed her own version of quietism, but she was always concerned to maintain a role for reason in religion. Coming out of a Calvinist dissenting tradition as she did, yet also influenced by the Cambridge Platonists, Rowe dealt with logical contradictions between Calvinist belief in human depravity after the fall and Platonic understandings of human nature as naturally good and human reason as capable of discerning God. The ancient quarrel between St. Augustine and Pelagius, who denied original sin and was branded a heretic, echoed in late-seventeenth-century and early eighteenth-century theological debates. The more Calvinist English dissenters and Anglicans charged Latitudinarian divines with Pelagianism and French Jansenists similarly accused the Jesuits.

Rowe was part of a late-seventeenth-century movement to create a Christian poetry that would transcend classical poetry in sublimity and truth. Boileau had translated Longinus in 1674, Milton had published his great Christian epic, *Paradise Lost* in 1688, and the English critic John

Dennis was preparing to argue in *The Grounds of Criticism in Poetry* (1704)
that "the greatest Sublimity is to be derived from Religious Ideas."[43]
Biblical paraphrase, eschatological poetry, moral poetry, devotional poetry,
and hymns all attracted serious Protestant English poets, including Rowe.
Rowe's first published poem, in the *Athenian*, was "A Pindarick Poem on
Habbakuk." She offers a paraphrase of what is essentially a psalm, indeed, a
passage much admired as Hebrew poetry, from one of the minor prophets.
The lines describe a theophany (the appearance of a god to a person or
persons), here the appearance of the enraged and mighty God of Israel to
smite his enemies. The picture of the Divine Judge coming in might is
sufficiently splendid and wonderful that the final couplet making a contemporary political application comes as a deflation.[44] Rowe is fascinated
by thoughts of divine judgment and apocalyptic moments.

Dutton published Rowe's *Poems on Several Occasions. By Philomela*
(1696), an important volume beginning with a poem celebrating "Plato-
nick Love," including biblical paraphrases and meditations as well as more
secular poems in honor of William and Mary and a few lesser contemporaries, and ending with "A Farewel to Love." A preface signed by
Elizabeth Johnson praises Rowe as a new female genius and champion
of her sex more virtuous than Behn, declares that this female poet loves
"*Virtuously* and *Reasonably*," that she manifests a "clear and unaffected
Love to *Virtue*" and "heighth of *Piety* and warmth of *Devotion* in the
Canticles, and other Religious Pieces." The volume sets up contests
between human and divine love and between classical and biblical narratives. Still unmarried, the poet represents herself as a young woman who,
like Philips, writes from a secure pastoral retreat. A few of the poems are
responses from the Athenians to Rowe, including one responding to her
paean to Platonic love by urging the merits of human love, said to have
the power to arm us against our vices and associated with God's command
to humans to increase and multiply. The female poet in the midst of the
volume confesses in a pastoral vein to love for a swain and offers one
striking pastoral, "By Despair," set at night, describing mournful grief at
having been abandoned by her swain. An adventurous series of biblical
paraphrases of the Song of Solomon allows Rowe to voice an intensity of
passion rare in women's poetry:

> I *Claspt* him, just as meeting Lovers wou'd,
> That had the stings of Absence understood:
> I held him fast, and *Centring* in his *Breast*,
> My ravish'd Soul found her desired Rest.[45]

The Song of Solomon was itself a kind of Hebrew pastoral partly in the form of a dialogue between a bridegroom and his bride; it was allegorized by Christians as about the love of Christ and his Church or Christ and the believer.

The general tenor of the volume suggests the superiority of spiritual to carnal love and the superiority of the biblical to the classical. A long version of Ovid's story of Phaeton from the *Metamorphoses* interestingly suggests parallels to the biblical versions of apocalypse and terror of the divine, dwelling on Ovid's account of the chariot of the sun plunging to earth. Like Astell, in "Paraphrase on Canticle 5.6" the poet wonders at those who worship the "false Idol" of the god of Love and are blind to the more intense, perfect pleasures offered by the worship of the true God.[46] She can contemplate the Day of Judgment with apprehension in "Thoughts on Death" and "Paraphrase of Malachy 3.14," but more often, as in "The Rapture," longs to escape the limits of the corporeal world for the wonders of permanent divine presence in Heaven:

> Lord! if one distant glimpse of thee
>   Thus elevate the Soul,
> In what a heighth of Extasie
>   Do those bless'd Sprits roll,
>
> Who by a fixt eternal View
>   Drink in immortal Raies;
> To whom unveiled thou dost shew
>   Thy Smiles without Allays?[47]

THE THEATRE

As I observed at the beginning of this chapter, during the reign of William and Mary many moralists attacked the earlier Restoration theatre as a nursery of libertinism and irreligion. While some critics urged the pious to avoid the theatre altogether, in both France and England in the very late seventeenth century some dramatists tried to invent new theatrical forms that would make the stage a handmaiden of piety and morality. In France, influenced by Jansenism, Jean Racine abandoned secular drama and wrote his two great biblical dramas, *Esther* (1689) and *Athalie* (1691), both for performance by the young women of Maintenon's Saint Cyr school. In England, two of three significant new women dramatists who emerge in this period, Trotter and Mary Pix, align themselves with the newer movements aiming to foster morality and religion; the third,

Delarivière Manley, continued the libertine tradition of Behn. Theatre historians have pointed out that the break up of the United Company in 1695 and the subsequent re-establishment of two theatres in London produced new competition and new opportunities for amateur and beginning playwrights, including women, to have their works performed. Competition between these two companies and the novelty value of a play written by a woman combined to produce the unique phenomenon of the 1695/96 season: seven new plays by women appeared, including Manley's *The Lost Lover, or the Jealous Husband*, a comedy, and *The Royal Mischief*, a tragedy; Trotter's *Agnes de Castro*, adapted from a Behn story by the sixteen-year-old prodigy; and Pix's *Ibrahim, the Thirteenth-Emperor of the Turks*, an heroic tragedy, and *The Spanish Wives*, a comedy.[48] After the death of Behn in 1689, no one new woman writer emerged as such a dominant figure, but a market developed for literary performances by "ladies." And we begin to see small groups of mutually supportive women writers like Manley, Trotter, and Pix in 1695/96, who wrote commendatory verses for each other's plays.

TROTTER'S *FATAL FRIENDSHIP*

Trotter, who also wrote philosophical works, was the most intellectual of the three dramatists. It was no doubt inevitable that the intellectual and literary ambitions of women of this period should have led them to attempt tragedy, a literary form second only to epic in prestige and one slightly more approachable. As Jacqueline Pearson said, Trotter "created austere and idealistic plays which eschew sex and violence, offer minute analyses of moral and emotional dilemmas, and create pure and strong heroines whose intelligence and chastity refute stereotypes of female lust and irrationality."[49]

The eighteen-year-old Trotter created a sensation in 1698 when her verse tragedy, *The Fatal Friendship*, opened at London's Lincoln's Inn Fields theatre and became a critical and popular success. It is probably not coincidental that *Fatal Friendship* premiered in the same month that Collier's attack on the alleged depravity of earlier Restoration drama, *A Short View of the Immorality and Prophaness of the English Stage*, was published.[50] The commendatory verses published with the play praise Trotter as a "Stage-reformer," one who checks "the rage / Of reigning Vice that has debauched the Stage." Behn had earlier followed Dryden into heroic drama, the usual Restoration form of serious drama that was essentially romance, not tragedy. Trotter in *Fatal Friendship* follows

Thomas Otway into a new kind of blank-verse domestic tragedy. Like some of the more successful women writers of tragedy who followed her, Trotter has enough ethical imagination to find the nature of virtue a genuinely interesting subject.

Fatal Friendship, while far from a masterpiece, is more coherent, more genuinely dramatic, and more intellectually interesting than most tragedies of the period. Neoclassical literary ideals promoted didacticism and discouraged the moral complexity usually found appropriate to tragedy; neoclassical ideals of language were also unfavorable to styles that have satisfied in English tragedy.[51] Most of the verse in eighteenth-century tragedies written by well-educated men is wooden; much of the verse in eighteenth-century tragedies written by women is incompetent, even execrable. Trotter was unable to write distinguished blank verse, but she was able to make her characters speak with some fluency and directness.

Fatal Friendship continues concerns of seventeenth-century aristocratic romance, but re-imagines them in a more realistic bourgeois mode. The male protagonist, Gramont, is a poor younger brother, a French soldier with dismal prospects; he loves Felicia and has secretly married her, knowing that her brother and guardian would not countenance their marriage. Gramont's father orders him to marry a rich young widow, Lamira, who loves him. Although he is at first willing to suffer the consequences of his father's rage for refusing the proposed match, Gramont consents to this second marriage when he discovers that his dear friend Castalio needs to be ransomed from prison and that his infant son needs to be ransomed from pirates. He convinces himself that it would be wrong to preserve his own sense of honor at the expense of his friend, his child, and his wife, who he fears will starve. Gramont soliloquizes:

> And shou'd I Sacrifice 'em all, to keep
> A little peace of mind, the pride of never straying?
> Walk on by Rules, and calmly let 'em perish,
> Rather than tread one step beyond to save 'em?
> Forbid it Nature, no, I'll leap o'er all,
> *Castalio*, my suffering Babe, and Lov'd *Felicia*
> See how dear you're to me, how strong my Love,
> When it can turn the Scale against my Virtue.[52]

Dilemmas that pit honor against love in romance and heroic drama typically provoke long speeches about the insolubility of the protagonist's dilemma, thus demonstrating the refinement of the protagonist's moral imagination, but are then typically resolved by discoveries or some *deus ex machina* that makes it unnecessary for the protagonist to compromise his honor. Gramont, however, does sacrifice his honor by marrying Lamira, although he angers her by scrupling to have intercourse with her.

Trotter explores Gramont's moral suffering to suggest fundamental difficulties posed by the aristocratic masculine code of morality. She is troubled by the level of violence associated with the masculine defense of honor. Felicia declares herself willing to suffer poverty and pleads with Gramont to escape with her to some distant land because she fears what appears an inevitable duel between Gramont and her brother. Gramont dreads the further humiliation that, by the masculine code, such apparent cowardice would entail. Felicia further torments him by challenging him to imagine himself forced to accept charity, but he agrees not to fight. The scene between the husband and wife is sufficiently prolonged and Felicia's moral challenges to Gramont sufficiently compelling that the audience experiences Gramont's intense self-loathing and cannot dismiss him as a fool or a coward.

Throughout the play Trotter contrasts the sudden violence of male/male confrontations with what happens when people delay long enough for conversation and mutual explanation, which defuses rage. When the freed Castalio learns how he has been ransomed and reveals that he loved Lamira himself, it looks as though Castalio and Gramont will kill each other, but Castalio pauses long enough for an explanation and ends by admiring Gramont's ability to restrain himself from exercising his conjugal rights over Lamira. In the end, Gramont intervenes to prevent Castalio and Bellgard from killing each other, interposing himself between them and beseeching them to "hear at least what each has to alledge."[53] Like Gramont, Lamira is a mixed character, capable of rage, but, very unlike the villainesses of heroic drama, surprising us at the end by recognizing that her rival, Felicia, is as "Innocent to me, as I to you," and deciding to devote herself to religious retirement.[54] The play explicitly insists that all characters are mixed:

> None know their Strength; let the most Resolute
> Learn from this Story to distrust themselves . . .[55]

Nevertheless, the play ends tragically. Gramont, attempting to separate Castalio and Bellgard, accidentally kills his friend Castalio, then stabs himself. Dying, Gramont, learns that both he and Castalio were about to be favored by the king, so that, had he waited upon Providence, he might have been happy. A more occluded meaning of the play may be that

Gramont is destroyed because he is caught between older ideals of masculine honor and an emerging ideal of a more cautious masculinity more tied to wife and children than to male bonds.

MANLEY'S *ROYAL MISCHIEF*

Not every writer during the reign of William and Mary was committed to the new movements for moral and religious reformation. Among the resisters, Delarivière Manley made an effort to continue the Restoration libertine tradition of Behn. Having been tricked or seduced into a bigamous marriage with her cousin and become the mother of an illegitimate child, Manley perhaps decided to make a virtue of necessity and to offer sympathetic portraits of women who had lost their chastity. In her first, unsuccessful intrigue comedy, *The Lost Lover, or the Jealous Husband* (1696), a cast mistress, Belira, is allowed to complain of her wrongs, to arraign the libertine Wilmore for his lack of truthfulness, and – despite the fact that the play is a comedy – to express her desire for revenge on Wilmore and even to attempt to stab her successful rival for his love. Some of the dialogue in *The Lost Lover* touches on what subsequently becomes a major theme of Manley's later scandal chronicles: the alleged hypocrisy of respectable people who pay verbal tributes to virtue but who in secret act as lasciviously as those they condemn.

Manley's early work frequently expresses solidarity with other women writers. She had, for instance, provided commendatory verses for Trotter's *Agnes de Castro*, and she seems to have been the organizer and editor of a volume of elegies on the death of Dryden, *The Nine Muses; or, Poems written by Nine Several Ladies, upon the Death of the famous John Dryden, Esq.* (1700), including poems by Manley, Trotter, Pix, Lady Sarah Piers, Sarah Fyge Egerton, and Susanna Centlivre.[56] But a hint of the way Manley later turned on other women writers, especially those with reputations for virtue, in her scandal chronicles, appears in *The Lost Lover* in the character of "Orinda, an Affected Poetess." Manley's Orinda is silly rather than vicious, and what she says "bears little resemblance" to the work or life of Katherine Philips.[57] Nevertheless, Manley begins her literary career as a daughter of Behn rather than a daughter of Philips.

Manley had more success with an heroic tragedy, *The Royal Mischief* (1696), a play spectacularly lurid and extravagant following the Restoration mode of Nathaniel Lee and Elkannah Settle; an exotic eastern setting allows the display of eunuchs and poisons. Cruel punishments include a choice between a bowl of slow-acting poison or strangulation by mutes and – mercifully off-stage – death and dismemberment by being shot from a canon.

The ideas and characters of *The Royal Mischief* are similar to the ideas and characters in the amatory fiction of Behn, Manley herself, and later, Eliza Haywood. Love, or rather lust, is a sudden, irresistible, if fleeting, "tyrannic power"; men and women are both capable of experiencing intense passion, but women are apt to be destroyed by passion. The female protagonist, Homais, chafes under the restriction of being married and confined by an old husband, the Prince of Libardian. (In Manley's source, *The Travels of Sir John Chardin into Persia, through the Black Sea and the Country of Colchis*, 1686, the prince is neither old nor sexually impotent.[58]) Homais has had an earlier affair with the libertine Ismael, an army officer and younger brother of the Chief Vizier. Now – prompted only by his reputation and the sight of a picture of him – Homais has conceived a grand passion for Levan Dadian, her husband's nephew, newly married to the virtuous Bassima. Relentlessly, she aims to gratify her lust for Levan Dadian: schemes with her eunuch and her former lover to seduce Levan Dadian, sleeps with him, has her husband drugged with opium, conspires to have Bassima poisoned, and orders the Vizier shot from the canon. Her husband finally runs her through with his sword. Dying, frustrated and enraged, she reaches out trying to strangle Levan rather than die without him; bleeding, she spits out a misogynistic curse upon her husband:

> Thus I dash thee with my gore,
> And may it scatter unthought Plagues around thee,
> Curses more numerous than the Ocean's Sand,
> Much more inveterate than Woman's Malice;
> And but with never ending time expiring.[59]

Manley has built on the characters of bold villainesses, like the Empress Nourmahal in Dryden's *Aureng-Zebe* (1675), who is also married to a sexually unsatisfactory old eastern ruler and who conceives an incestuous passion for her stepson Aureng-Zebe; such villainesses, however, are not normally the principal character in male dramatist's plays, as Homais is. At least one feminist critic has thought of Homais as a feminist heroine because of her pursuit of sexual gratification, her "devastating candor," and her boldness.[60] More subtly, Melinda Rabb finds that "despite her conniving and wrongdoing, she is a surprisingly genuine and compelling character," one who becomes wicked "in response to a world that has few constructive options." Rabb reads the play as a satiric variation on heroic tragedy, creating a "female mock heroic," one in which "Manley has literally and metaphorically exploded the heroes of her play and exposed the threat that the transgressive woman poses to the homosocial assumptions underlying political and sexual power."[61] Personally, I find *The Royal Mischief* energetic but ridiculous, even pathetic and misogynistic, and Homais, bereft of moral scruples or even moral consciousness, a repulsive character.

The Royal Mischief, nevertheless, does address the subject of virtue, invoking the word at least eighteen times; in her own way, Manley responds to the contemporary movement for moral and religious reformation. The libertine Ismael is confident that virtue is merely "platonic / Nonsense"; he urges Osman to seduce the married Bassima despite her apparent virtue, making a point that had become a libertine cliché:

> [women] like the forward and the bold,
> For Virtue in such Souls is like their form,
> Only exterior Beauty, worn to deceive
> The credulous World and buy Opinions
> From the common rout . . .[62]

In a reversal of the usual pattern of a man seducing a virtuous woman, Homais seduces Levan Dadian, a man "much renowned for virtue."[63] After he succumbs, he doubts that he ever did possess real virtue:

> Nor is there any [praise] due to my past Vertue.
> What praise to stand when no temptations near?[64]

Bassima, who has been touched by love for Osman before her marriage to Levan Dadian, resists acting – although not speaking – her desire for him. The plotters nevertheless cause her husband to believe that she has been unfaithful and she is sentenced to be banished and to have "her Eyes put out," "Her Hands, her Nose, her Lips, to be cut off."[65] Manley understands virtue as a social fact, identifying it with reputation. She makes even Bassima equate her virtue with her "glory" and, unjustly condemned as an adulteress, declare:

> Now should I fall 'till time has cleared my Vertue,
> My Fame must perish with me: The Standard
> Which the World condemns, or clears us by
> Is not our Innocence, but our Success.[66]

Ludicrously, the ambitious Ismael, who has no scruples about scheming to destroy any innocent character who gets in his way or about conniving to murder his brother, agreeing to murder the Prince of Libardian in exchange for a promise of more sex with Homais, asks her to "swear by this Kiss, / Which steals my Vertue from me. . ."[67] Here virtue, if it has any meaning at all, can only mean that he has not yet lost his reputation and been exposed as a liar, a schemer, and a traitor. Manley seems so traumatized by the loss of her own reputation for virtue that she is bent on exposing any other virtue as duplicitous appearance or, alternatively, on showing that it will be destroyed, as Bassima and Osman are.

PIX'S *BEAU DEFEATED*

Mary Pix, the third of these dramatists, was simultaneously the most prolific as a playwright and the one who has attracted the least critical attention. She is credited with six tragedies and six comedies written and produced between 1696 and 1706, the comedies considerably better than the tragedies. Feminist critics have generally found her less interesting than Trotter or Manley because Pix seems less concerned to provide strong new heroines than Trotter or to dramatize the unfairness of women's lives than Behn or Manley. Pearson went so far as to say that Pix had "no ideas about gender."[68] Derek Hughes finds her "a slavish upholder of male authority."[69] Nevertheless, Pix successfully wrote bustling multi-plot intrigue comedy and she offers nicely down-to-earth contemporary characters, anticipating Frances Burney's later genius in the representation of comic vulgarity. Although less rigorously high-minded than Trotter, she contributed to the development of the new, more moral and sentimental comedy. Like both Manley and Trotter, Pix also experimented with plots in which traditional gender roles are reversed.

Pix's *Beau Defeated; or, The Lucky Younger Brother* (1700) gives a sense of what it might have felt like, to a person whose own ideological commitments were not the strongest, to be living in a period of such sharp ideological (or moral) change. The play suggests that libertine vice and modest, sober virtue are both roles that can be assumed or cast off. Characters inhabit a world in which seeing another person is often like looking through a kaleidoscope: at one moment his or her character appears as a gaudy pattern of libertine vice, then suddenly, it has reconfigured itself as a sober pattern of virtue – or *vice versa*. Pix thus dramatizes this time of moral reformation, when old styles of libertinism were in the process of being discarded by many – certainly not all – and new styles of virtuous gravity were becoming fashionable.

A widow herself, Pix in *The Beau Defeated* makes her heroine, Lady Landsworth, a young widow too, taking advantage of the greater latitude of action socially permitted to widows than to unmarried young women. Lady Landsworth has been married to a very old man, "who, in his Youth, having been a Debauchee, and dealing only with the worst of our Sex, had an ill Opinion of all, [and] kept me like a Nun . . ."[70] This husband dead, she has determined to come to London, to enjoy "all the innocent Liberty my Youth, my Wealth, and Sex desires," and to find herself a new husband with new virtues: "He should be Gentile, yet not a Beau; Witty, yet no Debauche; susceptible of Love, yet abhorring lew'd Women; Learned, Poetical, Musical, without one Dram of Vanity; in fine, very meritorious, yet very modest."[71]

Happily, such a meritorious man exists: Clerimont, a younger brother in mourning for his father, although his father has died leaving him no money. In a reversal of the usual older sexual dynamics, this man's "modest air" and reputation for chastity attract the woman. As Margarete Rubik observed, women dramatists preceded male dramatists in finding rakes unacceptable partners for virtuous heroines; women writers prefer male heroes who are consistently virtuous to rakes who abruptly repent in the fifth acts of the new sentimental comedy.[72]

Pix makes an amusing comedy out of gender reversals and changing moral standards. Lady Landsworth tests Clerimont's virtue by pretending to be a libertine woman willing to give him money, even to keep him. He resists taking the money, but likes the woman and her wit. Mrs. Fidget, Clerimont's old-fashioned landlady, berates him for *not* entertaining lewd women in his rooms, behavior that has reduced her income. When Clerimont and Lady Landsworth meet again in the Park, he is torn between attraction and repulsion, then horrified when she claims to have been kept by several men and now to be the "Perquisite of a Country Gentleman; a Man of Gravity, and one of the pious Senators; a great Stickler against Wenching and Profaneness."[73] The situation is exacerbated when Clerimont's servant Jack decides to help his master win this rich libertine lady by spreading the story that Clerimont "is the veriest Libertine the whole Town affords; has tir'd Vice in every one of her shapes; and now, forsooth, for variety, turns Hypocrite, that he may find their pleasures out."[74] But despite his love for the woman he thinks a vicious creature, Clerimont remains true to his moral scruples.

In her turn, Lady Landsworth discovers that apparent libertinism in a husband kills desire. When she hears Jack's gossip that his master is a notorious libertine, she is disgusted. Then Clerimont simultaneously experiences desire and wonders whether a woman's appearance ever gives an adequate index to her true character: "And what know I but the coy Dame, who hides her Face at the least word a wry, and blushes to be gaz'd on, has in her heart looser fires than my gay Mistress."[75] Looking upon Clerimont, her mind filled with the account of his libertinism, Lady Landsworth finds him less attractive, seeming to have "lost that modest sweetness which caught my unwary Soul."[76] Nevertheless, she keeps up her libertine pretence, inviting him to taste the joys of love, then – on a sordid note – to help her deceive her keeper. Clerimont seems lost in the language of tragic romance, echoing Anthony in Dryden's *All for Love* (1677): "If there must be profusion, let it be in Love; there lay out all thy Stock; let days and nights and years serve only to count the acts of Love." This time, Lady Landsworth turns on Clerimont: "Oh I could Curse myself, my Follies, to believe there was Vertue in thy Sex, thou vile dissembler . . ."[77] Her exit convinces a relieved Clerimont that she is actually honest. The two, dropping their masks, agree to marry.

Another plot, from which *The Beau Defeated* derives its title, presents a foolish City widow, Mrs. Rich, who yearns to rise socially and to be loved by a fashionable beau. The characters in this plot are more traditional comic characters, sometimes a bit roughly handled, closer to the characters of Shadwell or Vanbrugh then to those of Cibber and the emerging sentimental drama. Mrs. Rich believes the man who purports to be Sir John Roverhead is a fine gentleman and wants to marry him.[78] He offers banal flattery and scraps of current song equally to Mrs. Rich, to her daughter Lucinda, and to Lady La Basset, a female gamester. His exposure begins when Mrs. Rich reads aloud banal verses he claims to have written to her. Lucinda and Lady La Basset realize that he has presented the same verses to them. Lady La Basset, it turns out, is no lady, but a cast mistress who has financed Sir John Roverhead's servant to impersonate his master and has taught him "the Modes and Manners" of London.[79]

Mrs. Rich escapes marriage to this servant, but her virtuous brother presses her to marry Clerimont's boorish elder brother, an early avatar of Henry Fielding's Squire Western, and one not likely to make a pleasing husband. The elder Clerimont has come to London to see sports like bearbaiting that he cannot see in Yorkshire. He makes his first entrance into Mrs. Clerimont's drawing room accompanied by his huntsman and by "two hounds coupled," saying "love me, love my dog." He has learned from observing two dogs coupled – later a favorite image of the artist William Hogarth for the miseries of marriage – to avoid marriage:

See this Couple now how they lear, how spitefully they look at one another. I tell thee Couz, this is *Jewel*, and this is *Beauty*; the bitch is *Beauty*, do yee mark me, Couz; there was not two Dogs in the whole Pack lov'd like these two, they play'd together like two Kittens . . . now they are join'd their hate is the same; one snarls, t'other bites, one pulls this way, t'other that; Gadzooks! They'd either venture hanging to be parted . . .[80]

Such ridicule of socially powerful gentlemen and of misogynistic and anti-matrimonial attitudes becomes a favorite theme of women writers, one that contributed to reducing the psychological power of patriarchal authority.

The Beau Defeated is a bit less good-natured than Pix's typical comedy, but it is typical of her in its reversing the gendering of standard comic plots. In *The Beau Defeated* the energetic, resourceful Lady Landsworth pursues the modest, romantic Clerimont. In Pix's first comedy, a farce, *The Spanish Wives* (1696), and in *The Deceiver Deceived* (1698), she reverses Cibber's sentimental plot of "an erring husband reclaimed by a forgiving wife," instead offering "an almost-erring wife prevented and reformed before actually yielding to temptation."[81] Pix's willingness to develop sympathetic female characters who are not paragons and not so perfectly virtuous that they do not struggle with temptation points forward to the eighteenth-century women writers who also give their sympathetic female characters more latitude than contemporary male writers did. Pix's dramatic career owed much to the example of Behn's success, and her tragedies continued to feature lurid assaults on female virtue, but her comedies, much less dark and much more genial than Behn's, became the model for the extremely successful comedies of her friend and protégée, Centlivre, as we shall see in the next chapter.

DRAKE'S *ESSAY IN DEFENCE OF THE FEMALE SEX*

Judith Drake was most probably the author of an anonymously published *Essay in Defence of the Female Sex* (1696); this *Essay* is at once a work of philosophy and a more belletristic entertainment. Drake sets out to confute the customary ideas of women's character defects by arguing that, in fact, men exhibit these defects as much or more than women do. She makes clear her allegiance to Locke, whose rationalism and empiricism, as we have seen, appealed to a number of his women contemporaries. Drake celebrates Locke as the great master of the "Art of Reasoning," and calls his *Essay on Human Understanding* (1689) an essential guide for women. In this willingness to consider the new philosophy and to publish on a philosophical subject, Drake followed the example of Astell. Unlike Astell, however, Drake makes only brief reference to religious arguments and announces that she will leave religion to the clergy.

Drake offers a variety of secular, mostly empirical, arguments to show that misogynistic claims about women are untrue. Among animals, she contends, male and female are equal: "a Bitch will learn as many Tricks in as short a time as a Dog, a Female Fox has as many Wiles as a Male."[82] Among the laboring classes, she notices, men and women seem more equal then they do among the upper classes. Drake also looks to foreign countries to see whether what appears in England "natural" may be only local custom. No further away than Holland, she discovers that Dutch tradeswomen demonstrate women's capacity for arithmetic and business.

Yet, although Drake has serious arguments to make about women's capacities, the *Essay* is not a treatise; it is closer to a philosophical entertainment, drawing on satire, relishing paradox, and aligning itself with drawing-room conversation. Her satire is akin to that in the Restoration comedy of Etherege and Wycherley, both of whom she praises explicitly, and of Behn, whose plays also contest misogynistic claims. Drake's satire uses "characters," types of contemporary men, including the pedant, the squire, the bully, and the beau (or fop). She mocks many of the supposed advantages of contemporary gentleman's education. Her all-too-recognizable version of the country squire has a classical education, but forgets it as soon as he leaves school; as a grown man he amuses himself with "stale Beer, and the History of his Dogs and Horses . . . he gives you a Pedigree of every one with all the exactness of a Herald . . ."[83] Men who have retained their classical learning, the pedants, she attacks as "Superstitious, bigotted Idolaters of time past . . . Children in their understanding all their lives . . ."[84] The time has come, she insists, for classicists and clergymen to give up their pretended "Monopoly of Learning,"[85] for the study of philology to yield to the study of things, and for people well-acquainted with modern languages, history, and politics to be called learned as well.

A key to Drake's intentions and methods in the *Essay* is in her concluding argument that men can benefit from the conversation of women. The preface explains that the book originated in a private conversation between some gentlemen and ladies and that it was written "for the Diversion of one Lady." In the body of the text, men are represented as often prone to useless violence, in need of being cajoled into good humor. Her Scowrer, for example, loves "Fighting for the sake of Blows" and is "as good as an Annuity to the Surgeon."[86] Left to themselves and to discussions of politics and religion, Drake argues, men are all too apt to become passionately disputatious. Trotter had shown the tragic potential of this aspect of upper-class male socialization; Drake suggests a remedy. By conversing with women, men can become better humored and argue more in a spirit of raillery, "to maintain a pleasant Argument, or heighten by a variety of Opinions an agreable Entertainment."[87]

Drake's own words seem offered in a similar spirit of pleasant raillery, aiming at entertainment, but also using the fluidity and tentativeness of conversation to play with paradoxes and to introduce new "Opinions." Because Drake does not demand full access to serious education for women and because she does not demand full public political or economic participation for women she does, to some extent, as Brenda Tooley has argued, "replicate the constructions of femininity upon which misogyny depends."[88] Yet it is possible to see the space of conversation Drake promotes not as the domestic sphere, as Tooley does, but as part of the emerging public sphere of Jürgen Habermas, here the space of the salon in which a rational critique of official state ideology and institutions could be developed. In any case, Drake wittily challenges the usefulness of the privileged male education that legitimized male authority and she demonstrates the intellectual capacity of at least one woman to make a trenchant critique of patriarchal privilege and patriarchal foolishness.

CONCLUSION

During the reign of William and Mary several women writers appeared self-consciously as women, writing not simply as individuals but often as "champions" of their sex. Although many of the works discussed in this chapter were initially published anonymously, in the sense that no individual author's name was attached to them, many nevertheless appeared clearly marked as the work of a woman. Thus, for example, Astell's *Serious Proposal* identifies its author as "a Lover of her Sex," Rowe's *Poems on Several Occasions* are by "Philomela," and Drake's *Essay in Defence of the Female Sex* tells the reader that it has been written "by a Lady." Frequently, also, the preliminary matter in these books celebrates the fact that the reader is about to encounter the work of a woman. Trotter's *Fatal Friendship*, for instance, appeared with a group of such commendatory poems, including one that lauds her as a champion of her sex who gives the lie to earlier representations of women as "Impotent of Mind."[89] Only the most commercial of these writers, Manley and Pix, were exceptions in more usually publishing under their own names.

Women writers in this reign developed an early feminist attack on the authority of a patriarchal culture that constructed women as less capable than men in order to legitimize their subordination. Most directly and elaborately, Astell and Drake use rational argument and empirical evidence to challenge assumptions that men were more able to think than women, with Drake making a particularly spirited satiric critique both of the truth-value of traditional university learning and of the empirical results of learned education in the typical scholar or the typical gentleman. Both Astell and Drake explicitly reject earlier patriarchal constructions of gender according to which women are by nature defective and marked by characteristic female vices, including lustfulness and vanity.

More positively, these women writers develop philosophical and theological grounds for women's entitlement to regard themselves and to be regarded by men as, at least potentially, as intellectually, spiritually, and literarily capable as men. Drawing on Cartesianism, Neoplatonism, and Christianity, feminist theoreticians maintain that the mind and the soul "have no sex." The dramatists make their own contribution by inventing intelligent, self-controlled heroines like Trotter's Felicia or Pix's Lady Landsworth, characters now embodied on the stage not by boy actors but by gifted actresses who could work collaboratively with women playwrights.

While certainly not unproblematic, the alliances many of these women writers forged with the forces of virtue and religion enabled them to justify their writing, and sometimes the publication of their writing, as contributions to the moral and spiritual welfare of their fellow subjects. As we have seen, virtuous and intellectually ambitious gentlewomen of this period were able to attract the support of decent learned and literary men who assisted them with their own intellectual and literary development and, sometimes, promoted their writing, as Norris and Hickes did for Astell or Bishop Thomas Ken (and later Isaac Watts) did for Rowe. It is not inconsequential that common commitments to virtue and religion meant that men like Norris, Hickes, or Ken would assist women like Astell, Hopton, or Rowe without expecting sexual favors in return. Especially in the cases of Anglican women writers like Astell, Burnet, or Hopton, the support of learned and pious clergy of the Church of England also meant that they could become approved role models for the large majority of English women who were also members of the Church and that they were having an effect on the established national

Church and on the newer, less formal associations for the reformation of manners and the advancement of religion. While to modern eyes this alliance women forged with the late seventeenth-century forces of religion and virtue may at first appear dreary or repressive or catastrophically sexless, Astell and many of her contemporaries judged it both intrinsically right and in the best interests of contemporary women. Given the real contempt for women of the older patriarchal ideology and the crucial role of theology in that ideology, and given the real dangers to seventeenth-century women posed by libertine philosophy and rakish practice, I find it hard to say that Astell judged wrongly.

CHAPTER 3

Politics, gallantry, and ladies in the reign of Queen Anne, 1702–1714

TEXTS

1703 Mrs. S. F. [Sarah Fyge Egerton]. *Poems on Several Occasions. Together with a Pastoral*

1703 Lady Mary Chudleigh. *Poems on Several Occasions. Together with the Song of the Three Children Paraphras'd*

1704 [Mary Astell]. *A Fair Way With the Dissenters and Their Patrons. Not Writ by Mr. L————y, or any other Furious Jacobite, whether Clergyman or Layman; but by a very Moderate Person and Dutiful Subject to the Queen*

1706 Catharine Trotter. *The Revolution of Sweden* (Haymarket)

1709 Susanna Centlivre. *The Busie Body* (Drury Lane)

1709 [Delarivière Manley]. *Secret Memoirs and Manners of Several Persons of Quality, of both Sexes. From the New Atalantis, an Island in the Mediteranean [!]. Written originally in Italian.* 2 volumes

1713 [Anne Finch, Countess of Winchilsea]. *Miscellany Poems, on Several Occasions. Written by a Lady*

1714 Susanna Centlivre. *The Wonder: A Woman Keeps a Secret* (Drury Lane)

1714 [Delarivière Manley]. *The Adventures of Rivella: or, the History of the Author of the Atalantis with Secret Memoirs and Characters of Several Considerable Persons Her Contemporaries*

INTRODUCTION

The accession of Queen Anne, Protestant daughter of James II, according to the plan Parliament had devised at the Glorious Revolution, meant that the Revolution settlement of the nation's affairs was increasingly secure. The political parties that had begun to emerge out of the Restoration Exclusion Crisis now began to take the shape of modern political parties.[1]

The Tory party had a majority of popular support in the country, as well as the enthusiasm of the Queen. Tories championed the interests of the Church of England and low levels of taxation; they were suspicious of government corruption and of the new financial revolution of the 1690s that had introduced the Bank of England, a national debt, and the beginnings of a stock market. The Whig party, a minority, included some who sought either a more comprehensive national Protestant Church or more political rights for Protestant dissenters. Whigs generally supported mercantile and financial interests and were associated with the increase in the size of the state and the higher levels of taxation that required. They most strongly supported the War of the Spanish Succession (1702–13) against France and Spain, a war caused in part by French threats to English trade. Although the parties did have different ideological positions and were beginning to develop organizations, alignments were fluid.

Contemporaries still overwhelmingly clung to the older belief that political opposition could only be produced by deplorable and seditious "factions." Tories repeatedly accused Whigs of being continuations of the seditious factions that had fought the seventeenth-century Civil War. Whigs accused Tories of being absolutist monarchists who rejected the model of mixed government represented by the Glorious Revolution settlement and of being Jacobites, loyal not to Protestant Queen Anne but to the Catholic Pretender living in France, the son of James II. Upon the death of James II in 1701, France recognized the Pretender as James III, King of England.

Political parties became an important source of patronage for writers. The discontinuance of the Licensing Act in 1695 meant that writers were free of prepublication censorship. (The threat of post-publication prosecution for subversive or libelous words continued to encourage anonymous publication of potentially questionable works: Delarivière Manley was arrested and held briefly for questioning after the publication of her *New Atalantis* in 1709.) Booksellers seized the opportunity of relative liberty to create public interest in political debates. The canonical male writers of this period – Jonathan Swift, Daniel Defoe, Joseph Addison, and Richard Steele – substantially participated in political journalism and hoped to be rewarded with patronage in jobs or money. While aristocratic women writers did not become political pamphleteers, some women writers from the gentry and middling classes did.

Like Swift, Astell supported what she believed to be the interests of the Church of England, insisting that maintenance of the Church's privileges as the state church was essential to true religion and good moral order.

Like Swift, she supported the Tory Bills Against Occasional Conformity (1702–05), proposed legislation aimed at dissenters who tried to hold political office and evade the requirements of the Test Act by attending services of the state church only "occasionally."[2] The Bills sought to impose high fines on men who had attended a Church of England service to qualify for political offices, high or low, and then been caught attending a dissenting meeting. Would-be government contractors would also have been affected, so that, for instance, a dissenter like Defoe would have become ineligible for contracts like the one he had to supply bricks to Greenwich Hospital.

Defoe attacked what he thought was the persecuting spirit of the Church of England in a number of pamphlets; Astell supported the Church and attacked Low Church and dissenting pamphleteers, including Defoe. Like most Tory writers, Astell supposes that Whigs and dissenters write out of some combination of venality and innate subversiveness. In *A Fair Way with the Dissenters and Their Patrons* (1704), she answers Defoe's *More Short-Ways with the Dissenters* (1704), suggesting that the dissenters should be destroyed as a party and that dissenting academies like the one in which Defoe was educated ought to be suppressed. Writers like Defoe, she says, should be treated "with all that Contempt that is due to little Scriblers and Busiebodies, who, either for Bread, and to deserve their Wages of the Party, or out of an innate Love to Mischief, alarm the Mob, and impose upon the Ignorant and Careless Reader . . ."[3] In addition to controversial pamphlets, Astell also published a substantial book, *The Christian Religion as Profes'd by a Daughter of the Church* (1705), directed against Locke as a philosopher, an advocate of rational religion, and a key Whig political theorist.

Opposed as she was to Astell on many matters of virtue, in the reign of Queen Anne, Manley also became a Tory political writer. She became notorious for a series of popular scandal chronicles that, under romance pseudonyms, attacked Whig leaders as corrupt, self-interested, greedy, and sexually rapacious. Paula McDowell has calculated that by 1714 Manley "was the author of at least six volumes of political allegories totaling some 1,500 pages in quarto, six political pamphlets, and as many as nine issues of the Tory *Examiner*" (the newspaper on which she collaborated with Swift).[4] Her letters to Robert Harley, a leading Tory minister, beseeching him to reward her services to the party, eventually earned her a rather paltry present of £50.[5] In the course of attacking the Whig Steele in her *Memoirs of Europe*, Manley gives a reasonably good summary of her own method: "*Stellico* shall make it his care to daub and misrepresent even the brightest and greatest Characters, to threaten and stigmatize with his Pen, those whom we fear and disapprove; he shall prepare Men's Minds for a favourable Approbation of our Proceedings, Vilafie to the Life those of our Enemies."[6]

There is less women's writing in support of the Whig minority. However, the playwright Susanna Centlivre made her allegiance to their principles and ministers clear in her plays, dedications, and occasional poems. Trotter's continued defense of Locke and his political ideology in a treatise and a serious verse drama, *The Revolution of Sweden* (1706), also aligned her with the Whigs. She lent support to the Church of England by converting from Roman Catholicism and publishing, albeit anonymously, a refutation of Roman Catholic arguments for the infallibility of the Pope and of the oral tradition of the Catholic Church in *A Discourse Concerning a Guide in Controversies in Two Letters. Written to One of the Church of Rome. By a Person Lately Converted from that Communion* (1707). These political allegiances and the development of intense partisanship during Anne's reign help explain why Manley, who had in the previous reign supported Centlivre and Trotter, now vilified them in her scandal chronicles.

Up to a point, churches and political parties wanted to publicize the fact that they had women adherents as well as men adherents, daughters as well as sons. Catherine Gallagher, in a consideration of Manley, has suggested that a gendered division of labor appeared in the political writers of this reign: male writers praise the politician's political virtues and women writers "attest to his personal attractions." In her analysis, problematically, male writers present themselves as competent to discuss policy, whereas what was desired from women writers "was desire itself, the introduction of the passions into a proto-political civil discourse, where their regulation might also be displayed."[7] This seems true of Manley, but not true of Astell or Trotter.

Alongside intensely partisan, sometimes vicious, political writing, writers also produced other texts that were studiedly non-political, or at least claimed to be. A new kind of belles lettres defined itself against the discourse of court or state. This new belletristic discourse laid claim to a calm disinterestedness and purported to be about more personal social matters. Addison and Steele in *The Tatler* (1709–11) and *The Spectator* (1711–12) urged their readers to consider quotidian issues of manners and *les petit morals*, fashions, psychology, and literary taste. Like Dunton's *Athenian Mercury* and other less famous periodicals of the 1690s and 1700s, the widely read and influential *Spectator* explicitly invoked an audience of both men and women and aimed to contribute to the development of a heterosocial polite society, one in which women would have some of the civilizing effects on men contemplated by Judith Drake. Explicit and fervent religious writing dominated the output of the press. Rowe, for example, compiled *Divine Hymns and Poems on Several Occasions . . . by Philomela and Several Other Ingenious Persons* (1704), including new Rowe poems, many of them hymns. But this newer kind of belletristic discourse Addison and Steele practiced focused more on the secular and tried to minimize theological and ecclesiastical quarrelling.[8]

Booksellers now decided that there was a market for texts that represented both men's and women's voices in heterosexual and heterosocial relationships. Particularly popular were letters that claimed the authenticity of documents. Many of these were love letters, but others offered varieties of intimate heterosocial friendships, often rife with tensions and ambiguities. Bernard Lintott published a set of letters from Katherine Philips (who had died in 1664) to Sir Charles Cottrell, Charles II's Master of the Revels, entitled *Letters from Orinda to Poliarchus* (1705). Philips writes about literary matters, including the revisions and publication of her plays and poems, as well as about family concerns. Lintott declares that these letters:

were the effect of a happy Intimacy between herself and the late famous Poliarchus, and are an admirable Pattern for the pleasing Correspondence of a virtuous Friendship: They will sufficiently instruct us, how an intercourse of writing, between Persons of different Sexes, ought to be managed, in Delight and Innocence and teach the World, not to load such a Commerce with Censure and Detraction, when 'tis remov'd at such a distance from even the Appearance of Guilt.[9]

No doubt having in mind volumes like Abel Boyer's *Choice Letters of Gallantry and Friendship, French and English. Collected out of the most Celebrated Wits of France* (1701), Lintott claims to be puzzled that the English reading public has been so reliant on translations of French letters, "when we have such Examples of Excellency among ourselves."

More typical of the published letters of literary ladies of the first decade of the eighteenth century are Centlivre's letters in several anthologies, *Familiar and Courtly Letters* (1700, the first publication of her writing), *Letters of Wit, Politicks, and Morality* (1701), and *Familiar and Courtly Letters* (1701).[10] The young Susanna writes to literary men including Abel Boyer, Tom Brown, and George Farquhar. Aiming to establish herself as a wit, she writes to Farquhar as Astrea, borrowing Behn's nom de plume.

The literary men respond with mixtures of gallantry and literary advice in performative letters that, like her letters, seem intended for publication.

The reign of Queen Anne inspired hope that the accomplishments of literary women might be fostered and honored. Her rule tended to inhibit some – certainly not all – naked expressions of misogyny. As Carol Barash has demonstrated, during Anne's reign, "repeatedly, we find a metonymic overlap between writing women's defenses of Anne's legitimacy and their defenses of their own legitimacy as authors."[11] In the nationalistic fervor coincident with the War of the Spanish Succession and Marlborough's brilliant victories over the French, English writers enjoyed celebrating England as a paradise for women in which no Salic law excluded women from the throne. Male writers often praised upper-class women writers like Lady Mary Chudleigh and Anne Finch, Countess of Winchilsea, in gallant style.

At the same time, male encomiums of women writers frequently suggested that the woman being praised was unique, as unlike any other woman as a Queen was unlike her subjects. For example, Pope's "Impromptu, To Lady Winchilsea" (written, c. 1714) insists that her poetry is so superior to the poetry of other women he praises that "To write their Praise you but in vain essay; / Ev'n while you write, you take that Praise away . . ."[12] Resisting this construction of herself as unique among women, Finch replied in "The Answer" with an explicit warning to Pope and a mock-epic reference to the fate of Orpheus torn apart by the Thracian Maenads. Women writers often resisted such encomiastic isolation, which threatened to make the individual a freak of nature and to make it impossible to imagine a continuing tradition of women's writing. Instead, they tried to create literary circles and female literary lineages for themselves.

It now seemed useful to publishers to publish women writers; in some literary circles, male writers were willing to include women in subordinate capacities. In this age of the Miscellany (usually a name indicating a volume of work by various hands), poems by women not infrequently appeared in collections of poems written predominantly by men. For example, Finch's important Pindaric ode "The Spleen" first appeared anonymously in *New Collection of Poems on Several Occasions* (1701) edited by Charles Gildon. Jacob Tonson's *Poetical Miscellanies. The Fifth Part* (1704) included eight new poems identified as by Elizabeth Singer. Tonson's *Poetical Miscellanies. The Sixth Part* (1709) featured the pastorals of Ambrose Philips and Pope, but also offered Rowe's new translation of a section of Tasso's *Jerusalem* and three poems of Finch, along with poems of Nicholas Rowe, Thomas Tickell, Swift, and others.

The power of the older assumption that any relation between men and women must be about sex and the pressure of the new style of fashionable gallantry between men and women complicated efforts at relationships between men and women writers and affected what women wrote. Cent-livre admired Farquhar's comedy and knew that she could use his support of her work. She was willing to send Farquhar encomiastic and occasional verse and to trade gallant banter and persiflage with him in a published correspondence. Bowyer appropriately remarked that this correspondence was in part "a literary exercise" for both of them. It seems to end with her rebuking him: "I guess our Acqaintance will be but of a short Longitude, if your *Pegasus* take such a Latitude in his Stile. I am sorry you misunderstand my Intent, which was only to divert you over a Bottle, and my self from the Spleen."[13]

Gallantry doomed the relationship between Elizabeth Singer and Matthew Prior, one of the most accomplished poets of Anne's reign. In 1703 and 1704 Singer, still single at twenty-nine, met Prior and began a correspondence with him; her letters to him have not been found and his to her were only published in the twentieth century.[14] One of her motives was to seek his assistance in improving her poetry and in communicating with the publisher Tonson about poems of hers and her friends that were to appear or not appear in Tonson's *Miscellanies*. The fact that Singer's poems appear in Tonson's *Miscellanies* with her name, whereas those of Prior, Swift, and some (certainly not all) other gentlemen authors appear anonymously, suggests that the publisher sees value in identifying her and perhaps also that the woman writer has a singularity. Prior writes to Singer in a gallant style, eventually declaring "I began with friendship, come off presently to Love, would be a reasonable Creature again if I could, yet must be unhappy unless I see you."[15] He tries to tease her about her dissenting religion in a fashion she almost certainly found offensive: "You want a quarrel mightily when you tell me I am a high Churchman, & I never knew before that you could like Cant & Nonsense in a Barn, rather than Harmony in a Cathedral . . ."[16] A master of polite style in verse and prose, Prior nevertheless makes a leitmotif of this correspondence the impossibility of finding a satisfactory style for it:

I have received a Letter from you full of real Wit, & affected Anger, I would answer it, if I knew what Stile would be agreeable to you, but to the different Key in which you Sing, it is impossible I should keep Consort . . . a desire of pleasing is condemned for Impertinence: So, not knowing the mind of my Goddess, I may mistake in the way of my Adoration, & whilst in one Letter we are to speak as plain as if we lived in the Golden Age, & in another we are to Disemble with each other & talk of Starrs & Destiny's, you must give me leave (with all the respect I have for you) to remember that I am writing to a Woman.[17]

Although this correspondence ended in 1704 and Singer married the more suitable Rowe in 1709, both Prior and she turned their relationship into minor literary capital. He did some literary favors for her and printed both her "Love and Friendship" and his "To the Author of Love and Friendship: A Pastoral" in his 1709 *Poems*, praising "the fineness of her genius" in his preface.

The unpoetical Locke, having discovered that Catharine Trotter was the author of *A Defence of Mr. Locke's Essay on Human Understanding* (1702), replied with a present of books and a letter cast in the gallant style that even a sober, philosophical gentleman apparently could not avoid in this period. Owning "you for my protectress" is "the greatest honour my Essay could have procured me," Locke implausibly wrote to Trotter: "Give me leave therefore to assure you, that as the rest of the world take notice of the strength and clearness of your reasoning, so I cannot but be extremely sensible, that it was employed in my defence. You have herein not only vanquished my adversary, but reduced me also absolutely under your power . . ."[18] A difficulty with this gallant style is that it makes it impossible for either the woman or us to know what the man actually thought of her work.

During the reign of Queen Anne, Astell, Trotter, and Lady Mary Chudleigh develop Astell's claims about women's capacity for rationality; several writers, including Trotter and Egerton, develop feminist analyses. The Queen's championing of the party of virtue especially emboldened writers like Astell and Chudleigh. In the theatre, Centlivre understood herself to be following the example of Behn, but profited from the examples of her friends Pix and Farquhar and allowed herself to be influenced by the moral revolution of the 1690s in producing notably genial, unlibertine comedies. Manley most obviously followed Behn, especially Behn's *Love Letters Between a Nobleman and His Sister*, in writing political fiction, although Manley's scandal chronicle fiction differs from Behn's in reflecting the impact of the relation between the new political parties and commercial writing. Manley also followed Behn in her construction of a narrative authority based on a woman's knowledge, especially knowledge of love.

POETRY

Bonamy Dobrée remarked that in the early eighteenth century people treated poetry as a "natural vehicle of expression that anybody was free to use, and which can be used for expressing anything";[19] consequently, a number of gentlewomen found verse an accommodating form. Individual poems and collections of poems continued to circulate in manuscript. The new periodicals and *Miscellanies* published individual poems. However, the shift from manuscript circulation to print publication is especially evident in three notable volumes that appeared during the reign of Queen Anne, volumes containing significant numbers of poems written earlier: Lady Mary Chudleigh's *Poems on Several Occasions* (1703), Sarah Egerton's *Poems on Several Occasions* (1703), and Anne Finch's *Miscellany Poems, on Several Occasions* (1713).

Writers aiming for public individual fame as poets typically published their own collections entitled *Poems on Several Occasions*, as Behn had done in 1684 and Rowe in 1696. *Poems on Several Occasions* was the usual title for a collection of poems by a single living author who was not yet an established poet; commonly, the poet aimed to demonstrate his or her talent in a range of genres and on a range of subjects.[20]

Significantly, no living woman writer in this period ventured to publish her *Works* under that title, which implied an assured literary reputation. Congreve was emboldened to publish his own *Works* in 1710 and the supremely ambitious twenty-nine-year-old Alexander Pope startled the literary establishment in 1717 with his *Works of Mr. Alexander Pope*, but the few *Works* of women poets published in the eighteenth century were normally published posthumously.[21] In early eighteenth-century collections of *Poems on Several Occasions* like those of Chudleigh, Egerton, and Finch, one typically finds commendatory and other occasional verse, *vers de société*, translations, songs, pastorals, and elegies, more or less loosely connected by the poet's particular thematic concerns and sometimes by threads of apparent autobiographical narrative.

Self-consciously building on the accomplishments of Behn, Philips, and Rowe, during the reign of Queen Anne, Chudleigh, Egerton, and Finch make major and successful efforts to write in clearly female voices. As Dorothy Mermin has argued, the success of a poet like Finch in speaking from a woman's point of view in lyric forms that conventionally had naturalized the male speaker was often to "give sharp contours to stories rubbed by long usage into featureless clichés."[22] The success of these poets in creating female speaking subjects in lyrics produced three remarkable books of brilliant, profoundly original poems.

Chudleigh, Egerton, and Finch were all interested in exploring and revising pastoral, a central subject of which was love. Their volumes include pastorals and reflect the heated contemporary debate over the status and character of pastoral. Pope began his poetic career with pointedly artificial classical *Pastorals* (1709), Gay tried a more realistic, more native, pastoral with some low dialect in *The Shepherd's Week* (1714), and the literary theorists, including Pope, debated the form in the pages of *The Guardian* and elsewhere. Annabel Patterson has contended that in this neoclassical pastoral energy shifted from the hermeneutics of pastoral to pastoral theory, with the consequence that the more complex kinds of pastoral were replaced by the "sweet, docile, and untroubling."[23] To the extent that this was so, pastoral, always a genre that invited inexperienced and modest poets, became even more inviting to women. Looking at the pastorals written by educated gentlemen in the early eighteenth century, Dobrée could only conclude that the form "seemed to be progressively dying of inanition."[24] Finch makes a male critic complain:

> Oh! stun me not with these insipid Dreams
> Th' Eternal Hush, the Lullaby of Streams.
> Which still, he cries, their even Measures keep,
> Till both the Writers, and the Readers sleep.[25]

Yet, as we have seen in looking at the libertine pastoral of Behn and the early pastorals of Rowe, the possibilities of pastoral from a female point of view had hardly been exhausted.

CHUDLEIGH'S *POEMS ON SEVERAL OCCASIONS*

Lady Mary Chudleigh's *Poems on Several Occasions* (1703) were dedicated to Queen Anne and prefaced by a statement that Lady Mary "chiefly design'd" her poems for "the Ladies" and intended them for their "Service."[26] The collection is framed by two poems, neither distinguished, that, in different ways, make the Queen their subject. A closing poem, "To the *Queen's* Most Excellent *Majesty*," celebrates Queen Anne as "A Heroin greater than Romance can frame."[27] The long and more original opening poem, "On the Death of his Highness the Duke of Glocester," laments the death of the Queen's son William, who, had he lived, would have succeeded her. Queen Anne is likened to Andromache, who mourned to see her son Astyanax thrown from the walls of Troy. The figure of St. George appears to console Britannia's mourners with a vision of the young prince embraced in heaven by former kings and queens of England, now "free from Care, and free from Pain." The speaker, nevertheless, is left torn between a feeling that it is wrong to express grief when the prince is secure in happiness and a feeling of sympathy with Queen Anne, whose "Tears forbid me to rejoice."[28] Chudleigh subsequently develops the wisdom, possibility, and propriety of stoicism as central issues in *Poems on Several Occasions.*

An admirer of the Neoplatonism of Norris and Astell, Chudleigh celebrates the pursuit of virtue as the only true pleasure and deprecates the value of material things, including beauty, as opposed to the mental or spiritual. In "To Almeystrea" (an anagram of Mary Astel), Chudleigh celebrates Astell's "bright Example" in breaking the shackles of tyrannical custom, leading the way to "Pleasures more refin'd / Than Earth can give," and, ultimately, to heaven, where souls enjoy the bliss of seeing and praising God.[29] Chudleigh's more optimistic poems celebrate the pleasures of the mind and even the possibilities of platonic love. One of the pastorals, "A Dialogue between *Alexis* and *Astrea*," begins as a Behn pastoral might, with a wooing shepherd and a suspicious shepherdess who desires love and honor:

> But Men, false Men, take Pleasure to Deceive,
> And laugh when we their Perjuries believe . . .[30]

But when this Alexis declares he must leave, this Astrea, instead of becoming distraught or accusing him of unfaithfulness, takes up an idea of Philips to reply that the separation of bodies is of no consequence so long as thoughts, which can never be confined, do meet. He agrees, and she concludes:

> A virtuous Passion will at a distance live,
> Absence to that will a new Vigor give,
> Which still increases, and grows more intense,
> The farther 'tis remov'd from the mean Joy of Sense.[31]

The longest poem in the main collection, "The Resolution," presents the speaker struggling against her suffering to render her soul "impassive"; in this struggle, books prove "the best Companion." An opening section pays tribute to contemporary divines of the Church of England, including Archbishop John Tillotson and Norris, whose books are useful. Most of the poem, however, celebrates the value of Greek and Roman heroes and philosophers, who can teach people how to follow virtue and restrain "Contending Passions." Like Bradstreet in the *Quarternions*, though on a smaller scale and with a sharper focus on those who have preferred virtue to survival or pleasure, Chudleigh demonstrates her acquaintance with the set of texts made prestigious by learned men. She admires Socrates and Epictetus, and, as Addison was soon to do in his controversial tragedy,

Cato (1713), she admires the stoic suicide who "reads with Pleasure of th immortal State, / And then with hast anticipates his Fate."[32] She finds a Stoic heroine in Arria, a Roman matron whose husband, charged with conspiracy against the Emperor Claudius, was "doom'd by his own Hand to die." Arria first tries to persuade her husband with reason, then offers her own example, stabbing herself with his dagger. Smiling, she tells him "Believe me, 'tis not difficult to die."[33] Theocritus, the Greek pastoral poet, is praised for his picture of "Love, unacquainted with deceitful Arts."[34] Although Chudleigh ventures to criticize Lucretius for atheism, finding it strange that such a strong thinker could suppose the world created without divine intelligence, she still, like many contemporaries, male and female, values *De Rerum Natura* for its power to diminish the fear of death.

Also of special importance to Lady Mary, as they were to many women writers, are Ovid's *Heroides*, the verse epistles supposed to be written by figures of antiquity, mostly women lamenting the loss of their lovers. Chudleigh singles out the epistles of Oenone (which Behn translated), Hypemnestra (who alone of the fifty daughters of Danaus disobeyed her father's orders to stab her husband on the wedding night), Laodamia (whose grief at her husband's death at Troy was so deep that the gods allow his ghost to return for three hours, after which she kills herself), and Sappho, represented in the *Heroides* as throwing herself from a rock after Phaon deserts her:

> And *Sappho* for her perjur'd *Phaon* burns:
> O Wondrous Woman! prodigy of Wit!
> Why didst thou Man to thy fond Heart admit?
> Man, treacherous Man, who still a Riddle proves,
> And by the Dictates of his Fancy moves,
> Whose Looks are Snares, and ev'ry Word a Bait,
> And who's compos'd of nothing but Deceit.[35]

Here Sappho's death is not an occasion for a tribute to the intensity of her passion but, instead, an occasion for reflecting on how love led to the waste of a talented woman.

Chudleigh's enthusiasm for the serious study Astell urged upon women is charmingly evident in "The Song of the Three Children Paraphras'd," an ambitious, if uneven, 2,065-line Pindaric poem printed separately at the end of *Poems on Several Occasions*. The title refers to three young men who sing praise to God in an apocryphal addition to the book of the prophet Daniel, but the poem is less a biblical paraphrase than a modern, scientific vision of the entire created universe, venturing into cosmology, geology, physics, and natural history, as well as the history of the world from creation on. Chudleigh complained in the preface to "The Song" and elsewhere that women were denied adequate access to scientific and other useful learning. However, she explicitly notes her own acquaintance with the books of Thomas Burnet, whose *Telluris Theoria Sacra* (Latin, 1684; English, 1689) advanced a remarkable theory of the material causes of the flood that inundated the earth in the time of Noah and of how the flood transformed the earth, and of John Ray, the great English naturalist, author of the popular *Wisdom of God Manifested in the Works of Creation* (1691) and *Three Physico-theological Discourses* (1692).

Chudleigh rejoices in the idea, advanced by Robert Boyle and Isaac Newton, as well as by Ray, that the discoveries of the new science would enhance humankind's appreciation of creation and of God the Creator. In her essay on "Knowledge," published in *Essays upon Several Subjects in Prose and Verse* (1710), she recommends the study of physics and other sciences to women because:

that will show us Nature, as she variously displays her self . . . instruct us heedfully to consider all her wonderful Productions, and trace infinite Wisdom and Power thro' the immense Space, from the Heights Above, to the depths Below; from the glorious Orbs which roll over our Heads, to the minutest Insect that crawls under our Feet; discover to us Beauties which Art can never imitate, and which common Spectators do not observe.[36]

Like Addison in "The Spacious Firmament on High" (1712), Chudleigh extols the created universe. She attends carefully to an enormous range of natural phenomena, even conventionally unattractive ones like those viewed by the inhabitants of the polar regions, who suffer "uncomfortable Darkness half their Days," "Seas Congealed," and "harden'd Earth [that] doth firm as Marble grow."[37] "A Song" anticipates James Thomson's *The Seasons* (1726–30) and even Christopher Smart's *A Song to David* (1763). While some of Chudleigh's moralizing and biblical history is tedious and too abstract, at its best the poem conveys acute curiosity and joyful fascination with novel images from nature. Thus, the poet sees whales praise the Lord:

> Ye Monarchs of the finny Race,
>   Who in the Northern Seas delight;
> Where your huge Bodies fill a mighty Space,
> And show like living Islands to the wond'ring Sight;
> As you your Heads above the Waters raise,
> Speak by your Gestures your Creator's Praise.[38]

Chudleigh's intellectual curiosity and her explicit concern that women take responsibility for developing their minds and souls show her commitment to the further development of Astell's ideas.

EGERTON'S *POEMS ON SEVERAL OCCASIONS*

Both Chudleigh and Egerton had earlier published assertive feminist poems, omitted from their 1703 volumes. Chudleigh had sharply critiqued reactionary patriarchy in her dialogue poem, *The Ladies Defence* (1701); there she responded to a dissenting minister's sermon that urged wives' strict duty of subjection to their husbands. Egerton in *The Female Advocate* (1687) had angrily rebutted the misogyny of Robert Gould's verse *Love given o're: or, a Satyr against the Pride, Lust, and Inconstancy, &c of Woman* (1682).[39] The omission of these poems from the 1703 volumes makes those volumes less confrontational, more belletristic.

Nevertheless, Egerton's *Poems on Several Occasions. Together with a Pastoral* combines pastorals, songs, and occasional poems with assertive feminist poems that further develop the position she had taken in *The Female Advocate*. In her dedication of *Poems on Several Occasions,* the poet emphasizes that her poems are the work of a young woman. She declares "Love seems the only proper Theme (if any can be so) for a Woman's Pen, especially at the Age they were writ in."[40] She hints at what the volume presents as the complicated and distressing situation of its poetic speaker. A woman has loved one man, Philaster, who no longer loves her; she now loves another man, Exalus, who does not love her either. She is married to still another man, who she does not love. Unlike Behn's libertine female speakers, however, Egerton's typically admire virtue, constancy, and chastity. The text suggests that the speaker's passion is not only involuntary but also that it has not led to adultery (and perhaps not even to fornication).

The world of Egerton's *Poems* is divided between, on the one hand, a recognizable scene of fashionable late-seventeenth-century London, its ideas, arts, and social mores, and, on the other, a timeless pastoral landscape. One poem celebrates Boyle's scientific contributions as having dethroned both Aristotle and Descartes, another fêtes Norris "on his Idea of Happiness," another Nathaniel Culverwell, the Cambridge Platonist, and three, reprinted from *Nine Muses,* eulogize Dryden. "To Marcella" plays with the paradox of an actress who is personally chaste but who can act desire. The speaker of *Poems* presents herself as an unusual person capable of true and constant love in a new age when loving has become the most superficial of affectations for many:

> In this soft Amorous Age now Love is grown,
> The modish Entertainment of the Town,
> And the fond Beau loves his half score aday,
> The Ladies too almost as Vain as they;
> Spare me, ye cruel Powers, let me not prove,
> The only Victim of a lasting Love.[41]

Fond of paradox, instead of wishing her lover to be constant, this speaker begs that she be made inconstant: were she to become one of the "shifting Fool[s] in Fashion," then she could escape the pain of her constant love.[42] This town world of fickle and meaningless "love" repels the poet, who, like Philips and Rowe, presents herself as having retreated to a rural, pastoral world of more authentic feeling.

Egerton invents an unusual plaintive shepherdess in the true spirit of pastoral in her ambitious "The Fond Shepherdess. A Pastoral," the longest and concluding poem in the collection. Two shepherdesses speak in this poem, but one speaks more briefly to draw her friend out and to sympathize. Like other women poets of the period, Egerton adapts the formal convention of pastoral in which two shepherds take turns speaking equal numbers of matched lines in a singing contest. Unsurprisingly, women poets find the topos of the singing contest problematic. When they transform the conventional shepherds into singing shepherdesses, the shepherdesses do not sing publicly before an audience or an umpire, but in private, for each other's ears alone.

"The Fond Shepherdess" avoids vapidity in part by imagining the scene of shepherding more concretely than most pastorals do, yet avoids sinking into vulgarity. Larinda describes the physical beauty of Exalus, who has now abandoned her, with unusual specificity. She tells of his kindnesses to her and of her gifts to him, ending with a suitably pathetic fantasy that she might will her sheep to him:

> To him a Crook and Beachen bowl I gave,
> (Did with my careful Hand the last Ingrave,)
> One side, with various Silvan Nymphs, I grac'd,
> And on the other *Pan* and *Flora* plac'd,
> Take these, said I; for all the generous Care,
> In which, so oft, my Flocks and I did share;
> And when I die, *Exalus* take them too,
> Tho' lost to me, they'll Joy to be with you . . .[43]

Exalus has abandoned her, while she is hopelessly constant in her obsessive love for him. She tries to sleep, but cannot; she tries to count her sheep, but forgets their number even as she counts. Desperate, she determines to fly to Ida's plains, where Exalus is, to find him out, and let him see her die:

> While I can gaze, it shall be on his Charms,
> And tho' not live; die in those lovely Arms . . .[44]

Unlike Behn's vengeful shepherdess in "The Return," who warns that a pitiless shepherd will in turn be humbled by some "hard hearted Nymph," Egerton's Larinda finds a generosity truer to the spirit of pastoral, uttering a long last prayer to the sylvan gods to bless Exalus and his sheep:

> From Fox and Wolf, preserve his tender Lambs,
> And with Twin-births, enrich the fruitful Dams.
> When his fair Flock the Sheerers care demands,
> Luxuriant Fleeces, tire their num'rous Hands.[45]

Imagining Exalus in a fecund landscape, still triumphing in singing contests, Larinda envisions nymphs strewing his path with pansies, anemone, and cypress. In an Ovidian moment, she exclaims:

> They too were Lovers once, tho' now transform'd,
> May I like them, to some kind Plant be turn'd.[46]

While some may prefer the hostility of Behn's shepherdess to the extremity of Larinda's tender abjection, Egerton brilliantly stays within pastoral conventions, yet invents a grieving figure who rises to remarkable heights of generosity and tenderness. Her plaintive shepherdess is also less narcissistic than the typical plaintive shepherd, who usually is less concerned to imagine his shepherdess than his own grief and much less forthcoming with generous wishes for her welfare. Pathos is an affect entirely proper in pastoral.

In contrast to this long pastoral, some of the most striking poems in Egerton's collection directly express anger; in some of them, she experiments with the curse, one of the most ancient kinds of poetry. "On my Wedding Day," an anniversary poem, apostrophizes the day as "Abandon'd Day" and asks accusingly, "why dost thou now appear?" The speaker attempts to command the day: "Oh! Rend thy self out of the circling Year."[47] "Satyr against the Muses" is a formal curse on her own muse; iambic tetrameter couplets with a high proportion of trochees and spondees and heavy use of consonants make the enraged poet seem to spit at her muse:

> Passion, that common Rage, I here refuse,
> Call Hell itself, to curse my Torturing Muse;
> Not the calm Author of blest Poetry,
> But the black Succubus of Misery:
> There let her sit, with her Infernal Chyme,
> And put the Shrieks and Groans of Fiends in Rhime.
> May their *Parnassus*, like *Vesuvius* burn,
> Their Laurels wither, or to Cypriss turn . . .[48]

"The Repulse to Alcander" forcibly expresses indignation at the power contemporary conventions of gallantry give men over women. Alcander has tried to use these conventions to seduce the married speaker:

> When a Salute [a kiss] did seem to Custom due,
> With too much Ardour you'd my Lips pursue;
> My Hand, with which you played, you'd Kiss and Press,
> Nay ev'ry Look had something of Address.[49]

The speaker has not wanted to "damn all little gallantries for vice," but realizing that Alcandor's persistent gallantries endanger her reputation, resolves to scorn and to shun him. The poet's rage at Alcandor's unwanted advances is heightened by her explicit awareness of a sexual double standard that allows men to behave badly without consequence and that sometimes punishes even innocent women. It is also heightened by her consciousness that the man she loved and the man she now loves make no such advances. Overall, in this volume Egerton creates a new variation on Petrarch, presenting a lover in torment, but one that is recognizably a married woman and an inhabitant of early modern England.

FINCH'S *MISCELLANY POEMS*

Anne Finch's *Miscellany Poems, on Several Occasions* (1713) is the most accomplished volume of poems published by a woman between 1660 and 1789. Although the title page of the first edition acknowledged only that the poems were "Written by a Lady," the volume was not prefaced by the kind of apology for the poet's lack of skill found in Egerton's earlier volume and many later volumes of women's poetry. Nor was there protest that the publication had been forced or was unwanted. Finch's husband wrote in a letter of 1714 that "though she owns itt, to our Friends, and all the Town know her to be the Author of it yett . . . she did not allow itt to be printed with her Name in the Title page."[50] The second edition appeared in 1714 as *Miscellany Poems on Several Occasion Written by the*

Right Honorable Anne, Countess of Winchilsea.[51] Finch's range, technical accomplishment in a variety of generic and metrical forms, and her originality are all impressive.

The normative speaker in Finch's *Poems* is a highly cultivated woman aware of the fashions and concerns of the court and town, but now withdrawn from them to a rural retreat. This retreat simultaneously invokes the poetic tradition of pastoral and offers a fresh and convincing vision of love in marriage. One of the longer poems central to the collection, "The Petition for an Absolute Retreat," asks "indulgent Fate" for the life the speaker seems presently to be enjoying: the satisfaction of bodily and aesthetic desires by a prelapsarian (but recognizably British) nature; sufficient quiet to permit contemplation; sociability provided by selected friends, notably the Countess of Thanet, to whom the poem is dedicated; and the love of a husband, "*A Partner* suited to my Mind."[52] Although connected to seventeenth-century garden poems like Marvell's, "The Petition" is Augustan in its willingness to notice contemporary events like the abdication of James II which precipitated the Finches' retreat from court. The poem is also Augustan in its invocation of classical stories like that of Marcus Licinius Crassus, one of Plutarch's noble Romans, but one who neglected his chance to retire from the pursuit of wealth and power and was murdered. Finch's pastoral idyll, with its Horatian comfort and sociability, is an aristocratic version of the decayed gentry farm idyll of so many eighteenth-century novels, for example, the Wilsons in Henry Fielding's *Joseph Andrews*. Finch altered the normative pastoral to suit her own desires by adding an intelligent and sympathetic husband, one elsewhere in the collection shown to delight in his wife's artistic and intellectual accomplishments, and also a woman friend who takes her "Wit, from an unmeasured Store, / To Woman ne'er allow'd before."[53] Her small circle of virtuous aristocrats shunning a corrupted court enjoy aesthetic pleasures richer and more complex than those available either to classic shepherds or to reduced gentry like Fielding's Wilsons. Thus Ardelia (the poet's nom de plume) visits her relatives and neighbors at a beautiful country house, Longleat, to produce a long poem admiring a tapestry created following Raphael's picture of St. Paul's blinding Elymis before Sergius Paulus, the Proconsul of Asia. Finch's imagination of an oppositional rural place from which the true poet critiques the public world of statesmen and false ambition anticipates what later became the common stance of mid-century and later poets, who abandoned panegyrics to the powerful and relinquished hope of speaking in a public voice.

Some of Finch's pastorals concentrate on giving more voice to shepherdesses and pay more realistic attention to their situations than conventional male pastoral does. Borrowing from a French poem, "La Passion
vaincue," she shows a despondent shepherdess abandoned by her lover
about to kill herself by plunging into the Severn river. Yet the anapestic
tetrameter of the poem belies depression. As the shepherdess reflects on
the horrors of death, the poem seems fittingly to conclude with a happier
ending:

> Some Scorn for the Shepherd, some Flashings of Pride
> At length pull'd her back, and she cry'd, Why this Strife,
> Since the *Swains* are so Many, and I've but *One* Life?[54]

Another poem features "A Pastoral Dialogue," not between the usual
shepherds (all of the speakers in Pope's pastorals, for example, are male),
but between "Two Shepherdesses" who talk about shepherds. Unlike
normative pastoral shepherdesses who are either young and beautiful or
dead, both of these shepherdesses are acutely conscious of aging and are
forced to notice that the shepherds who used to court them do so no
more.

Other Finch pastorals aim to make classical pastoral more recognizably
British and contemporary, and to do so without burlesque, so as to
produce that careful and affectionate observation of those new images
"of external nature" that later drew Wordsworth to her poetry. Willows,
oaks, and wild strawberries adorn the rural retreat of "The Petition."
Similarly, her much anthologized "A Nocturnal Reverie" delights in the
subtler sights and quieter sounds of a summer nightscape, "When fresh-
en'd Grass now bears it self upright, / And makes cool Banks to pleasing
Rest invite," when the foxglove seems to take on a "paler Hue," and when
the "loos'd Horse" can be heard chewing "torn up Forage." Like Cavendish, who seems to have written the first anti-field-sports poem in "The
Hunting of the Hare" (written from the perspective of the terrified
hare desperately trying to press its body into the earth), Finch has a
sympathetic eye out for the sportsman's trophies:

> When *Curlews* cry beneath the Village walls,
> And to her struggling Brood the *Partridge* calls;
> Their shortliv'd Jubilee the Creatures keep,
> Which but endures, whilst Tyrant *Man* do's sleep . . .[55]

Finch was exquisitely aware that marital love had no role in classical
pastoral or in French and English libertine pastoral. She looks back

instead to the Renaissance Protestant poetry of Sidney and Spenser, also favorites of Bradstreet, for inspiration in her project of inserting the celebration of married love into eighteenth-century pastoral. Ardelia's husband, sometimes under the pastoral name of Dafnis, is the subject, or rather the addressee, of several of her most brilliant poems. Dafnis, "the much lov'd husband of a happy wife," is he:

> [Who] to the world by tend'rest proof discovers
> They err, who say that husbands can't be lovers.[56]

In "To Mr. F. Now Earl of W.," Ardelia presents herself as desiring to write verses in "a *Husband's* Praise." Using a deft comic touch, Finch reimagines old poetic conventions put under the double stress of modern times and the changed gender of the speaker. Following the ancient custom of poets, she appeals to the Muses on Mt. Parnassus for assistance, although, instead of invocation, she employs the more modern and more worldly method of sending a "messanger" to the Muses "Court." The muses prove very like the fashionable great ones of Finch's day, profuse in their flattery of a lady and at first lavish in their professions of readiness to assist. Yet as soon as they hear that the subject of her poem is to be a husband's praise, they are amazed at the strangeness of her proposition. Hurriedly, they flee to take further counsel, and even – a nice comic touch – worry that they themselves will lose face with the fashionable folk of the Town should it ever get out that they are considering a proposal so outlandish. Like eighteenth-century great people denying favors to sup-pliants waiting at their levees, in refusing their aid these muses at least aim for politeness by attempting "plausible" excuses. Finch makes these ex-cuses wittily diminish the value of traditional high forms of poetry against which her proposed subject might be judged and labeled "low." Thus, joining her contemporaries Bernard Mandeville and Swift in disdaining panegyric, and characteristically reimagining the mythic winged horse Pegasus as a contemporary real horse, Finch has the muses plead:

> That *Pegasus* of late had been
> So often rid thro' thick and thin,
>   With neither Fear nor Wit;
> In *Panegyric* been so spurr'd,
> He cou'd not from the Stall be stirr'd,
> Nor wou'd endure the Bit.

Finch's comic reimagination of the muses and their horse as recogniz-ably contemporary English creatures makes the poetic tradition they represent less intimidating. This prepares for a conclusion in which the heavenly muse, Urania, breaking with her sisters, whispers helpful words to Ardelia, words that echo the opening of Sidney's *Astrophel and Stella*. Urania's words are a virtual charter for the women poet for whom a masculine literary past is too often a useless model:

> They need no Foreign Aid invoke,
> No help to draw a moving Stroke,
> Who dictate from the Heart.[57]

Thus empowered, the speaker determines to write her poem for the eyes of her husband alone. But she included it in *Miscellany Poems*, and, no doubt, expected her allusion to Sidney to be recognized.

Like "To Mr. F. Now Earl of W." many of Finch's poems address directly her situation as a woman poet. Perhaps the best known of these now is "The Introduction," designed as an introduction to a collection of her poems, but not published until 1903. Like a number of other poems she declined to publish, "The Introduction" engages in frank complaint. Here the poet complains that critics condemn women's poems as "insipid, empty, incorrect," allege that women writers "intrude" on the rights of men, and conceal the fact that earlier women excelled as poets (the Israelite Deborah in *Judges*, for example, also cited by Bradstreet and Astell). "The Introduction" also joins Astell's feminist lament that women are debarred from education, but concludes despondently, apparently eschewing hope of being rewarded with the poet's laurel crown.

The poems that Finch did publish in *Miscellany Poems* generally engage the situation of the woman poet more obliquely, often with humor, yet are perhaps more deeply provocative in their indirection. A number of them, like the poem she chose to open the collection, "Mercury and the Elephant," are fables. Originating from Aesop's Greek fables and Phaedrus's Latin ones, the fable was a recognized neoclassical form, one that was attracting renewed attention from literary theorists and poets. In *Miscellany Poems* Finch's elephant chats with a bored Mercury about his reputation, an unctuous cat fools an eagle from his tree, a rat mother fusses at her foppish traveling son, and even a lowly bramble talks back to a lord who plans to cut it down. Finch wonderfully combines their recognizable animal (or vegetable) qualities with the attitudes and language of contemporary people in narratives that exhibit the terminal morals required by the form, yet also leave the reader speculating on the range of their application. The elephant, distressed with what he believes to be the unfairness of the worldly narrative of his fight with a boar, inquires of Mercury what account the gods have recorded of him. He is chagrined to learn that the gods have paid no attention to his deeds, that it is news to Mercury that he has fought at all – just as Finch has learned that her poems prompt critics to no response more nuanced than surprise that she has "Writ!"

Finch's contemporaries rightly celebrated her as a gifted and innovative fabulist. She exploits the form's double traditions, its simultaneous orientation to power and powerlessness and its juxtapositions of paradox and platitude. As a former courtier and a countess, she knew intimately the world of privilege inhabited by the human versions of the fables' lions and eagles. Yet as a displaced courtier and as an ambitious woman in a patriarchal world, she also identified with the perspective of the lowly. As in traditional fable, in her fabular world diverse creatures live in fear; struggle for survival and power; eat one another; and often covet the bragging rights and security of being top animal. The fable becomes a discursive space in which the culturally invisible, even the culturally despised, find an opportunity to speak, and, sometimes, to demonstrate that they have strengths of their own. Thus, a self-satisfied lion in "The Lyon and the Gnat" no sooner congratulates himself on being the creature who feasts on fearful creatures, than he finds himself impotent against the sting of a tiny female gnat, who taunts and feeds on him.

"The Owl Describing her Young Ones" is a more complex fable of female writing. A mother owl attempts to protect her owlets, all female, from the ravenous hunger of an eagle. The mother owl agrees to entertain the eagle with a description of owlets in exchange for his promise not to eat them. Fondly, she paints an attractive verbal picture of her "Heiresses," still recognizable owls:

> I hope I have done their Beauties right,
> Whose Eyes outshine the Stars by Night?
> Their Muffs and Tippets too are White.[58]

One evening the hungry eagle returns to the owls' tree, scrupling to make a convenient meal of the young beauties. Soon enough, however, he finds his excuse in the failure of the mother's pretty description to correspond to another description he is able to formulate while gazing appetitively at them, a description that, though also recognizing authentic owl features, turns them into grotesque hags:

> What are these Things, and of what Sex,
> At length he cry'd, with Vultur's Becks,
> And Shoulders higher than their Necks?

> These wear no *Palatines,* nor Muffs,
> *Italian* Silks, or *Doyley* Stuffs,
> But motley Callicoes, and Ruffs.[59]

Thus salving his conscience, he gobbles them down, telling their grieving and reproachful mother that she has only herself to blame for lying "in every Word" she said. On one level, this fable can be read as having the concerns about the capacity of traditional poetic language to lie that Swift expresses in a poem like "The Progress of Beauty" (written in 1719 or 1720).

Yet the explicit and alarming moral Finch elects to draw in "The Owl" is pointed for women writers whose words were greeted with gallantry, especially for an aristocratic woman writer like herself, flattered both for her sex and for her rank:

> Faces or Books, beyond their Worth extoll'd,
> Are censur'd most, and thus to pieces pull'd.[60]

Like Astell and like Swift, Finch was suspicious of the language of romance and courtly love. As Swift does in "The Progress of Beauty," here she plays with different ways of describing in order to suggest that beauty may be a mere verbal construction overlying more naturalistic physical facts. For Swift, the realizations are literary ones about style and moral ones that constitute general lessons for women and their would-be admirers. So also for Finch, yet for her the applications are also threateningly personal. She had ample reason to know that the lady who was one day fulsomely praised might the next day be represented as a satiric grotesque.

MANLEY: SCANDAL CHRONICLE AND AUTOBIOGRAPHY

In sharp contrast to these poets' celebrations of retirement and virtue, during the reign of Queen Anne, Delarivière Manley continued her attack on what she considered the illusory character of virtue; in a famous series of prose scandal chronicles, she represented a contemporary social world of self-interest and uncontrollable desire for money and sex. She makes several women writers, including Egerton and Trotter, victims of her satire, insisting that they are virtuous only in reputation. Like the contemporary commercial publishers who tried to profit from the novelty value of women's writing, Manley did not scruple to engage in the unauthorized publication of other women's writing. In episodes of her *New Atalantis* (1709), itself something of a miscellany, Manley includes two poems of Finch's, "Life's Progress" (as "The Progress of Life") and "A Pindarick Poem Upon the Hurricane in November 1703" (as "The Hymn," apparently the first publication of the poem). *The New Atalantis* contrasts the majority of contemporary writers, like Manley, desperate for money, with Finch, "one of the happy few, that write out of Pleasure, and not Necessity," and comments that it is therefore Finch's fault, "if she publish any thing but what's good; for it's next to impossible to write much, and write well."[61]

The reign of Queen Anne was a crucial period for women's fiction, most notably because of Manley's scandal chronicles trafficking in court and political gossip. Manley's *Secret Memoirs and Manners of Several Persons of Quality of Both Sexes. From the New Atalantis*, usually referred to as *The New Atalantis*, created a sensation and was widely read. Along with Manley's other scandal chronicles, *The Secret History of Queen Zarah and Zarazians* (1705, possibly by Manley) and *Memoirs of Europe* (1710), *The New Atalantis* defined for many the potential dangers of women's writing and women's access to print in the new entrepreneurial marketplace.[62] Cultural fears about women's incapacity to keep silent about secrets seemed justified by *The New Atlantis*, which unsettled power in the state by contributing to the fall of the Whig ministry.

These English scandal chronicles descended from the French *chronique scandaleuse*, notably from Roger de Rabutin, Count de Bussy's *Histoire Amoureuse des Gaules* (1665) and, more directly, from Marie Catherine La Motte, Baronne d'Aulnoy's *Mémoires* of various European courts published between 1679 and 1695. The scandal chronicles were in important ways anti-romances; they presented upper-class characters who sported romance names, but who were motivated by lust and greed instead of by virtue and honor. In France, they contributed to a delegitimation of the monarchy and the aristocracy that prepared the way for the French Revolution.

In Queen Anne's England, Manley made the scandal chronicle an instrument of party politics. Writing on behalf of the Tories, especially Robert Harley, she targeted important Whig officials and politicians, including Sidney, Earl Godolphin, the Lord Treasurer, and Charles Talbot, Duke of Shrewsbury, Lord-Lieutenant of Ireland. Most insistently, she attacked John Churchill, Duke of Marlborough, General and commander of the British forces that won great victories over the French at Blenheim (1704) and Ramillies (1706) in the War of the Spanish Succession, and his wife, Sarah Churchill, Duchess of Marlborough, who had served the Queen in various household offices, including Keeper of the Privy Purse, and occupied the always dangerous role of "favorite." Perhaps because Manley's closest access to aristocratic gossip came from a brief period she spent in the household of the Duchess of Cleveland in the reign of William and Mary, many, although not all, of the alleged events alluded to in *The New Atalantis* date from that period. Beyond associating the Whigs with a love of money rather than a love of honor, *The New Atalantis* is less concerned with ideology or political issues than with purporting to offer shocking revelations of what went on in the bedrooms of the great and famous.

Manley purported to strip away what she claimed was the false veneer of virtue adorning contemporary great men and women, a veneer constructed by panegyric or even by the official government newspaper, *The Gazette*, in order to reveal their human vices. At one level, an appeal of *The New Atalantis* is to the early enlightenment sense that traditions and traditional modes of representation are false and that writers need to create new, less reverential modes of truth-telling representation. The title invokes Francis Bacon's call to empirical scientific investigation in his utopian fable, *The New Atlantis* (written 1624, published 1626). One of the early readers of *The New Atalantis*, the young Lady Mary Pierrepont (later Lady Mary Wortley Montagu), captured the general malaise with conventional panegyric and the yearning for something newer and more credible. Writing to regret the news that the authorities had detained Manley for her work (she was released after a week and charges were not pressed), Lady Mary commented:

I was in hopes her faint essay would have provoked some better pen to give more elegant and secret memoirs; but now she will serve as a scarecrow to frighten people from attempting any thing but heavy panegyric; and we shall be teized with nothing but heroic poems, with names at length, and false characters, so daubed with flattery, that they are the severest kind of lampoons, for they both scandalise the writer and the subject . . .[63]

Much of *The New Atalantis* is a dialogue between three female figures encouraging the reader to be skeptical about conventional morality and its maxims. The goddess Virtue and her daughter Astrea, goddess of Justice, have returned to earth "to see if Humankind were still as defective" as when Astrea, disgusted, fled earth at the end of the Golden Age.[64] In Atalantis, a country strongly resembling England, they recruit Intelligence to assist them in their inquiries. Intelligence knows and will recount the stories of the fashionable people Virtue and Astrea observe. Like the stories in the new newspapers, sometimes called "intelligencers," the stories

Intelligence narrates claim the authority of fact. What significance they have is a matter for debate among the interlocutors and for consideration by readers.

Intelligence herself typically suggests that the stories illustrate worldly maxims reminiscent of La Rochefoucauld's *Réflexions ou sentences et maximes morales* (1665), one of Manley's favorite books. For example, she suggests that one story illustrates the proposition that "Love sooner or later forces every Heart to acknowledge him Master." Another supports the claim that "the same unaccountable thing that cools the Swain, warms the Nymph: Enjoyment (the death of Love in all Mankind) gives Birth to new Fondness, and doating Extasies in the Women . . ."[65] Less stylish than La Rochefoucauld's spare formulations, Intelligence's maxims nonetheless share his antistoicism, his insistence that reason and will are weak and passion strong, and his misogyny. La Rochefoucauld declares, "Most virtuous women are hidden treasures, safe only because no one is looking for them."[66] Intelligence informs her interlocutors, "there is no surer a Defence against the Inconstancy of Woman, than their want of Charms and want of those that may make Application."[67] The French *Maxims* were adorned with a frontispiece showing a cherub stripping away a mask of impassivity from the face of the stoic philosopher Seneca, an advocate of reason and virtue, revealing a suffering face.[68] Behn had translated these maxims as "Reflections on Morality or Seneca Unmasqued," included in her *Miscellany* (1685). With La Rochefoucauld, and against Astell and Masham, Intelligence insists that reason is too weak either to control passion or to prevent suffering. Elegantly in La Rochefoucauld and less elegantly in Manley, we see the psychological realism that was to become so important in the worldly novels of the eighteenth century, especially those of Crébillon and Laclos.

Unlike La Rochefoucauld's, Manley's maxims are attached to stories crammed with tawdry particulars, indeed, with novelistic revelations about quotidian sexual oddities. Many of the stories are repetitive narratives of worldly male seducers or rapists taking advantage of less worldly wise women. To some extent, Manley distinguishes them from one another with sordid particulars. Some of these particulars are accusations of criminality – rape, incest, poisoning, theft, infanticide, treason – that might, differently treated, be at home in tragedy. But the tawdrier, more novel, revelations, designed to humiliate the satiric targets, create the sense that "real life" is being represented. Thus, the reader of *The New Atalantis* is told that the Earl Conningsby, in pursuit of a resisting Countess Scudamore, resorted to spiking her chocolate with an emetic in hopes

of keeping her confined to her room. Or that the Countess of Maccles-
field, possessed of a beautiful body but an unappealing face, allowed her
more finicky lovers to have intercourse with her while she draped "a
Gauze Handkerchief of *Turkish Embroidery*" over her face.[69] Or that
Egerton, living with her clergyman husband, talked incessantly, had
temper tantrums, and threw a hot apple pie in his face. The Reverend
Mr. Egerton is allowed to describe his wife as an ugly woman with a flat
nose and rotten teeth and to complain that she has had multiple affairs.
He voices the usual laments about learned women: "Deliver me from a
poetical Wife, and all honest Men for my sake! She rumbles in verses of
Atoms, Artick, and Antartick" (Of "Antartic and Arctic" actually, in "To
One who said I must not Love").[70]

Readers have disagreed sharply over the merits of Manley's scandal
chronicles. Most have found them tedious, dated, badly written, and
morally repellant. Manley follows Behn in helping to create the clichéd
prose of debased romance. For example, she describes the progress of an
affair between Don Tomasio Roderiguiz and Diana in these words:

the Lustre of her *Charms flash'd* full upon his Heart: He was wounded! He was
disarmed all at an instant! she had but to behold, to Conquer! He was surpriz'd at
the Suddenness of the *Invasion*! but, before he cou'd well reflect, he was
confirm'd in her *Victory*! . . . No sooner did she feel an Alteration of Mind,
but she (who tasted so few *refin'd* Delights) too easily gave into this. She never
examin'd whither the dangerous Guide would lead her, 'Twas all *new*! *sparkling*!
enchanting Brightness! no road could be displeasing in such agreeable Company.
Her killing Eyes now seem'd to lay aside their darts: Languishments usurp'd
upon the *Fire* and gave Don *Tomasio* unmolested leave to gaze . . .[71]

Bridget McCarthy memorably, and, I think, fairly, called Manley's prose
"elephantine" and filled with "blowsy euphemism."[72] Rejecting efforts to
recuperate Manley's writing as literature, William Warner has recently
argued that the true significance of Behn's and Manley's fiction is that
they created the first formula fiction and, in so doing, launched early
modern print entertainment and media culture. Against efforts to claim
Manley's fiction for feminism or to claim it as "feminocentric," he rightly
points out that the early secret histories in both France and England were
written and read by both men and women. What these narratives do,
according to Warner, is to use the "shell-like emptiness of their protagonists" to teach a "licentious ethical nihilism" to male and female readers.
Readers learn "to articulate desire and to put the self first," not to embrace
a particular class or political ideology, but only the ideology of "pleasure

itself."[73] (Whether these amorous narratives arouse readerly pleasure or provoke readerly disdain may be debated.)

Some recent feminist critics, however, have celebrated Manley's scandal chronicles as significant accomplishments in women's literature. The fact that Manley as a woman writer represents sexuality and the possibility of female sexual pleasure has recommended her to some as a brave, excitingly transgressive writer. That she exposes male sexual predation, its mentality and tactics, and protests explicitly against the sexual double standard also makes her seem to offer at least a proto-feminist protest against patriarchy.[74] Catherine Gallagher, recognizing that Manley represents herself as the new kind of hack writer, combining sexual scandal and venality, nonetheless finds that she makes scandal "a rich and complex experience" and credits her with a capacity for "humor" and conscious "self-parody."[75] Paula McDowell contends that Manley's combining the news function with modes of informal women's talk was a key contribution both to the development of the novel and to women's political writing. Yet, in my judgment, the absence of serious or interesting political thought in *The New Atalantis*, its highly personalized and sometimes unfounded attacks (coupled with servile panegyric of possible patrons), bad writing, and its acceptance of misogynistic ideas about women did more to reinforce resistance to women's entitlement to write than to advance the cause.

In addition to her scandal chronicles, Manley also published a fictional autobiography, *The Adventures of Rivella* (1714), a book in which she presents herself as a great mistress of the arts of love. Rivella is presented as a woman who, although deprived of conventional virtue and respectability, is to be understood by the reader as a good woman possessed of exceptional personal qualities: beauty, intelligence, generosity, and business sense. Manley seems to offer the story as that of an heroic woman. Rivella's qualities are expressed with superlatives. One admirer, for instance, describes her as, even at age twelve, "the Wittiest Girl in the World."[76]

Manley avoids the appearance of blatant narcissism by wrapping the narrative in several Chinese boxes, telling it from the points of view of Rivella's male admirers. The original account is supposed to have been written in French by Chevalier D'Aumont after he heard it told by his friend, Sir Charles Lovemore. Sir Charles describes how he fell in love with Rivella when she was twelve, then followed her adventures, continuing to love her, although she never returned his love. Lovemore is not so besotted with Rivella as to be uncritical; this has the effect of increasing his credibility. His supposed eyewitness testimony is used to refute contemporary hostile representations of her. Thus, when Lovemore hears Rivella's version of how she came to marry bigamously and thus be "ruined," he declares: "She told me all her Misfortunes with an Air so perfectly ingenuous, that, if some Part of the World who were not acquainted with her Vertue, ridicul'd her Marriage, and the Villany of her Kinsman, I, who know her Sincerity, could not help believing all she said. My Tears were Witnesses of my grief . . ."[77] Lovemore models the logic of the desired reader response: he, a gentleman, admires and loves Rivella; therefore, Rivella is admirable, even loveable, and pitiable.

As in Behn's amorous tales, in *Rivella* love is a passion irresistible to persons of sensibility; it is apt to lead, not to the noble deeds of romance, but to criminality. Rivella is only twelve when Lysander first makes her feel the power of love. Then, "she drank the Poyson both at her Ears and Eyes, and never took Care to manage or conceal her Passion . . . She knew not what she did, not having Freewill, or the Benefit of Reflection."[78] Without prompting from Lysander, the young Rivella steals money from her father to give to him. Once Rivella loses her "innocence" and reputation in the bigamous marriage to her guardian, she can no longer be a subject of normative romance, and Manley seems unsure how to develop her plot. Subsequent episodes mix the narrative of love with complex accounts of litigation over money. Despite his romance name, Rivella's lover Cleander is a lawyer she first encounters imprisoned in the house of the Sergeant at Arms. She begs him to join her scheme to make a large sum of money by engineering a settlement in the estate litigation between Lord Crafty and Baron Meanwell. Cleander quite properly resists joining the conspiracy, since he would have to betray Lord Crafty, who has been his client. Nevertheless, in this debased romance, Rivella's importuning has the power to make him chose love over honor. He declares: "no Lover either could, or ought to refuse what was ask'd him by the person he lov'd."[79]

Lovemore's narrative celebrates Rivella not only for her remarkable capacity to feel and inspire love, but also, perhaps more interestingly, for having an extraordinary understanding of love. He offers a clever apology for her lapses from chastity in an apogee of gallantry that concludes the story: she has "so peculiar a Genius" in relation to love, and "has made such noble discoveries in that Passion, that it would have been a *Fault in her, not to have been Faulty*."[80] The book dignifies Manley as the inheritor of a classical tradition, albeit a minor vein of that tradition, that of Ovid's *Amores* and *Ars Amatoria*.

Rivella's knowledge of love includes not only knowledge of conventional forms of passion, but also odder, more attenuated ways of being in "love" observable in her contemporary London social world. In both the scandal chronicles and *Rivella* Manley explores sexual desires that lead to a variety of behaviors, some strange, some sordid. Rivella flirts with Sir Peter Vainlove, a character based on Thomas Skipworth, MP and part owner in Drury Lane and Dorset Garden Theatres. Married and "towards Fifty," Sir Peter is obsessed with being "thought in the Favour of the Fair." For over ten years, he has kept a City mistress, Mrs. Settee, paying her £300 a year to dine with him one a week. Although he has never had intercourse with her, he says, "yet she never scrupled to oblige him so far, as to undress and go even into the Bed naked with him once every Week, where they found a way to please themselves as well as they could."[81] When Rivella has success as a playwright, Sir Peter begins to escort her about town and drives her wild by reading aloud to her from Mrs. Settee's love letters to him. Manley here creates a love triangle of two women and one man, reminiscent of Behn's love triangles. Rivella sends him a song characterizing him as a "dang'rous Swain" whose passionate words about another woman arouse her desire and make her vulnerable to ruin by him. Proud of this testimony of his power over women, Sir Peter boastfully sings the song "in all Companies where he came." When Mrs. Settee jealously demands he stop seeing Rivella, he capitulates but demands that, in return, Mrs. Settee have intercourse with him. She does, and he then advertises his success by going into "a publick Course of Physick," as though he needed treatment for venereal disease.[82] *Rivella* suggests that he was impotent. Sir Peter has some of the characteristics of the fops of Restoration comedy, as well as the impotence of Dryden's Mr. Limberham in *The Kind Keeper* (1678), but he is plausible as a mixed, novelistic character. Even when driven by a desire for revenge or a desire to profit financially from scandal, Manley's decision to represent contemporary people in her fiction sometimes produces a degree of psychological realism.

TROTTER AND TRAGEDY

Optimism about the possibilities for women's advancement during the reign of Queen Anne is particularly evident in the work of Catharine Trotter, whose *Fatal Friendship* we considered in the previous chapter. Trotter, as earlier noted, had burst upon the London literary scene in the 1690s as a precocious teenager with her novella, *Olinda's Adventures*, and then her tragedy, *Agnes de Castro*, based on a Behn novella. Trotter was unusually well educated, knowing not only French, but apparently also Latin, Greek, logic, and philosophy. During the reign of Queen Anne, she began to establish herself as a writer on philosophical subjects, notably as a defender of Locke in *A Defence of the Essay of Human Understanding Written by Mr. Lock* (1702). *A Defence*, first published anonymously, replied to Thomas Burnet's *Remarks upon an Essay Concerning Humane Understanding*, also published anonymously. Writing against objections that Locke's epistemology undermines morality, casts doubt on the immortality of the soul, and insinuates Deist views, she proceeds in a rational and perspicuous style. She maintains that innate knowledge of God is not required as a basis of ethical knowledge. Instead, "the Nature of Man, and the Good of Society, are *to us* the Reason and Rule of Moral Good and Evil: and there is no danger of their being less immutable on this Foundation than any other, whilst Man continues *a Rational and Sociable Creature*. . ."[83] In this and subsequent philosophical works, Trotter aimed to create a cultural space for undogmatic philosophical discussion. She considered that dogmatic defenses of religion, like Burnet's, supporting religion "upon Metaphysical Notions, upon false or abstruse Reasonings," only served to provoke more skepticism and atheism.[84]

Most of the seventeen original plays by women first performed during the reign of Queen Anne were comedies – and most of the comedies were by Centlivre – but the more intellectual women writers like Trotter persisted in trying to demonstrate their abilities in verse tragedy. In addition to the three verse tragedies she had written earlier, Trotter wrote a final verse tragedy, *The Revolution of Sweden* (1706). Overtly political, the play clearly articulates the Lockian and Whig understanding of the right relation between sovereign and people. It is cousin to John Dennis's *Liberty Asserted* (1704) and Joseph Addison's *Cato* (1713). *The Revolution of Sweden* tells the story of Gustavus Vasa, the sixteenth-century Swedish liberator of Sweden from Danish occupation. Vasa was a hero who, like George Washington, first served as a general of the army of liberation and then as a popularly elected executive. Trotter's source seems to have been René Vertot's *Histoire des révolutions du Suède* (1695), a sophisticated counter-Reformation history especially concerned with how the Church of Rome lost Sweden to the Lutherans during the reign of Gustavus. Trotter may well have consulted other sources, including Latin histories or the philosopher Samuel Puffendorf's *Complete History of Sweden from its Origin to this Time*, translated from the German in 1702. (Puffendorf was German and the son of a German Lutheran pastor, but in 1671 he went to Stockholm and became the Swedish historiographer royal.) Gustavus was a fascinating figure in European history, imaginable as a great democratic and a great Protestant hero. Later English accounts included Henry Brooke's play, *Gustavus Vasa* (1737), and Sarah Scott's *History of Gustavus Erickson, King of Sweden . . .* (1761), a history clearly indebted to Vertot and Puffendorf.

While not a great tragedy, *The Revolution of Sweden* presents vigorous, intelligent, and patriotic heroes and heroines. To some tastes at least, after the lust-crazed women in the work of Behn and Manley, it is refreshing to encounter Trotter's high-minded heroines. The verse is sometimes awkward and the style often prosaic, yet the language avoids absurdity and the play fits with an emerging democratic political aesthetic. Emphasis is on ideas rather than on verbal ornament. Trotter had earlier eschewed the florid style of heroic and sensational tragedy, writing in her preface to *The Unhappy Penitent* that Nathaniel Lee, aiming at the sublime, was not great but merely extravagant. At her best, she offers pointed political rhetoric.

The Revolution of Sweden is aggressively moral and political, using its plain style to articulate democratic and Lockian political values. Trotter reveals herself not only a student of Locke's *Essay on Human Understanding* but also of his *Second Treatise of Civil Government*. Gustavus fights for the rights of the Swedes against Danish oppression, conscientiously deferring to justice and law even when his self-interest is at stake. The play opens at a critical stage of the conflict between his Swedish army and the Danish occupiers. Nevertheless, when volunteer soldiers want to go home to harvest their crops, Gustavus overrules his more zealous lieutenant to let them go, insisting that the means they use in their struggle must be "strictly just and pious as our Cause":

> Suppressing Tyranny's an ill pretext
> For our becoming Tyrants.[85]

In act V, after Gustavus has been victorious in the field, he recognizes that the country has returned to a Lockian state of nature and immediately summons a legislature to select a new executive. When the senators offer to acclaim him King of Sweden, Gustavus insists that he will accept the authority of whoever they choose, at first declining but then bowing to their repeated pleas. (Vertot records two occasions on which Gustavus called such assemblies, but sees his first refusal to accept the Swedish crown as a ploy to avoid taking the coronation oaths that would have engaged him to preserve the Roman Catholic clergy in all their privileges

and immunities.[86]) Trotter thus endorses Locke's view that Parliament
had the power to confer legitimacy on William III.

Contrasted to Gustavus, the liberator and the democrat, are the Danish
Viceroy and his two Swedish collaborators, Beron and the Archbishop of
Upsala. The Viceroy is dissolute and irresolute; the Archbishop more
intelligent, urgent, and realistic about the danger Gustavus poses. Both
are absolutist, arbitrary, and self-seeking. When one of the heroines offers
the Archbishop a Lockian argument that an oppressed people seeking
redress of their grievances are not rebels, he exclaims, "Pernicious Principles," and opines that the problem is rather excessive clemency in the
Danish king, who should have killed Gustavus when he earlier held him
prisoner.[87]

Not one but two heroines in *The Revolution of Sweden* prize the public
good over their private pleasures; the play firmly insists that women are
capable of political virtue and that they can contribute to their country's
good. Indeed, in the dedication to *The Unhappy Penitent* Trotter had
doubted whether love were a proper subject for tragedy: "it seems to me
not Noble, not Solemn enough for Tragedy." For this play, Trotter found
in her historical sources an account of Peterson's wife, who becomes
Christina in her tragedy. Peterson was an old army friend of Gustavus's,
who offered him refuge when he returned to Sweden to fight the Danes.
But Peterson secretly planned to betray Gustavus. Peterson's wife warned
Gustavus and helped him escape to safety. As Christina, this heroine
appears in male disguise as a volunteer in Gustavus's camp, sentenced
to death by her husband, who, in the play, is called Beron. She worries
that her actions may be "interpreted" to her "dishonour," but is convinced
that she has done right in valuing the fate of her country over her
obligation to her husband:

> Many preserve their Virtue for a Name,
> But few for Virtue, wou'd abandon Fame.[88]

Taken prisoner by the Archbishop's army, she is shocked to discover that
Beron has branded her "a vile Adult'ress," since he can imagine no other
motive for her assisting Gustavus.[89] (Vertot similarly speculated, "she was
prompted by Pity, and perhaps by a more tender Passion, to discover her
Husband's Plot . . ."[90]) Christina remains true to the interests of Sweden,
however, and in act V discloses a new plot of her husband against an ally of
Gustavus's, resolving the play's conflicts. Stabbed by her villainous husband, she is the only virtuous character to die. Gustavus pronounces her
elegy:

Be our Generous Preserver
Never forgot, let Fame Record her Vertue,
With her Husband's Villany, to all
Who e'er shall hear of *Sweden's* great Deliverance;
And every Nation join in her just Praise.[91]

CENTLIVRE'S COMEDY

Trotter and other intellectuals liked tragedy, but eighteenth-century audiences preferred comedy, and eighteenth-century playwrights wrote better comedies than they did tragedies. Less strenuously intellectual than Trotter and more gifted as a dramatist, Susanna Centlivre was the most successful woman playwright between Behn in the seventeenth century and Hannah Cowley in the late eighteenth century. Like Chudleigh and Egerton, Centlivre was alert to the new ideas and manners, but she was more inclined – by temperament and perhaps by good fortune and the requirements of the commercial stage – to treat them humorously. She knew that she was following Behn's success in the commercial theatre, but she was not attracted to libertinism or to the bleaker, more mordant, elements in Behn's drama. Of her nineteen plays, the better comedies pleased contemporaries and still please audiences today.

Centlivre's heroines are unusually sunny, physically active, and inventive. When threatened with forced marriages, they resist with spirit, insist on the freedom to love whom they will, and successfully engineer or at least join in plots that defeat the desires of their fathers or guardians. They like their lovers to be honest and straightforward, neither fulsomely gallant or presumingly superior, neither, as one says, "Cringing or Correcting."[92]

Working in the line of English humors comedy staked out by Ben Jonson and later developed by Thomas Shadwell and then by her friend Farquhar, Centlivre is delightfully attentive to the topical, both to new kinds of social practices and to the odd new words and phrases that go with those practices. The art of her plays depends on a theatrical imagination that works through scenes and objects displayed on the stage rather than through witty dialogue. For example, Angellica in *The Gamester* (1705) puts on men's clothes to go after the gentleman she loves, a man obsessed with fashionable gambling. She pursues him to the gaming table, where the audience sees rakes and sharpers gather round the hazard table, a "Box-keeper" and "boxes for dice," and hears the argot of contemporary gaming: "Throw a Main then," "Five's the Main," "Now little Dice," and so on.

Also fetchingly topical, Valeria in *The Basset-Table* (1705), another play about gambling, is described in the dramatis persona as "a Philosophical Lady." Like Chudleigh, Valeria knows of Epictetus, Descartes, and Fontenelle and declares that only custom makes learning in a woman ridiculous. Especially interested in the new science, Valeria collects and dissects animal and insect specimens. The stage spectacle of a pretty young woman with a microscope eager to show her lover a tapeworm was both strikingly novel and humorous. When we learn that Valeria has dissected her pet dove to discover whether it had gall and witness her eagerness to exchange her jewelry for Lady Reveller's pet greyhound, the tenderhearted pet lover may shudder as well as laugh. Some critics have thought Centlivre meant Valeria as a satire on the learned woman and even as an attack on Astell. (Lady Reveller teases Valeria by saying that she should found a college for women.) To my mind, though, the portrait is more one of delighted, curious, fascination, than of condemnation. As other critics have pointed out, the plot of *The Basset-Table* requires the gambling ladies to repent, whereas Valeria does not have to renounce her interest in science in order to be matched with the attractive Lt. Lovely.

Centlivre's *The Busie Body* (1709), one of her best plays, combines a classic comic marriage plot with an original humors character, the eponymous Busie Body, Marplot. Centlivre invents a character quintessentially of the period: a person craving news and scandal – the ideal reader of the burgeoning newspapers and of Manley's scandal chronicle, *The New Atalantis*. As his name suggests, Marplot repeatedly threatens to spoil the lovers' plots. He acts not out of malice, but because he is obsessed with a desire to know the secrets of well-born men and to be seen to be their intimate friend. He is willing to pay money for an introduction to a notable man and to perform any service so that he can appear to be part of the public world, although, as a fool, he is spectacularly ill suited for such a part. "'[T]is a vast Addition to a Man's Fortune," says Marplot, "to be seen in the Company of Leading *Men*; for then we are all thought to be Politicians, or Whigs, or Jacks [Jacobites], or High-Flyers, or Low-Flyers [of the High Church or Low Church parties]; for you must know, we all herd in Parties now."[93] More or less inadvertently, when he does discover the gentlemen's secrets, he publishes them by blurting them out to the very people from whom they should be hidden.

Like the author of a scandal chronicle who claims to be a public-spirited satirist, Marplot can delude himself that his insatiable curiosity is a duty. When he follows one of the gentlemen lovers to the house of his beloved to spy on him, he soliloquizes: "I'll watch, it may be a Bawdy-House, and he may have his Throat cut; if there should be any Mischief, I can make Oath, he went in. Well, *Charles*, in spight of your Endeavour to keep me out of the Secret; I may save your Life, for ought I know . . . Gad, I love Discoveries."[94] (Centlivre's audience knew that members of the Society for the Reformation of Manners swore out many complaints against brothels and that lower-class young men, claiming the moral high ground, sometimes attacked brothels and got convicted of rioting.) What is funny about Marplot's speech here is that the audience knows he is spying because he loves to be in on secrets, not out of moral commitment. They know that, if he were an effectual and courageous friend of a man who was having his throat cut in a brothel, he would dash in and use his sword – not make a legal complaint after his friend's death. Yet Centlivre's comedy is genial, not severe. She reminds us that Marplot's voyeurism is not utterly unlike that of the audience. When a servant called Whisper speaks a low aside to his master, she lets Marplot ask the audience's question: what news does "*Whisper*" bring?[95] This desire to know the secrets of other's lives, cloaked with professions of moral duty, is also the formula for the Defoe's fiction; Defoe himself sought to serve greater men as a spy.

The love plots in which Marplot interferes show Centlivre's assured mastery of classic comedy and feature one of her inventive heroines, Miranda. Two nice girls, Miranda and Isabinda, love two nice young men, Sir George Airy and Charles Gripe. The blocking characters are modern versions of the Latin *senex*, two old men who want to control the marriages of the girls. Sir Francis Gripe loves money; he manages to get himself appointed executor of other men's estates and is the guardian of Miranda and Marplot. He wants Miranda and her fortune for himself. Sir Jealous Traffic also loves money; as a merchant living for a long time in Spain he has acquired a liking for the way the Spanish control their women. He confines his daughter, Isabinda, and declares that she must marry an aged, rich, Spanish gentleman. (Pix is the earlier woman dramatist Centlivre most resembles and this plot is perhaps homage to Pix's *Spanish Wives* [1696] – although Centlivre also takes advantage of the fact that England and Spain were antagonists in the current War of the Spanish Succession.)

Vivacious Miranda is the author of the principal plot and rightly prides herself on her invention. "Let the Tyrannt Man make what Laws he will," she tells her clever maid, "if there's a Woman under the Government,

I warrant she finds a way to break 'em."[96] Reversing the usual relation of man and woman to gallant flattery, Miranda flatters old Sir Francis and convinces him that she is in love with him and eager to marry him. Affectionately, she calls him "Gardy," puts up with his petting, and plays along with his insistence that young men are worthless fops and make bad husbands. Her intention is to get him to sign over her estate to her so she can marry Sir George. Sir Francis actually dotes on Miranda; the reality of his affection and his delight in what he thinks is Miranda's love for him softens the character. Perhaps Centlivre here gave Richard Sheridan a hint for his later Sir Peter Teazle in *The School for Scandal.*

Miranda's plot succeeds, but not before a series of events that prompted William Hazlitt, who knew *The Busie Body* as a repertory play, to praise "the ingenuity of the contrivance, the liveliness of the plot, and the striking effect of the situations." Centlivre, he observed, "delights in putting her *dramatis personæ* continually at their wits end, and in helping them off with a new evasion; and the subtlety of her resources is in proportion to the criticalness of the situation and the shortness of the notice for resorting to an expedient."[97] In the fourth act, for instance, Miranda thinks she has sent Sir Francis safely out of town and can at last enjoy an assignation with Sir George. But Sir Francis, doting on her, suddenly returns to take leave of his "dear *Chargee.*" Miranda stashes Sir George behind the chimney-board. Sir Francis is soon willing to depart, but, considerately, insists on neatly disposing of the peel from his orange under the chimney board so as not to "litter" Miranda's room. Miranda quickly improvises a story that she has a new monkey stashed under the chimney board and cannot have it let out until the man who tames monkeys comes. Sir Francis, whose trust in her is comic, accepts this and exits. But Marplot is there. He cannot resist anything hidden and so exposes Sir George, crying out in surprise "Thieves, Thieves, Murder!" – loudly enough to bring Sir Francis back again. Finally, for once, Marplot makes himself useful and says that, longing to see the monkey, he let it out, it scratched him and made him cry out, and then it escaped out of the window.

Centlivre's *The Wonder: A Woman Keeps a Secret* (1714), albeit in a relatively light-hearted way, joins in the contemporary feminist campaign waged by soberer writers like Astell, Masham, Egerton, and Chudleigh, the campaign designed to demonstrate that women have minds comparable to the minds of men and that they too are capable of exhibiting the range of human virtues, not only the virtue of chastity. The misogynist tradition represented women as more exclusively physical creatures than men, as more lascivious, and more loquacious. Women's speech in this tradition is associated, at best, with triviality and inconsequentiality, and, at worst, with disorder and sin. Eve's speech to Adam tempts him and dooms the human race to sin and death. In *The Wonder* Centlivre continues to insist that women are flesh and blood, but also has her heroine explicitly claim that ladies are as capable as gentlemen of loyal friendship and of the honor that consists in faithfully keeping promises. And she insists that women can hold their tongues when there is good reason to do so.

The Wonder is set in Portugal, mostly to make plausible the restrictive positions in which the heroines find themselves and to celebrate the superiority of British liberty over Peninsular tyranny. The sprightlier of the two heroines, Isabella, is threatened with a forced marriage to a rich, well-born, elderly man. In a memorable bit of stage business, when she pleads with her father, "I'll die before I'll marry *Guzman*," he offers her his sword, then laughs at her when she declines to use it on herself.[98] Locked in her room, she escapes by jumping out of the window – happily into the arms of one Colonel Britton, a Scottish officer on his way back to Britain from the Peninsular War. (Centlivre shows her support for the 1707 Act of Union between England and Scotland by making the Scot a hero and enlivens her scene by providing him with a servant who speaks in dialect and wears highland dress.) Isabella decides she would like to marry Colonel Britton, but asks her friend Violante to help by concealing her for a few days while she executes her plan. Violante, in love with Isabella's brother Don Felix, agrees that the secret must also be kept from him, since he would probably think his honor blemished by his sister's eloping and either return her to her father's confinement or (it is Portugal) kill her.

Violante's promise to keep Isabella's secret and her willingness to value a promise to a woman friend over her relationship with a male lover are sorely tested. Don Felix is a jealous lover whose suspicions are not unnaturally aroused by the flurry of tappings on his lady's window, noises in her closets and adjacent rooms, and her unwillingness to let him hide in the bedroom (where Isabella has already been hidden) when circumstances seem to demand it. Torn between jealousy and a sincere love for Violante, Don Felix is a fundamentally sympathetic character, one with more inwardness than is usual in comedy of intrigue. It is easy to understand why the brilliant actor David Garrick made this one of his favorite parts, resorting to it for his final performance in comedy in 1776.[99] Yet Don Felix is all too ready to see Violante as exemplifying the falseness and treachery of women. She declares her faithfulness despite the suspicious circumstances and beseeches him: "Oh think how far Honour can oblige your Sex – Then allow a Woman may be bound by the same Rule to keep a secret."[100]

Centlivre exploits the conventions of comedy of intrigue, especially those of hiding and disguise, to create variations on a theme that reveal how different the social expectations of women and of men are. In one scene, Don Felix rages that Violante could be hiding someone from him; in the next act, he depends upon a male friend to conceal him. (Don Felix is wanted for wounding a man in a duel; he is also hiding from his father, from whom he has fled to avoid accepting a woman other than Violente for his wife.) Violante pushes her way past a servant to confront Don Felix and to try to reason him out of his jealousy, to convince him that love without esteem is an impossibility and that "true love ne'er doubts the Object it adores."[101] While she speaks with him, a servant enters to get a cloak from the clothes press and discovers a woman hidden in it. Violante proposes that she will ask no questions about this woman if he will forget the man at her window. Haughtily, Don Felix declares, "I scorn Forgive- ness where I own no Crime . . ."[102] He insists that, despite the symmetry of the stage discoveries – a man at her apartments, a woman in his room – she must be guilty and he must be innocent.

Yet, since Don Felix's love is real, he repents and goes to Violante's house to clear himself and to seek reconciliation. Before this can be effected, Violante's father approaches, prompting Don Felix to try to hide in her bedroom (where Isabella's Colonel is already hiding) and prompting Violante and her maid to tell him that he must instead try to hide under a disguise. The disguise and role they thrust on him is an ignoble one, suitable comic punishment for a too proud, too jealous Don: he must pretend to be an old woman, mother to Violante's servant, deaf (so that he need not respond to Don Pedro's questions), and with such a "Defluxion in her Eyes" that she has to keep her hood pulled over her face.[103] Don Felix thus escapes from Don Pedro, but only retreats to another hiding place under the stairs, where he sees the Colonel come on stage from Violante's bedroom and exit. This time, though, his jealous rage is short-circuited. Violante calmly and inventively claims that she has played a trick on him to demonstrate how easily he will relapse into his "wonted error" of jealousy.[104] Isabella gratefully thanks Violante for keeping her secret despite the risks of losing both her own lover and her reputation, and promises that she will "to the World proclaim the Faith, Truth, and Honour of a Woman."[105]

Centlivre follows Judith Drake and joins her friend and contemporary Steele in attacking dueling, a key element of the older code of upper-class masculine behavior. She goes beyond Steele in representing the hair-trigger tempers of privileged men like Don Felix as consequences of their privileged and indulged lives and in arguing for more privileges for women. Despite Don Felix's declaration at the end of the fourth act that he will trust Violante rather than believe his eyes, at the beginning of the final act something he hears sets him to smoldering again and prompts him to draw his sword on the Colonel. Frederick, his merchant friend, interposes, insisting, "you shan't fight on bare Suspicion."[106]

Thus at least temporarily restrained, Don Felix goes to see Violante in a famous scene of the play, one that illustrates both the active determination of Centlivre's heroines and Centlivre's dramaturgical skill. Don Felix, surly and pacing irritably, tries to quarrel with Violante, yet his love for her and his realization that his accusations hurt her make him withdraw repeatedly from the brink of final rupture. Comparing this scene with the famous proviso scene in Congreve's *Way of the World* (1700), one is struck by Centlivre's representation of women's power over men and by her emphasis on her heroine's demand for freedom of locomotion – "I hope I may Walk where I please, and at what Hour I please, without asking you leave," Violante declares.[107] Like almost all conversations in this play, this lover's tête-à-tête is both overheard by another character in hiding (Isabella in the bedroom) and disrupted by the approach of yet another character dangerous to one of the interlocutors (Don Pedro). Still unwilling to discover Isabella to her brother, Violante cleverly saves herself by quickly inventing a tale of how a young lady pursued by a gentleman with drawn sword had just sought refuge in their house. Don Felix is forced further to embarrass himself by feigning drunkenness before he can finally hear the truth about Violante's concealing his sister. He marries Violante and ends the play proclaiming her virtues and the realization that women in general may be virtuous:

> No more let us Thy Sex's conduct blame,
> Since thou'rt a Proof to their eternal Fame,
> That Man has no Advantage but the Name.[108]

CONCLUSION

Of the women writers during the reign of Queen Anne, perhaps only Centlivre established herself as a professional writer. Between 1700 and her death in 1723, she produced a large body of work, most notably sixteen full-length plays and three shorter farces, almost all both produced in London and published. She was the most prolific playwright, male or female, of the early eighteenth century, and, very likely, the most popular woman dramatist in the entire history of English literature, including the twentieth century. During the eighteenth-century, three of her plays topped the list of most popular plays by women according to number of years produced: *The Busie Body*, produced in eighty-seven years, *A Bold Stroke for a Wife* (1718), produced in seventy-five years; and *The Wonder*, produced in fifty-three years.[109] Centlivre's plays also went through very large numbers of editions in Britain and America in the eighteenth and nineteenth centuries; several were translated into various European languages. Gotthold Lessing, the important German dramatist, reviewed the French translation of *A Bold Stroke for a Husband* and used *The Perjur'd Husband* (1700) as one of the sources for his domestic tragedy, *Miss Sara Sampson*.[110] As we shall see, Centlivre significantly influenced Hannah Cowley and Elizabeth Inchbald, major British dramatists of the second half of the eighteenth century.

As it had been during the Restoration, drama continued to be a lucrative genre for writers. This partly explains why so many eighteenth-century writers with small dramatic talent insisted on writing plays and why writers whose plays were rejected by theatre managers seem especially bitter. Dramatists normally received "author's benefits," profits from the third and sixth night's performances of a play's initial run, if the play managed an initial run that long. Authors could sometimes negotiate additional benefits, even for revivals. Records do not allow a reconstruction of Centlivre's income from author's benefit nights, but we know she enjoyed author's benefits both from several initial runs and from later revivals.[111] Many playwrights made little from such benefits since they depended on the length of a play's run, on the take of the house on the night, and on management's deductions for costs, but a successful play typically yielded more income to its author than a poem or book of poems or a pamphlet or a novel. After a production – or during a long-running one – a playwright could sell her copyright to a publisher. We know that Lintott paid Centlivre £10 each for the copyrights to *Love's Contrivance* and *The Busie Body*, more than Cibber got in 1696 for *Love's Last Shift*, although much less than the 50 guineas Addison got in 1716 for his unmemorable comedy, *The Drummer*.[112] Later, Curll paid her 20 guineas each for *The Wonder*, *The Cruel Gift*, and *The Artifice*.[113] The playwright also expected a third sum in the form of a present from the dedicatee.

When Centlivre dedicated *The Cruel Gift* to the writer Eustace Budgell he presented her with a diamond ring worth about 20 guineas. Steele's income as the author of *The Conscious Lovers* (1721) included £329 5s. from his author's benefit nights, £40 from Tonson for publication rights, and £500 from George I, to whom the play was dedicated.[114] These numbers are high, not representative, but they illustrate what a dramatist might strive for. Lock has guessed that Centlivre grossed from £100 to £150 each from her successful later plays.[115]

Like many authors of this reign, male and female, Centlivre vacillated on the issue of whether or not to appear publicly as the author of her work. A staggering number of early eighteenth-century texts appeared anonymously for a variety of reasons, including the worry about possible prosecution for libel or sedition that often motivated anonymity in Defoe, Swift, or Manley. Furthermore, what Michel Foucault called "the author function" was still relatively weak.[116] Yet it was important for women writers to appear publicly as authors of their own work if they were to provide the empirical evidence of women's capacities that early feminists like Astell desired.

Even the 1690s texts that came into the world as "by a Lady" or with another formula marking the author as a woman offered possibly dubious evidence of female capacity, since people realized that male writers could masquerade as female in printed texts. Indeed, the contemporary desire for the novelty of female voices encouraged such masquerading. Thomas Baker and Bernard Mandeville, for instance, seem to have taken it upon themselves to ventriloquize the female voices supposedly heard in *The Female Tatler* (1709).[117] George Berkeley not only edited the popular *Ladies Library* (1714), anthologizing Astell along with Jeremy Taylor, Fénelon, and Archbishop Tillotson, he also wrote the introduction to the volume, masquerading as a woman. On the other hand, women writers might masquerade as men, as Astell did when she selected "Mr. Wooton" as her pseudonym for her pamphlet *Bart'lemy Fair: Or, An Enquiry after Wit* (1709); Astell there attacked the Earl of Shaftesbury's *Letter Concerning Enthusiasm*, a plea for more religious toleration, but since the *Letter* had been published anonymously, Astell was not sure who she was attacking.

Only when writers like Astell, Rowe, Finch, Chudleigh, Trotter, and, especially, Centlivre appeared as the acknowledged authors of their own work was there more tangible evidence of what women could do. Astell seems to have recognized this to a degree, as in the reign of Queen Anne she permitted publication of the later editions of *A Serious Proposal* with her name. Chudleigh, Astell's follower, although she wrote more in terms of the older models of the seventeenth-century aristocratic learned lady than in the emerging model of commercial authorship, was perhaps also motivated to depart from the anonymity of her earlier publications to allow her name to appear with her 1710 *Essays* out of this desire to offer a model for women's emulation. Trotter signed the dedication to *Revolution of Sweden.*

Centlivre's career seems to illustrate a more general trend away from anonymity or from the kind of identification of the author by female gender only that we noted in the 1690s. Successful women authors increasingly used their proper names or at least some identifying formula that pointed to their individuality rather than simply to their gender. Frequently, subsequent works were advertised as "by the Author of" a successful earlier work; thus, Manley's title: *The Adventures of Rivella or the History of the Author of the Atalantis.* The three Finch poems in Tonson's 1709 *Miscellany* were marked as "By the author of the POEM on the SPLEEN."[118] Centlivre acknowledged authorship of her first two plays, but with *The Stolen Heiress* in 1702 concealed both her name and gender. In a 1706 preface to *The Platonic Lady* (published 1707) she complained that *Love's Contrivances* and *The Gamester* had succeeded because she had concealed her identity and the audience thought that a man had written them. However, *The Bickerstaff's Burying* (1710), a farce, was advertised in the theatre as "By the Author of *The Gamester*" and *A Bold Stroke for a Wife* was published as "By the Author of the *Busie-Body* and the *Gamester.*" An author who clung to anonymity deprived herself of the economic benefits of developing a public reputation, a valuable asset in negotiations for fees with theatre managers or publishers. By 1714, anyone with even a moderate interest in literature would have had good evidence that there really was a Susanna Centlivre living in London and writing successful plays.

Professional or amateur, these women writers of Queen Anne's reign sharply contested what the right understanding of love and gallantry ought to be. Albeit in different ways, most expressed suspicion of male gallantry and developed critiques of the falsity of conventional male flattery of women. Astell and Egerton inclined to see gallantry as mere pretended love, masking male contempt for women. Rowe, Astell, and Chudleigh looked to divine love and platonic love as superior to earthly love; with Trotter, they rejected the idea that a woman's identity ought to be determined by the roles of mistress or wife. I read the interest in the new science or the new political ideologies that Chudleigh, Egerton,

Astell, Trotter, and Centlivre express as, in part, an assertion of women's capacity to engage serious matters other than love. More the literary intellectual, Finch expressed concern that specious praise for women writers was itself dangerous. Finch also developed the Protestant celebration of married love in Sidney and Spenser, and – probably unknowingly, Bradstreet – in her original and accomplished poems on married love. In a lighter vein, Centlivre's independent heroines tease their male admirers about the conventions of flattery they employ and demand from lovers both more straightforward language and more authentic respect. From this perspective, Manley's writing often seems backward looking. She was sometimes alert to the dangerousness of a male gallantry that conceals male predation, yet desperately clung to a debased form of the old language of love, insisted that her heroines have power to compel male admiration, and grounded the woman writer's authority in her expertise as "mistress of the arts of love."

CHAPTER 4

Battle joined, 1715–1737

1736 Elizabeth Rowe. *The History of Joseph. A Poem. In Eight Books* (revised version in 10 books, published 1739)

INTRODUCTION

The death of Queen Anne on 1 August 1714 marked the end of the reign of the House of Stuart and the end of the reign of the only queen who ruled alone between 1660 and 1789. Hopes that the reigning queen might improve the condition of women by acting on proposals like Astell's for a female college had not been realized. By 1737 the monarch and the court had lost their cultural centrality to the more raucous and democratic worlds of party politics and the commercial marketplace. Amateur women writers in the country might look to local notables, especially ladies, for patronage, but in London women writers increasingly looked to the booksellers, who also served as publishers, for encouragement and employment. Two London writers, Eliza Haywood and Penelope Aubin, produced substantial numbers of prose works for this market. Although both had some involvement with the theatre, Haywood more than Aubin, drama ceased to be the only way to make a living from literature as fiction gained importance. Fiction, however, was still by no means the dominant literary form, even for women writers. Nor did women confine themselves to domestic subjects. Demonstrating considerable vigor, range, curiosity, and intellectual ambition, women writers of this period also experimented with satire, farce, epic, political writing, travel literature, translation, philology, and philosophy.

The most important women writers of this period – Lady Mary Wortley Montagu, Eliza Haywood, Mary Davys, and Elizabeth Singer Rowe – are in many ways quite different from one another. Montagu, daughter of an aristocrat and wife of an ambassador and Member of Parliament, had a well-deserved reputation as a wit; she wrote brilliant letters, satire, a periodical, *vers de société*, and Ovidian epistles. Davys, widow of a Dublin clergyman, moved to England, where she wrote plays, fiction, and autobiography; she used the profits from a successful play to open a coffee house patronized by the students and fellows of Cambridge University. Haywood, desperate for money, had a minor career as an actress and playwright, but is most important for her voluminous production of novels. Cheryl Turner noted Haywood's unique productivity:

The level and consistency of her output [of fiction] in the 1720s was unequalled by any other woman throughout the century, although . . . many of Haywood's works consisted of 100 pages or less, whilst a typical late eighteenth-century novel comprised three volumes of about 200 pages each. Haywood published fiction in almost every year of the third decade (with the exceptions of 1720 and 1721), producing at least 35 novels or approximately 70 per cent of the total output . . . by women in that period. Additionally, in most of those years she published more than one novel; for example, in 1725 (the peak year for novel output in the decade) she produced ten.[1]

Montagu and Haywood were frequent butts of contemporary satire, attacked as transgressive women writers and said to have compromised their reputations for chastity. Rowe, in contrast, in this period was celebrated as a religious poet and as a prose writer. (Singer had become Rowe on her marriage in 1710.) Hailed as the virtuous successor of Katherine Philips, she was much honored by her contemporaries and beloved by devoted readers for over one hundred years. Rowe's works, especially *Friendship in Death* (1728, 1731, 1732) and *Devout Exercises of the Heart* (posthumously published 1738), went through many editions in the eighteenth and early nineteenth centuries. *Friendship in Death* was re-issued thirty-three times between 1728 and 1814 and *Devout Exercises* thirty-seven times between 1738 and 1855.[2]

Nevertheless, despite their differences, Montagu, Davys, Haywood, and Rowe all had contestatory relations with their male contemporaries and all attacked dominant masculine ideologies. Montagu satirized both Swift and Pope and excelled at the "answer poem," a poem responding directly to a previous poem, or, alternatively, a poem giving voice to a previously silent figure in conventional lyric. Davys's novel, *The Accomplish'd Rake*, exposes the process of upper-class male socialization which results in a rather ordinary young country gentleman's feeling entitled to rape the daughter of his neighbor. Virtually all of Haywood's fiction may be considered as an attack on perfidious men and a defense of the "fallen" woman scorned by respectable society. Novel after novel represents powerful men as duplicitous and heartless schemers against female virtue and happiness. Even men specifically charged with the protection of female innocency, like the heroine's guardian in *The Rash Resolve* (1723), have no scruples about using patriarchal advantage to injure women. Late twentieth-century feminists particularly liked her *Fantomina, or, Love in a Maze* (1725), in which a well-born heroine, raped by the libertine Beau-plaisir, exacts a measure of satisfaction and revenge by disguising herself as different women, each of whom succeeds in evoking his desire.[3]

It is perhaps hardest to see the pious Elizabeth Rowe as engaged in a contestatory relationship with her male contemporaries, yet Rowe understood herself to be waging a righteous struggle with contemporary atheism and libertinism. Among the enthusiastic contemporary admirers of Rowe was Jane Turell, daughter and wife of Massachusetts ministers. In a poem published in Boston in 1735 Turell addresses Rowe:

> Inspir'd by Virtue you could safely stand
> The *fair Reprover* of a guilty Land.
> You vie with the fam'd *Prophetess* of old,
> Burn with her Fire, in the same Cause grow bold . . .
> A *Woman's* Pen strikes the curs'd *Serpents* Head,
> And lays the Monster gasping, if not dead.[4]

Rowe's success in developing cultural authority as a pious Christian laywoman provided a powerful model for later women writers and reformers like Hannah More and points forward to the ways in which nineteenth-century women in England and America claimed moral authority and justified their interventions in the public sphere by invoking the imperatives of Christian duty.

While relations between women writers and their male contemporaries seem more adversarial and women writers seem more independent in this period, it would be wrong to exaggerate the differences between the gallantry of the reign of Queen Anne and that of these early Hanoverian years. Montagu, as an aristocrat and a woman of some wealth and social position, was the recipient of commendatory verses and polite letters; indeed, Pope's letters and poems to her before about 1728 are notably gallant. (Lady Mary's letters to him, in contrast, offer a studied refusal to respond to his gallantries; she insists on focusing her side of the epistolary exchange on more sober topics like religion and poetry.) Later Montagu had Lord John Hervey as a close friend and occasional literary collaborator. Together they wrote the harsh satire of "Verses Address'd to the Imitator [Pope] of the First Satire of the Second Book of Horace" (1733). Davys was mocked in a *Grub-street Journal* essay as a writer of bawdy novels who instructed young men how to conduct amorous intrigue, but she was also generously supported by the Cambridge academics who frequented her coffee house when they paid to subscribe to her publications. Haywood was at first commended, though subsequently satirized, by Richard Savage; later in her career, she collaborated with her lover, William Hatchett, on an adaptation of Fielding's *History of Tom Thumb* as *The Opera of Operas* (1733), a satire on Italian opera. In 1715, Rowe's beloved husband, Thomas, died, and she withdrew into what has sometimes, rather misleadingly, been described as seclusion or rural retirement.

Her life as a widow nevertheless involved important relationships with Bishop Thomas Ken and Isaac Watts, both of whom encouraged her study and writing. Nevertheless, in these early Hanoverian years, more women writers published volumes under their own names, more women found women writers to celebrate as champions of their sex, and more women writers were emboldened to attack men.

THE DOMINANCE OF SATIRE

The greatest canonical literary works of this period are satires: Swift's *Gulliver's Travels* (1726), Gay's *Beggar's Opera* (1728), and Pope's *Dunciad* (1728f). While panegyric continued to be written, Swift and hordes of lesser writers increasingly insisted that panegyric was false and nakedly self-interested. (They were less likely to remark that satire might be equally self-interested, sometimes produced by writers hoping to curry favor with politicians by attacking their enemies, and occasionally produced by writers hoping so to terrify politicians that they would be bought off and paid to stop, either with money or places.) The attack on panegyric led to the cultivation of a variety of aggressively low styles and forms, all promising greater truthfulness. Thus, Swift cultivated iambic tetrameter couplet as the standard medium for his comic verse, Gay set off a vogue for ballad opera with *The Beggar's Opera*, and, between 1728 and 1737, Henry Fielding, naming himself "Scriblerus Secundus," dominated the London stage with farces, some of them politically topical. Satire prompted writers to represent the contemporary and the low. Sometimes satire's ostensible animus against its low targets modulates into neutrality or even affection, thus metamorphosing into something that looks increasingly like realism.

The government recognized the power of satire and farce when it passed the Licensing Act in 1737, closing the non-patent theatres like Fielding's Little Theatre in the Haymarket and bringing an end to this period by requiring pre-performance censorship. Haywood, also a minor actress, collaborated with Fielding at the Haymarket and collaborated with Hatchett on *The Opera of Operas*. She was appearing in performances of Fielding's *Historical Register* and *Eurydice Hiss'd* as a benefit for herself on 23 May 1737, the night before Walpole presented the Licensing Act to the Commons.[5]

The significant commercial success of Manley, Centlivre, and Haywood in fiction and drama, as well as the critical admiration for poets like Rowe and Finch, provoked hostile reaction in a number of male writers concerned about literary standards. The standards of high culture were threatened by uneducated women writers like Manley and Haywood – and by less educated male writers like Defoe. Elite male writers were also worried by women's increasingly significant challenges to male monopolies in literary reputation and market share. Pope's great satiric poem, *The Dunciad*, takes as its subject what Pope considered the death throes of high culture in the increasing triumph of low entertainments like farce, ballad opera, and popular fiction. Pope situates all the women writers he names, including Manley and Haywood, among the literary dunces. Following Pope's example, Fielding features Haywood as Mrs. Novel in his *Author's Farce* (1730).

Like other contemporary writers who aimed at literary immortality, Pope fretted that satire might be too particular and too topical to guarantee his own permanent fame; he suffered under accusations that his satire was merely an emanation of personal venom and spite rather than the cry of truth and justice he claimed it was. As a Roman Catholic ineligible for political preferment, Pope aspired to be the great poet of his age. Despite his worries about satire, his best poems are satires. He taunted his literary foes by boasting that their names would be known to posterity only because he mentioned them. Until very recently, some of the women writers of this period – including Haywood and Elizabeth Thomas – may have been best known for having been among the dunces of *The Dunciad*. The anxieties of male writers that satire was a problematic genre were shared by their female contemporaries, who labored under the additional burden that to publish satire seemed an unladylike activity.

Nevertheless, several women writers of this period joined in the satiric fray, sometimes on subjects remote from gender, sometimes in self-defense against attacks by male satirists, and often in their own attacks on particular men, types of men or men in general. Much has been made of the apparent misogyny and crudity of Swift's and Pope's satires on women, yet it is worth pointing out that women writers could be crude themselves. To Swift's famous "The Lady's Dressing-Room" (written about 1732), Montagu replied with *The Dean's Provocation for Writing the Lady's Dressing-Room* (1734), a retelling in which the sixty-year-old Swift goes to visit a prostitute only to be frustrated by his own impotence. He blames the girl's filth, demands his money back, and, seeking revenge, vows to write a poem describing her disgusting dressing room:

> I'll so describe your *Dressing-Room*,
> The very *Irish* shall not come;

> She answer'd short, I'm glad you'l write,
> You'l furnish Paper when I Sh—e.[6]

Pope had first admired, perhaps even loved, Lady Mary, but then turned on her with humiliating lines. Montagu responded to him with more protracted and bitter attacks, relentlessly depicting his parentage as low, his motives for writing as greed and the desire to rise socially, and his physical disabilities as monstrous outward signs of a vile soul.

It is hard to imagine any depths to which Haywood will not sink in her prose scandal chronicles. Following the example of Manley, she blackens not only the reputations of noblemen and politicians, but also those of her female rivals. Among the ostensibly depraved cast of characters in Haywood's *Memoirs of a Certain Island Adjacent to the Kingdom of Utopia* (1725–26) we find Gloatitia, the poet Martha Sansom, who is accused not merely of prostitution but of incest with her father.

THOMAS'S *MISCELLANY POEMS ON SEVERAL SUBJECTS*

Despite contemporary feeling that satire was not an appropriate form for women writers, some women during this period experimented with satiric forms, relishing the opportunity to paint elaborate portraits of idiotic fops and bad husbands as satiric butts. One of the livelier women satirists, Elizabeth Thomas, was influenced by the rationalist feminism of Astell and Chudleigh. Thomas's *Miscellany Poems on Several Subjects* (1722) offers a typical range of early eighteenth-century verse, including commendatory poems, translations and paraphrases, and religious poems. Instead of the usual love poems, however, in "The Defiance" the poet spurns "Vain Love!" and suggests that love is merely a cultural construction:

> Like Lovers Men, thy *Pow'r* adore,
> And worship what they made before . . .
> But *Vain Chimera* of the Brain!
> Whose Pow'r we by Tradition feign;
> Behold one to the *Muses* vow'd,
> Who never at thy Altar bow'd.[7]

Like Egerton, she offers her own version of Boileau's "Satire 2," the satirist's complaint about his compulsion to rhyme and his curse of his muse. The most striking poems in the volume are satires.

Thomas's "The True Effigies of a Certain Squire. Inscribed to Clemena" addresses a favorite topic of women satirists: the foolishness of men. She uses an important technique of contemporary satire, one also used by

Marvell, Waller, and Pope: imagining that the poet is speaking to a painter and giving directions how to paint a picture of the satiric object. Thomas's satiric target is a contemporary fop; she paints him from his shoes, to his pockets stuffed with "*Citron* Peel and Songs," to his giant powdered wig:

> The greasy Front press'd down with Essence lyes,
> The spreading Elf-Locks, cover half his Eyes;
> But when he coughs, or bows, what Clouds of Powder rise![8]

To the conventional misogynistic attack on women as empty-headed fashion-plates, Thomas responds with a recognizable picture of a type of contemporary man obsessed with fashion, as foolish and as superficial as any lady could be. This fop then speaks to express his distaste for women who try to read and educate themselves. His notion of how women ought to spend their time conjures up what many reflective eighteenth-century women felt were the horrors of time-wasting diversions like cards and chat, to which the rules of polite society sentenced them. Admitting that he never read six books in all his life, the squire reveals that on his wedding day he plans to order his bride to burn her books. Like Drake's earlier prose portraits of male folly, Thomas's ridicule of a privileged man is an important assertion of a female capacity for judgment. Most men and women in the early eighteenth century believed that men were naturally superior to women and most women lived in some awe of male superiority. This kind of female satire of male folly makes male authority less awe-inspiring, less terrifying, and prepares women to challenge it. It prepares women's minds for revolt in the same way that the Civil War satires on Charles I and the aristocracy or Thomas Paine's ridicule of George III and the aristocracy emboldened men's minds for revolution.

Several of Thomas's poems address another favorite topic of women satirists: marriage. She flirts with blasphemy in "A New Litany, Occasioned by an Invitation to a Wedding." Here the speaker appropriates the position of a priest presiding at a religious service. In the Anglican liturgy, the clergyman offers a series of prayer requests, for instance, praying for deliverance "From all evil and mischief; from sin; from the crafts and assaults of the devil; from thy wrath, and from everlasting damnation." The congregation replies to each supplication: "Good Lord, deliver us." Thomas adapts this form into a prayer for salvation from the miseries of marriage. She uses an anapestic trimeter meter associated with comic verse; the rapidity of anapestic tetrameter underscores her point that too many marry in haste and repent at leisure:

From a Mind so disturb'd that each Look does reveal it;
From Abhorring One's Choice, and not sense to conceal it:
Libera nos.[9]

Using the more common contemporary form of the verse epistle in heroic couplets, in "Epistle to Clemena. Occasioned by an Argument she had maintain'd against the Author," Thomas defends her satiric muse, attacks the sexual double standard, and offers a character of a contemporary husband, Nefario, who prefers drinking and gaming with his friends to conversation with his wife. She takes advantage of satire's openness to the undignified, the trivial, and the low to introduce realistic domestic dinner-table dialogue and action:

This *Meat's* too salt, t'other's too fresh, he cries,
And from the *Table* in a Passion flies:
Not, that his *Cook* is faulty in the least,
But 'tis the *Wife* that palls his squeamish Taste.[10]

Nefario's consorting with prostitutes infects his wife with venereal disease, an all-too-common misery for married women in the eighteenth century, when endemic venereal disease was both shameful and ineffectually treated:

Wretched *Nefario*! no Repentance shows,
But mocks those ills *Aminta* undergoes:
Ruin'd by him, with Pain she draws her Breath,
And still survives *an Evil worse than Death.*[11]

Inspired by the rationality of Astell and Chudleigh and by their advocacy of learning for women, Thomas makes resistance to female learning one of her satiric targets. In "On Sir J—S— Saying in a sarcastic Manner, *My Books would make me Mad.* An Ode," she insists that since book learning is the method men use to become wise, the same method would work for women. She ventriloquizes male claims that women are created to serve as "domestic Tools" and to amuse men with their "little *Follies*," leaving learning to men as their "great prerogative." Should a woman ask for a serious book, men are made to complain with an irrational nostalgia that exposes their valuing learning not for itself but as a male monopoly privilege:

Alas, poor *Plato*! All thy Glory's past:
What, in a *Female* Hand arriv'd at last![12]

Thomas dramatizes male misogyny to ridicule its foolishness and to refute it. She points out that the French permit women to improve their learning, without regarding them as monsters. In this poem, she ends by suggesting that greed leads men to want to retain their monopoly on learning and that fear makes them dread loss of their apparent superiority.

Thomas tried to help canonize Astell and Chudleigh. Her poems in their praise offer their accomplishments as evidence that women have intellectual and artistic capacities exceeding what the culture supposed were the limits of female nature. Thomas's poem to Astell, "To Almystrea, on her Divine Works," mentioned in chapter two, presents Astell as a British Protestant heroine who has outdone the Spanish Catholic Saint Teresa. Astell is figured as a champion of her sex, a heroine with the power to "Redeem the coming Age! and set us free / From the false Brand of *Incapacity*."[13] A poem to Chudleigh has the speaker long for a female champion to maintain women's right against the "brutal Rage" of men:

> What! all asleep!
> No *gen'rous Soul* with noble *Ardour* fir'd,
> No *free-born Muse* with Sense of *Wrong* inpir'd?
> Not one *Zenobia* to maintain our *Right*,
> And meet their *Champion* in an equal Fight.

(Zenobia was Queen of Palmyra, now Tadmur in modern Syria; she challenged the Roman Emperor Aurelian for hegemony in the region of Syria and Egypt, appearing in person with her army, but Aurelian defeated her army at Emesa and captured her in 272.) A swain appears in a dream vision to reveal that Chudleigh, with her "*Eloquence* divine" and "*strenuous* Proofs" has been that champion.[14]

Women's commendatory poems about other women writers frequently figure them as champions of their sex. It was, of course, not usual to claim in praise of a male writer that he was a champion of his sex, the male sex presumably not needing champions. Nor did men's poems in praise of women writers normally praise them as champions of the female sex. Just as Pope did when he celebrated Gay and Swift, Thomas understood that part of the process of gaining canonicity entailed being celebrated by other writers.

In her poems on Astell and her three poems on Chudleigh, Thomas created a written record that Astell and Chudleigh had been important and admired in her time. Similarly, in a collection of letters between Thomas and Richard Gwinnett, published as *Pylades and Corinna* (1731–32), Thomas also records her early admiration of Philips, whom she hoped to imitate, and Rowe. She cites *Letters from Orinda to Poliarchus* to support the possibility of friendship between a man and a woman, and *Pylades and*

Corinna aims to offer letters from a similar friendship. Praising Rowe for genius, learning, depth of thought, harmonious versification, and elegance of expression, Thomas urged Gwinnett to compose more commendatory verse on Rowe. But because Thomas herself did not become canonical, these gestures aimed at canonizing other women writers were historically ineffective.

LADY MARY WORTLEY MONTAGU'S POETRY

Unlike Thomas, Montagu never revised and gathered her poems together for a published volume; nevertheless, she earned her reputation as a satirist and dangerous wit. Montagu's verse is sometimes deft, sometimes original, sometimes powerfully sardonic; as in her prose, she uses wit to expose and penetrate the human comedy. Many of her poems were prompted by small events, remarks or letters from others; many were untitled. Like other women writers of this period, she engaged in raillery of the follies of both fashionable men and fashionable women. Thus, a little "Epigram to L. H." reads in its entirety:

> When Lycé enters so exactly dress'd
> My last year's Habit is her constant Jest,
> Lycé with reason you my cloaths upbraid,
> They are old fashion'd, but my Bills are paid.[15]

Montagu's reputation as a wit was firmly established by the unauthorized publication of three of her town eclogues in *Court Poems* (1716). Gay, as noted in the previous chapter, had experimented with adapting the classical pastoral to modern purposes in *The Shepherd's Week* (1714); there very English rural laborers conduct the business of their farms and of their loves. Like Pope's characters in *The Rape of the Lock*, though with more broadly comic effect, Gay's rural laborers express themselves in language often more portentous than the traditional decorums of matching style with the station of the speaker would justify. *The Shepherd's Week* is cousin to burlesque in mixing high style and low subject, although Gay's affection for his characters and the homey details of their lives – like Marian, the maid "that soft could stroke the udder'd Cow" – seems to remove satiric animus.[16] In one of the town eclogues published in *Court Poems*, "The Toilet," a stock shepherdess is transformed into a London lady, an aging beauty neglected by her lover but revived by her maid's flattery.[17] In Montagu's "The Basset-Table" two London ladies debate whether women suffer more from reversals of fortune at the card table or from the loss of lovers. In her "Roxana: or, the Drawing-Room" a censorious lady-in-waiting laments that she has sacrificed her reputation for strict virtue by attending a Princess who enjoys double-entendre in a "lewd" court.[18]

Not published in *Court Poems* but written at about the same time and in the same mode, "Tuesday. St. James's Coffee-house. Sillander and Patch," offers an arresting glimpse into the minds of two young men about town who make their way in the world by flattering ladies who give them presents. Like Swift – of whom she did not approve – Montagu was consistently suspicious of the language of romance, indeed, of any idealizing literary language, including that of pastoral. "Tuesday. St. James's Coffee-house" formally imitates the often-imitated shepherd's singing contests in Virgil's Eclogues 3 and 7. Sillander and Patch, however, instead of praising their mistresses or the gods and hoping to win a prize by exhibiting great artfulness, narcissistically boast of manipulating fashionable women into granting them favors, sexual and material. The ladies seem glad of discreet flirtation and toying, the fops puffed up by gifts of shoe buckles and snuffboxes. Fashionable slang and the names of contemporary things mingle with and deflate abstract and elevated language. Pastoral purity and sincerity are left far behind as Patch (identified as Algernon Seymour, later Duke of Somerset) boasts to his friend:

> My Countess is more nice, more artfull too,
> Affects to fly, that I may fierce persue.
> This Snuff box, while I begg'd, she still deny'd,
> And when I strove to snatch it, seem'd to hide,
> She laughed, and fled, and as I sought to seize
> With Affectation cramm'd it down her Stays:
> Yet hoped she did not place it there unseen;
> I press'd her Breasts, and pull'd it from between.[19]

None of these town eclogues was a poem a lady could unambivalently elect to publish. Several aimed at particular persons. Manuscript copies, however, were circulated and Edmund Curll, the quintessential entrepreneurial publisher, published them as having been found in a pocket book at Westminster Hall.

Montagu excelled at "answer poems," poems that reply to other particular poems or, alternatively, poems that respond to questions asked, but not answered, in conventional lyrics. Nothing was more common than the love lyric addressed to the coy mistress. Politer versions merely inquired why she was so coy; harsher versions threatened that the mistress's refusal of the speaker's sexual proposition would leave her bereft of any lovers, wretchedly ugly, old, and undesirable. The Earl of Rochester, in his menacing "Phillis, be gentler, I Advise," conjured up a parade of horribles, climaxing with:

> Then if to make your Ruine more,
>   You'll peevishly be Coy,
> Dye with the Scandall of a Whore,
>   And never know the Joy.[20]

The male speaker in the conventional address to the coy mistress usually assumes either that her reluctance is a coquettish charade or that she is unnaturally "cold." One of Montagu's more general "answers" to such male speakers attacks the narcissism of the conventional male speaker by asking a counter question:

> Why should you think I live unpleas'd
>   Because I am not pleas'd with you?
> My mind is not so far diseas'd
>   To yeild when pouder'd Fops persue.[21]

In these answer poems, Montagu enjoys showing that, far from being perverse, a resisting woman might well be more rational than the male lover issuing the conventional invitation, that his invitation does not constitute a good bargain for the woman. The unmarried woman speaker in "The Answer to the foregoing Elegy" concedes that she has feelings for the man who makes love to her, but recognizes that his resistance to marrying her would either plunge her into penitence and shame, or, if he did marry her:

> Then would thy Soul my fond Consent deplore,
> And blame what it sollicited before:
> Thy own exhausted, would reproach my Truth,
> And say, I had undone thy blinded Youth;
> That I had damp'd *Ambition's* nobler Flame,
> Eclips'd thy Talents, and obscur'd thy Name . . .[22]

More severely, in "An Answer to a Love Letter in Verse," a woman being importuned by a married man expresses her detestation of his "Artfull Falsehood, and designing Praise." She compares such men to robbers and, unfavorably, to dogs:

> Why should poor Pug (the Mimic of your kind)
> Wear a rough Chain, and be to Box confin'd?
> Some Cup perhaps he breaks, or tears a Fan
> While moves unpunish'd the Destroyer, Man.
> Not bound by vows, and unrestrain'd by Shame,
> In sport you break the Heart, and rend the Fame.

This woman has earlier been disappointed by an inconstant lover; she ends her epistle to the new would-be seducer with something between a wish for retributive justice and a curse:

> May soon some other Nymph inflict the Pain
> You know so well, with cruel Art to feign . . .[23]

Like most of her answer poems, Montagu's versions of the Ovidian epistle have women speakers; they are also answers to Ovid's *Heroides*. As we have noted in earlier chapters, women writers from Behn onwards were interested in Ovid's *Heroides* and the tradition of the *Heroides* because these poems represented women's speaking and women's experience. They suggested, as Gillian Beer put it, that "the experience of the slighted, the abandoned, the powerless, mattered."[24] Lady Mary at age twelve was already imitating the *Heroides* in her "Julia to Ovid." Her mature variations of the *Heroides*, "Miss Cooper to —" and "Epistle from Mrs. Y[onge] to her Husband," leave behind the usual mythological, historical, and literary women speakers to substitute contemporary women.[25] "Miss Cooper" is the poet Judith Cowper, whose husband Captain Martin Maden was unfaithful to her, and who herself had written "Abelard to Eloisa" (1720) in answer to Pope's "Eloisa to Abelard." Mrs. Y[onge] was Mary Heathcoate Yonge, whose libertine husband separated from her, sued her lover for criminal conversation damages, and finally sued in Parliament to gain a divorce based on her adultery.[26] The normative female speaker in the *Heroides* passionately longs for the lover who has abandoned her to return, desperately pleading with him even as she despairs that her words will have any power. The speaker in "Miss Cooper" seems at first to suffer the unassuageable passion usual in the tradition, weeping all night. However, she represents herself as faithful and intelligent and her husband as both faithless and superficial as he flits from the novelty of one mistress to the novelty of another:

> Harvey, How, Howard, please you in their Turn,
> You sigh for Ribands, and for Tippets burn.
> Where these are Merits, oh how vain I plead
> A tender Heart, and a reflecting Head!

Her husband's infidelity has prompted her to re-evaluate the value of female beauty:

> Take back, ye Gods, this useless pow'r to please,
> It gains no Glory, and it gives no Ease![27]

To the male lyricist's admiration of female beauty and insistence that beauty compels devotion, the woman poet replies that such admiration is so transient that it is not capable of yielding women substantial satisfaction. Whereas the most important word in conventional *Heroides* is the woman's cry to her lost lover to "Come," Miss Cooper says to her husband:

> Go Faithless Man, this wretched Victim leave,
> I cannot more be lost, or you deceive.

Whether she succeeds in ripping the image of this man, to whom she condescends as her "worthless Choice," from her breast is perhaps not clear; the poem ends with her despairing question whether there is in the world even

> One faithfull Partner to a tender mind,
> Gentle and Just, and without feigning, Kind?[28]

Still less conventional, the "Epistle from Mrs. Y[onge]" displaces Ovidian declamation to introduce a feminist argument about the sexual double standard. Mrs. Yonge writes in the painful consciousness that contemporary legal institutions provided a civil forum, in the criminal conversation suit, in which a husband could present public evidence of his wife's adultery without her having any standing to contest the process or to testify on her own behalf. (At the end of the century, Mary Wollstonecraft protests criminal conversation procedure in her novel *Maria; or, the Wrongs of Woman*, letting her adulteress heroine give a speech in her self-defense in open court – a turn of events which would not have been permitted outside fiction.) Nothing remains for the ruined and shamed Mrs. Yonge but the words she can utter in her epistle:

> But this last privelege I still retain,
> Th' Oppress'd and Injur'd allways may complain.[29]

The normative Ovidian epistle derives some of its claustrophobic intensity from its intimate address to the absent man who the female writer so desperately attempts to keep in her world. "The Epistle from Mrs. Y[onge]," in contrast, though formally addressed to Mr. Yonge, seems also designed to be read by the larger "Judging World" to which it refers.[30]

Mrs. Yonge claims for herself the Ovidian heroine's capacity for passion and sexual desire, but denounces a society that refuses to allow women in her position to satisfy that desire:

From whence is this unjust Distinction grown?
Are we not form'd with Passions like your own?[31]

As Astell had done at the end of the seventeenth century and as Mary
Hays was to do at the end of the eighteenth, Montagu has Mrs. Yonge
attack the logical contradiction of a patriarchal ideology that, on the one
hand, insists on the superiority of men to women, and, on the other
hand, excuses male infidelity while exacting severe penalties for female
infidelity:

> Our Sexes Weakness you expose and blame
> (Of every Prattling Fop the common Theme),
> Yet from this Weakness you suppose is due
> Sublimer Virtu than your Cato knew.

More firmly than Miss Cooper and with more contempt, Mrs. Yonge tells
her husband not to "Come," but to "Go; Court the brittle Freindship of
the Great."[32] Understanding that the purpose of allowing men to get
parliamentary divorces and to remarry was to allow them to continue their
legitimate family line despite their ill-luck in having married an adulteress, Mrs. Yonge concludes by imagining William Yonge becoming the
"Father" of a "Race" here sardonically called "Glorious," but which she
believes can be nothing but despicable. Montagu imagines her abandoned
women as capable of rejecting the men who abandoned them, of surviving
abandonment, then of reasoning through to a critique of the conventions
of love and the conventions of society that have failed to provide them
with happiness. Her female speakers do not claim a superiority based on
passion, but an intellectual and moral superiority.

DAVYS'S *SELF-RIVAL*

Although her late and most popular novel, *The Reform'd Coquet* (1724), is
more subdued and didactic than her earlier work, Mary Davys had the
interests, instincts, and talents of a satirist. The young widow of a Dublin
clergyman and schoolmaster, she wrote plays and novels to help support
herself. In her early, short, epistolary novel, *Familiar Letters Betwixt a
Gentleman and a Lady* (written 1716–18, published 1725), the heroine,
Berina, wishes that all soft-hearted ladies would read Francisco Gomez
de Quevedo's the "Casa de Locos de Amour" (1621). Included in Quevedo's *Visions of Loving-Fools*, this was a satire on the follies of male and
female lovers. The learned Quevedo was also the author of *El Buscón*,
which some have thought the greatest of all picaresque novels, and of

many satires that reveal his deep familiarity with classical satire, verbal brilliance, and wonderful powers of observation.

Davys's unperformed comedy, *The Self-Rival* (written 1716–18, published 1725), exhibits her satiric bent and explores satire itself. The heroine is the object of her father's forced marriage plot, but, instead of lamenting her fate, laughs at and ridicules the aged suitor her father produces. As lively as Centlivre's heroines and more willing to risk bawdy for a joke, this heroine, Maria Purchase, responds to old Lord Pastall's talk of wedded bliss by teasing: "I warrant, my Lord, you carry an Organ to bed with you every night, but I hate a Serenade."[33] The main plot of *The Self-Rival* is basically the same one Davys later used for her novel, *The Reform'd Coquet*: an attractive young male suitor of a coquette disguises himself as an old man with an eye to her reformation and in the end the young woman marries him. The later novel, however, requires more sobriety of its heroine, Amoranda. Maria also quickly sees through her lover's disguise and hatches her own counterplots, whereas Amoranda is unaware that her supposed guardian is a young man until the end of the novel.

The earlier play is less reverent toward marriage than the later novel. Maria and Mrs. Fallow, a good-natured old maid, entertain themselves making fun of married people, who, they claim, are "only fit Company for one another." Anticipating Jane Austen's satire on the tediousness of maternal gushing fondness, Mrs. Fallow complains of Lady Breeder, "who kindly entertains her Visitors with the Ingenuity of her Children: Master has a profound Invention, and has made a Scoop: Miss is so very Willey, that she puzzles the Parson . . ."[34] Davys's prologue to *The Self-Rival* describes the Muses as "Nine merry Girls," who "in the Laurel Shade / Fiddl'd and rhimed, and sung and danc'd, and play'd." Noting that none of the Muses themselves married – no doubt they were too poor – she concludes:

> But what of that! they liv'd the easier Life,
> Not clogg'd with the dull Duty of a Wife:
> They had more Time for sport, and so we find
> They wrote and did – what'er they had a mind . . .[35]

Davys uses a set of unmarried characters in *The Self-Rival* to explore the power of satire itself. Lady Camphire Lovebane, Maria's aunt, is an old maid who affects to loathe men; Verjuice is an irritable, cynical bachelor hating "Impertinence"; and Mrs. Fallows is an intelligent old maid. Like Pix, Davys creates interesting older women characters. Lady Camphire, with her affected aversion to men, is an updated version of the standard misogynist satire on old maids. She expresses envy for happy Amazons who were "govern'd by their own Laws!" – "Oh happy People! that there were such a State now!" – and Astell-like interest in spending her money to build a nunnery if she could get Parliament to consent.[36] For a standard satiric portrait of the love-crazed old maid Davys would have had to look no farther than Quevedo's misogynistic "Casa de Locos de Amour," where we find a set of single women:

one in consultation with a cunning man to know her fortune; another, dealing with a conjurer for a philter, or drink to make her beloved. A third was daubing and patching up an old ruined face, to make it fresh and young again; but she might as well have been washing a blackemoor to make him white. . . [W]ith their borrowed hair, teeth, eyes, eyebrows, [they] looked like fine folks at a distance, but would have been left as ridiculous as Aesop's crow, if every bird had fetched away his own feathers.[37]

Lady Camphire has no effective weapons against the satiric barbs aimed at her, but Mrs. Fallow does. In a remarkable scene, Verjuice hurls colorful misogynistic insults at both old maids. When Lady Camphire says her virtue provides a sufficient guard against raillery, he retorts: "Five and fifty's a better guard than all your Vertue; a Man must have a vast deal of Desire that can attempt a Person with no more Charms than a Skeleton, one that would damp his Desires more than the sight of a Charnel-House."[38] Mrs. Fallow, however, advises that the objects of this satire can simply move to higher moral ground and despise the satirist: "When there's neither Wit enough to say things entertaining, or Good-nature enough to keep a Man within the Bounds of good Manners: I think one may venture to despise such a Person, and bid him do his worst."[39] Yet Davys trespasses on the bounds of decorum to entertain her audience with vivid images of old women so like skeletons and charnel-houses that they make men impotent. Subsequently, Mrs. Fallows reveals that mere disdain will not satisfy; she wants revenge against Verjuice and is prepared to provide the plot and the cudgel to frighten and pummel him. When Verjuice thinks, wrongly, that he will be able to exact some counter-revenge, the punishment he imagines as appropriate for her is not beating, but the customary one for unruly women who speak against men: "A Woman's Tongue shou'd be used like a House on Fire, play it with Water till the Flames are quenched; ducking for scolding has been a custom long in Use, and there's a convenient Horse-Pond at the back of Sir *Ephriam's* Garden-Well."[40] At the end, though, Verjuice exits stamping in frustration. Mrs. Fallows is permitted to draw the moral: "use other People well, and it will be a certain means to make them use you so."[41] In *The Self-Rival* Davys exploits satiric conventions, including that of punishment on the body, to make explicit both the violence of misogyny and the desire for compensatory justice that it can provoke in women.

DAVYS'S *ACCOMPLISH'D RAKE*

Davys's best novel, *The Accomplish'd Rake: or, Modern Fine Gentleman* (1727), is unlike the amorous fiction of Behn, Manley, or Haywood; whereas that fiction derives from romance, and, sometimes, heroic tragedy, Davys's narrative is more cousin to the comedy of Sir John Vanbrugh and George Farquhar and to satire. Davys uses her familiarity with comic plotting and scene development to write a new, more realistic, kind of fiction with tighter, more unified plotting; more dialogue; and more fully realized contemporary scenes and characters. The story of *The Accomplish'd Rake*, like many of the amorous fictions, is a story of a male libertine who seduces and rapes. But Davys's Sir John Galliard is not glamorized, as these characters usually are in amorous fiction. He is not ravishingly handsome and he does not have remarkable powers to compel women to adore him. Instead, he is an ordinary young country gentleman, over-indulged by his mother after his father dies. At nineteen, he is shocked to discover his mother *in flagrante* with her footman. Traumatized and disillusioned with women, he determines to leave home to immerse himself in the life of "pleasure" in London. There, he, and the reader, discover contemporary phenomena like a gentleman's Hell Fire Club (where initiates pledge themselves to atheism, drink, and sexual adventure) and the bagnios, or baths, where, as Miss Wary explains, men of pleasure can bring women for sex and "for a small Sum" the proprietors "will find a Thousand Ways to avoid Discoveries, and prevent Disturbances."[42]

The tone of *The Accomplish'd Rake* hovers edgily between fairly raucous comic and satiric narrative of events and a more restrained, matter-of-fact narrator's voice, sometimes veering toward the wry or sardonic. Sir John's quest for pleasure becomes a series of comic mortifications, several of them entailing comic punishment on his body. When he attempts to climb stairs to an assignation with a married woman, he finds that her annoyed husband has laid firecrackers that turn the staircase into a trap. The resulting explosions scorch him and set his large wig on fire, making him look like "a smoked Flitch of Bacon."[43] When he tries to bed the mistress of one of his fellow rakes, Bousie, Bousie plays a version of the old bed trick on him, substituting a prostitute with venereal disease for the girl Sir John thought he was getting, thus sending him into weeks of confinement and medication in his lodgings. On the other hand, the narrator maintains a relatively sedate tone, seasoned with wry asides, allowing herself access to Sir John's consciousness in ways that keep him from becoming like a character in a farce. She exhibits his frequent unconcern, his various self-serving rationalizations, and his occasional reflection and remorse.

Davys's treatment of the rape avoids, on the one hand, tragedy or melodrama, and, on the other, comedy. Sir John's worst action is to drug and rape Nancy Friendly, the young daughter of his kindly country neighbor. Subsequently hearing that she has had his illegitimate child and that her father has fallen ill with grief, Sir John experiences some pity and remorse, yet chases those feelings away with alcohol and by repeating to himself a favorite libertine maxim: "is she not a Woman and was she not made for the Pleasure and Delight of Man . . .?"[44] Since Miss Friendly is a gentlewoman, one possible plot trajectory would be some combination of deaths: hers, her father's or Sir John's, perhaps in a duel. But this is clearly not a tragic narrative, and there is nothing demonic about Sir John, so the more likely trajectory would be the comic one of forgiveness and the happy ending of marriage. A series of events do increase Sir John's remorse. He is taken aback when Belinda, another gentlewoman he is pursuing, and whom he intends to rape, stings his class-pride and sense of self by angrily declaring that, though he appears to be a baronet by birth, his behavior is so dishonorable that his mother must have spawned him in adultery with one of her footmen. Knowing what he does about his mother's conduct, Sir John has to admit that what she wildly suggests is a possibility. Chastened, he desists, no doubt in part to demonstrate to himself that he is the gentleman society supposes him to be. What finally effects a kind of conversion in him, though, is a meeting with Mr. Friendly, reduced to misery by his daughter's shame, and listening to Mr. Friendly's expressions of distress.

Instead, however, of the euphoric repentance and forgiveness ending of the sentimental comedy Colley Cibber developed in the early eighteenth century, Davys offers a mordant negotiation between Sir John, who tries to save face by pretending that he is willing to marry Nancy out of altruism, and a very sober Nancy, who, once he is forced to confess to the rape, feels indignation. She agrees to marry him, but not happily:

The poor Lady trembled with Resentment, but recalling her Temper said as follows: Your barbarous Usage Sir *John*, might very well countenance a firm Resolution of seeing your Face no more, which I should certainly make were I only to suffer for it, but I have a Child which is very dear to me, and in pity to him I will close with your Proposals, provided you will order Matters so, that he may be the undoubted Heir to your Estate . . .[45]

Sir John, in some ways the butt of Davys's satire, thus ultimately becomes a character in something very like a realist novel. Nancy Friendly does, not what a tragic heroine would do, but what a sensible woman with a young illegitimate son in the 1720s might very likely have done. It is what most sensible characters in Richardson's later *Clarissa* tell Clarissa – raped by Lovelace but not the mother of an illegitimate child – she should do.

Davys claims a degree of authoriality in *The Accomplish'd Rake*, but she also relies on characters to exchange contradictory maxims with one another. Immediately before the rape, for instance, the narrator is willing to pronounce: "It is true, if we abstract bad Actions from Folly (which in my humble Opinion can hardly be done) Sir *John* was very free from the Imputation of a Fool, but then he had a double share of the Rake to make up his *Quantum*, and finish a very Bad Character."[46] Sir John himself throughout proposes a string of libertine maxims on the subject of women's nature. "Women," he tells the unwilling Belinda, "were made to be enjoyed . . ."[47] Yet, denying that there could be any comparison between his mother's actions and his own, he also reproaches his mother for her failure to instantiate a different feminine essence: "Women are naturally modest, Men naturally impudent."[48] The novel denies the purported validity of such male wisdom.

Davys, indeed, inaugurates a tactic of women's fiction: characterizing undesirable male characters by allowing them to pontificate foolishly on their mistaken ideas about women's nature. Mr. Teachwell seems closer to the narrator when he tries to tell Sir John: "Women no doubt, are made of the very same Stuff that we are, and have the very same Passions and Inclinations . . ."[49] What makes this novel both comic and chilling is how plausibly Davys demonstrates the connections between the sense of masculine entitlement the culture gives a gentleman and his capacity to rape.

HAYWOOD'S SCANDAL CHRONICLES

Haywood's most obvious satire is in the scandal chronicles; here she followed Manley, though Haywood's scandal chronicles were even less ideological and more simply personally libelous than Manley's. Her notorious scandal chronicles were *The Memoirs of a Certain Island Adjacent to the Kingdom of Utopia. Written by a Celebrated Author of that Country. Now Translated into English* (2 vols., 1725–26) and *The Secret History of the Present Intrigues of the Court of Caramania* (1727). Imitating Manley's allegorical framework, in *Memoirs of a Certain Island* Haywood makes an outraged Cupid the narrator who sees how contemporary islanders hypocritically pretend to venerate love but actually worship lust and avarice, sacrificing to the goddess Pecunia. John Richetti, comparing *The New Atalantis* and *Memoirs of a Certain Island*, finds Haywood's "vicious aristocrats . . . simply avaricious and lustful without any of the conspiratorial political motives that . . . Manley assigned to them. The stripping away of splendid surface to reveal vicious interiors is more plainly an expression of that envious hatred which we expect from middle-class exposés of aristocratic corruption."[50] Haywood's consistent interest in predatory male sexuality in *Memoirs of a Certain Island* reaches an apotheosis of horror dependent on familiar satiric images of corruption in the story of Bertoldus. Bertoldus is a libertine rapist whose outrages include the rape of his friend Anselmo's fiancée, Cipriana. Anselmo and Cipriana get revenge by substituting a woman with venereal disease for Cipriana. Ulcers that "devour his Flesh" and rottenness that "consumes his bones" punish Bertoldus.[51] *The Secret History of the Present Intrigues of the Court of Caraminia*, published in 1727 with a key, makes a rakish George II as "Theodore" its central character, showing him in relation to his faithful and wise wife, who knows how to manage his adulteries, and to a mistress, to whom he is attached but also unfaithful.

CENTLIVRE'S *GOTHAM ELECTION*

As we have seen in the previous chapter, given the newness of party and print journalism, it was not immediately obvious that women could not be political writers or write political satire. Manley had collaborated with Swift on the Tory *Examiner* in 1711. Astell had published pamphlets defending the Tory position on the right relation between Church and state. In Davys's *Familiar Letters*, the heroine firmly elaborates her Whig political position in a protracted debate with her Tory gentleman correspondent. Montagu anonymously brought out a short-lived weekly, *The Nonsense of Common Sense* (1737–38), in which she supported the Whig position of the Prime Minister, Sir Robert Walpole. The Tory Haywood attacked Walpole in *The Adventures of Eovaai* (1736).

However, Centlivre's farce, *A Gotham Election* (1715) makes clear the problems women confronted in imagining themselves as political satirists or writers on political subjects. Most political writing in the eighteenth century was produced by men attempting to progress from writing to wealth and office, often by moving from periodical journalism with a party slant through private secretaryships to public office. Satire was consistently used as a political weapon. Writers hoped to curry favor with politicians by savaging their enemies or, sometimes, by so terrifying politicians with their prowess that they would be bought off and paid to stop, with money or, preferably, with places. (A "place" was what con-temporaries called a government office, with its attached income. Patrons who had the power to appoint office holders typically expected political loyalty, so, especially when places were held by members of parliament, reformers railed against a too-powerful executive.) A happy example from the early eighteenth century is the case of Joseph Addison, who progressed from belles lettres and Whig journalism to a nice appointment in 1715 as Commissioner of Trade and Plantations, with a salary of £1,000, and in 1717 to the more exalted position of Secretary of State.

Given this developing pattern of writers looking to exchange their work for preferment to office in addition to smaller gifts of monetary value, there were almost no offices women could seek. Centlivre makes comedy out of this by imagining "places" women might win in exchange for helping candidates. Lady Worthy, campaigning for her husband who wants a seat in Parliament, thinks to promise Goody Gabble a place nursing a child if she will influence her husband's vote. Mr. Mallet goes through a long list of places he wants from Tickup, another candidate to represent the borough in Parliament, for his male relatives. Mallet's list is partly drawn from a printed list of "all the great Places" in the state of Gotham and includes positions in the army and navy, the courts of law, and the treasury, as well as the pleasingly archaic and silly-sounding post of "Groom of the Stole." Mallet finally thinks to ask for a place for his wife Joan, yet he cannot think what the name of such a place would be. Racking his brain, Tickup invents the post of "Oyster-Craker to the Court."[52] Presumably Centlivre designed this in part to get a good laugh of recognition from an audience who knew that she was married to the Yeoman of the Mouth, a court cook with a real job, not a sinecure. The audience was developing a sense that far too many "places" were archaic sinecures.

Centlivre's joke, however, underlines the gender asymmetry of the new political world. In this world, women may write about party politics in periodicals and elsewhere, as Manley and Montagu did, and may campaign for candidates, as women in *A Gotham Election* do, but the most important rewards for political activity, places and preferments, are in very short supply for women. Given these conditions, it is hardly surprising that most women in the generations immediately following Manley (who died in 1724) and Centlivre (who died in 1723) decided to write more directly for money by producing translations from the French for the booksellers, books of advice to women, plays, or novels.

COMMERCIAL PUBLISHING

Despite the continuing importance of the circulation of manuscript writing to some writers, including Montagu and Rowe, in this period, the shift from a manuscript literary culture to an entrepreneurial commercial culture was pronounced. Several women writers uninhibitedly brought their wares to market. Haywood, as already noted, dominated the market for amorous fiction. Despite occasional performances in Dublin and London between 1715 and 1737, she does not seem to have been a notably talented actress. It has plausibly been argued, however, that she used her notoriety as an author of scandal chronicles and amorous tales as a commodity on stage. She appeared, for instance, in 1730 at Lincoln's Inn Field's as Achilles' mistress, Briseis, opposite her lover William Hatchett, as Achilles, in his play, *The Rival Father*.[53] *The Rival Father* alternated at Lincoln's Inn Field's with Fielding's *The Author's Farce*, a topical satire about commercialism in literature. Bookweight, the bookseller, dominates and orders about his stable of hack authors, Scarecrow, Dash, Quibble, and Blotpage. Haywood is satirized as Mrs. Novel, a devotee of the Goddess Nonsense. In 1732, when she acted Lady Flame in the New Haymarket production of Samuel Johnson's *The Blazing Comet*, Haywood's name appeared in the cast list as "Madame de Gomez," the name of the author of *Les Journées*, which Haywood had translated as *La Belle Asemblée*. Minor theatrical appearances also functioned as advertisements for her books.

Pope makes Haywood the first prize in the booksellers' pissing contest in *The Dunciad* II: 149–57. Scriblerus's note glosses her appearance by explaining, "In this game is expos'd in the most contemptuous manner, the profligate licentiousness of those shameless scriblers (for the most part of that Sex, which ought least to be capable of such malice or impudence) who in libellous Memoirs and Novels, reveal the faults and misfortunes of both sexes, to the ruin or disturbance, of publick fame or private happiness."[54] Unlike Rowe, Pope did not scruple to write scandal and lampoons, or to attack George II, so it is worth considering why Pope felt authorized to criticize Haywood's practice. First, I think, Pope believed that his satire was aesthetically superior to Haywood's; most readers who accept aesthetic criteria at all, including me, have agreed with him. Second, Haywood's remarkable productivity and her commercial success, most notably with *Love in Excess* (1719–20), made Pope and other elite male authors worry both about the state of literature and about what might happen to their own market share of the reading public. Pope throughout his career was anxious to define himself as an important writer, a writer of great literature; he astounded many by publishing his own *Works* in 1717 at the age of only twenty-nine. He may have also been irritated by another fact that he reports in the *Dunciad* notes: "This Lady's Works were printed in four Volumes *duod.*, with her picture thus dress'd up, before them."[55] At a period when authors were becoming more present and individualized, the publication of an author's *Works* adorned by the author's picture looked like a bid for canonicity. Pope had caused his early *Works* to be printed in the formats of quarto and the grander folio and large folio. As a frontispiece, he had had a portrait of himself engraved by George Vertue from a flattering oil painting by Charles Jervas.

As we shall also see in subsequent chapters, the success of women writers prompted elite male authors to work on policing the boundaries of literature by suggesting that various forms were inappropriate for women, as Pope in the *Dunciad* note suggests that women ought to be without malice or impudence and ought not to write scandal, lampoon, or satire.

HAYWOOD'S *LOVE IN EXCESS*

The majority of Haywood's fiction was not scandal chronicle but in the mode of the Italian and French novellas earlier adapted by Behn and Manley. Haywood's success in publishing so many "novels" during this period contributed both to reinforcing the troubling association between women writers and transgressive sexuality and to normalizing the idea of the woman writer. *Love in Excess*, her first and most popular novel, effectively established Haywood's point of view on her central subject, "love," and on the battle between the sexes. The narrator writes from the perspective of one who has experienced the pleasures and the pains of love, one who has felt its "unspeakable joys" and "intollerable torments." She insists that true love is irresistible and that people who possess the capacity for passionate love constitute an elite. Those who say "we *ought* to Love with Moderation and Discretion" are "*Insipids*, who know nothing of the Matter":

> there is nothing more absurd than the Notions of some People, who in other Things are wise enough too; but wanting Elegance of Thought, Delicacy, or Tenderness of Soul, to receive the Impression of that harmonious Passion, look on those to be mad, who have any Sentiments elevated above their own, and either Censure, or Laugh, at what they are not refin'd enough to comprehend.[56]

Racine could make the irresistibility of passion and the move from passion to criminality into grand French poetry and tragedy, but Haywood's work is more erotic melodrama than tragedy.

Love in Excess offers examples of important types of characters who recur in Haywood's fiction. The hero, Count D'Elmont, is a man so beautiful and so charming that he repeatedly arouses uncontrollable desire in women who see him. The lovely Violetta, for one, with no encouragement from him, abandons her home, disguises herself as a page to follow him, then dies after declaring her love. Dying in his arms, she blasphemously wishes "to know no other Paradise than you, to be permitted to Hover round you, to form your Dreams, to sit upon your Lip all Day, to mingle with your Breath, and glide in unfelt Air into your Bosom . . ." The narrator remarks, "sure there are none who have liv'd in the Anxietys of Love, who wou'd not envy such a Death!"[57]

Part of Haywood's project in *Love in Excess* is to show Count D'Elmont changing from a man so driven by desire that he ruins and destroys the women who love him into a man so earnestly dedicated to matrimonial chastity that he deserves marriage to a virtuous woman. To show change in characters over time was one of the more difficult tasks of the early novel, often not attempted, sometimes attempted cursorily and awkwardly. As late as 1751 in *Amelia*, Fielding represents Booth's conversion to virtue by a sermon. The transformation of the indifferent and dangerous man into the adoring lover of a good woman is, of course, a favorite plot of popular women's romance, familiar in later works from Charlotte Brontë's *Jane Eyre* to the now best-selling romances of Danielle Steele. Haywood would seem to deserve some credit for establishing it. Toward the end of *Love in Excess*, she attempts to make a sharp distinction between a vulgar love, "that Passion which aims chiefly at Enjoyment" and is "fleeting," and a noble love of the soul, "immortal and unchangeable," where "Possession thus desired, and thus obtain'd, is far from satiating . . ."[58] Yet this seems inconsistent with the narrator's pervasive insistence on the irresistibility of love and on the inability of even the most "virtuous" characters to control acting on their sudden lusts.

OTHER HAYWOOD TALES

Much recent feminist fascination with Haywood has centered on shorter tales in which female protagonists self-consciously use their understanding of masculine assumptions to defeat men and to fulfill their own desires. In *Fantomina, or Love in a Maze* (1725), the female protagonist avoids being discarded by the libertine Beauplaisir, despite his inconstancy, by presenting herself to him in a series of disguises. First as a London prostitute, then as a country chambermaid, then as a sober widow, and finally as an upper-class Incognita, she continues to enjoy sex with him and to revel in having outwitted him. In *The City Jilt* (1726) – a tale reminiscent of Behn's city comedies – Glicera's father has pressed her into the arms of a man who subsequently deserts her when it is revealed that she has no portion. She revenges herself on men by flirting with a bevy of would-be lovers, extracting presents from each of them. From one suitor, an old alderman, she extracts the mortgage of the estate belonging to the man who jilted her. He joins the army in an effort to pay and is killed.

Some critics celebrate such tales as exposing the pathologies of patriarchal privilege and patriarchal economies of desire and as brilliantly imaginative, original, representations of female agency and subjectivity. Catherine Craft-Fairchild, for example, sees Glicera learning to be "a self-exhibiting subject rather than an exhibited object – she manipulates others rather than being manipulated herself . . ."[59] Considering *The British Recluse* (1722), in which two women ruined by the same man withdraw from society to live together, Jane Spencer finds that story a progressive feminist fable rejecting the idea of "woman as victim" to show the possibility of escape from heartbreak through female friendship.[60]

Other critics, however, have been struck by Haywood's inability – even in these tales that have something of the thought experiment about them – to escape from older cultural constructions of femininity that understand desirable femininity only in terms of its capacity to evoke male desire. Also considering *The British Recluse*, Cynthia Richards notes that its two heroines spend their time in retirement retelling their stories of loving the same man, making that man "central to the dialogue, the very source of their union." Because their two stories are one story, there is no "need for individual self-expression."[61] Rosalind Ballaster, in a deservedly influential reading of *Fantomina*, while finding that it challenges "the conventional plot structure and gendered subject positions of the amatory tale," also sees Fantomina's final masquerade as the Incognita as "the nadir of feminine representation": "She embodies the exchangeable female body, the empty sign into which both male and female readers can project their own fantasy and desire."[62] Craft-Fairchild herself, commenting on *The Masquerade: or, Fatal Curiosity* (1724, 1725), in which one woman adopts her friend's masquerade disguise and forges her handwriting in part to demonstrate her superior intelligence, notes that even in this tale, which seems to be about a woman's establishing her difference from another woman, the "'difference' that constitutes subjectivity, that could allow a woman being in her own right rather than as a man's mirror opposite, the difference that would separate one woman from another" collapses. The witty woman becomes equally concerned to capture the man's eye and indistinguishable from her friend. Indeed, it seems to me, that although some of Haywood's tales have intriguing plots, her characters remain rudimentary, limited by their recurrent obsessions with greed, revenge, and, especially, stereotypical passion. Haywood undoubtedly protested against the social realities of male power over women and articulated her sense that there was a battle between women and men – even in *The Fruitless Enquiry* (1727) imagining a woman's avenging her rape by castrating her rapist. Yet her fantasies of women's triumph over men often replicate in reverse the male libertine idea of sexual desire as desire for domination. They also often replicate traditional misogynistic stereotypes of women as uncontrollably avaricious, vengeful, and lustful.

Haywood thus aligns herself with a libertinism that was under attack by moralists in this period. Moreover, she sets herself against those women writers, like Astell in the previous generation and Rowe and Aubin in her own, who were attempting to establish the idea that properly educated women were capable of resisting the blandishments of seducers and the importunings of their own desires. Part of what a number of critics have thought an incoherence in Haywood's vision of love is that she seems simultaneously to insist on the irresistibility of love and to blame the victims of desire. Unlike Montagu and the later French libertine writers like Crébillon or Laclos, who analyze the complex operation of desire with cold amusement, Haywood offers what often seem reductively simple narratives. Her characters are first assaulted by sudden passions, then, in consequence, transgress rules of morality, and finally are condemned as reprobate by the narrator or suffer lurid condign punishments meted out by "poetic justice." Further incoherence in Haywood's narrative springs from her – alternately – forgiving and rewarding those made criminal by passion.

Second only to Haywood in productivity, Penelope Aubin set herself against the idea that love was irresistible and broke away from the often claustrophobic world of amorous passion by offering readers adventure set in exotic locales. In contrast to Haywood's frequently depraved and treacherous protagonists, most of Aubin's characters are attractively high-minded, polite, and generous. She offers them didactically as models for the reader's imitation and sets herself firmly against religious skepticism and libertinism. In *The Life of Charlotta DuPont* (1723), for example, the narrator declares:

> I wish Mankind would but reflect how barbarous a deed it is, how much below a Man, nay how like the Devil 'tis, to debauch a young unexperienc'd Virgin, and expose to Ruin and an endless train of Miseries, the Person whom his Persuasions hath drawn to gratify his Desire, and to oblige him at the expence of her own Peace and Honour. [He certainly merits death or] an eternal Infamy, who betrays the foolish Maid that credits his Oaths and Vows, and abandons her to Shame and Misery. And if Women were not infatuated, doubtless every Maid would look on the Man that proposes such a Question to her, as her mortal Enemy, and from the Moment banish him from her Heart and Company.[63]

Aubin's attacks on libertinism and plots of militant female virtue in distress influenced Samuel Richardson and other later novelists. When Aubin's heroines and heroes are shipwrecked or otherwise brought to extreme distress, they typically encounter eminently hospitable and pious strangers eager to feed and clothe them and to exchange stories. The happy coincidences in Aubin's tales owe something to romance, but she also explicitly theorizes them as manifestations of the workings of divine providence. Her theology is omnipresent and orthodox: we should trust in God to relieve our miseries if He will, secure in the knowledge that if he elects to have us suffer in this world, he will relieve us in the next. One question her characters debate is whether heroines ought to use lethal force against themselves or against their assailants in resisting rape. Some Christian scruples are expressed on these matters, yet several of her heroines do use lethal force against would-be ravishers.

Aubin's geographical range is remarkable, including not only most of western Europe, but also Africa, the Ottoman Empire, the Americas, and China. While the accuracy of her geography has been condescended to, the information – accurate and otherwise – that she offers about foreign places and foreign customs was part of her appeal. Contemporary readers were fascinated with factual and fictional versions of travel and with tales of English people taken captive in foreign lands, as we have seen in considering Rowlandson's narrative. Settlers in North America were sometimes made captive by Native Americans, but thousands of English and European people had also been captured at sea by pirates and sold into slavery in the Ottoman Empire. Montagu in *The Embassy Letters* reports meeting at Constantinople a well-born Spanish lady living in a seraglio. The lady, unlike Aubin's heroines, has decided that she prefers her Turkish lover to being ransomed and returned to life in a Spanish convent. While male captives produced factual versions of the oriental captivity narrative, Aubin delighted in producing fictional variations pitting resourceful women captives against lustful and despotic Arab and Turkish masters. Deprived of male protection, these heroines "assume some of the autonomous, improvisatory, and transgressive activities" of the male protagonists in the non-fictional Barbary captive narratives; their successful resistance has the effect of representing their Oriental captors as "abject and impotent."[64] Fanciful as Aubin's coincidences are, her narratives convey how hazardous travel and commence could be in this mercantilist age.

One of the most popular of Aubin's seven novels, *The Noble Slaves* (1722), flaunts its defiance of contemporary libertinism with militantly virtuous protagonists and seizes virtually the entire globe for its stage. Two principal married couples, one Spanish and one French, are captured at sea and sold into slavery in Algiers. The narrative moves back and forth from the adventures of the vigorous and resolute wives to the adventures and sufferings of their husbands, as the couples try to reunite. Suspense comes from how the protagonists can extricate themselves from myriad threats to their lives and virtue as their hopes for reunion and escape to Europe are repeatedly aroused and dashed. The reader is intrigued by mysterious figures they encounter, unknown humans, sometimes first apprehended by their groans or sighs and often strangely clad. Yet these unknown figures, unlike their counterparts in later gothic romance, when approached by Aubin's intrepid protagonists, usually prove reassuringly legible and friendly, quite willing to tell their own stories of sorrow and struggle.

Teresa de Avilla, one of the protagonists of *The Noble Slaves*, illustrates the vigor and resoluteness of Aubin's heroines. Daughter of the Spanish governor of Mexico, she is lost in a boating accident off the coast of

Mexico, first marooned on an island inhabited by a courteous and formerly shipwrecked Japanese merchant and his family. On this island, she finds and assists a second heroine, the French Emilia de Vendome, whose intended cross-class love-match with a marquis has been thwarted when his family has had her drugged and shipped to Canada. Here, presumably off the coast of Mexico, they stumble upon what seems to be an amazing Aztec ruin, with nearby pits and altars where sacrifices had been killed and offered. In their further adventures, Teresa and Emilia are captured at sea by Algerian pirates and separated from their beloved husbands. About to enter slavery, Teresa exhorts Emilia: "we'll go together, trusting in that God who is able to preserve our Souls and Bodies. Slaves we are doubtless doom'd to be, but our Minds can't be confined; our Lives must not end with our own hands, but may resist all sinful Acts till Life and Sense be lost."[65] Later, when the two hear cries of a woman in distress outside the house in which they have found temporary refuge, Emilia voices the female solidarity which is also characteristic of Aubin's heroines: "Shall we deny that Charity to another, which we were saved by in this Place? Shall we not relieve a Christian and one of our own Sex, in Distress?"[66] And they venture outside to drag the wounded woman in to safety.

Teresa bravely resists repeated assaults; like other Aubin heroines, she does not assume malign intent, but first appeals to the values of civilization and honor. Only if her appeals fail, does she resort to stratagems or force. Selim, the Governor of Algiers, buys her, but proves sufficiently compassionate to heed her pleas against rape (he does assault Emilia, who stabs him with his own dagger). Escaped from the seraglio, the heroines are not too delicate to contribute to their support by working at embroidery, which a kindly Algerian woman sells for them. Just as they get news of their husbands' whereabouts, the son of the Emperor of Morocco, Muly Arab, a man "very amorous and gallant," sees and captures them.[67] Rape is again averted and providence vindicated when a poisoned sherbet Muly Arab's jealous wife has prepared for the European women is mistakenly drunk by Muly Arab and the would-be poisoner. The heroines are next given to a court favorite, but contrive to escape by tying together sheets and curtains and sliding down to safety and the woods. Even after Teresa and her husband have finally been reunited and returned to settle at Barcelona, she repels a last attempt at rape by her husband's cousin. This time she surprises the assailant by tossing wine in his face, breaking a door lock, and rushing down the stairs, only to fall and fracture her leg: "the Shin-bone was Shiver'd, so that it had cut thro the Skin and Sinew, and appear'd."[68] The sight of this open fracture quenches the man's lust and arouses his concern, so Teresa is once again restored to her husband.

Earlier in the narrative, as Teresa and Emilia are starving in the woods, they discover one of the many strange human figures who dot Aubin's fictional landscapes. This man is apparently engaged in prayer: "a Man of middle Age, tall, well shaped, and would have been very handsome, had not Abstinence, Sickness, and Hardships alter'd his Face: He had a coarse Frize Coat, like a *Turkish* Dervise or Hermit, a Fur Cap, short Boots like an *Arabian*."[69] What could his story be? (These religious hermits and the proselytizing priests and passive noblemen who populate Aubin's novels are absent from the typical Barbary captive narratives, although there are similar kindly religious hermits in Tasso's epic romance, *Jerusalem Delivered*.) This mysterious figure turns out to be Andrea Zantornio Borgomio, a shipwrecked Venetian passing as Ismal the Hermit after having escaped the Turkish Governor of Tunis's attempt to make him his catamite. He lives by repairing watches and selling watercolors, giving alms to the poor and to Christians in distress. Like other hermits in Aubin, some of whom retire to seek forgiveness for their sins, Andrea is associated with forgiveness. The ladies are eventually able to reward his kindness to them by helping to reunite him with the Venetian woman he came to Barbary to seek, Eleonora. Unlike the principal heroines, who preserve their chastity, she has yielded to her master. But Aubin does not fetishize chastity, as many later writers were to do. Eleonora is "excus'd" because of the element of force and Andrea takes "her to his Arms with as much Joy as if she had been a Virgin."[70]

PROVINCIAL NOVELTIES

The commercial market willing to buy Haywood's amorous tales and Aubin's exotic adventures valued novelty. Here women writers had an advantage, since they themselves still were novelties. Representations of women's experience and the experiences of kinds of people not previously much represented in literature also appealed. Stephen Duck, an agricultural laborer, was celebrated for his "The Thresher's Labour" (1730) in heroic couplets. Robert Tatersal, a bricklayer, offered his *Bricklayer's Miscellany, or Poems on Several Subjects* in two parts (1734, 1735).

The increasing wealth and cultural activity of provincial towns meant that provincial women writers of the middling classes now appear to record provincial life. London remained the dominant center of British culture throughout the century, but more larger towns began to have their own newspapers, coffeehouses, assembly rooms, theatre companies, and book publishers. In 1700 there were no newspapers and few printers in provincial towns, but by 1730 every large town had a newspaper and a printer. The newspapers advertised books, the booksellers distributed London books, and, with other emerging provincial cultural institutions, dispensed the "knowledge and culture that went with education and a genteel mind."[71] The turn toward literary realism and the desire for literary novelty – sometimes coupled with local boosterism – encouraged provincial writers to depict towns different from London. Three of the livelier writers of this period wrote from important cities or towns: Mary Chandler from Bath, the spa and resort; Mary Barber from Dublin, then the second largest city in the English-speaking world; and Mary Davys, first from York, then from Cambridge.

MARY CHANDLER

Mary Chandler, who published a famous poetic *Description of Bath* in 1733 and then *Poems on Several Occasions* in 1734, might seem more likely to have become a satiric target for the Augustans than the good-humored provincial poet she did become. A dissenter and the proprietor of a milliner's shop in the growing spa at Bath, Chandler had a crocked back and never married. *The Description of Bath* is related to loco-descriptive poems like the Welsh poet John Dyer's *Grongar Hill* (1726), although most loco-descriptive poems celebrate country places. Chandler shares the loco-descriptive poet's interest in attentively observed beauties of landscapes, yet in *Bath* she celebrates a town situated in time with journalistic accuracy and with an enthusiasm that promoted tourism. The reader is led from Roman times into the bustle of the modern town with its various baths for various clienteles, including Cross Bath, where the "*tender Virgin*" may find a "*safe Retreat*":

> From *Sights* indecent, and from *Speeches* lewd,
> Which dare not there, with *Satyr-face* intrude.

There the tourist may observe a marble cross, relic of "Popish" times:

> Devoid *itself* of *Pow'r* to heal our Woes;
> Yet, deck'd with *monumental Crutches*, shows
> What *mighty Cures* this wond'rous *Pool* has done,
> And these the *Trophies* from *Diseases* won.[72]

Delights available to visitors include an *allée* of lime trees planted in adverse rows, the "Cross Post" invented by Ralph Allen, and a wonderful machine, "Self-*moving* downward from the Mountain's Heights."

Chandler makes the Bath bookshop of her own publisher, James Leake, especially enticing for women who yearn for education and culture:

> Heroes of *ancient*, and of *modern* Song,
> The bending Shelves in comely Order throng,
> Hither, *ye Nymphs*, attend the leading Muse,
> With her the *Labours* of the *Wise* peruse;
> Their *Maxims* learn, their *Precepts* be your Guide,
> Think *virtuous Knowledge WOMAN'S* truest Pride:
> *One* Hour thus spent, more *solid* Joys shall give,
> Than the gay *Idler* knows, or *Fools* conceive.[73]

Leake, whose shop was next to Chandler's, was Richardson's brother-in-law and one of those provincial booksellers who had good London connections. He was, therefore, able to see to it that the seven editions of *The Description of Bath* and Chandler's other poems published in his lifetime were published simultaneously in Bath and in London.

BARBER'S *POEMS ON SEVERAL OCCASIONS*

Mary Barber, the wife of a Dublin woolen draper, was able to begin her poetic career publishing short poems with Dublin printers, the Irish capital being earlier supplied with its own printers and other cultural institutions like theatres before English provincial towns were. A number of Barber's poems articulate her identification with Ireland or are addressed to or represent Irish people; a few venture to touch on Irish grievances. For instance, in an occasional poem to Edward Walpole, son of the Prime Minister, "An Invitation to *Edward Walpole*, Esq; upon hearing he was landed in *Dublin*," Barber warns:

> From the Lands of *Parnassus* the Rents are ill-paid,
> And *England* has cruelly cramp'd us in Trade . . .[74]

Other poems are set in the English spas of Bath and Tunbridge, where she traveled for her health.

Barber published *Poems on Several Occasions* by subscription, that is, published after would-be readers had paid in advance of publication to subsidize the cost of publication and to remunerate the author. Subscription publication had been used in the seventeenth century to facilitate publication of very expensive scholarly books likely to have a limited audience, for example, a polyglot Bible requiring several foreign language fonts, a collaborative project of thirty-two scholars, or Nehemiah Grew's *Anatomy of Plants*, featuring expensive illustrative plates.[75] The publication of Elstob's *An English-Saxon Homily on the Birthday of St. Gregory . . . translated into modern English, with Notes etc.* (1709) by subscription represented a similar subvention of scholarly publication. Barber's *Poems on Several Occasions*, however, exemplifies what was to become a more common use of subscription publication for women's books not intended for specialized audiences, especially books of poetry. Many of Barber's subscribers – 900, a high number, each paying a guinea a copy – paid in significant part because they understood Barber herself to be a worthy object of charity. Some, like Philips's Irish patrons, also paid because they were Irish or resident in Ireland and wished to support Irish cultural achievement. As has often been remarked, subscription publication allowed less wealthy people to become, at small cost, joint patrons of writers, and thus represented a transitional mode between older individual patronage and the fully anonymous commercial market.[76] As in other books published by subscription, the names of Barber's subscribers were published in a list in the front matter. The virtuous circle of subscription publication allowed writers and subscribers to draw luster from one another and humbler subscribers to bask in the light afforded by more illustrious subscribers.

Barber's list included political and social notables like the former Lord Lieutenant of Ireland and his wife, the current Lord Lieutenant of Ireland, and two Earls of Orrery, as well as Pope – who had laid the foundation of his fortune with the subscription publication of his Homer – Gay, and Swift. Swift, Dean of St. Patrick's Cathedral in Dublin, not only subscribed for ten copies, but was importantly responsible for the success of the subscription. He advised Barber on how to manage the subscription campaign, solicited subscriptions for her, and authorized her to use his name to support her applications to notables of his acquaintance, writing "[if they] who know me be told that it is by my request and earnest recommendation, I should fancy they will not refuse."[77] Swift here practices a new kind of patronage available to authors to exert on behalf of other authors, although he is also exercising Christian charity toward a worthy poor woman. As became customary in books by women published by subscription, a good number of women subscribed.

Barber in *Poems on Several Occasions* makes explicit both the element of literary patronage and the element of charitable subvention of a worthy poor person in some subscription publication. A number of her poems are panegyrics to individuals whose names also appear in the subscription list. More interestingly, some poems celebrate, encourage, and model charitable actions. In one, "The Widow Gordon's Petition: To the Rt Hon. the Lady Carteret," Barber composes a petition for aid to the Lord Lieutenant's wife from an impoverished officer's widow whose son is blind. The poet reminds rich women that the rich who are deaf to the cries of poor widows and orphans in this life will themselves weep in vain at the day of judgment. In another, "On seeing the Captives, lately redeem'd from Barbary by His Majesty," she praises King George's ransoming a group of Barbary captives. The final poem in the volume, "To a Lady who commanded me to send her an Account in Verse, how I succeeded in my *Subscription*," expresses gratitude to the good and great who have supported her, but mocks those who have refused to subscribe: an unpatriotic man who will subscribe to operas featuring Italian castrati but not to a British poet, one woman who insists women cannot write, another who claims that women should stick to needlework, and still another willing to spend money on gambling but not on poetry.

As Margaret Doody has argued, Swift's poetry proved a useful model for Barber and other women poets. Swift's colloquially rhymed tetrameter couplets were unpretentious, suited to a less educated woman poet, like Barber, who intended to stay in her social position as a tradesman's wife. Swift's comic, even awkward, poetic persona, the "critical grumbling impish voice that emerges not from the center of authoritative power but from somewhere on the sidelines," also was easier to adapt to Barber's uses than more conventional, more authoritative public personae.[78] In "To Mrs. Frances-Arabella Kelly" Barber adopts Swift's meter and witty, self-deprecating, even self-satirizing, humor in a presentation of herself as an old woman. At the same time, she hints that she might have more power than conventions suppose:

> Today, as at my Glass I stood,
> To set my Head-cloaths, and my Hood;
> I saw my grizzled Locks with Dread,
> And call'd to mind the *Gorgon's* Head.
>
> Thought I, whate'er the Poets say,
> *Medusa's* Hair was only gray:
> Tho' *Ovid*, who the Story told,
> Was too well-bred to call her old;
> But, what amounted to the same,
> He made her an immortal Dame.[79]

Slyly, Barber here aligns herself both with Ovid as a witty poet, and against Ovid, since she appears as a truth-telling plain speaker against what she claims is the Latin poet's genteel periphrasis. She also aligns herself with the Gorgon Medusa, possessor of magic powers. Yet, as she faces the Gorgon head in the mirror, a head with the power to turn men and beasts to stone, she herself, nevertheless, manages to chat amiably on. Indeed, Barber perhaps recalls that the hero Perseus, who succeeded in cutting off Medusa's head, did so, according to Ovid's *Metamorphosis*, by looking at her head only as it was reflected in the bronze shield he carried on his left arm.

Barber grounded writing and printing her *Poems on Several Occasions* (1734) in her duty as a mother. Her most notable poems were written for her son Constantine to speak on such homely occasions as "his first putting on Breeches" or getting a play-day at school. "I am sensible," Barber declared in her preface:

> that a Woman steps out of her Province whenever she presumes to write for the Press, and therefore think it necessary to inform my Readers, that my Verses were written with a very different View from any of those which other Attempters in Poetry have proposed to themselves: My Aim being chiefly to form the Minds of my Children, I imagin'd that Precepts convey'd in Verse would be easier remember'd, and . . . give early a proper and graceful Manner of speaking.[80]

Barber presents herself as a conscientious citizen's wife and mother, a plainspoken woman who knows her social place, yet solicits the attention and favors of the notable and the noble to her "innocent" and moral verse. "Nothing," she claims, "can be of more Use to Society than the taking early Care to form the Minds of Youth."[81]

The poems Barber wrote to be spoken by her son are less didactic than this declaration might imply, mingling pleasure in the supposed naiveté of the child's view with adult observations. In "Written for my Son, and spoken by him in School, upon his Master's first bringing in a Rod," for example, Con is first made to lament the "dreadful Birch!," the "instrument of Tryanny," and then to endorse Locke's *Thoughts Concerning Education*. Barber has fun with the idea that one of Locke's suggestions about preparing children to read "[b]y 'graving letters on the Dice" might simultaneously prepare them to gamble.[82] In "Written for my Son, and spoken by him, at a public Examination for Victors," Barber uses her son's voice to offer the socially radical suggestion that boys should be assigned roles on the basis of their talents rather than on the basis of their ancestry. Then not only would the talented contribute to their countries, but the untalented scions of the upper class, presumably including English officeholders in Ireland, would cease to be parasites on the body politic:

> And Boys of Genius to those Honours soar,
> Which high-born Dunces but disgrac'd before . . .[83]

(No doubt the fond mother was pleased when her Constantine, son of a mere woolen-draper, rose to become a physician, a professor at Trinity College, Dublin, and, later, President of the Dublin College of Physicians.)

Barber's tactic of putting words into her son's mouth leads to an unusual sequence of poems in which the authenticity of Con's poems is doubted and defended. In "A Letter for my Son to one of His Schoolfellows, Son to *Henry Rose*, Esq.," Con is made to describe his mother's complaining that the schoolmaster is turning her son into a poet instead of preparing him for the life of a shopkeeper. This is followed by a poem written by "The Rev. Dr. T —," "To Mr *Rose*; Sent in the Name of the Honourable Mr *Barry*, one of his Schoolfellows," insisting that Con's verses are actually his mother's, extravagantly complimenting her verse, and warning him:

> Presumptuous Youth! This dang'rous Art forbear;
> Nor tempt a Character beyond thy Sphere.
> Let meaner Flames thy tender Breast inspire;
> Touch not a beam of hers – 'Tis sacred Fire![84]

Then, in "Written for my Son, to Mr *Barry*, occasioned by the foregoing Verses," Con is made to complain that "Barry" injures him, seeming "to make my Praise your Aim, / With more success to wound my Fame."[85] Barber has thus reversed the standard situation in which the woman's writing is said not to be her own, the situation complained of, for instance, in Ann Killigrew's "Upon the Saying That My Verses Were Made by Another" (1686), here making the male complain that he is not believed to be the author of his own verses. And in this case, he is not. At the same time, identities are layered in these poems so that "Con's" complaint to "Barry" literally refers to the fact that "Barry's" has started by describing the "flowing Numbers," "easy phrases," "Wit," and "Humour" of "Con's" poems before declaring that "They ne'er could spring from his poor Baby head." Yet the lines also seem to hint that Barber finds "The Rev. T's" hyperbolic references to her "Sacred Fire" wounding to her Fame. "Praise undeserved is scandal in disguise," as Pope said.

Like Chandler and Barber, Davys was a woman of the middling classes with an eye for realist detail and an eagerness to represent the previously unliterary world of the mundane and the provincial. Her comedy, *The Northern Heiress; or the Humours of York* (1716) captures the tensions between the prosperous tradesmen in the northern county seat and the leisure class who gather there to spend money and to enjoy amusements including biweekly Assembly entertainments and horse races. Perhaps like Davys herself, the genteel protagonists take temporary lodgings in York because it has some culture but is cheaper than London. They are amused at what seem to them the pretensions of wives and widows of successful tradesmen, aldermen, and mayors, whose money comes from enterprises like manufacturing beer, soap, and gloves. Gramont, the visiting gentle-man hero, thinks these women "would be less ridiculous, were they less fond of being call'd Ladies, without which, you must never speak to 'em, tho' you may often see them going to Market in a blue Apron and a Bonnet, with a Basket for Butter and Eggs."[86]

The originality of *The Northern Heiress* lies in Davys's forceful repre-sentation of these York tradeswomen, who, although condescended to by the genteel as vulgar, are memorably depicted; they are also allowed to score occasional points at the expense of the more idle consuming classes. The society of the provincial town is small enough that these trades-women live in a degree of social intimacy with those who have traditional claims to gentility. Lady Greasy, widow of a grocer mayor, now superin-tends the business and lets lodgings. She is outspoken, even violent, in defense of her daughter and her own prerogatives. We see her at breakfast at the genteel Lady Ample's house, engaged in a conversation about local elections with the tradesmen's wives and widows. Stage directions call for the women to feast on "hot Ale and Ginger, Butter, Rolls, and a huge *Cheshire* Cheese."[87] They prefer this substantial, native food to more new-fangled, foreign tea. Their hearty tastes are endorsed by the pleasant and sensible Sir Jeffrey Ample, who testifies his approbation of their "good old-fashion'd Way of House-keeping." When poverty-stricken, pusillan-imous Captain Tinsel tries to enrich himself by seeking to marry Lady Greasy's daughter Dolly, Lady Greasy forthrightly souses Dolly with a mug of small beer; later, when they have married, she flies at Tinsel's throat, terrorizing him.

Both an object of satire and something of a satirist herself, the firmly materialist Lady Greasy confronts Tinsel with the hollowness of his claims to superiority based on gentle birth and military rank: "thou beggarly Dog! can any thing be a Gentlewoman that's tied to such a pitiful Scab as thou art? . . . what signifies your Family, unless you had something to uphold it with?"[88] She then proposes to consent to the marriage on the condition that he exchanges his "tawdry red Coat" for an apron and goes into business with her. Tinsel is horrified and Lady Greasy relents, but not before the audience has some opportunity to consider whether performing useful work renders a person beneath human notice. Davys, widowed at 24 in 1698, seems to have used her author's profits from *The Northern Heiress* to establish herself as the proprietress of a Cambridge coffeehouse.

PARADOXES OF PRINT

The opportunities for print revelations presented women with a double-edged sword. On the one hand, there was a market from which they could profit by offering revelations – or purported revelations – about themselves or others, as Manley had done in *Rivella*. Martha Fowke and William Bond published their verse epistles to each other, nicely described by Roger Lonsdale as "platonically amorous," as the *Epistles of Clio and Strephon* (1720, 3rd edn. entitled *The Platonic Lovers*, 1732).[89] Later, after her marriage to Arnold Sansom, Martha wrote a long autobiography touting her appeal to many men and defending her virtue; she most likely would have published this if she had not died in 1736.[90] Thomas, despite her efforts to cling to gentility, fallen on hard times, took a set of Pope's letters written to her friend Henry Cromwell and sold them to Curll for publication (enraging Pope). Haywood published *A Spy upon the Conjuror* (1724), containing a set of letters supposedly written by Duncan Campbell, the blind and mute "prophet," and apparently also *Some Memoirs of the Amours and Intrigues of a certain Irish Dean . . . with the gallantries of two Berkshire Ladies* (1718), a scandalous tale about Swift, Vanessa, Stella, and Martha and Patty Blount (Pope's women friends), with passionate letters.

On the other hand, the sword of publication a woman writer might use for her own profit or in her own defense could also be turned against her. Some booksellers were willing to engage in the unauthorized publication of writing that women preferred to have kept private; some writers were happy to produce writing that would be falsely attributed to particular women; and satirists were willing to attack both women in general and particular women.[91] Both sexes could play at these games. As I noted in the previous chapter, the anonymity and absence of a material author in print culture permitted writers of either sex to masquerade as the other. In a letter published in *The Flying-Post: or, Post-Master* of 11–13 September 1722, Montagu masqueraded as a Turkey merchant to advance her campaign for vaccination against smallpox. Many attributions of works written in the early eighteenth century remain insecure and many anonymous works remain unattributed. As an upper-class person and a famous wit, Montagu was an obvious target for humiliation through unauthorized publication. A Frenchman, Toussaint Rémond de Saint-Mard, tormented her by threatening to print her letters to him and got her to send him what was in essence blackmail money. Even the decorous and devout Rowe was not safe. Dunton threatened to publish her letters to him, and, against her express wishes, shortly after her death Curll republished her early Philomela poems.

TRANSLATION

Contemporaries joked that translation was one of the easiest ways to produce books for the market, that translators were mostly incompetent, that books which were actually translations were palmed off as originals, and that, in other cases, the label "translation" was used to sell books that were not, in fact, translations. As we saw in chapter three, Manley's *New Atalantis* claimed to have been "Written originally in Italian"; the second volume, tauntingly, added, "Written originally in Italian, and translated from the third edition of the French." Bookweight in Henry Fielding's *The Author's Farce* initiates one of his new hacks who applies to be a translator into the mysteries of the craft: "you will have more occasion for invention than learning here: you will be sometimes obliged to translate books out of all languages (especially French) which were never printed in any language whatsoever . . . Sometimes we give a foreign name to our own labor, and sometimes we put our own names to the labor of others."[92]

Translation of French prose, non-fiction and fiction, was the great resource of women concerned to write for money. Both Haywood and Aubin (who was born in London of French parents and probably had near-native fluency) alternatively produced translations from the French and original works. Among Haywood's most successful books was *La Belle Assemblée* (2 volumes, 1724–26), translated from Madeleine-Angelique de Gomez's *Les Journées amusantes* (8 volumes, 1722–31). Unlike Haywood's scandal chronicles or amorous fiction, *La Belle Assemblée* offers high-minded couples who entertain themselves in a country house with reading in the library, commenting on what they read, considering history and morality, and telling romance tales that have been described as smaller versions of La Calprenède and Gomberville, "love stories full of nobility and honor and fine sentiment, but given some degree of probability by their contemporary setting."[93] For professional writers like Haywood and Aubin, translation also served as something of a school exercise, increasing their familiarity with a range of literary techniques. Aubin's translations of French fiction in this period included *The Adventures of the Prince of Clermont, and Madam de Ravezan: a novel* (1722), by Luise Geneviève de Gillot de Beaucour; *The Illustrious French Lovers: Being the true Histories of the Amours of Several French Persons of Quality* (1727), by Robert de Challes; and *The Life of the Countess de Gondez* (1729), by Margurite de Lussan.

However, translation was not only a way of producing books to satisfy the appetite of a hungry market. As we observed in discussing Behn, translation also meant access to important literature, ancient and modern. Women writers continued to express gratitude to male translators of the Greek and Roman classics, who increasingly made these works accessible to women. Thomas enthusiastically celebrates Dryden's translation of Virgil and mourns – as have many – that he did not live to translate Homer as well. Like their male contemporaries, some women poets of this period offered translations and imitations of Latin poems, especially of Horace and Ovid; like Behn, those who did not know Latin used other translations as intermediary sources. This was, presumably, Thomas's procedure in her, quite free, imitation of one of Horace's *carpe diem* odes (Book I, II). Elizabeth Tollet, however, knew Latin as well as French and Italian; she includes in her *Poems on Several Occasions. With Anne Bolyn to King Henry VIII. An Epistle* (1724), a translation of one of Horace's odes and imitations of three others. Addressing herself to a modern text of intellectual interest, Rowe appended to her *Friendship in Death* "Thoughts on Death," her translation from part of the Jansenist Pierre Nicole's *Essais de morale* (4 volumes, 1671–78). Jansenism, the French counter-Reformation revival of Augustinian theology, critiqued the moral and spiritual laxity of the Jesuits and others; it appealed to many religiously serious English Protestants throughout the eighteenth century.

Women increasingly saw their own translations from the modern European languages as demonstrating literary powers and intellectual interests analogous to those that educated men sought to display in their translations from Greek and Latin. Montagu, after seeing a French company perform Pierre de Marivaux's wonderful comedy, *Le Jeu de l'amour et du hasard* (1730), wrote her English version, apparently without any intention of submitting it for production. Jane Robe did have produced at Lincoln's Inn Fields her blank verse version of Racine's *La Thébayde, ou les frères ennemis* (1664) as *The Fatal Legacy* (1723). Although Curll is most remembered for his publication of scandalous or unauthorized works, he also catered to the interest in serious works and had no objections to working with women writers. Thus, one finds Jane Barker as the translator of Fénelon's *Christian Pilgrimage*, published by Curll in 1718; to this she added "A Hymn on the Ascension" and fourteen Psalms.

AUBIN'S *GENGHIZCAN*

Penelope Aubin's translation of the *History of Genghizcan the Great, First Emperor of the Antient Moguls and Tartars; In Four Books . . .* (1727) is a very serious and fascinating scholarly book, a nice example of how translation could permit women to engage significant subjects conventionally thought beyond the purview of women. Its French author was François Pétis de la Croix, the elder, for forty years Louis XIV's secretary for Turkish and Arabic, author of a French–Persian dictionary, and also of a catalogue *raisonné* of the Turkish and Persian books in the King's library. *The History du grand Genghizcan* was posthumously published in 1710, edited by his son, who succeeded him as official interpreter and who also had an important diplomatic career in the orient. According to Pétis de la Croix, the younger, the idea for the history was originally suggested by Jean-Baptiste Colbert, Louis XIV's minister, as part of Colbert's program "of aggrandizing his Master's Glory," and putting France "in a condition of envying nothing which belonged to Strangers."[94] Pétis de la Croix, the elder, had also translated a history of Louis XIV into Turkish, thus publishing "the Grandeur" of French kings "to the farthest Parts of all *Asia*."[95] He labored for ten years on *Genghizcan*, collecting a wide array of sources, classical and oriental. The resulting French book displays this research, but also offers an engaging narrative constructed according to the modern historiographical methodology associated with Voltaire's later *Age of Louis XIV* (1751). The book was adorned with a state-of-the-cartographic-art map of northern Asia, drawn for the purpose by William de l'Isle, a member of the French Royal Academy of Science. The French preface, by the younger Pétis de la Croix, notes that in addition to the obvious value of the history for the learned and for geographers, it ought also to be read by merchants "who trade to *China*, the *East Indies*, *Persia*, or other Eastern Parts of the World, pursuant to the Treaty of Commerce renew'd and established [by Colbert in 1708 between Louis XIV and the Emperor of Persia.]"[96]

Reading *Genghizcan,* one can see that Colbert must have wanted an account of a superlative early conqueror who succeeded in building a great empire out of disparate elements, an account that would serve for comparing and contrasting similar achievements by the Sun King. Pétis de la Croix emphasizes the magnitude of Genghizcan's achievements as an empire builder: "This Prince laid the Foundation of a Monarchy greater in its Extent than those possessed by *Alexander* or *Augustus*; for he extended his Dominions to more than eighteen hundred Leagues from East to West, and above a thousand from North to South."[97] More surprisingly, Pétis de la Croix also celebrates Genghizcan as a lawgiver, devoting considerable attention to the military and civil codes he imposed on his empire, and as a ruler who proclaimed religious toleration. (Twentieth-century experts on the history of Mongolia agree that Genghizcan proclaimed religious toleration, although they say his motive was to prepare areas where there was religious conflict between Buddhists and Muslims for successful occupation, rather than because, as De la Croix claims, he was himself a Deist.) The French text sets up an implicit competition in which French kings are challenged to outdo Genghizcan as conquerors and rulers. Improbable as it may seem, Aubin dedicated her translation of *Genghizcan* to George Augustus, Prince of Wales. She claimed that he had all the fine qualities Pétis de la Croix discovered in Genghizcan and wished him and his posterity the same fame as conquerors. George is thus positioned not only to outdo Genghizcan, but, implicitly, Louis XIV as well (although exactly how wide-ranging conquest and general benevolence to mankind are to be reconciled is not explained).

ELSTOB AND ANGLO-SAXON

Another, very ambitious, translator in this period, Elizabeth Elstob, found a way to strike at the intellectual authority derived from elite male classical education. While she mastered Latin, she also saw that erudition in the modern languages might enable at least a few women to make their own contributions to knowledge, to demonstrate the kind of analytic power that learned men demonstrated in classical philology, and to attain a scholarly confidence sufficient to engage in controversy with educated men. Elstob had earlier translated Madeleine de Scudéry's *Discours de la gloire* (1708), a prize essay Scudéry had entered, anonymously, in a competition set by the Académie Française for the best essay on the set topic of glory. Without intending to, the Académie had established a gender-blind competition. That a woman could win, especially when the set topic was presumably a matter of masculine expertise, thrilled women intellectuals throughout Europe.

Elstob's access to higher learning came through her brother William, who was elected a fellow of University College, Oxford in 1696. Elizabeth became his collaborator in Anglo-Saxon studies, transcribing manuscripts, and producing scholarly editions and translations. In 1715 she published her own *Rudiments of Grammar for the English-Saxon Tongue . . .* (1715). Anglo-Saxon studies were at this time both pioneering and highly politicized, a major impetus for research coming from nonjuring clergymen like George Hickes, to whom Elstob dedicated her grammar. These nonjurors were looking for evidence consonant with their views on ecclesiastical polity and on the "ancient constitution" of Britain before the "Norman yoke."[98] Elstob's edition and translation of Ælfric's *Homily on the Birthday of St. Gregory* (1709) emphasizes the similarity of the Anglo-Saxon Church and the modern reformed Church of England, as opposed to the corrupt Roman Catholic Church. Thus, it is the Church of England not the Church of Rome that is continuous with primitive Christianity.

Although Elstob studied Latin, the originality of her work partly consisted in her willingness to abandon Latin as the medium and the model for English grammar. The first Anglo-Saxon grammars printed were Hickes's *Institutines Grammaticae, et Moeso-Gothicae* (1689) and *Linguarum Vett. Septentrionalium Thesaurus Grammaticu-Criticus et Archaeologicus* (1705). Elstob, having read Hickes, testified to the "Pleasure" she reaped from the knowledge she gained "from the original of our Mother Tongue" and proclaimed her desire to offer a grammar written in English "that others of my own Sex, might be capable of the same Satisfaction. . ."[99] Hers was the first Anglo-Saxon grammar written in English. Hickes and other contemporary learned men, having been schooled in Latin grammar all their lives, understandably used Latin grammar as a Procrustean bed into which they attempted to tuck Anglo-Saxon. Hickes, for instance, insisted that Anglo-Saxon had vocative and ablative cases. One modern scholar has observed that Elstob was less reliant on Latin paradigms than her male Saxonist contemporaries, using them, but also relying heavily on Ælfric's original native-speaker Anglo-Saxon grammar (also written in Latin), and, in cases of conflict between Hickes and Ælfric, favoring Ælfric.[100]

In "An Apology for the Study of Northern Antiquities," prefaced to the *Grammar*, Elstob directly attacks Swift's "A Proposal for Correcting,

Improving and Ascertaining the English Tongue" (1712). She enters contemporary debates about whether the teaching of English ought to continue to depend on Latinate grammars or to break free of them, arguing that the rules for English ought to be drawn only from English. Confident in her own unusual knowledge of "*Saxon, Gothick* and *Francick*, or old *Teutonick*," she ridicules Swift's admitted ignorance of and conventional prejudice against the northern languages.[101] Swift had complained that the northern languages are too monosyllabic and that English poets make this worse by "the barbarous custom of abbreviating words, to fit them to the measure of . . . verses; and this . . . so very injudiciously, as to form such harsh unharmonious Sounds, that that none but a *Northern* ear could endure." Against Swift, Elstob defends the simplicity of the northern languages and their use of monosyllables, producing a long list of monosyllabic lines from English poets from Chaucer to Swift.[102]

THE TRAVEL LITERATURE OF THE ENLIGHTENMENT AND MONTAGU'S *EMBASSY LETTERS*

Travel literature was an important genre in this period not only because it satisfied curiosity and desire for vicarious adventure, but also because it offered data for the new "science of man," both philosophy and what we now call the social sciences, including political science, economics, sociology, psychology, and anthropology. Locke's philosophical and political writings frequently cite travelers' observations in arguments designed to differentiate between practices that are merely local and customary as opposed to those deeply grounded in the nature of man. Enlightenment arguments about the nature of man were tightly bound to political arguments about the possibility of social and political change. If a particular practice or belief could be shown not to exist somewhere else in the world where there was recognizably civilized human life, for example, in China, then perhaps one could argue that that practice or belief was dispensable at home. On the other hand, other cultures might have invented practices that could usefully be imitated.

Like Pétis de la Croix's *Genghizcan,* Lady Mary Wortley Montagu's *Embassy Letters* is an original work redolent of the wide-ranging intellectual curiosity and analytic concerns of the enlightenment. Written while she was accompanying her husband on his embassy to Constantinople between 1716 and 1718, the *Letters* constitute, I would say, the most brilliant book by any women writer of the Restoration and eighteenth century and one of the best books written by a writer of either gender in this period. Circulated at first in manuscript form, made a little more widely known by the unauthorized publication in 1720 of one of her letters from Constantinople to the Abbé Conti, then posthumously published as a collection in 1763 after her death in 1762, the *Embassy Letters* made Montagu famous as a wit and as a woman who had the intellectual capacity to write a major volume of enlightenment travel. We know that Montagu had collected and prepared the letters as a book manuscript because in the 1720s Astell read the manuscript, urged its publication, and wrote a preface inscribed on Montagu's copy. Astell praised Montagu as an outstanding woman who could compete intellectually with men and suggested in a poem that the letters revealed "A genius so Sublime and so Complete, / [I] gladly lay my Laurels at her Feet."[103] Tobias Smollett, the important mid-century novelist and the author of his own *Travels through France and Italy* (1766), wrote in *The Critical Review* that Montagu's letters were "never equalled by any letter-writer of any sex, age, or nation." Voltaire pronounced the letters superior to Madame de Sévigné's and Madame de Maintenon's "(whose writing interests only their own nation) because they seemed written for all nations willing to be instructed."[104] The learned Edmund Gibbon, author of the monumental *Decline and Fall of the Roman Empire*, exclaimed, "What fire, what ease, what knowledge of Europe and Asia!"[105]

The most famous and practical example of Montagu's willingness to learn from foreigners was her description of the Turkish practice of inoculation to prevent smallpox (To Sarah Chiswell, 1 April 1717), her having her own children inoculated, and her campaign, upon her return to England, to have the practice generally adopted. Resistance to this innovation came from both clergymen and physicians. The fact that in Turkey old women commonly performed "the operation" of inoculation, as Montagu reported, helped inflame the resistance of an Englishman like the physician William Wagstaffe. Wagstaffe urged physicians not to allow amateurs to take over medicine and expostulated: "Posterity perhaps will scarcely be brought to believe, that an Experiment practiced only by a few *Ignorant Women*, amongst an illiterate and unthinking People, shou'd on a sudden, and upon slender Experience, so far obtain in one of the Politest Nations in the World, as to be receiv'd into the *Royal Palace*."[106] Understanding that one ground of opposition was misogyny, Montagu used the anonymity of print to pretend to be a male merchant who traded in Turkey for her essay, mentioned earlier, "A Plain Account of the Innoculating of the Small Pox," published in the *Flying Post* of 11–13 September 1722.[107]

Montagu's great subject in the *Embassy Letters* – and in many of her later letters – is the nature of human nature. Although she traveled to Turkey with her husband, who had been appointed English Ambassador charged with helping negotiate a peace between Austria and Turkey, her letters have virtually nothing to say about these negotiations. Instead, she pursues a set of themes that became characteristic of enlightenment travelers: the social institutions and customs of the people; their religion; the political, military, and legal systems of the Ottoman Empire; their poetry and art. She travels as a seeker, not as a censor. Because she shares the enlightenment belief that human nature is "every where the same," she shares enlightenment optimism about the possibility of gaining insight into human nature from studying the customs and beliefs of other peoples.[108]

Montagu is especially brilliant when she observes some apparently odd custom, then analyzes it carefully to discover how it is actually, if surprisingly, a reasonable response to different social or legal rules than those familiar to her and her readers. She conveys a passionate curiosity, a hunger for knowledge. Frequently she argues that Turkish behavior has been misinterpreted, that others have seen particular Turkish practices different from western European ones and too hastily concluded that those practices proceed from a natural inferiority of the Turks. She often admits that the Turks do what others claim, but looks more deeply, like a sociologist, to discern why, given the conditions in which they live, their behavior is functional, even perfectly reasonable, the same as what western Europeans would do were their own circumstances similar. Thus, she writes to Miss Thistlethwayte on Turkish houses:

I suppose you have read in most of our Accounts of Turkey that their Houses are the most miserable pieces of building in the World. . . 'Tis true they are not at all solicitous to beautify the outsides of their houses, and they are generally built of Wood, which I own is the cause of many inconveniencys, but this is not to be charg'd on the ill taste of the people but the Oppression of the Government. Every House upon the death of its Master is at the Grand Signor's disposal, and therefore No Man cares to make a great Expence which he is not sure his family will be the better for. All their design is to build a House commodious and that will last their Lives, and are very indifferent if it falls down the Year after.[109]

These analyses are energized by her sharp sense that laws and customs at home are by no means perfect and her optimism that her travels might lead her to knowledge of new practices, like inoculation for smallpox, and new ideas that could usefully be imported to improve England.

Throughout the *Embassy Letters* Lady Mary insists that her representations of life in the Ottoman Empire are more accurate than the representations offered in earlier French or English books like Richard Knolles's *The Turkish History from the Original of the Nation to the Growth of the Ottoman Empire with the Lives and Conquests of their Princes and Emperors* (1603), Jean Du Mont, Baron de Carlscroon's *Nouveau Voyage au Levant* (1674), Sir Paul Rycaut's *The Present State of the Ottoman Empire* (1668), or Aaron Hill's *Full and Just Account of the Present State of the Ottoman Empire in all its Branches of Government, Policy, Religion, Customs and Way of Living of the Turks in General* (1709), all of which she had read. She constructs her authority partly on empirical grounds, insisting that she tells what she sees and hears directly rather than relying on what others have said in books. Thus, in another letter to a woman friend, she scorns to repeat the conventional historical facts about Constantinople, declaring:

I'll assure you 'tis not want of learning that I forbear writeing all these bright things. I could also, with little trouble, turn over Knolles and Sir Paul Rycaut to give you a list of Turkish Emperours, but I will not tell you what you may find in every Author that has writ of this Country.

I am more enclin'd, out of a true female spirit of Contradiction, to tell you the falsehood of a great part of what you find in authors; as, for example, the admirable Mr. Hill, who so gravely asserts that he saw in Santa Sophia a sweating Pillar very Balsamic for disorder'd heads. There is not the least tradition of any such matter, and I suppose it was revealed to him in Vision during his wonderfull stay in the Egyptian Catacombs, for I am sure he never heard of any such miracle here.[110]

She also derives authority from her privileged access as an aristocrat and an ambassador's wife to audiences with those members of the elite who have political and intellectual understanding of their culture.

As she was to do on later occasions, Montagu attempts to trump the gender privilege of her male rivals with her class privilege as an aristocrat. "'Tis certain we have but very imperfect relations of the manners and Religion of these people," she tells the Abbé Conti, "this part of the World being seldom visited but by merchants, who mind little but their own Affairs, or Travellers who make too short a stay to be able to report any thing exactly of their own knowledge. The Turks are too proud to converse familiarly with merchants etc., who can only pick up some confused informations, which are generally false, and can give no better an Account of the ways here, than a French refugée lodging in a Garret in Greek Street, could write of the Court of England." Giving the Abbé a long account of religion in the Ottoman Empire, she boasts, "I had the advantage of lodging 3 weeks at Belgrade with a principal Effendi, that is to say, a Scholar." There "an intimate daily conversation . . . gave me an opportunity of knowing their Religion and morals in a more particular manner than perhaps any Christian ever did."[111] On the basis of these conversations, she feels empowered to declare: "Sir Paul Rycaut is mistaken (as he commonly is) in calling the sect *Muserin* (i.e., the secret with us) Atheists, they being Deists, and their impiety consists in making a jest of their Prophet."[112]

Since the previous western accounts of the Ottoman Empire had been written by men, Montagu further legitimately boasts that a unique merit of her book is that, as a woman, she had an access to the life of women, including women confined to harems, that no earlier western traveler ever had. Again, she contrasts male ignorance to her knowledge, exclaiming, "Now I am a little acquainted with [the ways of the Turkish ladies], I cannot forbear admiring either the exemplary discretion or extreme Stupidity of all the writers that have given accounts of 'em."[113] Rebutting the common western assumption that Turks are inferior "barbarians," she particularly stresses the courtesy of Turkish women to her, since a fundamental feature of civilization is courtesy to strangers.

Montagu's treatment of women in the *Embassy Letters* is rich in complex ironies, in its way as rich in irony as Gay's *Beggars' Opera*. She plays her realistic observations off against the polite convention that English women are virtuous and free, while foreign women (particularly women in the Ottoman Empire) are depraved and enslaved. Her persona is that of a very sophisticated, very witty, female philosophe – Voltaire's sister. Implicitly, she revels in the knowledge she shares with her sophisticated female correspondents that, despite the popular belief in the superiority of English virtue, "immorality" is common enough at home. A central paradox in the *Embassy Letters* is the suggestion that Turkish women "have more Liberty than we have," indeed, that Turkish women are "the only free people in the Empire." This declaration comes as the climax of a passage describing the veils Turkish women wear and claiming that the anonymity of veils permits Turkish women to make sexual assignations free from the fear of discovery either by jealous husbands or by their lovers (who "can very seldom guess at her name they have corresponded with above halfe a year together").

You may easily imagine the number of faithfull Wives very small in a country where they have nothing to fear from their Lovers' Indiscretion, since we see so many that have the courage to expose them selves to that in this World and all the threaten'd Punishment of the next, which is never preach'd to the Turkish Damsels. Neither have they much to apprehend from the resentment of their

Husbands, those Ladys that are rich having all their money in their own hands, which they take with 'em upon a divorce with an addition which he is oblig'd to give 'em. Upon the Whole, I look upon the Turkish Women as the only free people in the Empire.[114]

Given the western view of the Ottoman Empire as the quintessential locus of servility and tyranny and of its women as the slaves of slaves, Montagu knows that her use of the words "liberty" and "free" in this context will shock; these are the sacred terms of Whig political pride and she was a good Whig. As in Swift's *Argument to Prove that the Abolishing of Christianity in England May . . . Be Attended with Some Inconveniences* (1708), satire here is directed at the hypocrisy of conventional polite English society, where women profess Christianity but act as though they did not believe adultery would be punished by damnation and hell. Montagu then glances back at Turkish women and men, making precisely the sort of shrewd economic point characteristic of her analyses. Here she suggests that economic interest often rules behavior. Given a family law that permits divorce but requires a husband who wishes to divorce his wife to return her dowry and more should he send her back to her family, simple avarice inspires husbands to ignore being cuckolded.

In the wake of Edward Said's *Orientalism* (1978), much criticism of the *Embassy Letters* has been preoccupied with trying to decide whether or to what extent Montagu produces the kind of Eurocentric, exotic account of an imaginary orient to which Said objected.[115] In particular, the scene in which Montagu visits the women's baths at Adrianopole, sees the women naked, and compares them to Eves and goddesses painted by Titian, has provoked debate over whether Montagu voyeuristically makes the woman into sexualized others, synecdoche of a supposedly effeminized orient, constructing her own authority to speak of scopic and aesthetic pleasure at their expense. More recently, noting the number of Turkish women who engage in dialogue with Montagu and the extent to which Montagu "presents her own shifting location as an object of inquiry," Mary Jo Kietzman has argued that Montagu preserves "the dynamism of her subjects" and makes interpretation "ongoing collaborative work," fashioning "a hybrid subjectivity through acts that transform by means of displacement or destabilization."[116]

There certainly were limits to Montagu's knowledge of Ottoman cultures she encountered. Moreover, she was eager to find in those encounters ammunition for battles in which she was already engaged. For example, she uses her meetings with Muslim scholars to reinforce her disdain for Roman Catholicism and her sympathy with deistic rational religion, insisting that whatever superstitious common people might believe, Muslim intellectuals and Christian intellectuals are both essentially deists. Nevertheless, her encounter with the Ottoman Empire prompts her to contemplate questions of religion, social organization, and sexuality in a broader context and at a more general level of analysis than those of most British writers who stayed at home. She escapes from narrow doctrinal disputes within Christianity to the philosophical consideration of religion itself that we see in early deists like John Toland and later in David Hume. From the perspective of Constantinople, she sees sexuality not simply as sinfulness or as irresistible natural desire but rather as part of the "economy of nature" subject to radically different expressions in different societies with different political and economic bases.[117] Montagu uses her reading, her observation, her unusual perspective as a woman, and her remarkable analytic power to challenge not only many of the existing western assumptions about the inhabitants of the Ottoman empire, but also many of the fundamental assumptions of her own English society.

ROWE: THE VOICE OF RELIGION AGAINST THE LIBERTINE

While the canonical work now most critically admired from this period is satiric and comic, it is important to remember that contemporaries were also pursuing soberer subjects and that religious writings continued to compel attention. As I observed in the previous two chapters, biblical paraphrase, eschatological poetry, moral poetry, devotional poetry, and hymns all attracted serious poets of the early eighteenth century, including Rowe. While we now remember Matthew Prior for his *vers de société*, his contemporaries were impressed with his long *Solomon, or the Vanity of the World* (1718); Rowe paid her tribute in "To Mr. Prior, On his Solomon." Rowe also explicitly admired Thomas Parnell's "A Night Piece on Death" and "A Hymn on Contentment" (1714), both well-known to readers in England and America for over one hundred years. Parnell's "Hymn" develops the seventeenth-century tradition of meditative poetry about retirement familiar in Philips and further developed in a more explicitly religious way by Rowe. Two major religious poets of the period important to Rowe were clergymen. Edward Young, a clergyman of the Church of England, was author of "A Poem on the Last Day" (1713), a *Paraphrase of Part of the Book of Job* (1719), and later *The Love of Fame* (1728) and *Night Thoughts* (1742–45). Isaac Watts, a learned Congregationalist minister, was famous as a hymnist ("When I Survey the Wond'rous Cross") and as the author of the elegant "The Day of Judgment: Attempted in English Sapphick" (1706) and *Horae Lyricae* (1706). In "To Mr. Watts, on his Poems sacred to Devotion," Rowe, as she does on several occasions, renounces pastoral for sacred poetry. She declares that Watts's poetry allows her to gain "Seraphic heights" and to feel "sacred transports." Rowe rejoices that Watts's poetry has had evangelical impact in missions abroad:

> With such a grateful harmony
> Thy numbers still prolong,
> And let remotest lands reply,
> And echo to thy song.[118]

The intellectual ambitiousness of Rowe's religious poetry should not be underestimated. For a woman to publish the biblical paraphrase of *The Song of Solomon* (as *Canticles*), of verses from *Exodus* and *Job*, and a series of poems on the attributes of God and the four last things (Death, Heaven, Hell, Judgment) was daring. As a religious poet, Rowe had some advantages in not being a clergyman obliged to uphold denominational orthodoxy. Since she was grounded in the Calvinist orthodoxy of the Independents and stayed within that sect, it is perhaps least surprising that she was fascinated with Pascal's Jansenism, yet she was also attracted to the Cambridge Neoplatonists, to the mysticism of Henry More, and to Quietism. Rowe was well aware of the logical contradictions between, on the one hand, Calvinist belief in human depravity after the fall, and, on the other, Platonic constructions of human nature as naturally good and of human reason as capable of discerning God. The ancient quarrel between St. Augustine and Pelagius, who denied original sin and was branded a heretic, echoed in late seventeenth-century theological debates between more Calvinist English Protestants, Anglicans and dissenters, who charged the Latitudinarians with Pelagianism. It also echoed in the quarrels between French Jansenists and the Jesuits, who they similarly accused of Pelagianism. Rowe's tact in negotiating these theological minefields ensured that her religious poetry appealed to a wide spectrum of Christian readers.

At the same time, Rowe's persistent Calvinist concern with sin and God's judgment of sinners gives her condemnation of vice a vigorous, eschatological edge. In "The Conflagration. An Ode" she imagines a Day of Judgment filled with stunning ecological, geological, and even astronomical catastrophe. Molten rock pours "in sulph'rous waves" from the center of the earth:

> And where
> Tall mountains stood, prodigious chasms appear.
> With wilder fury here
> The fierce materials outward rush,
> And where, ev'n now, a level plain was spread,
> Vast rocks and frowning steep erect their hideous head;
> From where dark entrails and livid torrents gush,
> And glowing cataracts spout:
> Like *Ætna* now the new *Volcano* roars,
> Unweildy stones, and burning crags throws out,
> With show'rs of sand, and seas of melted ores . . .
> Now mightier pangs the whole creation feels;
> Each planet from its shatter'd axis reels,
> And orbs immense on orbs immense drop down,
> Like scatt'ring leaves from off their branches blown.[119]

As the saved souls confront the conflagration with "a calm assurance," the damned plead in vain. Finally, "Opprest with shame, confusion and despair," howling, they sink through waves of molten lava, as "hell extends itself on ev'ry side."[120]

Rowe's "Upon the Death of her Husband" (1717) grapples with a theological dilemma posed by intense mourning. This affecting, touchingly plain elegy for a good man and a beloved husband begins with the usual invocation of the muses and graces of pastoral elegy. Quickly, however, in a move familiar in Finch's "To Mr. F. Now Earl of W," the speaker determines instead to follow only "the dictates of my heart."[121] The mourner experiences her position as problematic because she is forced to ask whether, given her religious faith, her grief is excessive. Even as she declares, "For all that knew his merit must confess / In grief for him there can be no excess," the reader is invited to consider that grief can be excessive and that the refusal to be consoled can be evidence of a failure to trust in the promises of the Lord to his faithful.[122] Her husband's virtues seem to instantiate virtue itself, to be like a Beatrice to her Dante, and thus to excuse adoration of him as not merely personal, but as love of Virtue itself:

> Practis'd by him, each virtue grew more bright,
> And shone with more than its own native light.

When the speaker turns from the more public character of her husband to his intimate character as her "lover" and her "tender husband," the problem of excess returns, this time as a question of whether her passion for him when he was alive – a virtuous man, but still only a creature – was excessive:

> Whate'er excess the fondest passion knew,
> I felt for thee, dear youth; my joys, my care
> My prayers themselves were thine, and only where
> Thou wast concern'd, my virtue was sincere.

This bold confession of what looks like a blasphemous love for a creature instead of the Creator is coupled with an expression of such dependency on her husband that, in his absence, her own self and virtue seem not to be authentic. The second verse paragraph of the elegy begins by raising the questions of why she should have loved so intensely and why heaven should have "dissolv'd the tie so soon," but quickly moves to intense images of hearing and seeing her husband when he was alive, and, finally, to dreadful images of him in his death throes.[123]

As Rowe knew, there was a long tradition of believers longing for the voice and sight of God in biblical and devotional poetry. These longings are major themes in *The Song of Solomon*, some of which she translated, and in her own original devotional poetry. Of her husband, she remembers:

> For he could talk – 'twas ecstasy to hear,
> 'Twas joy, 'twas harmony to ev'ry ear:
> Eternal musick dwelt upon his tongue,
> Soft and transporting as the muses song . . .
> I hear the lov'd, the melting accent still,
> And still the warm, the tender transport feel . . .[124]

Thus the Bride in *The Song of Solomon* exclaims: "The voice of my beloved! behold, he cometh leaping upon the mountains, skipping upon the hills . . . My beloved spake, and said unto me, Rise up, my love, my fair one, and come away."[125] In "Devout Soliloquy XXXVI," the speaker experiences euphoria in praising the Lord, but still longs for the sight of his countenance and the sound of his voice, a sound sweeter than the music of angels:

> Thy voice is music, harmony it self
> In its transporting charms – Ye golden harps
> Which angels tune, for ever silent lie;
> Let me but hear my Lord's sweet, gentle voice,
> Breathing celestial Solace to my soul,
> And peace ineffable, the peace of God.[126]

The degree to which Rowe's passion and longing for the beloved husband and her passion and longing for the beloved God could interpenetrate one another have had the power to disturb readers from Isaac Watts on. Yet, as the allegorical readings of *The Song of Solomon* in both the Hebrew and the Christian traditions indicate, and mystical poetry like that of Dante and St. John of the Cross shows, spiritual ardor has long been comprehended through experience and images of more thoroughly human longing.

In her religious poetry, though she does have some sense of divine presence in the natural world, Rowe generally understands herself to be separated from God so long as she lives; she thus longs more intensely for death as the necessary prelude to enjoying divine presence in heaven. Instead of a Platonic idea of the soul as simply immaterial, she returns again and again to a contrast between a worldly body that impedes the soul's contact with God and a transfigured, resurrected body that will finally enhance the soul's perception of God. In the Devout Soliloquies, her spiritual self-discipline is rigorous enough that she at one point can declare:

> Let God himself, to whom I dare appeal,
> Let God, my glorious judge, be witness here!
> Unfold my inmost soul, for thou shalt find
> No rival form, no image but thy own.[127]

Nevertheless, so long as she lives, the sense of separation is painful. It is particularly well expressed in "The Submission," which begins with the speaker's willingness to accept God's "terms" "however hard," acknowledges his justice, expresses her hope of adoring God in heaven, yet ends with a lament about separation:

> But oh! how long shall I thy absence mourn?
> When, when wilt thou, my sun, my life, return?
> Thou only can'st my drooping soul sustain
> Of nothing but thy distance I complain.[128]

In the most explicitly meditative poetry, notably the Devout Soliloquies, Rowe creates a poetic persona of the Christian actively seeking God, contemplating creation, sometimes troubled by doubts and weaknesses, yet offering her experience as model for other believers and articulating her praise of and trust in God. As Madeline Marshall observed, "the apparent privacy of any soliloquy is eminently public," and Rowe offers herself and was accepted by many readers as a spiritual guide.[129]

Rowe's ambitious long narrative poem, *A History of Joseph* (1736, 8 books; 1737, 10 books), uses biblical history to develop narratives of heroic chastity and to further the attack on libertinism. Her poem continues the line of English narrative and philosophical poems reimagining scripture inaugurated by Milton's *Paradise Lost*, and continued, for example, by Sir Richard Blackmore's *A Paraphrase on the Book of Job* (1700) and Matthew Prior's *Solomon, or the Vanity of the World* (1718). Recognizing that the usual subject of male epic was heroism in war, the poet of *Joseph* apparently cedes such traditionally high subjects to others, while at the same time deprecating the ungoverned passions typical of epic heroism as unworthy:

> Let others tell, of ancient conquests won,
> And mighty deeds, by favour'd heroes done;
> (Heroes enslav'd to pride, and wild desires,)
> A virgin Muse, a virgin theme requires;
> Where vice, and wanton beauty quit the field,
> And guilty loves to stedfast virtue yield.[130]

Rowe elaborates on and supplements the story of Joseph in Genesis, adding colorful detail from her reading in biblical and Near Eastern history and mythology. Apparently taking a hint from Milton, she opens her poem not in hell but in the hellish Temple of Molock where "wanton damsels" engage in "Detested Orgies" to pay tribute to pagan deities including Astarte, the goddess of fertility (Ashtreth in the Bible). Mithra, "whom all the *East* adores," hatches a plan designed to destroy the Hebrews by implanting a "mad desire" for Jacob's daughter Leah in Shechem in order to bring down the wrath of the Canaanites on Israel.[131] Throughout, the powers and spells of the pagan gods and their followers prove impotent against Joseph. The biblical narrative suggests several captivity narratives, including that of Jacob's daughter Dinah, made captive and raped by the Canaanite Shechem, and, of course, Joseph himself, whose jealous brothers sell him into captivity in Egypt. Additionally, Rowe interpolates into the biblical narrative the story of Semiramis, legendary founder of Babylon, which she adapted from Diodorus Siculus's first-century *Bibliotheca Historica*. Dropping the supernatural elements in Diodorus, she instead critiques pagan mythology and priestcraft.[132] Rowe preserves the episode of Semiramis's donning male armor to accompany her general husband to war, although she otherwise reduces Semiramis's participation in battles; she also alters her source by making Semiramis chaste.

In Joseph, Rowe finds a masculine hero whose resistance to unlawful love she can celebrate. She adds to the Genesis narrative by supplying him with the protection of the angel Gabriel, who links his chastity with the welfare of his nation, prophesying:

> A great and grateful nation yet unknown,
> Sav'd by thy care, shall thee their patron own;
> But let thy breast inpenetrable prove
> To wanton beauty, and forbidden love:
> This heav'n enjoins.[133]

As in Genesis 39, Potiphar, a captain of the Egyptian guards, buys Joseph. Potiphar's wife attempts to seduce Joseph, then, when he resists, charges him with rape, and has him jailed. The wife, called Sabrina by Rowe, resorts to charms and to astrology. When these fail to influence Joseph, she offers philosophical arguments about the naturalness of sexual desire more familiar from seventeenth-century libertine philosophy than from scripture. Sabrina upbraids a resisting Joseph for his fear of an avenging God:

> What God, alas! does cruelty command?
> Or human bliss maliciously withstand?
> Such thoughts as these the heav'nly powers arraign,
> Efface their goodness, and their justice stain.
> Would they the gen'rous principle controul,
> Who gave this am'rous byass to the soul?
> What nature is, they make it: nor can bind
> With servile laws the freedom of the mind . . .[134]

Rowe thus puts in a woman's mouth libertine arguments typically addressed by men to women or male characters to female characters. Once Joseph is jailed, the biblical narrative drops Potiphar's wife, but Rowe allows her to experience remorse and repentance and to confess her crime to Potiphar on her deathbed. By making chastity the virtue of a male hero, indeed, of a biblical patriarch understood to be a type of Christ, Rowe seeks to make it a serious virtue. Translated into German, *Joseph* influenced Johann Jacob Bodmer, the Swiss poet and literary critic who resisted French neo-classicism, and Friedrick Klopstock, the German poet now most famous for his lyrics but in his own time celebrated as the author of a biblical epic, *Messias* (1749f), also influenced by *Paradise Lost*.

Rowe's prose *Friendship in Death. In Twenty Letters from the Dead to the Living . . .* (1728) offers letters from the virtuous dead, happy in heaven, but concerned to communicate with still-living friends and relations. In the preface Rowe expresses concern that too many of her contemporaries are not firmly convinced of the immortality of their souls and hopes that her imaginative exercise might assist to make minds "familiar, with the Thoughts of our Future Existence, and contract, as it were, unawares, an

Habitual Persuasion of it, by Writings built on that Foundation, and address'd to the Affections and Imagination . . ."[135] The heavenly spirits are solicitous. One explains to a fearful living person, "There is not a Spark of Guilt or Malignity, left in virtuous Minds, when releas'd from their earthly Prison, all is gentle and kind, and their Concern for Human Welfare is more tender and disinterested than before."[136]

The letters are generally short, often addressed to situations contemporaries debated as moral dilemmas; they thus have perhaps more kinship with the periodical essay than with the novel proper, although their concern with problematic dilemmas and right responses links them to romance. Some have little narrative interest, concentrating on simple situations like that of the two-year-old son of a Countess who writes to rebuke his mother for her excessive grief and to console her with testimony of his enjoying greater happiness in heaven than he could ever have enjoyed on earth: "Instead of the thoughtless Thing you lately smil'd on and carres'd, I am now in the Perfection of my Being, in the Elevation of Reason: Instead of a little Extent of Land, and the Propriety of so much Space to breathe in, I tread the starry Pavement, make the Circuit of the Skies, and breathe the Air of Paradise."[137]

Other letters recall novelistic situations like those familiar from Manley, Aubin, and Haywood, but resolve the situations differently. Amintor has lost his life defending his love from Algerian Corsairs, who take him prisoner and make her slave to a pasha. He writes to assure her of his happiness in heaven, to tell her that the pasha is unlikely to use violence against her, but also to urge her not to resort to poison (and thus be guilty of the crime of murder) if he does. A father writes to his son who has sent a challenge for a duel, urging him to retract it:

What is the Vertue of this fine Lady, in defence of whom you are going with such Bravery to die? What is this Honour you are giving up your Life, and all your hopes of Salvation to maintain?

This guiltless lovely Woman, is only perjur'd to her Marriage Vows: this Angel, this divine Creature, does but deceive, does but expose to Infamy, the best of Husbands: she does but return his unequal'd Tenderness, and constant Affection to her, with artful Fondness, and dissembled complaisance . . .[138]

Throughout, Rowe attacks all the elements of libertinism, including the ideas of the amatory fiction of Behn, Manley, and Haywood that passion is irresistible, and that passionate, transgressive love is a sign of a superior nature. Instead, Rowe characterizes such passions as sordid, cruel (to others who have legitimate conjugal ties), and stupid (against the soul's long-term interest). Rowe's heroines, instead of succumbing to the temptations of passion, retire into the country, think about what they ought to do, meditate, and successfully resist. They anticipate Jane Austen's Elinor Dashwood in *Sense and Sensibility*, not Marianne. Considering both *Letters from the Dead to the Living* and their later companion *Letters Moral and Entertaining*, Richetti has called attention to Rowe's construction of an opposition between religion and infidelity, between belief in immorality and skepticism, and between dedication to conjugal love and cynical libertinism. This, he argues, is the key ideological matrix for the English novel, the matrix "in which Richardson's *Clarissa*, for example, may be said to achieve a heroism close to sainthood."[139]

CONCLUSION

The burgeoning commercial literary marketplace of this period, with its appetite for novelty and controversy, created opportunities for women writers, including Chandler, Centlivre, Rowe, Aubin, and Haywood. While Haywood continued the practice of Behn and Manley of grounding the authority of a woman writer in her superior knowledge of human love, Barber more originally developed her novel persona as a mother. As we shall see, the special authority of a woman writer as a mother was soon to be elaborated upon to produce new kinds of advice literature and children's literature. From this point on, it became possible for some women writers, like Chandler, to develop primarily as local, provincial celebrities, never becoming London writers. Unlike Chandler, but like Davys and Barber, such writers might be partially supported by local subscribers who underwrote the publication of their books. The more professional London writers, like Haywood and Aubin, developed Behn's career pattern of writing in various genres and using translation from the French for various purposes, including making relatively quick money, expanding the repertory of literary techniques and kinds, and engaging in the contemporary world of ideas. No other woman in this period was able to come close to Centlivre's exceptional success in the theatre, and, increasingly, women turned to fiction rather than to drama.

The dominance of satire encouraged women writers to develop their own critiques of masculine authority and emboldened them to ridicule forms of masculinity and individual men possessed of prestige and authority. The straightforward attacks of early eighteenth-century satirists like Thomas and Montagu on foppish beaus, foolish suitors, and wretched husbands led, mostly, not to more verse satire, but to more muted complaints in later women's fiction. The essential list of complaints, however, had been formulated. Satire also invited women to imagine punishments for men who, in the real society of the eighteenth century, could too often injure women with impunity. Thus, Davys can imagine Sir John Galliard scorched with firecrackers and infected with venereal disease. Although I do not see Haywood fundamentally as a satirist, some of her novels, like *The City Jilt*, invoke the satirist's pleasure in wreaking fantasy punishments on those who otherwise, as Pope said, "'scape the law."[140] Of equal importance, supported by the convictions of their class or their party or their learning, individual women stepped forward to ridicule prestigious individual men, as Montagu felt free to ridicule earlier male writers on the Ottoman Empire and Elstob felt free to ridicule Swift's ignorance of the history and nature of language.

In the 1730s, by the time of the passage of the Licensing Act and the death of Rowe, both in 1737, we see not only a persistent celebration of Philips as the type of the virtuous woman writer, but also some solidarity among women writers who attack what they see as the libertinism (male and female) of the dominant culture, defend religion, and insist that women are capable of morality, learning, and reasoning. Trotter, having married a Scottish clergyman, Patrick Cockburn, in 1708, no longer wrote plays, but published a *Vindication of Mr. Locke's Christian Principles* (1727) and, in *The Gentleman's Magazine*, a poem, "Verses, occasion'd by the Busts in the Queen's Hermitage . . . and Mr Duck being appointed Keeper of the Library in Merlin's Cave" (1737). Cockburn praised Queen Caroline for her patronage of Newton, Samuel Clarke (a theologian whose most important work was *A Discourse Concerning the Being and Attributes of God*, 1704–5), Locke, and Stephen Duck, yet wished that the Queen would extend her patronage to women, who have been denied learning and rewarded with infamy instead of fame when they attempt "exalted themes." Should the Queen champion Cockburn's philosophical writing, she suggested, then other women might be inspired to emulate her:

> The female world wou'd bid their toys farewell.
> T'approve themselves to thee, reform their taste:
> Nor all their time in trifling pleasures waste;
> In search of truths sublime undaunted soar,
> And the wide realms of science deep explore.[141]

This enthusiasm for virtue and piety did not entail a lack of curiosity or intellectual range and these writers certainly did not confine themselves to matters domestic.

Rowe's success as a writer of prose and verse, her militant Christianity, and her unblemished personal reputation made her an appealing model for other women writers. Her death in 1737 was widely mourned. Watts, complying with her wishes, revised and published her meditations as *Devout Exercises of the Heart* (1737). Rowe was a particularly important figure to the later bluestockings, who refer to her works in their letters. The most learned of the bluestockings, Elizabeth Carter, was twenty when Rowe died. Her elegy for Rowe constructed a history of women's writing as an earlier dark age of licentiousness and misogyny, of female wits enthralled by "Th'intriguing novel and the wanton tale," ended by the triumphant career of Rowe, who used her talents:

> From trifling follies to withdraw the mind,
> To relish pleasures of a nobler kind.[142]

While Rowe continued to be popular with serious readers, and Theophilus Rowe's posthumous publication of her *Works* prefaced by a laudatory biography helped keep her before the public, the strenuous intellectualism of an Elstob or a Montagu and the raucous satire of a Thomas or a Davys were about to give way to the more decorous virtues of the next generation of women writers. These women, I will argue in the next chapter, negotiated new places for themselves as members of a tamer "literary family."

CHAPTER 5

Women as members of the literary family, 1737–1756

TEXTS

1739–62 (written) Eliza Lucas Pinckney. *Letterbook*

1744 [Mary Collyer]. *Felicia to Charlotte. Being Letters from a Young Lady in the Country, to her Friend in Town* . . .

1744 [Sarah Fielding]. *The Adventures of David Simple: Containing An Account of his Travels Through the Cities of London and Westminster, In the Search of a Real Friend.* 2 volumes

1748 Mary Leapor. *Poems upon Several Occasions*

1748 (Dublin). Laetitia Pilkington. *The Memoirs of Mrs. Lætitia Pilkington, Wife to the Rev. Mr. Matth. Pilkington. Written by Herself* . . . 2 volumes

1748 *An Apology for the Conduct of Mrs. Teresia Constantia Phillips* . . . 3 vols.

1749 [Mary Collyer]. *Letters from Felicia to Charlotte. Volume the Second*

1749 Sarah Fielding. *The Governess: or, Little Female Academy, Being the History of Mrs. Teachum, and her Nine Girls, With their Nine Days Amusement: Calculated for the Entertainment and Instruction of Young Ladies in their Education*

1751 Mary Leapor. *Poems upon Several Occasions. By the Late Mrs. Leapor*

1751 [Frances Anne Holles Vane, Lady Vane]. "Memoirs of a Lady of Quality"

1752 [Charlotte Lennox]. *The Female Quixote; or, The Adventures of Arabella.* 2 volumes

1753 [Sarah Fielding]. *The Adventures of David Simple. Volume the Last, In which his History is Concluded*

1755 Charlotte Charke. *A Narrative of the Life of Mrs. Charlotte Charke: youngest Daughter of Colley Cibber, Esq., Written by Herself*

228

1756 [Eliza Haywood]. *The Wife. By Mira, one of the Authors of the Female Spectator, and Epistles for Ladies*
1756 [Eliza Haywood]. *The Husband. In Answer to the Wife*

INTRODUCTION

After the Licensing Act of 1737, the number of new plays by either men or women fell off significantly; at mid century, with the exception of women who were already actresses, women more rarely wrote for the theatre. Like Fielding after the Licensing Act, Eliza Haywood also abandoned the stage to write fiction. Haywood's turn away from the romance and scandal of her earlier fiction to the moral advice of her periodical *The Female Spectator* (1744–46), her conduct books, and her more moral novels, including *The Fortunate Foundlings* (1744) and *The History of Miss Betsy Thoughtless* (1751), is particularly clear evidence of the emergence of a new kind of popular women's writing designed to be less provoking and easier to accept.

Satire against women writers diminished and women writers who exemplified certain qualities were increasingly accepted as members of the literary family, albeit subordinate members. Several commentators, including Felicity Nussbaum, have noted a mid-century decline in overt misogyny.[1] Jane Spencer, in an important chapter, "The Terms of Acceptance," in *The Rise of the Woman Novelist: From Aphra Behn to Jane Austen*, argues that a group of mid-century women novelists escaped the hostility earlier directed at Behn, Manley, and Haywood, but did so only at the cost of exemplifying the supposedly "'feminine' qualities of delicacy and propriety."[2] The woman writer's eschewal of romance for more sober morality is also, as we will see, thematized in Charlotte Lennox's *Female Quixote* (1752). Moreover, Spencer points out, the mid-century "praise of the 'feminine' literary qualities was given in such a way to limit the women writers' acceptable scope, and often to imply that for all its virtues her work was weak."[3]

Although the literary history of women's poetry has been less studied than the history of the women's novel, a roughly similar shift to acceptability seems to have occurred, conveniently memorialized by the editorial tone and selections found in George Colman and Bonnell Thornton's *Poems by Eminent Ladies* (1755). John Duncombe's *Feminiad* (1754) also celebrated the union of female virtue and female literary talent. Duncombe rejects Behn, Manley, and Centlivre as "Vice's Friend's" and celebrates Philips, Finch, Trotter Cockburn, Carter, and Mary Leapor.[4] The most successful mid-century women's poetry is exemplified by the less religious, more amusing – although not immoral – verse of Mary Jones, admired by a number of recent commentators including Eric Rothstein, Roger Lonsdale, Margaret Doody, and Claudia Thomas.[5] Indeed, I would argue, the accomplishment of some of Finch's non-confrontational comic poems and of Lady Mary Wortley Montagu's *vers de société* may have helped a number of mid-century women poets to understand that polished and witty poetry in lighter veins might be perceived as suitably self-deprecating and not as a challenge to higher masculine ambitions.

What is particularly striking about this mid-century shift is the way women writers won acceptance by playing the roles of daughters, sisters, or wives to literary men. And they did so at the moment when the culture was celebrating the properly hierarchical family as the source of the highest human pleasure and the basis for right social order. At mid century, earlier hostility toward women writers modulated into ostensibly friendly correction and assistance. As we shall see in this chapter, women writers, amateur and professional, who were willing to develop suitable feminine personas were likely to be encouraged and praised. Through sometimes complex and tense negotiations with male mentors and patrons, both Sarah Fielding and Charlotte Lennox were able to establish significant literary careers and to produce well-received work in a variety of genres.

Moreover, women took advantage of and promoted the mid-century turn to the family itself as significant subject matter, claiming special authority on matters domestic, including not only relations between parents and children and husbands and wives, but also masters and servants. As the novel turned from the wide-ranging adventures of Defoe or Aubin to the sometimes claustrophobic domestic interiors of Richardson and to sentiment, Mary Collyer succeeded in using the epistolary form to show how conflicts between parents and children might be resolved and to portray an ideal husband and wife living a model domestic life. Sarah Fielding published the first long didactic story for children, *The Governess* (1749), inaugurating a long line of women who succeeded in writing children's literature. Haywood ventured into the realm of conduct literature with her companion volumes, *The Wife* (1756) and *The Husband* (1756). In a still humbler realm of nonfiction, we see the emergence of the first famous and wildly successful women writers on cookery and home economics, Elizabeth Moxon and Hannah Glasse.

On the other hand, a more defiant tradition of women's writing continued, particularly in new variations on the scandal chronicle earlier

made infamous by Manley and Haywood, but now taken up in autobiographical narratives by other women who had lost their own reputations
for chastity: Laetitia Pilkington, Teresia Constantia Phillips, Lady Vane,
and Charlotte Charke. The experiences of these writers challenged the
emerging ideology of the sentimental family as offering adequate love and
protection for women.

FAMILIAR LETTERS NOT INTENDED FOR PUBLICATION

Letters, as I have said, were a form in which women were actually encouraged to write. While a commercial bookseller like Curll might purchase the
letters of women notorious for sexual scandal, eminently respectable girls
and women were expected to write letters for a variety of private purposes.
Letters of news to distant family and friends were supposed to be, at least,
informative, and, at best, entertaining or affecting. Often, women were
expected to carry on correspondences that maintained and developed
relationships within the family and that cultivated appropriate networks
of "friends" (in the eighteenth-century sense of "those engaged in mutual
benevolence" and in patronage relationships). Committed amateur letter
writers might study the appropriate rhetorics of various sorts of letters at
school, in published collections like Philips's *Letters from Orinda to
Poliarchus* or in manuals like Richardson's *Letters Written to and for
Particular Friends, on the Most Important Occasions. Directing not only the
Requisite Style and Forms to be observed in Writing Familiar Letters; But
How to Think and Act Justly and Prudently, in the Common Concerns of
Human Life* (1741). Many such letters were merely instrumental and
have little interest for readers today who are not social historians.

Yet other private letters were written with care by women with talent,
and, sometimes, offer narratives of women's lives that seem fresher, more
original, and less restricted by emerging sentimental convention than
many contemporary novelistic narratives produced for the public market.
Frances Boscawen, later associated with the bluestockings, wrote early
letters in the 1740s and 50s to her husband who was serving as a naval
officer, taking careful note of her own abilities as an estate manager and a
parent.[6] Several critics have remarked, and I agree, that some mid-century
women's letters not intended for publication reveal more acute and
original intelligences than are apparent in the works of literature and
literary criticism they published. For example, in the case of Sarah Scott,
who published her first novel, *The History of Cornelia*, in 1750, and who
had a high reputation for piety, critics have noticed that the wit and satiric

humor characteristic of her still unpublished letters do not appear in her published fiction.[7] Occasionally, letters written by women with no apparent ambition for literary fame, letters intended to serve purposes within private circles of family and friends, construct epistolary personae more lively and intriguing than those of most of the heroines of novels in this period.

PINCKNEY'S *LETTERBOOK*

Eliza Lucas Pinckney (1722–93), born in the West Indies and educated for a few years in London, was one of the more intelligent and curious mid-century letter writers who wrote for her own family and friends. Selections from her letters were not printed until 1850, and the surviving *Letterbook* (1739–62), including summaries of some letters and full texts of others, did not appear until 1972. Letters, of course, are usually prompted by physical separation. The circumstances of Lucas Pinckney's colonial life made her separations from beloved members of her family protracted and difficult: her father, a British army officer, was stationed in Antigua while she was in the Carolinas on the family plantation; her brothers were being educated in England. Most wrenchingly, after her marriage to Charles Pinckney, a Carolina planter, and his death, she felt that she had to manage the Carolina plantations, keeping her daughter with her, but leaving her two young sons in England to complete their educations.

In the face of such geographical distances, Lucas Pinckney's letters are dedicated to promoting a common family vision of how to live worthy lives in the world and to maintaining close and affectionate family relationships. Still a teenager herself, as older sister to her fifteen-year-old brother George, just entered into the British army, she writes a long letter expressing her fear that he may succumb to the fashionable vice of religious skepticism. She attempts to buttress his belief in a version of rational Christianity with an argument drawn from Robert Boyle. Separations in this world are inevitable trials to be born patiently and with faith in the ultimate beneficence of God. Writing to her sickly younger brother Tom, who had apparently barely survived a serious illness, she says, "Surely one of the greatest – if not the very greatest – of human evils is the seperation of Dearest friends, but it is one that must certainly happen for as sure as we are born we must dye."[8] In her anguish over her husband's death after fourteen years of a happy marriage, she writes movingly from Carolina to her mother in Antigua to announce the death and her hope that, one day, the pain of these separations will end:

. . . the fatal day . . . deprived me of all my soul held dear and left me in a distress that no language can paint. For his Virtues and aimable quallities are deeply imprinted in my heart, his dear image is ever in my Eye, and the remembrance of his affection and tenderness to me must remain to my latest moment – a remembrance mingled with pleasure and Anguish. The remembrance of what he was sooths and comforts me for a time . . . This pleases while it pains and may be called the Luxury of grief . . . what anguish is in the reflection that these that were my greatest delights and blessings are taken from me for Ever in this world – for in the next I hope there is a Union of Virtuous souls where there is no more death, no more separation, but virtuous love and friendship to endure to Eternity![9]

What helps her recover from her grief is the "attention and activity" required to manage the Carolina plantations and her commitment to seeing her two young sons – who have to be told of their father's death in a letter – grow up to be men worthy of that father.[10]

For Lucas Pinckney, her family's Carolina plantations offered freedoms and opportunities for female self-development and service to society only imagined by Astell. She read Milton, Locke, Addison, Parnell, and Richardson, and happily took music lessons, much as a genteel woman in London might have done. But the novelty of her situation in the Carolinas arouses her intelligent curiosity about the natural world, which she studies as a naturalist, enjoys as ornamental, and – to use her word – "schemes" to make profitable. Her vision of her plantation anticipates, on a larger scale, the aesthetic *ferme ornée* later popularized by the poet William Shenstone. Reading Virgil's pastorals and georgics, she decides that "tho' he wrote in and for Italy, it will in many instances suit Carolina."[11] Promptly, she determines to plant a cedar grove: "I intend then to connect in my grove the solemnity (not the solidity) of summer or autumn with the cheerfulness and pleasures of spring, for it shall be filled with all kind of flowers, as well wild as Garden flowers, with seats of Camomoil, and here and there a fruit tree – oranges, nectrons, Plumbs, &, &."[12] She writes too of planting a large fig orchard with the intention of drying and exporting figs. Her "love" of the "vegitable world" and her enthusiasm for turning it to use earned her fame for importing indigo seed from the Caribbean, experimenting successfully with its cultivation in Carolina, distributing seeds to fellow planters, and, eventually, turning it into a successful export crop.[13]

A true Briton, Lucas Pinckney felt a special fondness for the oak. Like Pope's at the end of *Windsor-Forest*, her heart leapt up at the idea of trees (turned into ships) leaving their forests to rush into waters bearing

"*Britain's* Thunder . . . / To the bright Regions of the rising Day."[14] Unlike Pope, she had access to enough land to plant her own forest: "I am making a large plantation of Oaks which I look upon as my own property, whether my father gives me the land or not; and therefore I design many years hence when oaks are more valueable than they are now – which you know they will be when we come to build fleets."[15] (Her editor notes that Carolina live oak was especially valued in shipbuilding.) As a widow of fifty, Lucas Pinckney declares: "Being a sort of anthusiaste in my Veneration for fine trees, I look upon the destroyers of Pyrford Avenue as sacrilidgious Enemies to posterity, and upon an old oak with the reverencial Esteem of a Druid."[16]

Like most eighteenth-century letter writers, Lucas Pinckney was well aware that letters might be read aloud to circles of friends and that they could be treasured for their news value. Her own letters offer notable vignettes of Carolina plantation life, as well as news of the fortunes of war on her frontier of the growing empire. The still "untamed" Cherokee Indians appear in Lucas Pinckney's letters like the New England Indians in Rowlandson's captivity narrative, as terrifying savages. Her privileged access to news of political and historical importance and news of colonial novelties is something of value she has to offer to English friends in exchange not only for the English news she values, but, more importantly, in exchange for the care those English friends take to look out for the interests of her family, especially the care they take in helping to superintend the education of her two sons at school in England.

To some extent, the rise of newspapers and magazines during the century had a chilling effect on letter writers' commitment to offering narrations of news. While the Stamp Act and costs of postage kept newspapers generally down to four, or less often, six, sheets, printers learned to cram more news into each issue by using larger sheets and smaller type. The number of provincial newspapers increased dramatically. Annual newspaper sales in England have been estimated at 2.5 million in 1715, rising to 7.3 million in 1750 and to 10.7 million by 1756.[17] Henry Fielding, not a very interesting letter writer – indeed, one who seems to have felt that if he were going to work at writing entertaining narratives he might as well do it for the booksellers – writes to a friend in the tense days of the Young Pretender's invasion of England in 1745: "For news I recommend y^o to the public Papers with wch I doubt not y^o are supply^d, at the same time y^o receive this . . ."[18]

Unlike Fielding, an amateur letter writer like Lucas Pinckney was unlikely to feel she was wasting time writing news to friends, yet awareness of the rival narratives available in newspapers could still sometimes inhibit correspondents. Frances Boscawen sometimes comments on news, but several times also refers to dispatching bundles of newspapers to her husband along with her own letters. Lucas Pinckney's accounts of the colonists' struggles with the Cherokee, for instance, are intriguing but frustratingly brief. It does not occur to her that the Cherokee have any right to defend their land; her accounts mainly reflect her pride in British military prowess:

> Gov. Lyttleton with our army are safely returned from their Cherokee Exped-ition, where they went to demand satisfaction for the murders committed on our people – the first Army that ever attempted to go into that wild Country. They had been very insolent and committed several Murders and Outrages in our back settlements, nor ever expected white men would have resolution to march up their Mountains. Mr. Lyttleton has acted with great spirit and conduct and gained much honour in the affair, and obtained from them what Indians never before granted: such of the murderers as they could then take and Hostages for the rest till they could be taken. If you have any curiosity to know more particulars Mrs Morley to whom I inclose it can furnish you with the Carolina Gazett.[19]

She doubts that the "barbarian" Cherokee could pose such serious chal-lenges to the Carolina settlers were it not for the fact that the French were assisting them with arms and ammunition. Inconsistently, perhaps, she is quite happy to admire the fighting prowess of the "Mohocks," northern native Americans the British import to Carolina to fight as mercenaries on their side: "for the Mohocks are very fine men . . . and they are looked upon by the rest of the Indians with both dread and respect for they think them the greatest warriors in the world."[20] Apparently without ambition to publish any of her letters, Lucas Pinckney left a lively record of the mind and experiences of an intelligent woman on one of the many challenging margins of the growing British empire at mid century.

NOVELS

In part because letter writing was such a sanctioned activity for women, women novelists often found the letter form accessible. While many of the earlier epistolary fictions were amatory (for example, the influential *Lettres portugaise* [1669] or Behn's *Love Letters Between a Nobleman and his Sister*), later epistolary fiction, including Rowe's *Friendship in Death* and *Letters Moral and Entertaining* and Richardson's *Pamela* (part 1, 1740; part 2, 1741) and *Clarissa* (1747–48) powerfully demonstrated that episto-larity might be used in the service of virtue. Inspired to some extent by

Rowe and Aubin, as well as by Richardson, spiritual autobiographies, and contemporary theology and moral philosophy, English fiction of the 1740s and 1750s was much concerned with the problem of how to be virtuous in a contemporary world of real evils. Many fictions purported to be authentic memoirs or historical biographies of contemporary people, high and low, catering to a desire for topicality, contemporary relevance, and empiricism. Short tales and frame narratives were still published, but the new novel was generally, if tentatively, becoming longer and more ambitious.

French fiction continued to be an important influence on English fiction. After 1737, however, the influence of the French romances and *nouvelles* was supplanted by the influence of later French writers, including Prévost, Crébillon, and Marivaux. As fiction became a more important genre in this period, more women published novels; a good many of them also published translations from French fiction. For women writers, these translations served as convenient ways to add to their incomes by satisfying public demand for fashionable French fiction; although they were typically not lavishly rewarded, translations could usually be completed more quickly than original works. Translation also afforded women literary education that they could apply to their own original work. Thus, Mary Collyer began her literary career in 1742 by publishing her important translation of Marivaux's *La Vie de Marianne, ou les avantures de Madame la comtesse ---* (1731), entitled *The Virtuous Orphan or, the Life of Marianne, Countess of ·····*. Marivaux's novel significantly influenced novelists of sentiment and novelists of manners, including Collyer herself, Laurence Sterne, and Frances Burney.[21] Haywood's translation of Marivaux's *Le Paysanne parvenue* (1735–37) as *The Virtuous Villager; or Virgin's Victory* (1742) no doubt assisted her in writing her own more sentimental fiction, especially *The Fortunate Foundlings* (1744) and *The History of Jenny and Jessamy* (1753). The latter also shares some elements with Prévost's *Memoires et avantures d'un homme de qualité* (1728–31), which she translated as *Memoirs of a Man of Honour* (1747). Besides Collyer, two other novelists who began their careers in this period, Charlotte Lennox with *The Life of Harriot Stuart* and Sarah Scott with *The History of Cornelia*, both published in 1750, also translated French fiction, although fiction of less distinguished writers.[22]

COLLYER'S *FELICIA TO CHARLOTTE*

One of the most interesting of the epistolary novels of the 1740s or 1750s is Mary Collyer's *Felicia to Charlotte. Being Letters from a Young Lady in the*

Country, to her Friend in Town . . . chiefly tending to prove, that the Seeds of Virtue are implanted in the Mind of Every reasonable being (1744) and *Letters from Felicia to Charlotte. Volume the Second . . .* (1749). Collyer's husband Joseph was a London printer and translator from the German. He published her translation of Marivaux's *La Vie de Marianne* and the first volume of her original novel, *Felicia to Charlotte*. This is a novel of ideas, linking some of the aspirations of writers like Astell and others I described in chapter two as belonging to "the party of virtue" to those of the later bluestockings and aiming to reimagine the amatory novel as the novel of sensibility.

In the first volume of *Felicia to Charlotte*, the intelligent and high-minded Felicia describes, in a series of letters to her friend in London, her romance with Lucius, a virtuous and philosophical young man. The only obstacle to their union is her father's objection to her marrying a man with a fortune smaller than her own. In the second volume, Felicia and Lucius are married and devote themselves to constructing a satisfying domestic life, one that promotes their own happiness and the happiness and virtue of others in their community. Collyer self-consciously rejects the novel of intrigue; her virtuous protagonists all place a very high value on openness and candor. Repeatedly, in *Felicia to Charlotte*, situations that in the novel of intrigue or even in comedy or tragedy would drive a plot by creating misprision are quickly resolved. In this novel characters have some confidence in the goodness of other characters; apparent evidence to the contrary, instead of sending them into fits of jealousy or rage, leads them to make prompt, direct inquiries of the persons concerned, and quickly clears up misunderstandings. Both explicit discussions and plot events advance the idea that events and appearances may be misleading. Collyer values psychology over plot events, so true understanding requires appreciation of another's intentions.

In contrast to the rakish heroes of Restoration comedy and amatory fiction, Lucius is a new kind of masculine hero, an early example of the man who is desirable because of his virtue and his sensibility. Felicia begins to love him, not when she sees him, but when, walking in the countryside, she overhears him, unseen, soliloquizing about the beauties of nature and "the bounteous author of all goodness who thus distributes his favours to men, and thus teaches us to concur with him in promoting the universal good."[23] Repudiating the convention of love at first sight dear to amatory fiction, Collyer has Felicia write to Charlotte as she recounts this episode, ". . . I shall forbear giving a description of his person, till I can give you that of his mind, and that must not be till

I know him better . . ."[24] Among Lucius's other charms, from Felicia's point of view, is his avoidance of conventional flattery of women; "He is too good a christian to deify his mistress," she notes, "and has too good an opinion of me to think I should be pleased with such senseless homages."[25] She finds his silent looks of tenderness or joy more authentic evidence of his feelings than "flattering phrases" would be. More intellectual than Richardson's later virtuous Sir Charles Grandison, Lucius argues explicitly against Calvinist ideas of innate human depravity and for the existence of a moral sense.

Pointing out that "virtue and vice have names in all languages," Lucius defines the moral sense as "that distinguishing faculty of the mind which makes us *feel*, – sensibly and strongly feel, – the harmony and discord of actions. It is the *touch*, the *ear* of the soul; while reason is the *eye* to regulate the exertions of this sympathetic faculty."[26] Lucius thus aligns himself with the arguments of Anthony Ashley Cooper, the third Earl of Shaftesbury, in *An Enquiry Concerning Virtue and Merit* (1699) – subsequently volume two of the more famous *Characteristics of Men, Morals, Opinions, Times* (3 volumes, 1711) – and Frances Hutcheson in *An Inquiry into the Original of our Ideas of Beauty and Virtue* (1725) and *An Essay on the Nature and Conduct of the Passions and Affections with Illustrations upon the Moral Sense* (1725). These philosophers were, in part, heirs to the Cambridge Platonists who inspired the party of virtue in the 1690s. They were, however, more secular. Inspired by Locke's epistemology, they sought to show that individuals could have an adequate knowledge of ethical principles grounded in their own experience, independent of external authority. Their insistence that feeling has a crucial role in morality and moral discourse was philosophically significant; it was also key to the emphasis on feeling in the literature of sensibility.

Lucius and Felicia both excel in filial piety and, in the second volume, become devoted parents. Dramatic demonstrations of filial piety and family affection become hallmarks of sentimental drama and fiction. Although Felicia does correspond with Lucius knowing that her father will probably disapprove of him – female behavior that in conventional epistolary fiction would make her a victim of seduction – she is confident that he will not take advantage of her and firm in her resolve not to marry without her father's approval. Her resolve is based more on feelings of love and gratitude to her father than on an abstract sense of duty. When her father discovers the courtship and is outraged, Lucius meets him to declare, "I have never presum'd to harbour a thought of obtaining your daughter without your consent; I love her too tenderly to injure you, or to think of depriving her of your affection, by persuading her to forget her duty."[27]

Lucius's extreme demonstrations of filial piety resolve the plot in the first volume. His own father has ruined his estate through libertinism and extravagance. As this father is about to be confined in a debtor's prison, endangering not only his own welfare but also that of Lucius's mother and sister, Lucius sacrifices £3,000 of his own small fortune to save him. Apparently, he thus ruins his chance at marriage with Felicia should her father discover this. Scorning to conceal his misfortune, however, Lucius candidly discloses his loss of the money to Felicia's father and renounces his pretensions to her. The spectacle of such virtue so affects her father, who has become less mercenary, that he exclaims, "Generous youth . . . I shall think myself happy in being allied to a person of such worth . . . Actions like these . . . spread a lustre that can never be equal'd by all the pride of wealth."[28] Throughout the novel, the spectacle of virtuous action and benevolence, as well as the force of rational argument, have the power to improve the characters of others who have been weak and thoughtless. Collyer thus reinvents older romance as bourgeois sentiment. Instead of noble birth being the essential ground of heroism, the new ground is the capacity for virtuous feeling and action, a capacity conceivably present in ordinary people.

In so far as *Felicia to Charlotte* has a villain or villainess, she is Prudella, an older woman in whom the predatory female sexuality of heroic drama or amatory fiction becomes comic and grotesque. Prudella first appears as a scandalmonger convinced of the truth of Calvinist theology. When the more progressive characters praise Locke and talk of the naturalness of the moral sense and the social affections, she reminds them that this philosophy challenges the orthodox Christian doctrine of original sin. In fact, many theologically orthodox contemporaries considered the moral philosophies of Shaftesbury, Hutcheson, and Hume guilty of the Pelagian heresy. Felicia, however, finds it incredible that God could be so "false, malevolent, and cruel" as to predestine many to damnation. She laments that some clergy "declaim against morality"; so long as they do, "such gloomy representations of religion . . . must needs corrupt the minds of the multitude, and fix the strongest prejudices against every thing sacred; make our duty looked upon as a burthern; and the most pleasing exercises of grateful piety, regarded as an irksome drudgery."[29] For a reason that at first seems obscure, Prudella tries to destroy the romance between Felicia and Lucius by writing an anonymous letter to Felicia's father revealing that she is keeping company with a man of unequal fortune and implying that she has lost her chastity. This behavior contrasts sharply with the behavior of Felicia's aunt, her cousin Amelia, and Lucius's sister Marilla, all of whom are notably sympathetic to and supportive of one another. While Felicia's father credits the letter and responds with rage, her aunt immediately believes Felicia's protestations of innocence and helps to unravel the mystery. Prudella, it surprisingly appears, lusted after Lucius herself.

The second volume of *Felicia to Charlotte* represents a model domestic life in which the reader sees husband and wife continue their consideration of various contemporary theological and philosophical issues, as well as discuss and solve many of the dilemmas aired by writers of conduct books. Felicia buttresses her insistence on the naturalness of virtue with a long quotation from Henry Coventry's *Philemon to Hydaspes. Relating a conversation to Hortensius: upon the subject of False Religion, Part* II. *In which is asserted the general lawfulness of pleasure; and the extravagant severities of some religious systems are shown to be a direct contradiction to the natural appointment and constitution of things* (1737). Lucius, given an estate by Felicia's father, devotes himself to managing it well, ascertaining the characters of his tenants, and benevolently assisting the virtuous farmers who, through no fault of their own, have suffered losses from agricultural disasters. Felicia agrees to his proposal for family prayer twice a day, delights in managing her household, and joins in acts of local charity. Since Lucius and Felicia are themselves relentlessly rational and benevolent, some drama is provided by the misguided behavior and distresses of relatives, tenants, servants, and acquaintances whom they reform and assist. For instance, one of their maidservants, Dorothea, is observed crying when she thinks she is unobserved and seems to have stolen a valuable gold snuffbox. Investigation reveals that she is also in possession of a crucifix set with diamonds and a mass book in Latin and English. Daughter of a Roman Catholic mother and a Protestant father, she has fled her home after her mother's death when her father refused to let her practice her Catholicism; she has stolen nothing. In Collyer's novel, this becomes an occasion for observing how "prejudice" once awakened "changes the color of objects, and shapes them to our fancy" and for discussing the truth of Locke's arguments in the *Letter on Toleration* in favor of religious liberty being the "birthright of every reasonable being."[30] Lucius and Felicia permit Dorothea to practice her religion, reconcile her with her father, and convince her that she should use her reason and study to discern truth from error. In time, "mildness and freedom" accomplish "what severity and restraint" could not, and Dorothea becomes a Protestant.[31]

Collyer pays attention to issues involving children. In the first volume, Felicia's aunt cites her own "experience" as a mother as evidence against that "natural turpitude which is the subject of so many pompous harangues . . ."[32] Once Felicia has a son, instead of sending him to a wet nurse, she agrees that a mother's nursing her child herself is "one of the indispensible obligations of nature."[33] The obligation of a mother to nurse her own child and the pleasures to be derived from maternal nursing are increasingly insisted on in the literature of sensibility. Husband and wife devote themselves to reading "the best authors" on education, including Locke. They agree on the desirability of having a children's book that would "dress up morality, and the sublimest truths of natural religion, in the easy language of infancy, and by degrees to pour in more and more light as the understanding enlarges."[34] A footnote informs the reader that such a book already exists, the *Christmas Box*, a collection of moral stories for children. The note does not mention that Collyer herself published this book in 1748–49.

Whereas in the amorous novel female beauty incites male admiration, in sentimental fiction a wife's virtuous, altruistic behavior evokes her husband's admiration and love. Felicia, it turns out, surprisingly, in an interesting if awkward and perhaps risible turn of the novel, has an illegitimate stepdaughter. Behavior toward stepchildren becomes a touchstone of sentimental virtue. Prudella, dying of consumption, reappears in the second volume to confess that, unbeknownst to Lucius, she has had intercourse with him and born his child. While Lucius was sleeping, she came to his bed, and he awoke and had intercourse with her; she left, leaving behind a token of one of the housemaids. Like one of Haywood's heroines, Lucius in an ambiguous state of consciousness has been ravished, though Prudella's brother makes it clear that a man cannot "Get a child in his sleep!"[35] Lucius is ashamed of himself and repentant, but here the emphasis is on what to do about the child. Conduct-book writers generally agreed that stepchildren provoked domestic discord. Haywood in her conduct book advises that stepchildren be sent out of the house immediately after their parent's remarriage least they make false insinuations; they should not go to relatives, but to strangers competent to educate them. Nevertheless, like Richardson's *Pamela* confronted with a similar situation, Felicia determines to love the child and care for her for Lucius's sake, conduct that, since he feels paternal affection for his daughter, inspires him with "the highest admiration and gratitude."[36]

Collyer was a more ambitious writer than the early reception of her novel acknowledged; indeed, although favorable, the review in *The*

Monthly Review already demonstrates what was to become the standard reviewers' approach to women's fiction. *The Monthly Review* was founded by Ralph Griffiths in 1749. (Its important rival as a judge of belles lettres, *The Critical Review*, was not founded until 1756, and hence did not pronounce on *Felica to Charlotte*.) Both magazines consisted primarily of substantial summaries and evaluations of serious books, including books of poetry, philosophy, criticism and translation of classical and modern literature, theology and biblical criticism, political works, and history and memoirs. Thus, the first issues of *The Monthly Review* feature long articles on Henry Grove's *System of Moral Philosophy*, Montesquieu's *Sprit of the Laws*, and Gilbert West's translation of Pindar. With some exceptions, notably *Tom Jones* in the 1740s, reviews normally noticed novels only very briefly at the back of each issue, along with topical pamphlets. *The Monthly Review*'s brief notice of *Felicia to Charlotte* relegates Collyer's book to a realm imagined as populated by female readers who are not interested in the serious books attended to in the body of the magazine. Yet, as I have indicated, Collyer's book engaged the serious philosophical issues of the day; in her later career, she translated from the German Salomon Gessner's *The Death of Abel* (1761) and part of Friedrick Klopstock's *Messiah* (the latter interrupted by her death in 1763 and completed by her husband). The reviewer finds the second volume of *Felicia to Charlotte* "not inferior to the first," predicts that it will be "as well received" as that volume, which met with "so favourable a reception from the public": "But we forbear entering into more particulars concerning a work that is more peculiarly calculated for the ladies than [for] the majority of our readers."[37] A similarly brief notice of Mrs. Hooper's Haymarket entertainment, *Queen Tragedy Restor'd* (1749), demonstrates the explicit double standard by which most reviewers decided to evaluate women's writing: "the piece is not without humour enough to do honour to a female pen, notwithstanding some inaccuracies and little faults, which the good-natured and generous will not look upon with too severe an eye."[38] In a study of the reviews and literary careers, Frank Donoghue concludes that from 1749 until the late 1780s, the reviewers consistently granted women writers "critical lenity but not more enthusiastic praise" and that they "indiscriminately rendered all women's writing, regardless of specific merits or weaknesses, as second-rate."[39] As we shall see, although reviewers were generally indulgent, indeed, frequently gallant or chivalric, toward women writers, this was typically so only as long as reviewers could construe what women wrote as suitably feminine.

A GENDERED DIVISION OF LITERARY LABOR

Although there was significant overlap between the kinds of writing done by men and those done by women in this period, we begin to see a more pronounced gendered division of literary labor. Admittedly, such generalization must be cautiously made because a very large number of works were published anonymously and, in many cases, we still do not know who wrote them or whether they were written by a man or a woman. And we do know that the practice of writers of one sex masquerading as writers of the other continued. Haywood wrote as a man in her Jacobite pamphlet, *A Letter from H— G—, Esq.* (1750), although authorities pierced her disguise, detained her for a few weeks, and destroyed the copies. The Reverend Archibald Arbuthnot, writing as the mistress of the Pretender, composed the anti-Jacobite *Memoirs of Miss Jenny Cameron* (1746). John Hill was the author of *The Conduct of a Married Life. Laid down in a Series of Letters, written by the Hon. Juliana-Susannah Seymour, to a Young Lady, her Relation, Lately Married* (1753). Christopher Smart conducted his serial, *The Midwife*, as Mother Midnight. (The adoption of female pseudonyms by male authors – when they are not simply parodic or ironic – suggests that the female point of view had acquired a market value.) Nevertheless, as far as we can identify authors, certain important kinds of contemporary writing were predominantly masculine, whereas other kinds of writing were either imagined to be especially suitable to women or were being developed by women as female specialties.

Both serious theological writing and more secular enlightenment philosophy, like that of David Hume, the most important writer of philosophical treatises and essays in this period, were masculine provinces. Questions about the nature of human nature, about whether humans were born depraved or born with intrinsic capacities and desires for virtuous action, were widely debated not only by philosophers but also, as Collyer's *Felicia to Charlotte* suggests, in drawing rooms. Yet Catharine Trotter Cockburn, born in 1679, seems to have been the only woman in this period writing serious philosophical prose dealing with philosophical issues; when she died in 1749 she had no apparent female successor.[40] Nor did women poets publish the ambitious, long, philosophical, and didactic poems characteristic of this period, the finest examples of which are Edward Young's *The Complaint; or, Night-Thoughts on Life, Death, and Immortality* (1742–46) and Mark Aikenside's *The Pleasures of the Imagination* (1744).

Historical writing was another masculine province, increasingly so with the rise of parliamentary politics and philosophical history. Classical history and biography, like Conyers Middleton's *History of the Life of Marcus Tullius Cicero* (1741), required the classical education normally possessed only by elite men. Sarah Fielding, who had more classical learning than all but a few other women, tried an experiment with fictionalized classical biography in *The Lives of Cleopatra and Octavia* (1757), pairing an imagined letter from Cleopatra from the shades below with one from Octavia. Her characters, however, are too simplistically opposed to one another to arouse much interest as psychological studies and the work also lacks the interest in critical historiography of a book like Middleton's.[41] The public continued to be interested in courtiers' and statesmen's memoirs. Although discretion saw to it that neither was published until the next century, the two best memoirs written in this period were *Memoirs of the Reign of King George II* of the courtier, John Hervey, Baron Hervey of Ickworth, Montagu's friend, and *Memoirs of the Reign of George II* of Horace Walpole, son of the Prime Minister and himself Member of Parliament. Men had an advantage as historical writers in their access to experience of political and military affairs. The only women's court memoir published in this period, Sarah, the Duchess of Marlborough's *An Account of the Conduct of the Dowager Duchess of Marlborough From her first coming to Court in the Year 1710* (1742), looks back to the second decade of the century. This features the complex story of the relations between the Duchess and Queen Anne as Lady Masham displaced the Duchess as the Queen's favorite.[42] Once Parliament and the political parties gained power at the expense of the King and the court, the significance of the courtier point of view also diminished. Moreover, as the philosophical history of Voltaire increasingly supplanted the memoirs and chronicles of the late seventeenth century, women were encouraged to read history as a source of moral edification but not to write it.

Books of travel and adventure were a third masculine province. Although perhaps less intrinsically forbidding to women writers than philosophy or history since they required less formal education or knowledge of public affairs, the significant books of travel and adventure of this period, like George Anson's *Voyage Round the World* (1748) were written by male travelers.[43] A few women novelists, however, are alert to the topical appeal of contemporary travel. Lennox, who was in New York as a girl, includes New York scenes and encounters with Mohawk Indians and Spanish privateers in her first novel, *The Life of Harriot Stuart* (1750). A fourth, more markedly subliterary popular genre, the criminal

biography, also – as far as we know, since many of these were anonymous –
seems to have been a masculine province.

Some women did translate men's works of philosophy, history, and
travel, evidence both of the attraction of these works to the reading public,
and of the interest of at least some women in these important enlightenment forms. Both men and women, of course, translated nonfiction
prose, yet such translation, I think, had special importance for women.
To translate seemed less presuming than to write an original work, more
consonant with emerging ideas of proper femininity. At the same time, as
the parameters of what kind of writing was appropriate for women began
to narrow, translation was a significant way that women could demonstrate at least their understanding of intellectual provinces from which the
culture was trying to exclude them. As a narrower domestic sphere was
marked out as the only one appropriate for women, women could escape
merely domestic confines in translation. Elizabeth Carter translated *An
Examination of Mr. Pope's Essay on Man* (1739) from the Swiss philosopher
J. P. Crousaz's French; she also published *Sir Isaac Newton's Philosophy
Explained, for the use of the Ladies* (1739) from Algarotti's Italian. Her
letters, unpublished in her lifetime, and her translation of Epictetus,
which I will discuss in the next chapter, demonstrate her continuing
interest in theology and philosophy, but she did not attempt an original
philosophical work. Charlotte Lennox is now remembered principally as a
novelist, author of *The Female Quixote* (1752), but she also translated
nonfiction from French. Contemporaries paid more attention to her
translation of *Memoirs of Maximillian de Bethune, Duke of Sully, Prime
Minister to Henry the Great. Containing the History of the Life and Reign of
that Monarch* (1755, 3 vols.) than to any other work of hers.[44] Sully (1560–
1641) fought in the Protestant army in the French civil wars, then served
Henry IV as a minister who improved the finances and administration of
the French state, encouraged agriculture, promoted public works, and
helped put down insurrections of the nobles. His memoirs, edited and
rewritten in 1745 by the Abbé de l'Élose, are an important source of
French history. Carter had already read Sully's book in French, writing
in 1751 to her friend Catharine Talbot to recommend it as "extremely
worth reading. I know none that shews one the world in a more entertaining and instructive manner, and numberless are the reflections that
every page suggests to me."[45] Lennox translated a number of serious
nonfictional works from French, but, as Carter did not attempt an
original work of philosophy, so Lennox did not attempt an original work
of history.

Both men and women wrote conduct and advice books, but women were making a bid to claim special relevant experience in books of advice to women about how to conduct themselves and how to manage their families and books about or for children. Male writers certainly did not abandon their sense of entitlement to instruct women on how to conduct themselves; for the clergy, in fact, this was part of their professional duty. Yet women writers increasingly took advantage of the culture's growing belief that subjective experience could be a ground of authority to claim special understanding and knowledge relevant to women's lives. Britain's increasing wealth and the increasing reading public also permitted a larger literary market where there was more room for the development of special audiences.[46] Haywood founded and edited a monthly, *The Female Spectator* (1744–46), described as "the first English periodical written by women for women."[47] Haywood's persona, "Mira," described herself as a sister to Addison's Mr. Spectator. Frances More Brooke followed with her essay periodical, *The Old Maid* (1755–56), her first publication; she made her persona "Mary Singleton," an older, unmarried woman. Haywood also published three conduct books on the duties of various members of the eighteenth-century family: *A Present for a Servant-Maid* (1743) – servants were crucial parts of all but poor families and domestic service was a major occupational category – *The Wife* (1755), and *The Husband* (1756).

Haywood was right to think that dispensing advice about domestic life was going to be one of the provinces in which women's writing would be accepted. Later women writers avoided presuming to dispense advice for husbands. Elizabeth Moxon, Penelope Bradshaw, and, with spectacular success, Hannah Glasse cultivated the pragmatic, subliterary realm of cook books and books of household management. Humble as these works were, they prepared the way for some nineteenth- and twentieth-century women writers on domestic economy like the American Lydia Maria Child (1802–80), who succeeded in combining the pragmatic advice of her *The Frugal Housewife* (1829) with a broad program of social reform and the writing of women's history.

HAYWOOD'S CONDUCT BOOKS: *THE WIFE* AND *THE HUSBAND*

Like the original *Spectator* of Addison and Steele, Haywood's periodical and conduct books of this period mingle abstract advice with short narratives designed to illustrate the advice; the narratives are usually said to be true stories, sometimes of events directly witnessed by the writer, but they are probably often invented fictions. Haywood's *The Wife* and *The Husband* address many issues of proper conduct in family life that were much discussed in the period; contemporary novels also frequently consider these issues. For instance, to what degree a wife should appear at public amusements was much debated. Like other writers of conduct books who were also playwrights, Haywood argues for the legitimacy of women's attending the theatre, despite worries of some other moralists. Indeed, she claims that seeing "those propensities which we feel within ourselves lively represented in the actions of another" on the stage in the sentimental comedy of Cibber will have a more efficacious moral effect than "some discourses from the pulpit."[48] She also defends attendance at oratorios (this was the period of Handel's great oratorios), but attacks the farces at the Haymarket Theatre (where she formerly worked), ridottos and masquerades (a *bête noire* of almost every moralist), and the pleasure gardens at Vauxhall and Ranelagh (the latter opened in 1742). *The Wife* instructs that a woman must love her husband most and not be "over-fond" of other creatures newly bidding to be seen as members of the family: pets. "Of late years," Haywood laments, "a fondness for the brute creation" has "become so general, that a monkey, a dog, a squirrel, a dormouse, or a squawling paroquet, are almost always part of the appendages of a fine lady."[49]

   Like other mid-century conduct books, *The Wife* takes a pessimistic view of marriage, especially of the likelihood that husbands will have adulterous affairs and that their wives will consequently suffer. Most secular writers, including Haywood, advise a wife who discovers her husband's unfaithfulness to avoid reproaches and anger and to try to make herself and her home greater sources of pleasure than any rival mistress could offer: she "must endeavour" to get "often to her house, the most witty, gay, and spirituous of her acquaintance, who will sing, dance, tell pleasant stories, and take all the freedoms that innocence allows . . ."[50] More than most, Haywood recommends stratagems and concealment to both spouses. Not only should the wife with an unfaithful husband "conceal the agonies of a bleeding breaking heart beneath a face of smiles," at any point in the marriage she should realize that, sleeping in a common bed with her husband, "she has a full opportunity to urge all the arguments she can, and by her endearments to win him to attention," and to ask for favors.[51] The husband is told that, while no prudent wife would attempt to infringe his authority, if he insists on his authority imperiously and in a "haughty" way, rather than using "tenderness and complaisance," a good wife will be rendered less good and a bad one worse.[52] Such secular pragmatism, hedonism even, shifts the responsibility for domestic success from the husband, who was responsible for domestic good order in older, more religious versions of patriarchy, onto the wife.

In *The Husband*, Haywood demarcates the husband's proper sphere and the wife's, enforcing her points with a little story. Women, she writes, are "both by nature and education . . . best suited for the management of household affairs," including the kitchen and the laundry, so husbands ought not to interfere in these areas. According to her supposedly true story – offered as such stories typically are in this conduct literature as empirical proof of the truth and usefulness of the writer's advice, as well as to liven up the abstractions of advice – one clever lady annoyed by her husband's interfering in the kitchen succeeded in breaking him of this habit. She did not reproach him or argue with him. Instead, she went to the stable to talk with the groom about managing the horses. When her husband reacted with surprise, she replied: "it becomes me full as well to enquire how many oats your horse eats in a week, as for you to examine how many eggs I order my maid to put into a pudding!"[53] *The Husband* accepts that husbands will have control of family financial assets, but lobbies for the concession of a weekly housekeeping allowance to the wife, from which she ought to be entitled to dispose of any savings she can make without stinting family needs. (Contemporary law would not have given a wife property even in such savings.) Haywood campaigns against kinds of masculine expenditure that threatened husbands' ability to support their families, including gambling and risking assets by standing surety for male friends, both common topoi of conduct literature and novels of the period. Haywood's concerns about domestic economy reveal an unusually sharp anxiety about masculine expenditures, as she warns also against men's wasting money on lotteries, dangerous investments, and collecting the sorts of natural or antiquarian curiosities that appealed to contemporary gentlemen.

NEGOTIATING A GENDERED DIVISION OF LITERARY LABOR WITH A FAMILY MODEL

As I have said, what seems especially striking about the successful women writers who aimed to publish their works at mid century is the way in which a gendered division of literary labor got negotiated. Complex cultural negotiations in this period produced a model of literary labor in which women generally ceded the highest, most impressive peaks of ambition and accomplishment to elite male writers, while accepting certain lesser foothills, pleasant and useful enough in their smaller way, as their proper province. Hume wrote challenging, original works of philosophy; Young and Aikenside produced long philosophical poems; and Henry Fielding attempted to recreate the popular romance as a neoclassical, learned "comic epic in prose," a literary rather than a subliterary form. At the opposite extreme, Glasse pioneered in books of cookery and household management and Collyer and Sarah Fielding pioneered in the creation of children's books. Writing for children henceforth becomes one of the literary, or, rather, subliterary, arenas women are permitted to dominate. Because the canon of early modern English literature that was fixed in the nineteenth century was almost exclusively male, it is easy not to notice the struggles between male and female writers in the eighteenth century for the prizes of professional prestige. The canonical novelists, for instance, turned out to be Richardson, Fielding, Smollett, and Sterne; Behn, Manley, Haywood, Sarah Fielding, Charlotte Lennox, Frances Brooke, Frances Sheridan, Elizabeth Griffith, Frances Burney, Charlotte Smith, and Elizabeth Inchbald had virtually disappeared until the last decades of the twentieth century.

In the middle of the eighteenth century, however, male writers were quite conscious of the rivalry of their female predecessors and contemporaries; it was by no means obvious that literature, even serious or high literature, would continue to be a male monopoly. Moreover, the change from a Renaissance system of literary patronage to an early modern system of commercial book selling posed special challenges to traditional ideas of authorship as an occasional activity or as a learned and disinterested calling. The exclusion of women from the schools that provided rigorous classical literary education and from the universities did provide considerable protection for the male monopoly on literary prestige, despite an occasional woman like Carter who acquired classical languages and learning through private education. Nevertheless, the increased importance and prestige of modern languages and learning challenged the relevance and importance of classical learning. Contemporary French literature was deservedly admired and accessible to the many educated women who had studied French, as is evident in the women writers mentioned earlier who translated contemporary French fiction. A smaller, but significant number of women knew Italian literature. Lennox used her Italian to produce a significant work of comparative literature, *Shakespear Illustrated: or the Novels and Histories, On which the Plays of Shakespear are Founded, Collected and Translated from the original Authors. With Critical Remarks. In Two Volumes* (1753). The growth of literacy and the practices of

commercial booksellers combined to make it possible for relatively unlearned individuals, including women, to publish, and even, in a few
cases, to publish enough to make genteel livings. Just as certain medical
men in this period had to exert themselves to secure social and intellectual
positions distinct from and superior to those of midwives, so literary men
had to struggle to distinguish themselves from, to borrow a contemporary
phrase, "scribbling women."

The emerging model of literary productivity has different and special
roles for men – figured as fathers, brothers, and husbands – and women –
figured as daughters, sisters, and wives. Contemporary negotiations over
this gendered division of literary labor are dramatically evident in the
careers of Henry and Sarah Fielding, literally brother and sister. Henry's
efforts to distinguish his work from that of his sister Sarah and also from
that of Behn, Manley, and Haywood illustrate the tactics of a male writer
struggling to create a hierarchy of writers that elevates male writers like
himself possessed of classical educations and supposedly superior rationality above the women who, supposedly, can write only out of limited
personal experience. Throughout his career, Fielding devoted acute attention to the state of literature, sometimes in his own literary works, like *The
Author's Farce*, sometimes in separate critical essays. As a novelist and as a
critic, he exerted himself with considerable success to erect a great moat
between the high literature produced by gentlemen and the alleged sub-
literature of Grubstreet, much of it produced by women writers. One of his
powerful tactics was to ignore the women writers, while mentioning and
discussing male writers of whom he approved. When, unusually, in 1752 in
his *Covent Garden Journal*, Haywood's lively novel, *The History of Miss
Betsy Thoughtless*, is brought to judgment, the title of the novel is reduced to
initials, B– T–, Haywood is not named, and in a three page trial of the text,
absolutely no mention is made of its contents. Instead, B– T– is indicted
"on the Statute of Dulness," then acquitted because the Covent-Garden
Court of Censorial Enquiry "hath no Jurisdiction over any of the Subjects
of Grubstreet, unless in Cases of Blasphemy, Sedition, Scurrility and
Indecency"; B– T– is merely dull, and Grubstreet is found to have "the
Privilege of being dull." Shakespeare, Jonson, Dryden, Swift, and Pope –
all named as subjects of the rival Kingdom of Wit and all part of the canon
Fielding is in the process of establishing – are said to have had to pay tribute
to the rival "great Power of Grubstreet."[54]

If we could imaginatively approach the narrator's discussions of the
novel as a literary form in *Tom Jones* with only the reading experience of

the decades before its publication in 1749, we would be more astonished than we now are by the virtual erasure of the women novelists who preceded Fielding. These earlier unnamed writers, so Fielding's narrator tells us, were practitioners of the lower, "monstrous" form of romance, not of the high form of novel writing that he is inventing. With notable candor, he admits that were it not for their earlier practice and for the contempt cast on romance, he himself "might otherwise have been well enough contented" to be called a writer of romance. The serious literature of the novelist, he claims, is to be understood as the work-product of a learned profession; the popular literature of romance is the product of lower, mechanical, artisanal work. Novelists like himself produce a genuine truth about the world. They require "a good Share of Learning" (including literary and historical learning), and the kind of experiential knowledge of the world that is to be obtained only by access to "all Ranks and Degrees of Men." Romance writers, mere mechanics, require nothing "but paper, Pens and Ink, with the manual Capacity of using them." The demand that the novelist be learned and that he have access to "all Ranks and Degrees of Man" functions to exclude women, who are barred from classical learning at school and university. Moreover, since respectable upper-class women cannot converse with lower-class men and lower-class people lack access to conversation with those in high life or to university education, it also functions to exclude both women and lower-class men.[55]

The popular earlier female novelists are present in the text of *Tom Jones* collectively and implicitly as powerful rivals and individually as near-buried trace elements, momentary jokes. Like Fielding's earlier Shamela, Mrs. Fitzpatrick, the wife who elopes with her lover in *Tom Jones*, reads Manley's *Atalantis*. At the very center of *Tom Jones*, in the scene at the Upton Inn, Mr. Maclachan lies in bed reading an – unnamed – novel by Behn. Maclachan is an impoverished Irish younger brother, on his way to Bath to try his luck with cards and women. A friend has told him, "that he would find no more effectual Method of recommending himself to the Ladies than the improving his Understanding, and filling his Mind with good Literature."[56] Fielding thus invites the reader to laugh at the impecunious Irish gallant, at the appropriateness of reading the erotic Behn in bed, and at the confusion of Grubstreet trash with serious literature. Yet Behn herself, as we saw in chapter one, had understood that the production of novels and comedy did not necessarily require the education of a gentleman.

SARAH FIELDING

While Henry Fielding expressed mixtures of amused condescension and contempt for Behn, Manley, and Haywood, he encouraged the literary career of his sister Sarah. The siblinghood of Henry and Sarah was artistic as well as biological. It is now generally believed that Sarah contributed sections to several of Henry's works, including the letter of Leonora to Horatio in book 2, chapter 6 of *Joseph Andrews* (1742) and the narrative of Anna Boleyn that constitutes the last chapter of *A Journey from this World to the Next* (1742).[57] Henry, it has been noticed, turned to Sarah for certain first-person female narratives, and, in general, "usually appropriates the virtuous lives of his heroines to his own authorial discourses, while regulating minor characters with racier pasts to the 'other' discourse of self-portrayal."[58] Conversely, Sarah occasionally relied on Henry for contributions to her books where specifically masculine authority seemed required, for example, for at least two prefaces and for five letters in her *Familiar Letters between the Principal Characters in David Simple* (1747), some of them ostensibly written by the hero's male friend Valentine. Henry's preface to Sarah's *Familiar Letters* explicitly supports the appropriateness of this gendered division of literary labor, in which women specialize in women's points of view and men in men's: "In the conduct of women, in that great and important business of their lives, the affair of love, there are mysteries, with which men are perfectly unacquainted."[59]

Although I have no doubt that Henry loved Sarah or that he attempted to assist his sister in her career as a writer in various ways (including correcting her grammar and style as well as writing congratulatory prefaces), the relationship was not without significant tensions. Sarah resented the fact that their father had not provided adequately for his daughters, and also, I think, the fact that when her brother acquired money, he did not make up for their father's derelictions. Her work is cluttered with examples of fathers and brothers who behave selfishly and inconsiderately to daughters and sisters who, left without fair shares of the family patrimony, are reduced to poverty and dependency. Further tension developed when Sarah, like several other women writers, became a member of "the family of Richardson." Richardson worked with women on their fiction, promoted it, and happily accepted tributes from ladies, including Sarah's remarkable critical essay praising *Clarissa* in 1749. It was Richardson who lent Sarah 10 guineas when she needed to go to Bath for her health. Moreover, like many serious-minded women of the period, Sarah wanted to know much more about classical literature, history, and languages than was provided in a typical lady's education. Henry did not approve of learned ladies, and, in any case, was not adept at Greek. According to an anecdote of Hester Thrale Piozzi – one not universally believed by Henry Fielding scholars – once Sarah became a competent in classical languages, "the Author of Tom Jones began to teize and *taunt* her with being a literary Lady &c. till at last she resolved to make her whole pleasure out of Study, and becoming justly eminent for her Taste and Knowledge of the Greek language, her Brother never more could perswade himself to endure her Company with Civility . . ."[60] Arthur Collier – brother of Sarah's friend and Sometime Collaborator, Jane Collier – acted as Sarah's classics tutor; later, for assistance with her translation of Xenophon's *Memoirs of Socrates* (1762), she turned to James Harris, a good scholar and clergyman.

As Janet Todd claimed, Henry helped provide his sister with "the acceptable image of the woman writer."[61] That ordinary readers might not see such a gulf fixed between the learned writing of a Henry and the unlearned work of his sister is evident in the fact that some attributed *David Simple*, published anonymously, to Henry. Henry's preface to the second edition did double duty: denying the attribution to himself and puffing the work of his sister. Like many prefaces written by men in support of women's work, Henry's mixes condescension and praise and invokes the idea that the work of women ought not to be subjected to rigorous criticism. That Sarah has committed stylistic errors, not all of which he has had leisure to correct, he admits, but he praises her unity of action, her characters, her "delicate" sentiments, and her good heart. As Todd has said, "The Sarah Fielding he created (with her assistance) appealed to male readers and literary promoters through the humility and gratitude of the stance, as well as through subject matter and style."[62]

FIELDING'S *ADVENTURES OF DAVID SIMPLE*

Sarah Fielding's *Adventures of David Simple: Containing an Account of his Travels Through the Cities of London and Westminster, In the Search of a Real Friend* (1744, 1753) analyzes dependency and the physical and psychological tortures endured by those lacking money enough to support themselves. In part, it is a philosophical tale (albeit a long one) about a virtuous and compassionate young man, who, cheated out of his patrimony by his younger brother, determines to search the world for a "Friend that he could live with," one "who could throw off all separate Interests . . ."[63] (Fielding herself called the book a "moral romance"; in it she cites Fénelon's *Télémaque* [1699], a useful model for a quest romance more interested in philosophy than adventure, although Fénelon was writing a mirror for princes about virtues for public men and Fielding a mirror for private persons about more domestic virtues.) The egalitarian friendship David seeks, like the friendship celebrated in Philips's poetry, is the antithesis of those hierarchical relationships of domination and subordination that the narrative represents as characteristic of both patronage and families. Fielding stigmatizes these hierarchical relationships not only as inhumane and unjust, but worse, as destructive and sadistic. Like Collyer's Lucius, David is a benevolent man of sensibility. However, unlike the sensibilities of Lucius and Felicia, the sensibilities of David and his eventual wife make them unsturdy, vulnerable. Their sensibility is expressed not only in compassionate feelings and benevolent actions, but also in tears, fainting, and, ultimately, inability to survive in a fictional world dominated by other characters animated by avarice, pride, and – a major emotion in Fielding – envy. Fielding's sober concern with morality and psychology anticipates Samuel Johnson's similar concerns in *The Rambler* (1750–52), which also moves back and forth between abstract, highly generalized reflections and illustrative fictions. Her hero, similarly, anticipates Johnson's Rasselas (1759), another innocent young man who travels in hopes of making a wise choice of life.

David's goodness, like the goodness of Mr. Heartfree in Henry Fielding's *Life of Mr. Jonathan Wild the Great* (1743), makes him vulnerable to exploitation by a parade of worldly villains, who function to expose the debased moral standards of society and of the legal profession. Carolyn Woodward has suggested that Fielding's bestowing upon her hero a set of typically feminine virtues ("innocence, passivity, privacy") defamiliarizes them and exposes them as weaknesses, useless in the contemporary world.[64] Despite the speciousness and self-interest of would-be fashionable friends like Mr. Orgueil (French for "pride") and Mr. Varnish, by the end of the first part David has gathered about himself not one but three friends: Valentine and Camilla, a brother and sister he has rescued from extreme poverty, and Cynthia, a young woman he rescues from the cruelties of a lady she has been forced to live with as a companion. Valentine has married Cynthia, David has married Camilla, and all four prepare to settle down to the simple, virtuous country life that captivated the eighteenth-century moral imagination and that proved so satisfying to Mary Collyer's Lucius and Felicia.

Fielding's arraignment and analysis in *David Simple* of the sadism of the powerful and the misery of the powerless overlaps significantly with the black and brilliant comedy of *The Art of Ingeniously Tormenting* (1754), usually attributed to Sarah's friend, Jane Collier. David falls in love with Cynthia, seeing her first as a humble, teased lady's companion, silent in the face of humiliation, only her face expressing "Indignation and Shame at being thus treated."[65] Like Collier, Cynthia calls attention to sadistic pleasure employers and patrons derive from demeaning those forced into economic dependence. Cynthia articulates how those who have power fiendishly create situations that simultaneously produce in their dependents shame, which silences them, and indignation, which makes them want to cry out. More exquisite mental torment is added when dependents are in relationships where gratitude and/or family feeling produce affection, along with shame and indignation. Thus, Cynthia laments that her lady "had raised my Love, by the Obligations she had confer'd on me, and yet continually provoked my Rage by her Ill-nature . . ."[66] Mordantly, Cynthia observes, "I know not to what Malignity it is owing, but I have observed, in all the Families I have ever been acquainted with, that one part of them spend their whole time in oppressing and teazing the other; and all this they do like *Drawcansir*, only *because they dare*, and to shew their Power: While the other Part languish away their Days, in bemoaning their own hard Fate, which has thus subjected them to the Whims and Tyranny of *Wretches*, who are so *totally void of Taste, as not to desire the Affection of the very People, they appear willing to oblige.*"[67] The power of a malign stepmother who falsely tells their father that they are guilty of incest reduces Camilla and Valentine to abject poverty and Valentine to near death. When Camilla begs at the houses of gentlemen who have not heard the scandal, she finds they give money at first, but quickly expect sexual favors in return. Desperate, she reports:

I made myself a Hump-back, dyed my Skin in several places with great Spots of Yellow; so that, when I look'd in the Glass, I was almost frighten'd at my own Figure. I dress'd myself decently, and was resolved to try what I could procure this way . . . If I began to speak of my Misery, they laugh'd on one another, and seem'd to think it was no manner of Consequence what a *Wretch* suffer'd, who had it not in her power to give them any *pleasure*.[68]

This outré image of the woman driven to masquerade as a hunchback emblematizes what it could feel like for a woman to be in any patronage relationship: if she reveals herself as the fully human person she is and speaks what is in her mind, she arouses feelings in the patron (whether desire or anger) that are unwanted; if she disguises herself by masquerading as a crippled and limited inferior and silences herself, then she risks becoming alienated from herself and so invisible and inaudible that she cannot be seen or heard by the very people whose aid she requires. The need to disguise oneself provokes rage at those who demand it, panic at the prospect of losing oneself, and self-disgust at the repulsive, cowardly spectacle one has allowed oneself to become. David's attraction is that he has found ways to give, or rather, to share, that recognize the objects of charity as humans equal to himself; instead of envying Cynthia's superior intelligence, he treasures it.

In *The Adventures of David Simple. Volume the Last* (1753), when the utopian community of friends David and Cynthia have created is destroyed, the horrors of dependency are rendered still more melodramatically. Cynthia's daughter is so ill that she requires a trip to the spa at Bath, but the family cannot afford to send her. Mrs. Orgueil offers to take her as a companion for her spoiled, obnoxious, and wonderfully named daughter, Henrietta-Cassandra. Little Cynthia is reduced to a servant, cruelly relegated to a damp bedroom, and dies. David cannot resolve the double binds his would-be friends and patrons create for him. The narrator pronounces authoritatively:

Such Dependance is Slavery, worse than working in the Gallies: all Endeavours to please are vain: if you exert yourself, and take any one Step without previously consulting these Patrons, this they condemn as throwing them off, and seeking other Protection: and if you entirely depend upon them, they accuse you of Imprudence, in that you seem to think them bound to provide for you. And the true Source of all this odd Behaviour seems to be, that such Friends do not desire that a Man they chuse for a Slave, should be provided for; but that he should be kept on in a dependent State, with only barely enough to prevent his being starved, and by that means escaping their Power.[69]

Fielding's exploration of the relations of domination and subordination in the contemporary family model illuminate the high practical and psychological costs it could entail.

FIELDING'S *GOVERNESS*

Sarah Fielding's *The Governess: or, The Little Female Academy* at once exemplifies the experimental character of her work and the way in which women writers began to establish themselves as specially qualified for an important new role in the literary family, the authorship of children's books. Children had previously read chapbooks recounting versions of stories like the old romance of *Guy of Warwick*, but a combination of new enlightenment attention to education and the entrepreneurial zeal of mid-century publishers, notably John Newbery, for new markets created a favorable climate for *The Governess*. Fielding's book is now said to be the "first sustained fictional narrative specifically written to amuse children."[70] Newbery's *The Renowned History of Little Goody Two-shoes* was not published until 1765.[71] Mrs. Teachum, the eponymous governess, presides over a girls' boarding school; she is offered as an ideal grown-up guide for the moral development of her pupils. Within a frame, different girls recount the small stories of their own lives and a set of narratives from different genres, including fairy tales, romances, and a fable. Despite Sarah Fielding's own dedication to the study of classical languages and literatures, the curriculum of this model girls' school is limited to reading, writing, needlework, morality, and good behavior. Formal instruction is not represented, as we see the girls entertaining themselves after classes and on a supervised excursion to a dairy farm. Recounting narratives, listening to narratives, and drawing explicit morals from narratives are the primary actions of the book.[72] The explicit morals Mrs. Teachum and the girls draw emphasize the dangerousness of self-indulgence and passions and the countervailing value of self-abnegation and self-control.[73] Whereas Locke's educational theory, developed with boys in mind, stressed the importance of children's experience, these girls are apparently to learn more vicariously.

The Governess became a popular children's book for the rest of the century, constructing and celebrating a self-denying, self-controlling femininity. In its final fable, "The Assembly of Birds," the winner of a contest for the most admirable and happiest bird is the female dove, who stays in her nest, minding her young, and has "no Ambition for a public Preference."[74] Sarah Fielding herself never married, had no children, and never opened a school, yet the success of *The Governess* contributed a model of female authority in the education of girls and helped lay a foundation for later women writers of children's books and books on the education of children, as well as for women who set up boarding schools.

SERVANT AUTHORS

As I noted earlier, servants were commonly part of the eighteenth-century family. A few newly literate women from the laboring classes now appeared to write their stories, notably Mary Collier and Mary Leapor. Collier, the first woman poet of the laboring classes, answered Duck's "The Thresher's Labour" with her *The Woman's Labour. An Epistle to Mr. Stephen Duck* (1739), printed in a little pamphlet selling for sixpence.

Collier complains that Duck had not fairly represented the hard work that women did in the fields and that he ignored their domestic work and the hard labor of women like herself who served as washerwomen for others' households:

> Heaps of fine Linen we before us view,
> Whereon to lay our Strength and Patience too;
> Cambrics and Muslins, which our Ladies wear,
> Laces and Edgings, costly, fine, and rare,
> Which must be wash'd with utmost Skill and Care . . .[75]

For this form of day labor, Collier writes, mistresses unconvincingly plead their own poverty to keep servants' wages down, tell them to be sparing of the soap and fire, and remain oblivious to the poor women's cracked and bloody hands that were the result of long immersion in water and caustic soaps. "For all our Pains," Collier concludes, "no Prospect can we see / Attend us, but *Old Age* and *Poverty*."[76] Yet Collier, like other poets now dubbed laboring-class or "occupational poets," was claiming some cultural authority for herself based on her occupational experience, her literacy, and her willingness to write about her experience. To represent household labor in poetry, as Collier and Leapor did, was to assert its value.

Newly literate women writers from the laboring classes were doubly novel by virtue of both gender and class. As did women writers and laboring-class writers generally, they profited from the enlightenment turn to empiricism and its corollary valuation of the different experiences of different people. Men and upper-class people, it was coming to be understood, could on the basis of their own experience tell only partial truths about the world. A fuller story required the testimony of women and of lower-class people about their experiences – even if persistent doubts about authorship suggested residual incredulity about the power of either women or laboring-class writers to offer representations.

LEAPOR'S *POEMS UPON SEVERAL OCCASIONS*

A more ambitious and accomplished poet than Collier, Mary Leapor was the daughter of a gardener, with whom she sometimes worked, and also sometimes a housemaid. Two volumes of her *Poems upon Several Occasions* were posthumously published in 1748 and 1751 after her untimely death from measles at twenty-four. Leapor's volumes contain a considerable range of poems, including biblical paraphrases and prayers, pastorals, Hudibrastics (comic tetrameter couplets in the manner of Samuel Butler and Swift), dream visions, allegories resembling Edward Young's, didactic verse, feminist protest, and moral essays and epistles in heroic couplets inspired by her favorite poet, Pope. Leapor chose "Mira" as her poetic persona; strikingly, and in sharp contrast to Egerton with whom she has other affinities, Leapor has little to say about love and her volumes do not chronicle dramas of Mira and her lovers. Indeed, in "The Temple of Love" she offers a memorable allegorical image of love as no more than deceitful artifice. The poet is reading Nicholas Rowe's *The Tragedy of Jane Shore* (1714), a she-tragedy, when she falls asleep and dreams of Cytheria (another name for Aphrodite, Goddess of Love) with Cupid on her knee:

> On the bright Walls, around her and above,
> Were drawn the Statutes and the Arts of Love:
> There taught the silent Language of the Eye,
> The broken Whisper and amusing Lye . . .
> The graceful Anger, and the rolling Eyes:
> The practis'd Blush and counterfeit Surprise,
> The Language proper for pretending Swains;
> And fine Description for imagined Pains . . .[77]

Mira's important relationships figured in these volumes are not with lovers, but, most extensively, with "Artemesia," the local gentry woman who encouraged her writing, with other women patrons and a woman friend, and with the spirit of Pope.

Contemporaries expected that a gardener's daughter might be able to make a contribution to revivifying the pastoral, at this point sinking into vapidity. Leapor's pastorals only partially satisfy this expectation, often, as in "Beauties of Spring," repeating well-worn clichés. They sometimes exemplify the bathetic "infantine" Pope defined as "when a Poet grows so very simple, as to think and talk like a child" and mocked in *Peri Bathos*.[78] Occasionally, though, her pastorals offer more originality. In "Colinetta – Autumn," the virtuous shepherdess Colinetta lies on Lydia's lap to sing her own pastoral elegy, mingling the naive infantine with better touches of homey rural realism:

> When I am gone, I leave to sister *Sue*
> My Gown of Jersey, and my Aprons blue,
> My studded Sheep-hook *Phillida* may take.
> Likewise my Hay-fork and my Hazel Rake:
> My hoarded Apples, and my winter Pears
> Be thine, O *Lydia*, to reward thy Cares.[79]

In "The Charms of Anthony," two shepherdesses, Lucy and Phebe, engage in the alternate song of classical pastoral, admiring a shepherd whose virtues are moving away from pastoral toward a more practical, recognizably English, georgic. Leapor breaks the decorum of the pastoral when Phebe compares Anthony's "curling Locks" favorably to "the white Wig on Squire *Fopling's* Brow," and then, more radically, when Phebe and Lucy, not faithful to Anthony, end by adjourning to a contemporary-sounding tavern with Colinet and Rogerio.[80] One critic has pointed out that in two volumes Leapor "refers to more than eighty specific types of trees, flowers, plants, and vegetables."[81] "The Month of August" suggests what Leapor might have been able to do if she had lived to cultivate the georgic. Sylvanius, a courtier, tries to tempt Philis, a country maid, into his formal garden, adorned with dwarfed and espaliered pears. Philis rejects him:

> In vain you tempt me while our Orchard bears
> Long-keeping Russets, lovely Cath'rine Pears,
> Pearmains and Codling, wheaten Plumbs enough,
> And the black Damsons load the bending Bough.[82]

Leapor's most admired poem is now "Crumble Hall," a revision of the country-house poem from the servant's perspective. Unlike a gentleman poet celebrating his patron's estate – Marvell in "Upon Appleton House" or Pope in the "Epistle to Burlington" – Mira is a servant unimpressed with things like architectural ornaments or grand tapestries. Instead, half-way through the poem, Mira leads the viewer into a place not considered in the earlier country-house poems: the kitchen. For the celebration of the order and beauty achieved without visible signs of labor by the great estate in the conventional country-house poem, Leapor substitutes a disenchanted, more democratic view of the household as constituted by the people who labor below stairs.

Critics have disagreed over Leapor's precise tone in "Crumble Hall," especially over whether she is satirizing the servants. Her descriptions have features of mock epic, using formal features of the epic language she knew from Pope's Homer, including the heroic couplet, apostrophe, high diction, epithets familiar from epic, and inverted word order. Thus, she describes the housekeeper in language that mixes some epithets familiar from epic ("pliant," "*Ambrosial*," and "baneful") with language more typical of the subliterary cookery books:

> *Sophronia* sage! whose learned knuckles know,
> To form round Cheese-cakes of the pliant Dough;

> To bruise the Curd, and her Fingers squeeze
> *Ambrosial* Butter with the temper'd Cheese:
> Sweet Tarts and Pudden, too, her Skill declare;
> And the soft Jellies, hid from baneful Air.[83]

In my judgment, while there is certainly comedy in the incongruity of high and low elements in "Crumble Hall," the overall effect is not to satirize the servants. Instead, more in the way of Gay's use of mock-heroic in *Trivia*, the poem conveys an affection for the low, even a respect for craft skills like the housekeeper's, and challenges the literary conventions that ban the low from serious representation.

A number of Leapor's better poems address the problems of a servant who writes poetry and the problems of a self-taught poet of the laboring class who requires gentry patronage. Leapor craved more learning, more poetic craft, and more time to develop her art. She never met Pope or corresponded with him, yet, touchingly, she laments his death in 1745 in part as her loss of a mentor:

> Unpolish'd Souls, like *Codrus* or like mine,
> Fill'd with Ideas that but dimly shine,
> Read o'er the Charms of his instructive Pen,
> And taste of Raptures never known till then . . .
> Ah! who shall now our rustick Thoughts refine,
> And to grave Sense and solid Learning join
> Wit ever sparkling, and the Sweets of Rhyme?[84]

Hoping to acquire more poetic "polish," Leapor nevertheless has ambivalent attitudes toward criticism. Sometimes she eagerly seeks it, usually to be disappointed by the unwillingness, triviality, or wrong-headedness of the better educated whose assistance she asks. In "To Grammaticus," after her poems have apparently wounded a gentleman critic's delicate ears, she first graciously and humorously seeks a herbal remedy for him. At the end, however, she declares that what he really needs is "good nature."[85] In "An Epistle to Artemisia," inspired by Pope's "Epistle to Dr. Arbuthnot," a parade of gentry men and women fitfully and unhelpfully attend to Mira's verse. Of the more promisingly literary, Vido spurns her pleas for him to correct her verse, plying her with flattery she thinks is false:

> But Mira, tho' too partial to the Bays,
> And like her Brethren, not averse to Praise;
> Had learn'd this lesson; Praise, if planted wrong,
> Is more destructive than a spiteful Tongue.[86]

Showing considerable penetration, Leapor appreciated that she was dealing with a culture in which a stubborn refusal to believe laboring-class people could develop literary capacity coexisted with a primitivist enthusiasm for discovering "natural genius" amongst the lower orders. Johnson noted and deplored this enthusiasm, remarking of James Woodhouse, the poetical shoemaker, "it was all vanity and childishness: and . . . such objects were, to those who patronized them, mere mirrours of their own superiority . . . He may make an excellent shoemaker, but he can never make a good poet."[87] At the same time, plebian poets like Duck and Leapor not only found patronage but also benefited from some of the largest sets of subscribers of any writers. Leapor had about 600 subscribers to her first volume, which one scholar calculates should have resulted in a profit of about £75.[88]

We do not know whether Leapor had read Finch's "Circuit of Apollo," in which Apollo is too nervous to create a hierarchy of women poets, but Leapor's "The Proclamation of Apollo" offers an Apollo who disapproves of hierarchy on principle. The poem escapes from worries about poetic faults and inferiority into a fantasy of infinitely generous patronage and appreciation for all kinds of poets. To develop this distinctly unPopian idea, Leapor turns to Swiftian Hudibrastics. Apollo summons all poets to Parnassus to enjoy a holiday feast. (Leapor is as interested in the details of food as she is of plants.) Critics, "Much like *Parnassian* Grenadiers / With surly Eyes and sour Faces," appear to put each poet in "his proper Place," on "Laurel Benches all a-row." The poets rapidly turn angry and surly, ceasing to enjoy the fine refreshments Apollo has provided. Apollo then declares that contention and envy among poets distress him and insists on a truce:

> Let Wits shake Hands with one another,
> And ev'ry Dunce embrace his Brother.
> From batter'd Bards with ne'er a Shoe
> To those who strut about with two;
> From Poets doom'd to whittle Sticks,
> To Rhimers in a Coach and Six.[89]

Departing thus boldly from the aesthetic principles of the author of *The Dunciad*, Leapor has Apollo say:

> So shines the Muse on ev'ry Creature,
> Who tags his humble Lines with Metre.[90]

Once poets promise to obey Apollo, delicious food and nectar appear. For a parting present, Apollo provides the poets with a magic "Ink that into

Metre runs, / And charms against the Fear of Duns," and a magic bath that has the power to immunize a dunce "against sharp Satyr's Pain," giving him or her "Confidence to push / Through the world without a Blush."[91]

One of Leapor's fables and some of her other short poems about writing play with fantasies of female artists improbably turning the tables on apparently more powerful male figures. "The Inspir'd Quill" is one of those eighteenth-century poems in which an inanimate object is the speaker, an experiment with extending the range of imagined subjectivities that also extended to novels, for example, *The Travels of Mons. Le Post-Chaise. Written by Himself* (1753) or the *History and Adventures of a Lady's Slippers and Shoes. Written by themselves* (1754). Leapor's quill has undergone a Pythagorean transmigration of souls, beginning as a rich, usurious country squire, then descending through a beau, a lapdog, a lawyer, and a crow. While a lapdog, he suffers from what seems to have been a common problem of eighteenth-century lapdogs: the envy and malicious acts of servants who resent the fact that an animal is better treated than people who are servants. A servant tosses him into the river and drowns him. Now a crow quill, he is still not entirely purged of his avarice and so does not want to belong to a poet and be doomed "to scrawl unprofitable Rhymes." We do not learn whether the poet accedes to his begging that he be recommended to a place with an attorney so he can write bills. In the fable, "The Sow and the Peacock," a witty sow, learned enough to have read Seneca, suddenly falls in love with a peacock. She jumps up from her dunghill couch, washes, then, in an authentically porcine fashion, rubs "her Sides against a Tree," the better to cleanse herself, preparatory to inviting the handsome peacock into her hut. The sow promises the peacock that in her he will find "an open Heart and honest Mind."[92] However, the peacock refuses her invitation, worrying that the narrow pigsty door might tear his feathers or scent them with "unsav'ry Fumes / And what am I without my Plume?" Offended, the witty sow resolves in future to "take it as a Rule, / The shining Case contains a Fool."[93] This overt moral emphasizes a common Leapor theme of the – apparently almost universal – discrepancy between beautiful outsides and worthy insides. At the same time, the witty sow also seems a self-representation of Leapor, the unattractive barnyard creature who is nevertheless studious and intelligent, and who, though, pained by rejection from her beautiful betters, bravely continues to assert her own self-worth.

CHARLOTTE LENNOX

Charlotte Lennox's negotiations over what was to be her place in the mid-eighteenth-century literary family were at least as complex as Sarah Fielding's, although none of the men upon whom Lennox depended for advice and assistance were tied to her by blood or marriage. Lennox's financial circumstances drove her to try to make money by writing and publishing, so she was eager for whatever aesthetic or practical assistance established male writers might be able and willing to offer, and she was prepared to become a kind of surrogate daughter to both Richardson and Johnson. Having spent her childhood in New York where her father was stationed as a British army captain, Charlotte Ramsey came to England after his death. In 1747, when she was about eighteen, she published *Poems on Several Occasions*, dedicated to the Countess of Rockingham and Lady Isabella Finch; she also married Alexander Lennox, a Scot who proved unable and unwilling to support his family.

In part because a substantial set of letters between Lennox, Johnson, and other literary men survive, we have an unusually detailed knowledge both of Johnson's literary assistance to Lennox and of her attitudes about her dependence on male luminaries like Johnson and Richardson.[94] When Lennox in 1750 published her first novel, *The Life of Harriot Stuart*, Johnson gave a famous all-night party at the Devil Tavern to celebrate. According to Sir John Hawkins's account of this event: "Johnson had directed that a magnificent hot apple-pye should make a part of it, and this he would have stuck with bay-leaves, because, forsooth, Mrs. Lenox was an authoress, and had written verses; and further, he had prepared for her a crown of laurel, with which, but not till he had invoked the muses by some ceremonies of his own invention, he encircled her brows."[95]

In orchestrating this celebration, Johnson undoubtedly intended, as we might say today, to be supportive. Margaret Doody has commented, "This affair seems a good piece of advertising, as well as a pleasant festivity."[96] At the same time, Johnson's ritual artifice was bound to strike many contemporaries as containing elements of the absurd and parodic, as Hawkins's "forsooth, Mrs. Lenox was an authoress" hints, and as I believe Lennox appreciated. For any living author to allow himself to be crowned with a laurel wreath had elements of presumption; when that author had written only two books of no great distinction, when the second of those books was a mere novel, and when the author in question was a young woman, absurdity was piled upon presumption. Yet a young author desperate for success could hardly say no to an invitation to be honored by the author of "London" and "The Vanity of Human Wishes."

Johnson, of course, had thought much about literary patronage and had, in various ways, rejoiced in the death of the old patronage system that freed authors like himself from dependency on unimpressive and annoying aristocrats. The booksellers, Johnson had declared with satisfaction, are the new "patrons of literature."[97] One of Johnson's activities in support of women writers of whom he approved was to introduce them to booksellers and use his influence with booksellers to get their work published. Johnson, for instance, took Lennox to see Richardson, who read and liked her *Female Quixote* and then persuaded Andrew Millar to publish it.

Prominent authors like Johnson, indeed, especially Johnson, began to be a new kind of patron, upon whom lesser writers were dependent. The dynamics of this new kind of patronage were in some ways like the older aristocratic patron/author relationship, but, in other ways, different. Author patrons like Henry Fielding or Johnson were likely to dispense favors to their lesser author clients in the form of favorably mentioning them in their works; writing prologues or prefaces to clients' works; or writing favorable reviews (now that evaluative reviews were part of the new magazines). Johnson wrote dedications for Lennox's works – more than once apologizing for the author's sex – and wrote favorable reviews, for instance, a review of *The Female Quixote* for *The Gentleman's Magazine* and one of her translation of the *Memoirs of the Duke of Sully* for *The Literary Magazine*.[98] On occasion, older aristocratic patrons had suggested revisions in works to be dedicated to them, but the range of suggestions, the scope of revisions, and the aesthetic weight of such suggestions, when they came from an author patron, were all likely to be greater. When the author patron was as well educated as Henry Fielding or Samuel Johnson and the author client as informally educated as Sarah Fielding or Charlotte Lennox, the line between patronage and collaboration was particularly likely to blur and the client's dependency likely to become peculiarly intimate and intense. When the author patron happened also to be a brother of his author client (as Henry Fielding was of Sarah), or a father (as Richard Edgeworth was of Maria), or a husband (as Richard Griffith was of Elizabeth and Thomas Sheridan was of Frances), the intimacy stood a chance of seeming relatively comfortable. But when the author patron had no literal familial relation to a female author client, as Johnson had no such relation to Lennox, then the inadequacy of the male patron/male client model to fit a male/female relationship was likely to be starkly exposed.

LENNOX'S *FEMALE QUIXOTE*

The question of whether or not Johnson wrote the crucial penultimate chapter, "Being in the Author's Opinion, the best Chapter in this History," of Lennox's most important original work, *The Female Quixote* (1752), is still being debated. Despite the resistance of many professional Johnsonians to including this chapter in the canon of the master, I am inclined to think that he did. No one seems to doubt that he wrote the dedication "To the Right Honourable the Earl of Middlesex," in which, writing as Lennox, he makes her characterize herself as timid, as dreading public censure, and as "impressed by the Consciousness of Imbecility."[99]

The premise of *The Female Quixote* is simple: the heroine Arabella reads seventeenth-century French romances in social isolation and understands them to be true descriptions of the world. Since the characters she encounters in the novelistic world of contemporary England are animated by different motives and behave differently than the romance characters, Arabella consistently, ludicrously, misreads them. Like the premises in Aristophanes or Molière, Lennox's premise is a ground for complex comedy. The book resembles Augustan satires like Swift's *Gulliver's Travels* (1726) or *The Memoirs of Martinus Scriblerus* (1742), the collaborative Scriblerian "biography" of a nonexistent pedant whose father makes his small son speak classical Greek and eat the letters of the Greek alphabet formed from gingerbread. Thomas Macaulay was right to say "*The Female Quixote* has undoubtedly great merit when considered as a wild, satirical, harlequinade . . ."[100] Unlike more topical earlier satire and like Johnson's own satire, Lennox's generally avoids attacking particular individuals, focusing instead on more generalized types. Arabella persists in her conviction about the truth of romance until the penultimate chapter, when she is suddenly converted.

Lennox's method in the satire can be illustrated by an episode in which Arabella notices Edward, a handsome young gardener working on her father's estate. She quickly decides that he must be a man of rank, a lover who has disguised himself to be near her. An intelligent girl, she notices a variety of ways in which the expectations she derives from romance about the likely behavior of such a person do not, in fact, match her further observations. Thus, "She often wondered, indeed, that she did not find her Name carved on the Trees, with some mysterious Expressions of

Love . . ."[101] Yet, because she is so well read and inventive, she can usually discover what appear to her plausible reasons why such disappointing observations do not necessarily require her to abandon her original romance-based hypotheses. When Edward is discovered lurking about the fishpond, the head gardener accuses him of intending to steal carp to sell and beats him. Horrified, Arabella insists that he, as a despairing lover, must have been intending to drown himself. She will barely listen to the head gardener's explanation, which offers a fully novelistic economic motive, and rebukes him: "tell me no more of these idle Tales."[102] The larger debate in the narrative turns on the question of precisely what kinds of narratives deserve to be stigmatized as "idle," "trifling," or "false," and what kinds are entitled to be celebrated as significant and as true histories. A fundamental question in *The Female Quixote* is, What counts as true history?

Many have remarked that by the 1750s the vogue of French romance in England had considerably abated and wondered why it should be so central in *The Female Quixote*. A hidden term in the satire is the English amatory romance of Behn, Manley, and Haywood, less idealizing than the earlier French romance, but sharing its concentration on love. Lennox wants to go back to reclaim the concern of romance with virtue (which is not a concern in English amatory fiction), and, at the same time, like Collyer and Sarah Fielding, to construct a new women's fiction against that of the earlier transgressive women writers. Her contemporaries, including Johnson and Richardson, thought she had succeeded in both these aims. Even Henry Fielding, less the moralist, in reviewing *The Female Quixote*, said "our Author hath taken such Care throughout her Work, to expose all those Vices and Follies in her Sex which are chiefly predominant in Our Days, that it will afford very useful lessons to all those Young Ladies who will peruse it with proper Attention."[103] In fact, Lennox moves to attack ordinary women like the coquette Charlotte Glanville; French romances are not interested in such attacks. Lennox defines her heroine as exceptional by characterizing her against developed portraits of ordinary women, who she represents as unappealing; this is a disturbing and common feature of the subsequent women's novel.

The emerging women's novel wishes to define itself against romance, French and English; at least as urgently, it needs to differentiate itself from the scandal chronicle, exemplified by Manley's *New Atalantis* and Haywood's *Memoirs of a Certain Island*, but given new and powerful life by women writers of Lennox's own generation, Con Phillips, Lady Vane, and Laetitia Pilkington, whose books we will consider later in this chapter. Unlike the romance, the scandal chronicle claims verisimilitude and to be true history. Indeed, Montagu labeled the scandalous anecdotes in her own letters "small histories," ironically, but, I think, also seriously meaning to contrast them with the larger, more public histories filled with the lies of panegyric. The longer scandal chronicles are generally animated by anger at the falsity of more decorous, public, authoritative histories and narratives. Their characters are revealed to be motivated by lust and greed – low, novelistic motives – rather than by honor and benevolence.

Lennox's confronting the scandal chronicle is clear in the rich comedy of Arabella's encounter with Miss Groves and Miss Groves's servant, Mrs. Morris. Conscious of her own social isolation and regretting it, Arabella has yearned for "an agreeable Companion of her own Sex and Rank."[104] Seeing a young woman, "very magnificently dressed," at her country church one Sunday, she rejoices at the prospect of a romance heroine for a friend. When the lady, Miss Groves, proves reluctant to narrate her own adventures, Arabella turns to her servant Mrs. Morris, who recounts them in a chapter entitled "*The History of Miss* Groves, *interspersed with some very curious Observations.*" Miss Groves, we learn, is the daughter of a rich merchant who left his widow rich enough to marry a Duke. A wild teenager, Miss Groves was seduced by a writing master, ran away from the Duke's home, and launched herself into a career as a kept mistress. Her adventures feature greed, illegitimate children, gambling, debt, and repudiation by "the Honourable Mr. L—, Brother to the Earl of —," in short, the basic stuff of scandal chronicles.[105]

One might assume a virtuous innocent like Arabella would be shocked and appalled to have entertained such a creature in her father's house. Instead, in a delicious comic surprise, Arabella sheds tears of pity at this woman's plight and tells the astonished Mrs. Morris:

Your Lady's Case . . . is much to be lamented; and greatly resembles the unfortunate *Cleopatra's*, whom *Julius Cæsar* privately marrying, with a Promise to own her for his Wife, when he should be peaceable Master of the *Roman* Empire, left that great Queen big with Child, and, never intending to perform his Promise, suffered her to be exposed to the Censures the World has so freely cast upon her; and which she so little deserved.

Arabella, the narrator remarks, "seemed so little sensible of the Pleasure of Scandal . . . as to be wholly ignorant of its Nature; and not to know it when it was told her."[106]

Arabella's ability to renarrate Miss Groves's story in the language and formulas of romance, like many such moments in *The Female Quixote*, calls attention to the non-transparency and manipulability of language, highlighting not only the conventionality of romance narratives but also the conventionality of anti-romance narratives. At the same time, Arabella's move illuminates something high romance and scandal chronicle have in common: a vision of female characters as significant and as targets of male predation.

Lennox's awareness of the similarities between scandal chronicles and "true histories" is highlighted when Arabella ventures into the Assembly Room at Bath. Surrounded by strangers, she asks Mr. Tinsel to relate their "Histories," announcing that she hopes to hear "something which may at once improve and delight me; something which may excite my Admiration and engage my Esteem, or influence my Practice." Tinsel boasts of the freshness and accuracy of his "Intelligence"; Intelligence, it will be recalled, is one of the principal characters in Manley's *New Atalantis*. He proceeds to relate a series of scandalous anecdotes. Arabella rejects these narrations, insisting that they cannot rightly be denominated "Histories": "I think they do not deserve that Name, and are rather detached Pieces of Satire on particular Persons, than a serious Relation of Facts."[107]

Like the scandal chronicles, early novels also claimed to be true histories, sometimes as actual or virtual hoaxes, but in a more sophisticated way in Henry Fielding. Fielding in book 2, chapter 1 of *The History of Tom Jones, a Foundling* (1749), "Shewing what kind of a History this is; what it is like, and what it is not like," invokes the ancient idea that poetry is more philosophical than history. Fielding attacks the language of romance as "pompous" and artificial, not capable of being truth-bearing. Fielding's move to outlaw romance is like the tactic employed by the good Doctor to convert Arabella at the end of *The Female Quixote*; the Doctor demands the renunciation of "the Authority of Scribblers, not only of Fictions, but of senseless Fictions; which at once vitiate the Mind, and pervert the Understanding."[108] Both Henry Fielding and the Doctor undertake to demonstrate that romances are not histories but fictions.

In contrast, Arabella's enthusiasm for romance is related to romance's representation of women as heroines, and as consequential persons capable of exalted virtue. The scandal narratives disgust her in part because they record what she considers trivial deeds. She rejects even the less sensational activities of fashionable life as empty, "trifling amusements":

What room, I pray you, does a Lady give for high and noble Adventures, who consumes her Days in Dressing, Dancing, listening to Songs, and ranging the Walks with People as thoughtless as herself? How mean and contemptible a Figure must a Life spent in such idle Amusements make in History? Or rather, Are not such Persons always buried in Oblivion, and can any Pen be found who would condescend to record such inconsiderable Actions?[109]

To record precisely such "inconsiderable Actions" is, of course, a project of the canonical English novel from Jane Austen to Henry James and beyond, albeit these novelists insist that small, hidden, private lives can be endowed with moral consequence.

SCANDALOUS MEMOIRISTS

Like the familiar letter, the *Memoir*, either as first-person autobiography or as third-person biography, continued to be an important form at mid century. In contrast to the Restoration women, Cavendish and Hutchinson, who wrote biographies of their husbands, notable women writers of memoirs at mid century chronicled their own lives. To publish an account of one's own life was not the act of a modest woman. Duncombe in *The Feminiad* notices Con Phillips, Lady Vane, and Laetitia Pilkington in the same verse paragraph with "Vice's" other "friends," Behn, Manley, and Centlivre, remarking in a note, "These three ladies have endeavour'd to immortalize their shame, by writing and publishing their memoirs."[110] It is unsurprising that the mid-century women autobiographers were generally driven to publication first by the loss of their reputations for chastity and then by consequent financial distress. The resulting narratives challenged the public stories that branded them as bad women; they also usually excoriated the men in their lives who, unlike the good men in Lucas Pinckney's life, had failed to protect and support them. The women hoped to defend their own conduct and to humiliate or punish their oppressors, as well as to make needed money. These narratives thus resemble Manley's *Rivella*, but the best of them are freer from debased romance formulas and more adventurous than contemporary fiction in bringing into representation the wide range of experiences that at least some eighteenth-century women had. Related to the longer memoirs are a set of shorter, occasional pamphlets in which women with particular grievances use print in defense of their positions in public or private controversies, as, for example, the actress Kitty Clive did in *The Case of Mrs. Clive* (1743) against the managers of the Covent Garden and Drury Lane Theatres.

PHILLIPS'S *APOLOGY*

Teresia Constantia Phillips in *An Apology for the Conduct of Mrs. Teresia Constantia Phillips, more particularly that part of it which relates to her Marriage, with an eminent Dutch Merchant* (1748) blamed one "Thomas Grimes" for having intercourse with her before she was married to another man at thirteen and for abandoning her to her later life as the kept mistress of many aristocratic men. Her rapist had been widely identified as Lord Chesterfield, but has now convincingly been identified as Sir Thomas Lumley Sanderson, third Earl of Scarborough.[111] It seems reasonable to regard the *Apology* as a collaborative effort, not only because of the male narrator, but also because the text includes many letters supposedly from and to Phillips and documents presented as evidence in Phillips's litigation with Muliman, the Dutch merchant who married her and then obtained a judgment that their marriage was invalid.[112] The *Apology* appeals to readers to judge between, on the one hand, those who have accused Phillips of immorality and, on the other hand, her presentation of herself as a woman, gravely injured, who tried to defend herself and to survive. Most readers were prepared to sympathize with a young teenager who fled an abusive stepmother, only to fall prey to the blandishments of a gentleman who turned her head with talk of being a "great Lady," lured her to his rooms, plied her with alcohol, and raped her. Phillips's emphasis on her position as a vulnerable "Child" contributed to the emerging concern for children in the age of sentiment; Hogarth similarly appeals to this sentiment in his "Visit to the Quack Doctor" (1743–45), depicting a libertine Viscount who brings his child mistress to the quack so that she can be treated for venereal disease. In the *Apology* account of the rape and elsewhere, the male narrator models the desired reader response, commenting that "to hear her relate the melancholy Scene, even at this Distance of Time, one is scarce able to refrain from Tears."[113] Phillips argues forcefully against a predatory and hypocritical male sexuality that ascribed moral blame to its female victims. The nineteenth-century utilitarian philosopher Jeremy Bentham later testified that Phillips's *Apology* had significantly influenced his thought as a reformer: "It was the first, and not the least effective, in the train of causes in which the works by which my name is most known had their origin."[114]

The accounts of Phillips's later conduct, however, present her not as a pitiful victim, but as a tough, resourceful, often unscrupulous and avaricious combatant. Still a teenager, after the rape, she runs up £500 in debt in a few months, then, to avoid debtors' prison, takes advantage of the

legal rule that husbands are responsible for their wives' debts by contract-
ing a marriage with a man paid to marry her and then disappear. Aware of
the conventions of sentimental, weak femininity, she glories in fooling
men who take those conventions for reality. When she realizes that the
Dutch merchant who has married her has filed for annulment on the
ground of her previous marriage and is about to turn her out of doors,
she packs her jewels and valuables and sends them for safekeeping to a
banker. Mr. Muliman and "3 or 4 ruffians" he brings along to terrify her
attempt to force her to tell where these valuables are or be sent to prison
for theft. Coolly, she reports, she would not be terrified by menaces or by
ruffians brought "on purpose to terrify her out of her Senses, expecting
nothing but Tears, Swooning, and Lamentations from her."[115] The novelistic miseries of marriage represented in Haywood's *History of Miss Betsy
Thoughtless*, where a bad husband quarrels with his wife's household
expenses and kills her pet squirrel by throwing it against a wall, here
become still darker, as Muliman draws his sword, threatens to kill Con,
and, perversely, beats and strips her for his male friends to look at.
Throughout the *Apology*, Phillips reports making her own threats to
men: either they pay her sums of money she considers adequate or she
will humiliate them by publishing her account of their relations with her.
Her claim that she exposes the corruption of great men – libertines who
exploit women and court officials who accept bribes – coexists with
monetary demands that seem very like blackmail. Phillips is not to be
placated by smaller sums that would have kept a country clergyman and
his family in genteel poverty, nor does she express the religious penitence
that was becoming a staple of Methodist spiritual autobiographies and
sentimental fiction.

The *Apology*'s scandalous revelations and its invitation to readers to
judge Phillips's "case" for themselves produced impressive sales and
pamphlet controversy. Rebuffed by publishers possibly fearing litigation,
Phillips kept the copyright herself, became her own publisher, and sold
copies out of her house, retailing over 8,000 copies before the Dublin
printing to earn gross proceeds at that point estimated as over £2,400.[116]
(Compared to the £10 or £20 a beginning contemporary novelist might
get from her publisher, the wages of sin here proved staggeringly lucrative.) For a public already fascinated with Colley Cibber's *Apology for the
Life of Mr. Colley Cibber, Comedian* (1740), Phillips's *Apology* escalated his
brisk impertinence into shocking effrontery.

While Phillips's *Apology* boldly critiques the injustice of patriarchal
domestic and legal systems, the text also invokes existing female types,

including the pathetic victim, the loquacious woman whose tongue is uncontrollable, and the avaricious whore whose greed ruins men. However, neither Phillips nor other women writers of scandalous memoirs in this period evoke the type of the lustful woman or the woman supremely knowledgeable in the arts of love, as Manley had in *Rivella*. Phillips's character, perhaps, bears some resemblance to the villainesses of heroic drama, like Homais in Manley's *Royal Mischief,* although in her avarice exists not only without lust but also without ambition to rule, and it leads to small crimes rather than great ones. (Phillips was accused of attempted murder, but acknowledges only firing a pistol with harmless squibs in it at her husband and his cohorts.) Her conduct thus partially fits patterns established in misogynistic stereotypes of women. Despite apparent similarities between her conduct and that of stereotypically bad women, Phillips struggles to maintain a sense of her own worth. As Rousseau was later to do in his *Confessions* (1782–89), she insists on her worth and on her superior truthfulness, despite society's condemnation of her conduct. In the process of this struggle, she emerges as a woman with "character" and suggests the need for more complex constructions of female character.

LADY VANE'S *MEMOIRS*

One of the best mid-century scandalous autobiographies is "Memoirs of a Lady of Quality," by Frances Anne Holles Vane, Lady Vane, but published in Tobias Smollett's novel, *The Adventures of Peregrine Pickle* (1751). Contemporaries, rightly believing that Smollett published the memoirs with her approval, were astonished that an upper-class woman would venture to print such a thing. Still more astonishingly, her husband apparently did not protest. Lady Luxborough wrote to Shenstone to wonder: " What was ever equal to this fact, and how can one account for it?"[117] Yet print had already been used by others, including Lord Vane, to brand Lady Vane a scandalous woman; she saw publication of the "Memoirs" as a way to set the record straight by offering justification of her conduct. In accounts of her happier love affairs, Lady Vane follows in the footsteps of French women memoirists, celebrating the pleasures of passionate love with upper-class lovers who treat her with respect and delicacy. The language is that of well-worn romance formulas: "Never was passion more eager, delicate, or unreserved, than that which glowed within our breasts."[118] Like Behn, Manley, and some of the French women, she treats passion as a natural fact, ultimately irresistible, although one might struggle against it.

The "Memoirs" are more brilliant in the character she develops of her second husband, William Hollis, 2nd Viscount Vane. Here truth is stranger and more intriguing than most fiction. He marries her because he desires her, yet proves sexually impotent; when she elopes and has one affair after another with more attractive men, he continues to pursue her, again and again pressuring, even forcing, her to return to live with him. At one point, he puts an advertisement in the newspapers offering £100 for her return. (Of this, Lord Egremont commented, "One would think he had lost some favorite spaniel bitch . . . But the advertisement makes sport to the town. He is a very silly young man, half mad, half fool."[119]) Like Pope quoting Cibber's *Apology* in his notes to *The Dunciad*, Lady Vane relishes such evidence of her husband's condemning himself by his own publication. Implicitly, his prior publication works to justify her own.

Lady Vane's descriptions of William make him as repulsive as Solmes in Richardson's *Clarissa*, and more ludicrous. He arrives in a carriage bizarrely stuffed with hay, having paid a fat man to sing his praises: "he was a thin, meagre, shivering creature, of a low stature, with little black eyes, a long nose, sallow complexion, and pitted with the small pox, dressed in a coat of light brown frize, lined with pink-coloured shag, a monstrous solitaire [diamond] and bag [wig], and (if I remember aright) a pair of huge jack-boots."[120] Pressured by friends and family, she says, to marry this creature at eighteen, very soon after the death of her beloved, handsome, and passionate first husband, Lady Vane does not come to the wedding night without sexual experience. Unlike her first husband, Lord Vane on the wedding night huddles in a corner: "when, after a long hesitation, he ventured to approach me, I trembled as if I had been exposed to the embraces of a rattlesnake. Nor did the efforts of his love diminish this antipathy; his attempts were like the pawings of an imp, sent from hell to teize and torment some guilty wretch . . ."[121]

Lady Vane's exploration of her husband's peculiar psychology rivals the classic case histories of psychopathology. She never claims to understand him, but continues to record the empirical data of his irrationality even as his jealous and obsessive pursuit of her becomes increasingly wearisome and frightening. Thus, she reports, he is angry when she refuses to lie in bed for "a whole hour every morning, with my neck uncovered, that by gazing he might quiet the perturbation of his spirits."[122] She struggles to maintain her image of him as a ridiculous and cowardly creature, in part as a strategy to diminish her fear. When one night he startles her by coming into her bedroom with his sword drawn, she acknowledges that she affected to ignore him, "because I was ashamed to acknowledge, even to my own heart, any dread of a person whom I despised so much."[123] About as close as she can get to penetrating the motives of this "perverse humorist" and "self-tormentor" is to speculate that, despite all her expressions of dislike and all her elopements, he is "so ridiculously stocked with vanity and self-conceit . . . that . . . he is still persuaded, that at bottom, I must admire and be enamoured of his agreeable person and accomplishments . . ."[124]

Like other authors of scandal memoirs, Lady Vane tries to substitute her new narrative for the public narratives that have already condemned her. In her case, these included Dr. John Hill's hostile *The History of a Woman of Quality; or, the Adventures of Lady Frail* (1751). In addition to dramatizing the loathsomeness of her husband – which serves as a partial explanation for her conduct – Lady Vane also constructs herself as a character with her own private morality and her own scruples. Candidly acknowledging her unchastity, she declares that she has regarded her ties to her lovers – one at a time – "as sacred as any nuptial tie, and much more binding than a forced or unnatural marriage."[125] During divorce proceedings initiated – but, characteristically, not completed – by her husband, her affairs have become hopelessly public. Philosophically, she renounces "the world with the most perfect resignation," considering that reputation, "ceremonial visits, and empty professions" are worth much less than peace of mind and "the more substantial enjoyments of life," enjoyments clearly including sensual pleasure.[126] On occasion, she condemns herself for behaving badly, usually because she listened to advice rather than following her own heart and her own judgment. When she determines to leave Lord Berkeley, for whom she feels only tenderness and esteem, not passion, she later admits that she was "generally extravagant" in her "notions of happiness" and that she construed tranquility as "insipid languor and stagnation."[127]

Lady Vane insists on her remaining virtues: truthfulness, integrity, sensibility, energy, generosity, and courage. Like all the scandalous memoirists, she denies the simplistic proposition that chastity is the only consequential virtue in women. She outlines scruples that prevented her from behaving in ways she would condemn, as when, despite her need, she returns money to a lover upon leaving him. Despite her animus against her husband, she disdains opportunities to ruin him financially. Yet she succumbs to the ancient sexist idea that women are the weaker, the vainer, and the more foolish sex, sometimes pleading feminine weakness and naiveté as excuses for her elopement and illicit affairs. Her version of love is sentimental and refined, like Crébillon's, although more tender.

Unlike the more combative, angrier Phillips, Lady Vane represents herself as unmercenary, confident of a certain superiority because she understands the pleasures of the heart. She accedes to lovers she fancies out of a tenderness that cannot bear to perpetuate their suffering and to demonstrate her own "sincerity and love."[128] Like other scandalous memoirists, Lady Vane declines to offer the spectacle of an unchaste woman – like Collyer's Prudella – driven by fear and self-loathing to repentance. Conventional ideas about women are so false, Lady Vane claims, that only her insights into her private motives can enable readers to judge rightly of her character and conduct: "So little is the world qualified to judge of private affairs!"[129]

CHARKE'S *NARRATIVE*

Perhaps still more outrageously, Charlotte Charke, Colley Cibber's daughter, in *A Narrative of the Life of Mrs. Charlotte Charke . . . Written by Herself* (1755), told of her life as impresario of a puppet theatre, in male dress as "Mr. Charles," as grocer, sausage seller, and valet. Once actresses had been introduced to the English stage in the Restoration, a brilliant actor and established theatre manager like Cibber could think of bringing up both sons and daughters to take places in the theatre. Cibber prepared his son Theophillus and his youngest daughter Charlotte to be actors and carefully introduced them to the theatrical public. At seventeen, with her parents' approval, Charlotte married a violinist friend of her brother's. Richard Charke, however, soon proved to be a dreadful husband who had married Charlotte only hoping to advance his theatrical career and to profit from her prospects as a potential heiress to her very successful father. Cibber's biographer thinks that, of all his children, the flamboyant Charlotte was the one most like her father, but the one he least understood.[130]

As a young actress Charlotte managed simultaneously to imitate her father and to defy him in peculiarly irritating ways. She defected from the Drury Lane company and started a company of her own, staging her original farce, *The Art of Management* (1735) transparently ridiculing the Drury Lane managers, her father's friends and employers, before she failed and returned home. Worse, she then went over to the company of one of her father's enemies, Henry Fielding, appearing as Lord Place in Fielding's hit *Pasquin* (1736), a satirical farce that included her father among its targets. Cibber, although one of the more tolerant and easygoing fathers of the period, never spoke to her again.

Charke's *Narrative* takes her father's earlier *Apology for the Life of Mr. Colley Cibber* (1740) for a model, attempting to claim for herself a similarly winning candor and taking a similarly perverse pride in what she hopes will be her delightful oddity. Her father's *Apology* never mentions her, but her *Narrative* is in part addressed to him as a desperate plea for understanding and reconciliation. As his *Apology* is a valuable document of theatre history, hers offers intriguing glimpses into the lives of strolling players. Among its best scenes is one in which she and her colleagues attempt to perform Farquhar's *Beaux Stratagem* before a set of drunken butchers and their wives. Provoked by the cacophony of the inattentive audience, Charke, who has begun in breeches playing a male role in Farquhar's comedy, switches to speeches belonging to the hero of Otway's tragedy, *Venice Preserved*, "making Love from Jaffeir" to her fellow actress. This actress, despite being dressed for a female part, responds with a soliloquy of Addison's famous tragic hero, Cato.

While Cibber, as an eminently successful man, in his *Apology* is able to create "a unified professional persona" and "breezily" to "admit his follies," Charke lurches from persona to persona, switching suddenly from plaintive repentant daughter to energetic strolling player and back again.[131] Charke's efforts to appeal to the public by playing standard feminine repertory roles are disrupted by her also playing more vigorous masculine roles, so that "the very communication of her worthy attempts at self-support might deprive her of readers' patronage by turning her into an inappropriate object of support – an unnatural, energetic woman."[132] As much as Cibber's *Apology* struck many contemporaries as appallingly undignified, he never sank to the wretched level of Charlotte's intermittent begging for pity and charity in the *Narrative*.

Charke brings her father into the text of her *Narrative* in more literary ways by her many references to characters from plays he wrote or to theatrical roles he played. These references bring her personal experience to challenge the optimistic view of the power of women his sentimental drama projected, even, to some extent, created. She alludes more than once to his famous comedy, *The Careless Husband* (1704), in which the heroine's refusal to upbraid her husband with his adultery leads to the husband's repenting and newly adoring his wife; this became a popular sentimental plot. Charke's husband had early shown himself a notorious "whoremaster"; he had decamped for Jamaica, leaving her and her child with no support. Charke, complaining that her husband uses prostitutes in the first year of their marriage, declares: "This, consequently, raised in me both Aversion and Contempt . . . not having Years enough to afford me much Reflection, nor Patience sufficient to sit down like Lady *Easy* [in *The Careless Husband*] contented with my Wrongs, 'till Experience might by Chance have made him wiser."[133] Overtly offered as self-criticism, this contrast between her father's fictitious married couple and her own marriage covertly raises questions about the claims to realism of Cibber's sentimental art. At other points, she seeks sympathy by aligning herself with male characters created and/or played by her father. Thus, commenting on the "oddity" of her own youthful disposition, she quotes Cibber's hero's self-description, "for, as Sir *Charles Easy* says to his Lady, *he is often rude and civil without Design*: the same Inadvertency had an equal Dominion over me, and I have avoided or committed Errors, without any premeditation either to offend or oblige."[134]

Charke's relatively short narrative is closer to picaresque than the other women's autobiographies discussed here, trafficking in low, farcical adventures, sometimes in sketchily realized scenes. Given her own conduct, she seems disingenuous – or perhaps excessively in the thrall of sentimental paradigms – professing to find her father's rejection of her inexplicable. Particularly disappointing is her failure to explain her motives for adopting male clothes offstage or for adopting the name Mr. Brown, telling the reader that these motives must remain secret. We can forgive the autobiographer almost anything except lack of candor.

PILKINGTON'S *MEMOIRS*

Charke's *Narrative*, explicitly pleading with her father to restore her to her rightful position as his daughter, failed in that effort; however, Cibber took on another female protégée, not an actress, but a poet eager to play the role of surrogate daughter: Laetitia Pilkington. The relationship between Cibber, poet laureate from 1730 until his death in 1757, and Pilkington, an Irish poet and memoir writer, offers a touching, absurd, and illuminating variation on the theme of male author patron and female author client. Cibber and Pilkington first met in 1739. Cibber at 66 had essentially retired from his long and brilliant career as actor, playwright, and theatre manager, but he continued to have a lively, typically good-natured, interest in young talent. Cibber's original comedies, including *She Wou'd and She Wou'd Not* (1702), *The Careless Husband* (1704), and *The Double Gallant* (1707), still were regularly performed. Pope had not yet crowned Cibber King of the Dunces, although he was soon enough to brand him "This arch Absurd, that wit and fool delights; / This Mess, tos'd up of Hockley-Hole and White's . . ."[135] Pilkington had recently come to London from Dublin, taking lodgings directly across the street from White's chocolate-house, an exclusive club frequented by aristocrats, gamblers, and literary men. Her Irish clergyman husband, Matthew, had just divorced her, presenting evidence that he had discovered her *in flagrante* with Robin Adair. Both Matthew and Laetitia had been young friends and protégés of the aging Jonathan Swift in Dublin, but, for different reasons, Swift had at this point dropped both of them.

Pilkington's *Memoirs of Mrs. Laetitia Pilkington, wife to the Rev. Mr. Matthew Pilkington. Written by herself. Wherein are occasionally interspersed, all her Poems, with Anecdotes of several eminent persons, living and dead. Among others, Dean Swift, Alexander Pope, etc.* (2 volumes, 1748), was an immediate sensation, not quite as staggeringly successful as Phillips's *Apology*, but like it provoking further pamphlet literature, having excerpts printed in the magazines, and going through multiple editions.[136] It has continuously been valued for offering accurate and vivid pictures of Swift during his later years; William Makepeace Thackeray relied on it for his account of Swift in *The English Humourists of the Eighteenth Century* (1853). Swift's twentieth-century scholarly biographer, Irvin Ehrenpreis, declares that she "gives by far the fullest account of Swift's social behavior in late middle age" and that "she had a most extraordinary memory, and has proved reliable whenever I could verify her facts – except for natural evasions concerning her shady liaisons."[137] The book is an astonishing combination of memoir, literary history, scandal, and verse miscellany – a sort of unholy marriage between Manley's *Rivella*, Richard Savage's *An Author to be Lett* (1729), and Cibber's *Apology*.

Pilkington represents her relationship with her husband, also a poet, as having degenerated into a destructive sibling rivalry, the two of them struggling for recognition from their fatherly but taunting patron, Swift. She insists that she knows her place, recognizes her inferiority, and acknowledges Matthew's superior natural talent and learning. Yet, at the same time, she cites Swift as authority for her intellectual superiority over Matthew. At least two of her early poems, not very good ones, take the stance of the good wife toward a loved husband. More interestingly, when her husband is first apart from her in London, she elects to paraphrase an Horatian ode (book 3, ode 7) in which the poet speaks to separated lovers telling the woman to trust her husband's constancy and warning her to avoid temptation herself. Swift, Laetitia testifies, was her first and best teacher, though an eccentric and an ungentle one: "if I have any Merit, as a Writer, I must gratefully acknowledge it due to the Pains he took to teach me to think and speak with Propriety; tho', to tell the Truth, he was a very rough sort of Tutor for one of my Years and Sex; for whenever I made use of an inelegant Phrase, I was sure of a deadly Pinch . . ."[138] The more favor Swift shows toward her, the more envious Matthew becomes. When Matthew decides to wile away a winter evening writing an Horatian ode, she writes one more quickly, claiming that she expected to please him but found instead that he became angry. "Here," she says, "let me seriously advise every Lady who has the Misfortune to be poetically turn'd, never to marry a Poet, but remember *Swift's* lines":

> What Poet wou'd not grieve to see
> His Friend cou'd write as well as he;
> And rather than be thus out-done,
> He'd hang them every Mother's Son.[139]

Matthew eventually published not only *Poems on Several Occasions* (1731) and various religious works, but an important *Gentleman's and Connoisseur's Dictionary of Painters* (1771).

In London, divorced, Laetitia attracts Cibber's attention by publishing an Ovidian verse fable, *The Statues: or, The Trial of Constancy. A Tale for the Ladies* (1739).[140] A Queen, finding a handsome stranger, informs him that the man who wins her hand and fortune must be faithful for the single day each month that she is required to descend into the sea to visit her father, Neptune. The young man vows enthusiastically, yet on the first night is unfaithful. Before he is turned into a statue to join the twenty men who had failed before him, the Queen rebukes him and his sex, transferring to men epithets traditionally attached to women:

> Thy changeful Sex in Perfidy delight,
> Despise Perfection, and fair Virtue slight,
> False, fickle, base, tyrannic, and unkind,
> Whose Hearts, nor Vows can chain, nor Honour bind:
> Mad to possess, by Passion blindly led;
> And then as mad to stain the nuptial Bed . . .[141]

Reversing the genders, Pilkington's story recalls the premise of *The Arabian Nights*, in which the King, having caught his first wife in adultery, resolves henceforth to wed virgins whom he will kill on the morning after their wedding nights. More directly, as she notes, she has adapted a story from Thomas-Simon Gueullette's *Mille et une heures, contes péruviens* (1733), translated as *Peruvian Tales, Related, In One Thousand and One Hours. By One of the Select Virgins of Cusco, To the Ynca of Peru* (1734).

Cibber undertakes to assist Pilkington in finding subscribers for her poems and suggests that, to counter rumors that her poems were actually written by her husband, she write a new poem upon "some Subject, that has never yet been touched upon."[142] Cleverly and insinuatingly, she writes a panegyric to the much-ridiculed Cibber, praising his truthfulness and benevolence, concluding:

> If, which I know these Facts are true,
> Confess, at least, the Verse is new,
> That publicly speaks well of you.[143]

Cibber responds by including her verses in his pamphlet, *The Egotist, or Colley upon Cibber* (1743), and promises hints for her *Memoirs*.

Like Charke, Pilkington follows Cibber's *Apology* in representing her own character humorously as unique and odd; Pilkington, however, oscillates between representing herself as a witty humorist and representing herself as a more sentimental, wretched, and pitiable woman. In a truly Cibberian moment, she boasts that she is like Falstaff, "not only witty myself but . . . the Occasion that wit is in others."[144] In this most literary of the scandal memoirs, Pilkington supports her character as a wit with copious poetical quotations and by printing her poems, many of which, she reveals, she has written for hire at the behest of gentleman would-be-wits who passed them off as their own. Although at points she explicitly renounces satire, she also quotes Pope's late satires to suggest that, like Pope, she is revealing and scourging vice, and imitates Pope's practice in the late satires of cryptically writing names of targets as initials and dashes. Chief among the vices she rebukes is the alleged hypocrisy and stinginess of well-placed Churchmen who refuse to give her money or give only small sums. (Considering that she had been officially divorced for adultery in the Church court and that she was consorting with men not known for virtue, it is not clear to me that these clergy ought to have considered themselves obliged to support her.) Other offenders are married men who solicit her sexual favors; these she threatens to expose – unless they subscribe to her poems. Like Manley, then, Pilkington aspires to be thought a wit.

Yet Pilkington claims no expertise or interest in the arts of love and seeks to dissociate herself sharply from Manley, Haywood, and Con Phillips. Pilkington declares that she is a "modest Woman," that she was innocent of adultery, that she has been distraught over the loss of her reputation and the loss of her children, indeed, that she was on the brink of suicide.[145] In "Sorrow," written "from my heart," she is the picture of grieving sensibility:

> While sunk in deepest Solitude and Woe,
> My streaming Eyes with ceaseless Sorrow flow,
> While Anguish wears the sleepless Night away,
> And fresher Grief awaits returning Day . . .[146]

Drawing a distinction between herself and Manley and Haywood, Pilkington disclaims "the wicked Art of painting up Vice in attractive Colours, as too many of our Female Writers have done to the Destruction of Thousands, amongst whom Mrs. *Manley*, and Mrs. *Haywood* deserve the foremost Rank."[147]

Acutely aware of her anomalous place as one officially exiled from a proper family, Pilkington still tries to appeal for support on the basis of her sex, seeking the male protection she cannot get from a father or a husband. When she visits Dr. Richard Meade to ask for money to publish her poems, he skeptically inquires whether she supposes her poems are as good as Pope's. She replies, ". . . I did not presume to put myself in any Degree of Comparison with so justly an admired Writer, but that perhaps, on Account of my Sex, I might find a little Favour."[148] Pilkington seems aware that in soliciting support for the printing of her work she is simultaneously appealing to people's desire to be amused by her wit and to a charitable obligation to support a poor woman who has encountered difficulties. She thus reinforces the reviewer's idea we noticed at the beginning of this chapter that women's literary work was not to be judged by the more severe standards appropriate to men's and that men had a duty to be generous and indulgent toward women writers.

Pilkington teases the reader with contradictions between her stance as a bold wit and her stance as a pitiable woman. She undercuts her own claims of innocence with levity and with simultaneous justifications for her adultery (should she actually have committed adultery). As one critic suggests, Pilkington boasts of turning "lubricious attempts on her person into donations for her writing," yet uses innuendo to "leave room for a kind of erotic ambiguity."[149] Whereas Charke simply withholds her secrets, Pilkington engages in verbal slight of hand, seeming to collude with an implied reader who can recognize her need to claim respectability, wink at their shared knowledge of the sexual realities of life in the world, and admire her ability to transform her pariah status into an entertainment for which she will be paid.

CONCLUSION

Instead of Astell's strenuous vision of women's intellectual and moral capacities, in this period most women writers reinforce the idea that God and nature created women as different from men, more tender, weaker, properly subordinated to men and dependent upon male admiration and male protection. Women grasped opportunities afforded by the idea that women had special knowledge of those subjects most appropriate for women. Thus, Sarah Fielding staked out the field of children's literature, Hannah Glasse earned her fame in cookery and domestic economy, and Eliza Haywood and Frances Brooke created women's magazines.

It is significant that the more transgressive women writers – Con Philips, Lady Vane, and, especially, Laetitia Pilkington, with her more obvious literary interests and ambitions – were essentially one-book authors. Inventive as they were in developing forms for the narration of their lives and their critiques of the hypocrisies and injustices of patriarchal society, the personas they created did not command much cultural authority. Despite their insistence that women's characters were about much more than chastity, they remained focused on sexuality and gender and contributed to reinforcing sexist stereotypes. Having invoked self-defensive comedy to make their own personas farcical, both Charke and Pilkington experimented with farce, but (sympathetic as I am to farce) neither created anything trenchant or memorable. Charke did write four moralistic fictions, including *The History of Henry Dumont* (1756), which attacked male homosexuality, but she also failed to develop a successful literary career.

The increased acceptance of women as members of the literary family and as worthy of literary patronage and literary approval benefited primarily those women writers like Mary Collyer, Sarah Fielding, and Charlotte Lennox who supported virtue and who could at least be perceived as staying within the bounds appropriate to women. Cultivation of sentiment offered certain advantages to women. Jettisoning the amorous novel, with its heroines incapable of resisting passion, as Collyer showed, could mean imagining a heroine capable of self-control without also insisting that she was incapable of sexual desire. Novelists like these seized the opportunity to continue women's campaign against male libertinism by representing male libertines as not only atheistical and immoral but also as lacking in sensibility; they created new kinds of male heroes, more moral and more respectful of women.

For all groups subordinated by gender or by class, sentimental values offered more democratic ideas of human worth against which the privileged could be judged and found wanting. Thus, Fielding could elevate her sensitive impoverished women over the rich people who sadistically torment them, Leapor could claim human and moral superiority to employers who unfeelingly denied her human capacities, and the African Briton Philis Wheatley could invoke sentiment in the service of the campaign to abolish slavery. Sentimental glorification of tender, considerate husbands and fathers constituted a propaganda campaign to transform male characters. Some writers begin to imagine a less hierarchical world, as Fielding does in her emphasis on sharing wealth and on mutuality in *David Simple* and as Leapor does in "The Proclamation of Apollo."

On the other hand, uncritical celebration of tenderness and of "natural" feeling in the family, products of sentiment, threatened to become a disabling orthodoxy, replacing older religious and moral conceptions of duty with less thoughtful, more clichéd, more psychologically ensnaring, reverence for pity and "natural" affection. Hence, the glorification of filial and wifely abjection, the desperate, implausible representations of evildoers suddenly converted by the spectacle of virtue, as in *Felicia to Charlotte*, or the more obviously despairing stories of sentimental heroes and heroines, like David Simple and his friends, too fragile to survive in a real world. Sentiment's discouragement of wit as hostile and cruel was disabling to literature, but perhaps especially so for women, who were more stringently debarred from wit and who had more to be critical about. As Pilkington not very kindly said of Haywood's reformed style in *The Female Spectator*, "Mrs. *Haywood* seems to have dropped her former luscious Stile, and, for Variety, presents us with the insipid: Her *Female Spectators* are a Collection of trite Stories, delivered to us in stale and worn-out Phrases . . ."[150]

Although the 1740s and 1750s are often thought of as the crucial period of the "rise of the novel," and more women wrote more "novels," it is more useful to see this period as dominated by interpenetrating prose forms, including essay, letter, memoir, pseudo-memoir, biography, and fictional story. The scandalous memoirists probably garnered more cultural attention and more money for their individual books than the woman novelists did. Acute fascination with claims to historicity or journalistic truth fueled the response to Phillips, Vane, Charke, and Pilkington. They also often prompted fiction writers to model their narratives on nonfictional forms and to appeal to readers by representing current events, as Lennox does in making her *Life of Harriot Stuart* (1750) like a biography and including scenes of the negotiations between the Mohawks and the British in New York. On the one hand, Sarah Fielding's invocation of Fénelon's *Telemachus* as a model for *David Simple* highlights the extent to which she understood the story as a convenient scaffold to which she can attach moral essays. On the other hand, Haywood's didactic writing in *The Female Spectator*, *The Wife*, and *The Husband* consistently supports its essayistic analysis and injunctions with illustrative stories. Phillips's *Apology* combines biographical narrative with a developed essayistic critique of corruption and injustice in the legal system. The best "novel" of this period, I think, is Lennox's *Female Quixote*. But its accomplishments are not the more novelistic ones of character development or creating a fully developed social and economic world; instead, they arise from Lennox's sophisticated meditation on a central literary problem of the day: the competition among modes of narrative representation and their contested claims to truth value.

CHAPTER 6

Bluestockings and sentimental writers, 1756–1776

1773 [Hester Chapone]. *Letters on the Improvement of the Mind. Addressed to a Young Lady.* 2 volumes

1774 Hannah More. *The Inflexible Captive: A Tragedy* (published Bristol, 1774; performed Bath and Exeter, 1775)

1774–76 (written) Abigail Adams. *Letters*

INTRODUCTION

In 1756 England's rivalry with France for trade and control in America, the Caribbean, Africa, and India began the Seven Years War (1756–63), the first modern world war. British victory in 1763, and the new territorial acquisitions secured by the Peace of Paris, laid the foundation of an extended empire. After the peace, in the 1760s and 1770s, the British struggled with the problems of establishing functioning ministerial control over an expanded state, the division of spoils among office holders, and the difficult fiscal issues posed by the larger state. The empire required managing India affairs, working out conflicts between the East India Company and the state, and confronting conflict with the American colonies that exploded with the American Declaration of Independence in 1776. Ironically, British victory in the Seven Years War, by driving France off the North American continent, reduced the British American colonists' need for protection from a hostile European power and thus facilitated their revolution.

Although women did not play military or major political roles in these great events, and although battle and high political tension did not come as close to most English households as they had in the English Civil War of the seventeenth century, most women of the literate classes in 1756–76 knew that they were living in times of great historical significance. Patriotic feelings were intense over the rivalry with France and over the prospect of Britain's becoming an imperial power that might outdo even ancient Rome. Many women's letters show their concern with the fortunes of the British army, with challenges to ministerial policy, and with popular challenges to government power by the radical John Wilkes and his followers. Most women writers now refrained from publishing political pamphlets, but the radical Catharine Macaulay tangled with Edmund Burke in her pamphlet *Reply to Mr. Burke's Pamphlet, entitled, Thoughts on the Causes of the Present Discontents* (1770). She argued for more frequent parliaments, urged an extension of the franchise to men who did not meet the property qualifications of the existing acts, and attacked "place men," members of Parliament who held profitable offices from Crown patronage and who were consequently expected to vote in support of Crown measures. In *Address to the People of England, Scotland, and Ireland, on the Present Important Crisis of Affairs* (1775) Macaulay supported American complaints about ministerial injustices in the colony, including colonial resistance to taxation without representation.

History was the dominant literary genre, as fascinated readers and writers compared ancient history, French history, and British history. William Robertson of Edinburgh, an important Scottish enlightenment historian, first traced the transition from feudal to commercial society in his *History of Scotland* (1759). He then studied the same transition on the continent in *The History of the Reign of Emperor Charles V* (1769), the sixteenth-century Habsburg Emperor and King of Spain. Robertson sold the copyright of the latter for £4,000. Gibbon wrote his magnificent and enduring *Decline and Fall of the Roman Empire* (6 volumes, 1776–88) for a public accustomed to discussing parallels between Roman history and British history. As Karen O'Brien has pointed out, during this period the public considered history "a nationally important form of writing"; publishers, who sometimes paid research expenses or conceived projects themselves, used "patriotic rhetoric" to attract subscribers and purchasers.[1] Elizabeth Montagu and Elizabeth Carter read their way through Thucydides, Livy, and Tacitus, as well as many historians of modern Europe, writing back and forth to discuss their judgments of characters, the relative merits of ancients and moderns, and historiographical method. Readers eagerly devoured the memoirs that served as primary documents of French history, sometimes in French, sometimes in English translation.

Women translated historical works from French and wrote original histories. To her earlier translations of *The Memoirs of the Duke of Sully* and Voltaire's important *Age of Lewis XIV* (1752), Charlotte Lennox added *Memoirs for the History of Madame de Maintenon and of the last Age* (1757), a book, as we shall see, of special interest to women readers.[2] Sarah Scott wrote original works on three subjects in European history: *History of Gustavus Erickson, King of Sweden* (1761), the hero who liberated Sweden from Danish rule and under whose rule Sweden became a Protestant country; *The History of Mecklenburg, from the First Settlement of the Vandals in the Country to the Present Time* (1762), intended to satisfy British curiosity about the country of Charlotte, Princess of Mecklenburg, who was to become the wife of George III; and *The Life of Theodore Agrippa D'Aubigné, Containing a Succinct Account of the most Remarkable Occurrences during the Civil Wars of France . . .* (1772), the French Huguenot hero who lived in the sixteenth and seventeenth centuries.

Scott's *Gustavus* and *Theodore Agrippa D'Aubigné* illustrate the kind of character-based historical writing using literary techniques also used in fiction that helped expand the audience for historical writing. To David Hume's most popular and widely read work, *The History of England* (6 volumes, 1754–62), Catharine Macaulay replied with her own, radical, *History of England* (8 volumes, 1763–83), arguably the most impressive book written by a British woman writer during the period covered by this chapter.

As compared to the novel, especially the kind of domestic novel thought suitable to lady writers that we considered in the previous chapter, history offered a much less claustrophobic discursive space in which women could contemplate human actions in a wider world and consider human behavior and human motives of a darker, more complex, kind. This was true even though historical writing was impelled by a didacticism of its own. The gendered division of labor in the literary family discussed in the last chapter had quite effectively restricted women's writing in the novel to a rather narrow domestic sphere and to observations about life suited to virtuous young ladies. Moralists', and even novelists', attacks on novel reading and writing as trivial wastes of time helped contribute to legitimating women's interest in history, regarded as a sober, improving subject. Since mid-century historians were now generally simply well-educated writers, rather than great men participant observers like the earlier Earl of Clarendon, historical writing was becoming somewhat more accessible to women. Few objected to women's reading history, although women's writing history was more controversial. When Scott published her history of Gustavus, she took the precaution of using a male pseudonym. The reception of Macaulay's *History* combined celebration of her as the "British Thucydides" with complaints that she had trespassed in a genre properly reserved for male writers. Significant novels continued to be written, including domestic novels by Sarah Fielding, Elizabeth Griffith, and Frances Sheridan, but good histories yielded authors more money and more literary prestige than novels. Histories were likely to be the subjects of long lead articles in the literary reviews that still relegated reviews of novels to brief, usually condescending, paragraphs at the back of the magazine.

The women writers who dominate this period are the bluestockings, famous for their intellectual discussions in salons and on paper, often militantly virtuous, and, in the tradition of Astell, concerned about developing the minds and characters of women. The "Queen of the Blues" was Elizabeth Robinson Montagu. Married to a grandson of the

Earl of Sandwich, she was a very wealthy woman who used her wealth to support a London salon and an extensive network of patronage and charity. Among the women writers Montagu patronized was Elizabeth Carter, who in 1769 amazed the world with her translation of the Greek philosopher, Epictetus. This book seemed to contemporaries the most dazzling evidence of female intellectual capacity. The bluestockings were closely associated with Church of England clergymen, none more so than Carter's friend Catharine Talbot, who lived with the family of Thomas Secker, Archbishop of Canterbury from 1758 until his death in 1768. Carter published Talbot's religious *Reflections on the Seven Days of the Week* in 1770 shortly after Talbot's death. Distributed by the Society for Promoting Christian Knowledge, *Reflections* sold over 25,000 copies between 1770 and 1809.[3] Montagu also encouraged Hester Chapone, niece of the Bishop of Winchester, and widow of a lawyer; Chapone, in her turn, celebrated Carter by contributing "An Irregular Ode. To Mrs. Elizabeth Carter" to Carter's *Epictetus*. Hannah More, once she came to London in 1773 or 1774, frequented Montagu's salons, and, in this early phase of her career at least, was also considered one of the bluestockings. Loosely associated with the bluestockings, Sarah Scott, Montagu's sister, and Sarah Fielding, were both patronized by Montagu. The success of Carter's *Epictetus* encouraged Sarah Fielding to complete her own translation from the Greek, *Xenephon's Memoirs of Socrates, with the Defence of Socrates before his Judges*, published by subscription in 1762 with the names of Carter, Montagu, and other bluestockings in the subscription list. Fielding probably earned over £200 for *Xenephon*, the only book she published with her name on the title page.[4]

The bluestocking writers were aware of following the earlier women writers described in chapter two as "the party of virtue," especially Rowe and Trotter Cockburn. Talbot in an early letter to Carter had referred to Rowe as "our favourite," and later reported, "I scarce know a greater pleasure than reading over a book one is fond of with persons of taste and candour, to whom it is entirely new. A great deal of this pleasure I have had lately. Mrs. Rowe's works were an undiscovered treasure to Mrs. Berkeley, and she values them as they deserve."[5] We earlier noted Carter's poem "On the Death of Mrs. Rowe" (1737), and Carter cared enough about Rowe to make a pilgrimage to Frome, the town where Rowe had lived. A fourth edition of Rowe's *Works* with the *History of Joseph* was published in 1756. Talbot and Carter eagerly anticipated Thomas Birch's publication of *The Works of Mrs. Catharine Cockburn, Theological, Moral, Dramatic, and Poetical* before it appeared in 1751. When it did appear,

Carter commented, "she seems to have had a most remarkable clear understanding and an excellent heart." Talbot replied, "What a pity that her last years were in a manner lost in obscurity so little suited to her genius."[6]

CHAPONE'S *LETTERS ON THE IMPROVEMENT OF THE MIND*

Hester Chapone's much read and often reprinted *Letters on the Improvement of the Mind. Addressed to a Young Lady* (1773), dedicated to Elizabeth Montagu, lays out a challenging program of reading and discussion designed "to gain some insight into the general history of the world."[7] *Letters* was written in the first instance for Chapone's fifteen-year-old niece; the published version preserves Chapone's persona as a concerned aunt, thus relying on the kind of familial model discussed in the previous chapter to legitimate her authority. Like Astell's *Serious Proposal to the Ladies*, Chapone's *Letters* offer instructions about how to develop one's mind and nurture one's soul. Greek and Roman history, Chapone explains, will be deeply interesting and highly entertaining both because they are intrinsically great and because they are models for modern emulation:

As Greece and Rome were distinguished as much for genius as valour, and were the theatres, not only of the greatest military actions – the noblest efforts of liberty and patriotism – but of the highest perfection of arts and sciences, their immortal fame is a subject of wonder and emulation, even to these distant ages; – and, it is thought a shameful degree of ignorance, even in our sex, to be unacquainted with the nature and revolutions of their governments, and with the characters and stories of their most illustrious heroes. – Perhaps, when you are told that the government and the national character of your own countrymen have been compared with those of the Romans, it may not be an useless amusement, when you read Roman History, to carry this observation in your mind, and to examine how far the parallel holds good.[8]

Of modern European histories, the history of France is most closely connected with the history of England and is the most important for British readers: "The extent of their dominion and influence – their supposed superiority in elegance and politeness – their eminence in the Arts and Sciences – and that intercourse of thought – if so I may call it – which subsists between us, by the mutual communication of literary productions – make them peculiarly interesting to us . . ."[9] But the stories of the dramatic – if sometimes morally disturbing – modern conquests in the West Indies, in America, and in India are now also relevant to a British young lady:

You may pass to every quarter of the earth, and find yourself still in the British dominion: – this island, in which we live, is the least portion of it – and, if we were to adopt the stile of ancient conquerors, we might call it the throne, from which we rule the world – To this boast, we are better entitled than some of those who formerly called themselves *Masters of the Globe*, as we possess an empire of greater extent, and from the superior advantages of our commerce, much greater power and riches; – but we have now too many rivals in dominion, to take upon us such haughty titles.[10]

Chapone's *Letters on the Improvement of the Mind* was the most widely read work of the first generation of bluestockings; between 1773 and 1851 it went through fifty-seven editions or reprintings.[11]

ROME AND FRANCE

Neither the meaning of Rome nor the meaning of France was unambiguous. The image of Rome was Janus-faced: one face offered the model of a great imperial power for British emulation; the other offered a crucial model of republican virtue and resistance to tyranny in the name of freedom that inspired English radicals like Macaulay and American revolutionaries like John and Abigail Adams.

The complexity of the Roman paradigm is evident in the work of Philis Wheatley, an African poet educated while she was a slave in Boston. Wheatley was the author of *Poems on Various Subjects, Religious and Moral* (1773), first published in London, the first book of poetry by an African Briton or African American. The opening poem in this collection, "To Mæcenus," addresses her patron under the name of the Roman who patronized Virgil and Horace. Her list of gifted writers includes the Roman playwright Terence, who, she correctly reminds readers, was born at Carthage, in Africa. Now, Wheatley implies, other Africans may become poets of the British empire, following the model of Terence, himself once a slave, but finally a free man and a great writer in Rome. Wheatley's poem on George III, "To the King's most Excellent Majesty, 1768," hails the King as ruler of an empire of "num'rous nations" and hopes – after the 1766 repeal of the Stamp Act, which the colonists had characterized as an act of imperial tyranny and enslavement – for a new pax Britannica.[12] On the other hand, Wheatley uses republican ideology not only to align herself with the American colonists' lamentations over alleged British tyranny, but also to confront the Americans with the contradictions between their demands for republican freedoms for themselves and their unwillingness to permit Africans enslaved in America to be free. Addressing the Earl of Dartmouth, the Secretary of State responsible for North America, in 1772, the poet grounds her authority to speak about the cruelty of enslavement in her own literal enslavement. Shortly after her manumission, in 1774 Wheatley wrote a letter published in the *Connecticut Gazette* and other New England newspapers supporting the abolitionist activities of a Native American (and Presbyterian minister); she yoked biblical language of liberation with the republican language of natural rights and liberty to assert an inherent love of liberty in all humans.[13]

France could stand for either libertinism and absolutism in contrast to British virtue and democracy or for laudable refinement and cosmopolitanism. Some women saw themselves as champions of English culture, as Elizabeth Montagu did in her *Essay on the Writings and Genius of Shakespeare* (1769), written to counter Voltaire's championing of Corneille and his attacks on Shakespearian drama as barbarous. At the same time, most women writers, including Montagu, even during the Seven Years War, maintained a lively interest in French history and an appreciation of French literature and learning; they valued French enlightenment writers in part for their cosmopolitanism, their efforts to rise above national prejudices. Thus, Frances Brooke introduces her translation of the Abbé Claude François Xavier Millot's *Eléments de l'histoire d'Angleterre* (1769) by remarking that the translator "knows how difficult it is to break the ties of education, to change an habitual mode of thinking, and to become absolutely a citizen of the world. She has only to wish, that she may . . . have read, translated, and observed, in the same spirit of universal charity and philosophic candor, in which her author wrote."[14]

LENNOX'S *MEMOIRS FOR THE HISTORY OF MADAME DE MAINTENON*

Writing by or about French women presented a special set of issues to English women. In general, the achievements of French women, including their achievements and the recognition they had gained as writers, were an inspiration and a challenge to their English sisters. Often, when English women writers contemplate their French sisters, their response is, implicitly or explicitly, if French women can display such talent and be honored for it, why cannot the English?

Among the most significant French heroines celebrated by an English translator was Madame de Maintenon. Charlotte Lennox published *Memoirs for the History of Madame de Maintenon and of the Last Age* in four volumes in 1757. This was a feminist exercise in recovering a heroine whose name and fame had suffered, not oblivion, but infamy. Maintenon was widely believed to have been one of the mistresses of Louis XIV, as well as the woman partly responsible for his decision to revoke the Edict of Nantes, thus ending toleration for French Protestants. She had been the subject of numerous satires and scandal chronicles, including, and available in English, *The Cabinet Open'd, or, the Secret History of Madame de Maintenon, with the French King* (1690). Nevertheless, according to twentieth-century scholarship, the scandal was unfounded.[15] Lennox elected to translate a French book, first published in Amsterdam in 1755–56, one using Maintenon's own letters and other original documents. The French book refutes the attacks on Maintenon, offering evidence that she was chaste and married to Louis in a morganatic marriage. It argues that for thirty years she had more influence at the French court "than it is common for queens or even mistresses to possess," that she used this influence for the good, and that she was a heroine who added to the glory of France.[16]

Like many *Memoirs* published in the eighteenth century, the *Mémoires pour servir à l'histoire de Madame de Maintenon, et à celle du siècle passé* (1755–56) is a complex book. Its author, Laurent Angliviel de La Beaumelle, although born in France, lived at various times in Scandinavia and Germany. He was a contentious character, perhaps most remembered for tangling with Voltaire over *The Age of Louis XIV*.[17] When he wrote the *Memoirs of Madame de Maintenon*, he was a professor of French literature at the University of Copenhagen. An important set of letters and papers by and about Madame de Maintenon was in the possession of Louis Racine, son of the dramatist, presumably because the dramatist and Madame de Maintenon had been friends. Louis Racine intended to use them to write a biography, but, as he had not done so, passed them on to the eager Danish professor, who did. La Beaumelle's biography celebrates Maintenon as a woman of extraordinary piety, charity, and intelligence. For instance, he stresses that, unlike most people who experience poverty and are then elevated to wealth, Madame de Maintenon "looked upon her elevation as a burden which the practice of benevolence could alone enable her to bear."[18]

La Beaumelle devotes much attention to Maintenon's project of getting the King to establish and to endow a boarding school for about 250 girls, and to her involvement with the administration and even day-to-day operations of the school over a long period. This school, subsequently called St. Cyr, was established in 1686, eight years before Astel's proposal for a similar institution in England. La Beaumelle reports that many opposed its establishment and that it was even rumored to be a seraglio for the King, but that Maintenon triumphed over all opposition and despised all rumors. Reading the French book shortly after its publication, Montagu wrote of her admiration for Maintenon's prudence and wisdom and wished that an institution like St. Cyr were established in London.[19]

It is reasonable to suppose that Lennox translated this book, intended by La Beaumelle to be a defense of the glory of France, at least in part because she understood it as historical evidence of the intelligence and virtue of women, and as evidence of the capacity of at least some women to play important roles in their countries. Some scholars have believed that Samuel Johnson wrote the preface to Lennox's translation, but the preface she prints is clearly her translation of La Beaumelle's preface to his book; some of his ideas about historical writing happen to overlap with Johnson's.[20]

Lennox, like Elizabeth Griffith and Charlotte Smith after her, generally dealt with racier and worldlier material in her translations from the French than she did in her original work. Nonfiction, or at least ostensible nonfiction, books about or by celebrated French mistresses, played a special role for English women writers. Griffith, most known for her sentimental novels and plays, also translated *The Memoirs of Ninon de L'Enclos, with her Letters to Monsr. de St. Evremond and to the Marquis de Sevigné* (1761) and Marthe-Marguerite, Madame de Caylus's *Memoirs, Anecdotes, and Characters of the Court of Lewis XIV* (1770).[21] One could hardly write about French history without encountering mistresses, including royal mistresses. Despite La Beaumelle's insistence on Maintenon's chastity, he necessarily also deals with Louise de La Vallière, Louis's first major mistress, whose *Meditations and Penitential Prayers* Lennox translated in 1774. La Beaumelle also considers Madame de Montespan, the King's second major mistress, since Maintenon was tutor to the illegitimate children of both La Vallière and Montespan.

In their moralized original work, respectable English ladies were not supposed to notice that revered kings, like many other men, had mistresses, and that some mistresses, far from being hounded out of society and suffering condign punishment, were most politely treated. Given this, they must have been relieved to have found in translation at least one discursive space where they were not obliged to pretend utter ignorance about such matters. Indeed, looking back at *The Female Quixote*, which defines the respectable novel not only against romance but also against the scandal chronicle, one can notice a tiny allusion to the Hanoverian mistresses in the story of Miss Groves. Lennox's publisher, Andrew

Millar, resisted publishing the History of Miss Groves, and the manuscript version of this episode may well have been more scathing than the
surviving printed version.[22]

LETTERS

Even more than in translation, in familiar letters written with no intent to
publish, women writers of this period show themselves far more engaged
in public and in worldly matters than the representation of women in the
contemporary domestic novel would suggest. As in earlier periods, some
women's letters written with no intent to publish offer especially engaging
personae and lively, candid accounts of events, feelings, and ideas. Accomplished letter writers of this period include, in addition to the bluestockings already mentioned, Mary Delany, who from 1743 to 1768 lived
in Ireland with her husband, the Dean of Down in the Church of Ireland,
and Frances Boscawen, wife of an admiral and a bluestocking hostess.
Self-censorship in writing intended for publication probably became more
severe as newer standards of propriety and of sentimentalism combined to
make women concerned about their reputations very careful. Fears of
being thought "wits" could terrorize even aristocratic women of this
period. Some lamented the alleged looseness of Montagu's *Embassy
Letters*, posthumously published in 1763, although the *Monthly Review*
was relieved to find no sentimental femininity in them: "There is no
affectation of female delicatesse, there are no prettynesses, no Ladyisms in
these natural, easy familiar Epistles."[23] Self-censorship in the novel by
writers committed to Richardsonian and Johnsonian theories of the
novel's responsibility to provide moral exemplars was especially rigorous;
it has led more than one critic of these novelists to lament, as Betty Rizzo
does of Sarah Scott, that the fiction lacks "the humor and satiric wit so
prevalent in her letters."[24] On the other hand, the wide popularity of
collections of letters, including those of Madame de Sévigné, Ninon de
L'Enclos, Katherine Philips, and Lady Mary Wortley Montagu herself –
and the wide popularity of the epistolary novel – gave even those women
writers who were not intending to publish their letters valuable models
and, sometimes, useable insights into the aesthetics of letter writing.

Two fine sets of letters not meant for publication, one written in
England by Sarah Byng Osborn and the other in Massachusetts by Abigail
Adams, capture some of the differences between the London metropole
and the unhappy American colonies. As was the case in the English Civil
War, women writers normally take the points of view of their families, feel

empowered and motivated to write by the sense that they had useful "intelligence" to offer their relatives, and often write to advance what they understand to be the interests and entitlements of their families. Newspapers still sometimes made men and women correspondents alike wonder whether they could have any valuable intelligence to add to newspaper accounts of events, but the better correspondents recount events not covered, offer motives not publicly admitted, and otherwise fill gaps in official accounts. The better correspondents are also sensitive to the relational dynamic of letters, adjusting and varying the selves they present to suit different recipients, and, where appropriate, allow correspondences to develop complex and intimate relationships.[25]

SARAH OSBORN'S *LETTERS*

Sarah Byng, born in 1693, was the daughter of Admiral Sir George Byng, created Viscount Torrington in 1721; she sees the world from a perspective that is both uniquely her own and that of a woman within the British establishment. In 1710 she married John Osborn, a descendant of the Dorothy Osborne famous for her seventeenth-century love letters to Sir William Temple. John died in 1719, leaving his widow with three sons. Unlike the less worldly heroines of contemporary sentimental novels, Sarah learned about the management and improvement of the heavily encumbered estate so that when her eldest son, Sir Danvers, attained his majority, the estate was solvent and flourishing. Scattered sets of the long-lived Sarah's letters written between 1721 and 1773 survive, including fond letters written to Sir Danvers, who died in 1753 as governor of the colony of New York.

Osborn exercised her rhetorical skills in a letter-writing campaign attempting to save the life of her brother. Days after the English declaration of war against France on 15 May 1756, her brother, Admiral John Byng, arrived with an inadequately equipped fleet to defend the British base at Minorca. When he failed to repel the French and retreated to Gibraltar, Minorca was lost. He was court-martialed for cowardice, disaffection, and negligence; acquitted of the first two charges; convicted of negligence, and shot. (He was the Admiral of whom Voltaire famously wrote in *Candide*: in England "it is good now and then to put one admiral to death in order to encourage the others."[26])

As during the Civil War, the writing of petitions continued to be one of the few forms of political activity open to women. Indeed, convention dictated that women were especially appropriate petitioners on behalf of their family members and may even have permitted some additional freedom in argument on the grounds that women were not political actors whose views could have dangerous consequences. Admiral Byng's court-martial immediately became a domestic political issue. The ministry defended the necessity of conviction and punishment under the Articles of War and in the interest of military effectiveness, while the opposition claimed that an incompetent administration was scapegoating and martyring Byng. Voltaire, characteristically, saw the conviction of Byng as a human rights issue and wrote to the imprisoned Byng, enclosing a testimonial to his good conduct from the opposing French officer. Sarah hoped the court martial board's recommendation for mercy would lead to a pardon. In pursuit of this hope, she wrote to the Duke of Bedford to gain his support should the case be referred to the cabinet council, of which he was a member; she also directly petitioned the Lords of the Admiralty. A wonderfully ambiguous "perhaps" in her petition allows her both to occupy the position of helplessness designed to inspire the mighty to offer relief and to make a substantive legal argument about the injustice of the government she addresses:

The court-martial, My Lords, seem to have acquitted my unhappy brother of cowardice and disaffection, and therefore it is presumed he stands sentenced under the head of negligence. It is not fitting perhaps that a wretched woman as I am should offer any arguments in my brother's behalf to Your Lordships, who are masters of the whole, but what criminal negligence, My Lords, can there have been in which neither cowardice nor disaffection have had a part? . . . I must submit to Your Lordships whether it be the meaning of the law that every kind of negligence, wilful or not, should be punished with death: if so, it is not for me to make an observation on the laws; if not, and negligence arising neither from cowardice, disaffection, nor wilfulness, ought not according to the spirit and intention of the law to be deemed capital, why, my Lords, should my poor brother suffer . . .?[27]

Neither the deaths of her husband and children nor the disgrace and execution of her brother John could destroy Sarah Osborn's lively interest in the events of the great world or her determination to aid her family. One attractive set of her letters are those she wrote between 1766 and 1768 to her grandson John when he was in his twenties, at the British Embassy in Naples, trying to make a public career, diplomatic or otherwise, for himself. This grandmother is uninhibited about giving her grandson the latest news about the ladies, whether about Lady Amelia Stanhope, whose marriage has had to be postponed because her groom is under treatment for venereal disease, or, more lightheartedly, about a new bride whose high head-dress "is built up like a rock with diamonds," and who is "so much covered with jewels, that they compare her to a lark wrapped up in crumbs."[28] More elaborately, she gives him a vivid and useful picture of this period of unusual ministerial confusion, turmoil, and turnover, filled with difficulties over raising revenue, dissatisfaction with colonial policy, food shortages, unemployment, and riots in London by a more radical popular opposition, sometimes led by John Wilkes.

Osborn's letters to her grandson explain the peculiarities of the times, the characters of significant political actors, and the mechanisms of the political patronage system that its enemies called "old corruption." Of William Pitt, asked by King George in July 1766 to form a government, she writes:

Pitt is quite a harlequin: one day appears in one shape, the next quite contrary: roasts all sides; says there is not an honest man to counsel with; therefore will stand alone. The mongrel curs of the present times shrink and creep, and fall down at his footstool, watch his nod, and would show implicit obedience to his will, but he does as all great minds should do, – despises sycophants.[29]

Often her observations register tough-minded economic realism and realpolitik calculation remote from the tender sensibility officially approved for people, especially ladies, of refinement. Of Pitt she reports – cold bloodedly, if usefully – "Pitt has the reversion of Lady Grandison's £9,000 a year, if young Villiers, her son, dies under age. He is inclined to be wild, and has not had the small pox, and Pitt is lucky. Therefore everyone concludes the boy is to die."[30]

Osborn's distinctly unofficial account of the elections of 1767 reveals the facts behind the more flattering public fictions. So-called "female politicians" were stock figures of ridicule in this period, even in comedies and novels written by women, but Osborn usefully informs her grandson about the processes, customary and novel, of electioneering. In 1768 both Sir George Osborn, John Osborn's brother, and the more famous radical John Wilkes won their respective contests for parliamentary seats. The landed interest, with which the Osborns identify, was being challenged by the possessors of new money, who were better able to bribe the electors: "'Tis said two millions will be spent in elections; £20,000 and £30,000 comes out of every purse. Nabobs, [army] contractors, silversmiths, bankrupts, are in high luck: there will hardly be two hundred real gentlemen in the House."[31] Fortunately, from the perspective of the Osborns, Lord Northampton and Lord Halifax, the local magnates, have for years settled between themselves who will be the Member of Parliament for Northampton, the constituency Sir George wishes to represent, and they have agreed on Sir George, Lord Halifax's nephew. As there will thus be no contest, Sir George's expenses in "feasting and canvassing" the electors will be "a trifle in comparison of what others are: perhaps four or five thousand pounds. Sir Robert Barnard says he has £45,000 in his banker's hands, and will spend it all in opposition to Hinchinbroke and Carisfort for County Huntington."[32] She notes that in the course of this election, which became known as the "Spendthrift Election," Sir George has been victorious, but that Lord Spencer, who has spent £50,000 and lost, is petitioning the House of Commons to overturn the result. When he presents his petition, she reports: "We have most of the leading interest with us. Ladies enter into this affair, and Lady Spencer obtains all the *belles esprits* to fight their cause, as she thinks the men cannot resist them . . ."[33]

Letters like Osborn's testify to the interest of some upper-class women in contemporary politics and to their knowledge. However, they did not publish political pamphlets or treatises, presumably in part because they could not entertain the ambition for office of many of the upper-class men who did publish on such subjects. Electoral politics and political economy were not supposed to be feminine subjects. In the lonely case of Charlotte Forman, who for many years did publish serious newspaper essays on such matters as the financing of the Seven Years War and diplomatic relations between Britain and continental states, she was driven to write for money and successfully buried her gender under the pseudonym Probus.[34]

ADAMS'S *LETTERS*

Like Osborn, Abigail Adams, daughter of a Massachusetts congregational minister, had an interest in politics and wrote many letters over many decades. Here I want to focus on those she wrote to her husband between 1774 and 1776, the years immediately before the revolutionary war when he was often away as a Massachusetts representative to the Continental Congress. In 1764 Abigail Smith married John Adams, in 1776 a signer of the Declaration of Independence and eventually, in 1797, President of the United States. Abigail's letters deeply sympathize with the revolutionary cause and offer her husband useful intelligence of events in the countryside south of Boston.

Her descriptions of events are writing to the moment of a high order, conveying not only vivid local detail but also her own excitement, her determination to put public good over private ease, and her euphoria at the magnitude of events which promise to make her family actors on a world stage. While she dreads bloodshed, she is riveted by the spectacle and reality of combat:

I have just returned from P[enn']s Hill, where I have been sitting to hear the amazing roar of cannon and from whence I could see every shell which was thrown. The sound I think is one of the Grandest in Nature, and is of the true Speicies of the Sublime. 'Tis now an incessant Roar. But O the fatal Ideas which are connected with the sound. How many of our dear countrymen must fall?[35]

No statesmen challenged by public duty could wish for a wife more prepared to applaud his efforts and more willing to manage private concerns. "You cannot be, I know, nor do I wish to see you an inactive Spectator," she wrote, "I must intreat you to be as careful as you can consistent with the Duty you owe your Country . . . I wish you may be supported and devinely assisted in this most important crisis when the fate of Empires depend upon your wisdom and conduct."[36] Recognizing her inexperience, Abigail presents herself as pleasantly surprised at her own courage. "I would not have you distressed about me," she urges, "Danger, they say, makes people valient. Heitherto I have been distress'd, but not dismayed. I have felt for my Country and her Sons, I have bled with them, and for them."[37] Her republican enthusiasm ran, perhaps, higher even than her husband's.

Adams's letters could have been used in a treason prosecution against either her or her husband, so she frequently suggests that he burn them and usually either leaves them unsigned or signs them "Portia." Portia (or Porcia) was the daughter of Cato of Utica, the Roman republican (celebrated in Addison's tragedy) who killed himself rather than suffer Caesar's rule, and the wife of Marcus Brutus, one of the assassins of Caesar. For Adams, the events of 1774–76 are in part to be understood as a repetition of Roman history: the virtuous American republicans risk their lives and fortunes in an epic contest against imperial tyranny. Moments of Greek and Roman history are constantly in her mind as possible parallels, sometimes as possible warnings. As the moment of war comes nearer and nearer, lines from Shakespeare's version of Brutus's story, *Julius Caesar*, flood her mind. She almost certainly also knew Plutarch's "Life of Marcus Brutus" in which Porcia tests her own fortitude by wounding herself with a knife before she asks to be admitted to his counsels "that require secrecy and trust."[38] Adams consistently presents herself as cheerfully willing to make whatever sacrifices are necessary to establish a virtuous republic. As provisions become scarce because of the British blockade of the port of Boston, she vows, "I hope by degrees we shall be innured to hardships and become a vi[r]tuous valient people, forgetting our formour Luxery and each one apply with industery and frugality to Manufactory and husbandery till we rival all other Nations by our Virtues."[39] More practically, when the numbers of men drafted into the colonial militia and engaged in privateering have reduced the supply of agricultural labor, she declares herself prepared to pick and husk corn.

While Roman history provides Adams with one source of parallels for the events of 1774–76, biblical history provides another. As, in the seventeenth century, Hutchinson and the English revolutionaries and Bradstreet and the earliest generations of New England colonists had drawn upon the Puritan idea of themselves as Israelites under special divine protection, so Adams in this later generation rebuffs discouragement and defeat by recourse to the Old Testament, which assures her, though Charlestown is laid in ashes, "The race is not to the swift, nor the battle to the strong, but the God of Israel is he that givith strength and power unto his people."[40] That the American Revolution was in some ways a repetition of the English Civil War seemed obvious to many contemporaries. When the British capture one of John Adams's letters to General James Warren, President of the Provisional Congress, Abigail reports, they publish a parody of it entitled, "a paraphrase upon the Second Epistle of John the round Head, to James the prolocutor of the Rump parliament."[41]

One thinks of Cromwell's righteous soldiers in the new model army when Adams is pleased to report of a visit on board a Connecticut ship that "no private family appeard under better Regulation than the Crew" and "not a profane word among any of them."[42] Very early on, as soon as the British General Thomas Gage gives orders to seize the colonists' stores of gunpowder, 200 local Braintree men "preceeded by a horsecart . . . marched down to the powder house from thence they took the powder and carried [it] into the other parish and there secreted it." They demand of the sheriff his warrants for summoning juries and put it to a vote whether they ought to burn them. Having voted yes and burnt the warrants, "they then call'd a vote whether they should huzza, but it being Sunday evening it passed in the negative."[43]

In contrast to Hutchinson and Bradstreet, however, for Adams religious concerns command less attention than secular history. Adams, indeed, is also well read in contemporary poetry, appositely citing Dryden, Collins, Goldsmith, and many others. She is wonderfully able to integrate curiosity, patriotism, religion, fortitude, belles lettres, and tender affection for her husband in letters of enduring interest.

BLUESTOCKINGS

Neither Osborn nor Adams thought of themselves or were thought of by their contemporaries as "authors." Most notable among the women literate contemporaries would have thought of as "literary ladies" in 1756–76 were the bluestockings I mentioned at the beginning of this chapter: Elizabeth Montagu, Elizabeth Carter, Catharine Talbot, Hester Chapone, and others associated with them, including Sarah Scott and Sarah Fielding. These bluestockings shared a hunger for learning, firm commitments to the Church of England and virtuous living, and a determination to improve themselves and their society.

Like the French *salonnières*, of whom she was well aware, Montagu extended her hospitality to men and women of talent and accomplishment. Conversation at her houses included David Garrick; Samuel Johnson; George, Lord Lyttelton; Edmund Burke; and Sir Joshua Reynolds – as well as scholars, clergymen, and other bluestocking women, a principal point of the salon being to promote rational conversation between men and women. Participants in her salon or in the salon of her friend Elizabeth Vesey did not indulge in the fashionable amusements of dancing, card-playing or drinking. But conversation was intended to be both polite and easy, allowing speculation, exploration of ideas and sentiments, friendly mutual support, and more informality than was customary in the great drawing rooms of the day. Montagu conspicuously remitted the usual tributes due to a person of her high rank and great wealth from lowlier ladies and gentlemen of talent, insisting, with complex and subtle tact, on constructing friendships based on reciprocity in which she professed to be the inferior person.[44] Unlike a number of the French *salonnières*, Montagu entertained no lovers; she set herself and her salon against fashionable libertinism.

The term "bluestocking" first appears in Montagu's correspondence in 1756, applied to a poor gentleman scholar, Benjamin Stillingfleet, who wore cheaper blue worsted stockings instead of fashionable white silk. Sylvia Myers has shown that Montagu and her friends first used the word to describe, not women, but "men with intellectual interests whose friendships were valued by the women as helping to develop their own studies through conversation and correspondence." Next the women begin to use the word to indicate "a point of view – 'blue stocking doctrine' or 'blue stocking philosophy,'" apparently a stoic acceptance of a virtuous life apart from the world of ambition and politics. By 1774 Montagu is using the word to refer to both men and women in her circle, although the later use of the word to refer exclusively to intellectual women appears by the late 1770s.[45] Thus, what began as a friendly little female joke about a social difference between the wealthy upper-class and shabby genteel gentlemen friends became a word later used to mark gender difference and to ridicule the supposed pretensions of intellectual women.

The bluestockings typically thought of themselves more as women who studied and tried to learn and improve themselves and those around them than as the deliberate producers of literary works. The core group of Montagu, Carter, and Talbot wrote large numbers of letters, which have survived and were published in the nineteenth century, but few works were published in their own time. The familiar letter was a crucial medium for these writers: they used it to create a mutually reinforcing female community, encouraging each others' intellectual and spiritual development, networking to provide economic and other kinds of support for those in need, and taking advantage of its intimacy to express themselves more candidly than they thought appropriate to more public forms.[46] Sarah Scott and Sarah Fielding, often desperately poor, became authors as a way of making needed money and thus were more prolific in print, but were not very eager to be authors either. Montagu was a patron to all the other women, giving them access to other writers, lending and giving them books, soliciting opportunities and subscriptions for them, sometimes inviting them to her town or country houses or taking them on trips to other places they could not have visited on their own, and, for Scott and Fielding, providing money. The two most important published works that best characterize the bluestockings are Montagu's *Essay on the Writings and Genius of Shakespear* and Elizabeth Carter's translation of *All the Works of Epictetus.*

MONTAGU'S *ESSAY ON THE WRITINGS AND GENIUS OF SHAKESPEAR*

Montagu's *Essay on the Writings and Genius of Shakespear, Compared with the Greek and French Dramatic Poets* (1769) directly addressed Voltaire's attacks on Shakespeare. Although French culture clearly dominated English culture in the early eighteenth century, by mid century, English culture was beginning to have significant influence in France. Voltaire, a refugee from France in the 1720s, had celebrated English achievements, including literary achievements, in *Letters Concerning the English Nation* (1733). However, he became increasingly disturbed that French Anglophilia was going too far, especially in the theatre, where the influence of George Lillo and Denis Diderot had led to a new, bourgeois *drame*, a sentimental form neither comic nor tragic. In 1760 the *Journal encyclopédique* published, as translated from the English, a series of parallels between Shakespeare and Corneille, Otway and Racine, and Horace, Boileau, and Pope, in each of which the English author was preferred. This was the sort of event that incited Voltaire's polemical *Appel à toutes les nations de l'Europe des jugements d'un écrivain anglais, ou manifeste au suject des honneurs du pavillon entre les théâtres de Londres et de Paris* (1761). Voltaire celebrated the perfection of French culture and language in the age of Louis XIV and the perfection of dramatic poetry in Corneille. Shakespeare, by contrast, he attacked as emblematic of a more barbaric English taste, "an aberrant sport alien to the mainstream of European cultural progress."[47]

Voltaire went on to support his position with a monumental work of literary criticism and scholarship, his twelve-volume edition of the *Théâtre de Pierre Corneille, avec des commentaires*, published in 1764. In addition to presenting all the plays of Corneille, Voltaire offered French translations of analogous scenes from plays by Calderón and Shakespeare, discussing French, Spanish, and English drama comparatively, but clearly preferring French neoclassical theatre. Conscious of waging war on the cultural front while French armies and navies were fighting England in the Seven Years War, Voltaire wrote to one literary friend as French defeat in the war was imminent: "Il n'est pas mal de rabattre un peu l'orgueil des Anglais qui se croient souverains du théâtre comme des mers et qui mettent sans façon Shakespear au dessus de Corneille."[48] David Williams has convincingly argued that Voltaire intended the Corneille edition to re-establish the prestige of French neoclassical theater throughout Europe and to show that French taste established a universal standard while English taste was merely local. Further to demonstrate this, Voltaire saw to it that the edition appeared with a large subscription list of nearly 1,200 subscribers representing nineteen countries.[49] Voltaire's work on this edition clearly parallels Samuel Johnson's work on his edition of Shakespeare (8 volumes, 1765), a project for which Lennox had been engaged to work on Shakespeare's Italian sources and which had led to the publication of her *Shakespeare Illustrated* (3 volumes, 1753–54).

Montagu's *Essay* uses Voltaire's *Corneille* as the occasion for her appreciative criticism of Shakespeare, by mid century recognized as Britain's greatest dramatist. Her published *Essay* extends her part of the conversations of her salon into a printed book and extends the circle of participants beyond London to include Paris. Montagu had long had an interest in Shakespeare; about 1762, encouraged by Lord Lyttelton and Elizabeth Carter, she began to consider publishing a book of her own criticism. As her correspondence with Carter makes clear, she also studied Greek drama as seriously as she could without knowing Greek. She was able to use Pierre Brumoy's *Le Théâtre des Grecs* (1730), *The Greek Theatre of Father Brumoy*, edited and partly translated by Lennox in 1759.[50] Carter assisted by translating Plato's discussion of drama from the *Republic* for her. The appearance of Johnson's edition of Shakespeare in 1765 gave Montagu pause, but she rightly decided that she had something additional to say. Her *Essay* pays polite tribute to the several eighteenth-century editors of Shakespeare, who included not only Johnson, but also Nicholas Rowe, Pope, Lewis Theobald, Thomas Hanmer, and William Warburton. These editors have "corrected and elucidated" Shakespeare's works, she notes gratefully. Yet she suggests that the more "learned, deep, and sober critics . . . whose acquaintance with the characters of men is formed in the library" rather than in "the busy walks of human life" may misjudge a writer not himself learned but one who faithfully represented living people.[51]

Montagu is especially interested in celebrating Shakespeare's accomplishments in the history plays and in developing, as Johnson did not, a set of principles appropriate to this kind of writing. Aristotle, she observes, never encountered history plays and therefore offered no *Poetics* appropriate to them. Johnson's defense of Shakespeare's generic impropriety in allowing comic scenes in tragedy perhaps assisted her thinking. Yet, as she tries to define the special excellence of history plays, Diderot's dramatic theory, which praised (and helped invent) the new bourgeois *drame*, may have influenced her sense of their desirability. Shakespeare, Montagu argues, "broke down the barrier that had before confined the dramatic writers to the regions of comedy, or tragedy. He perceived the fertility of the subjects that lay between the extremes; he saw, that in the historical plays he could represent the manners of the whole people, give the general temper of the times, and bring in the incidents that affected the common fate of his country."[52] She prefers drama to other literary forms in part because its immediacy, its power to create sympathy and to move the passions, produces the strongest moral effect on an audience. Shakespeare chose subjects from the wars of York and Lancaster when they were still fresh in men's minds. These stories engaged his audience more deeply than fables or myths could have done. "If it be the chief use of history, that it teaches philosophy by experience," historical drama "must be allowed to be the best preceptor."[53] That Shakespeare could use the available sources, "a mere heap of rude undigested annals, coarse in their style, and crouded with trivial anecdotes," and transmute them into coherent actions of complex, recognizably human characters, was strong evidence of his genius: "No Tacitus had investigated the obliquities of our statesmen, or by diving into the profound secrets of policy had dragged into light the latent motives, the secret machinations of our politicians: yet how does he enter into the deepest mysteries of state!"[54] Comparing Sir Thomas More's account of Richard III, which presents Richard's deformity as an omen of his later villainy, with Shakespeare's, in which deformity does not presage but instigates Richard's cruel ambition, Montagu admires and finds more plausible Shakespeare's psychological presentation of character.

Montagu's extensive discussions of anachronism reveal the later eighteenth-century's pervasive concern with historical truth. Johnson in his "Preface to Shakespeare" had treated these concerns rather blithely, confident of the constancy of human nature. He had observed that "Dennis and Rymer think [Shakespeare's] Romans not sufficiently Roman," but famously dismissed these and related concerns as "the petty cavils of petty minds": "a poet overlooks the casual distinction of country and condition, as a painter, satisfied with the figure, neglects the drapery."[55] Yet historicist thinking was having so profound an impact that in 1777 the painter Benjamin West revolutionized history painting by abandoning classical drapery. In a picture exhibited at the Royal Academy, West dressed a modern general, the dying General Wolfe, slain at the battle of Quebec, in his very modern red English uniform.

Montagu argues that Shakespeare was truer to historical fact than Corneille and that he consequently wrote plays of greater significance. Voltaire had elected to compare Corneille's *Cinna* with Shakespeare's *Julius Caesar*, both plays set in Rome and taking as their subjects conspiracies to assassinate the ruler. Shakespeare treated the conspiracy that killed Julius Caesar in 44 BC, Corneille a failed conspiracy against Augustus in the first century. Among Montagu's arguments for the superiority of *Julius Caesar* to *Cinna* is that Shakespeare's characters are much more plausible as republican Romans than Corneille's. Corneille, as she correctly maintains, was heavily indebted to seventeenth-century French romance for his character types, just as Dryden, Behn, and Manley were indebted both to the romances and to Corneille for the Almanzors and

Homais of their heroic drama. Indeed, it will be remembered from chapter five, Arabella in *The Female Quixote* still admired the romance heroes and heroines, although Lennox, like Montagu, considered them ludicrously unrealistic. Like the writers of *romans historique*, Montagu points out, Corneille does not scruple to add purely fictitious characters to historical ones, especially when the historical record affords no evidence of love intrigues. Shakespeare follows Plutarch's life of Marcus Brutus reasonably faithfully and keeps the motives political, whereas Corneille invents Emila demanding Cinna kill Auguste to earn her love. Shakespeare transports his audience to republican Rome, makes us "become Romans," teaches us "to adore the images of Junius Brutus, the Horatii, Decii, Fabii, and all who had offered dear and bloody sacrifice to the liberty of their country."[56] Corneille's love-obsessed characters, in contrast, appear to her silly and trivial:

> It is a common error in the plan of Corneille's tragedies, that the interest of the piece turns on some unknown [to history] person, generally a haughty princess; so that instead of the representation of an important event, and the characters of illustrious persons, the business of the drama is a love-intrigue of a termagant lady, who, if she is a Roman, insults the Barbarians, if she is a Barbarian, braves the Romans, and even to her lover is insolent and fierce. Were such a person to be produced on our theatre, she would be taken for a mad poetess escaped from her keepers in Bedlam, who, fancying herself a queen, was ranting, and delivering her mandates in rhyme upon the stage . . .[57]

Montagu's *Essay* not only demonstrates the impact of historicist thinking on literary criticism in this period, but is also important as woman writer's bid for literary critical and aesthetic authority. Behn, as we saw in chapter one, claimed that her woman's experience of the world could offer a better preparation for a writer of comedy than the university man's knowledge of dramatic rules. Montagu follows the French *salonnières* in claiming that her sophisticated knowledge of the world is a better basis for understanding Shakespeare than the knowledge possessed by university men "formed in the library."

In this period, after Edmund Burke's *Philosophical Enquiry into the Origin of our Ideas of the Sublime and Beautiful* (1757) an age of aesthetics as well as an age of history, other women besides Montagu laid claim to aesthetic taste, a claim women generally made more successfully than they did claims to historical expertise. For example, Anna Miller, who presided over a literary salon at her house outside of Bath, published the remarkable *Letters from Italy, Describing the Manners, Customs, Antiquities, Paintings, &c. of that Country, in the Years* MDCCLXX and MDCCLXXI . . . (1776).

These *Letters* offer very detailed descriptions of and judgments upon enormous numbers of paintings, examples of architecture, landscape architecture, and interior decoration. She obviously traveled with copies of Charles-Nicolas Cochin's *Voyage pittoresque d'Italie, ou recueil de notes sur les ouvrages de peinture et de sculpture . . .* (1756) and of Jérôme de La Lande's *Voyage d'un François en Italie, fait dans les années 1765–1766* (1769) and does not hesitate to take issue with either of them. Miller, traveling to Italy with her husband, often separates her discussions of art from passages on political economy supposedly contributed by him. As Kathleen Turner has argued, within the developing discourse of aesthetics and consumption, "women's public display of good taste" can be sanctioned.[58] Montagu and Miller both published their books anonymously, waiting for the generally positive receptions they got before allowing their authorship to be known; both then used the reputations they acquired for knowledge and taste to enhance their power as *salonnières*.

CARTER'S *ALL THE WORKS OF EPICTETUS*

It is hard to overestimate the importance to women's writing of the appearance in 1758 of *All the Works of Epictetus, Which are Now Extant; Consisting of his Discourses, Preserved by Arrian. In Four Books, The Enchiridion, and Fragments. Trans. from the original Greek. By Elizabeth Carter. With an Introduction, and Notes, by the Translator*. Classical scholarship still held sway as the highest, most intellectually demanding and learned kind of literary work. Carter's translation was immediately recognized as well-informed and skillful. It went through many editions; even in the twentieth century, W. H. D. Rouse chose it for the Everyman's Library. In the contemporary culture wars with France, England could now declare that it had produced a rival to the famous Anne Dacier, translator of Homer in 1699 and 1708. Lord Lyttelton boasted to Montagu: "The English ladies will appear as much superior to the French in wit and learning, as the men in arms."[59] That a woman could master a difficult Greek philosophical text amazed literate Europe. Notice was taken as far as Moscow, where an account of Carter appeared in the press and a copy of *Epictetus* was presented to Catherine the Great. For women who harbored intellectual and literary ambition, Carter's achievement inspired them to venerate her and to dream of challenging themselves to go beyond the boundary markers being put in place to fix the proper limits of women's intellectual and literary ambition.

Carter's earlier accomplishments, including her translations of Crousaz on Pope from Latin and Algarotti on Newton from Italian, noted in the previous chapter, as well as her *Poems upon Particular Occasions* (1738), had already made her a celebrated figure. Penelope Aubin had dedicated her *History of Genghizcan* to Carter. But the major accomplishment of the *Epictetus* provided secure evidence of the intellectual capacity of women. Especially to the bluestockings, it offered a rock upon which they could rest their claim that women ought to be taken seriously as citizens of the republic of letters.

Why did Carter elect to translate Epictetus? The simple answer is that her friend Catharine Talbot asked her to. Talbot was the posthumous child of a clergyman who, with her widowed mother, had been taken into the household of Thomas Secker, the clergyman who successively became Bishop of Oxford in 1737, then in 1758 Archbishop of Canterbury. Carter was the daughter of the Reverend Nicholas Carter, DD, a clergyman living in Deal, on the Kentish coast, who was also one of the six preachers in the Cathedral Church of Canterbury. Thanks to the survival of extensive correspondence between Talbot and Carter, we know much about the reading habits of both families and know that Secker's family regularly spent evenings listening to books read aloud. Selections ranged from Pliny's *Letters*, through many volumes of French memoirs, to Richardson's *Sir Charles Grandison*, but since Mrs. Talbot understood only English, they chose only books available in English. Wishing to add Epictetus to the family readings, Catharine asked Elizabeth to prepare an English translation. Over the years between this request and publication in 1758, Talbot continuously encouraged the completion of the translation, helped engage assistance and support from learned men, including Secker, and pressed a reluctant Carter to publish.

In an early letter to Carter prompted by her reading a new translation of Pliny, Talbot captures some of the significances translation had for contemporaries. She explains why translation could seem a modest, self-effacing literary role for women, one that cut against the satirical stereotypes of hysterical, narcissistic literary ladies like Phoebe Clinket in *Three Hours after Marriage* (1717), the farce by Pope, Gay, and John Arbuthnot. According to Talbot:

... a faithful and elegant translator is a character of the highest virtue in the literary republic. It implies public spirit the most void of ostentation; a kind regard for the illiterate; a love of our own native country, shown by enriching its language with valuable books; a just regard for merit of whatever country, by placing the merit of some valuable foreigners in the truest and fairest light; a care, a judgment, and exactness that original writings do not require, and some degree of humility in scarce aspiring to the name of an author.[60]

A very unusual father, Dr. Carter gave his daughter the same classical education he gave her brothers and told her that he thought it was right she should earn money by publishing her work.

But this support of a woman's translation of a classical text does not explain the peculiar value of Epictetus to Carter. Epictetus was a Greek-speaking Roman stoic philosopher who lived from roughly AD 50 to 130. He was born in Asia Minor of a slave woman and lived for years as a slave himself. After studying with an early stoic teacher and being banished from Rome by the Emperor Domitian in 89 or 93, Epictetus taught his philosophy in Greece to disciples who came to him from many countries. His version of stoicism taught that a person could control and develop his own mind and character so as to make himself a worthy moral subject, no matter how minimal his resources, no matter how challenging, even how horrifying, his external circumstances. This, I believe, was a philosophy that seemed relevant to a powerless, portionless woman like Carter.

Carter admired the continuing moral effort Epictetus recommended and hoped for the human dignity he claimed for himself. The root of human dignity Epictetus discovered in man's existence as "a distinct Portion of the Essence of God" and as a creature capable of philosophical reflection: "Being, then, the Formation of such an Artist, will you dishonour him; especially, when he hath not only formed, but intrusted, and given the Guardianship of you, to yourself? . . . You are a Citizen of the World, and a Part of it: not a subservient, but a principal, Part. You are capable of comprehending the divine Oeconomy; and of considering the Connextions of Things."[61] The task of a human being is to look to God as a pattern and to "expell . . . Grief, Fear, Desire, Envy, Malevolence, Avarice, Effeminacy, Intemperance, [from your Mind]." The good student of philosophy ought to proclaim: I desire to live "free from Passion, and Perturbation" and to learn "Duty to God, to my Parents, to my Relations, to my Country, and to Strangers."[62]

Like Socrates, whom he admired and frequently cited, Epictetus did not write but taught through dialogues; Arrian, a Roman senator and one of his followers, committed his teachings to writing. But Epictetus is often sardonic, rougher and brusquer, with his interlocutors than Socrates was. Secker encouraged Carter not to polish or refine Epictetus's style. As Carolyn D. Williams has aptly observed, "To her eternal credit, Carter abandoned her ladylike scruples and gave the world a translation that conveyed, as faithfully as her contemporary notions of decency would permit, Epictetus' abrupt manner, his predilection for concrete references and imagery, his penchant for blistering personal insult, and his reckless disrespect of persons."[63] Carter articulates her attraction to his unladylike style in her introduction, although her description presents it as less cutting than her translation does: "There is such a Warmth and Spirit in his Exhortations; and his good Sense is enlivened by such a keenness of Wit, and Gaity of Humour, as render the Study of him, a most delightful as well as profitable Entertainment."[64]

Despite his call for rigorously disciplining the passions, for unwhimpering acceptance of frugality and hardship, and for strenuous moral self-cultivation, a principal aim of Epictetus' philosophy is to secure happiness for the individual. At the same time that he urges his followers to cultivate *autarkia*, the independence of the virtuous mind from external circumstances, he also points to the pleasures of freedom, of virtue, and of life. Epictetus' invocation of extreme situations in which the prospect of happiness would seem remote to an ordinary observer has a gleeful triumphalism. Consider, for instance, this dialogue in the chapter on "Intrepidity," a dialogue illustrating the difference between externals and the internal subject that depends only on the exercise of moral choice:

> when a Tyrant threatens, and sends for me; I say, Against what is your Threatening pointed? If he says, "I will chain you;" I answer, it is my *Hands* and *Feet* that you threaten. If he says, "I will cut off your Head;" I answer, "It is my *Head* that you threaten . . ."
> Does he not threaten *you*, then?
> If I am persuaded, that these Things are nothing to me, he doth not; but, if I fear any of them, it is *me* that he threatens.[65]

The person with the best principles is always superior to a person who has worse principles. Epictetus' very position of utter powerlessness over externals, combined with his euphoric sense of self-sufficiency and internal dignity, constitute his charm for Carter.

While the melodrama of depraved Roman emperors, conjured up by Epictetus' examples, might seem remote indeed from the tribulations that were the lot of genteel Englishwomen in the eighteenth century, Carter nevertheless imaginatively identified with her stoic philosopher. Her "Ode to Wisdom," famous in part because Richardson inserted it in *Clarissa* as a poem written by Clarissa, disdains the gifts of fortune and ambition, and asks instead:

> To me thy better Gifts impart,
> Each moral Beauty of the Heart
> 　By studious Thought refin'd;
> For Wealth, the Smiles of glad Content,
> For Pow'r, its amplest, best Extent,
> 　An empire o'er my Mind . . .
>
> By thee protected, I defy
> The Coxcomb's Sneer, the stupid Lie
> 　Of Ignorance and Spite . . .[66]

Many of her poems are addressed to women friends and apply stoic philosophy to their situations, insisting that happiness and content are not to be found in externals valued by society (including suitors) but in a woman's cultivation of her own mind. Nor is happiness denied to us in life, reserved only for the future, and located only in Heaven, as some pious people suppose.

> To temper'd Wishes, just Desires
> 　Is Happiness confin'd,
> And deaf to Folly's Call, attends
> 　The Music of the Mind.[67]

One theme in the correspondence between Carter and Talbot is Talbot's recurrent depression over feeling that her life is trivial and insignificant. Carter responds by insisting that the small duties of domestic life are moral duties, that Talbot is doing good by caring for others and by taking the necessary exercise to care for her own health, and that we all have an obligation to make the best of our circumstances and to be pleased. Among the attractive aspects of Carter's own character was her capacity to delight in nature, expressed both in letters where she revels in long walks – sometimes as long as the sixteen miles between Canterbury and Deal – and in poems celebrating the delights of aspects of nature not conventionally thought delightful. "Written at Midnight in a Thunder Storm" boldly declares:

> Let coward Guilt with pallid Fear
> 　To shelt'ring Caverns fly,
> And justly dread the vengeful Fate,
> 　That thunders thro' the Sky . . .
> In the thick Clouds tremendous Gloom,
> 　The Light'ning's lurid Glare,
> [Intrepid Virtue] views the same all-gracious Pow'r,
> 　That breathes the vernal Air . . .[68]

Once the decision was made to publish *Epictetus*, however, Carter's ideas about the significance and purpose of her work began to clash with those of her friends at the Bishop of Oxford's, notably Talbot and Secker himself. Secker reviewed Carter's drafts, suggested corrections, and played a crucial role in soliciting subscriptions for the splendid large quarto volume published by Richardson. The remarkably long and distinguished subscription list eventually numbered 1,031; the names of the Prince of Wales and the Princess Dowager of Wales came first, followed by names of many aristocrats and clerical dignitaries. Carter would have been content to publish the translation unadorned by any apparatus; the Bishop of Oxford's circle wanted to see a handsome large volume in which the pagan text was surrounded by Christian commentary that made clear the superiority of Christian theology and Christian morality. Carter, against her own inclinations, was pressured to step forward as a champion of the intellectual and moral excellencies of British womanhood and of the superior truth of British Christianity. While she never published her own letters, she organized and preserved those letters that record her debates over these issues with Talbot, acting as spokeswoman for herself and for the Bishop and his circle. Talbot expresses terror that Epictetus may support infidels and libertines in their evil ways, unless the text is "sufficiently guarded with proper notes and animadversions."[69] Carter responds that the light-minded and unchristian are unlikely to read her large book, and that, even if an infidel were to read it, he would find no "great comfort in the study of Epictetus, unless he is perverse enough to take comfort in finding himself obliged to practise the morality of the Gospel without its encouragements and supports."[70] (Epictetus, it is worth noting, was severe on adulterers.) Talbot disagrees: "Fine gentlemen will read [your book] because it is new; fine ladies because it is yours; critics because it is a translation out of the Greek; and Shaftesburian Heathens because Epictetus was an honour to Heathenism, and an idolator of the beauty of virtue."[71] Carter insists: "I never had the least apprehension that an author who enjoins so strict a morality, who censures even the fashionable vices which fine gentlemen at present consider as mere trifles, and who discovers so deep a sense of religion, could be studied by bad people; or if he was, that the effect would be any other than convincing them that there was nothing to be gained, though an infinite deal to be lost, by their turning Heathens."[72] Nevertheless, Carter bowed to the desires of the Bishop's circle, wrote an introduction and notes, and, apparently, incorporated some notes they provided for her. Some of the apparatus, as requested, animadverts on Epictetus' errors; on occasion, notes point to similarities between his ideas and those of the gospels, also observing that the gospels more perfectly express the sentiment in question.

MONTAGU–CARTER LETTERS

The letters of Elizabeth Montagu and Elizabeth Carter to one another can be read as an original work by both of them on the subject of female friendship, a subject they knew Philips had earlier considered. Friendship, as we have seen, differed from the other common relationships of parent/ child, husband/wife, and master/servant because it promised equality instead of hierarchy and a freedom that accompanied the absence of hierarchical constraint. This relationship between Montagu and Carter began as a sort of patronage relationship, in which the much richer, more socially prominent Montagu offered herself as Carter's patron. The letters show Montagu continued to do the sorts of things a patron might do for a writer: she bought books for Carter, invited her to meet other writers and intellectuals at her salon, took her on trips to places she could otherwise not have seen, and solicited subscriptions for her books. What is remarkable, and original about the correspondence, however, is the way both writers work to construct this apparently hierarchical relationship of patron and client as an egalitarian relationship of female friends. Each encourages the other to write and to publish, partly by recourse to Astell's idea that women need female models to emulate.

Montagu, acutely aware of the capacity of her wealth and fame to intimidate a Kentish clergyman's daughter, delicately constructs herself as the one who has the most to gain from the relationship; she works to encourage from Carter a degree of candor and intimacy that Carter would otherwise not have been able to produce. Early in their relationship, Montagu writes to Carter, "I have long been deprived of the pleasure of wandering amongst the aromatics of Parnassus; when I have my full range I only sport like the butterfly; you are the honey bee, and extract the precious essence, and I desire you would continue to send me of your honey."[73] Over many years of the correspondence, she demonstrates the sincerity of this desire by eagerly questioning Carter about matters literary and moral and by enjoying Carter's assistance with her study of tragedy for the *Essay on the Genius and Writings of Shakespear*. Montagu's rare reproofs of Carter are prompted only by manifestations of deference or withholding intimacy. "Send me a better letter," Montagu teasingly scolds, "yes, I say a better letter; you think I care for your wit and wisdom, when you won't tell me how you do? direct your next to Madame Sevigné, in the shades, or to Madame Maintenon's spirit in the cloisters of St. Cyr, they will admire your language, they will approve your sentiments, and being no longer of earth's mould, will fear none of the fears, the cares, that haunt a mortal woman for a mortal friend."[74]

Carter gradually accepts Montagu's warm professions of friendship and admiration and becomes emboldened to define her own singularity, even to the point of refusing Montagu's invitation to stay at her great London house on the ground that her own peculiar "spirit of liberty is strangely untractable and wild."[75] As Harriet Guest has argued, Carter finds that her learning makes her eccentric and strange, yet at the same time "gives her the kind of claim to independence that is . . . in these decades, becoming more typical of the liberal professions."[76] Her liberty and independence, which Montagu acknowledges, are the rewards of her industry. Both writers display refined politeness as they work to create this extraordinary, affectionate, and mutually supportive textual record of friendship between two women intellectuals. Both follow Astell in their concern for the advancement of "the sex." But Montagu was able to contrive more dramatic, more public demonstrations than Astell of the advantages to both women and men of the kinds of homosocial and heterosocial friendships that her salon and her correspondence displayed.

HANNAH MORE'S *INFLEXIBLE CAPTIVE*

Carter and Montagu were both in their fifties in 1774 when the twenty-nine-year-old Hannah More, who was to become one of their most enthusiastic admirers, came to London with the manuscript of her first full-length play, *The Inflexible Captive*. More was the daughter of a schoolmaster who had given her an unusually good education. Hannah and her sisters became proprietresses of their own girls' boarding school in Bristol. In a remarkably short time, More became a young friend and protégée to Montagu, Edmund Burke, and Garrick, who produced *The Inflexible Captive* at Bath in 1775. Her early letters record her astonished delight at the warmth with which Montagu, Garrick, Johnson, Sir Joshua Reynolds, and Frances Boscawen include her in their circle and praise her talent. Invited to dine at Hill Street, Berkeley Square, Montagu's London house, More exclaimed: "Mrs. Montagu received me with the most encouraging kindness; she is not only the finest genius, but the finest lady I ever saw: she lives in the highest style of magnificence; her apartment and table are in the most splendid taste . . ."[77]

The Inflexible Captive, a verse translation of Metastasio's *Attilio Regolo*, evinces high literary ambition; it is a kind of late eighteenth-century serious play different from traditional tragedy, but apt to be mistaken for botched tragedy. Metastasio's poetry most famously provided eighteenth-century opera composers over 800 settings of his verse dramas, but he also gave readings of his poems, considering them autonomous verse dramas. We overlook at our peril the attraction of his kind of poetry and opera for English writers and audiences of the eighteenth century. One of the casual remarks Charles Burney makes in passing about a Metastasio libretto for *Siroe* (set by Handel) would surprise most eighteenth-century drama specialists: "The opera of *Siroe*, which at present every one acquainted with the Italian language almost knows by heart . . ."[78] The interest in a Metastasio libretto is an interest in a spectacle of virtue; a famous example is Mozart's *opera seria, La Clemenza di Tito* (1791). Roger Parker nicely describes Metastasio's appeal:

To his mind, the two-stanza aria provided a perfect forum for the inner psychological struggles between duty and inclination, between reason and desire, that constitute the central moral conflict in nearly all of his libretti. In the mellifluousness of his verses, the stylized decorum of his poetic lexicon, and the finesse of his emotional palette Metastasio has never had his equal in the history of opera . . . He articulated with a gratifying and refined sensuality the essential qualities that ought to define nobility and the exercise of authority in an age of reason.[79]

The hero of *The Inflexible Captive* is the historical Marcus Atilius Regulus, a Roman leader captured and held by the Carthaginians in the First Punic War. In 251 BC the Carthaginians sent Regulus back to Rome to arrange for peace or at least for an exchange of prisoners; he promised to return to Carthage to be executed should he fail. In Rome, instead of suing for peace, Regulus heroically urged Rome to continue fighting; he then returned to Carthage where he was put to death. More uses Regulus to develop a philosophical stoicism that would be recognizable to readers of Carter's Epictetus. Her blank verse employs studied antithesis, a legacy from the heroic couplet, and paradox. Rejecting compromise, Regulus declaims:

> 'Tis not *to-day* I learn that I am mortal.
> The foe can only take from Regulus
> What wearied nature would have shortly yielded,
> It will be *now* a voluntary *gift*,
> 'Twould *then* become a necessary *tribute*.[80]

We can see More beginning to develop her ideas of public obligation and glimpse what will be her own later role as author, public intellectual, and evangelical activist who played out a version of Astell's vision of the single Christian woman who takes the whole world for her family:

> *That* man was born in vain, whose pow'r of serving
> Is circumscrib'd within the wretched bounds
> Of *self* – a narrow miserable sphere!
> Glory exalts, enlarges, dignifies,
> Absorbs the *selfish* in the *social* feelings,
> And teaches virtue how to charm mankind.[81]

More creates acute dramatic and philosophical interest in the clashes between virtuous Regulus and his virtuous children, his son, Publius, and his daughter, Attilia. The children want to save their father from death. The play poses serious questions about how obligations a person has as a citizen ought to be related to obligations he or she has as a member of a family. It also asks whether virtue in a woman would lead to different conduct than virtue in a man. From the perspectives of Publius and Attilia, what Regulus understands by virtue and duty begins to look not only cruel but unnatural, even monstrous. In an effort to persuade Publius to consent to his father's death, Regulus cites the heroic examples of Brutus, Virginius, and Manlius, all fathers who killed their children in the name of virtue. Publius replies in a speech that, like the play as a whole, uses paradox to provoke thought about what virtue is:

> Rome 'till now
> Boasts not a *son* of such *surpassing virtue*,
> Who, spurning all the ties of blood, and nature,
> Hath labor'd to procure his father's death.[82]

It should not be surprising that, following in the footsteps of Astell and Trotter and their insistence on the possibility of female virtue, some later women playwrights would be drawn to a dramatic form that encouraged the presentation of heroically virtuous heroines, called for the exploration of feelings, and made problems of conscience in choosing between two goods central to its plots. We ought to explore more seriously the aesthetics and the philosophical interest of this Metastasian form, although I would concede that it is probably most successful in good opera and that it is dependent upon either good music or good poetry. The ability to write good serious verse was admittedly in short supply among women writers.

The best volume of poems published by a woman in this period was probably Anna Letitia Aikin's *Poems* (1772). Born in 1743, two years before More, at this point Aikin was barely in her twenties and had not yet married Rochmont Barbauld. Although published in London, *Poems* strongly reflects the local northern places and dissenting culture of Lancashire, where she lived with her father, a Presbyterian clergyman and schoolmaster at the important Warrington Academy, a center of advanced scientific and political thought. Among the prominent intellectuals in her family's circle was Joseph Priestly, famous then as a writer on electricity and now for the discovery of oxygen. "Verses on Mrs. Rowe" invokes Rowe as "bright pattern" of her sex and hopes for her inspiration as the young poet's muse.[83] Like Rowe's, Aikin's poems include spiritual meditations and hymns; one of the hymns, "Praise to God, immortal praise," is still sung by many Protestant congregations. Other poetic influences include Young, Collins, Parnell, Finch, and Carter. "On the Origin of Song-Writing" and several songs show the contemporary revival of interest in song, although that is perhaps more powerfully evident in the Scottish women collectors and adaptors of traditional songs and in the Cumbrian poet, Susanna Blamire.[84]

Earlier in the century, some literary theorists had urged poets to discover new sources for poetic originality in modern science and natural history – and we have seen Chudleigh's interest in natural history – but early and mid-eighteenth-century poets had generally not ventured far from conventional pastoral and georgic images of nature.[85] Some of Aikin's poems use tired poetic clichés, but she also proves capable of fresher observation, especially of lowlier creatures less attended to by earlier poets. Thus, in "To Mrs. P[riestly], With some Drawing of Birds and Insects," a beetle is seen refracted by epic language and in polished heroic couplets, but precisely and at close range, perhaps as with a naturalist's magnifying glass:

> See the proud giant of the beetle race;
> What shining arms his polish'd limbs enchase!
> Like some stern warrior formidably bright
> His steely sides reflect a gleaming light;
> On his large forehead spreading horns he wears,
> And high in air the branching antlers bears;
> O'er many an inch extends his wide domain,
> And his rich treasury swells with hoarded grain.[86]

"The Mouse's Petition" uses a humble stanza form of alternating iambic tetrameter and iambic trimeter short lines to express a mouse's plea to Priestly that the "free-born" mouse not be sacrificed to his experiments with gases:

> The well taught philosophic mind
> To all compassion gives;
> Casts round the world an equal eye,
> And feels for all that lives.[87]

This amusing, though kindly, poem probably influenced Robert Burns's more famous "To a Mouse."

Unlike Rowe, but like Chandler and other local poets before her, Aikin brings the unique features of her place into representation. The elegant "On the Backwardness of the Spring 1771" captures a northern spring, unlike the southern spring, which "call'd the Tuscan Muses to her bowers":

> Her opening breast is stain'd with frequent showers,
> Her streaming tresses bath'd in chilling dews,
> And sad before her move the pensive hours,
> Whose flagging wings no breathing sweets diffuse.[88]

Strikingly, in a verse epistle, "The Invitation: To Miss B*****," she describes one of the new technological engineering wonders near Warrington, the Duke of Bridgewater's canal that allowed coal to be delivered from the mines:

> The traveler with pleasing wonder sees
> The white sail gleaming from the trees.[89]

Poems demonstrates Aikin's early commitment to poetic craft, study, moral seriousness, and progressive politics. The strong opening poem, "Corsica," celebrates the Corsican revolt against Genoa and the long struggle for liberty against imperial domination. Yet, like most members of what can be thought of as a more dispersed second generation of bluestockings, Aikin here is more torn between ambition and a modest acceptance of female limitations than Montagu or Carter. She draws distinctions between herself and what she imagines as a more astringent bluestocking or religious asceticism, insisting in "Wisdom" that if wisdom leads to gloom or the death of passion she will embrace pleasure, and, in "Verses Written in an Alcove," calls not for a solemn Muse wreathed with laurel but for her "smiling sister," singing "in a lighter measure," "All unknown to fame and glory."[90]

MACAULAY'S *HISTORY OF ENGLAND*

A political radical, Catharine Macaulay was not a frequenter of Montagu's salons or a close friend of either Montagu or Carter; she presided over her own more political salon where she received radicals like Abigail's husband John Adams. Nevertheless, contemporaries sometimes thought of her as another bluestocking. Richard Samuel's 1778 painting "The Nine Living Female Muses of Great Britain" includes her with Montagu and Carter. Macaulay published far more than the normative bluestockings. It could be argued that no book written by a woman between 1660 and 1789 was more impressive or more influential than her *History of England from the Accession of James I to that of the Brunswick Line*, published in eight volumes between 1763 and 1783.[91] Unlike most contemporary women writers who confined themselves to genres supposed to be suited to ladies (letters, translations, poems, novels, and, perhaps, comedies), Macaulay dared to write in a prestigious genre, history, which most people still considered exclusively the proper province of male authors. Despite advice literature's frequent admonitions to ladies that they ought to read fewer novels and more history, and despite the introduction of history into approved curricula for ladies, few people had contemplated the possibility that a woman who could read history might also write it.

As Natalie Zemon Davis has suggested, a would-be historian needed "a sense of connection, through some activity or deep concern of her own, with the areas of public life then considered suitable for historical writing, namely, the political and the religious."[92] As we have seen in chapter one, the traumatic events of the English Civil War inspired writers like Cavendish and Hutchinson to write what could be described as works of family history, designed, as they saw them, to correct the historical record in so far as it failed properly to record the virtues of their husbands. I would agree with Davis that such family histories continued to be popular and that they "undoubtedly had some significance in the formation of the historical consciousness among learned women."[93] Macaulay knew Hutchinson's life of Colonel Hutchinson and bestirred herself to get it published, although she failed to do so.

Like Edmund Gibbon, Catharine Sawbridge (Macaulay after her marriage) was the grandchild of a South Sea Director punished by Parliament for "breach of trust" by expropriation of his assets. The Sawbridges were more successful than the Gibbons in reversing their fortunes after the South Sea Bubble, partly through marriages with heiresses. Catharine's elder brother John became a wealthy London Alderman, a Wilkite, a radical Member of Parliament in 1774, Mayor of London in 1775, and a founder member of the Society for the Support of the Bill of Rights. Throughout her life, Catharine was close to John, a sharer in his political point of view, and an enthusiastic participant in radical circles. Certainly her brother's political engagement helped give her that "sense of connection" with public life Davis finds crucial to forming an ambition to be an historian.

However, Macaulay's *History of England* was in no sense a family history or what Cavendish described as a "particular history," like her *Life of the Duke of Newcastle*; instead, Macaulay's was an ambitious national history that took for its subject the complex events of the seventeenth century, from the accession of James I in 1603, through the escalating struggle between the Crown and Parliament, to the English Civil War, regicide, Cromwell's Protectorate, the Restoration of King Charles II to the throne, ending finally with the abdication of James II and the Glorious Revolution of 1688. Like most European historians of their own countries in the eighteenth century, eager to have national histories that could rival those of Greece and Rome and that could supplement or even replace those histories in the education of citizens of modern nation states, Macaulay understood her history as a patriotic work. Just as Voltaire in *The Age of Louis XIV* had elected to treat the period he considered the apogee of French greatness in an age of absolutism, that period in which the achievements of France were most characteristic of the nation and best distinguished it from Greece and Rome and from other European countries, so Macaulay elected a period of her national history during which those she believed to be the greatest champions of English liberty had lived and struggled.

It was an embarrassing fact that one of the most important histories of England written during the first half of the eighteenth century – one Macaulay used and respected – was the Frenchman Paul Rapin de Thoryras's *Histoire d'Angleterre*, published in Holland in ten volumes between 1724 and 1727 and quickly translated into a fifteen-volume English version. Even in her 1773 *Letters on the Improvement of the Mind* Chapone is reduced to advising the young lady who needs to learn English history: "If you have courage and industry enough to begin so high as the invasion of Julius Caesar . . . you may set out with Rapin, and proceed with him to William the Conqueror. From this era there are other histories of England more entertaining than his, though I believe none esteemed more authentic."[94]

Macaulay wrote aware that the seventeenth century furnished copious parallels to the struggles of the later eighteenth century, when Crown and

Parliament, Parliament and people, once more so intensely contested their relative prerogatives and rights that revolution and civil war again seemed possible. Hers was an engaged history that intended to contribute both to knowledge of the past and to the political understanding of a present crisis. As she saw it, the Crown, an aristocratic oligarchy, and hordes of rapacious placemen again threatened the liberty and property of Englishmen. The present government of England in the 1760s, the ruling Crown "faction," she declared, "has not only prevented the establishing any regular system to preserve or improve our liberties; but lie at this time in wait for the first opportunity which the imperfections of this government may give them, to destroy those rights, which have been purchased by the toil and blood of the most exalted individuals who ever adorned humanity . . ."[95] Governmental apologists had succeeded in convincing the nation that the system of corruption was a good thing and liberty a danger.

Moreover, Macaulay complained, the history of the nation's past had been so perversely narrated that Englishmen have "lost a just sense of the merit of the men by whose virtues these privileges [unpossessed by other nations] were attained; men that, with the hazard and even the loss of their lives, attacked the formidable pretensions of the Stewart family, and set up the banners of liberty against a tyranny which had been established for a series of more than one hundred and fifty years . . ."[96] Her heroes include Sir Thomas Fairfax, John Lilburne, John Hampden, Sir Henry Vane, Algernon Sydney, and Milton (though not Cromwell). Instead of being taught that these men were champions of liberty, children in the eighteenth century have been brought up to believe that they were dangerous "disturbers of the peace of mankind."[97] This distortion of history has been accomplished at the behest of "men to whom tyranny is in some measure profitable," men who enjoy illicit privilege and the spoils of a corruption that a better educated public would know enough to censure.[98]

Of particular interest to literary history is Macaulay's treatment of freedom of the press. She gives detailed accounts of punishments meted out to seventeenth-century authors, accounts designed to arouse indignation at what she labels the "cruelty" and "unconstitutionality" of those punishments. Like the seventeenth-century radicals, English radicals in the 1760s and 1770s struggled, albeit more successfully, to establish legal rights to freedom of speech and freedom of the press. Thus, as Macaulay makes clear, her narratives of the Crown's repression of speech and printing in cases like those of Sir John Eliot, Alexander Leighton, John Lilburne, William Prynne, and others had continuing relevance for her readers. They followed, among others, the prosecution for seditious libel of Wilkes and his printers for the publication of number 45 of *The North Briton* (1762), an attack on the government ministers who negotiated the Treaty of Paris. Macaulay thinks some of the prosecuted seventeenth-century writers were foolish and fanatical, but she considers government prosecution of speech and writing more foolish and more wrong: "There is not a more certain mark of an ill-designing or impotent administration, than attempts to restrain the liberty of speaking or writing."[99]

Macaulay's treatment of the case of William Prynne, author of the famous Puritan attack on plays, *Histrio Mastix: The Players Scourge, or Actors Tragodie* (1633), illustrates her advocacy of freedom of the press and her participation in the enlightenment campaign against cruelty, particularly state torture. Prynne's views on the theatre she finds foolish, remarking that Prynne was "as obstinate, as zealous, and as limited in his opinions" as his antagonist Archbishop William Laud.[100] Nevertheless, she tells the story of the Crown's dealing with him to highlight the dangers of allowing government officials to decide when the words of their opponents are dangerous. Prynne, she points out, had a license to publish *Histrio Mastix* granted by Laud's chaplain. Yet Laud subsequently took advantage of Queen Henrietta Maria's appearing in a court masque to suggest to King Charles I that Prynne's words, "Women-actors notorious whores," referred to the Queen. The Star Chamber prosecution of Prynne transformed Prynne's "general invectives against plays" into "a treasonable libel, of dangerous consequence to the realm and state."[101] The "cruel sentence," the "illegal, barbarous" punishment meted out to Prynne disbarred him as a lawyer, fined him £5,000, required him to stand in the pillory, and ordered both his ears cut off. (These kinds of Star Chamber sentences, including the enormous fine, which threatened to keep the offender perpetually imprisoned for inability to pay, are the classic instances of what the authors of the American Bill of Rights had in mind in Article 8 when they forbade "cruel and unusual punishments" and "excessive fines.")

Macaulay devotes most of four closely printed pages of notes to recording the idiocies of the Crown prosecutors, rather like Pope in *The Dunciad* allowing her dunces to condemn themselves in their own words. She records their unctuous and irrelevant flattery of the Queen and the revolting mélange of pettiness and bloody-mindedness of the Earl of Dorset's argument for Prynne's perpetual imprisonment: ". . . I should be loth he should escape with his ears, for he may get a perriwig, which he now so much inveighs against, and so hide them, or force his conscience to make use of his unlovely love-locks on both sides; therefore, I would have him branded in the forehead, slit in the nose, and his ears cropt too, my lords."[102] (Dorset mockingly glances back at Prynne's earlier *The Unloveliness of Lovelocks* [1628], an argument that men's wearing long hair was unseemly and unlawful for Christians.) With characteristic disdain for sycophancy, Macaulay relates that the Attorney General and other lawyer courtiers prevailed upon their colleagues in the Inns of Court to spend £21,000 to offer their own masque to the Queen, presumably by way of apology and reassurance that not all lawyers were dangerous. "To the ridicule of every person of common sense in the kingdom," she reports sardonically, "the four grave societies of the inns of court threw aside their law studies, and attached themselves with earnestness to the important business of a mask . . ."[103]

As Macaulay follows Prynne's further adventures, she shows her interest in the legal tactics of resistance to state authority that Wilkes, the radicals of his circle, and the early campaigners for the abolition of slavery like Granville Sharpe all cultivated. Imprisoned, Prynne writes *Prynne against Prelates* (1637), inveighing against innovations in worship. At this point, Prynne and some fellow sufferers try suing the bishops, "charging them with usurping upon the royal-prerogative."[104] This innovative tactic of defendants suing the prosecution did not work for Prynne, but was brilliantly successful for Wilkes. In 1763 Wilkes sued Robert Wood, an Under-Secretary of State, who had been part of the group who came into his house to arrest him and seize his papers, for trespass; he won £1,000 damages. He also encouraged printers who had been arrested to sue officials for damages and they also won generous judgments from sympathetic London juries.[105] Subsequently, in the important case of *Entick* v. *Carington* (1765), the judges ruled that the "general warrants" the government had used to discover the printers and publishers of the *Monitor* were invalid. (This case essentially established a new right, one that lies behind the prohibition in Article 4 of the American Bill of Rights against warrants that do not particularly describe "the place to be searched, and the persons or things to be seized.") Convicted again, Prynne is sentenced to another enormous fine, perpetual imprisonment, the loss of the remaining parts of his ears, and to be branded "in each cheek with S. L. for a seditious libeller."[106]

Macaulay points out that other historians have not been "particular" in their accounts of the Star Chamber punishments, "either from tenderness to the character of the government, or from motives of abhorrence to the nature of the offence given by the wretched sufferer."[107] Her narrative, however, burns with an indignation at torture worthy of Voltaire: "The hangman performed his bloody office with an approved barbarity . . . Prynne's [ears] were hacked barbarously; he lost a large part of his cheek with the remainder of his ears, and the executioner applied the burning iron twice to the branding of one cheek." Amazingly, from the scaffold, Prynne reviews the applicable statutes to demonstrate to a large and sympathetic crowd that "there was no law in the realm that authorized such tyranny."[108]

Macaulay insists that ignominious punishments like the pillory and mutilation are "slavish corrections" "incongruous to the privilege of a free man."[109] As she recounts, the English revolution abolished the Star Chamber and the Court of High Commission and neither of them was restored in 1660. Nevertheless, reminding her readers that the government still has recourse to criminal sanctions including the pillory, whipping, and long imprisonment for putative sedition in speech or writing, Macaulay comments: "The constitution of this country has never been purged from the venom with which it was infected by the erection of the Star-chamber: Its infamous doctrine and servile discipline have in many instances been adopted in the courts of common law."[110]

The question of whether a good historian can be politically engaged or whether he or she is required to write from a position of "scientific objectivity" was debated in this period, as it is still debated. Enlightenment historians not only repudiated the older chronicle for a newer, more philosophical narrative, they also set themselves against older court panegyric and aimed to develop critical positions. While important French and English enlightenment historians wanted to contribute to the honor of their nations, they made efforts to avoid some kinds of partisanship. Macaulay's most important rival was the Scottish philosopher David Hume, whose six-volume *History of England* had appeared from 1754 to 1762. Hume wrote and published in reverse chronological order, beginning with his first two volumes on the seventeenth century and ending with his two volumes covering the earliest period from the invasion of Julius Caesar to the accession of Henry VIII. Writing about the seventeenth century in the 1750s, before the more divisive political climate of the 1760s, he attacked earlier eighteenth-century English historians for distorting their narratives with Whig or Tory partisanship, devoted careful – and philosophical – attention to restating the arguments of each side in the seventeenth-century debates he discussed, and claimed to rise above party and "faction" to appeal to readers he described as "impartial reasoners."[111] With justice and evidence, he attacked the favorite Whig belief that there was an "ancient constitution" in place before the Norman invasion of 1066, a constitution that could be appealed to as the guarantor of English liberties. He also complained that earlier Whig history had too exclusively prized liberty; to Hume, desire for liberty was "a laudable passion," but one that "ought commonly to be subordinate to a reverence for established government."[112] At the same time, more liberally, he made the gradual attainment of the liberties of the subject – including habeas corpus and the freedom of the press – a central theme of his narrative and a chief ground of British greatness.

Nevertheless, in the 1760s many English readers, including Macaulay, were not prepared to grant Hume's claim that he was impartial. His *History* was frequently denounced as distorted by conservative ideology; some labeled it a Tory history. Hume had certainly written as a *philosophe*, following those Roman sages who understood philosophy as esoteric and comprehensible only to a small elite and who were content to leave the common people with traditional customs and beliefs. Discussing the validity of republican principles on the right of resistance to tyrants in his narration of the trial and death of Charles I, Hume commented:

If ever, on any occasion, it were laudable to conceal truth from the populace; it must be confessed, that the doctrine of resistance affords such an example; and that all speculative reasoners ought to observe, with regard to this principle, the same cautious silence, which the laws, in every species of government, have ever prescribed to themselves. Government is instituted, in order to restrain the fury and injustice of the people; and being always founded on opinion, not on force, it is dangerous, by these speculations, to weaken the reverence, which the multitude owe to authority, and to instruct them before-hand, that the case can ever happen, when they may be free'd from their duty of allegiance.[113]

Such elitism was repugnant to the radicals of the 1760s, who were more democratically engaged in educating the people about their rights, and who organized resistance to such abuses of liberty as the press gangs that seized civilians and mustered them into the navy. Although Macaulay's *History* was originally published in impressive large volumes selling for £4 10s. each, she also arranged for inexpensive serial publication, dividing each volume into fifteen numbers, each priced at one shilling to accommodate a popular audience.[114]

Contemporaries immediately recognized the publication in 1763 of the first volume of Macaulay's *History*, the volume treating 1603–28, as an unprecedented and significant intellectual and literary event. Attention was divided between the achievements of the *History* and the fact that a woman wrote it. While, as I have earlier noted, the leading reviews of the day, *The Critical Review* and *The Monthly Review*, normally devoted perfunctory and often condescending attention to novels, both this first and many successive volumes of Macaulay's *History* were considered as major works in long leading articles. *The Critical Review*, not associated with radicalism or even liberalism, correctly saw that the grand subject of the volume was "the great lines of the constitution" and declared that she had succeeded in offering "a judicious and connected account of those famous debates and arguments concerning the liberty of the subject, the power of princes, the prerogative of the king, and other capital points, upon which the constitution of England may be said to hinge."[115] Her character of James I was "masterly in the highest degree, and built on the best authorities," and her style "every-where animated, yet correct, varied but not irregular . . ."[116] In a review of a later volume in 1769, the *Critical* went so far as to praise her contrast between the behavior of the King's army and Parliament's army after the battle of Naseby as a passage "at least equal to any we meet with in Tacitus."[117]

Macaulay's use of manuscript materials and seventeenth-century pamphlets as sources was an historiographical advance in the treatment of this period. While Rapin had cited some original sources extensively, Hume made no pretense of doing so. Macaulay uses footnotes citing her sources. She cites manuscripts in the British Museum, first opened to the public in 1759, and also seventeenth-century tracts (some of which were bought for her by admirers of her work). *The Critical* decided that her use of primary documents contributed to producing a history that would "remain unanswered in point of fidelity . . . unless the public record of the kingdom shall be proved to have been vitiated, and the hand-writings of our princes and great-men to have been forged."[118] While Hume mocked the petitioning of "seditious" common people who approached Parliament, Macaulay finds the texts of the petitions and tells her readers exactly what they said their grievances were.

Moreover, despite the real strengths of Hume's *History*, they did not include sympathetic attention to religion or much willingness to grant sincerity or even sanity to persons animated by religious motives. Hume consistently ridiculed Puritans, Presbyterians, Quakers, and the host of what he calls "fanatics" whose beliefs and actions are so central to seventeenth-century English history; not infrequently, he professed to find their positions and words unintelligible, and hence not worth recording. Duncan Forbes perceptively observed that as a Scotsman and a target of the opprobrium of religious people himself, "Hume did not regard the excesses of those dangerous visionaries, as he saw them, as a phenomenon safely confined to the past."[119] The Presbyterian Covenanters had risen up to support Jacobite invasion and insurrection as recently as 1745, posing a threat to what Hume valued as the emerging good order of modern Britain. But that only suggests one of the many ways in which Hume's *History* had its own present relevance and engagement. Macaulay, though a member of the Church of England, treats dissenting religion with more respect.

As Macaulay proceeded to the volumes dealing directly with the Civil War and interregnum, her republican principles became clearer to readers, and, as the political atmosphere became tenser and more contentious, the reception of her work became more qualified. Yet her substantive arguments and evidence continued to evoke substantive discussion even from reviewers who were worried that she advanced principles inimical to monarchical government. Even at the moment when the loss of America, in part as a consequence of the dissemination of republican principles, had become a reality, *The Critical Review* acknowledged on the publication of her eighth and last volume: "This volume completes a work which must afford one of the most signal instances ever known to the literary world, of the extraordinary abilities and persevering exertion of a female writer."[120] Much of the reception of the *History* was clouded by tortured gallantry, befuddlement over female accomplishment, and even alarm from some men and women about the implications of such a precedent. Yet Macaulay established herself as a significant historian and as a defender of liberty, in the words of her young admirer Mary Scott in *The Female Advocate* (1774):

> A name, to every son of freedom dear,
> Which patriots yet unborn shall long revere.[121]

Macaulay's *History* circulated in Britain, France, and America. In Britain, it was especially valued by radicals and dissenters and served as their standard history until William Godwin's *History of the Commonwealth of England* (1824–28) supplanted it. In France, the Comte de Mirabeau, a leader in the Constituent Assembly in the first year of the French Revolution, saw that it was translated into French by 1791–92 so that her contribution to revolutionary thought might be a corrective to Hume's counter-revolutionary narrative.

For Americans, the *History* became a key book among the books that made their Revolution possible. John Adams in 1770 wrote to Macaulay that the *History* was "calculated to strip off the Gilding and false Lustre from worthless Princes and Nobles, and to bestow the Reward of Virtue, Praise, upon the generous and worthy only."[122] Macaulay supported the colonists' grievances against the British government, corresponding with American leaders and propagandists and advocating their positions in her pamphlet, *An Address to the People of England, Scotland and Ireland on the Present Important Crisis of Affairs* (1775). While Johnson supported Lord North's ministry and belittled the colonists' grievances in his pamphlet *Taxation no Tyranny* (1775), Macaulay criticized the Stamp Act, the closing of the port of Boston in retaliation for the Boston Tea Party, and the Quebec Act. Evidence abounds that major figures of the American Revolution including John and Samuel Adams, Benjamin Rush, Benjamin Franklin, Thomas Jefferson, and George Washington read and admired the *History* and personally met or corresponded with her.[123] In 1771 Abigail Adams wrote to her uncle, a Boston merchant then in London and acquainted with Macaulay, asking for information about "one of my own Sex so eminent in a tract so uncommon." Later, in 1774, responding to a desire Macaulay had expressed to John Adams to become acquainted with American women, Abigail wrote her a long letter discussing the grievances of the colonists, their growing sense of common cause against the British government, and their republican resolution to scorn "the livery of Britain" by dressing themselves not in imported "gaudy trappings that adorn slaves" but in "the coarse and plain vestures of our own Manufacturing."[124]

SENTIMENTAL PLAYS AND NOVELS

Given that only two London theatres and one or two in Dublin were licensed to produce new plays, that the theatre managers of this period generally preferred the safety of tested repertory to the hazard of a new play, and that women had an even harder time having play manuscripts accepted than men, it is not surprising that women in this period wrote and published many more novels than plays. Two women who did have some success as playwrights both had the advantage of previous association with the theatre, providing them with valuable knowledge and contacts. Frances Sheridan was married to Thomas Sheridan, an actor and sometimes theatre manager; her husband performed one of the principal roles when her first sentimental comedy, *The Discovery*, premiered at Drury Lane in 1763. Elizabeth Griffith had a short career as an actress, beginning at the Smock Alley Theatre in Dublin in 1749, then playing minor parts at Covent Garden in London from 1753 to 1755, before the first of her five comedies, *The Platonic Wife*, was performed, also at Drury Lane, in 1765, with her brother in a supporting role.

Most women's plays and novels in this period were sentimental. As we saw in the previous chapter's consideration of Collyer's *Felicia to Charlotte*, a very early sentimental novel, a philosophical ground of the sentimental was the insistence by Shaftesbury and Hutcheson that humankind had a "moral sense" and that feeling had a crucial role in morality and moral discourse. After 1756, philosophers continued to argue that humankind had a natural capacity to be virtuous; increasingly, they addressed themselves to the psychology of sympathy. In *A Theory of Moral Sentiments* (1759), Adam Smith analyzed the apparently irrational possibility that the recollection and recounting of pain and grief could be a source of pleasure:

How are the unfortunate relieved when they have found out a person to whom they can communicate the cause of their sorrow? . . . by relating their misfortunes they in some measure renew their grief. They awaken in their memory the remembrance of those circumstances which occasioned their affliction. Their tears accordingly flow faster than before, and they are apt to abandon themselves to all the weaknesses of sorrow. They take pleasure, however, in all this, and, it is evident, are sensibly relieved by it; because the sweetness of [the listener's] sympathy more than compensates the bitterness of that sorrow . . .[125]

Sentimental writers usually understood themselves as members of the party of virtue, although as Carter's criticism of sentimental fiction as "destructive" suggests, not everyone agreed. Their heroes and heroines were characters who felt distress at the sufferings of others and whose tears flowed freely. These protagonists suppose that by listening to tales of sorrow they help to alleviate the griefs of the tellers. Spectators at sentimental drama and readers of sentimental novels, in turn, were expected to enjoy what Anna Letitia Aikin (later Barbauld), in her essay "An Inquiry into the Kinds of Distress which excite agreeable Sensations," called the "sweet emotion of pity."[126] Aikin thought that the most effective sentimental representations connected misery with "the display of some moral excellence or agreeable quality," as in Richardson's *Clarissa*. She observed that fictitious representations of distress "are generally thought to improve the tender and humane feelings."[127] In her view, however, repeated literary evocations of compassion risked decreasing the emotion – creating what is now called "compassion fatigue" – and evoking compassion when there was no actual object for charitable action. Moreover, since objects of pity in sentimental literature are imaginatively pleasing, even elegant,

Aikin thought that they were unlike the people in real life who needed charity, people who were apt to be vulgar, even disgusting, but people true charity should help.

One paradigmatic sentimental plot in drama or fiction shows a protagonist, understood to be fundamentally good and possessed of a capacity for sensibility, nevertheless guilty of some error. The action and the articulated "sentiments" of other good characters eventually enlighten the protagonist, who then successfully reforms. For example, the heroine of Griffith's sentimental comedy, *The Platonic Wife* (1765), is guilty of two errors. Already married, Lady Frankland nevertheless makes such extravagant demands for romance from her husband that she forces a separation. Then, while separated, she attempts to demonstrate that a married woman can have male friends. The plot – based on Jean-François Marmontel's sentimental moral tale, *L'Heureux divorce* (1761) – overtly teaches Lady Frankland that she is not entitled to have her demands for ardent romance within marriage met and that men other than her husband regard her as sexual prey. However, as is typical of sentimental plots, the protagonist's misery, abject repentance, and protestations of undeservingness immediately produce lavish rewards. As soon as Lady Frankland relinquishes her demands for romance as an entitlement, her husband rewards her with romantic adulation.

FRANCES SHERIDAN'S *THE DISCOVERY*

Also common in sentimental plots are paragon characters who offer to make dramatic sacrifices, demonstrating their extraordinary virtue – only to find that their proffered sacrifices will not be required. We saw this in *Felicia to Charlotte*. In Sheridan's sentimental comedy, *The Discovery*, Lord Medway has been so selfish and extravagant that he cannot provide for his children, who want to marry. Further indulging himself, he tries to have an affair with an unhappy young married woman and loses so much money gambling that he creates an immediate cash flow crisis. He wants his paragon son, Colonel George Medway, who has already relinquished his right to a future share of the family estate to help his father, also to relinquish his paragon lady love to marry a rich widow whose money can help repair the family fortunes. Unlike such fathers in older comedy, who might simply have demanded obedience from their children, Lord Medway reproaches himself for his bad behavior. This son's compliance is secured not by paternal command but by his father's making himself a spectacle of pathos. However, George's proffered sacrifice turns out not to be required by the "discovery" that gives the play its name: the rich young widow his father had wanted him to marry is discovered to be Lord Medway's illegitimate daughter, a girl he fathered when he was an army officer serving in Portugal but of whose birth he was ignorant.

Like the heroes and heroines of romance, sentimental paragons never act on mercenary motives yet are rewarded with wealth. George has shown his willingness to sacrifice his financial interests and his love to rescue his family from distress. He rejects the idea that his lady love, Clara Richly, could feel compensated by money, uttering one of the "senti-ments" or moral maxims characteristic of sentimental comedy: "it is not in the power of riches to heal a wounded mind!"[128] Nevertheless, all is mended when Mrs. Knightly, the rich widow now revealed to be Lord Medway's illegitimate daughter, herself is sentimental enough to revere her newly acquired parent and generous enough to share her fortune with the Medways.

Instead of showing the scene of discovery and reconciliation between father and illegitimate daughter as a stage tableau, the obvious choice in sentimental drama, Sheridan decides to have Lord Medway narrate it to his son:

Mrs. Knightly's agitations are not to be described. She wept and wrung her hands. I mixed my tears with her's; and, while she fell on her knees before me, I involuntarily dropped on one of mine, and begged of her to accept a blessing from her repentant father. She strained me to her bosom; then rising with a noble air, she made a sorrowful and silent motion with her hand that I should leave her.[129]

Whether this scene is shown or narrated, the spectator is invited to take pleasure in the double distress of father and daughter. Because each demonstrates both a sense of shame for himself or herself and pity for the other, revealing intrinsic goodness, the spectator may enjoy what Adam Smith described as sweet sympathy that more than compensates for sorrow. Sheridan's decision to have Lord Medway narrate the scene instead of dramatizing it tightens the focus on his feelings of tenderness and remorse. By interposing the further spectacle of his painful recollec-tion between the audience and primary scene, she shows his developing capacity for reflection and offers the audience a layering of scenes of heightened emotion.

The sentimental idea that bad behavior is the result of mistaken ideas that can be corrected by analysis and reasonable speech – an idea equally fundamental to the political reform campaigns of the enlightenment and to later psychotherapy – is illustrated by a slightly edgier subplot involving Lady Medway and a young married couple, Sir Harry and Lady Flutter. They heedlessly immerse themselves in London's fashionable amusements and quarrel with one another over trivia. Lady Medway overhears Lord Medway attempting to seduce Lady Flutter by fueling her discontent with her young husband. Going beyond the conduct-book injunctions for wronged wives to forbear reproaching their husbands, she says nothing to her husband but sits down for long talk with Lady Flutter. Once, she acknowledges, she might have been jealous, but now she has "out-lived . . . so selfish a passion"; "pity" for the younger woman and "tenderness and duty" toward her husband motivate her to try to save Lady Flutter from "ruin."[130] Lady Medway promises that she can show Lady Flutter a way for the Flutters to be happy with each other and persuades her to try a three-day "experiment" of not contradicting her husband. This works like a charm, disrupting the neurotic patterns into which they have fallen. Almost immediately, Sir Harry vows never to contradict his wife either and the couple express their fondness for each other. Since, like Richardson's Pamela and many real good women then and now, Lady Medway is also willing to receive her husband's illegitimate child as a treasured member of her own family, and since Lord Medway is thoroughly repentant, he rewards his wife with admiration for her virtue and embraces her, declaring, "best of women, receive my hand a second time; and with it an assurance, which I could never make before, that you possess my heart entire."[131]

The sentimental comedy of Griffith and Sheridan and their contemporaries ultimately descends from Cibber's comedy, but sentimental comedy in this later period also is indebted to the developments in moral philosophy represented by Smith's *Theory of Moral Sentiments*. It also owed much to Diderot's bourgeois *drame*, *Le Fils naturel, ou les épreuves de virtue* (1757) and *Le Père de famille* (1758), and to his essays defining and defending the form; Griffith, significantly, worked on translating Diderot's *drame*, although she failed to get that translation performed.

NOVELS

Neither Macaulay nor Adams evince interest in novels; most of the more typical bluestockings were appreciative readers of Richardson, but they too spent most of the large amounts of time they devoted to reading to history, to "works of the intellect," to religion, and to poetry. Chapone, while admitting in *Letters on the Improvement of the Mind* that a few novels join "excellent morality" with "the most lively pictures of the mind," warns against most fiction. She condemns sentimental fiction as especially apt "to vitiate your stile, and to mislead your heart and understanding."[132] Carter, despite an occasional good word for a particular novel, thinks novels generally "wretched books, by which the understanding, the taste, and the heart are in danger of being vitiated." She sees sentimental novels as especially deplorable: "those which are writ in the most specious manner, with great appearance of delicacy, and high pretensions to virtue, are of all others the most destructive; they form a jumble of right and wrongs, so entangled together, that it requires an exactness to separate them, which seldom or never belongs to young people . . ."[133] Carter achieved fame and considerable fortune from *Epictetus*; the more than £1,000 she earned from its publication enabled her to buy her own house and yielded income that added to her independence. Macaulay certainly earned more than £1,000 from her *History*. When she changed publishers midway through the volumes of the *History*, Dilly agreed to pay her £900 for the rights to an octavo edition of her works and £1,000 for the copyright of each subsequent volume she should write.[134] Writers of novels, on the other hand, even though the novel was becoming a more established literary commodity, were lucky to get about £20 or £30 or so for the outright sale of the copyright to a bookseller.

Between 1756 and 1776, identifiable women published about eighty-seven novels, roughly four each year.[135] Lennox and Sarah Fielding both continued to write novels; after 1756 they were joined by Frances Brooke, Griffith, and Sheridan, each of whom also had success as a novelist. Less important novelists who published more than one novel include Mrs. Woodfin, whose *Northern Memoirs, or the History of a Scotch Family* (1756) was the first of five novels; Phebe Gibbes, who wrote several novels for the new circulating libraries; and Sophie Briscoe, author of *Miss Melmoth; or, the New Clarissa* (1771) and *The Fine Lady: A Novel* (1772). (Briscoe earned 20 guineas for the copyright of *The Fine Lady*.)[136] In addition to the eighty-seven novels produced by identifiable women writers, other novels published anonymously or with some variation on the formula "By a Lady" were certainly by women who have not yet been identified. Most novels, in fact, were published anonymously or pseudonymously and have not been securely attributed. Contemporaries sometimes had the impression that women were beginning to dominate the novel. A reviewer in the *Monthly Review* of 1773, for example, claimed that "this branch of the literary *trade*" was "almost entirely engrossed by the Ladies."[137] Nevertheless, James

Raven is probably correct to estimate that women during this period produced less than 15 percent of all the novels published. These women novelists generally continued the Richardsonian tradition, often now affected by French influences; they did not engage in the learned wit or bawdy of Sterne's *Tristram Shandy* (1760–67) or the satiric adventure mode of Richard Graves's *Spiritual Quixote* (1773).

French influences are evident in the fiction of Frances Brooke, daughter of a Lincolnshire clergyman, and Griffith, the Irish actress who became a London-based playwright and novelist. Both Brooke and Griffith read widely in French literature, published translations of French books, and wrote novels of sensibility in the new mode fashionable in France and England and most brilliantly exemplified by Rousseau's *Julie: ou, la nouvelle Héloïse* (1761). Both, in turn, saw their novels translated into French. After futile efforts to have theatrical pieces of various kinds produced in London, and after editing a weekly periodical entitled *The Old Maid* (1755–56), Brooke published a successful translation of Marie-Jeanne Riccoboni's *Lettres de Milady Juliette Catesby à Lady Henriette Campley, son ami* (1759) as *Letters from Juliet, Lady Catesby, to her Friend, Lady Henrietta Campley* (1760). (Riccoboni's characters are English, a not too uncommon choice in French novels and plays of this period.) Riccoboni was an important translator of English plays into French and a close friend of Garrick's, as well as an important novelist. Juliette writes her grief after having been suddenly and without coherent explanation abandoned by her fiancé, Lord Ossory. Shortly before they were to be married, he quickly married another woman. While behaving properly, Juliette is far from attempting to cultivate stoicism or to eliminate love and passion as central to her life. She is uninhibited in expressing her feelings, her pain, and her complaints to her woman friend, the recipient of her letters. As Lorraine McMullen argued, from Riccoboni's *Letters*, Brooke "learned how to construct a tightly knit novel of sensibility."[138]

Brooke went on to write a number of original works of drama and fiction, including, in this period, two epistolary novels of sensibility, *The History of Lady Julia Mandeville* (1763) and *The History of Emily Montague* (1769). A hero and a heroine of sensibility in *Lady Julia* come to a tragic end like that of Romeo and Juliet, not because of quarreling family dynasties but because the too-impetuous hero mistakenly believes Lady Julia is going to marry a richer man and gets killed by his supposed rival in a duel. Voltaire praised *Lady Julia Mandeville* as perhaps the best novel of the kind that had appeared in English since *Clarissa* and *Grandison*.[139]

BROOKE'S *EMILY MONTAGUE*

Emily Montague expresses Brooke's patriotic enthusiasm over British acquisition of one of the important prizes of the Seven Years War, Canada; it successfully appealed to the proprietary interest of the British public in its new territories. Brooke was the wife of a Church of England clergyman, John Brooke, chaplain to the British army in Canada, where she joined him in October 1763, after the Peace of Paris ended the war and made Canada British. *Emily Montague* is set in Canada and has frequently been called the first Canadian novel, indeed, the first North American novel (leaving Behn's *Oroonoko* with the title of the first South American novel). Unlike Riccoboni's novels of passion or the typical English senti- mental domestic novel, which have generalized, lightly specified settings, *Emily Montague* carefully describes the Canadian landscape. The novel's appeal is partly that of the travel books that were favorites of enlighten- ment readers. Rivers, Brooke's hero, finds the aesthetic sublimity Burke had defined in *A Philosophical Enquiry into the Origin of our Ideas of the Sublime and Beautiful* in the Canadian landscape:

> On approaching the coast of America, I felt a kind of religious veneration, on seeing rocks which almost touch'd the clouds, cover'd with tall groves of pines that seemed coeval with the world itself: to which veneration the solemn silence not a little contributed; from Cape Rosieres, up the river St. Lawrence, during a course of more than two hundred miles, there is not the least appearance of human foot-step; no objects meet the eye but mountains, woods, and numerous rivers, which seem to roll their waters in vain.[140]

All the correspondents in Brooke's epistolary novel are British and view the French and Indian inhabitants of their new territory from the British perspective, but Brooke uses the form of the epistolary novel to divide the work of observation along gendered lines. Sir William Fermor's letters provide the serious accounts of political economy and public policy issues in the new territory that one would expect from an upper-class male traveler. He sees French Canadians as an inferior people, weakened by laziness, vanity, and Popish superstition, but has hopes that providing free English-language schools might in time make them "happier in them- selves, and more useful members of the society to which they belong" and that they might, eventually, "acquire the mild genius of our religion and laws, and that spirit of industry, enterprize, and commerce, to which we owe all our greatness."[141] Sir William deplores that the French have been unable to "civilize" the Native Americans and, worse, that they have reportedly imitated them in their cruelties – including offering rewards for scalps in the war and even cannibalism. This behavior serves to demonstrate that the French ought to be subjected to the British. Rivers offers instead something closer to soft primitivism in his description of the Huron Indians, who he describes as free and egalitarian, hospitable (when not at war), and essentially deists. Writing to his sister, he reports that the Huron women elect the chiefs, commenting jocularly: "I am pleased with this last regulation, as women are, beyond all doubt, the best judges of the merit of men; and I should be extremely pleased to see it adopted in England . . . In the true sense of the word, *we* are the savages, who so impolitely deprive you of the common rights of citizenship, and leave you no power but that of which we cannot deprive you, the resistless power of your charms."[142]

Courtship and love occupy the women correspondents more than politics; they have an eye for the picturesque in the landscape as well as the sublime. Unlike Lady Julia Mandeville, Emily Montague fares more happily with a gentler hero of sensibility, the proto-feminist Rivers, whose eventual marriage to her is temporarily blocked by his concerns about supporting his mother. Arabella Fermor, the heroine's lively friend, is at first attracted by the apparent freedom the Huron women enjoy, but recants her enthusiasm when she discovers that Huron girls do not enjoy the liberty of selecting their husbands.

Modern critics have been divided over whether to read *Emily Montague* as a feminist novel, some seeing Brooke as supporting such radical ideas as women's suffrage. She is clearly interested in such ideas, yet, as Heinz Antor points out, "the greatest weight of the oppositional feminist dis- course is ironically to be felt when produced by a man."[143] Moreover, even Arabella, seen by some as challenging sentimental ideology and suspicious of sentiment as weakening women, nevertheless on occasion produces sentimental, essentialist constructions of femininity that would have horri- fied either Astell or the bluestockings. Brooke's strongly gendered points of view in the novel, though, do raise questions about gendered competencies and, of course, Brooke herself was the author of the men's letters.

In both Brooke novels, a livelier friend on the model of Richardson's Anna Howe counterpoises the heroine of sensibility. Brooke increasingly emphasized this character type in her fiction, and such friends often prove a resource to women novelists of this period when heroines are so stiflingly correct and genteel that they threaten to bore readers. As Ann Messenger has argued, Arabella Fermor is probably also Brooke's revision of the coquette heroine of Pope's *Rape of the Lock*, a revision "using the possibilities for psychological intimacy offered by the epistolary novel." In this reading, Brooke takes Pope's Belinda "and, while retaining the frivolous character perceived by the outside observer," turns her inside out to show "the mind, the motives, the wit, and the wisdom of the artful coquette."[144] Arabella and Rivers offer occasional critiques of the unfairness of the situation of British women that are very characteristic of the women's novels of this period. However, *Emily Montague* has a cheerfulness and interest in the wide external world uncharacteristic of most sentimental novels.

FIELDING'S *COUNTESS OF DELLWYN*

Most better women's novels of this period are notably grim. Their writers embrace the obligation to inculcate virtue in their readers and accept the rule that respectable women novelists should confine themselves to matters domestic. At the same time, perhaps in part as a consequence of these constraints, Fielding, Griffith, and Sheridan produce dark novels in which marriage is revealed to be a state of suffering, even torment. Instead of offering protection and love, the husbands in these novels leave wives few options but to try to achieve the stoic heroism available to women who can learn "to suffer without repining."[145] Much more than the male novelists, these women novelists turn away from the courtship plot to make the relationship of husband and wife within marriage an important subject.

Fielding's fiercely didactic *History of the Countess of Dellwyn* (1759) is more novelistic than her earlier, more fable-like, *Adventures of David Simple*, discussed in the previous chapter. Unlike most women's fiction of this period, it is not epistolary. Instead, it has the features of "overt authoriality": "substantive prefaces, generalizations in the narrator's voice, explicit allusion by the narrator to literature or history, direct addresses to a public narratee, and explicit reference to the narrating subject or the narrative act."[146] Fielding's substantial preface, adorned with discussion of Virgil, Plutarch, Horace, and Bossuet, declares: "nothing can give us so strong an Idea of the Misery of a Woman, as to suppose her under the Power of her own Passions . . ." Inflamed female passions, we are told, eradicate "that Gentleness which is the characteristic Beauty of the female Mind."[147] Fielding lacks sympathy for her protagonist, the Countess, treating her as something between a case in a conduct book and a satirical butt. The appeal of the novel is not so much in the characters, who are seen from an almost *Rambler*-like distance, but in the mordant observations of the narrator, who looks on the follies of fashionable life with scornful insight. The narrator's maxims and cold accounts of tortuous mental states sometimes recall La Rochefoucauld or anticipate Choderlos de Laclos's *Les liaisons dangereuses* (1782).

In an intriguing variation on the standard bad father who wants his daughter to marry for money, the father of the future Countess, Mr. Lucum, is obsessed with politics. He has held places, but lost power because he changed sides so often that he "at length became the Contempt of all Parties."[148] Fielding further blackens his character – and insists on the obligation of good women to confine their conversation to private subjects – by noting, "He was often the Subject of Coffee-house Debates, and was generally introduced to the Tea-table Conversations of female Politicians."[149] Out of place, Mr. Lucum is tormented by newspapers: "A Paragraph, beginning with the Words, *We hear his Majesty has been pleased to appoint*, was sufficient to raise a Tumult in his Breast."[150] His political ambitions are re-arroused when Lord Dellwyn hints that Miss Lucum might be exchangeable for lucrative employment.

Lord Dellwyn, in his sixties, is ingeniously repulsive; the marriage is doomed from its inception. His body, diseased as a consequence of his intemperate, luxurious life, is wheeled about by attendants in a "Machine, so artfully contrived, that he could vary his Postures, either lay himself almost at length, or sit upright, as his various Pains required . . ."[151] Miss Lucum's initial, eminently proper, refusal of marriage to this grotesque specimen of manhood is eventually overcome. Her father and Lord Dellwyn scheme together to immerse her so completely in London's fashionable amusements that she loses the "Power of Reflection."[152] This power of reflection was precisely what the serious reading and intellectual self-cultivation so strenuously advocated by the bluestockings was supposed to produce; it was the capacity to split one's consciousness between felt impulses and a mental awareness of disembodied principles. Unreflecting, Miss Lucum succumbs to envy of the rich and to piqued vanity when Lord Dellwyn affects to ignore her and pretends that he will marry Fanny Fashion instead.

Besides succumbing to the unlovely passions of envy and vanity in marrying Lord Dellwyn, Miss Lucum also sins in ignoring the obligation of virtuous women to combine to help enforce high moral standards for men, a frequent theme of women's writing in this period. Miss Lucum, the narrator comments, failed to reflect that if Lord Dellwyn were really engaged to Fanny Fashion, "he must necessarily now act a most dishonourable Part; and that, therefore, she had no Reason to place any Confidence in him; but must be certain, that his Conduct was solely regulated by his own whimsical wavering Inclinations."[153]

Fielding makes her Countess just good enough to be ashamed of herself. Once married to this man, who inspires disgust more than love, she has sufficient decency to feel the burden of being "under an Obligation to live a Lye" and that she has reason for "Self-condemnation."[154] When she learns that her father and husband conspired to provoke her vanity, she is indignant and so "Husband-sick" that her physician sends her to the spa at Bristol.

The narrator carefully analyzes the psychological dynamics of the Countess's fall into adultery, suggesting that she becomes lost in the rapt contemplation of pleasing images of herself. At the spa, Lord Clermont begins to flatter her with his attentions. Motivated not by lust but by insatiable vanity, she basks in his flattery, but is more intensely thrilled by the "Self-admiration" of her virtuous resistance.[155] Instead of resisting when Lord Dellwyn asks her not to see Lord Clermont any more, she willingly complies. But, warns the narrator, offering a maxim à la Rochefoucauld, "One fancied Virtue is more dangerous than many acknowledged Vices . . ."[156]

Fielding explores the pathology of a marriage in which mutual torment offers the only pleasure. Like Jane Collier in *The Art of Ingeniously Tormenting* (1753) or Jane Austen, she exposes the possibilities for sadism available in the full light of the drawing room. She is especially attentive to the deployment of what passes for polite language. Frank hatred becomes the dominant passion between the Dellwyns after each humiliates the other at a dinner party in which neither raises his or her voice and neither directly addresses the other. Lord Dellwyn praises Mrs. Saunders, an exemplary married woman; the company, rightly understanding this as an implicit reproach to his own wife, merely look "down at their Plates."[157] The Countess retorts by telling the story of soldiers who lose a battle under one general, cowardly or incompetent, but who would willingly fight the battle again under another commander; all the company understand the "Application."[158] Even the pleasure of publicly humiliating his wife pales as Lord Dellwyn begins to understand that he has been imprudent in marrying and that he has not purchased his wife's affections. When he begins refusing her requests for money, she soon grasps "that she had not, by marrying a Man of a large Fortune, obtained any great Proportion of Property she could call her own, or command at her Pleasure."[159] Thus humiliated, disappointed, and hated, the Countess falls relatively easy prey to Lord Clermont's seduction.

Refusing to accord any dignity to the Countess's passion, Fielding deprives her of Lady Vane's construction of passion as heroic truthfulness. Instead, she subjects her to a public separation and divorce, ridicules her efforts at reform, and denies her even the dignity of death. One exemplary good woman, her character so established "that she did not burden herself with any unnecessary Terrors, that her conversing with Lady *Dellwyn* could cast any Blemish on her spotless Reputation," temporarily convinces the Countess of the pleasures of a simple life in retirement.[160] Again striking a pose designed to evoke her own admiration, the Countess rents a small cottage and decks it "with Symbols of Sorrow and Penitence."[161] Harshly, the narrator mocks her hysterical theatricality and her effort to cloak her suffering in the language and signs of she tragedy: "Had Lord *Clermont* been slain abroad, it is probable she would have endeavoured to obtain his Body, and lamented over it with all the Pomp of *Calista* in the *Fair Penitent*."[162] Boredom with retirement and repentance soon drive her to Paris. Exposed there, she returns to London and to a life of "continual Mortification," barred from good company, loath to associate with bad, "for, tho' infamous, she was not impudent."[163] Lord Dellwyn is punished by marriage to his housekeeper, who rules him "as an Infant," and forces him to leave his fortune to her, "to the Scandal of his Name."[164]

A more sentimental subplot ostensibly provides some relief from the selfishness and misery of the principal characters in *The Countess of Dellwyn*. In this subplot, a virtuous wife, Mrs. Bilson, replays the virtuous conduct of Henry Fielding's Amelia until she finally reclaims her husband's affections and reforms him. Unlike her brother, who provides a male rescuer for the unhappy couple in *Amelia*, Sarah Fielding creates good women to come to the aid of her heroine. Her landlord's wife sets her up in the millinery business. Unlike more delicate heroines in sentimental fiction, she is able to work productively for a year and a half, "her Beauty, and the Gracefulness of her Person, giving a Dignity even to so low an Employment."[165] (Very likely, Fielding here recollects the similar good works in real life of her friends Sarah Scott and Lady Barbara Montagu, whose active charity provided means of employment for destitute women of various classes.) A charitable lady of higher rank also appears, Lady Dently, disgusted with fashionable life, where people "live in the World like Squirrels in a Cage hung with Bells, in a Round of Noise, without Variety, till their heads are too giddy to think on the future, or reflect on the past."[166] She pays the Bilsons' debts, retires into the country with them, then conveniently dies leaving them a fortune. They demonstrate their worth by using it to found a utopian community that includes schools where unfortunate children learn trades, a house for poor gentlewomen, almshouses for the aged, a community where "the Old spun and knitted for the Young; and those who were not decrepid served for Nurses to the Sick."[167]

Only in the Bilson subplot in *The Countess of Dellwyn* do we begin to see what a more typical sentimental novel of the period might be like, since the main plot is so fiercely didactic and satiric. Fielding partly moved in Richardson's orbit and partly occupied the position of a poor bluestocking living on the edge of Montagu's circle, friendlier with Scott than with her richer sister. Her vehement contempt for anything fashionable and her fervid asceticism align her with Scott, Talbot, and Carter, the poorer bluestockings, for whom the novel remained a problematic and dubious form.

GRIFFITH'S SENTIMENTAL NOVELS

Elizabeth Griffith was a commercial writer not personally associated with the bluestockings; like Brooke and Sheridan, she followed Richardson and French models to produce feminocentric novels of sensibility. Her early work included *The Memoirs of Ninon d'Enclos* (1761), a translation of what she believed to be the memoirs of the seventeenth-century French courtesan. Like many contemporary readers, she did not realize that much of the text she translated was an epistolary novel of 1750 by Louis Damours; like Brooke, she thus began her career as a novelist by translating a mid-eighteenth-century French novel, a useful way to learn. Later she translated Claude Joseph Dorat's sentimental novel *Les Malheurs de l'inconstance, ou lettres de la marquise de Circé et du comte de Mirbelle* (1772) as *The Fatal Effects of Inconstancy* (1774). Griffith's first original novel, *The Delicate Distress* (1769), is a sentimental epistolary narrative. The high-minded Lady Woodville controls her sad recognition that her husband is tempted by adultery, until, moved by awe and admiration of her restraint, he learns to love her more intensely. It firmly rejects the old myths and stories that characterize women as passionate and impulsive and men as rational, capable of controlling themselves and others.

Griffith's second original novel, *The History of Lady Barton* (1771), is tragic. This time adulterous desires tempt the wife. Lady Louisa Barton is a scrupulous woman who finds that she loves a meritorious man not her husband; unlike the Countess of Dellwyn, she does not commit adultery. She explores her feelings and considers her responsibilities in letters to her sister. The husband, Sir William, is a very ordinary gentleman, well behaved by ordinary standards, and guiltless of adultery. But he is not a man of sensibility. He refuses to let Louisa give £10 to rebuild burnt out cottages belonging to his tenants. This denies her the partnership with her husband in virtuous charity that makes Felicia's marriage in Collyer's *Felicia to Charlotte* so happy. Worse, it threatens to make it impossible for Louisa to perform the charitable actions required to maintain her own virtue. Sir William expresses illiberal sentiments about women, including the view that "female friendships are a jest." Although he allows his wife to correspond with her sister, one of his favorite maxims is "that women should be treated like state criminals, and utterly debarred the use of pen and ink . . . those who are fond of scribling, are never good for any thing else . . ."[168] In contrast, Lord Lucan, the man Lady Barton begins to love, talks of the need for Astell-like refuges for women, including ill-treated wives. When an apparently illegitimate child is abandoned on Sir William's doorstep, he wants to turn it over to the parish officials who administer poor relief; Lord Lucan, like a more handsome Squire Allworthy, volunteers to adopt the infant.

Lady Barton's situation raises the kinds of questions of love inherited from the seventeenth-century French romance, questions that were debated in the salons that gave birth to those romances and that continued to be interesting to mid-eighteenth-century women: is a woman who marries at her family's prompting, before she experiences love, guilty of dishonoring marriage? Ought a woman expect to learn to love a husband after marriage? Can a woman who begins to experience an illicit passion prevent its growth and resist acting on it?

Lady Barton considers herself in a double bind: on the one hand, she has vowed to love, honor, and obey her husband, and she considers that vow a serious obligation, but, on the other hand, although she can obey Sir William, she cannot make herself feel love or esteem for him. Were she to succeed in doing so, that would entail a coarsening of her sensibility. Griffith effectively uses the epistolary form to show the motions of Lady Barton's mind as she struggles with her dilemma. Older justifications for erotic transgression, familiar from Behn and Manley, and the violated contract arguments from plays like Thomas Southerne's *Wives Excuse* (1691) flood into her consciousness, but she challenges them:

If passion is involuntary, it cannot be criminal; 'tis consequences only that make it so . . .

Flattering sophistry! Alas! I would deceive myself, but cannot! Have I not vowed, even at the altar vowed, to love another? yet can that vow be binding, which promises what is not in our power, even at the time we make it? But grant it were, the contract sure is mutual, and when one fails, the other should be free.

Wretched Louisa! strive no more to varnish o'er thy faults – Thou wert a criminal, in the first act, who wedded without love; and all the miseries which proceed from thence, too justly are thy due . . .

I . . . will patiently submit to those corosive chains, which I myself have rivited.[169]

Lady Barton's capacity to arraign her own conscience keeps her a sympathetic character.

Lady Barton's female correspondents – her sister, Miss Fanny Cleveland, and a woman friend, Lucy – are less sentimental, indeed, rigorous. Lucy responds to Louisa's hint that she does not love Sir William by warning, "It is dangerous to sport with such sentiments; you should not suffer them to dwell even upon your own mind, much less express them to others – we ought not be too strict in analyzing the characters of those we wish to love . . ."[170] However valid such advice might be, even contemporary readers committed to virtue may have blanched at the thought that a woman's virtue might require her to so dull her awareness that it ceased even to register her husband's deficiencies. The plot of *Lady Barton* is also rigorous. Lady Barton goes no further than permitting Lord Lucan to make a declaration of his feelings – knowing she could prevent him – but her husband suspects her of adultery, she is disgraced, and dies.

SHERIDAN'S *SIDNEY BIDULPH*

The most powerful, if also the most painful, woman's novel of this period is *The Memoirs of Miss Sidney Bidulph. Extracted from her Own Journal, and now First Published* (1761) by the Anglo-Irish writer, Frances Sheridan. Sheridan most successfully adapts high-minded seventeenth-century romance into the realistic novel, producing especially well-realized characters and scenes. The heroine's journal entries, the first one dated 2 April 1703, addressed to her sister, offer detailed accounts of the operations of her mind written at moments of her struggling to make moral choices with the information (sometimes faulty) that she has at the time. As in some of Riccoboni's novels using a similar technique limiting the point of view to a single woman character, what these *Memoirs of Sidney Bidulph* lose from the variety of multiple correspondents they gain in intensity.

Sheridan was aware of contemporary theories of the novel that novelists ought to exhibit virtuous characters and that they ought to show virtue rewarded, theories exemplified in Richardson's *Sir Charles Grandison* (1753–54), one of the few novels bluestockings applauded. *Sidney Bidulph* is dedicated to Richardson in tribute to his "exemplary Goodness and distinguished Genius" and as the author of *Clarissa* and *Grandison.*[171] However, Sheridan frames her novel with a debate over John Home's tragedy *Douglas* (1756) and over whether works of art ought necessarily exhibit poetical justice. The editor of the memoirs rejects the poetical justice requirement, arguing that experience teaches virtue is not always rewarded in this world (a point few defenders of the theory would have denied) and, more importantly, that while pagans might require reward in this world to incite them to virtuous actions, Christians should not. Echoing the Christian stoicism of Carter and Talbot, the editor argues that for Christian readers an absence of poetic justice in works of art "should serve to confirm that great lesson which we are all taught indeed, but which we seldom think of reducing to practice, *viz.* to use the good things of life with that indifference, which things that are neither permanent in their own nature, nor of any estimation in the sight of God, deserve."[172] The editor declares that this narrative will be about a woman of "exemplary virtue" who was nevertheless "through the course of her whole life, persecuted by a variety of strange misfortunes" and "unhappy."[173] (A perfected philosophical stoicism was supposed to guarantee happiness no matter how great the misfortune was; even Carter expressed skepticism over that.) Given this frame, we read Sidney's journal entries written in moments of hope knowing that all her efforts may preserve her virtue but cannot ensure her good fortune or her happiness.

Like La Fayette's Princess of Clèves, Sidney Bidulph consistently prefers what she understands to be virtue to self-indulgence. She finds Orlando Faulkland the handsomest man she has ever seen and is enormously attracted to him as he begins to court her, yet struggles to control her feelings and rejects the idea of uncontrollable passion:

certain as the event of our marriage appears to me at present, I still endeavour to keep a sort of guard over my wishes, and will not, give my heart leave to center *all* its happiness in him; and therefore I cannot rank myself amongst the first-rate lovers, who have neither eyes, nor ears, nor sensations, but for one object . . . I think we women should not love at such a rate, till *duty* makes the passion a virtue . . . I think we ought always to form some laws to ourselves for the regulation of our conduct: without this, what an impertinent dream must the life be of almost every young person of our sex?[174]

She thus rejects the primacy of passion in the earlier erotic fiction of Behn and Manley. The very form of the journal encourages that "reflection" Fielding satirizes the Countess of Dellwyn for lacking. When it appears that Faulkland has had an affair with a Miss Burchell and has had a child by her, Sidney refuses to marry him.

The revelation of Faulkland's fornication leads to a family fight. Sidney's mother, who had been jilted by a man who suddenly announced he had seduced another woman and felt obligated to her, decides that Faulkland is a "monstrous libertine."[175] Moreover, she takes the position that Sidney ought not to marry Faulkland because both morality and female solidarity require her to refuse him. Mrs. Bidulph tells Faulkland that he has an obligation to marry Miss Burchell and that she will never "purchase [her daughter's] worldly prosperity at the expense of the shame and sorrow of another woman . . ."[176] On the other hand, Sidney's brother, Sir George, dismisses Faulkland's fornication as trifling, the sort of thing any man might have done. He tells his mother and sister that if they are going to insist on male chastity, Sidney will never find a husband. Sidney allows herself to be influenced by her mother's strong feelings.

How to conduct oneself when confronted by male unchastity was one of the most frequent questions debated in the literature of this period, fictional and nonfictional – and probably also by women themselves. For unmarried women, the question was sometimes framed as to whether women had an obligation to provide disincentives to male unchastity by refusing to accept "male libertines" in marriage. This, of course, is a central question in *Clarissa*. The hero in Riccoboni's *Juliet Catesby* turns out to have abandoned the heroine out of a sense of obligation to a humble woman he seduced in a drunken episode; after he marries this woman and she dies, Juliet takes him back. Griffith's most successful comedy, *The School for Rakes* (1769), is an adaptation of Beaumarchais's first play, *Eugénie* (1767), in which the male protagonist tricks the heroine into an invalid marriage. When he repents his treachery, the question becomes whether the heroine ought to forgive him and marry him. Changing his mind on the question of whether reformed rakes make acceptable husbands, the heroine's father declares: "the man who sincerely repents of error, is farther remov'd from vice, than one who has never been guilty."[177] Sentimental fiction and sentimental drama liked these plots of repentance and reform for men.

The hard-core bluestockings were apt to be more severe and became interested in the possibilities of holding men to standards of good conduct and chastity as strict as those said to be appropriate to women. According to her nephew and biographer, Carter was supposed to have rejected an otherwise unexceptionable suitor to whom she was attached because he "published some verses, which, though not absolutely indecent, yet seemed to shew too light and licentious a turn of mind: and of these he was afterwards sincerely sorry."[178] Sylvia Myers believed that this gentleman was the Reverend John Dalton, a pleasant, literary man, who, according to Horace Walpole, had an affair with Lady Luxborough that lead to Lady Luxborough's separation from her husband and to the birth of an illegitimate daughter in 1736, and that it was his conduct not his verses that made Carter refuse him.[179] However impracticable a widespread rejection of unchaste men as husbands was in the eighteenth century – given the acceptance of the sexual double standard and male entitlements and the general economic dependence of women on men – the bluestocking stand on this matter was a double assertion of female power: first, in the *Lysistrata*-like denial to men of access to the bodies of good and desired women, and, second, as a display of women's power over their own desires.

Again, like the Princess of Clèves, Sidney allows herself also to be persuaded by her mother that it is wise to marry another man, Mr. Arnold, who appears virtuous and kind and who wants to marry her. Sidney's marriage to Mr. Arnold, Mrs. Bidulph urges, will cause Faulkland to despair of ever having her and help precipitate his doing Miss Burchell the justice of marrying her. Sidney's marriage thus becomes simultaneously an act of obedience to a beloved parent and a generous gesture toward an unfortunate woman; it has nothing to do with the gratification of her own desires. Early in the marriage it appears that her devotion to what she understands to be a right rule of conduct will be rewarded. She feels gratitude to her husband for his "assiduity and tenderness" and declares: ". . . I am convinced it is not necessary to be passionately in love with the man we marry, to make us happy. Constancy, good sense, and a sweet temper, must form a basis for a durable felicity."[180] This was certainly the dominant view of moralists in the early eighteenth century (and Sidney's story is supposed to begin in the first decade of the century).

Yet, as is usually the case in this sort of woman's novel, indeed, as is the case in *The Princess of Clèves* and *The History of Lady Barton*, a woman who marries without being "in love" with her husband is in an unstable marriage. After several good years and the birth of two children to the Arnolds, Sidney discovers that her husband has been having an affair with their neighbor in the country, Mrs. Gerrarde, and that Mrs. Gerrarde has also been poisoning Mr. Arnold's mind with suspicions that Sidney still loves Faulkland.

We thus enter into what contemporaries found a peculiarly "interesting" situation, that of a married woman who discovers that her husband is committing adultery, a situation frequent not only in the plots of plays and novels, but also in the advice literature. Haywood's *The Wife*, considered in the previous chapter, offers the standard advice to a wife who discovered her husband's adultery: avoid reproaching him, suffer in silence, redouble efforts to be attractive, hope that in time he will see the folly of his ways. While this attitude may seem masochistic to us, it reflects the contemporary view that masculine lapses from chastity are virtually inevitable and that wives are nevertheless required to "love, honor, and obey" their husbands according to the religious vows they took in the marriage service.

Sidney responds to her husband's adultery with Christian stoicism that conforms to this standard of proper wifely conduct; simultaneously, she expresses the sentimental hope that the spectacle of her suffering will have the power to transform his conduct and his heart. She resolves: "let me not aggravate my own griefs, nor to a vicious world justify my husband's conduct, by bringing any reproach upon my own. The silent sufferings of the injured, must, to a mind not ungenerous, be a sharper rebuke than it is in the power of language to inflict."[181] However exquisite the wife's pain, and Sidney's is intense, she derives consolation and self-respect from a sense that she is acting well, indeed, exhibiting heroic patience. And, since an accidental meeting with Faulkland provides her husband with an excuse to banish her, in disgrace, from their house, Sidney suffers the additional humiliation of public disgrace to try her patience and to challenge her ability to maintain her self-respect.

Sheridan's variation on the plot of the wife who patiently endures her husband's adultery takes a plot that expresses a cultural sense of the greater value of men and turns it into an expression of the superiority of women. In Sheridan, men seem weak, women strong; men seem incapable of impulse control or reflection, women able to exert heroic self-control. Mr. Arnold is eventually reduced to abjection. Men are in need of forgiveness; women, Christlike, have the power to redeem. Advice books and sermons on the patient wife admit that no matter how well a wife in such circumstances behaves, her husband may not repent and society may not offer much consolation; her consolations are in the internal sense of doing right and the hope of heavenly reward. In contrast, in the sentimental versions of the story, as in Sidney's, the "silent sufferings" of the wife, often visible on her body, have a transformative power and a power to compel admiration.

Mr. Arnold's mistress, Mrs. Gerrarde, a type of the passionate woman associated with Behn and Manley, speaks of herself as a great soul. However, she is exposed as the mere daughter of a country innkeeper, brought up in a Dublin convent, more motivated by avarice than lust. She is finally a comic figure, posturing and affecting tenderness. Faulkland punishes her in the way of Restoration comedy by a trick marriage to a French servant. Mr. Arnold, now £7,000 in debt, has impoverished himself by catering to her pleasures, saving one of her brothers from hanging for forgery, and credulously supplying the needs of other supposed relatives, at least one of whom has instead been a lover. Reconciliation between the Arnolds is facilitated by Lord and Lady V—, who find Mr. Arnold repentant and abashed, unwilling to involve his wife in his "beggary." He recognizes Sidney as a unique heroine: "I know I have wronged her so, that were she any other than the woman she is, I could never hope for forgiveness . . ."[182]

Sidney's silent tears and her husband's sobs mark the reconciliation, presented as a more authentic marriage. Here, as is characteristic of the fiction of sensibility, tears substitute for articulated sentiments and are signs of valued capacity for feeling. Weeping like Sidney's is offered as a sign of overflowing and refined feeling. Her tears come unbidden, so her allegiance to stoic silence can be overridden by her body's revelation of capacity for intense feeling. Here the tears do not proceed from grief, but from a kind of pleasure that the novelist refuses to name or define. In the reconciliation scene between the husband and the wife, words are, as much as possible, banished. Abjuring all desire to require apology or spoken contrition, Sidney begs Lady V— to tell her husband "not to mention any thing that was past, but let our meeting be, as if the separation had been only occasioned by a long journey."[183] Sheridan offers a wordless tableau of sensibility in which Arnold falls into his wife's extended arms, sobbing, and both shed plentiful tears. Now husband and wife experience authentic, if problematic, feeling, and both seem truly to love. Mrs. Bidulph, as a kind of surrogate for Sidney, receives Arnold's kneeling repentance; she joins the couple's hands in a new marriage, which she blesses. She pointedly distinguishes between an unmarried woman's obligation not to forgive male unchastity and a wife's duty to forgive her husband. Yet Sheridan offers a more worldly way of describing the reconciliation. Brother George says ironically, "no doubt . . . we all [have cause to rejoice] that your husband has been graciously pleased, after beggaring you and your children, turning you out of doors, and branding you with infamy, to receive you at last into his favor."[184]

Yet, as the reader has known from the beginning, Sidney's periods of happiness will be brief. In the third volume, after Mr. Arnold's death, although Faulkland is eager to marry Sidney, she prevails upon him to do what she supposes is the honorable thing: marry Miss Burchell and give his child a father. Married, Faulkland discovers his wife was never an innocent. When he finds her *in flagrante*, her lover shoots at Faulkland, who kills him in self-defense, and, apparently, kills his wife. Partly to prevent Faulkland's killing himself from despair, and partly because her male relatives recommend it, Sidney at last marries Faulkland. Almost immediately, they discover that his wife lives and that their marriage is therefore bigamous. Sidney separates from Faulkland, who dies.

Given that Sidney's apparent devotion to virtue produces such florid disasters and harrowing suffering, some readers have understandably wondered whether Sheridan could have wished to recommend so self-sacrificial a virtue. Both Lady Bidulph's initial harsh judgment of Faulkland and Sidney's own favorable judgment of Miss Burchell prove mistaken and both lead to unfortunate marriages. The impotence of women to judge – and the disabling effects of protecting female delicacy – are underlined by a very late revelation from Sir George that he has known all along that Miss Burchell was a girl of bad character. Patricia Spacks finds that while "the institutionalized self-suppression of the female" has become "an article of faith for the virtuous woman," several of the women in the novel who are more self-willed than Sidney, including Mrs. Gerrarde, "seem more likely to get what they want." In her reading, the "reiterative disaster" of the plot "established outrage at the female situation of helplessness" and "lends bite to Sheridan's version of sentimentalism."[185]

SCOTT'S *MILLENIUM HALL*

Scott's *A Description of Millenium Hall* (1762) links the bluestocking concerns of the writers considered in the earlier parts of this chapter with those of the domestic novel of sensibility. The sentimental novels of Griffith and Sheridan offer isolated heroines whose sufferings in bad marriages are private. *Millenium Hall* (1762) imagines good gentry women, most of whom are refugees from bad marriages, but these women reject marriage to establish a utopian female community where women pursue learning and the arts and where women work to provide models for the transformation of their society.

The frame narrative, ostensibly by "A Gentleman on his travels," describes the present operation of the utopian community. Long interpolated accounts by a woman member of the community narrate the previous "histories" of the individual gentlewomen before they made their decisions to enter the community. The women pool their money to live on an estate in the country and establish rules for their own society. All the ladies share equally in the society's benefits, take turns running the household, and have equal access to the society's books, musical instruments, and materials for artistic creation. All participate in the society's elaborate charitable work in the community. It seems very likely that Scott knew of Astell's *Serious Proposal to the Ladies* for a similar community of women dedicated to Christian principles.[186]

As in Astell's community, in Scott's women seek to escape from male predation and from what they consider the intellectual, cultural, and spiritual vacuity of the fashionable social world. Astell suggests a curriculum that aims at a higher level of philosophical thought, whereas Scott's women, in keeping with the greater interest in the aesthetic in this period, have more interest in cultivating the arts. In the different discursive space of a fiction, and writing later when "political economy" was attracting interest, Scott also offers a more elaborate account of what the women's charitable work entails.

Scott aims to give the lie to earlier comic representations of female communities, which assume that, since women require male supervision, such communities are unstable and ultimately impossible, that women without men will inevitably be turbulent and jealous rivals of one another. The earlier female utopian communities in John Fletcher's *The Sea Voyage* (1622), Edward Howard's *Six Days Adventure* (1671), and Thomas D'Urfey's *Commonwealth of Women* (1686), for instance, dissolve as the women succumb to desires for men. Scott, in contrast, represents a stable, self-supporting female community, one that even at the end of her narrative has the capacity to provide happiness for its women inhabitants and to influence for the good the behavior of the gentlemen who observe it. Moreover, Scott's heroines are devoid of those characteristics misogyny found natural to women, especially vanity, jealousy of other women as rivals, and turbulent passion. Although the gentlewomen do find some of the poor women they take into their wider community given to quarrelsomeness, they consider this a defect of their socialization rather than of their natures. They resocialize them so that they too can enter into supportive rather than rivalrous relationships with other women.

The interpolated histories paint a picture of the fashionable world as so profoundly unsatisfactory that good women are virtually required to withdraw from it. Biological families are indifferent or malicious rather than protective or educative for their female members. An apparently generous man raises a young orphan only as a secret scheme to make her his eventual mistress. Scott's sharp distaste for "the world" and her enthusiasm for religious piety and active charity – in the novel and in her own practice – link her with the Evangelicals within the Church of England, including those like Mary Bosanquet. Some of these women later became Methodists.

The one member of the Millenium Hall society who does not begin as a paragon, Lady Mary Jones, spends some years in the household of a character resembling Elizabeth Montagu. Called, not flatteringly, Lady Brumpton, this highly educated woman displays her elegant taste in the furnishings of her house. She aims at making this house "a little academy," inviting "all living genius's . . . from the ragged philosopher to the rhiming peer."[187] On the one hand, Scott credits Lady Brumpton with intelligence and generosity and recognizes that people who were in fact "most desirous of being in her parties" ridicule her as a "learned lady."[188] On the other hand, she indicts Lady Brumpton for worldliness and vanity, commenting: "The adulation which she received with too much visible complacency, inspired her with such an opinion of herself, as led her to despise those of less shining qualities . . . and called her real superiority into question."[189] Lady Brumpton is made to succumb to a nervous fever, to lose all her ostensible friends when she can no longer amuse, and, immediately before her death, to repent her vanity. She confesses that what she had thought "dullness" was in truth "the religious life" and that what she thought "meanness of spirit or affectation" was "the humility and calmness of a true Christian disposition."[190] It speaks well of the real Elizabeth Montagu's generosity that she persevered in her own kindnesses toward her poorer sister after the publication of this portrait.

As in seventeenth-century French romance, in these interpolated histories the virtuous ladies struggle with puzzling dilemmas about love which have no obvious solutions. We know that the ladies are virtuous, but suspense comes from the difficulty of knowing what a virtuous person would do in the problematic circumstances that the narrative poses. Such a dilemma confronts Louisa Melvyn when a bad stepmother plots to discredit her with her father. The stepmother produces an old man, Mr. Morgan, a man for whom Louisa can feel nothing but disgust, as a proper husband for her. At the same time, the stepmother accuses her of having an affair with a young farmer. All of Louisa's efforts to deny this slander to her father fail. She is thus presented with a choice between marrying

Mr. Morgan and being "exposed to shame, in being publicly disclaimed by her parents" as an immoral girl.[191] Both choices entail what she recognizes as positive moral evils: if she marries Mr. Morgan, she understands it to be "the highest injustice to marry a man whom she could not love, as well as a very criminal mockery of the most solemn vows."[192]

By a logic that will be far from obvious to modern readers, Louisa considers the other alternative even more immoral. Focusing not on the practical difficulties of supporting herself should she be turned away by her parents or on the embarrassment she would experience, Louisa decides that she has a duty to other people not to allow herself to be falsely and publicly branded unchaste. Like Scott herself, she reasons that "Example is the means given universally to all whereby to benefit society."[193] Louisa fears contaminating society should she appear to add herself to the already too large number of vicious persons in the world. She reasons: "Every vicious person abates the horror which [vice] would naturally excite in a virtuous mind. There is nothing so odious, to which custom will not in some degree reconcile us . . ."[194] That a young woman, indeed, any non-aristocratic woman, should imagine her own behavior of such high public consequence is remarkable. Yet this is the feminist lesson Scott teaches. Louisa thus elects to become Mrs. Morgan and suffers the exquisite torment of fulfilling her obligation to honor and obey her husband without complaint. She finds her virtues "refined," and takes comfort from the knowledge that God, "whom she most wished to please, would graciously accept her endeavours . . ."[195] After six years of this marriage, Mr. Morgan awakes to his wife's merits. The novelist promptly kills him off, leaving Mrs. Morgan with their estate, which becomes Millenium Hall, as well as her jointure and an extra £2,000.

Within the utopia of Millenium Hall, the ladies benefit their community by their example and by providing others with the means of production so that they too are relieved from the horrors of dependency and grinding poverty. The ladies follow the injunctions of the Christian gospel "to feed the hungry, cloath the naked, to relieve the prisoner, and to take care of the sick."[196] Abjuring the fashionable display of an Elizabeth Montagu, they each take only £25 a year for clothes and personal expenses, enough to provide dresses that are "plain and neat," though not uniforms. They thus avoid the conspicuous consumption by which the rich, Scott worried, increasingly "infect the whole community."[197] With money saved from such personal expenditure, the ladies educate orphaned gentlewomen, provide schools for poor children, supply nurses and medicine for the sick, and assist newly married couples with home furnishings and "some sort of stock, which by industry would prove very conducive towards their living in a comfortable degree of plenty."[198] Among their other charitable enterprises is a carpet "manufacture" employing several hundred people, most of whom could not otherwise find work.[199] At a time when new national subscription charities, like the famous Magdalen Hospital for the reformation of prostitutes, were directed by men, and political economists were offering new plans for managing the poor, Scott insists on women's capacity to conceptualize and to manage charities, indeed, that women "who are themselves models of industry and cleanliness . . . are the best guardians and governors of the poor."[200]

The carefully calculated economy of this utopia entails spreading benefits by example and by the related practice of making as many expenses as possible simultaneously "donation[s]." Thus, when they purchase commodities, they "endeavour so to apply all they spend, as to make almost every shilling contribute towards the support of some person in real necessity. . ."[201] As the narrator points out, this practice can be imitated by anyone, even a poor person, so that even "the poorest may thus turn their necessary expenses into virtuous actions."[202]

Scott was caught in conundrums posed by her allegiance to competing moral imperatives. On the one hand, she was committed to the principle that talented and virtuous women have a duty to offer their talents and the spectacle of their virtue as a model that others might emulate. Thus, she lived a notably virtuous life and published books like her history of Gustavus, the Protestant hero, *Millenium Hall*, and her later novel, *The History of Sir George Ellison* (1766), which was filled with everything from complaints about candidates for Parliament bribing electors with alcohol to ideas about ameliorating the conditions of Africans enslaved in the West Indies. On the other hand, Scott disdained ambition, public display, and wealth, insisting that these bespeak a lack of proper Christian humility. She satirized her sister Montagu's public accomplishments. Even more fiercely than Fielding, Scott in part identified with the poor and humble and scorned the privileged as morally blind. Indeed, one critic, Betty Rizzo, disagrees with the majority critical view that Scott was politically and socially conservative, arguing that Scott offered "sly hints" of a radical agenda and that her positions only appear to be meliorist because she carefully calculated "those reforms she could safely advocate (and still hope to be influential) and those she could not."[203] Yet Scott's consistent idea that people without privilege – whether poor English people or enslaved Africans in the West Indies – can be improved by education and opportunity coexists with her equally consistent idea that good women and men of genteel birth are the only appropriate governors of women and men of ungenteel birth and her apparent conviction that such subordination will maximize the happiness of the ungenteely born. Scott's model reform schemes, moreover, depend on significant amounts of inherited wealth for their enactment. However, the extremities of misery that characters in her sentimental fiction endure, and from which they need to be rescued, reflect the widening gap between the typical conditions of people's lives and bluestocking aspirations. The miseries of Scott's characters are also consistent with sentimentalism's reaching for more and more intense affect, a subject we will explore in the next chapter.

CONCLUSION

Between 1756 and 1776 women writers continued to claim and to develop the special kind of authority concerning the education and socialization of children and women that the family paradigm discussed in chapter five had conceded to them. Chapone's *Letters on the Improvement of the Mind*, as we have seen, invoked the persona of the concerned aunt to her teenage niece to voice her opinions on the proper ways of educating and socializing young women. Hannah More first began to establish her literary reputation with the circulation of her manuscript pastoral play written for school girls, *The Search After Happiness*, written when she was sixteen, published in 1773 and many times thereafter.

In contrast to the bluestockings Chapone and More, most women writers of advice literature in this period stressed the importance of domesticity for women and developed more elaborate, more marked notions of gendered character. In a vein more plaintive and pathetic than Chapone's, Lady Sarah Pennington produced another of the most popular conduct books of the period in *An Unfortunate Mother's Advice to her Absent Daughters; in a Letter to Miss Pennington* (1761). Lady Pennington turned to print after she was separated from her husband and lost custody of and contact with her children. She combined a brief defense of her character against her husband's allegations with more lengthy advice to her daughters, much of it concerned to instruct them on how to avoid the misery that befell her. She used her duty as a mother to trump the taboos against wives speaking ill of their husbands or violating the privacy of the family. While she was emphatic about the importance of religious education and observation, of good French, and some history for young ladies, she said bleakly that a sensible woman would realize "that all the Learning her utmost Application can make her Mistress of will be, from the Difference of Education, in many points inferior to that of a School Boy"; this will ensure her humility.[204] Household economy, which she claimed requires little study to master, "is the only proper temporal Business" Providence assigns to women.[205]

As magazines became more numerous, Lennox became the proprietress of *The Ladies Museum: Consisting of a Course of Female Education and Variety of other Particulars for the Information and Amusement of Ladies* (1760–61). This offered fiction, some of it Lennox's original fiction, some her translations, but also included essays and translations of essays on the education of women, including Fénelon's ever popular *Education des filles* (1687). *The Ladies Museum* eschewed the more strenuous kinds of philosophical, philological or historical study advocated and practiced by Astell, Carter, or even Chapone. Its presiding persona, the Trifler, claimed her chief design was to amuse and published repeated injunctions to women to avoid pedantry. The Trifler fretted that exposure to "the depths of literature" would be tiresome for women, and declared her "wish to render the ladies though learned not pedantic, conversable rather than scientific."[206] Most of the historical narratives in the magazine, many of them translated from French, featured women: the Roman Vestal Virgins; Joan of Arc; and the Duchess of Beaufort, mistress of Henri IV, the late sixteenth-, early seventeenth-century King of France. As Katherine Shevelow has argued, *The Lady's Museum* and similar magazines contributed to the construction of the new model of domestic and sentimental femininity.[207]

Like many of their male contemporaries, women dramatists and novelists wrote sentimental drama and sentimental fiction. Here the relation between English and French literary culture was especially close. Richardson inspired Diderot, Diderot in turn theorized the sentimental and inspired Beaumarchais, Rousseau, and English sentimental writers. Thus, for example, we find Griffith making plays by translating Diderot and adapting Beaumarchais and several of Griffith's novels being quickly translated into French and published in France. Or Brooke beginning her career as a novelist with a translation of Riccoboni. Or Sheridan's *Sidney Bidulph* being translated into French by no less a personage than the Abbé Prévost.

Women's sentimental drama and fiction typically offered portraits of extravagantly virtuous women who displayed kinds of self-sacrifice, even abjection, that now make us uncomfortable. Thus Lady Medway in Sheridan's *Disappointment* forbears to reproach her husband for his adultery or gambling and welcomes his illegitimate daughter into the family. More remarkably, Sheridan's Sidney Bidulph ignores her love for Faulkland to marry Arnold because she believes it will make her mother happy and because she is convinced her marriage to another man will make Faulkland more likely to marry the young woman he has seduced. Sentimental women writers offered their extravagantly virtuous heroines in part to counter traditional misogynistic representations of women – although these more traditional representations lingered in their portraits of secondary "bad women" characters like the deceitful Miss Burchell in *Sidney Bidulph*.

When they chose the epistolary form, as Griffith did in all her novels, or the journal form, as Sheridan did in *Sidney Bidulph*, the novelists often used the virtuous heroine's first-person narrative to dramatize not only a woman's capacity for suffering, but also her capacity for careful moral reflection. As in seventeenth-century romance, much of the interest of these narratives derived from the characters' extended debates over problematic moral questions. Among the most recurrent of these questions – one common to *Lady Barton* and *Sidney Bidulph* – was the question of whether a woman who married at her family's urging, but without experiencing love for the man she married, was guilty of dishonoring the sacrament of marriage. That these debates could arrive at casuistical levels of complexity is evident in Louisa's surprising arguments in Scott's *Millenium Hall* that she is right to marry Mr. Morgan, who disgusts her, rather than to allow her stepmother to blacken her character by false public accusations of fornication.

Contemporaries generally found sentimental spectacles of suffering both moving and pleasurable and most literary intellectuals supposed that such spectacles had the power to lead audiences to virtue. The bluestockings, however, were often skeptical about sentimentalism's conviction that feeling rather than reason was the best guide to life and suspicious that sentimentalism too often entailed moral incoherence. They were apt also to be skeptical about sentimentalism's representation of the power of a good woman to transform male character, although inclined to agree, in Scott's phrase, that good women made "the best guardians and governors of the poor." Perhaps most modern readers are likely to find the extreme examples of enlightenment optimism about the ease of moral reformation unconvincing, even risible. For modern readers, it is likely to be the darker women's novels which raise doubts about the power of virtue in the world, present bleaker pictures of women's experience in marriage, and analyze the capacity of patriarchal domination to warp character that are especially compelling. These would include *Sidney Bidulph* and *Lady Barton*, as well as Fielding's predominantly unsentimental *The Countess of Dellwyn*. Yet most women's novels of this period, sentimentally optimistic and bleak alike, suggest that women are distressed by nervous anxiety over how to behave and confined to a domestic private life strangely outside of history. Only rarely does women's fiction of this period look to the wider world and remind us that the eighteenth-century novel generally still drew upon the enlightenment's interest in travel literature, as Brooke's *History of Emily Montague* does.

Happily, many of the best women's letters that survive from this period, including those of Sarah Osborn, Frances Boscawen, Lady Mary Wortley Montagu, Elizabeth Montagu, and Abigail Adams, remind us of the artificiality of representations of women in the sentimental literary modes and make it clear that some women were capable of engaging with the world in ways very remote from abjection. Although the Seven Years War was fought abroad rather than at home, as the Civil War had been, now women could be aware of military news – as well as news of domestic politics – not only from their relatives and friends, but also from more extensive reporting in newspapers and magazines. Many women's letters show how engaged they were with public events.

For the bluestockings, the familiar letter was at once a discursive space where they permitted themselves more candor than they thought suitable to more public forums and a medium that they used to create a mutually reinforcing female community. Elizabeth Montagu's letters reveal the energy and skill she applied to build her salon and the rhetorical tact with which she could alternately encourage the diffident Carter or write more playfully to Dr. Messenger Monsey. In this period of fairly sharp political polarization, Montagu and other salon hostesses took advantage of the fact that women, lacking access to political office, were less politically polarized than men and, hence, in a position to view politics with some detachment and to make their salons places where public men could mingle away from the pressures of party. They prided themselves on accomplishing one of the goals earlier proposed by Drake in *An Essay of the Female Sex*, namely, using female conversation and the model of female socialization to increase male politeness and diminish male violence. At the same time, Montagu's salon was itself a quasi-public space that she used to publicize the writers, especially the women writers like Carter and Chapone, who she thought deserved fame.

Women's ambition to shine beyond the domestic sphere was even more evident in works of literary criticism and history like Montagu's *Essay on*

the Writings and Genius of Shakespear and Macaulay's *History of England.*
Montagu cast herself as a patriotic champion of British culture in its
rivalry with French culture, demonstrated the impact of historicist thinking on literary criticism, and made a successful bid for aesthetic authority.
Her example helped prepare the way for other women writers of literary
criticism and literary history, including, in the generation immediately
following, Mary Wollstonecraft, Elizabeth Inchbald, Clara Reeve, Anna
Seward, and Ann Thicknesse, and, in the nineteenth century, Charlotte
Yonge, George Eliot, and Harriet Martineau. Still more ambitiously,
indeed, so ambitiously, that she had no direct women imitators in the
eighteenth century or even the nineteenth century, Macaulay wrote a
multi-volume national history of England that tied her narrative of
seventeenth-century events to enduring issues of constitutionality and
freedom. The many nineteenth-century women writers of history typically elected explicitly feminine topics, as Agnes and Elizabeth Strickland
did in their *Lives of the Queens of England.* The idea that decent women
should not concern themselves with matters beyond the state of their own
souls and the proper functioning of their families and households utterly
failed to impress either Abigail Adams or Catharine Macaulay. While
Macaulay's radical politics were the reverse of Astell's Tory commitments,
Macaulay in a way extended the reach of Astell's injunction that "the
whole World is a single Ladys Family"; for Macaulay, willing publicly to
condemn government repression of free speech in England or troops
firing on civilians in the Boston Massacre, there was nothing, even
marriage, which put public matters beyond the purview of a lady.

Translation, generally a more modest enterprise than literary criticism
or history, continued to be an important form of women's writing.
Indeed, as we noted in considering Lennox's translation of the *Memoirs
for the History of Madame de Maintenon*, as the constraints of the kind of
domestic femininity thought suitable to the novel grew more severe,
translation of more worldly texts may have seemed an increasingly welcome relief from those constraints, as well as a continuingly useful source
of income. Critics' vigilance as to whether a novel was suitable for quite
young ladies – novels often being judged as adolescent literature – did not
extend to translations of books everyone understood were for adults.
Although most women's translations continued to be from French, the
rarer women's translations from classical languages – notably Fielding's
Xenophon's *Memoirs of Socrates* and Carter's *All the Works of Epictetus* –
were understood to make especially strong statements of women's

capacity to go beyond the boundary markers being put in place to fix the supposedly proper lines of women's literary and intellectual ambition.

Montagu and the other bluestockings were self-conscious about having a gendered group identity and a duty to represent its interests. This prompted not only Montagu's active patronage of women writers like Carter and Scott, but reciprocal tributes to Montagu and other bluestockings from women writers who had less personal access to money and social power. Thus, More in the fifth edition of *Search after Happiness* (1774), adds a dialogue epilogue in which one lady's deprecation of learned ladies as lacking in virtue is responded to by another lady's declaring that, although that might have been the case "When SAPPHO's and CORINNA's tun'd their lays," now, all can see that "female *virtue* joins with female *sense*":

> When moral *Carter* breathes the strain divine,
> And AIKIN's life flows faultless as her line;
> When all-accomplish'd MONTAGUE can spread
> Fresh gather'd laurels round her SHAKESPEARE's head.[208]

We observed a briefer but similar showing of mutual support among women writers in the 1690s and in 1700 at the time of Manley's *Nine Muses*. However, as we have seen, the amount of women's writing produced was much smaller in the late seventeenth century than it was in this later period. Moreover, in the second half of the eighteenth century a significant canon of women writers was beginning to be available, allowing new women writers to recognize the achievements of their predecessors as well as of their contemporaries. For example, in 1757 interested readers could find works of Cavendish, Astell, Behn, Centlivre, Leapor, Finch, and Rowe advertised in the catalogue of William Bathos's London circulating library, one of the earliest such libraries, available for borrowing at two or three shillings a volume.[209] The 1690s also lacked other mechanisms for publicizing the accomplishments of writers that had developed by the second half of the eighteenth century. These included biographical compilations like the *Biographium Femineum* (1766) and magazines that offered reviews, literary anecdotes, engravings of authors, and reprinted literary works or excerpts from literary works. The earlier period also lacked a female patron as powerful as Montagu.

CHAPTER 7

Romance and comedy, 1777–1789

INTRODUCTION

From the point of view of literary history, the American Revolution, begun with the Declaration of Independence in 1776 and ended by the American defeat of General Charles Cornwallis at Yorktown in 1781, meant that women writers in the former North American colonies from henceforth would be part of another national literature. The American women writers of the early Republic period, including Mercy Otis Warren, historian of the American Revolution and disciple and friend of Macaulay, therefore, play no role in British literary history. It is worth noting, however, that Judith Sargent Murray, a Bostonian who can reasonably be called the first American feminist, in 1779 wrote an essay "On the Equality of the Sexes." She explicitly praised Masham and Astell for the accuracy of their reasoning. She also included Philips, Chudleigh, Finch, Lady Mary Wortley Montagu, and Macaulay in her later account of writers who demonstrated the capacities of women.[1]

Like Englishmen, Englishwomen writers were divided in their attitudes toward the war with America. Macaulay, who supported all the revolutions that occurred during her lifetime, continued to support the Americans. The last three volumes of her *History* (VI and VII in 1781 and VIII in 1783) continue to suggest the relevance of seventeenth-century English history to the later eighteenth century. The final volume urged Parliament to extend the limited democracy of the Glorious Revolution of 1688 by electoral reforms, including the extension of the franchise. Carter, demonstrating that her own extensive reading of Athenian and Roman history yielded insight, wrote to Elizabeth Montagu in July 1777: "I am no American, but every reader of history must be convinced, that colonies are always, after a certain time, destructive to the mother country, whenever there is a contest; and that when they wish for independence, the truest policy is at once to give up the point."[2] Even for those who supported it, the war with America exacerbated concerns that England had become a dangerously luxurious imperial state and concomitant anxieties that women's pursuit of frivolity and luxury constituted a special danger.

Carter's letters, like the letters of other women of this period, also express concern over the fates of Englishmen at war, mourn the deaths of those who die in combat, and grieve for their widows and orphans. Beginning her literary career, Anna Seward became famous for her *Monody on Major André* (1781), an elegy on a friend who was a British spy hanged by the Americans. Harriet Guest reads this poem as constructing an important form of patriotism identified with ideas of "loss and bereavement, and best expressed in elegiac consolation."[3] Guest sees Seward and some other women writers inventing models of a more private, sentimental patriotism based in familial affection that contest models of public patriotism as exclusively male.

As it often is in times of national crisis, the theatre was simultaneously a target of attack for those concerned about frivolity and dangerous luxury and a preferred venue for rousing calls to patriotism. Hannah Cowley's comedy, *Which is the Man?* (1782), shows Englishwomen capable of an older, more republican patriotism, albeit in the service of empire. The heroine, Lady Bell Bloomer, is an attractive, intelligent young widow courted by Lord Sparkle, a fashionable wit, gambler, and manipulator of local elections by bribes. Lady Bell spurns this epitome of luxury for a poor soldier, Captain Beauchamp ("beautiful battlefield"). Within days of leaving for America, Beauchamp appears on stage dressed in his regimentals. In the fifth act, a Welsh booby, Bobby Pendragon, asks for a commission. The virtuous Fitzherbert, a benevolent guardian character, denies his request and reproves him in a speech designed to elicit a loud patriotic clap from the audience: ". . . the requisites of a soldier are not those of pertness and assurance. Intrepid spirit, nice honor, generosity, and understanding, all unite to form him – It is these which will make the British soldier once again the first character in Europe – It is such soldiers who must make England once again invincible, and her glittering arms triumphant in every quarter of the globe."[4]

The loss of the American colonies intensified concern over the remaining parts of the empire, including the West Indies and India. Of the West Indian islands lost to the French and the Spanish during the War of American Independence, the British managed in the 1783 Treaty of Versailles to retrieve the Bahamas, Grenada, St. Kitts, St. Vincent, and Montserrat, losing only Tobago to the French. Doubts about the legitimacy of the slave trade, apparently crucial to the manufacture of sugar in the West Indies, led to the formation in 1787 of an Abolition Committee and to serious parliamentary investigations into the atrocities of the trade. For many British writers, the West Indies continued to be merely a convenient off-stage source of wealth that could resolve plot dilemmas – as it had been for Frances Sheridan in *Sidney Bidulph* – but others engaged in the abolitionist campaign. Aikin Barbauld's *Hymns in Prose for Children* (1781) aimed to inculcate pity for an enslaved African mother. Carter, Sarah Trimmer, and Mary Scott all subscribed to the Abolition Society. This Society, recognizing More as the most authoritative contemporary serious woman writer, invited her to contribute a poem that might help to sway public opinion toward abolition, which she gladly did in *Slavery. A Poem* (1788).

Debates over the parliamentary regulation of the East India Company and concern over political power in England being acquired by men enriched by service in India also absorbed the attention of a public increasingly familiar with the geography and politics of India. Many thought the parliamentary debates over Fox's India Bill in 1783 outdid the theatre in interest and eloquence. Edmund Burke, as a Member of Parliament and opponent of the Company, painted with special plangency the sufferings of the Indian people at the hands of what he characterized as a cruel and rapacious Company. Burke in 1788 also began the parliamentary impeachment of Warren Hastings, the first British Governor General of India, for extortion and murder in India. In one of the best diaries of the eighteenth century, Frances Burney describes her experience of several days of this trial. She was acquainted with both Hastings and Burke and, although she thought Hastings innocent, she paid tribute to Burke's eloquence:

When he narrated, he was easy, flowing, and natural; when he declaimed, energetic, warm and brilliant. The sentiments he interspersed were as nobly conceived as they were highly colored; his satire had a poignancy of wit that made it as entertaining as it was penetrating . . . and the wild and sudden flights of his fancy, bursting forth from his creative imagination in language fluent, forcible, and varied, had a charm for my ear and my attention wholly new and perfectly irresistible.[5]

Griffith's *The Times* (1779) is one of many plays to consider the returning English "nabobs," Englishmen returned from India with great wealth, and the impact of their wealth on English society. Cleverly, Elizabeth Inchbald began her long and very successful career as a playwright by capitalizing on the public's fascination with India in a farce, *The Mogul Tale, or the Descent of the Balloon* (1784), imagining what might happen if three very ordinary English people were suddenly to arrive in the seraglio of the Grand Mogul.

Despite the stress of major war and the sharpness of disputes over India, English culture between 1777 and 1789 is obsessed with entertainment, conspicuous consumption, and luxury. In addition to the usual dramatic performances at Covent Garden and Drury Lane, audiences also relished performances of Italian opera at the King's Theatre, ballad opera at Sadler's Wells, and concerts at Ranelagh and Vauxhall Gardens. These pleasure gardens offered landscaped walks, refreshments, and entertainments.

Between 1773 and 1778 Frances Brooke, with Mary Ann and Richard Yates, managed the King's Theatre, where the Italian operas were produced. Burney, daughter of a musician and perhaps the best woman novelist of the century, writes in her diary of the famous Italian singers who call at her father's London house. Her novels include scenes that take place in the pleasure gardens, at the theatres, and at the opera. The luxuries that fascinated contemporaries included not only the diamonds and exotic fabrics the nabobs helped introduce, but exotic servants and slaves from India, the West Indies, and Africa.

The social origins of the most important women writers of 1777–1789 were generally lower than those of the earlier bluestockings; several of them had fathers from the more humble ranks of knowledge and culture workers. The numbers of booksellers, schoolmasters, actors, and musicians had been increasing, partially as a consequence of the growth of culture in provincial towns discussed in chapter five. Three of the books discussed in this chapter were first published at provincial presses. Just as Cibber had been able to imagine his daughter also becoming an actor, some of these families educated their daughters in ways that encouraged them also to become knowledge and culture workers. These women writers wrote in part for money to support themselves and their families and tended to have longer, more productive careers than their more genteel, more amateur sisters. More's father, a schoolmaster, trained his daughters to be school-mistresses. The father of Cowley, the most successful woman dramatist since Centlivre, was a Tiverton bookseller and her husband was a London newspaper writer. Burney's father was a musician and musicologist. Sophia Lee's father and mother were both actors and she became a schoolmistress. Anna Aikin Barbauld's father was a distinguished dissenting clergyman and schoolmaster, who taught her both modern and ancient languages; she also married a dissenting clergyman and schoolmaster and taught pupils herself. Inchbald, following Cowley as an even more successful play-wright, had the least likely family background: her father was a Suffolk farmer. But even Inchbald as a girl read plays at home in a family circle and visited provincial theatres at Norfolk and Bury St Edmunds. Of the new major women writers in this period, only Clara Reeve and Charlotte Smith claimed genteel origin. Reeve's career in the 1770s and 1780s conformed more to the bluestocking pattern than to that of a commercial writer. Smith, however, made a disastrous marriage to a wastrel husband that left her as the sole supporter of twelve children, and she tried to maintain her family's gentility. Consequently, she was driven to write for money even more earnestly than her more humbly born contemporaries.

Poetry, translation, the domestic novel, sentimental comedy, children's books, and books of advice to women continued to be important forms for women writers in this period. Smith, for example, began her career with a volume of poems, *Elegiac Sonnets and other Essays* (1784), a translation of Prévost's *Manon Lescaut* (1753) as *Manon L'Escaut* (1785), and another translation of stories drawn from Gayot de Pitaval's compilation of French legal cases, *The Romance of Real Life* (1787). The total number of novels published rose dramatically in the late 1780s. In the last half of the 1780s, for the first time, the number of identifiable female novelists exceeded the number of identifiable male novelists. (Many novelists continued to remain anonymous.) Identifiable women novelists published a total of 224 novels between 1777 and 1789, a staggering 118 appearing in 1789 alone.[6] Typical payments to novelists continued to be low, and it was much easier to sell a novel than to have a play accepted for production; nevertheless, London managers produced thirty-two plays by women on the public stage between 1777 and 1789, nine of them by Cowley and ten of them by Inchbald.[7] Some women writers now specialized in children's literature. Dorothy Kilner, for example, wrote the charming *The Life and Perambulation of a Mouse* (1783), as well as other stories and religious books for children. Hannah More in *Sacred Dramas* invented a new kind of school play derived from the Bible. At the same time her identification with the biblical prophets like Daniel suggests how, increasingly influenced by Evangelicalism, More will overcome any lingering feminine modesty to become a strong social critic. Witnessing young Daniel rebuke Belshazar's luxury and pride, one character wonders at his "holy boldness" and another responds, "Such is the fearless confidence of virtue":

> And such the righteous courage those maintain
> Who plead the cause of truth![8]

Concern with the representation of place and sometimes with place at a specific historical time frequently characterizes the literature of this period, across genre. In part, this seems a result of the British public's experiencing so much exposure to news of foreign wars and colonial issues. Inchbald, for example, set her very successful five-act comedy, *Such Things Are* (1787), in contemporary "Sumatra, East Indies," using sets for British colonial residences, the Sultan's palace and Council Chamber, and the Sultan's prisons. Attention to foreign places simultaneously provoked efforts to articulate what was distinctive about British places.

Interest in the representation of place was also a consequence of the development of a post-Burkian aesthetic that valued the sublime and beautiful in landscape and, increasingly, after William Gilpin's *Observations on the River Wye, and several parts of South Wales, &. relative chiefly to picturesque beauty* (1782), the picturesque as well. The woman's poetry of this period, reflecting this aesthetic – as well as building on James Thomson, the graveyard poets, and the earlier poetry of sensibility – often explores particularized landscapes either as reflections of psychic states or as contrasts to them. An overlap in experiments with the function of landscape in poetry and in the novel is most explicit in the work of Seward, who published *Louisa: A Poetical Novel* (1782), and in that of Smith, who composed sonnets for characters in her novels that she later published in the various editions of her *Elegiac Sonnets*. Place and time also become key elements in Ann Radcliffe's gothic novels, the first of which, *The Castles of Athlin and Dunbayne*, appeared in 1789. To the accounts of art and the analysis of foreign societies readers had come to expect from books of European travel, Hester Thrale Piozzi now added elaborate descriptions of landscapes, both cultivated and wild, in her *Observations and Reflections Made in the Course of a Journey through France, Italy, and Germany* (1788). Responsiveness to the aesthetics of landscape became a firmly established hallmark of sensibility.

A sense that the old British landscape was disappearing because of increased commerce and new manufacturing also prompted a nostalgic valuation of the older "unspoiled" landscape. Cowley makes this particularly clear in her poem, *The Scottish Village: Or, Pitcairne Green* (1786), prompted by a newspaper story about a manufacturing facility to be built in a Scottish village. A weeping Genius of the Place nostalgically evokes a peaceful landscape unchanged through centuries, as a "motley crowd" of "Mechanics, Pedants, and Traders" invades.[9] Then, in a more optimistic, progressive vein, a mortal replies, insisting that "sullen vegetation" and "sterile nature" must inevitably yield to commerce and to the social blessings of commerce.[10] These, in Cowley's reading, include more learning and the hope that Scotland can produce its own Sewards, Barbaulds, and Burneys. (Cowley seems unaware that Scotland had already produced Lady Mary Walker.)

By the late 1770s enthusiasm for the virtues of sensibility still ran high, yet many contemporaries were bored with what had become sentimental conventions. Reviewers had good reason to bemoan, as they regularly did, the tired sentimental clichés retailed by many poets, novelists, and playwrights. As we shall see in considering the comedy of this period, comic dramatists and comic novelists paid acute attention both to established sentimental conventions and to a multiplicity of new variations on them. Of particular interest to literary history, sensibility's versions of the inexpressibility topos, a cause of weakness in the literature of sensibility, proved a rich target for satire and comedy.

Other thoughtful observers worried that, however sensibility might legitimately be a ground of virtue, fashionable sensibility was a hazard to morality. Praise for melting tenderness persisted, yet increasingly mere tenderness, sympathy, and pity seemed too tame. Writers ratcheted up the emotions produced by sensibility to extreme melancholy, despair, even terror and horror, and offered characters of sensibility who progressed to madness. These more extreme manifestations of sensibility become hallmarks of a romantic poetry like that of Smith's *Elegiac Sonnets* and of the new gothic fiction, like that of Radcliffe or Sophia Lee in *The Recess* (1783–85).[11]

Hannah More, while continuing to regard sensibility as an affective ground of virtuous conduct, was particularly alert to its dangers; her critique yields insight into the complex struggles with sensibility characteristic of this period. Like other critics, More sometimes attacked affectations of sensibility and, at other times, attacked excesses of sensibility or sensibility unregulated by rational principles. The sensibility More invokes in her important poem, "Sensibility. A Poetical Epistle to the Hon. Mrs. Boscawen" (1782), is most immediately a sensibility associated with melancholy and mourning. She mourns for Garrick, who died in 1779. Frances Boscawen, who bends "in anguish o're the frequent urn," lost her husband, Admiral Boscawen in 1762, a son in the navy in 1769, and another son in 1774; when More wrote the poem, Boscawen was anxious about a soldier son serving in America. Sensibility, for More and many others, is simultaneously the basis for pain and for pleasure. Without it, a person would live in "joyless apathy" and be incapable of feeling "transports of pleasure."[12] Even the pain experienced by the person possessed of sensibility can sometimes be experienced as pleasure, a paradox that led contemporaries to formulate many quasi-Petrarchian oxymorons. Thus, More reminds Boscawen:

> Ev'n the soft sorrow of remembered woe,
> A not unpleasing sadness may bestow.[13]

Indeed, More, at the moment when she praises the "noble few" in whom heightened sensibility most properly leads to active charity, invokes Petrarch directly:

> Ye, who with pensive *Petrarch* love to mourn,
> Or weave fresh chaplets for Tibullus' urn . . .
> Would you to 'scape the pain the joy forgo,
> And miss the transport to avoid the woe?[14]

As I said in the previous chapter, one appeal of sensibility to members of the middling classes was that it offered a basis of human merit not dependent on birth and class. More, daughter of a schoolmaster and herself a schoolmistress as a teenager, was aware of this attraction. Furthermore, with her increasing attention to the laboring classes, she envisions the possibility of a kind of Christian democracy in which poor people might themselves show sensibility and be virtuous benefactors of the afflicted. Not all good works require wealth:

> Heav'n decrees
> To all, the gift of minist'ring to ease.
> The gentle offices of patient love,
> Beyond all flatt'ry, and all price above.[15]

This was the vision that helped make charitable activists out of working- and middling-class Evangelical members of the Church of England, including the so-called Methodists.

However, More correctly perceived that sensibility in her culture too often became an excuse for foolish and destructive behavior. A major turn in "Sensibility" comes when she declares:

> Yet, while I hail the Sympathy Divine,
> Which makes, O man! the wants of others thine:
> I mourn heroic JUSTICE, scarcely own'd,
> And PRINCIPLE for SENTIMENT dethron'd.
> While FEELING boasts her ever-tearful eye,
> Stern TRUTH, firm FAITH, and manly VIRTUE fly.[16]

Since sensibility is significantly imagined as inherent in the body, one problem is that its physical manifestations – tears, sighs, tremblings, and faintings – can be counterfeited. And its virtuous maxims can be uttered insincerely, as they were most amusingly by Richard Sheridan's Joseph Surface in *The School for Scandal* (1777). More attacks those who offer the now conventional external signs of sensibility without engaging in acts of charity to fellow humans:

> So exclamations, tender tones, fond tears,
> And all the graceful drapery Pity wears;
> These are not Pity's self.[17]

In *Essays on Various Subjects, Principally Designed for Young Ladies* (1777), More associates true sensibility with virtue – and romance – and warns against false sentimentality:

I will even go so far as to assert, that a young woman cannot have any greatness of soul, or true elevation of principle, if she has not a tincture of what the vulgar would call Romance, but which persons of a certain way of thinking will discern to proceed from those fine feelings, and that charming sensibility without which a woman may be worthy, yet she can never be amiable.[18]

Yet, in what she identifies as "the age of sentiment," sentiment has become "the varnish of virtue to conceal the deformity of vice."[19] Sentimental books, especially novels, will mislead their young readers, who must learn instead that "Sentiment suggests fine harangues and subtle distinctions; principle conceives just notions, and performs good actions in consequence of them."[20] How to claim and to express those "fine feelings" tied to "greatness of soul" and "true elevation of principle" without merely parroting the now conventional language of sensibility or succumbing to the foolishness or selfishness of fashionable sensibility became one of the main challenges for many women writers of this period.

Two valuable legacies of the bluestockings to some of the women writers who immediately followed them were a degree of confidence that women might usefully write on modern literary subjects and a continuing desire to promote the work of women writers and the interests of women. Women writers thus participated in the strong interest in literary criticism, literary biography, and editorial projects characteristic of the last decades of the eighteenth century. Among the important works of literary scholarship and literary history by male writers were Thomas Warton's *History of English Poetry* (1774–89), Johnson's *Lives of the Poets* (1778–81), and James Beattie's *Dissertations Moral and Critical* (1783). Beattie, a poor Scot, benefited from Montagu's patronage. Griffith used her literary reputation to promote a *Collection of Novels, Selected and Revised by Mrs. Griffith* (3 volumes, 1777), which she introduced and edited. She includes Aphra Behn's *Agnes de Castro* and *Oroonoko*, Penelope Aubin's *Noble Slaves*, and Eliza Haywood's *Fruitless Enquiry*. Clearly, Griffith wants to make a place for these women writers in the emerging canon, although she finds they have faults that require expurgation for a modern audience. Jane Spencer suggests that Griffith here represents the situation of a new generation of women writers who "no longer needed to define themselves in relation to Behn" and who could afford "a new detachment" in their attitudes toward the transgressive women writers of the

Restoration and early eighteenth century; they could regard their "faults" as consequences of their historical situation and consider that there was "no danger" of their "contaminating a new generation of women writers."[21] Ann Ford Thicknesse, also a talented musician, dedicated her *Sketches of the Lives and Writings of the Literary Ladies of France* (3 volumes, 1778, 1780–81) to Carter. These volumes combined literary biography and criticism with an anthology of work by French women writers. They were explicitly designed not only to praise the achievements of French women but to inspire English women to comparable accomplishment. After Johnson's death in 1784, Hester Thrale, instead of simply selling her Johnson materials or turning them over to a publisher for a male writer to use, or to Boswell for his prestigious projected biography, was emboldened to use them herself to write her *Anecdotes of the Late Samuel Johnson* (1786). She followed this with her edition of *Letters to and from the Late Samuel Johnson* (1788), including twenty-eight letters of her own. Carter's legacy of literary scholarship and translation from ancient languages was perhaps most memorably continued by Elizabeth Bowdler, a student of the Hebrew scriptures, translator of the Song of Solomon, and author of commentaries on the Song of Solomon (1779) and Revelation (1787). As we shall see, Susannah Dobson's translations of French works on Italian and French literary history made significant contributions to the revival and rehabilitation of romance in this period.

I. ROMANCE

A number of male and female writers between 1777 and 1789 turned away from the contemporary to explore the distant European past, through scholarship, through works of the imagination, and in works that mingled or conflated scholarship and imagination. Scholars debated the historical origins of romance, some maintaining that it came to Europe from eastern tales at the time of the Crusades or before, others finding its origins in Celtic or Norse sources. We perhaps think most readily of the so-called northern revival evident in Thomas Chatterton's *Poems* (1777) or James Macpherson's *Poems of Ossian* (1784) and in the debates over the historicity of those poems. Scholars also insisted on the importance of historical elements in romance, challenging the apparent epistemological bright line between romance as the discourse of the imaginary and history or realist fiction as the genres of the real. The crusades, strongly associated with romance in part because of Tasso's great sixteenth-century romance epic, *Jerusalem Delivered*, became the period setting for novels like Reeve's

Champion of Virtue (1777), dramas like More's *Percy* (1777), and poems like Cowley's *Maid of Aragon* (1783). In the argument prefaced to her verse "Edward and Laura. A Legendary Tale" (1783), Miss R. Roberts remarks: "The time of the Crusades was an æra as favourable to the romantic passion of love as it was to the enthusiastic spirit of religion; the like ardent zeal animated the heroes souls in both these glorious causes; and if it sometimes carried them to excess, it was, however, an error on the side of virtue . . ."[22] Reeve's *Progress of Romance* (1785) uses this eighteenth-century scholarship to consider romance from its ancient origins, through the middle ages and the Renaissance, to the contemporary novel.

Contemporary conflict over North America, the West Indies, and India helped inspire self-conscious and wide-ranging inquiry into comparative history, including cultural and literary history. This is evident in Gibbon's *Decline and Fall of the Roman Empire* (1776–88), in Burke's speeches on India affairs, and in Sir William Jones's founding of the Bengal Asiatic Society in 1784. There was also significant interest in England in earlier periods of Italian, Spanish, and French literature and culture. Cervantes was treated to a serious six-volume scholarly edition of *Don Quixote* by John Bowle in 1781. For his edition, published entirely in Spanish, Bowle read his way through all the Spanish romances mentioned in the novel.[23] A common theme in both orientalist and medieval scholarship was that some things that might seem fantastic from the perspective of British realism or empiricism nevertheless had elements of true history.

Women writers, as we have seen, had already insisted that, for women, scholarship and imitation in the romance languages was a vehicle for displaying the kind of literary capacities learned men had traditionally displayed in scholarship and imitation of Greek and Latin literature. In this period we see women continuing to use their knowledge of romance languages to participate in belles lettres – and to defend romance. The debate over the value and historicity of romance was simultaneously an historiographical debate and a debate over literary history and theory.

DOBSON'S *LIFE OF PETRARCH*

New serious attention to Petrarch revealed him to be a gifted humanist poet who offered something that looked very like the "worship" of a woman. In 1757 no less a sage than David Hume in "Of the Standard of Taste" had disparaged Petrarch and included his poetry in the category of work so marred by "eternal blemishes" that it could not produce pleasure: "It must for ever be ridiculous in PETRARCH to compare his mistress,

LAURA, to JESUS CHRIST."[24] Nevertheless, in 1775 Susannah Dobson had translated a *Life of Petrarch*, first published in French by Jacques-François-Paul-Aldonce de Sade, uncle of the notorious Marquis de Sade. The older Sade was a libertine but learned Abbé who did research on Petrarch's Laura (from whom the Sades believed themselves descended). Dobson was interested in Petrarch's engagement with philosophy, with literary manuscripts, with European courts, and, especially, in his insistence that he learned from Laura. She translates his declaration: "I bless the happy moment . . . that directed my heart to Laura. She led me to see the path of virtue, to detach my heart from base and grovelling objects: from her I am inspired with that celestial flame which raises my soul to heaven, and directs it to the Supreme Cause as the only source of happiness."[25] Perhaps surprisingly, at this point only a small number of Petrarch's sonnets had been translated into English. John Nott, classical scholar and physician to the Duchess of Devonshire, supplied this lack with his *Sonnets and Odes Translated from the Italian of Petrarch*, published in 1777, offering 317 sonnets in Italian and English translation on facing pages. Nott offered only a cursory sketch of Petrarch's life, referring the reader to "that more laborious but excellent work of Mrs. Dobson's."[26]

DOBSON'S *LITERARY HISTORY OF THE TROUBADOURS* AND *MEMOIRS OF ANCIENT CHIVALRY*

Dobson went on to translate two additional works of serious scholarship concerned with the early history and literature of France, both significant defenses of romance: *The Literary History of the Troubadours* (1779), edited by the Abbé Millot from materials given to him by Jean-Baptiste de La Curne de Sainte-Palaye, and the *Memoirs of Ancient Chivalry* (1784) by Sainte-Palaye. Sainte-Palaye was a great French scholar, a member of the Académie des inscriptions et belles-lettres and of the Académie Française. He dedicated his life to producing a history of medieval France that would be at once a triumph of modern scholarly method and a contribution to the glory of France. On the occasion of Sainte-Palaye's election to the Académie Française in 1759, the Abbé Alary observed that in the Renaissance only Greek and Latin learning had been regarded as erudition, but that Sainte-Palaye had had the "courage needed to go against the prejudice and into the impenetrable forest" of the Old Provencal manuscripts and romances that were the archive of the early history of their nation.[27] Having collected the necessary manuscripts on trips to Italy and the south of France and done the difficult philological work necessary to make his way through what he called "the dark labyrinth of the language,"[28] Sainte-Palaye produced not a dry chronicle, but an engaging account of the laws and customs of the early French people and "the political and military establishment that was ancient chivalry." The work Dobson translated Sainte-Palaye first presented in the form of papers read before the Académie des inscriptions et belles-lettres between 1746 and 1755; the papers were published in the proceedings of the Académie and then collected in three volumes published in 1756, 1759, and 1781. Like Montesquieu, whose *Espirit des lois* was published in 1748, he tries to discern the internal coherence of the system he studies, its relation to monarchical government, and the causes of its decline.[29] While Sainte-Palaye is concerned to make out a nationalist case for the superiority of the French to the Greeks and Romans, he does not wish to exalt medieval chivalry over the civilization of modern France. On the contrary, he considers medieval chivalry, despite its elements of superstition, folly, and barbarism, as the beginning of a long progress to modern refinement. As Lionel Gossman has said in an excellent book on *Medievalism and the Ideologies of the Enlightenment*:

Sainte-Palaye's standards and values remained resolutely those of the unheroic nobility of his own time, the new aristocracy of the monarchical state – urbanity, civilized behavior, law and order, comfort, enlightenment and, latterly, the good of humanity. The superstitious piety and the gross sensuality of the knights, as he described them in the fifth *Mémoire*, were genuinely repulsive to him. The very style of his book, however – limpid, persuasive, almost weightless – as well as the elegant presentation in neat duodecimos, demonstrated amply his allegiance to his own civilization and to the modern and educated aristocracy of which he was a member.[30]

Sainte-Palaye's work was eagerly read by Englishmen seriously interested in the middle ages, including Thomas Gray, Thomas Percy, Thomas Warton, and Richard Hurd. Hurd's *Lectures on Chivalry and Romance* (1762), commonly said to have "helped to initiate the Romantic movement," is heavily indebted to Sainte-Palaye.[31]

For Sainte-Palaye and his French admirers, part of the point of his history was to demonstrate that, when one compared the histories of the Greeks and the Romans with the history of the French people at a similar stage in their development, the French, thanks to their system of chivalry, were in some respects superior. "No other *human* laws inforced, as Chivalry did," he argues, "sweetness and modesty of temper, and that politeness which the word *courtesy* was meant perfectly to express."[32] He attaches particular importance to the tournaments of chivalry because, he claims, in them the vanquished were not humiliated, and the victors learned, not to boast, but to attribute their success to "fortune and the fate of arms." As a consequence of schooling in chivalry, he believes, the French and the English in later times "ever used such humanity and faith towards their prisoners, that they have been mutually the firmest supporters of its laws, and have persevered in proving the spirit of them, when their neighboring nations have given horrid examples of barbarity and treachery to their unhappy prisoners."[33]

Dobson, while recognizing that there would be an English market for a book so important and so engaging as *The Memoirs of Ancient Chivalry*, probably had little interest in it as a contribution to French national glory; instead, she deployed the authority of this distinguished academician to maintain that romances were not merely the idle tales and useless fictions their English critics claimed and that their vision of women as heroines worthy of male worship was not merely a fictive illusion. Sainte-Palaye was well aware that other serious readers had dismissed romance as childish and frivolous, as we have seen the learned Doctor do in Lennox's *Female Quixote*. The first French edition of *Memoirs* contains an advertisement by Bougainville attempting to rebut the proposition that romances are monotonous and insipid fictions and claiming, with Sainte-Palaye, that they are crucial sources of the history of France. Another authority is cited to say that "however the study of the old romances may be censured by the ignorant . . . it would be a disgrace to a man of learning not to have read them; or having read, not to profit by them."[34] Sainte-Palaye, of course, was arguing for the historical importance of the medieval romances. Dobson happily translates these defenses, and, invoking the usual latitude eighteenth-century translators permitted themselves, also tosses into her version of the preface an additional defense of the seventeenth-century French romance: "the romances of Astrea, Cyrus, Cleopatra, the Princess of Cleves, Zayde, were wrote to paint the manners of the courts of Henry the Fourth, Lewis the Thirteenth, and Lewis the Fourteenth, as characteristic novels; and for their delicacy (though somewhat prolix) they are far from deserving the neglect they are fallen into."[35]

Dobson elected to translate works about the European middle ages that exalted women as capable of imparting valuable knowledge to men and that exalted love as a serious passion; such representations, in Petrarch, in troubadour poetry, and in romance provoked resistance in many eighteenth-century male readers. Dobson, on the other hand, rejoices at these spectacles of women being extravagantly praised and exercising apparent control over men. "Women," she writes in her preface, "ought to hold these ancient writers in high esteem, for the deference they pay to modesty, and the fame they so liberally bestowed on virtue. They taught generous firmness, judicious observance of superiors, and constant love, to unite in the same hearts. . ."[36] On some occasions when Sainte-Palaye acknowledges that the pure ideals of chivalry became corrupted and led to licentious behavior, she declines to translate such qualifications. In *The Literary History of the Troubadours* and *Memoirs of Ancient Chivalry* Dobson deployed the authority of French academicians against that of English authorities like the Johnsonian "Pious and Learned Doctor" in *The Female Quixote* who dismissed romances as "senseless Fictions, which at once vitiate the Mind, and pervert the Understanding" and that "teach Women to expect . . . Worship."

HANNAH MORE'S *PERCY. A TRAGEDY*

In *Percy* (1777) More used a romantic medieval setting for what might be called a sentimental tragedy. With the assistance of David and Eva Garrick, More wrote a blank verse drama that impressed her contemporaries as a moving work of high art; it was an important keystone of More's growing reputation. Henry MacKenzie, author of *The Man of Feeling* (1771), was only one among the many who confessed to shedding tears over this play. The action of *Percy* takes place in a British gothic castle in the time of the Crusades. Although the heroine Elwina loves and has been engaged, with her father's permission, to Percy, Earl of Northumberland, a petty quarrel has led her father, Earl Raby, to force Elwina to marry Earl Douglas instead. Percy has gone off to the Crusades. Douglas combines jealousy with a morbid desire to pick at Elwina's wounds. Elwina devotes herself to being a dutiful wife, but Douglas – more a man of the late eighteenth century than of the middle ages – scorns

> Cold, ceremonious, and unfeeling duty,
> That wretched substitute for love . . .[37]

He will not be satisfied with his wife's obedience and physical chastity, but requires that her heart dote only on him. Percy, having distinguished himself in the Crusades, returns.

Unlike many other contemporary writers who treat the Crusades as a virtuous Christian enterprise, More suggests that to use violence in the name of religion is unholy and perhaps even that aggressive war itself is unholy. Earl Raby rejoices that Palestine has been subdued and that "the hated cresent" has yielded to the cross. Elwina, though, declares that God abhors the "bigot rage" of the Crusades:

> When policy assumes religion's name,
> And wears the sanctimonious garb of faith,
> Only to colour fraud, and license murder,
> War then is tenfold guilt.[38]

Jesus, she says, "Abhors the sacrifice of human blood."[39] We know from one of More's letters that she expected her audience to apply this passage to the current American war. She reports that when the Prime Minister's wife took a stage box for one of her benefit nights and she suspected that the Prime Minister, Lord Frederick North, himself was in the theatre, she was frightened and "trembled when the speech against the wickedness of going to war was spoken."[40] More tries to save the romance of knight errantry from the violence of the Crusades and to move her hero closer to a modern ideal of a man of sensibility by having Percy's friend and fellow knight report, improbably, of Percy:

> [He] bore his banner formost in the field,
> Yet conquer'd more by mercy than the sword . . .[41]

The central action of the tragedy turns on a suitably theatrical chivalric token, a scarf Elwina has given Percy as a pledge of their love. The sight of this on Percy's breast convinces Douglas that his wife is unfaithful. Percy and Elwina attempt to make the plot a romance of their heroic renunciation of passion for virtue. Elwina tells Percy she envies the fact that he can shed tears which are not criminal, while, since she is married,

> mine are criminal.
> Are drops of shame which wash the cheeks of guilt,
> And every tear I shed dishonours Douglas.[42]

Percy declaims in response: "To triumph over Douglas, we'll be virtuous."[43] But Douglas's jealousy and his pathological drive to dissimulate so that he can arrange scenes in which he experiences spectatorial superiority over Elwina force the action to tragedy. Douglas has his knights falsely report to Elwina that Percy has killed him. Elwina seizes the opportunity to drink the poison Douglas has ordered his knights to administer to her should he die. As she is dying and raving in a kind of madness, Douglas enters and admits he sent the false report:

> To give thy guilty breast a deeper wound,
> To add a deadlier sting to disappointment . . .[44]

Douglas displays the scarf Percy swore Elwina would never see without him unless he were dead, reveals that he has killed Percy, and triumphs in satisfied "revenge."[45] When Douglas realizes Elwina has taken the poison, he stabs himself.

More invokes sensibility to explain how Elwina could have betrayed her love for Percy. In the first act, Elwina offers her father's cruelty and her own weakness as the explanations for her marriage. "My barbarous father," she pleads,

> . . . Dragg'd me trembling, dying, to the altar,
> I sigh'd, I struggled, fainted, and – complied.[46]

In her third-act scene of reunion with Percy, in the castle garden, Elwina calls the marriage "her father's deed" and pleads:

> I cou'd withstand his fury; but his tears,
> Ah, they undid me! Percy, dost thou know
> The cruel tyranny of tenderness?[47]

As we have seen from sentimental novels like Collyer's *Felicia to Charlotte* and sentimental plays like Sheridan's *The Discovery*, self-sacrifice for a parent, especially for a badly behaved father, was a standard trope of sentimental plots. Normally, such sentimental plots reward the child's willingness to sacrifice himself or herself and do not push beyond mere willingness. In *Percy*, however, Elwina has guilt for betraying her vows to Percy and for marrying without love. Placing the action back into the middle ages makes Elwina less guilty and more sympathetic, but does not seem in More's judgment to leave her entirely guiltless. The medieval world More depicts in *Percy* is more a nightmare of cruel patriarchy in Earl Raby and sadism in Douglas than a paradise of chivalry in which women are worshipped. At the end, though, all acknowledge Elwina's "unequall'd virtues," Douglas begs her forgiveness, and Earl Raby blames himself for murdering his daughter. Still, More seems to want to insist that Elwina cannot elude responsibility for her own acts; hence, the tragic conclusion. One might argue that More imagines Elwina's tragic flaw as her inability to separate her own will from the wills of her father and husband.

REEVE'S *CHAMPION OF VIRTUE*

One of the original English novels of this period, Clara Reeve's *The Champion of Virtue. A Gothic Story* (1777), subsequently in 1778 called

The Old English Baron, features chivalry and a knightly tournament, but has a more complex relation to women's defense of romance than Dobson's translations do. Reeve was a militantly virtuous daughter of the Church of England, both literally and metaphorically. She was the granddaughter of the Reverend Thomas Reeve and the daughter of the Reverend William Reeve. In her father's house, Reeve learned enough Latin so that her first published work was a translation of a Latin verse romance, John Barclay's *Argenis* (Paris, 1621), published as *The Phoenix; or, the History of Polyarchus and Argenis* (1772), in four volumes. *The Old English Baron* is often cited, along with Horace Walpole's *Castle of Otranto* (1764), as a pioneering gothic novel, but to a reader familiar with the later gothic novel, it feels more like an historical romance than a gothic novel. As J. M. S. Tompkins remarked, in their origins the gothic novel and the historical romance "are not easily distinguishable."[48] Reeve described her book as designed:

to unite the most attractive and interesting circumstances of the ancient Romance and modern Novel, at the same time it assumes a character and manner of its own that differs from both: it is distinguished by the appellation of a Gothic story, being a picture of Gothic times and manners . . . [To unite the various merits and graces of the ancient Romance and modern novel] . . . there is required a sufficient degree of the marvellous to excite the attention; enough of the manners of real life to give an air of probability to the work; and enough of the pathetic to engage the heart in its behalf.[49]

The Champion is set in England in the fifteenth century, or, as its first sentence more closely specifies, "In the minority of Henry the Sixth King of England . . ."[50] "Gothic" at this time "meant primarily barbarous, antique" and was often applied to anything from the medieval period through the sixteenth century – and sometimes beyond.[51]

One central figure in *The Champion of Virtue* is Sir Philip Harclay, recently returned to England from the Crusades. He intends to devote himself to a retired life of "works of piety and charity" to prepare himself "for a better state hereafter." First, though, he desires to see his old friend, Lord Lovel. The old Lovel castle he finds inhabited not by Lord Lovel, who has died, but by one of his kinsman, his heir, Baron Fitz-Owen. The Baron has been raising his own sons, his nephews, and Edmund Twyford, a remarkable son of a cottager, all to be proper knights, seeing to their training at crossbow and riding as well as to their study of languages. Sir Philip is so struck by Edmund's virtues – and by a strong resemblance that he bears to Lord Lovel – that he volunteers to adopt him and to provide for him more lavishly than Fitz-Owen can afford to do. Edmund, however, proclaims his gratitude to Fitz-Owen and his unalterable attachment to the Lovel "house and family." Touched by Edmund's loyalty and gratitude to his first benefactor, Sir Philip makes an alternative offer: "If you ever want a friend, remember me; and depend upon my protection, so long as you continue to deserve it."[52] We also learn that Emma, Fitz-Owen's only daughter, loves Edmund, in preference to her better-born cousins. Given Reeve's deployment of these romance conventions, the reader is not surprised when Edmund is revealed to be the true son and heir of the late Lord Lovel, who has been murdered by a younger brother hoping to enjoy his estate and his wife.

Overtly, the moral of the tale is that vice will be outed and punished and patient virtue acknowledged and rewarded. As the champion of Edmund, Sir Philip challenges the murderous brother, who has assumed the title Lord Lovel, to a trial by combat, administered by the warden of the marches. A Christian hero, Sir Philip wounds but refrains from killing the villain. Edmund is restored to the title and allowed to marry Emma. A secondary moral emphasizes the conservative virtues and pleasures of proper subordination.

Contemporaries found *The Champion of Virtue* attractive, calling for at least ten editions before 1800, and Sir Walter Scott recognized it as an avatar of his own historical romance. However, some twentieth-century commentators have found the story bland and even vapid. Bridget MacCarthy complained of Edmund: "He is too good, too long-suffering and too humble . . . He has all the virtues, but no vigour. He wins through all his difficulties simply by being harmless – an affecting but rather improbable circumstance."[53] It is thus worth considering precisely what interests Reeve in her romance. A few recent critics have found socially progressive subtexts in the novel, but I am inclined to agree with James Watt's conclusion that its politics are conservative, that it is what Watt nicely describes as "loyalist gothic," part of a larger conservative project to refashion national identity in the wake of the loss of the American war and the imperial crisis. As Blackstone and Burke were doing, Reeve develops an idea of an old English wisdom "largely unexaminable yet prescriptively authoritative."[54]

Considered as a hero, Edmund is admittedly oddly unexciting. His physical courage is tested briefly in France and he is willing to spend three nights in a castle room said to be haunted, listening to moans from beneath the floor, where he discovers blood-stained armor. Yet he awaits his fate passively and is remarkably concerned about behaving correctly.

When it has become clear that jealous rivals in Fitz-Owen's household aim to blacken his reputation and even to kill him, and when he has also had several good hints that he is probably Lord Lovel, he recalls Sir Philip's promise of protection, journeys to his house, waits outside until summoned in, then, "seized with an universal trembling," kneels down at Sir Philip's feet, takes his hand, kisses it, and presses it to his heart in silence.[55] Here we have the tableau favored by the sentimental drama of the 1770s and 1780s. Encouraged to speak, Edmund sighs deeply and finally says, "I am come thus far, noble sir, to throw myself at your feet, and implore your protection. – you are, under God, my only reliance!"[56] Unlike the bold Almanzors of Dryden's romance, even with some consciousness of his own noble birth, Edmund will not presume to act without the explicit authorization of his superiors and defends himself with forms of passive resistance. Sir Philip, not Edmund, fights for Edmund's title, challenging the false Lord Lovel as the murderer of Arthur, Lord Lovel, Edmund's father. The narrator gives Edmund's character:

> The notice and observation of strangers, and the affection of individuals, together with that inward consciousness that always attends superior qualities, would sometimes kindle the flames of ambition in Edmund's heart, but he checked them presently by reflecting upon his low birth and dependent station – he was modest, yet intrepid; gentle and courteous to all, frank and unreserved to those that loved him, discreet and complaisant to those who hated him, generous and compassionate to the distresses of his fellow-creatures in general; humble, but not servile, to his patron and his superiors.[57]

When he is directly accused of giving the lie to one of the young gentlemen with whom he has been brought up, he replies "with equal spirit and modesty," "not in words sir . . . but I will behave so that you shall not believe them."[58]

Edmund's situation, character, and conduct echo in significant ways the situation, character, and conduct of a late eighteenth-century religious woman like Reeve herself. Both combine "an inward consciousness . . . of superior qualities" with modesty and proper deference to superiors; both have the self-discipline to "check" ambition that is not properly authorized. The frisson in *The Champion of Virtue* is not the later gothic frisson of terror at being pursued by a malevolent supernatural being; instead, what frisson there is comes from abjection before a venerated and benevolent superior or superiors, as one waits to discover whether one's virtue will be recognized. The revelation that Edmund, who has appeared not to be a member of the Lovel family, is indeed a member of a noble family seems an allegory for Reeve's conviction that as a woman she has appeared not to be a full member of her learned and genteel family, coupled with a hope for fuller recognition of female excellence. Edmund's behavior seems odd as the behavior of a gothic or even seventeenth-century man, but more normal as the behavior of a pious gentlewoman in a plot of sensibility in the late eighteenth century. Restored to his castle and greeting his two foster fathers, Fitz-Owen and Sir Philip, he behaves like Burney's Evelina meeting her lost father, Sir John Belville:

> Edmund threw himself at their feet, and embraced their knees, but could not utter a word. – they raised him between them, and strove to encourage him, but he threw himself into the arms of sir Philip Harclay, deprived of strength, and almost of life. – they supported him to a seat, where he recovered by degrees, but had no power to speak his feelings. – he looked up to his benefactors in the most affecting manner, he laid his hand upon his bosom, but was still silent.[59]

Edmund's virtue consists of his modesty, his refusal to presume, his capacity to check his ambition, and his gratitude and deference to his superiors – all virtues within the grasp of a pious gentlewoman. Reeve's heroine is slightly represented and is not the object of anything that could be stigmatized as florid worship, yet, through Edmund, Reeve has contrived to make feminine modesty and feminine virtue subjects of celebration in her romance. At the same time, she inaugurates a female gothic novel more concerned with domesticity and less reliant on supernatural horrors than the male gothic was.

REEVE'S *PROGRESS OF ROMANCE*

Reeve went on to write an explicit defense of romance in *The Progress of Romance, through Times, Countries, and Manners; with Remarks on the Good and Bad Effects of It . . .* (1785). While somewhat constrained by the rigor of her adherence to virtue, her qualms about "amorous fables," and the concern typical of the period about the morals of youth, *The Progress* is nevertheless an ambitious work of literary history ranging from ancient Greek and oriental romances, through medieval European romance, to seventeenth-century French romance and the contemporary novel. Reeve demonstrates willingness to engage in original thought. She criticizes James Beattie's discussion of romance in *Dissertations Moral and Critical* for inattention to significant works and she treats women writers Beattie and other contemporaries ignored, including Behn, Manly, Haywood, Griffith, and Brooke (a particular favorite). In her preface, Reeve observes that the majority of learned Englishmen "have in general affected a contempt for this kind of writing, and looked upon Romances, as proper furniture only for a lady's Library."[60]

Reeve explains that she decided to cast her book in the form of a dialogue so that "arguments and objections might be more clearly stated and discussed" and that dry material might become livelier.[61] The twelve dialogues are a textual version of the kind of conversation enlightenment salons aimed to foster, with the three interlocutors candidly exchanging information and opinions in a polite search for truth. The main debate occurs between Euphrasia, a female defender of romance who has made a serious study of it, and Hortensius, a well-educated gentleman who has read little romance but imbibed typical prejudices against it. The third interlocutor is a less learned lady who likes good contemporary fiction. This dialogue itself might be said to imitate romance in its presentation of a virtuous and learned lady to whose wisdom a gentleman defers.

Like Dobson, whom she cites with admiration, Reeve notes that contemporary French and Italian learned men have taken a different view from that of most Englishmen. Throughout, she emphasizes that at many times and in many cultures learned and virtuous men, far from condescending to romance, have themselves read and even written romances. Thus, she notes that Heliodorus, author of the third-century Greek romance of *Theagenes and Chariclea*, was the Bishop of Tricca in Thessaly and that Jean de Meun, who continued *The Romance of the Rose*, was a Dominican friar and a Doctor of Divinity. Cervantes, she rightly observes, had more attachment to romance than simplistic readings of *Don Quixote* as an anti-romance indicate; after *Don Quixote* he wrote the ambitious romance *Los trabajos de Persiles y Sigismunda*. Euphrasia views the Elizabethan period with special affection, praising Sidney's *Arcadia* and Spenser's *Faerie Queene*. She celebrates Queen Elizabeth for presiding over a court where heroes wrote and read romances and for being herself "an Heroine, worthy to command such men."[62]

Reeve considers the complex question of the degree of historicity of various kinds of romances. As E. J. Clery points out, in the 1780s "the very idea that romance could 'progress' was contentious; the two words had not previously been used together."[63] Behn, Euphrasia remarks, wrote in an age of "licentious manners" and so is especially unsuited to youthful readers, although "there are strong marks of Genius in all this lady's works."[64] In Reeve's analysis, romance may be found in the literature of any country, eastern or western, and in any historical period. Euphrasia effectively and amusingly attacks Hortensius's simplistic assumption that classical epic is historical and romance merely fictitious. Thus, when Hortensius pontificates, "The Epic poem is always derived from some Historical fact, though perhaps remote and obscure," Euphrasia exclaims, "Remote and obscure indeed," and proceeds to offer a comparative reading of Homer's *Odyssey* and *Sinbad the Sailor* from *The Arabian Nights*. Her reading demonstrates that Homer's story is "far more wild and extravagant, and infinitely more incredible."[65] Reeve's book thus significantly intervenes in the developing history of prose fiction, repudiating the overly simple idea of progress from the primitive and superstitious romance to the enlightenment of the realist novel. She also insists on the presence of women writers in literary history.

WALKER'S *MUNSTER VILLAGE*

Reeve defends romance as offering models of virtuous action that inspire virtuous action in readers and as inculcating respect for women – a virtue conspicuously lacking in classical epic; she does not develop the more aggressively utopian element of romance we see in Lady Mary Walker's *Munster Village* (1778). (Walker, daughter of a Scottish Earl, married Dr. James Walker in 1762; after his death, in the 1780s, she was known by the name Hamilton.) *Munster Village* is doubly a romance: it is a feminist utopia like Scott's *Millenium Hall*, but unlike *Millenium Hall*, it uses heterosexual romance plots for its frame. The heroine, Lady Frances Munster, inherits a large estate in Shropshire when her brother dies. She is in love with the "amiable" Lord Darnely, but self-sacrificially decides not to marry him so that she can devote herself to bringing up her orphaned niece and nephew and to the development of the estate.[66] Over a period of ten years, she turns the estate into a center for learning, the arts, and new manufactures.

Walker's utopia organizes male learning as well as female learning and makes frequent comment on national deficiencies as well as local ones, thus in some ways making it more cousin to Cavendish's *Blazing World* than to Scott's *Millenium Hall*. Lady Frances establishes an academy with "able professors," two hundred scholars liberally supported, and an additional twenty women admitted with "funds for their perpetual maintenance."[67] This is imagined as an institution from which authoritative cultural pronouncements can be made. It becomes, we are told, "a seat of the muses, and place to which many resorted for the solution of literary doubts."[68] While London of the 1770s has no proper public library, the extensive library of this institution is to be open to the public "at stated times; (like that of the Vatican, and the French king's) with every proper accommodation to all strangers."[69] The British Museum, though "rich in manuscripts," is "wretchedly poor in printed books" and "not sufficiently accessible to the public . . ."[70] This narrator comments on a wide range of public policy matters, marking deficiencies with the confidence of a modern writer of editorials in a national newspaper.

The visual arts, including architecture, are cultivated at a level more ambitious than the drawing and painting of the ladies of *Millenium Hall*; again, the explicit ambition is to transform the national arts scene, not simply the lives of individual women. Walker was concerned that England was still behind Italy and France in the visual arts and strategizes about ways to change that. Lady Munster determines to provide not only a public library but also a public picture gallery "to afford our youth ready access to good pictures."[71] Walker wants the import duty on pictures abolished and lobbies for Sir Joshua Reynolds to be allowed – as he had offered to do – to adorn the interior of St. Paul's in London. Lady Munster hires Capability Brown to design her gardens and consults with "Mr. Adams" (presumably the famous Scottish architect, Robert Adam) about designs for houses on her estate. Then she admits the public to view the house and gardens, believing that "People accustomed to behold order and elegance in public buildings, and public gardens, acquire urbanity in private."[72] The hospital she erects for the reception of 200 incurables, like other buildings she commissions, is both a charitable institution and an architectural work "of national magnificence."[73]

Although Walker's politics in some ways are conservative, she advocates enlightenment causes and promotes the kinds of practical improvements fostered by the Society for the Encouragement of Arts, Manufactures and Commerce, known as the Society of Arts. This Society, founded in 1754, awarded prizes to inventors who agreed not to patent their inventions and for things like drawings for patterns to be used on textiles. As is evident in James Barry's 1777 picture, "The Distribution of the Premiums in the Society of the Arts," the Society gave prizes to girls and women as well as to boys and men.[74] Instead of sending her son, young Lord Munster, on the usual Grand Tour, Lady Munster sends him to study trade at Amsterdam, "as the best school for learning, temperance, œconomy, and every domestic virtue."[75] Artisans who excel at their crafts are invited to live rent free on the estate for two years so they can sell their products "at moderate rates" and establish businesses. Artificers from Tuscany who excel at porcelain manufacture are also invited to settle on the estate.

Foreign animals and crops are imported, including buffaloes, Norwegian sheep, Indian corn, and rice. Superstition has been banished from the village, astrology is not taught, and religious toleration is praised.

Walker in her fictional utopia documents the historicity of heroism. Young Lord Munster goes to Scandinavia, where he takes note of the Queen Dowager of Sweden, "perfect mistress of Latin, as well as the modern languages," "an exalted character . . . the avowed protectress of letters, and encourager of merit," who "during her husband's life possessed an almost unlimited influence over affairs of state."[76] This was Louise Ulrica, the sister of Frederick the Great, active in Swedish politics and an important patron of the arts in Sweden. Denmark, Lord Munster learns, boasts Margaret, the fourteenth-century Queen who united Denmark, Sweden, and Norway into one kingdom lasting for over a hundred years. This is the Margaret described in Voltaire's *History of Charles XII* as the Semiramis of the North.

Most importantly, I suspect, Walker has in mind as inspiration for the bold experiments of Munster Village Catherine the Great's still bolder program for enlightenment reform in Russia. Catherine began ruling in her own right in 1762 and launched a staggeringly ambitious program that included founding a Society for the Translation of Foreign Books and the Russian Academy of the Language, and founding a boarding school for noble girls on the model of St. Cyr, as well as free state coeducational schools in provincial towns. Catherine promoted neoclassical architecture and decorative arts, and bought foreign collections of painting and sculpture (including Sir Robert Walpole's) that laid the foundation of the present Hermitage collection. Catherine also invited foreign artisans to establish themselves in Russia, offered settlers temporary exemptions from taxes, and declared freedom of economic enterprise.[77] *Munster Village* mentions Catherine explicitly as one whose "name will be immortal," who "gave a code of laws to her empire, which contains a fifth part of the globe; and the first of her laws was to establish universal [religious] toleration."[78] Here we have come very far from the paradigmatic woman of *The Female Quixote*'s realist fiction in which women have no power and no adventures. Walker's challenge to the supposed epistemological bright line between fictive romance and factual history is particularly bold. She uses the form of the romance to imagine a woman so powerful than she can positively transform national culture, creating a fiction that defies the laws of novelistic verisimilitude, then reminds her readers of a living historical figure who seems to have precisely that power.

SMITH'S *EMMELINE: THE ORPHAN OF THE CASTLE*

More typical of the women's novels of this period than the utopian *Munster Village*, Charlotte Smith's first novel, *Emmeline: The Orphan of the Castle* (1788), might be called a sentimental romance. Smith subsequently was known as a gothic novelist, but *Emmeline*, despite its Welsh castle, is set in contemporary Great Britain and Europe and has no mysterious gothic villains or supernatural phenomena to evoke terror. Taking hints from Burney (whose novels we will consider in the second part of this chapter), and developing a form of the romance plot that was becoming a mainstay of women's fiction, Smith tests a virtuous, genteel, but financially insecure heroine with a series of marriage proposals that offer her a secure place in the world but that come from men she cannot love or admire. Initially, Emmeline understands herself to be the illegitimate daughter of Henry Charles Mowbray. Her uncle, Lord Montreville, has had her brought up by servants in a remote castle in Wales and seems prepared to give her only the meagerest of allowances. Considering herself born into an upper class and possessed of mental superiority, Emmeline first indignantly rejects her uncle's idea that she should marry the castle steward, Mr. Maloney. "Believe I have a mind," she tells Lord Montreville, "which tho' it will not recoil from any situation where I earn my bread by honest labour, is infinitely superior to any advantages which such a man as Malone can offer me."[79] Distressed as her material circumstances continue to be, Emmeline subsequently rejects three more serious marriage proposals: one from Humphrey Rochley, a middle-aged businessman who has a portfolio of stocks and bonds worth £60,000, in addition to his business and real estate; another from the Chevalier de Bellzane, a Swiss nobleman and officer in the French army who has fought on the side of the Americans, but who is a coxcomb; and, the most serious temptation, the proposal of her cousin Frederick Delamere, Lord Montreville's only son. Delamere is passionate and impulsive, pursuing Emmeline as she moves from place to place trying to avoid him and to honor her promise to her uncle not to encourage him. When Emmeline has rejected these offers of marriage from men not worthy of a heroine, she wins her reward by marriage to Captain William Godolphin, younger brother of the Earl of Westhaven, and a man of extraordinary virtue, sensibility, and considerable wealth. Although the novel does not invite the public collective clap that Cowley solicits when her heroine in *Who's the Man?* chooses a serving British officer, Smith's hero is also proud of his profession of arms.

How is Smith's very late eighteenth-century romance different from romances of the late seventeenth and early eighteenth century? The plot of romance in which virtuous characters display their virtues, are tested, and rewarded persists, but Smith and other late eighteenth-century writers redefine virtue. Older aristocratic romance indissolubly linked physical virtues, including beauty and courage, with spiritual and mental virtues, and with upper-class birth. Smith, strongly identified with the gentry and in the 1780s socially conservative, persists in coupling virtue and birth. Emmeline is ultimately revealed to be the legitimate daughter and heiress of the eldest Mowbray brother, and thus, finally, the owner of the castle. However, Smith diminishes the significance of Emmeline's beauty, eschewing the traditional blazon, the formal and detailed description of the heroine's beauty that is a standard feature not only of seventeenth-century high romance but also of the debased romance of Behn and Manley. Men are attracted to Emmeline, but her physical beauty has a vestigial role compared to the role of her mental and spiritual virtues.

In this sentimental romance, the hero and the heroine of sensibility fall in love with one another not because of beauty or sexual desire but because they witness one another performing notable acts of charity. Emmeline takes it upon herself to care for Lady Adelina Trelawny, a pregnant but repentant adulteress she discovers in a remote cottage in Woodbury Forest. While women writers often shared with men concern over other kinds of distressed people – maimed soldiers, poor children, and slaves, for example – for respectable women writers fallen women were probably the most "peculiarly interesting" objects of charity. Pale, delicate, and ill, Lady Adelina makes an attractive melancholy sentimental object: "If it were possible to personify langour and dejection, it could not be done more expressively than by presenting her form, her air, her complexion, and the mournful cast of her beautiful countenance."[80] As we saw in *Millenium Hall*, strong-minded women sometimes declared that a truly virtuous woman could and even should risk assisting a fallen woman, confident that her own virtue was secure from contagion and undeterred by possible damage to her own reputation. But the matter was controversial. An adulteress was seen as a more dangerous character than a naïve unmarried young girl who had been seduced. As an unprotected and unmarried young woman daring to befriend an adulteress, Emmeline puts herself in exceptional jeopardy. Not surprisingly, her sudden disappearance in order to assist Lady Adelina give birth to her child in discreet Bath lodgings gives rise to rumors that Emmeline herself is ruined. Later, when Delamere finds Emmeline holding Lady Adelina's infant son, Delamere concludes Emmeline must be the mother and denounces her. Captain Godolphin, however, is Lady Adelina's brother. When he returns from naval duty to witness his sister desperately ill, "frequently deranged," but tenderly attended by Emmeline, Godolphin falls in love with Emmeline. His superior sensibility is immediately evident in the sentimental tableau of his visit to his sister: Lady Adelina "still lay without any signs of existence, and . . . her brother still knelt [by the bedside] in speechless agony."[81]

Emmeline comes to love Godolphin because of his tenderness toward his sister, his love of poetry, and his active charity. In one romantic encounter, before Godolphin, loving Emmeline, is aware that she can love him, Emmeline is on a deck chair, at night, on board a ship crossing the English channel: "a declining moon only broke thro' the heavy clouds of the horizon with a feeble and distant light. There was a solemnity in the scene at once melancholy and pleasing."[82] She sees a male passenger, "muffled in a great coat," hears him utter a "deep sigh," then recite "in a voice low, but extremely expressive," a sonnet "addressed to Night."[83] (Like other sonnets Smith first printed in her novels, she later printed this one in subsequent editions of her *Elegiac Sonnets*.) Emmeline then learns that Godolphin has just rescued the wretched Lt. Stornaway, a naval officer he knew in the West Indies, who was dying in a French debtor's prison for debts he incurred nursing his wife through smallpox. With the sententiousness characteristic of the heroes of sentimental drama, Godolphin declares: "It was a trifle. I blushed to think, that while Englishmen were daily passing thro' the place in pursuit of pleasure, a gentleman, an officer of their nation, languished for such a sum in the horrors of such a confinement."[84]

Emmeline and Godolphin prefer moderately wild landscapes to the attractions of cities. In one of the most notable descriptive passages of the novel, Emmeline, leaving the Welsh castle, looks back on it with regret:

It's venerable towers rising above the wood in which it was almost embosomed, made one of the most magnificent features of a landscape, which now appeared in sight.

The road lay along the side of what would in England be called a mountain; at it's feet rolled the rapid stream that washed the castle walls, foaming over fragments of rock, and bounded by a wood of oak and pine; among the ruins of the monastery, once an appendage of the castle, reared it's broken arches; and marked by grey and mouldering walls, and mounds covered with slight vegetation, it was traced to it's connection with the castle itself, still frowning in gothic magnificence . . . Farther to the West, beyond a bold and rocky shore, appeared the sea . . . [85]

A key scene in which Emmeline eventually meets her dead father's old servant, who helps to unlock the mystery of her birth, takes place amidst a craggy landscape in the south of France. As Emmeline silently admires "this beautiful and singular scene," elaborately described by the narrator, she wishes she could be with Godolphin, the only person she knows "who had taste and enthusiasm enough to enjoy it."[86] Godolphin's house, East Cliff on the Isle of Wight, has dramatic ocean views.

At the end of the novel, after the impetuous Delamere is killed in a duel (not by Godolphin), Emmeline and Godolphin occupy Mowbray Castle. Although the castle is off-stage during most of the novel, Lorraine Fletcher has argued that it is the first novelistic castle or great house "intended to be read as a precise emblem of England," and that *Emmeline* and Smith's later novels treat questions "about who should own the great house and how it should be run" as questions about "England's ownership and government," influencing later novelists including Austen and Dickens.[87] However, it seems more accurate to say, as J. M. S. Tompkins did, that while Smith in *Emmeline* first began to explore the possibilities of the gothic castle and the contrasts between a beautiful heroine and a grim castle, it was Radcliffe who first put the castle at the heart of her novels.[88]

SEWARD'S *LOUISA. A POETICAL NOVEL, IN FOUR EPISTLES*

Although Reeve in *The Progress of Romance* rightly considers prose romances, it might be argued that the most satisfying forms of romance are in verse. Since romance represents ideal value, the heightening of verse has seemed appropriate to romance. Anna Seward in *Louisa. A Poetical Novel, in Four Epistles* (1784) used heroic couplets to produce a narrative more intense than that of the contemporary sentimental novel, which she was aiming to supplant. Like Lady Mary Wortley Montagu earlier, Seward adapted the Ovidian epistle to her own purposes, but unlike Montagu, combined the shorter Ovidian epistle with the longer form of the epistolary novel. She acknowledged an interest in imitating at least one accomplishment of Rousseau's *Julie, ou la nouvelle Héloïse*, the use of scenic description to paint psychic states. For example, when the hero Eugenio has apparently deserted Louisa, she describes her desolation:

> one barb'rous deed,
> That kills my hopes, like Eurus' fierce career
> On the bright foliage of the early year;
> Which turns, while premature its buds disclose,
> To livid yellowness the damask Rose.[89]

The setting of Seward's poem is ostensibly contemporary England, yet it mingles the contemporary with a kind of abstracted ballad-like medievalism and a dark orientalism. Thus Eugenio rescues a beautiful and richly attired woman from would-be ravishers in a wood:

> Her taper waist the broider'd zone entwines,
> Clasp'd by a gem, the boast of Orient Mines;
> On as we pass, on ev'ry side it gleams,
> And to the Moon, in trembling lustre, streams![90]

Louisa struggles with the despair and abjection typical of the traditional abandoned woman, but overcomes them with a feminist and Christian sense of her own independent self-worth, and is finally rewarded by marriage to the virtuous hero.

In *Louisa* the chaste heroine who loves rural England is threatened by commerce and by the luxuriousness and sensuousness associated with the Indies. Eugenio, we eventually learn, married Emira, the diamond-adorned woman he saved in the wood, not because he cared for her but to save his trader father from the shame of bankruptcy and his mother and sisters from poverty. The father laments that he pursued "gay commercial visions, false, and vain."[91] Like Sheridan in *The Discovery*, and many, many other sentimental writers, Seward thus makes her hero willing to sacrifice his own happiness, even to make a loveless marriage, to benefit his suffering parents. Emira proves a Lamia, epitomizing sensuality and the fashionable opulence associated with the Indies. Married and living in London, she dresses like the "wanton Inmate" of a seraglio, in a high turban, silver Plume, and diamond, a costume that might realistically have been worn by a fashionable woman of the 1780s:

> The snowy Veil, in soft disorder thrown,
> The bosom, rising from the loosen'd zone,
> And limbs, by golden muslin ill conceal'd,
> Whose clinging folds their perfect form reveal'd.[92]

(Muslin, a fine-woven cotton fabric, derives its name from the Arabic word for the city of Mosul; expensive muslins were generally imported in the 1780s.) Seward thus displaces onto Emira the female sexuality of her literary models, the Ovidian epistle and Pope's "Eloisa to Abelard." Louisa writes of her feelings to a female friend "exil'd" to the East Indies, but Emira is not allowed to voice her subjectivity in any of the poem's epistles.[93] Emira bears Eugenio a child but is unmaternal. She commits adultery with a libertine lord and dies of a fever, but not before beseeching

Louisa to marry Eugenio and care for her child. Emira's sordid eastern wealth thus passes into ostensibly pure British hands.

BROOKE'S ROSINA

Opera is a form of late eighteenth-century romance too often neglected by literary historians. After 1700, the verse romance of Dryden's heroic dramas appears in opera. Handel's London Italian operas – *Guilio Cesare* (1724), *Rodelinda* (1725), and *Ariodante* (1735), for instance – are romances. *Guilio Cesare*, indeed, does exactly what the seventeenth-century romances complained of in *The Female Quixote* do: it combines historical characters with invented episodes. In the later period we are now considering, important Italian opera was again being performed at the King's Theatre and the elite theatre-going public was again in raptures over Italian singers, as is memorably documented by the Burneys. As I mentioned, between 1773 and 1778 Brooke was one of the managers of the King's Theatre, where Italian operas were produced. Her tragedy, *The Siege of Sinope*, presented at Covent Garden in 1781, is based on Giusseppi Sarti's Italian libretto for *Mitridate a Sinope*, first produced in Florence in 1779.[94] In the last quarter of the eighteenth century, of the twelve most performed main pieces, six were operas, and of the nine most popular afterpieces, all were operas.

Metastasio's twenty-seven poetic and moral librettos for *opera seria* were set again and again by composers all over Europe, including Pietro Alessandro Guglielmi in *L'Olimpiade* (1763, but in the Theatre Royal repertory in the 1780s) and Mozart in the great *La Clemenza di Tito* (1791). More's version of Metastasio's *Attilo Regulo, The Inflexible Captive*, discussed in chapter six, is one among many tributes to Metastasio's moral dramas in which nobly born characters triumph over passion and uphold their moral visions against the challenges of morally weaker characters. Although women were attracted to the romance and morality of the Metastasian formulas, they were not notably successful in producing good literary works based on them. It would have taken a very gifted poet to produce a great verse drama based on a Metastasio libretto; neither More nor Brooke were great poets in the higher registers.

On the other hand, Brooke had a remarkable success with the related but less exalted form of the pastoral romance opera in *Rosina* (1782). *Rosina* is cousin to Rousseau's *Le Devin du village* (1752), an experiment in producing a French "intermede" in the spirit of the new Italian comic opera; Charles Burney adapted it as *The Cunning Man* (1766). Comic opera had become popular in England with Thomas Arne and Isaac Bickerstaff's *Thomas and Sally, or, the Sailor's Return* (1760) and *Love in a Village* (1762), but Brooke's immediate source for *Rosina* was French, Charles-Simon Favart's *Les Moissonneurs* (1770).[95] Although Favart was most famous for his *opéra comique* libretti, he also worked in the sentimental mode derived from Diderot's *drame* and developed in Marmontel's moral fables. According to the *London Stage's* calculations of the popularity of afterpieces between 1776 and 1800, *Rosina*, performed 201 times, was second only to Milton's *Comus* (as adapted and performed with Arne's music). It was still popular in the English-speaking world in the nineteenth century; Edgar Allen Poe's mother appeared in it in America.

Thanks in part to effective use of scene and music, *Rosina* has the charm essential to good pastoral romance. Rosina, who has been orphaned and lost her fortune, lives in a northern village in a cottage with an old woman, her foster mother. She is innocent and content to support herself and her aged foster mother by gleaning in the fields, though she cannot help sighing with fondness for the local benevolent squire, Mr. Belville. In keeping with this period's increased interest in setting and landscape, very specific stage directions call for a cottage to be set next to a little hill, with a spring of water rushing from the side and falling "into a natural basin below." The action takes place over twenty-four hours, beginning at dawn, with the light "imperceptibly" changing: "In the first act the sky clears by degrees, the morning vapour disperses, the sun rises, and at the end of the first act is above the horizon . . ." In the second act, the sun progressively declines.[96] We see Rosina gleaning in the wake of a jolly chorus of rustic reapers who sing:

> As we reap the golden corn,
> Laughing Plenty fills her horn.
> What would gilded pomp avail
> Should the peasant's labour fail?[97]

In *Rosina* the idealization of the English countryside common in the poetry of this period is reinforced by visual spectacle and by music.

Brooke collaborated on the song texts with her friend the Reverend Richard Gifford; the music, composed by William Shield, was a pastiche of songs from Italian operas, Scots songs and ballads, and original melodies. Shield was a member of the King's Theatre orchestra and learned to orchestrate from playing the operas of Antonio Sacchini and Giovanni Paisiello, so the music is closer to that of Italian opera than one might expect by imagining *The Beggar's Opera* or Arne's *Love in a Village* as a norm. (Paisiello was court composer to Catherine the Great in 1782 when he composed his famous comic opera, *Il barbiere de Siviglia*.)

Mr. Belville acts with special kindness toward Rosina, but has a predatory brother, Captain Belville who tries – ineffectually, of course – to seduce her. When the Captain offers to make it possible for her to spend her days in idleness, Rosina replies, "I only wish for so much leisure as makes me return to my work with fresh spirit." When he presses "charity" upon her, she tells him to give to the aged woman instead. As he demurs, she raises a laugh at his expense by remarking, "I understand you, Sir; your compassion does not extend to *old* women."[98] In a nice pastoral moment, the bashful Rosina spies Mr. Belville asleep in a grove, approaches to shade him from the sun by tying two branches together with a ribbon drawn from her bosom, then flees as he awakes. The Captain has Rosina abducted by a gang of men led by his French valet, but she is rescued by brave Irish reapers laying about with their "shilelays." The abashed and repentant Captain is rebuked by his brother, who tells him, "You have dishonor'd me, dishonor'd the glorious profession you have embraced."[99] He offers to marry Rosina, but Rosina – who turns out to be a Colonel's daughter – is to marry Mr. Belville, signing her assent not with words but with tender glances and blushes.

As Brooke observed, English taste was less purely sentimental than the French, so she adds more to a comic rustic subplot – although she certainly does not reach the potentially revolutionary "low" view that was to explode out of comedy and comic opera in Beaumarchais's *Le Marriage de Figaro* (1784) and Mozart's *Le nozze di Figaro* (1784). Brooke's low rustics, like Rousseau, celebrate the superior virtues of simple country living over the decadent opulence of the city. William reassures Phoebe of his love by singing:

> See high-born dames, in rooms of state,
>   With midnight revels pale;
> No youth admires their fading charms,
>   For beauty's in the vale.[100]

He offers appropriately humble versions of pastoral simile: "Do I love thee? Do I love dancing on the green better than threshing in the barn? Do I love a wake, or a harvest-home?"[101] It is a nice and generous touch when the Irish guest workers, at first condescended to as lazy by their English brethren, turn out to be the brave rescuers of Rosina and are awarded the purse of gold with which the Captain tried to seduce Rosina.

Like the plot, mingling the genteel sentimental with the humble rustic, the music also mingles *galant* Italian-style songs with British folk music. Shield's overture ends with "a tune he orchestrated to suggest bag-pipes."[102] One of the Scottish tunes he orchestrated became widely known as a tune from *Rosina*, but now we know it as the melody of "Auld lang syne."

CHARLOTTE SMITH'S *ELEGIAC SONNETS*: FROM ROMANCE TO ROMANTICISM

The most important volume of women's poems of this period, Charlotte Smith's *Elegiac Sonnets* (1784, Chichester and London; 5th expanded edition London, 1789), yields insight into how earlier romance and sensibility became what we now recognize as "romantic." It is also useful to consider the relation of these sonnets, famously praised by Wordsworth for their "true feeling for rural nature," to earlier pastoral. Although Smith's volumes have a small number of panegyrics, an "Ode to Despair," a translation of a French *carpe diem* poem, a translation of a Metastasio poem, and a 123-line poem on "The Origin of Flattery," most poems are original sonnets whose speakers are melancholy or anguished. *Elegiac Sonnets* thus differs from the more miscellaneous volumes of *Poems on Several Occasions* typical of earlier periods, making a more focused and stronger impression of a single affect. In the 1789 volume Smith translates four Petrarch sonnets that give voice to the torments of a male lover; she imagines five original sonnets as spoken by Werther, the suicidal protag-onist of Goethe's *The Sorrows of Young Werther* (1774). Smith's most characteristic sonnets, however, the majority of the poems, present a sorrowing female poet in a carefully realized English landscape, indeed, in a Sussex landscape featuring the South Downs and the River Arun. This landscape is often seen at twilight or at night by moonlight and in autumn as well as spring. The poet invokes the contemporary city and the world of commerce only as contrast to this more valued rural world, explicitly called "romantic" in "To the River Arun":

> Be the proud Thames, of trade the busy mart!
>   Arun! to thee will other praise belong;
> Dear to the lover's, and the mourner's heart,
>   And ever sacred to the sons of song!
>
> Thy banks romantic, hopeless Love shall seek,
>   Where o'er the rocks the mantling bindwith flaunts,

And Sorrows drooping form and faded cheek,
Choose on thy willow'd shore her lonely haunts![103]

Smith subtly orchestrates a blend of tones from traditional pastoral, from eighteenth-century graveyard and loco-descriptive poetry, and from more prosaic natural history, all compressed into sonnets. As some early eighteenth-century pastoral theorists had urged, and as we saw Egerton do (probably unbeknownst to Smith), Smith makes her nature firmly English. The willows and riverbanks in "To the River Arun" were well established in classical pastoral, but *Elegiac Sonnets* provides a botanical gloss for the more novel "bindwith": "The plant Clematis, Bindwith, Virgin's Bower or Traveller's Joy . . . towards the end of June begins to cover the hedges and sides of rocky hollows, with its beautiful folliage, and flowers of a yellowish white of an agreeable fragrance . . ."[104] Such native, realistic images do not challenge but instead are assimilated into a decorous poetic world, one in which personifications like "Love" and "Sorrow" may be found, and one described in an English diction ultimately descended from Milton through Gray.

With equal subtlety, Smith discovered ways to make the apparently contemporary romantic. The older convention figured the scene of romance as long ago and far away. Thus, Tasso's sixteenth-century *Jerusalem Delivered* is set at the end of the eleventh century in the Holy Land. Cowley's long blank verse narrative, *The Maid of Arragon. A Tale* (1780), exemplifies this understanding of romance, choosing Spain in the time of the Crusades as a setting for its heroine, Osmida. At first glance, Smith's sonnets, some of which, like "Sonnet 31. Written on Farm Wood, South Downs, in May 1784," have contemporary dates and English place names in their titles, seem strikingly lacking in these characteristics of romance. Yet the poems develop a sharp contrast between an idealized past time, that of the poet's childhood when she lived in happy enjoyment of this local nature, and the more realistic present time of the melancholy, suffering speaker, now irrevocably severed from that happiness. Smith thus personalizes the abstract nostalgia for distant childhood of Gray's "Ode on a Distant Prospect of Eton College" (1747), one of several Gray poems that influenced her profoundly. This reverence for childhood links the sentimental with later Romanticism; childhood itself becomes the long ago and far away. Probably the increasingly historicized consciousness of the late eighteenth century and the sense of gentry-identified readers like Smith that an older order was under attack by increasingly self-confident commercial sectors of society contributed to readers' accepting that the relatively few years between childhood and adulthood might constitute significant time.

In classical, Renaissance, and neoclassical pastoral, the poet conceals himself or herself in the character of the shepherd. In Smith's transformation of pastoral, in contrast, the lyric speaker and the occasional shepherd in the landscape are antithetical; the shepherd is figured as insensible, incapable of the poet's suffering:

> Blest is yon shepherd, on the turf reclin'd,
>   Who on the varied clouds which float above
> Lies idly gazing – while his vacant mind
>   Pours out some antique tale of rural love!
> Ah! *he* has never felt the pangs . . .[105]

Similarly, the "hind" in Sonnet 31, "All his hours / To wholesome labour given, or thoughtless mirth," is capable of enjoying spring, whereas the speaker, burdened by "sorrow past" and "coming dread" cannot:

> Ah! what to me can those dear days restore,
> When scenes could charm, that now I taste no more![106]

Also in classical, Renaissance, and neoclassical pastoral, the ideal harmony of shepherd and nature produces the pathetic fallacy. Pope's Hylas, for example, laments his absent Delia in "Autumn. The Third Pastoral": "For her, the Lillies hang their heads and dye." Typically in Smith's sonnets, as is not the case in earlier pastoral, neither shepherds nor landscape are capable of expressing the poet's feeling. Instead, reversing the pathetic fallacy, the natural scene the poet observes sharply contrasts with her psychological state. Here she has taken a hint from Gray's only sonnet, the fine "Sonnet on the Death of Mr. Richard West," beginning, "In vain to me the smiling mornings shine . . ." (1775) and perhaps from William Cowper's "The Shrubbery. Written in a Time of Affliction" (1782).

Smith inventively constructs the turns in several of her best sonnets around such contrasts, thus heightening the pathos of the speaker's solitary, suffering isolation, at the same time using the inexpressibility topos to insist on the intensity of that suffering. "Sonnet 2. Written at the Close of Spring" in the octet paints a fetching picture of spring flowers just disappearing:

> Till Spring again shall call forth every bell,
>   And dress with humid hands her wreaths again.–

The sestet, though, laments a human happiness that has "no second Spring."[107] "To the South Downs" describes the "beechen shade" of the South Downs and the "limpid waves" of the Arun, only to ask if the hills can "soothe the sense of pain" or the river bestow a "kind Lethean cup," despondently concluding:

> Ah! no! – when all, e'en Hope's last ray is gone,
> There's no oblivion – but in death alone.[108]

"Sonnet 44. Written in the Church Yard at Middleton in Sussex" conjures up an arresting and moonlit scene of bodies of the village dead torn from their seaside graves by an ocean storm:

> With shells and sea-weed mingled, on the shore
> Lo! their bones whiten in the frequent wave . . .

Yet even this image of desolation and misery will not suffice as an objective correlative for this speaker's suffering. Her response is to envy the dead:

> But vain to them the winds and waters rave;
> *They* hear the warring elements no more:
> While I am doom'd – by life's long storm opprest,
> To gaze with envy, on their gloomy rest.[109]

The poetic logic here anticipates that of Cowper's affecting "The Castaway," only posthumously published in 1803, made famous in the twentieth century by the repetition in Virginia Woolf's *To the Lighthouse* of Cowper's lines, "But I beneath a rougher sea / Am whelmed in deeper gulphs than he."

Elegiac Sonnets withholds explanation of what has caused the speaker's suffering. Caroll Fry has suggested that Smith knew perfectly well that the conventional subject of a sonnet sequence was romantic love, yet because this was a topic forbidden to her as a woman she substituted the theme of hopeless melancholy.[110] In the earlier sonnets, two things offer at least transient relief from despair: the friendship of a few named women and thoughts of poetry itself, sometimes through contemplation of two other suffering poets associated with the Arun, Collins and Thomas Otway, occasionally through the knowledge that her own poetry has won praise. In Sonnet 36, however, the speaker declares that even these have failed, leaving no refuge from misery but death, "that tranquil shore, / Where the pale spectre Care, pursues no more."[111] In the 1789 volume, illustrated with engravings on which Smith consulted, this sonnet is highlighted by an accompanying image of "sickening Fancy," who has laid her "pencil" on the ground, and "weary Hope," reclining on a tomb.

SOME CONCLUSIONS ABOUT ROMANCE

Even in the age of sentiment and sensibility a number of women writers resisted efforts to confine them to the allegedly realistic claustrophobic sphere of modern domesticity. More ends her poem on slavery with a vision of Mercy coming to Africa to breathe manumission. Mercy causes the chains and fetters to drop from the captives and proclaims the Africans' land, labor, and loves from henceforth their own, safe from plunder. Walker uses utopian romance to imagine a transformation of national culture. A move back in time or to a remote place could authorize the representation of grander passions and stranger visions, as it does in More's *Percy* and as it increasingly was to do in the gothic novel. Concern with remote and exotic places also led to efforts to describe them and to heightened, if often nostalgically tinged, descriptions of English settings in many genres, including poetry, fiction, and comic opera.

One of the stronger forms of this resistance to the confinement of modern domesticity was the invocation of history by Dobson, Reeve, and Walker against emergent literary realism. In contrast to some of the bolder bluestockings of the immediately preceding period, however, the women of 1777–89 tended to be still more socially conservative and more indirect in their resistance. Dobson deploys the authority of Sainte-Palaye, Millot, and Sade to make her case, although she does not scruple to edit them to her advantage. Reeve avoids the direct representation of heroinism in *The Champion of Virtue*, rendering it through Edmund, and in *The Progress of Romance* combines the representation of a woman of wisdom with a complicated series of gestures invoking and resisting male literary authority.

The women writers of this period – especially Smith, Seward, Lee, and Brooke – offered a less rigorous, less ascetic feminism than that of the earlier bluestockings like Scott and Carter who withdrew from heterosexuality. Their versions of feminism, which rewarded suffering but self-respecting women with idealized heterosexual love, had more popular appeal. On the one hand, one rejoices to see their development of female self-respect and a moral and intellectual autonomy partially independent of patriarchal authority. On the other hand, one can see this less ascetic feminism modulating into the annoying nineteenth-century paradigm of the domestic woman as the angel in the house.

II. COMEDY

By 1777 the vogue of pure sentiment had, mercifully, abated. The "laughing comedy" of Oliver Goldsmith and Richard Brinsley Sheridan dominated the stage. Late eighteenth-century theatre audiences much preferred comedy to tragedy, and Thomas Harris, manager of Covent Garden, proved unusually willing to produce new comedies. George Colman, the Elder, playwright and manager of the Haymarket summer theatre from 1777 to 1788, also was unusually hospitable to new plays, both the farces traditionally associated with Haymarket and five-act comedies. During his twelve seasons as manager, William J. Burling points out, Colman "mounted more new plays than all of his summer managerial predecessors combined for the previous century."[112] He extended the summer season and initiated daily performances during the season. In Burling's view, Colman's infusion of "creative energy . . . elevated the little Haymarket to the *same* level as the patent theaters as a viable venue for new playwrights."[113] As it had to Behn and Centlivre earlier, stage comedy continued to appeal to women writers looking for income and reputation. Cowley, Lee, and Inchbald benefited from the willingness of Harris and Colman to deal with new playwrights and new work. Cowley began her long career with *The Runaway* in 1776, the first of thirteen plays, most of them comedies, produced between 1776 and 1795. Cowley's *Runaway* earned her an estimated £500 and her *More Ways than One* yielded profits to her of £485. Lee's profit from *The Chapter of Accidents* was sufficient to allow her to establish a girl's school at Bath, a school that provided her main source of income between 1781 and 1803. Inchbald's *Such Things Are* earned her £601.[114]

In this period women comic dramatists were generally concerned both to make their audiences laugh and to maintain their own reputations as decent ladies. Sentimental comedy was more easily congruent with the persona of a delicate lady than laughing comedy. Significantly, Burney, whose diaries and novels reveal a sharp satiric observer, at first welcomed Sheridan's invitation to write a comedy, but then, having written "The Witlings" in 1779, acquiesced in suppressing it. Indeed, one of the main themes of Burney's writing is the tension between an acute and observant intelligence, capable of being amused at the follies of the world, and the decorums of femininity, which appear to her to require prodigious degrees of female silence and a female consciousness incapable of harboring critical thought. Cowley also felt constrained by feminine decorums, although she usually managed to negotiate these treacherous shoals quite nicely. Cowley and Inchbald were both freer of the inhibitions of genteel ladyism than Burney; both had the advantage of having been married (and so were not constrained to conform to maiden decorums). Inchbald was amazingly able to retain her satisfaction with her low middling social rank, and a certain plain-spokenness that permitted, all the while enjoying the access to the clever and the great that her literary success afforded her. As another caution against being too deeply impressed with the repressive power of conduct-book-like feminine inhibitions in the women of the 1770s and 1780s, it is worth noting that both Inchbald and the venerated Sarah Siddons played Hamlet in breeches in this period.

Hannah More had a talent for comic verse, evident in "Bas Bleu," her tribute to the bluestockings, although as her commitment to Evangelical Christianity strengthened during the 1780s, she relinquished the pleasures of theatre and those of comedy; after 1789 she wrote no more plays and no more comic verse. Some of the minor women poets of the late eighteenth century still liked the kind of occasional comic verse Lady Mary Wortley Montagu and Mary Barber wrote. Amidst more earnest offerings in Mrs. Savage's *Poems on Various Subjects and Occasions* (2 volumes, 1777), for instance, we find "Nothing New," Hudibrastics mocking sentimental and emerging gothic clichés, "The Reason why Cuckolds go to Heaven," a comic narrative in anapestic tetrameter couplets; and a fabliau-like " The Living Reading Desk, From a Verbal Translation of a French Tale." The living desk is a naughty boy of olden times, the seat of whose breeches is repaired with a piece of parchment from a missal; monks try to sing a mass from his "bum" but cannot finish because he gets stung by a wasp and runs away. In fiction, Burney's *Evelina, or a Young Lady's Entrance into the World* (1778) significantly disrupted the tearful sentimentality of the mainline of women's fiction of the 1760s and 1770s, delighting critics and readers alike with a cornucopia of sharply observed comic characters.

Burney, Cowley, and Inchbald catch the "vulgar" speech of ungenteel middling sorts of people, some of them aspiring to gentility. They often juxtapose this more energetic and vivid language against what can sound like the enervated language of the genteel. All three have good ears for many new, intriguing fashions in language. In an age when obsession with fashion extended to fashions in language, as these comic writers see, the quest of sensibility for sincerity could be challenging indeed.

Sophia Lee's deservedly popular and controversial comedy, *The Chapter of Accidents* (1780), invented an appealing mix of comedy and sentiment, emphasizing progressive sentiment. Colman's prologue reports that sentiment is under critical attack, but defends sentiment as flowing from "genuine *feelings*" and nature, and congratulates Lee on creating a viable comic formula:

> Smiling in tears – a serio-comic play –
> Sunshine and show'r – a kind of April-Day![115]

What made Lee's play controversial in 1780 was its premise: the heroine, Cecilia Harcourt, "possesses ev'ry virtue" but chastity.[116] Lee thus questions the traditional assumption of romance that heroines must be chaste. As Richard Cumberland had done in making despised types like the West Indian and the Irishman heroes of his sentimental comedy, so Lee appeals for sympathy for her fallen woman. She takes a hint from one of Marmontel's *Moral Tales*, "Laurette," in which the Count de Luzy seduces a graceful peasant girl but then marries her. Before the play begins, Cecilia has allowed herself to be seduced by the sentimental hero, Frank Woodville. She laments: "My sensibility first ruined my virtue, and then my repose." Woodville, however, far from being a libertine, is a man of sensibility who genuinely fell in love with a girl he mistakenly thought was merely "a lovely country maid," not a gentlewoman. Indeed, when he was falling in love with Cecilia he felt himself to be a lover in a pastoral romance: thinking "romances the only true histories; all the toilsome glories recorded by Livy, phantoms of pleasure, compared with the mild enjoyments described by Sir Philip Sydney . . ."[117]

Some suspense is created in *The Chapter of Accidents* by an early dispute between Lord Glenmore, father of the hero and a man of sensibility, and Lord Glenmore's curmudgeonly brother-in-law, Governor Harcourt, recently returned from India, on what system of education is best designed to produce virtuous young people. The modern Lord Glenmore insists that young people need freedom, an opportunity to experience the world, and to cultivate "that innocent elegance, which renders ev'ry rank easy, and prevents pleasure from seducing the heart, or ignorance the senses."[118] Old-fashioned Governor Harcourt is so convinced that only rural retirement can breed virtue that he has had his daughter, ignorant of who she is, brought up in Wales by a poor curate and his wife. Harcourt plans to marry this daughter to his nephew and to bestow his fortune on the couple. Lord Glenmore demurs: "I . . . am far from wishing the chief accomplishments of Woodville's Lady should be making *cream cheeses*, *goats whey*, and *alder wine*." Harcourt retorts that "women were never better than when those *were* their chief accomplishments"; he shocks his brother-in-law with the revelation that his son is keeping a mistress whom he intends to marry.[119] It does not take the spectator long to guess that Frank's mistress will turn out to be Harcourt's daughter.

Insisting that despite her lapse of chastity Cecilia nevertheless possesses virtue, Lee organizes the action of the play as a series of tests of that virtue, as is usual in romance. One test is contrived by a friend of the hero's, who falsely tells Cecilia that Woodville is going to marry another woman, but that a rich nobleman is eager to take her into keeping. Cecilia's indignant rejection of this sordid proposal, her tears, and her air of injured delicacy convince the friend of her virtue and prompt him to offer her a safe asylum. In a more challenging test, despite Woodville's willingness to marry her, the repentant Cecilia vows not to injure Woodville by marrying him. She vows never to accept him without "the joint consent of both our fathers" and declares she considers that "an eternal abjuration . . ."[120]

Another test, in which Lord Glenmore and Governor Harcourt undertake to visit Cecilia in her lodgings to ascertain her character, goes comically amuck when they encounter not Cecilia, but Bridget, her country-bred maid who has dressed herself in Cecilia's clothes and talks enthusiastically, if ungrammatically, about the pleasures of the town. Appalled at her vulgarity, they decide to shut her up in a room above Lord Glenmore's stable to keep her away from Woodville. When the asylum provided for the real Cecilia turns out to be Lord Glenville's house, he promptly falls in love with the melancholy, fainting, stranger, exclaiming: "Tears were her only answers to my questions, and blushes to my looks, yet those only heighten a curiosity they have softened into love."[121] Final revelations clear all confusion and leave both fathers blessing the union of their wayward children. Cecilia's foster-father, the virtuous curate, has come in search of her, like Goldsmith's Parson Primrose after his lost Olivia; he ends the play claiming that her return to virtue after a lapse is a more heroic virtue than simple chastity could be.[122]

The Chapter of Accidents performs the progressive political work characteristic of the sentimental project. Just as Cumberland's sentimental plays attack hostile stereotypical views of Irishmen and Jews that understand them as less than fully human, so Lee works to show that a young woman who has had premarital sex may nevertheless be worthy of marriage and a respectable place in society. The boldness of her position is apparent from a hostile review in *The Westminster Magazine*. Their reviewer found that Lee's originality had violated both social norms and generic norms. Although he professed approval of "the author's motive for attempting to gloss over the most venial of all frailties," he insisted that "the characters of frail women cannot be the principal subject of comedy, consistent with the general apprehensions of decency."[123] Yet Lee succeeded in overturning this convention.

Lee and Inchbald were skilled in inventing scenes that suited the new acting styles of the period. This theatrical style sought to engage the feelings of the audience by offering displays of emotion flooding through the characters. Lee's script offers stage directions for affecting tableaus. For example, Cecilia "bursts into tears, and sinks into a chair, without minding Harcourt, who watches her with irresolution."[124] It was an age of performers, and, in Cecilia, Lee created one key role that made Elizabeth Farren a great star.

COWLEY'S COMEDY

Turning more firmly away from sentiment than Lee, Hannah Cowley followed the example of Centlivre, becoming a very successful author of comedies featuring lively, resourceful heroines. Her best comedies were *Who's the Dupe?* (1779, a farce), *The Belle's Stratagem* (1780), *Which is the Man?* (1782), and *A Bold Stroke for a Husband* (1783). *Who's the Dupe?* adapted one of the plots of Centlivre's *Stolen Heiress; A Bold Stroke for a Husband* took its hint from Centlivre's *Bold Stroke for a Wife* (1718), but made the ingenious wooer the woman instead of the man. *Who's the Dupe?* was performed 126 times in twenty-two seasons between 1779 and 1800, then continued to be performed and anthologized in the nineteenth century. Similarly, *The Belle's Stratagem* was performed 118 times in London between 1780 and 1800; it ranked fourth in number of performances between 1776 and 1800 among mainpieces written in this period and eleventh among the most popular mainpieces (by women or men, no matter when originally written).[125]

Cowley's comedy – even her farce – breathes the gentle, sympathetic spirit of the age of Goldsmith and Sheridan, although, like Goldsmith and Sheridan, she aligns herself with what Goldsmith called "laughing comedy," rather than with sentimental comedy. Like Goldsmith and Sheridan, she often allows her comic characters, even some of the ridiculous ones, a degree of self-awareness that makes them partially sympathetic. As her willingness to write farce as well as five-act comedies suggests, Cowley was even more ready than Goldsmith or Sheridan to venture into the realms of the "low" or "vulgar" so ruthlessly banished from works of sentiment. Not fully genteel herself, Cowley joins enthusiastically in the late-eighteenth-century critique of the uselessness of the aristocracy and expresses sympathy for the points of view of those who work. She had a talent for rendering a great variety of different kinds of speech and used that talent to excellent dramatic effect.

COWLEY'S *WHO'S THE DUPE?*

Who's the Dupe? displays one of the vulgar entrepreneurs whose efforts amassed a fortune in trade and money lending, despite his being "bred . . . in a Charity-school."[126] Deprived of learning himself, old Abraham Doily decides that his daughter Elizabeth, upon whom he dotes, must marry a scholar. He scorns empty-headed men of fashion, declaring vigorously, "Oh! before I'd give my gains to one of these puppies, I'd spend 'em all in building hospitals for lazy Lacquies and decay'd Pimps."[127] Elizabeth, however, is secretly in love with the fashionable Captain Granger, who is about to be sent out to fight with the army in India; she strategizes to defeat her father's plan. The scholar, Gradus, dutifully comes down from the University to commence his awkward wooing. Elizabeth tells Gradus that she will not listen to him until he abandons his grave, oratorical manner and turns himself into a fashionable gentleman. Gradus does his best to comply, albeit with relapses into learned allusion. Doily, adamantly opposed to fashionable "Puppies," is appalled at Gradus's transformation and willing to consider a rival, supposedly another scholar but actually Granger, solemnly dressed in black. Doily demands the two compete for Elizabeth's hand by demonstrating their learning for him; Gradus offers a nice Greek epigram, Granger utters learned gibberish worthy of Molière and wins. As Elizabeth promised Granger at the beginning, "if you'll be guided by me, my father shall give me to you at St. James's Church, in the face of the world."[128]

The father's desire must be and is defeated, but not before he has been allowed to score points at the expense of useless men of fashion whose gaming debts have driven them to borrow money from him. In a moment of comic pathos, he confides that he thinks his lack of learning caused his humiliation at a local meeting when he tried three times to give a little speech, failed, and was forever after laughed at and nick-named "Dummy, through the whole Ward."[129]

Cowley has the dramatist's skill of creating sympathy for contradictory positions; she uses this skill to expose how highly contested "femininity" was in this period. New opportunities for women to learn and to partake in public cultural pleasures like the theatre and the opera may have contributed to a conservative backlash, provoking the construction of sentimental femininity, particularly its emphasis on modesty, weakness, and privacy. Cowley makes fine comedy by playing with some of the contradictions and absurdities of contemporary ideas about what women are and ought to be. One feels the impact of the burgeoning literature about ideal femininity. Older, unsentimental, ideas of women's nature as best suited to practical "huswifery" still had considerable force, as Lee's General Harcourt's plan of having Cecilia brought up simply in Wales suggests. Indeed, the frivolity of the new fashionable, consumption-oriented femininity reinvigorated these older ideas as commonsensical and moral correctives to fashionable excesses. However, the new, senti-mentalized femininity of modesty, delicacy, and restriction to a private sphere was gaining ground. Various versions of this sentimental feminin-ity had been advocated by Rousseau in *Émile* (1762), James Fordyce in *Sermons to Young Women* (1765), and John Gregory in *A Father's Legacy to his Daughters* (1774). Women writers of conduct books in this period replied to and revised male versions of sentimental femininity, yet repro-duced its main outlines. This is true of More's *Essays on Various Subjects, Principally Designed for Young Ladies*, Griffith's *Essays Addressed to Young Married Women* (1782), and Wollstonecraft's *Thoughts on the Education of Daughters with Reflections on Female Conduct in the more important Duties of Life* (1787). Donna Victoria in Cowley's *A Bold Stroke for a Husband*, masquerading as a man to woo her husband's mistress, remarks that she has succeeded by *not* following the advice of "*Essayists* on the female heart."[130]

Cowley's characters confront one another with these contesting con-structions of femininity, often in language that begins as something that might be unremarkable in a contemporary conduct book. Frequently they present their positions so hyperbolically that the spectator has to laugh, not necessarily unsympathetically, yet can locate no alternative construc-tion that seems securely satisfactory. Cowley's adroit use of comic disguise and her excellent ear for fashions in speech reinforce a spectator's sense of how performative and how labile feminine identities may be.

In the broad comedy of *Who's the Dupe?*, characters' statements about what women know and are achieve a kind of dramatic irony. Gradus ineptly compliments Elizabeth by telling her he is happier to meet her than he would be to meet even Graevius, Gronovius, or the elder Scaliger, all famous scholars. Elizabeth replies politely, "I believe all you have said to be very fine, Sir; but, unfortunately, I don't know the Gentlemen you mention. The education given to Women shuts us entirely from such refined acquaintance."[131] Her apparently obvious remark about what women know is undercut by the fact that a woman playwright has written Gradus's part for him and put his learned allusions in his mouth. Gradus's efforts to recover quickly lead him to a position that seems absurdly archaic and useless as a standard for contemporary women: "The more simple your education, the nearer you approach the pure manners of the purest ages. The charms of Women were never more powerful – never inspired such achievements, as in those immortal periods, when they could neither read nor write."[132] Cowley knows her London audience of 1779 does not seriously expect upper-class Englishwomen to return to spinning, as Doily would like, yet she also knows that there is enough worry about the dangers of luxury, the possible parallels between Roman luxury and loss of empire and British luxury and the threat of losing British colonies, to give Gradus's vision of republican female virtue some appeal: "Ah! – it was at the Loom, and the Spinning-wheel, that the Lucretias and Portias of the world imbibed their virtue; that the Mothers of the Gracchi, the Horatii, the Antonines, caught that sacred flame with which they inspired their Sons, and with the milk of their own pure bosoms gave them that fortitude, that magnanimity, which made them Conquerors and Kings."[133] (Cowley, of course, did not know that Abigail Adams was corresponding with John as "Portia," although she might have known that American female patriots, including Adams, were urging a return to home production and taking pledges of "non-importation" in order to preserve their virtuous republic from imperial domination and the contamination of European luxury.)

COWLEY'S *THE BELLE'S STRATAGEM*

Both plots of *The Belle's Stratagem* display conflicts over what kinds of feminine identity are desirable. In the main plot, Doricourt returns from France and is supposed to marry Letitia Hardy, an heiress his family has known since her childhood. At their initial meeting, his indifference so distresses her that, caring for him as she does, she vows never to be his wife until she can touch his heart. Letitia fixes upon a paradoxical strategy: she will appear as a naive, babbling rustic girl (like Congreve's Miss Prue in *Love for Love*) in order to disgust the elegant Doricourt, on the theory, as she explains, that "'tis much easier to convert a sentiment into its opposite, than to transform indifference into tender passion."[134] Doricourt listens in horror to what seems the very "simplicity," "naturalness," "innocency," and lack of "affectation" that so many contemporary moralists claimed they wanted to see in the ideal English women.

LETITIA: Laws Papa, how can you think he can take me for a fool! when every body knows I beat the 'Potecary at Conundrums, last Christmas-time? and didn't I make a string of names, all in riddles, for the Lady's Diary? – There was a little River and a great House – that was Newcastle. – There was what a Lamb says, and three letters, that was *Ba*, and *k-e-r*, ker Baker. There was –[135]

Appalled at the prospect of marriage to a girl who seems a virtual idiot, Doricourt takes another leaf out of Congreve and determines to try to avoid marrying her by feigning madness (as Valentine does in *Love for Love*).

In the subplot of *The Belle's Stratagem*, Mrs. Rackett, a sophisticated London widow, determines to transform Lady Frances Touchwood, a naive new bride just come to London from the country, into a woman of fashion. Mrs. Rackett and Sir George Touchwood, an uxorious but also a jealous husband, articulate dueling definitions of what constitutes a "Fine Lady":

SIR GEORGE: [A fine lady] is seen every where but in her own house. She sleeps at home, but she lives all over the town. In her mind, every sentiment gives place to the Lust of Conquest, and the vanity of being particular. The feelings of Wife, and Mother, are lost in the whirl of dissipation. If she continues virtuous, 'tis by chance, and if she preserves her Husband from ruin, 'Tis by her dexterity at the Card Table!
MRS. RACKETT: . . . Now, Sir, hear my definition of a Fine Lady: – She is a creature for whom Nature has done much, and Education more; she has Taste, Elegance, Spirit, Understanding. In her manner she is free, in her morals nice. Her behaviour is undistinguishingly polite to her Husband and all Mankind; – her sentiments are for their hours of retirement. In a word, a Fine Lady is the life of conversation, the spirit of society, the joy of the public! – Pleasure follows wherever she appears, and the kindest wishes attend her slumbers . . .[136]

Given her name, one might expect Mrs. Rackett to be simply a satiric butt. "Racket," meaning a large and noisy fashionable social gathering, was a new coinage in the second half of the eighteenth-century and was often used disparagingly. Richardson in a *Rambler* essay complains that modern women had given themselves over to dissipation: "now they are too generally given up to Negligence of domestick Business, to idle Amusements, and to wicked Rackets without any settled View at all but of squandering Time."[137] But in *The Belle's Stratagem* the audience is encouraged to agree that Sir George's insistence on confining his wife from society requires, as Mrs. Rackett says, some humbling and that the "Education," "Spirit," and "Conversation" Mrs. Rackett praises and exemplifies do look like desirable female qualities.

In a later comedy, *Which is the Man?* (1783), Cowley makes an intelligent, fashionable widow, fond of rackets and routs, Lady Bell Bloomer, the heroine who chooses which man to marry. Lady Bell even dares to be witty at the expense of English gentlemen, who, she says, have been ruined for conversation:

[English gentlemen] make themselves members of Clubs in the way of business; and Members of Parliament in the way of amusement: all their passions are reserved for the first, all their wit for the last . . . [In Paris] 'tis quite another thing! . . . Devoted to elegance, they catch their opinions, their wit, and their bon mots, from the mouths of the ladies – 'Tis in the drawing-room of Madame, the Dutchess, the Marquis learns his politicks; whilst the sprightly Countess dispenses taste and philosophy to a circle of Bishops, Generals, and Abbés.[138]

COWLEY'S *BOLD STROKE FOR A HUSBAND*

Cowley's appealingly high-spirited and imaginative heroines are unconstrained by sentimentality and its frequently constrictive and depressive effects. Olivia in *A Bold Stroke for a Husband* cleverly foils her father by making the unwanted suitors he produces not want to marry her. Cowley knew very well that female "docility and gentleness," so recommended by conduct-book writers, on the stage or in life, could seem tedious insipidity. (Don Garcia in *A Bold Stroke for a Husband* rings changes on these words.) Olivia cultivates a reputation as a termagant and playfully challenges the relevance of Shakespeare's *Taming of the Shrew*. She claims kinship with Socrates' Xanthippe and reproaches Shakespeare's Kate as not having the spirit "of a roasted chestnut – a few big words, an empty oath, and a scanty dinner, made her as submissive as a spaniel. My fire will not be so soon extinguished."[139] As Behn, Pix, and Centlivre had done earlier, Cowley sets her comedy in Spain in part so that an autocratic Spanish father and threats of being perpetually immured in a convent serve to make the English Protestant audience more sympathetic to a rebellious daughter.

Olivia entertains herself and the audience with pretended compliance with her father's orders; the literalness of her compliance exposes the fact that most men have been so inattentive to women and to their own desires that the rules for female conduct are incoherent and badly designed to elicit desirable female behavior. Thus, when the frustrated father Don Caesar tells his daughter, "you are always charming enough, if you would but hold your tongue," we understand what he is trying to achieve and what one of his models of female excellence is.[140] Almost at once, however, we also realize that society does not really find mute women "charming." Dimly grasping this, Don Caesar thrashes about to produce some polite conversation that his daughter might speak: "*bless me! I hear Lucinda has run away with her footman, and Don Phillip has married his housemaid!,*" he suggests. Pleased with this, he observes, "That's the way agreeable ladies talk . . ."[141] Now we laugh not only because we recognize that his sentences are fair representations of fashionable polite conversation and because they are far from "charming," but also because the father's confusion exposes how little serious attention he has ever paid to what precisely constitutes "charm" in a woman, and, therefore, how incompetent he is to offer rules for female behavior.

Cowley's willingness to use some of the topicality and hyperbole of farce in her five-act comedies gives them a colorfulness and energy that pleasantly contrasts with the frequent dull abstraction of sentimental comedy, as the action between Don Vincentio and Olivia illustrates. Like many fashionable upper-class Englishmen in the 1770s and 1780s, Don Vincentio is devoted to music: he attends concerts, composes plays, and even has his own small orchestra. Olivia says "he ought to be married to a Viol de Gamba."[142] The pretence that the comedy is set in Spain is at its flimsiest when Don Vincentio rattles on about the performers and composers who were then all the rage in London. He adores Gasparo Pacchierotti, the Italian castrato soprano who made his London debut in 1778, of whom Charles Burney wrote, "there was a perfection so exquisite in tone, taste, knowledge, sensibility and expression, that my conceptions in the art could not imagine it possible to be surpassed."[143] His favorites also include Sacchini, an Italian resident in London who composed as many as seventeen operas for the King's Theatre between 1772 and 1781, one of whose airs William Shield used in Brooke's *Rosina*. Charles Burney regarded him as equal to any composer in Europe. When Don Vincentio justifies his musical obsession and his efforts at composition by remarking "A young man of rank shou'd not glide through the world without a distinguish'd rage, or, as they call it in England – a hobby horse!," at least some members of the audience must have thought of the fabulously rich William Beckford, now most remembered as the author of the gothic *Vathek* (1787), but also a celebrity musical connoisseur.[144] Beckford wrote a short opera for his widely talked of coming-of-age party in 1781, then composed the music for another opera, *The Arcadian Pastoral* (1782), libretto by Lady Elizabeth Craven, also given in a much-talked-of private performance. English musical enthusiasts like Beckford or the Burneys, however, were not willing to sacrifice body parts to art, as Don Vincentio apparently is when he declares: "This recreant finger fails me in composing a passage in E, octave: if it does not gain more elastic vigor in a week, I shall be tempted to have it amputated, and supply the shake [i.e., trill] with a spring."[145] Cowley invites us to think of castrati like Pacchierotti who had sacrificed more important body parts for art.

Cowley produces inspired silliness and fun with musical vocabulary in Don Vincentio's speeches. He is so pleased to meet Olivia that he offers an extempore lyric: "her presence thrills me like a cadenza of Pachierotti's, and every nerve vibrates to the music of her looks":

> Her step *andante* gently moves,
>   *Pianos* glance from either eye;
> Oh how *largetto* is the heart,
>   That charms so *forté* can defy![146]

Don Vincentio charms by his enthusiasm and his sweet anticipation of pleasing Olivia through introducing her to the full range of musical delights. The very reverse of a stiff Spanish grandee, who might expect unthinking compliance in a wife, he reacts with pleasure when Olivia agrees with him that a "*mark'd* character" is best and makes her own imaginative suggestions about how the two of them might heighten his eccentricities. His eagerness to please survives even Olivia's devastating response to his promise that their married life will be filled with wonderful concerts. "Concerts!," Olivia replies, "Pardon me there – My passion is a single instrument . . . my nerves are so particularly fine, that more than one instrument overpowers them."[147] Undeterred by this profession of exquisite sensibility, Don Vincentio gamely inquires the identity of her favored instrument, vowing to master it. Only the revelation that she adores the Jew's harp – a small crude instrument, precursor to the harmonica – makes him finally despair.

Women characters in *A Bold Stroke* use acting to get what they want and the play values wit in women. In a more sentimental subplot, Donna Victoria pretends to be a gentleman in order to make love to her husband's mistress. The mistress has got Donna Victoria's husband's property in her hands, so Donna Victoria successfully plots to get it back and makes her husband repent. In the main plot, Don Caesar, frustrated by Olivia's not marrying, decides at sixty-three to get an heir for himself by marrying nineteen-year-old Marcella, a daughter of his friend. Cowley is not squeamish about including a traditional joke about the likelihood of his being cuckolded. But Marcella refuses to "enter in a league with a crass old father against a daughter," writes to Olivia that she will only pretend to acquiesce in the marriage, and helps Olivia.[148] Olivia pretends to be a vixen or anything else that seems strategically useful in order to avoid marriages she dislikes, because she would like to marry Don Julio. Happily, Don Julio thinks too much sweetness in a wife "wou'd be downright maukish": "I like the little acerbities which flow from quick spirits, and a consciousness of power. – One may as well marry a looking-glass as a woman who constantly reflects back one's own sentiments, and one's own whims."[149]

FRANCES BURNEY'S *EVELINA, OR, A YOUNG LADY'S ENTRANCE INTO THE WORLD*

Burney's first, phenomenally successful novel, *Evelina, or, a Young Lady's Entrance into the World* (1778), contrives to find a way to communicate her comic sense of the world without hopelessly compromising her reputation for propriety. Cautiously, Burney published *Evelina* anonymously, keeping the secret of her authorship even from her fond father. She waited to observe the reception, carefully recording in her diary and letters everything she read and heard about it. *The Monthly Review* quickly greeted *Evelina* as "one of the most sprightly, entertaining, and agreeable productions of this kind, which has of late fallen under our notice," praising its "great ease and command of language" and its "great variety of natural incidents, some of the comic stamp."[150] The formidable *Critical Review* virtually admitted the neophyte writer into the canon when it proclaimed that this "amusing and instructive" novel "would have disgraced neither the head nor the heart of Richardson."[151] As the secret leaked out, Burney recorded her experience of being received as a talented writer in a social circle that included Johnson, Reynolds, Burke, and Hester Thrale, famous as Johnson's friend and hostess. Johnson, then sixty-nine and celebrated as the greatest critic in England, alternately lauded and teased Burney, treating her as something between a protégée and a grandchild. Writing to her sister Susanna, Burney described an occasion at the Thrale's house at Streatham in September 1778 when Hester Thrale inquired whether she wanted to meet Elizabeth Montagu. "*Wants*," Burney politely replied, ". . . I had *none* at Streatham, but

I should be the most insensible of all animals, not to *like* to see our sex's Glory."[152] Montagu is duly produced and Thrale turns the conversation to a discussion of *Evelina,* which she urges Montagu to read by reporting that Burke "sat up *all night* to read it." Claiming to find her own situation "inexpressibly awkward," Burney nevertheless recorded every word of the exchange between the two famous *salonnières* about her book:

"And Mr. Johnson, Ma'am, added my kind *Puffer* [Hester Thrale], says *Fielding* never wrote so *well,* – never wrote *equal* to this Book; – he says it is a better picture of Life & manners than is to be found *any* where in Fielding."
    "Indeed?" cried Mrs. Montagu, surprised, "*that* I did not expect, for I have been informed it is the work of a Young lady, – & therefore, though I expected a very pretty Book, I imagined it to be a work of mere Imagination; & the *Name* I thought attractive; – but *Life & manners* I never dreamt of finding."
    "Well, Ma'am, what I tell you is literally true; – & for my part, I am never better pleased than when good Girls write clever Books; – & that *this* is clever – But, all this Time, we are *killing* Miss Burney, who wrote the Book herself!" –[153]

Burney followed Richardson in writing *Evelina* as an epistolary novel, yet her concern is not so much the profound psychological analysis of character and subjectivity of Richardson as the more "objective" portrait of society of a comic novelist like Fielding or Smollett. Only seventeen when she first comes to London, the naive Evelina, brought up in the country by a virtuous clergyman, confronts the awkward facts of her birth. Sir John Belmont, her father, married her mother clandestinely and has refused to acknowledge the marriage or Evelina. Her maternal grandmother, Madame Duval, began life as a tavern maid. Although she comes to London as the guest of the dignified Mrs. Mirvan, Evelina is soon plunged into what is, to her, the excruciatingly vulgar and embarrassing world of her grandmother, Madame Duval, and her relations, the brilliantly rendered Branghton family, proprietors of a silversmith shop. The Branghtons are everything that the genteel, modest Evelina finds horrifying: bold, impertinent, intrusive in their curious questioning, frank about money. Evelina lives in dread that others, especially the elegant Lord Orville, with whom she falls in love, will see her with the Branghtons and think that she belongs among them. Because the comedy and satire are contained within the frame of a sentimental romance plot, although Lord Orville does repeatedly see Evelina in embarrassing, even compromising circumstances, he nevertheless recognizes, even adores, her purity and delicacy. In the end, Lord Orville proposes, her father acknowledges her as his daughter, and all concludes happily.

England in the 1770s and 1780s offered a variety of places of amusement where people of various classes could commingle, so long as they could pay the price of admission; the detailed portraits of such places in Burney's novels are characteristic of the topicality common to journalism, classic comedy, and realist fiction. In *Evelina* the Branghtons eagerly, if awkwardly, avail themselves of these new pleasures, traipsing off, with Evelina, to the little theatre in the Haymarket to see Samuel Foote in his farces *The Minor* and *The Commissary*, to White-Conduit House, the opera, a ball in the long room at Hampstead, a concert and fireworks display at Marylebone Gardens, and Kensington Gardens. On a pleasant June evening they take a boat down the Thames to Vauxhall Gardens, which Evelina finds pretty, if too formal:

The trees, the numerous lights, and the company in the circle around the orchestra made a most brilliant and gay appearance; and, had I been with a party less disagreeable to me, I should have thought it a place formed for animation and pleasure. There was a concert, in the course of which a hautbois concerto was so charmingly played, that I could have thought myself upon enchanted ground, had I spirits more gentle to associate with.[154]

With an acute ear for the social provenance of language and a morbid fascination with "vulgarity," Burney records the Vauxhall conversation of the Branghtons and their slightly better-off lodger, Mr. Smith:

About ten o'clock, Mr. Smith having chosen a *box* in a very conspicuous place, we all went to supper. Much fault was found with every thing that was ordered, though not a morsel of any thing was left; and the dearness of the provisions, with conjectures upon what profit was made by them, supplied discourse during the whole meal.

When wine and cyder were brought, Mr. Smith said, "Now let's enjoy ourselves; now is the time, or never. Well, Ma'am, and how do you like Vauxhall?"

"Like it!" cried young Branghton, "why, how can she help liking it? she has never seen such a place before, that I'll answer for."

"For my part," said Miss Branghton, "I like it because it is not vulgar."

"This must have been a fine treat for you, Miss," said Mr. Branghton; "why, I suppose you was never so happy in all your life before?"[155]

Burney in passages like this anticipates Jane Austen, whom she influenced. She records the malaise and the solecisms in grammar and gentility of the insufficiently genteel and communicates her own distaste for their attitudes, manners, and speech. The reader is invited to sympathize with the delicate Evelina as she squirms under the humiliations of being associated with such people.

At the same time, *Evelina* invites the reader to laugh – quietly – at the ignorance and presumption of characters like these; the reader can do so in part because the structure of the novel affords reasonable assurance that Evelina's sufferings will be temporary. As Evelina occasionally remarks, even in the midst of painful situations, she "could almost have laughed."[156] She does so when Sir Clement Willoughby, the bad baronet, abashes the presuming Mr. Smith, causing him "to lose at once all his happy self-sufficiency and conceit; looking now at the baronet, now at himself; surveying, with sorrowful eyes, his dress . . . he gazed at him with envious admiration, and seemed himself, with conscious inferiority, to shrink into nothing."[157] Unlike Evelina and Lord Orville, the indelicate characters engage in loud laughter themselves. As Ruth Yeazell observed, Burney's allegiance to late eighteenth-century conventions of propriety, coupled with her "immodest desire to look and to laugh," almost drove her to writing, especially to writing in her journal, where she could secretly record for her own delectation (and the delectation of a few trusted confidants) all the absurdities of the people she encountered – without violating the rules that enjoined near silence on modest young women.[158] No doubt her sense of how constricting these rules were for her helped fuel her fascination with the behavior of people like the Branghtons who appeared so perfectly oblivious of them.

Elements of romance remain in Burney's *Evelina*, albeit sometimes rather vestigially and sometimes strangely transformed. Evelina is beautiful and virtuous and she has the romance heroine's power to compel men to admire and desire her. Against his more prudent judgment, Lord Orville proposes marriage before the mysteries of her relations with possible rivals are all resolved and before the cloud of bastardy is lifted from her birth. He kneels to declare, ". . . I revere you! I esteem and I admire you above all human beings!"[159] Although not the marrying sort, the libertine Sir Clement Willoughby pursues Evelina, at last flinging himself at her feet, begging her from henceforth to govern all his actions and to new-model his character. Young Mr. Branghton thinks of Evelina as a suitable wife for himself. The semi-genteel Mr. Smith more politely courts her, as does the better born but foppish Mr. Lovel. Evelina's having multiple admirers has a different effect than the virtual catalogue of smitten men offered by women writers in the early eighteenth century, for example, by Manley in *Rivella* or Martha Sansom in *Clio: or, a Secret History of the Life and Amours of the late celebrated Mrs. S—n—m. Written by Herself. In a Letter to Hillarius* (1752; Sansom died in 1736). Apparently barely aware of her own beauty, and utterly lacking the self-possession of a

Rivella or any consciousness of female power, Evelina finds the attentions of these men, except Lord Orville, annoying, frightening or ludicrous. Burney oscillates between revealing the power of men to terrorize young women and showing even a young woman's capacity for finding patriarchal presumptions absurd.

Readers are presumably supposed to join Lord Orville in finding Evelina admirable because of her earnest wish to be good and her firm repudiation of the low and sordid even when lowness appears to be her natural station, but real readers may be more inclined to like Evelina because of the relish for the ludicrous she shares with her author. As a character, Evelina generally adheres to the decorums that prohibited laughing out loud, decorums that amused Burney the journal writer. At her first ball, the spectacle of the ugly but foppish Mr. Lovel advancing "on tiptoe" toward her "with a kind of negligent impertinence" and the flourish of his hand as he invites her to dance prompt Evelina to laughter that she must turn away to conceal. As a narrator, however, Evelina is free to relish absurdities. At the end of the novel, in one of the passages some critics have found excessively brutal, Mr. Lovel, having condemned himself out of his own misogynistic mouth by pronouncing his "insuperable aversion to strength, either of body or mind, in a female," is condignly punished for his foppishness and his presumption.[160] Captain Mirvan, a sea-captain satirist descended from Manly, the protagonist of Wycherley's *Plain Dealer*, dresses a monkey to resemble Lovel and releases it in the drawing room. Frightened and angry, Lovel strikes the monkey with his cane, provoking the animal to sink its teeth into Lovel's ear. Most of the characters laugh uproariously at this contretemps, although Orville benevolently unfastens the monkey and Evelina piously records her sorrow "for the poor man, who, though an egregious fop, had committed no offence that merited such chastisement."[161] Burney, in inventing such a scene, literalizes her own relation to satire – which, when effective, does bite – and seems to achieve a kind of vicarious revenge on those social rules that encourage pompous male idiots to talk on while clever girls are supposed to keep their mouths shut.

BURNEY'S "THE WITLINGS"

Burney's comedy "The Witlings" (1779) can be painful for a modern feminist to read, but it illuminates how problematic the position of being a public woman writer felt to Burney in the 1770s. The principal satiric target in "The Witlings" is Lady Smatter, an ignorant, unintelligent woman who has set up a literary salon and who fancies herself a critic. Burney's Lady Smatter is presented even less sympathetically than Hugh Kelly's Lady Rachel Mildew, the aging female playwright in *A School for Wives* (1773). Other members of Lady Smatter's salon include Dabler, a talentless male poet, and Mrs. Sapient, another ignorant woman. Dabler lives in lodgings provided by Mrs. Voluble, who prates incessantly, and who prides herself on familiarity with the gentry. Mrs. Sapient utters thoughts so staggeringly banal and tautologous that one is sometimes reminded of Harold Pinter dialogue: "in *my* opinion, to be injudicious is no mark of an extraordinary understanding."[162] Censor, an intelligent man-about-town, observes that she marks her observations "as a Discovery resulting from her own peculiar penetration and Sagacity."[163] Standard proper sentiments, uttered by Mrs. Sapient, become ridiculous simply because she insists that they are her unique views and that she has newly invented them. Thus, she confides that she always wears whatever the milliner sends her: "for I have a kind of maxim upon this Subject which has some weight with *me*, though I don't know if any body else has ever suggested it; but it is, that the real value of a Person Springs from the *mind*, not from the outside appearance."[164]

Burney exploits conventional misogynistic stereotypes of women as incapable of serious learning and as possessed of uncontrollable tongues. Her satire follows earlier portraits of would-be literary women like Kelly's and like Phoebe Clinket in *Three Hours After Marriage* (1717) by Pope, Gay, and Arbuthnot, although even the Scriblerians grant Clinket more energy and antic imagination than Burney grants Lady Smatter. Lady Smatter functions as a blocking character to the match between Beaufort, her nephew and heir, and Cecilia Stanley, a virtuous, quiet, young lady who declines to join the literary club. Lady Smatter yearns to be as public as possible, having apparently no capacity for reflective subjectivity: "if my pursuits were not made public, I should not have any at all, for where can be the pleasure of reading books, and studying authors, if one is not to have the credit of talking of them?" Cecilia, in contrast, modestly prefers privacy: "My pursuits, whatever they may be, are too unimportant to deserve being made public."[165] As is evident from her diary, the young Burney clearly struggled with contradictions between her own desire, on the one hand, to conform, like Cecilia, to the social demands of modest femininity, and, on the other hand, to enjoy the pleasures of articulating, sometimes very publicly, her own satirical observations.

Burney's father Charles and their friend the Reverend Samuel Crisp warned that Lady Smatter would be taken as a portrait of Elizabeth

Montagu and urged Burney to suppress the play, which she did. Hester Thrale wrote in her journal that "none of the scribbling Ladies have a Right to admire [the play's] general Tendency" and thought Lady Smatter might be a portrait of herself.[166] Lady Anna Miller, with her salon at Batheaston encouraging light and occasional verse, might have had still more reason to see Lady Smatter as aimed at her. "The Witlings" was not performed and has only recently been published from the manuscript in the Berg Collection of the New York Public Library.[167] I am inclined to agree with Catherine Gallagher that the men in this instance better grasped what would be best for Frances's literary reputation than she did. It is possible, as Gallagher suggests, that Frances "on first entering the world of the wits, anachronistically associated it with personal satire" and imagined that she might gratify her principal patroness, Hester Thrale, by satirizing a woman who was in some sense her rival, Elizabeth Montagu.[168] As Gallagher argues, Charles Burney understood that the earlier literary economy of patronage which had promoted scandal and lampoon had given way to a different literary economy of booksellers and more diffuse networks of influence that valued politeness and civility. He could also have grasped that misogyny itself was increasingly frowned upon in polite belles lettres, however vigorously it may have held on in other venues.

INCHBALD AND THE THEATRE

Elizabeth Inchbald, farmer's daughter, actress, and playwright, cared about her own reputation for respectability, but was mercifully free from the severe anxieties about gentility that Burney suffered. Following Cowley, Inchbald became an even more prolific and commercially successful playwright. Born in 1752 the daughter of a Suffolk farmer, Elizabeth Simpson could nevertheless be drawn to the theatre because of the greater availability of books and theatres in provincial towns, discussed in chapter five. She grew up reading and reciting from plays in her family reading circle and visiting the theatres in nearby Bury St. Edmunds and Norfolk with her family. At sixteen, she tried, unsuccessfully, to become a member of the Norfolk company; at seventeen, she ran away intending to become an actress, leaving her mother a letter saying "be not uneasy: – believe the step I have taken, however indiscreet, is no ways criminal . . ."[169] Soon Elizabeth married Joseph Inchbald, an actor and painter, and became a member of various provincial touring companies. In 1780, a young widow, she made her debut in London at Covent Garden.

Inchbald's constant presence in the theatre as a professional actor gave her a practical knowledge of acting and stagecraft. Before her own first play premiered, she had acted in the plays of several earlier women dramatists: as Violante in Centlivre's *Wonder*, as Miss Mortimer in Lee's *Chapter of Accidents*, and as Lady Rackett and Lady Touchwood in Cowley's *Belle's Stratagem*, Lady Touchwood being one of her favorite parts. Inchbald met Cowley at a rehearsal when she was cast in Cowley's new farce, *The World as it Goes: or a Party at Montpelier* (1781). Although the two never became close and this particular farce of Cowley's did not succeed, Ellen Donkin seems right to suggest that the younger Inchbald cannot have failed to absorb "the fact of a woman playwright's occupying a legitimate space in the theatre."[170] Ambitious and hardworking, Inchbald used her access to theatre managers to submit her manuscripts and to work collaboratively with them and with other playwrights, actors, and literary friends on revisions. Inchbald seems to have been a better actress than Griffith, but was not as gifted as her close friends Sarah Siddons and John Philip Kemble.

Inchbald understood that playwriting in the 1780s could prove a lucrative profession. Cowley, as I noted earlier, had made over £500 from her first play, *The Runaway*. Prices to authors were generally rising in this period, but, unlike Smith with *Emmeline*, most novelists had to be satisfied with about £10 a volume. Susanna Rowson, for example, earned £30 for the three volumes of her second novel, *The Inquisitor: or, Invisible Rambler* (1788), while both Burney and Anna Maria Cox parted with the copyrights to three-volume novels – *Evelina* (1778) and *Retribution: A Novel* (1785) – for a mere £20.[171]

INCHBALD'S *THE MOGUL TALE; OR, THE DESCENT OF THE BALLOON*

In the summer of 1784, Inchbald's first farce, *The Mogul Tale*, was performed at the Haymarket. Colman paid her 100 guineas, an unusually high price for a two-act farce by an untested author, but the play was a great success and helped give Inchbald bargaining power with the managers for her subsequent work. As she did in much of her comedy, Inchbald took her inspiration for this farce from a contemporary novelty much written about in the newspapers, in this case, from the Montgolfier brothers' hot air balloon that in 1782 had proved capable of flight. Inchbald sends three ordinary English characters up in a new balloon and lands them in the Mogul's seraglio. Anxious about their safety, the Doctor balloonist pretends to be the British Ambassador; his humbler companions, Johnny the Cobbler and his wife Fanny, pretend to be the Pope and a nun.

In *The Mogul Tale* Inchbald turns the stereotypes of savage oriental despotism and western enlightenment topsy-turvy. Her Mogul and his chief eunuch are clever and inventive, the English dim. This Mogul is a philosophical fellow who has kept abreast of European developments; his eunuch has traveled to England. In fact, as contemporary supporters of the East India Company complained, Indian elites were reading newspaper and pamphlet reports of English politicians' attacks on the Company, including Burke's parliamentary speeches, thus undermining English control in India. The Mogul decides to have fun with his invaders, to scare them by conforming to western stereotypes of the Orient. He instructs his eunuch to tell them that he is "the abstract of cruelty, the essence of tyranny."[172] The primary plot of the farce is his: "For tho' I mean to save their lives, I want to see the effects of their fears, for in the hour of reflection I love to contemplate that greatest work of heaven, the mind of man."[173] The English hear of horrible punishments, including racks and being burnt alive or in caldrons of boiling oil; the Doctor is brought handcuffed to a place of execution decorated with a wheel. In a nice use of costume for comic effect, the cobbler's wife is dressed in oriental splendor and invited to join the ladies of the seraglio.

Unlike more fashionable couples, Fanny and Johnny are very fond of one another, low but loving and lovable. In the midst of India's warmth and the splendors of the Mogul's court, Fanny makes us laugh when she reminisces over her days with Johnny in a tiny Wapping room as happier days: with "one child a crying on my knee, and one on yours; my poor old mother shaking with the ague, in one corner of the room – the many happy mornings Johnny that we have got up together shaking with the cold . . ."[174] Her sentimental nostalgia is funny because of the presumed unattractiveness of chilly Wapping poverty, but her affection for her family makes her lovable. Johnny's subsequent lament that her "straw hat and linen gown" have disappeared and his patriotic declaration that "one morsel of British beauty, is worth a whole cargo of outlandish frippery" also suggest the popular idea that anything British must be better than anything Indian – or French, for that matter.[175] The Doctor instructs the Mogul that although the balloon is "a Machine of French invention," it is based on English science, on Boyle's experiments and laws of gases.[176]

In the end, the Mogul's little experiment playing on the fears of the English certainly seems no worse that the Doctor's experiments, which seem to stand for western science more generally. Before letting them go, the Mogul rebukes the English for their lies to him and for the barbarism of the English to the Hindus: "know that I have been taught mercy and compassion for the sufferings of human nature; however differing in laws, temper and colour from myself . . . For, your countrymen's cruelty to the poor Gentoos has shown me tyranny in so foul a light, that I was determined hence forth to be only mild, just and merciful."[177] The Doctor has decoyed the poor cobbler and his wife into this dangerous journey for a mere 5 guineas. Moreover, he has tried to get Johnny to kidnap one of the Indian women of the seraglio to take back with Fanny in the balloon so as to see "which can live longest in the air, the women of this country, or our own," an experiment that envisages the death of at least one of the women.[178] An amused reviewer in *The European Magazine* remarked that the play's "admonitions . . . on India pecularions and cruelties . . . will be nearly as effectual in remedying the evils as the celebrated India Bills of Mr. Fox and Mr. Pitt."[179]

Quickly, Inchbald followed the success of *A Mogul Tale* with a five-act comedy about divorce and remarriage: *I'll Tell You What* (Haymarket, 1785), and two more farces: *Appearance is Against Them* (Covent Garden, 1785) and *The Widow's Vow* (Haymarket, 1786). Like many of the plays of her contemporaries and like several of the ten plays Inchbald wrote between 1784 and 1789, *The Widow's Vow* was adapted from a French source.

INCHBALD'S *SUCH THINGS ARE*

Inchbald's fifth play, *Such Things Are* (1787), one of her best, displays her characteristic mix of laughing comedy, satire, and sentiment. Boaden captured her technique: "Mrs. Inchbald alternates, even mixes her gaity with her pathos; and the tear is scarcely dry, when you are summoned and willing to join in the most irresistible merriment."[180] The action is said to take place in "Sumatra," in the very contemporary East Indies. The characters include a powerful local Sultan; Zedan, an imprisoned native; Elvirus, who is descended from both indigenous people and Europeans; and long-resident and newly arrived English people. "Sumatra" appears to be a place of Asiatic cruelty and arbitrary tyranny. Several scenes are set in the Sultan's prison, where indigenous people and Europeans are confined, some on mere suspicion of being subversive. Zedan complains of a miserable prison diet of "sour rice, and muddy water."[181] Other scenes are set in the Sultan's palace and council chamber. These might seem more appropriate settings for a tragedy or an heroic play than for farce or sentimental comedy, and, as we have seen, in the Restoration and early eighteenth century, Asiatic and eastern settings were typically associated with those genres. Earlier, for example, we considered Manley's *Royal Mischief*, set in Persia; Dryden's heroic drama *Aurung-Zebe* (1676) shows the Mogul empire in India. Inchbald, however, writes at an imperial moment when India has become, in a way, part of Britain's own domestic scene, no longer so exotic, but now a place where members of English families go to live and work. (To look no further than the families of women writers, for instance, Griffith's son Richard went to India and returned by 1784 rich enough and generous enough to enable his mother to retire from writing; Smith in 1786 sent her seventeen-year-old son William to Bengal as a writer in the East India Company; and Cowley's husband went out as an employee of the East India company in 1783, remaining there until he died in 1797.)

A thoughtful spectator at *Such Things Are* might wonder whether he or she is laughing simply at the vices and foibles of those English people who go out to the Indies or laughing also at the vices and foibles that these adventurers have in common with their fellow countrymen who can afford to stay at home. Some of the jokes are clearly targeted at Anglo-Indians, who, everybody knew, would not have risked life and health going to the Indies if they could have afforded to stay at home. Cowardly Sir Luke Tremor is apparently in the Indies because he fled from his regiment in the midst of a battle and was cashiered. His young wife, who he met and married in the Indies, is the daughter of a grocer and the niece of a noted wig maker. Twineall, a new arrival, is a fashionable young gentleman desperate for a place.

Inchbald makes Twineall an incarnation of principles taught in Lord Chesterfield's famous but controversial *Letters . . . to his Son* (1774). Twineall is determined to advance himself by flattery, so he importunes Meanwright for information about everyone's secrets: "for when I once become acquainted with people's dispositions, their little weaknesses, foibles and faults, I can wind, twist, twine, and get into the corner of everyone's heart . . ."[182] Put off by this, Meanright sets up one line of the comedy by misinforming Twineall. He instructs him, for example, that Sir Luke prides himself on his bravery and that Lady Tremor prides herself on her high birth and on an ancient wig worn by her ancestor Malcolm when he was crowned King of Scotland. (The Scots, given the poor economy of Scotland, were vastly overrepresented among the British in far flung outposts.) Duped, Twineall proceeds with his plan of flattery, only comically to discomfit nearly everyone he engages. Twineall's efforts to flatter Lady Tremor about her high birth are doubly funny, first because the audience knows she is ashamed of her grocer and wigmaker progenitors, and second because Twineall's hyperbolic reverence for rank makes such reverence ridiculous. "I wish I may suffer death," Twineall tells pretty Lady Tremor, "if a woman, with all the mental and personal accomplishments of the finest creature in Europe, wou'd to me be of the least value, [*Snapping his fingers.*] if lowly born." Sir Luke, who often has lines that invite the audience to laugh with him as well as at him, remarks: "I sincerely wish every man who visits me were of the same opinion."[183]

Twineall's speech, as hyper-fashionable as his dress, represents an important mode of inarticulacy different from the more obvious inarticulacy of sentimental sighs and tears, but perhaps ultimately deriving from it. He explains the new London mode to his new friends, who have been away from England for many years:

> we have now a new fashion, in England, of speaking without any words at all . . . for instance, when a gentleman is asked a question which is either troublesome or improper to answer, you don't say you *won't* answer it, even tho you speak to an inferior – but you say, "really it appears to me e-e-e-e-[*mutters and shrugs*] – that is – mo-mo-mo-mo-mo-[*mutters*] if you see the thing – for my part – te-te-te-te- that is all I can tell about it at *present!*"[184]

While this may be partly a topical jab at the expense of young Chesterfield, whose indistinct speech and mumbling Lord Chesterfield constantly reprimanded, it also gets at a more general affectation of languorous and muttering speech among fashionable gentlemen of the day. Burney mocks similar patterns in *Cecilia*, where the yawning Mr. Meadows affects apathy to all conversation, answers Cecilia's questions with irrelevant non-sequiturs, or instead of responding looks about, pretending to be lost in thought. These fashionable gentleman are insisting that their birth rank and fashionable clothes should be sufficient to maintain their high social standing and class privilege, that they have no obligation to perform in newer arenas where other kinds of merit clamor for recognition or to engage with any people other than aristocratic men. At the same time, the middling-class women who satirize them sense that the languor fashionable men offer as a sign of ease and entitlement masks a real enervation and despair that the days of their unquestioned privilege are over and masks a cowardly refusal to make a rational case for themselves. Inchbald heightens the comedy of Twineall by having Sir Luke try to draw him into uttering seditious thoughts to be overheard by the Sultan's agents.

Twineall succumbs, uttering words like "suspicious," but never formulates a coherent sentence.[185] He is arrested anyway.

Inchbald's portrait of John Howard, the prison reformer, as Haswell in *Such Things Are* is equally topical but more in the sentimental line. One of the devoted enlightenment reformers of the late eighteenth century, Howard suffered as a prisoner in France after a ship on which he was a passenger was captured by a French privateer in 1756. When he became High Sheriff of Bedfordshire in 1773 he carefully examined the conditions in the county jails and houses of correction. He reported his findings about abuses in *The State of Prisons in England and Wales, with Preliminary Observations and an Account of Some Foreign Prisons* (1777, and later expanded editions) and in testimony before parliamentary committees that led to legislation abolishing some jailer's fees and attempting to improve sanitary conditions. Howard was particularly concerned about the jail fevers that killed many unconvicted prisoners held for trial and many convicted of minor offenses. (He carried on his investigations at great risk to himself, ultimately dying in 1790 of a camp fever in Russia, where he had gone to investigate reports of sickness among the Russian army and where he attended personally to some sufferers.) Inchbald's title, *Such Things Are*, anticipates the titles of radical and reformist plays and Jacobin novels of the 1790s, like Robert Bage's *Man As He Is* (1792) and *Hermsprong, or Man as He is Not* (1796) or her friend Godwin's *Things As They Are; or, the Adventures of Caleb Williams* (1794).

In *Such Things Are* Inchbald drafts existing sentimental conventions into the service of institutional political reform, a crucial tactic for the Jacobin novels of the 1790s, as well as for the abolitionist campaign. Haswell in Sumatra has personally been providing medical care to sick soldiers and charity to their widows and orphans. The Sultan summons him to the palace to offer him a reward. Haswell wishes for justice to all the Sultan's prisoners: "The justice which forbids all but the worst of criminals to be denied that wholesome air the very brute creation freely takes . . ."[186] Touring the Sultan's prison, Haswell has his pocket picked by one of the morose prisoners, Zedan. Zedan resents the misery he endures from "men who spurn me – who treat me as if (in my own Island) I had no friends that loved me – no servants that paid me honour – no children that revered me. – Taskmasters who forget I am a husband – a father – nay, a *man*."[187] Later Haswell responds to Zedan's lament that he is separated from his wife and children by giving him money. This benevolence not only moves Zedan to return Haswell's pocketbook, but to exclaim: "the love of my family was confined to them alone, but this makes me feel I could love even my enemies."[188] Boaden, present at the opening night of *Such Things Are*, described James Fearon as Zedan throwing himself upon his knees before Haswell, holding his heart, and with "a convulsive emotion," returning the pocketbook. Fearon's acting, Boaden reported, struck his speech about love "into every heart" and the applause "never was exceeded in a theatre."[189]

BURNEY'S *CECILIA*

Burney's *Cecilia; or, Memoirs of an Heiress* (1782), though still relying on some sentimental conventions, is the most ambitious and brilliantly successful book of this period. She was able to sell the copyright of its five volumes for £250, according to surviving records apparently the highest price paid for the copyright of any novel of this period.[190] Reviewing it for the *Mercure de France*, Laclos immediately ranked it below only *Clarissa, Tom Jones*, and *Julie, ou la nouvelle Héloïse*.[191]

The sheer length of *Cecilia*, 1,647 pages in the first edition, suggests Burney's more epic ambition. The novel, indeed, can be read as Burney's meditation on cultural norms of heroism and on the possibilities of female heroism. From a classical perspective, according to which epics were to celebrate military prowess and statecraft, an effort to compose an epic with a female hero would inevitably be comic, as Pope knew when he wrote "The Rape of the Lock." By the end of the eighteenth century, however, despite the continuing importance of military heroism to England, writers increasingly attacked older heroic norms as barbaric and cruel and struggled to articulate new norms of greatness, less dependent on physical qualities and physical courage and more dependent on mental, psychological, and moral qualities. Thus, James Boswell in his epic-length *Life of Samuel Johnson* (1784) celebrates the ungainly, bookish writer as a new type of English hero: a man of learning, intellectual strength, piety, and compassion, who has battled and overcome his own psychological demons in order to bring his wisdom and useful moral precepts to mankind. As I suggested in chapter six, these new norms of heroism were more accessible to men of the middling classes than the older aristocratic norms were, and they were more accessible to women. In 1782 Burney is able to write a novel in which heroism is taken seriously, without the need for the kinds of Augustan ironies Pope and Lennox use to deal with their ambivalences about representing "trivial" subjects in "The Rape of the Lock" or *The Female Quixote*.

Cecilia Beverley is a twenty-one-year-old heiress with three guardians as diverse from one another and as at odds with one another as the three guardians in Centlivre's *Bold Stoke for a Wife*. As did sometimes happen in real life, she is to inherit an estate with a provision that, if she marries, her husband must take her name, thus allowing the Beverley family to perpetuate its name in the absence of male heirs. Cecilia falls in love with Mortimer Delville, the only son of one of her guardians, a man possessed of a castle and obsessed with the high rank of his ancient family. The elder Delville nicely illustrates the decayed and useless aristocracy attacked by anti-aristocratic writers of this period; he is adamantly opposed to a marriage in which his son would have to abandon the Delville name.

Burney constructs Cecilia's heroinism in part around her desire to create for herself a life more meaningful than the "frivolous insipidity" of the fashionable men and women she sees about her. On coming to London, Cecilia formulates for herself a "plan of conduct" not too far from the bluestocking agenda. She vows to select only such friends "as by their piety could elevate her mind, by their knowledge improve her understanding, or by their accomplishments and manners delight her affections," as well as to engage in active works of charity to benefit the poor.[192] Events then expose how sharply such a female desire for a worthy life clashes with contemporary manners and with society's expectation for women. In London Cecilia lives with another guardian and his wife, Mr. and Mrs. Harrell, both extravagant and absorbed in the attractions of fashionable assemblies, masquerades, auctions, and the pleasure gardens of Vauxhall. Ignorant of the ways of the world and the depths of unscrupulousness to which a man like Harrell can sink, Cecilia is prevailed upon to devote some of her fortune to the impossible project of staving off his inevitable bankruptcy.

While the realism of the novel prevents Cecilia from accomplishing much in the way of her *Millenium Hall*-like plans, and while the conditions of her life block her efforts at self-cultivation and useful charity, she does display a crucial quality of heroinism: mental fortitude, especially the ability to control strong feelings. This heroinism does not rest on an absence of feeling, but on a combination of strong feeling and adamantine rational control over that feeling. Like some other serious contemporary women writers, Burney rejects the old dichotomy between male capacity for reason and female capacity for feeling and passion, a dichotomy that legitimates male control of women, since they cannot control themselves. As Cecilia begins to be attracted to young Delville, she monitors her feelings carefully; she is able to control her passions, as so many of the heroines of Behn and Manley are not. As the narrator puts it, "she was not of that inflammable nature which is always ready to take fire, as her passions were under the controul of her reason."[193] In the midst of the novel, at Delville Castle, when Mortimer, formerly attentive, behaves with reserve and even avoids her, Cecilia resolves "to use every method in her power to conquer a partiality so ungratefully bestowed." She then executes "this task" with "constancy of mind."[194] Horrified by the sound of a gunshot when Harrell commits suicide in Vauxhall Gardens, she nevertheless presses through the crowd to try to come to his aid and then assists the widow. Her conduct evokes from Mrs. Delville that admiration proper to a romance heroine, the admiration Lennox's Arabella seeks for conduct that, in her story, provokes laughter:

Charming Miss Beverley! how shall I ever tell you half the admiration with which I have heard of your conduct! The exertion of so much fortitude at a juncture when a weaker mind would have been overpowered by terror, and a heart less under the dominion of well-regulated principles, would have sought only its own relief by flying from distress and confusion, shews such *propriety of mind* as can only result from the union of good sense with virtue. You are indeed a noble creature![195]

The somberness of Cecilia's difficult journey to marriage with Mortimer is much relieved by a Dickensian plenitude of comic characters, acutely registering not only material but also psychological fashions. We meet, for example, Mr. Meadows, cousin to Inchbald's Twineall, a man so exquisitely the quintessence of fashion that "his decision fixes the exact limits between what is vulgar and what is elegant."[196] His guiding rule is that "the first study of life is ease."[197] Sitting next to Cecilia at a concert at the Pantheon, where they might well have been hearing C. P. E. Bach or Italian opera arias, Mr. Meadows lolls, yawns, and complains. No art can entertain him. "I hate," he declares, "every thing that requires attention."[198] Cecilia's intelligent friend, Mr. Gosport, explains that Meadows, having realized that "devotion to the fair sex, had given way to a more equal and rational intercourse," determined to innovate, creating a new fashion of positive rudeness toward women. The labor of talking to women, Meadows protests, is worse than the labor of a galley-slave.

One of Burney's comic vulgarians in *Cecilia*, Mr. Hobson, a bricklayer, is a man of sufficient intelligence to articulate home truths about the social world he inhabits. The narrator describes Hobson as "a fat, sleek, vulgar-looking man, dressed in a bright purple coat, with a deep red waistcoat, and a wig bulging far from his head with small round curls, while his plump face and person announced plenty and good living, and an air of defiance spoke the fullness of his purse."[199] No diffidence prevents him, in the midst of Vauxhall, from dunning Harrell for the money he is owed; he responds to efforts to snub him not by cringing but by feeling provoked and retorting that he is "a man of as good property as another man."[200] Burney makes the reader feel the new power of a man like this, power that comes from earning money, pride in honest work, and refusal any longer to perpetuate the genteel fictions of humble dependency. Burney herself is still repelled at the idea of putting money first and makes grim comedy out of Hobson's objection to debtors like Harrell killing themselves: "A man has a right to his own life, you'll tell me; but what of that? . . . it does not give him a bit the more right to my property; and a man's running in debt, and spending other people's substances, for no reason in the world but just because he can blow out his own brains when he's done . . . why it's . . . a great hardship to trade . . ."[201] Yet when Hobson continues, defending the justice and legal right of creditors to seize a deceased debtor's household goods despite hardship to his widow, the narrator remarks that "the truth of this speech" palliated its "sententious absurdity."[202] Hobson, insisting that there is nothing to be despised about business, pleases himself with his economic independence. Sensibly, he advises a linen draper's wife of the folly of her dream that her Eton-educated son might become an ambassador: "Those sort of great people keep things of that kind for their own poor relations and cousins."[203]

Burney considered herself a creature of a different order from formid-able grand dames like Elizabeth Montagu or Hester Thrale or from learned ladies like Elizabeth Carter or even the Latin-reading Hannah More. In life and in her journal she could be diffident and timorous. Yet, as the author of *Cecilia*, Burney profited from the bluestocking tradition's insistence on the intellectual capacities of women. Using an omniscient narrator, she revealed her capacity for penetrating observation and analysis of her social world and her willingness to judge it. Her gifts for creating character and dialogue bring that world vividly to life. Jane Austen, who learned much from Burney, rightly pronounced *Cecilia* a "work in which the greatest powers of the mind are displayed, in which the most thorough knowledge of human nature, the happiest delineation of its varieties, the liveliest effusions of wit and humour are conveyed to the world in the best chosen language."[204]

PIOZZI'S *ANECDOTES OF THE LATE SAMUEL JOHNSON*

Hester Thrale Piozzi's *Anecdotes of the Late Samuel Johnson, LL.D. during the Last Twenty Years of His Life* (1786) is not formally a comedy;

nevertheless, it suggests the importance of the anti-authoritarian, anti-sentimental stance of comedy for women writers. Piozzi's shorter *Anecdotes* scooped Boswell's monumental *Life of Johnson*, not published until 1791. As a biographer, Piozzi had the advantage of Johnson's having lived for many years as an intimate in the house she shared with her husband, Henry Thrale. Her book, like Boswell's, is committed to recording the sayings of a great man who had died in 1784, and, like Boswell's, insists that Johnson was a great moralist and a great man of letters. Piozzi's account, however, reveals some problematic and some simply "low" aspects of Johnson's character and personality that are not in Boswell's more reverential *Life*. Indeed, Piozzi creates Johnson as a comic character more humanly complex than any character in the novels of Smith, Burney, or Radcliffe. Her Johnson, as she explicitly says, is a creature "at once comical and *touchant*," comical and affecting.[205]

Like many literary biographers, Piozzi is both a disciple and a rival of her subject. As a disciple, she celebrates Johnson's literary critical genius, the wisdom of his ethical pronouncements, and the importance of his example of Christian piety. Since Johnson was himself a biographer and close student of human nature, Piozzi can represent herself as following her master in her choice of biography as a significant literary form, pursuing the enlightenment concern with the nature of human nature. She quotes Johnson's definition of a story – or biographical anecdote – as "a specimen of human manners" that "derives its sole value from the truth," and praises Johnson's conversational anecdotes of people as "exquisitely amusing and comical."[206] Yet even as Piozzi pursues her master's concern with the vagaries of human conduct, as a rival, she contests the truthfulness of Johnson's self-representations. Although as befits its genre *Anecdotes* is desultory, Piozzi persistently develops what she sees as comic contradictions between Johnson's verbal pronouncements about his own virtues and her observations of his conduct. Her comedy is not primarily the satiric animus against hypocrisy, but a more Johnsonian comedy of sheer wonder at the human capacity for irrationality and self-delusion. To this is added a less Johnsonian capacity for finding Johnson's blindnesses and self-torment *touchant*.

Piozzi's Johnson relentlessly universalizes his own experience, even when his experience is ludicrously unrepresentative of most people's. Unable to enjoy painting or landscape because his eyesight is so poor, and unable to enjoy music because his hearing is so bad, Johnson retreats into a strict utilitarianism and treats both arts with "utter scorn." When Frances Brooke tries to tell him of the sublime and beautiful landscape she saw traveling up Canada's St. Lawrence river (the landscape we saw her describing in *Emily Montague*), Johnson reproves her: "Come Madam . . . confess that nothing ever equalled your pleasure in seeing that sight reversed; and finding yourself looking at the happy prospect DOWN the river St. Lawrence." Scoffing at "prospects and views," Johnson says he values only gardens that produce "the most roots and fruits."[207] When Johnson travels about England or France with the Thrales and Mr. Thrale attempts to point out beautiful prospects, Johnson retorts: "Never heed such nonsense . . . a blade of grass is always a blade of grass, whether in one country or another."[208]

Johnson was famous for his animadversions against various kinds of wit, including the metaphysical wit he had attacked in his "Life of Cowley," yet Piozzi astutely discerns how much of Johnson's conversation was driven by his desire to surprise his auditors with paradox and the superiority of his own wit. Johnson, she observes, delighted in wrong-footing and teasing his interlocutors. "It was not very easy," she writes, "for people not quite intimate with Dr. Johnson, to get exactly his opinion of a writer's merit, as he would now and then divert himself by confounding those who thought themselves obliged to say to-morrow what he had said yesterday . . ."[209] Even Garrick is discombobulated to find his old friend Johnson suddenly confuting what anyone would think safe praise of Dryden, as Johnson makes Garrick "look silly at his own table."[210] Nor is Piozzi's Johnson above teasing with what amounted to literary practical jokes. To get back at Mrs. Piozzi's mother, who annoyed him by talking about contemporary politics – which Johnson insisted were uninteresting – Johnson writes fictitious stories about plots and international diplomacy and plants them in the newspapers to draw her out and confound her.

Piozzi finds Johnson profoundly contradictory on the subject of manners: he repeatedly proclaims his deep reverence for politeness and, as repeatedly, outrageously insults inoffensive people – many of them the Thrales' guests. *Anecdotes* highlights these contradictions, sometimes finding light comedy in them, sometimes revealing Johnson's capacity for egoistic cruelty. One of the lighter occasions finds Johnson traveling in a coach with the Thrales, descanting upon how studiously he had always sought not to make enemies, then turning to reading a book. A Mr. Ch—lm—ley stops to pay his compliments, "desirous not to neglect Dr. Johnson." Since Johnson is rapt in his book and half-deaf, they tap him on his shoulder to get his attention. "'Tis Mr. Ch—lm—ley, says my husband; –'Well, Sir! and what if it is Mr. Ch—lm—ley!' says the other sternly, just lifting his eyes a moment from his book, and returning to it again with renewed avidity."[211] Among Johnson's many practices that made him a trying house guest, his reading in bed with lighted candles threatened incineration. It also led to his appearing at dinner with "the fore-top" of his wig "burned by the candle down to the very net-work." The Thrales appoint one of their valets to assist the sage: to keep a spare wig "always in his own hands, with which he met him at the parlour-door when the bell had called him down to dinner . . ."[212]

More seriously, Johnson was at his most insulting when his theological convictions were threatened. On one occasion, his belief that no person was happy was challenged by a gentleman who insisted that his sister-in-law was happy. When the lady, who was present, confirmed that she was, in fact, happy, Johnson retorted: "If your sister-in-law is really the contented being she professes herself Sir (said he), her life gives the lie to every research of humanity; for she is happy without health, without beauty, without money, and without understanding."[213] As Piozzi develops Johnson's character, his drive to dominate by his intellect and wit and his refusal to credit the experience of others can make him blind and cruel. Piozzi does not explicitly draw out the feminist implications of her observations of Johnson's assumptions of male privilege, but it is worth remarking that one intended female victim of Johnson's wit, Macaulay, later, in *Letters on Education with Observations on Religious and Metaphysical Subjects*, 1790, diagnosed Johnson's talking for victory as a consequence of defects in elite male education.

Piozzi presents Johnson as militantly, even hyperbolically anti-sentimental in his pronouncements, yet as often feeling the sentiments he attacked. Johnson will pity material distress, but "he did not even pretend to feel for those who lamented the loss of a child, a parent, or a friend.—'These are the distresses of sentiment (he would reply) which a man who is really to be pitied has no leisure to feel.'"[214] Johnson seems partly motivated by an understandable disdain for the absurd excesses of contemporary sentimentality, but also, more deeply, by a religious view of human nature as so darkened by sin and selfishness that to accept a human capacity for disinterested sympathy would be to fall into the Pelagian heresy. Nevertheless, Piozzi repeatedly finds Johnson sorrowing over the deaths of his friends. She reports, "The truth is, nobody suffered more from pungent sorrow at a friend's death than Johnson, though he would suffer no one else to complain of their losses in the same way; 'for (says he) we must either outlive our friends you know, or our friends must outlive us; and I see no man would hesitate about the choice.'"[215]

Piozzi's boldest criticism of Johnson finds error at the heart of his religion. While she honors his efforts to be a good Christian and his charities to the poor and the sick, she reveals his terror that he might not be among the saved. It had led him so bitterly to lament "the horrible condition of his mind" to the Thrales that when one morning they overheard him begging the Reverend Dr. John Delap to pray for him, they decided to try to rescue him by having him come live with them.[216] This spiritual terror fuels Johnson's notorious fears of madness and death and his unwillingness to sleep. It leads him to demand that she stay awake to keep him company and make him tea until four o'clock in the morning. Johnson's own edict that "life is made up of little things," after all, authorizes her attention in this narrative to the mundane world of providing wigs for the careless and tea for the distraught; it makes her "repeated acts of beneficence towards him" a more authentic Christianity than his egoistic torments.[217] Piozzi is touched by Johnson's spiritual suffering and does her best to alleviate it, recognizing its kinship to the intensities of feeling Johnson the anti-sentimentalist did his best to deny and also to the Calvinist elements in Anglican theology, of which Johnson could also be critical. But in the end Piozzi dares to judge that "his fears for his own salvation were excessive" and that the religion of this most celebrated wise and pious man "ended in little less than disease."[218]

Anecdotes derived some of its initial fame from its author's ability to reveal secrets about a famous writer, just as Laetitia Pilkington's *Memoirs* was sought after for its account of another famous writer, Swift. Pilkington and Piozzi both bring the conversation of their famous subjects vividly before the reader, but Piozzi offers a deeper study of her subject's character and a still more fascinating window into the alternately affectionate and tense relationship between a supremely ambitious literary man and a literary woman emboldened to follow his example to become a biographer and a critic.

CONCLUSION

Both romance and comedy were important modes for women writers of this period. Perhaps most clearly in Walker's *Munster Village* we can see the continuing appeal of the ideal and utopian elements of romance to feminist writers dissatisfied with the realities of patriarchal society. Other texts, less utopian, offer heroines whose idealized virtues are strikingly different from those of their Restoration and early eighteenth-century counterparts. Unlike Manley's earlier Rivella, for example, celebrated for her passion and her genius in the arts of love, Smith's Emmeline excels at controlling her own desires and firmly resists Delamere, the passionate, uncontrolled, aristocratic lover. Seward in *Louisa* is especially explicit in showing that her heroine can, if fate and virtue direct, live a life without the love of a man, although in the end she rewards Louisa with her lover. Seward, Walker, Cowley, Inchbald, and even Burney were heiresses of the tradition stretching from Astell through the bluestockings when they made the heroines of their romances reflective, intelligent, gifted with exceptional fortitude, and capable of controlling their own desires.

The serious consideration of the history of romance in this period, most evident in the work of Dobson and Reeve, changed and complicated the traditional understanding of romance. The historicist argument that the sources of early romance were historical made romance something other than merely the poets' imagination of ideal value. For some women writers, this meant that the modern state of gender relations was not natural and unchangeable, but that chivalric respect for virtuous women had once been an historical reality and that it could therefore be so again. The invitation to explore the historical past of romance most simply prompted writers to invent new settings, as More does in *Percy* and Reeve does in *The Champion of Virtue*. Often, as in Reeve, the move backwards in time is in the service of a conservative politics of nostalgia. Sometimes, as in *Percy*, it can prompt more critical comparative looks at medieval and modern societies and states.

Many of the sentimental romance plots of this period are signs of a crisis in women writers' understanding of female virtue. On the one hand, they embrace a desire for more learning and for more autonomy, based on the idea that women are capable of self-control. On the other hand, they engage in a desperate effort to imagine a kind of moral heroism not based on recourse to physical violence and an equally desperate effort to claim that female longings for more opportunities and more autonomy will not undermine family feeling and family stability. We see this both in the new-style male heroes of sensibility in Reeve, Seward, Radcliffe, and Burney and in their heroines. Protagonists in these sentimental romances turn that aspect of sensibility that is love and reverence for family into orgiastic self-abnegation before parents and siblings. Elwina in *Percy* marries Douglas abject before her father's "flowing tears." Eugenio in *Louisa* marries the Lamia-like Emira to try to save his father from bankruptcy and his mother and sisters from poverty. Mary in *The Castles of Athlin and Dunbayne* offers to marry the villain in order to free her brother from captivity. Mortimer Delville in *Cecilia* renounces his love for

Cecilia when his mother demands that he not change his name; she cries "My brain is on fire!," and collapses on the floor, covered with blood. Sometimes the desire for a heroine who is both morally autonomous enough to be responsible for herself and willing to sacrifice her own judgment for her family becomes simply contradictory. In *The Castles of Athlin and Dunbayne*, for instance, Mary both professes that she will never give her hand in marriage without her heart and volunteers to marry the villain, for whom she feels nothing but fear and loathing. In *Percy*, as we have seen, More makes the contradiction tragic.

The conventions of comedy, which sanction irreverence, provided welcome relief for women writers in this age of sentiment. Cowley and Inchbald produced heroines who speak their desires and plot to achieve them, heroines who lack the timorous modesty conduct-book writers were claiming was a hallmark of femininity and the concomitant anxiety found in many heroines of novels and in Burney's diary. Cowley, as we have seen, made the new models of modest femininity a target of her satire. As Pix had before them, Cowley and Inchbald also sometimes abandoned the young unmarried heroine for more sophisticated married and widowed heroines. Against all the novelistic versions of women terrorized into silence at the prospect of jealous men dueling over them – indeed, it is the possibility of duel between two men over Burney's Cecilia that makes her first speechless and then temporarily mad – it comes as a relief to see Inchbald's Lady Euston in *I'll Tell You What* have no qualms about telling her husband about Major Cyrus's attempts to seduce her and to see her deal with such attempts herself by ridiculing the offender. While Burney stuck to less bold unmarried virgins for heroines in her novels, she joined Cowley and Inchbald in taking full advantage of comedy's concern with the topical. Here comedy becomes cousin to journalism, revelling in an amazing abundance of novelties tossed up by what was not only an age of sentiment but an age of new wealth and cultural expansion: Burney's newly self-confident prosperous man in the business of bricks; Cowley's Don Vincentio, besotted with Italian music and creating his own orchestra; or Inchbald's balloonists and prison reformer.

Stage comedy was certainly not considered the highest form of art, yet it had an advantage over the novel in being considered a form of entertainment for adults. Unlike novelists, writers of stage comedy were not subject to reviewers relentlessly asking whether their plays were suitable surrogate conduct books for teenage girls. Inchbald thus in *I'll Tell You What* felt free to explore the very topical modern comedy of what happens when divorced people remarry and men are supposed to be civil to rivals who have cuckolded them. She did not think she was writing primarily for fifteen-year-old girls, nor did her audience or the reviewers suppose that she should have been. Often, what modern critics have supposed were omnipresent constraints on women writers in this period were only the conventions of a certain kind of novel.

Contemporary understanding of the capacities of women writers, including women writers' self-understanding, ranged over a broad spectrum of opinion. At one extreme, some saw no difference between the intellectual and artistic capacities of men and women, other than that made by education. This was not only Macaulay's view, it was also the view of a male writer in the *Monthly Review* of 1782 who found Macaulay's *History* excellent evidence for the equality of male and female abilities and for the proposition that genius is not confined to either sex.[219] In the broad middle, many were trying to articulate gendered models of human capacity, for instance, finding men stronger in judgment, women stronger in fancy and sympathy. At the other extreme, much older ideas of women's inferiority continued to be voiced – providing material for comic portraits like Lee's Governor Harcourt and Cowley's Gradus.

A good, if complex, sign of the extent to which women's writing had become a normal part of literary production by 1789 is the fact that between 1777 and 1789 we begin to see women writers reviewing the work of other women writers. Restoration and early eighteenth-century women writers, we have seen, occasionally celebrated one another's literary accomplishments in commendatory verses, typically in prologues to plays or celebratory verses in the preliminary matter of published volumes. At mid century, when prose reviews published in magazines became a dominant mode of criticism, the first reviewers were male. Women, however, did take advantage of the open editorial policies of these magazines to take literary critical positions about the writing of other women, as we have seen Carter do in her poem on Elizabeth Rowe first published in *The Gentleman's Magazine*. In the later eighteenth century, when something approaching a critical mass of women writers exists, we begin to see newspapers and magazines used as venues for disputes among women writers and women writers try to take a role in shaping the reception of other women writers through literary history and criticism. More and Cowley exchanged letters in *The Saint James's Chronicle* in 1779 on the subject of whether More's play, *Fatal Falsehood*, was indebted to Cowley's *Albania*. Seward, who aspired to be a literary critic, proffered an overwritten, anonymous, and rather nasty attack on Reeve's *Progress of Romance* that was printed in *The Gentleman's Magazine* in 1786. Professing admiration for Reeve's *Old English Baron* and solicitude for Reeve's fame, Seward attacks Reeve's preference for Richardson's *Pamela* over his *Clarissa* and *Sir Charles Grandison*. In significant books of literary history and criticism, Thicknesse evaluates French women writers and Reeve finds places for women writers in her history of romance.

By the 1780s women writers also begin to appear as reviewers. Seward rejected an invitation to become a reviewer for *The Analytical Review*, but Mary Wollstonecraft wrote for it regularly, albeit anonymously. Like Reeve and Seward, Wollstonecraft was eager that women writers succeed, but, like them too, she refused to suspend her critical judgment simply because a work had been written by a woman. Less influenced by sensibility as a reviewer than as a novelist, Wollstonecraft allowed herself to be annoyed that in *Emmeline* Smith had offered up the "theatrical contrition" of Lady Adelina and mocked the stereotypical sentimentality of "hair freed from its confinement to shade feverish cheeks, tottering steps, inarticulate words, and tears ever ready to flow, white gowns, and black veils, and graceful attitudes." Finding Lady Adelina an example of "romantic notions and false refinement," Wollstonecraft instead praised the "rational resignation" of Lady Stafford, an ill-used wife who serves as Emmeline's mentor.[220] Unlike Manley's personal attacks on Trotter and Egerton in *The New Atalantis*, the criticism Seward and Wollstonecraft offer is directed at the substance and style of other women's literary work. This is in part a product of the development of the history and criticism of English literature in the late eighteenth century, development fostered by Johnson, Warton, and Hugh Blair among the elite writers, but also evident in humbler manifestations like the improvement of theatrical criticism in *The Westminster Magazine* of the 1780s and the longer, more analytical reviews of novels Wollstonecraft wrote for the *Analytical Review*.

The women writers of the first bluestocking generation and of this group that next flourished between 1777 and 1789 established a base upon which subsequent generations of feminist critics could build. Most of them had a special eagerness to know what other women had written, a certain prejudice in favor of the works of their own sex (as Montagu Pennington described Carter's attitude), and an eagerness to advance the reputations of women writers. At sixty-one in 1778 Carter had only mild interest in novels or in young girls just entering the world, but she still wrote to Montagu "Have you read Evelina, a novel, of which I hear a very high character; I am wishing much to see it . . ."[221] When Hester Thrale in 1784 married a Roman Catholic Italian musician, becoming Hester Piozzi, the bluestockings did not approve, partly because, as Chapone put it, the marriage "has given great occasion to the Enemy to blaspheme and to triumph over the Bas Bleu Ladies."[222] Nevertheless, Piozzi carefully documented what evidence she could find of Johnson's respect for the work and the literary judgment of women writers, including the bluestockings. She reports Johnson's saying that Montagu's *Embassy Letters* was the only book "which he did not consider as obligatory" that he read from cover to cover in his entire life.[223] She also reports that Johnson was delighted by Elizabeth Montagu's praise of his work, commenting, "That such praise from such a lady should delight him, is not strange; insensibility in a case like that, must have the result alone of arrogance acting on stupidity."[224] When Boswell wrote in his *Tour to the Hebrides* that Johnson and Hester Thrale agreed that they could not get through Montagu's *Essay on Shakespeare*, Piozzi wrote to deny that she had ever said such a thing and to testify that she had always commended the book.[225] Showing still stronger enthusiasm for the work of a sister writer, Wollstonecraft in *A Vindication of the Rights of Woman* (1792) described Macaulay as undoubtedly the most able woman England had ever produced and an "example of the intellectual acquirements supposed to be incompatible with the weakness of her sex."[226] In a touching letter, only discovered in the 1990s, Wollstonecraft sent Macaulay a presentation copy of her *Vindication of the Rights of Men* (1790), declaring, "You are the only female writer who I coincide in opinion with respecting the rank our sex ought to endeavour to obtain in the world. I respect Mrs Macaulay Graham because she contends for laurels whilst most of her sex seek only for flowers."[227]

While they were generally eager to support the work of their sister writers, these late eighteenth-century women writers also exercised critical judgment. They described what faults of substance or style they discerned in other women's writing and they reserved the right to differ over important matters of religion, politics, or class. Fascinated as they were with Macaulay's accomplishments in the *History*, nothing could induce Carter or More to agree with her political agenda. More's protégée Ann Yearsley, the so-called Bristol milkwoman, in her *Poems on Several Occasions* (1785) pays tribute to More in "Night. To Stella," commending her power to arouse conscience and beseeching her assistance. However, after a quarrel over More's having put the subscription money raised from the volume in a trust for Yearsley, independent of her husband's control, Yearsley in a second volume of *Poems on Various Subjects* (1787) angrily attacked More as unjust and condescending; she offered a poem to rival and debate More's poem on sensibility. Yearsley, apparently dismissing More as one of the "self-confounding sophists," claims that the highest sensibility is to be found, not in the educated and the socially privileged, but in a laboring person like herself who has known acute suffering:

> Does Education give the transport keen,
> Or swell your vaunted grief? No, Nature feels
> Most poignant, undefended; hails with me
> The Pow'rs of Sensibility untaught.[228]

Modern feminist critics who try to build on the accomplishments of these eighteenth-century women writers still struggle with the relative allegiances they ought to owe to gender, on the one hand, and to a competing range of other values, still including religion, politics, class, and aesthetic value, on the other. We do well to follow our late eighteenth-century predecessors in their enthusiasms for the works of women and their zeal for improving the condition of women. We might especially take a leaf from Reeve's notebook to acknowledge that women of periods other than our own sometimes had other values. Ruthlessly interrogating the works of earlier women writers primarily to fault them according to whether they commit solecisms in terms of modern feminist or democratic political standards is not the best way to construct a feminist literary history or a feminist canon. Nor do tortured readings of their works that reinvent earlier women writers as modern feminists contribute to good feminist literary history. It is true that canons require usable models, which is one reason why Radcliffe was happy to pay homage to Reeve's *Champion of Virtue* and why feminist criticism can never entirely escape its obsession with the qualities of heroines. At the same time, it cannot be a sin against feminism to find that some women wrote well and others badly. Whether we agree or not with Seward's complaint that Smith's *Elegiac Sonnets* were "ever-lasting lamentables" and "hackneyed scraps of dismality" – and I have not agreed with this judgment – Seward was right to consider whether or not they were hackneyed.[229] In a history of literature, women writers must be judged by what they accomplished in their work, not merely sympathized with because they suffered from patriarchy or from misogynistic critics. We may continue to disagree about the merits of many of these works, but literary criticism does need to focus on the works. That is what I have tried to do.

Notes

INTRODUCTION

1 David Perkins, *Is Literary History Possible?* (Baltimore, Md.: Johns Hopkins University Press, 1992), 17, 4.

2 Clare Brant, "Varieties of Women's Writing," in *Women and Literature in Britain, 1700–1800*, ed. Vivien Jones (Cambridge: Cambridge University Press, 2000), 302.

3 Sharon M. Harris, *American Women Writers to 1800* (Oxford: Oxford University Press, 1996), 5–6. Addressing the situation of English women's texts of this period, Isobel Grundy says simultaneously that she wishes "to champion women's writing chiefly on account of its literary qualities" and that "the argument from literary quality is doomed to get bogged down in the incompatibility of subjective judgments." "(Re)discovering Women's Texts," in *Women and Literature in Britain*, ed. Jones, 184.

4 Harris, *American Women Writers*, 21.

5 Allen Wood, "The Objectivity of Value," *New Literary History* 32 (2001), 872.

6 Faith Beasley, "Altering the Fabric of History: Women's Participation in the Classical Age," in *A History of Women's Writing in France*, ed. Sonya Stephens (Cambridge: Cambridge University Press, 2000), 69.

7 I am indebted to a conversation with Susan Lanser for this suggestion.

8 Margaret J. M. Ezell, *Writing Women's Literary History* (Baltimore, Md.: Johns Hopkins University Press, 1993).

9 Perkins, *Literary History*, 185.

10 *Ibid.*

11 William Warner, *Licensing Entertainment: The Elevation of Novel Reading in Britain, 1684–1750* (Berkeley: University of California Press, 1998), 92.

12 Perkins, *Literary History*, 182.

13 Rita Felski, *Beyond Feminist Aesthetics: Feminist Literature and Social Change* (Cambridge, Mass.: Harvard University Press, 1989).

14 John Butt, *The Oxford History of English Literature: The Mid-Eighteenth Century, 1740–1789*, ed. and completed by Geoffrey Carnall (Oxford: Clarendon Press, 1979), 7.

15 *Ibid.*

16 Housman's review originally appeared in *The Cambridge Review* (27 January 1915). Here quoted from A. E. Housman, *Selected Prose*, ed. John Carter (Cambridge; Cambridge University Press, 1961), 108–09. He was reviewing the *Cambridge History of English Literature*, ed. A. W. Ward and A. R. Waller, 14 vols. (Cambridge: Cambridge University Press, 1907–27), XI: *The Period of the French Revolution*, 1914. All the contributors to this volume were men, except Mrs. H. G. Aldis, who wrote the penultimate chapter on "The Bluestockings."

17 Christine Blouch, "Eliza Haywood and the Romance of Obscurity," *Studies in English Literature* 31 (1991), 540.

18 See, for example, the recent collection of essays edited by George L. Justice and Nathan Tinker, *Women's Writing and the Circulation of Ideas: Manuscript Publication in England, 1550–1800* (Cambridge: Cambridge University Press, 2002).

19 Catherine Gallagher, *Nobody's Story: The Vanishing Acts of Women Writers in the Marketplace, 1670–1820* (Berkeley: University of California Press, 1994), 327.

20 Perkins, *Literary History*, 46.

21 *Ibid.*, 41.

22 Norma Clarke, *The Rise and Fall of the Woman of Letters* (London: Pimlico, 2004), 338.

23 Perkins, *Literary History*, 33.

24 George Sherburn and Donald Bond, *A Literary History of England: The Restoration and Eighteenth Century (1660–1789)*, ed. Albert C. Baugh (1st edn. 1948; revised 1967; reprint London: Routledge & Kegan Paul, 1975).

1 PUBLIC WOMEN: THE RESTORATION TO THE DEATH OF APHRA BEHN, 1660–1689

1 *The Memoirs of Anne, Lady Halkett and Ann, Lady Fanshawe*, ed. John Loftis (Oxford: Clarendon Press, 1979), 24.

2 Keith Thomas, "Women and the Civil War Sects," *Past and Present* 13 (1958), 42–62. For a feminist treatment covering 1640 to 1700, see Phyllis Mack, *Visionary Women: Ecstatic Prophecy in Seventeenth-Century England* (Berkeley: University of California Press, 1992).

3 Margaret Fell, *A Declaration and an Information from Us the People of God Called Quakers to the Present Governors, the King and both Houses of Parliament, and all whom it may concern* (London, 1660).

4 My calculation from data provided in Patricia Crawford, "Women's Published Writings, 1600–1700," in *Women in English Society, 1500–1800*, ed. Mary Prior (London: Methuen, 1985), 211–82. For an important consideration of this body of writing and an argument that ecstatic Quaker women's writing functions as *écriture féminine*, see, Margaret J. M. Ezell, "Breaking the Seventh Seal: Writings by Early Quaker Women," in *Writing Women's*

Literary History (Baltimore, Md.: Johns Hopkins University Press, 1993), 132–60.

5 Katharine Evans, *This is the Short Relation of some of the Cruel Sufferings (For Truth's Sake) of Katharine Evans and Sarah Cheevers, in the Inquisition in the Isle of Malta* (London, 1662), 13. Wing Film 1532: 17.

6 *Ibid.*, 20.

7 *Ibid.*, 41.

8 George Ballard, *Memoirs of Several Ladies of Great Britain who have been Celebrated for their Writings or Skill in the Learned Languages, Arts and Sciences*, ed. Ruth Perry (Detroit, Mich.: Wayne State University Press, 1985), 327–31.

9 Packington was widely thought to have written the enormously popular, though anonymous, *Whole Duty of Man* (1658) and *The Ladies Calling* (1673). Ballard argues strenuously for her authorship (*Memoirs*, 290–301), although Richard Allestree and/or John Fell have more frequently been said to have written *The Whole Duty of Man*. *The Ladies Calling* was published as by the author of *The Whole Duty of Man*.

10 Alice Thornton, *The Autobiography of Mrs. Alice Thornton of East Newton Co., York*, ed. Charles Jackson (Durham: Pub. for the Surtees Society, vol. LXII, 1875); Ann Fanshawe, *The Memoirs of Ann, Lady Fanshawe, Wife of the Right Honorable Sir Richard Fanshawe* (written 1696, published 1829); Brilliana Harley, *Letters of Lady Brilliana Harley*, ed. Thomas Taylor Lewis (London: Camden Society, no. 58, 1854), Halkett cited in note 1 above, Cavendish and Hutchinson notes 11 and 22 below.

11 Margaret Cavendish, Duchess of Newcastle, *The Life of the Thrice Noble, High, and Puissant Prince William Cavendishe, Duke, Marquess, and Earl of Newcastle* (London, 1667), [(b2)].

12 *Ibid.*, [(c2)].

13 *Ibid.*, [(c2)].

14 C. H. Firth, ed., *The Life of William Cavendish, Duke of Newcastle . . .*, 2nd edn. (New York: George Routledge & Sons and E. P. Dutton, 1906), viii–xi.

15 Cavendish, *Life*, 50.

16 *Ibid.*, 32.

17 *Ibid.*, 110.

18 *Ibid.*, 67.

19 Edward Hyde, Earl of Clarendon, *The History of the Great Rebellion*, ed. Roger Lockyer (London: Oxford University Press for the Folio Society, 1967), 219, 221. Clarendon is also severe on Prince Rupert's conduct.

20 Cavendish, *Life*, 50–51.

21 Jasper Ridley, *The Roundheads* (London: Constable, 1976), 76.

22 James Sutherland, in Lucy Hutchinson, *Memoirs of the Life of Colonel Hutchinson with the Fragment of an Autobiography of Mrs. Hutchinson*, ed. James Sutherland (London: Oxford University Press, 1973), xiv. Her title was *The Life of Colonel Hutchinson*. Sutherland restores substantial cuts made in earlier editions. Editing a manuscript, he engages in some limited normalization.

23 *Ibid.*, 45.
24 *Ibid.*, 224.
25 *Ibid.*, 223.
26 *Ibid.*, 169.
27 *Ibid.*, 32.
28 *Ibid.*, 13.
29 *Ibid.*, 28–9.
30 *Ibid.*, 207.
31 *Ibid.*, 33.
32 *Ibid.*, 10.
33 N. H. Keeble, "'The Colonel's Shadow': Lucy Hutchinson, Women's Writing, and the Civil War," in *Literature and the English Civil War*, ed. Thomas F. Healy and Jonathan Sawday (Cambridge: Cambridge University Press, 1990), 230, 232.
34 Hutchinson, *Life*, 114.
35 *Ibid.*, 114.
36 *Ibid.*, 128.
37 *Ibid.*, 189.
38 *Ibid.*, 229.
39 The text of the petition, upon which my characterization is based, is in an appendix of Sutherland's edition of the *Life*. Her own description in the text of the *Life* is much vaguer; she refers to a letter to the Speaker "to urge what might be in his favor."
40 Hutchinson, *Life*, 230.
41 *Ibid.*, 263.
42 *Ibid.*, 272.
43 David Cressy, *Coming Over: Migration and Communication between England and New England in the Seventeenth Century* (Cambridge: Cambridge University Press, 1987), 68. Cressy discusses the motives of the emigrants, acknowledging the importance of religion, but also considering a range of other motives, including economic.
44 *Complete Prose Works of John Milton*, ed. Don M. Wolfe, 8 vols. (New Haven: Yale University Press, 1953–82), I: 585.
45 Hutchinson, *Life*, 46.
46 Barbara Keifer Lewalski, *Writing Women in Jacobean England* (Cambridge, Mass.: Harvard University Press, 1993), 120. The first substantial volume of original poems published by an Englishwoman, according to Lewalski, was Aemilia Lanyer's *Salve Deus Rex Judaeorum* (1611); despite the title, the poems are in English.
47 A Gentlewoman in New England [Anne Bradstreet], *Several Poems: Compiled with a great Variety of Wit and Learning . . .* (Boston, 1678), [a3v]. Wing Film 759: 15.
48 *Ibid.*, 196.
49 *Ibid.*, 200–01.
50 *Ibid.*, 239.

51 *Ibid.*

52 This manuscript poem was not included in either the 1650 or the 1678 volume. It may be found in *The Complete Works of Anne Bradstreet*, ed. Joseph R. McElrath, Jr. and Allen P. Robb (Boston: Twayne, 1981), 232–33. This edition offers a useful discussion of the textual history of the poems.

53 Bradstreet, *Poems*, 226.

54 On this tradition in the literature of the period, see Maren-Sofie Røstvig, *The Happy Man: Studies in the Metamorphosis of a Classical Ideal*, 2 vols. (Oslo: Akademisk Forlag, 1954–58).

55 Margaret Cavendish, Duchess of Newcastle, CCXI *Sociable Letters* (London, 1664), Letter XXVII, 52.

56 Katherine Philips, *The Collected Works of Katherine Philips: The Matchless Orinda*, ed. Patrick Thomas, 3 vols. (Stump Cross, Essex: Stump Cross Books, 1990), I: 9.

57 Katherine Philips, *Poems. By the Most deservedly Admired Mrs. Katherine Philips, The Matchless Orinda* (London, 1667), 88–89. This is the posthumous edition compiled by Philips's friend, Sir Charles Cotterell; there was an unauthorized 1664 edition, with fewer poems, that was withdrawn after protests. Thomas provides good bibliographical descriptions and discussion in his edition.

58 Philips, *Poems*, 28.

59 Earl Miner, *The Cavalier Mode from Jonson to Cotton* (Princeton, NJ: Princeton University Press, 1971), 298.

60 *Ibid.*, 301.

61 Philips, *Poems*, 51.

62 This point is made by Elizabeth Susan Wahl, *Invisible Relations: Representations of Female Intimacy in the Age of Enlightenment* (Stanford, Calif.: Stanford University Press, 1999), 130.

63 Philips, *Poems*, 95.

64 *Ibid.*, 83, 85.

65 Arlene Stiebel, "Subversive Sexuality: Masking the Erotic in Poems by Katherine Philips and Aphra Behn," in *Renaissance Discourses of Desire*, ed. Claude J. Summers and Ted-Larry Pebworth (Columbia: University of Missouri Press, 1993), 225.

66 *Ibid.*, 229.

67 Deborah Shugar, "Excerpts from a Panel Discussion," in *Renaissance Discourses of Desire*, ed. Summers and Pebworth, 272.

68 Philips, *Works*, ed. Thomas, I 19.

69 For an analysis of the translation, see Michel Adam, "Katherine Philips, traductrice du théâtre de Pierre Corneille," *Revue d'historie littéraire de la France* 85 (1985), 841–51. Adam concludes: "dans l'ensemble, le *Pompey* de Katherine Philips pourrait servir de modèle à bien des traducteurs de Corneille, et reste sans conteste le meilleure version de l'œuvre en langue anglaise" (847–48). On the reception of Corneille in England as well as on

Philips, see Dorothea Frances Canfield, *Corneille and Racine in England* (New York: Columbia University Press, 1904).

70 Katherine Philips, *Pompey. A Tragœdy* (Dublin, 1663), 74. Wing Film 1684: 29.

71 *Ibid.*, 57.

72 *Ibid.*, 57.

73 Mary Rowlandson, *A True History of the Captivity and Restoration of Mrs. Mary Rowlandson, A Minister's Wife in New England* (London, 1682), 33. The Boston edition of 1682, entitled *The Soveraignty and Goodness of God, Together, With the faithfulness of his Promises displays; Being a Narrative of the Captivity and Restauration of Mrs. Mary Rowlandson,* has been lost.

74 "The Preface to the Reader," *Captivity,* [A2v]. The author of the preface was probably Increase Mather.

75 Rowlandson, *Captivity,* 11.

76 Nancy Armstrong and Leonard Tennenhouse, *The Imaginary Puritan: Literature, Intellectual Labor, and the Origins of Personal Life* (Berkeley: University of California Press, 1992), 208, 209.

77 Kathryn Zabelle Derounian, "The Publication, Promotion, and Distribution of Mary Rowlandson's Indian Captivity Narrative in the Seventeenth Century," *Early American Literature* 23 (1988), 239–61.

78 Rowlandson, *Captivity,* 23.

79 *Ibid.*, 22.

80 *Ibid.*, 13.

81 *Ibid.*, 19.

82 *Ibid.*, 28.

83 *Ibid.*, 20.

84 *Ibid.*, 29.

85 *Ibid.*

86 Dawn Henwood, "Mary Rowlandson and the Psalms: The Textuality of Survival," *Early American Literature* 32 (1997), 171.

87 *The Complete Works of William Wycherley,* ed. Montagu Summers, 4 vols. (Soho, [London]: Nonesuch Press, 1924), III: 155. A much-cited article on Behn by Catherine Gallagher goes further to argue that Behn embraced the equation of women writer and prostitute and flaunted her "self-sale." (Catherine Gallagher, "Who Was that Masked Woman? The Prostitute and the Playwright in the Comedies of Aphra Behn," *Women's Studies* 15 [1988], 23–42.) Derek Hughes has sharply attacked Gallagher's position: "The Masked Woman Revealed: or the Prostitute and the Playwright in Aphra Behn Criticism," *Women's Writing* 7 (2000), 149–64.

88 Aphra Behn [spelled Bhen on title page], *The Dutch Lover; A Comedy* (London, 1673), "An Epistle to the Reader," a, [A3v], [av]. Wing Film, 445: 32.

89 Judith Phillips Stanton, "'This New-Found Path Attempting': Women Dramatists in England, 1660–1800," in *Curtain Calls: British and American Women and the Theater, 1660–1820,* ed. Mary Anne Schofield and Cecilia

Macheski (Athens: Ohio University Press, 1991), table 5. "Most popular plays staged by number of years produced," 353. Stanton also notes nine editions of *The Rover* published between 1677 and 1757.

90 Aphra Behn, *The Rover: or, the Banish't Cavaliers* (London, 1677), 30. Wing Film 446: 3.

91 *Ibid.*, 11.

92 *Ibid.*, 80.

93 Elizabeth Howe, *The First English Actresses: Women and Drama, 1660–1700* (Cambridge: Cambridge University Press, 1992), 133–36.

94 Behn, *Rover*, 20.

95 *Ibid.*, 60.

96 *Ibid.*, 75.

97 Aphra Behn, *Poems upon Several Occasions: With a Voyage to the Island of Love* (London, 1684), 53. Wing Film 525: 2. The earlier version published in Creech's volume offers a more pious version. (*T. Lucretius Caro . . . De Natura Rerum* [Oxford, 1683]). It is possible Behn wrote both versions or, as Todd suggests, that Creech may have changed Behn's lines out of fear of their effect. *The Works of Aphra Behn*, ed. Janet Todd, 7 vols. (Columbus: Ohio State University Press, 1992–96), 1: 383.

98 For a fine essay on the *Heroides* and English poems descended from them, see, Gillian Beer, "'Our Unnatural No-voice': the Heroic Epistle, Pope, and Women's Gothic," in *Modern Essays in Eighteenth-Century Literature*, ed. Leopold Damrosh, Jr. (New York: Oxford University Press, 1988), 379–411.

99 Behn, *Poems*, 139.

100 Trans. Guy Lee, *Ovid's Amores* (New York: Viking Press, 1968), 145.

101 Richard E. Quaintance, "French Sources of the Restoration 'Imperfect Enjoyment' Poem," *Philological Quarterly* 42 (1963), 190–99.

102 Behn, *Poems*, 75.

103 *Ibid.*

104 Reprinted with a continuation as *Le Voyage et la conqueste de l'isle d'amour*, 1685.

105 Behn, *Poems*, 8.

106 *Ibid.*, 10.

107 Dorothy Mermin, "Women Becoming Poets: Katherine Philips, Aphra Behn, Anne Finch," *ELH* 57 (1990), 335–55.

108 Behn, *Poems*, 98–99.

109 *Ibid.*, 99.

110 Earlier versions of this poem, "Song: I led my *Silvia* to a grove," appeared in the *Covent Garden Drolery* (1672) and in Behn's play, *The Dutch Lover* (1673). Poems of this period were likely to have many versions, variously appearing in manuscripts, published miscellanies, and in an author's collected poems. Bernard Duyfhuizen offers a model exercise in exploring the relationships of such versions using this poem as an example in "'That which I dare not name': Aphra Behn's 'The Willing Mistress,'" *ELH* 58 (1991), 63–82.

111 Behn, *Poems*, 45.

112 *Ibid.*, 102.

113 *Ibid.*, 63.

114 Renato Poggioli, *The Oaten Flute* (Cambridge, Mass.: Harvard University Press, 1975), 16.

115 Bruce K. Smith, *Homosexual Desire in Shakespeare's England: A Cultural Poetics* (Chicago: University of Chicago Press, 1991), 82.

116 Aphra Behn, ed. *Miscellany, Being a Collection of Poems by Several Hands. Together with Reflections on Morality, or Secena Unmasqued* (London, 1665), 207. Wing Film 190: 11.

117 Frank Kermode, *English Pastoral Poetry from the Beginning to Marvell* (London: George G. Harrap, 1952), 18, 16.

118 Behn, *Miscellany*, 210.

119 *Ibid.*

120 *Ibid.*, 211.

121 Aphra Behn, *Sir Patient Fancy. A Comedy* (London, 1678), [92].

122 Janet Todd, *The Secret Life of Aphra Behn* (New Brunswick, NJ: Rutgers University Press, 1997), 298.

123 Aphra Behn, *A Pindarick Poem on the Happy Coronation of His most Sacred Majesty James II and his Illustrious Consort Queen Mary* (London, 1685), 4. For a more sympathetic view of Behn's public poetry generally and this poem in particular, see Carol Barash, *English Women's Poetry, 1689–1714: Politics, Community, and Linguistic Authority* (Oxford: Clarendon Press, 1996), ch. 3.

124 Rosalind Ballaster, *Seductive Forms: Women's Amatory Fiction from 1684 to 1740* (Oxford: Clarendon Press, 1992), 52.

125 Aphra Behn, *The Fair Jilt; or, the History of Prince Tarquin and Miranda* (London, 1688), 44–45.

126 *Ibid.*, 1, 6.

127 *Ibid.*, 45.

128 *Ibid.*, 84–85.

129 See, for example, Jacqueline Pearson, "Gender and Narrative in the Fiction of Aphra Behn, I," *Review of English Studies* 42 (1991), 40–56, and "Gender and Narrative in the Fiction of Aphra Behn, II," *Review of English Studies* 42 (1991), 179–90.

130 Aphra Behn, *Oroonoko, or, the Royal Slave. A True History* (London, 1688), 17.

131 *Ibid.*, 187.

132 Aphra Behn, *Emperor of the Moon: A Farce* (London, 1687), 48. Wing Film 203: 4.

133 *Ibid.*, 59.

134 Stanton, "This New-Found Path Attempting," table 5, 333.

135 Margaret Cavendish, Duchess of Newcastle, *The Description of a New World, Called The Blazing World* (London, 1668), 139.

136 On Cavendish and science, see Lisa T. Sarasohn, "'A Science Turned Upside Down': Feminism and the Natural Philosophy of Margaret Cavendish,"

Huntington Library Quarterly 47 (1984), 289–307, and Anna Battigelli, *Margaret Cavendish and the Exiles of the Mind* (Lexington: University Press of Kentucky, 1998). Both agree that what previous commentators found to be very eccentric ideas in Cavendish were within the realm of contemporary scientific discourse. Battigelli argues that Cavendish "made lasting contributions to atomism itself" and that she was "one of the first to transmit Gassendi's revival of Epicurean atomist into England" (48–49). The evidence for Cavendish's influence on others seems weak to me, and I am inclined to agree with Sarasohn's view that, however interesting Cavendish's thought was, it did not significantly influence the science or philosophy of her own time. Cavendish's access to such thought was limited by her inability to read Latin and, more surprisingly considering her long residence in Paris, French.

137 Samuel I. Mintz, "The Duchess of Newcastle's Visit to the Royal Society," *Journal of English and Germanic Philology* 51 (1952), 174.

138 Cavendish, *Blazing World*, 15.

139 *Ibid.*, 54. I have emended "contagions" to "contagious."

140 This point is made by Sarashon, "A Science Turned Upside Down," 292–93.

141 Although I cannot agree with Carol Barash's enthusiasm for Behn's court panegyrics, there was no doubt political value in Behn's writing in her explicitly female persona on the occasion of James II's controversial accession in 1685; it made the group of poets heralding the accession of James and his Queen seem more diverse and representative of the nation as a whole. Barash, *English Women's Poetry*, 129–45. Barash is especially interested in Behn's poems representing Queens and argues that these poems construct the Queens as figures of authority and desire for the female poet, creating a community of heroic women.

2 PARTISANS OF VIRTUE AND RELIGION, 1689–1702

1 This Rawlinson manuscript was first published as Appendix D in Ruth Perry, *The Celebrated Mary Astell: An Early English Feminist* (Chicago: University of Chicago Press, 1986). "Judgement" is on pp. 413–29.

2 *Devotions in the Ancient Way of Offices . . .* (London, 1700), "To the Reader." Hickes refers to Josiah Woodward's *Account of the Rise and Progress of the Religious Societies in the City of London and of the Endeavours for Reformation of Manners which have been made therein* (1698), an important contemporary account. The SPCK distributed throughout the country many thousands of copies of this and Woodward's other works against vice. Hickes does not identify the adapter of the 1700 volume in that volume or reveal her sex. He does describe the adapter as "one that hath a mighty genius for Divinity" and as a person who has "attained to a Skill in the Sacred Science, not much inferior to that of the best Divine."

3 Dudley W. R. Bahlman, *The Moral Revolution of 1688* (New Haven: Yale University Press, 1957), 17.

4 Jeremy Collier, *A Short View of the Immorality, and Profaneness of the English Stage, Together with the Sense of Antiquity upon this Argument* (London, 1698), 1.

5 [Catharine Trotter], *The Fatal Friendship*, (London, 1698), "Dedication," and "To the Author of the Fatal Friendship."

6 Calculations of Quaker titles from Hilda L. Smith and Susan Cardinale, *Women and the Literature of the Seventeenth Century* (New York: Greenwood Press, 1990), xii. Barbara Blaugdone, *Account of the Travels, Sufferings, and Persecutions of Barbara Blaugdone. Given forth as a Testimony to the Lord's Power, and for the Encouragement of Friends* (London, 1691), 15. Wing Film, 2204: 3.

7 François Poullain de La Barre, *The Woman as Good as the Man: Or, the Equality of Both Sexes*, ed. Gerald M. MacLean (Detroit, Mich.: Wayne State University Press, 1988). On the impact of Descartes on French women, see, Erica Harth, *Cartesian Women: Versions and Subversions of Rational Discourse in the Old Regime* (Ithaca, NY: Cornell University Press, 1992).

8 Moira Ferguson, ed., *First Feminists: British Women Writers, 1578–1799* (Bloomington: Indiana University Press and Old Westbury, NY: Feminist Press, 1985), 5. See also Hilda L. Smith, *Reason's Disciples: Seventeenth-Century English Feminists* (Urbana: University of Illinois Press, 1982), ch. 4.

9 [Hopton, Susannah], *Devotions in the Ancient Way of Offices with Psalms, Hymns, and Prayers for every day of the week, and every holiday in the year* (London, 1700), "To the Reader," [A12]. Wing Film, 842:3. Wing and other modern sources give the original author of *Devotions* as "William Birchley"; this was Austen's pseudonym.

10 Flora Isabel MacKinnon, *The Philosophy of John Norris of Bemerton*. Philosophical Monographs 1, Oct. 1910 (Baltimore, Md.: Review Publishing, 1910), 81–82.

11 Later, in *Occasional Thoughts in Reference to a Vertuous or Christian Life* (1705), she again replied to Norris, and to Astell's *The Christian Religion as Professed by a Daughter of the Church* (1705), expressing concern that they undervalued the role of reason in religion and arguing that "our knowledge of God is obtained demonstratively from knowledge acquired by the operations of sensation and reflection." Sarah Hutton, "Damaris Cudworth, Lady Masham: Between Platonism and Enlightenment," *The British Journal for the History of Philosophy* 1 (1993), 37–38.

12 Latitudinarianism was an informal movement within the Church of England that aimed to downplay divisive theological controversy in favor of promoting Christian morality, clear preaching, and a degree of theological toleration. Among its leaders was John Tillotson, in 1689 Dean of St. Paul's and in 1691 Archbishop of Canterbury.

13 [Damaris Cudworth Masham], *A Discourse Concerning the Love of God* (London, 1696), 83.

14 *Ibid.*, 82.

15 *Ibid.*, 27, 126.

16 Francis X. J. Coleman, *Neither Angel nor Beast: The Life and Works of Blaise Pascal* (New York and London: Routledge & Kegan Paul, 1986), 37–38.

17 Masham, *Discourse*, 31.

18 Patricia Springborg, "Astell, Masham, and Locke: Religion and Politics," in *Women Writers and the Early Modern British Political Tradition*, ed. Hilda L. Smith (Cambridge: Cambridge University Press, 1998), 109–17.

19 [Mary Astell], *A Serious Proposal to the Ladies, for the Advancement of their True and Greatest Interest, By a Lover of her Sex* (London, 1694), 61, 146. This is Part I.

20 *Ibid.*, 89.

21 *Ibid.*, 73–74.

22 *Ibid.*, 86.

23 *Ibid.*, 49–50.

24 [Mary Astell], *A Serious Proposal to the Ladies. Part II: Wherin a Method is Offer'd for the Improvement of their Minds* (London, 1697), 122.

25 Alessa Johns, "Mary Astell's 'Excited Needles': Theorizing Feminist Utopia in Seventeenth-Century England," in *Female Communities: Literary Visions and Cultural Realities*, ed. Rebecca D'Monté and Nicole Pohl (New York: St. Martin's Press, in association with the Institute of English Studies, School of Advanced Study, University of London, 2000), 139.

26 Astell, *Serious Proposal, Part II*, 211–12.

27 Perry, *Mary Astell*, 233–43.

28 George Ballard, *Memoirs of Several Ladies of Great Britain who have been celebrated for their writings or skill in the Learned Languages, Arts, and Sciences*, ed. Ruth Perry (Detroit: Wayne State University Press, 1985), 347.

29 E. J. F. and D. B., "George Berkeley and *The Ladies Library*," *Berkeley Newsletter* (Dublin), no. 4 (December 1980), 5–13; and Patricia Springborg, ed. *Mary Astell, A Serious Proposal to the Ladies, Parts I & II* (London: Pickering & Chatto, 1997), xviii–xix.

30 Astell, *Serious Proposal, Part I*, 51, 53.

31 This point is made by Christine Mason Sutherland, "Mary Astell: 'Reclaiming Rhetorica' in the Seventeenth Century," in *Reclaiming Rhetorica: Women in the Rhetorical Tradition*, ed. Andrea A. Lunsford (Pittsburgh, Pa.: University of Pittsburgh Press, 1995), 102.

32 Elizabeth Thomas, *Miscellany Poems on Several Subjects* (London, 1722), 219. Many of these poems probably date from an earlier period.

33 On this point more generally, see, Susan Staves, *Player's Scepters: Fictions of Authority in the Restoration* (Lincoln: University of Nebraska Press, 1979), 111–90.

34 Mary Astell, *Some Reflections upon Marriage. The Third Edition. To which is added a Preface, in answer to some objections* (London, 1706), [A4v].

35 Patricia Springborg, "Introduction," in *Astell: Political Writings*, ed. Patricia Springborg, Cambridge Texts in the History of Political Thought (Cambridge: Cambridge University Press, 1996), xxviii.

36 Perry, *Mary Astell*, 155.

37 [Mary Astell], *Some Reflections upon Marriage. occasion'd by the Duke and Dutchess of Mazarine's Case; Which is also consider'd* (London, 1700), 4.

38 *Ibid.*, 66–67.

39 Sutherland, "Reclaiming Rhetorica," 105.

40 Astell, *Reflections upon Marriage*, 66.

41 Gilbert McEwen, *The Oracle of the Coffee House: John Dunton's Athenian Mercury* (San Marino, Calif.: Huntington Library, 1972), 107.

42 As rector of Bemerton, Norris was aware that he lived in the same house Herbert had had when he was rector of Bemerton.

43 David Morris, *The Religious Sublime: Christian Poetry and Critical Tradition in Eighteenth-Century England* (Lexington: University Press of Kentucky, 1972), 14.

44 Rowe cut the final couplet in versions of the poem in subsequent editions.

45 [Elizabeth Rowe], *Poems on Several Occasions. By Philomela* (London, 1696), "To One that Persuades me to Leave the Muse," "A Paraphrase on the Canticles, Chap. 3," 42.

46 *Ibid.*, 13.

47 *Ibid.*, 35.

48 On this season, see Paula Backscheider, *Spectacular Politics: Theatrical Power and Mass Culture in Early Modern England* (Baltimore, Md.: Johns Hopkins University Press, 1993). The seventh play has not yet been attributed to a named woman.

49 Jacqueline Pearson, *The Prostituted Muse: Images of Women and Women Dramatists, 1642–1737* (New York: St. Martin's Press, 1988), 170.

50 Constance Clark, *Three Augustan Women Playwrights* (New York: Peter Lang, 1986), 78.

51 On this point, see, Susan Staves, "Tragedy: Orphaned by the Enlightenment?," in *Cambridge Companion to British Theatre, 1740–1830*, ed. Jane Moody and Daniel O'Quinn (Cambridge: Cambridge University Press, forthcoming).

52 Catharine Trotter, *Fatal Friendship. A Tragedy* (London, 1698), 20.

53 *Ibid.*, 54.

54 *Ibid.*, 41.

55 *Ibid.*, 56.

56 John Wilson Bowyer, *The Celebrated Mrs. Centlivre* (New York: Greenwood Press, 1968), 32–33.

57 Jane Spencer, *Aphra Behn's Afterlife* (Oxford: Oxford University Press, 2000), 151.

58 Melinda Rabb, "Angry Beauties: (Wo)Manley Satire and the Stage," in *Cutting Edges: Postmodern Critical Essays on Eighteenth-Century Satire*, ed. James E. Gill (Knoxville: University of Tennessee Press, 1995), 148.

59 Delarivière Manley, *The Royal Mischief, a Tragedy* (London, 1696), 45–46.

60 Fidelis Morgan, *The Female Wits: Women Playwrights of the Restoration* (London: Virago, 1981), 210.

61 Rabb, "Angry Beauties," 147, 153.

62 Manley, *Royal Mischief,* 10.

63 *Ibid.,* 3.

64 *Ibid.,* 26.

65 *Ibid.,* 38.

66 *Ibid.,* 36.

67 *Ibid.,* 30.

68 Pearson, *Prostituted Muse,* 167.

69 Derek Hughes, *English Drama, 1660–1700* (Oxford: Clarendon Press, 1996), 419.

70 Mary Pix, *The Beau Defeated; or, The Lucky Younger Brother. A Comedy* (London, 1700), 4.

71 *Ibid.,* 4–5. I have supplied a comma after "Musical."

72 Margarete Rubik, *Early Women Dramatists, 1550–1800* (Basingstoke: Macmillan; New York: St. Martin's Press, 1998), 80.

73 Pix, *Beau Defeated,* 19.

74 *Ibid.,* 20.

75 *Ibid.,* 34.

76 *Ibid.*

77 *Ibid.,* 35.

78 Pix indicated that her play was partly translated from the French. John Harrington Smith identified Florent Carton Dancourt's *Le Chevalier à la mode* (1687) as the source of this plot. "French Sources of Six English Comedies," *Journal of English and Germanic Philology* 47 (1948), 390–94.

79 Pix, *Beau Defeated,* 46.

80 *Ibid.,* 17.

81 Lynda R. Payne, "Mary Pix," *Dictionary of Literary Biography,* vol. 80 (Detroit, Mich.: Gale Research, 1989), 180.

82 [Judith Drake], *Essay in Defence of the Female Sex. In which are inserted the Characters of a Pedant, a Squire, a Beau, a Vertuoso, a Poetaster, a City-Critick, &c.: in a Letter to a Lady* (London, 1696), 13–14.

83 *Ibid.,* 32.

84 *Ibid.,* 29.

85 *Ibid.,* 46.

86 *Ibid.,* 64–65.

87 *Ibid.,* 138.

88 Brenda Tooley, "'Like a False Renegade': The Ends and Means of Feminist Apologetics in *A Dialogue Concerning Women* and *An Essay in Defence of the Female Sex,*" *The Eighteenth Century: Theory and Interpretation* 36 (1995), 174.

89 "To the Ingenious Author, on her Tragedy, call'd Fatal Friendship," in *Fatal Friendship.*

3 POLITICS, GALLANTRY, AND LADIES IN THE REIGN OF QUEEN ANNE
1702–1714

1 A useful discussion may be found in J. H. Plumb, *The Growth of Political Stability in England, 1675–1725* (London: Macmillan, 1967).

2 For the perspectives of various contemporaries on these Bills, see: Irvin Eherenpreis, *Swift: the Man, his Works, and the Age*, 3 vols. (Cambridge, Mass.: Harvard University Press, 1967), II: 114–21, 283–84; Paula R. Backscheider, *Daniel Defoe: His Life* (Baltimore, Md.: Johns Hopkins University Press, 1989), 84–105; Mary Astell, *Astell: Political Writings*, ed. Patricia Springborg (Cambridge: Cambridge University Press, 1996), 123–87, offers an introduction to *A Fair Way* and is heavily annotated.

3 [Mary Astell], *A Fair Way With the Dissenters and Their Patrons . . . by a very Moderate Person and Dutiful Subject to the Queen* (London, 1704), 2. EC Film, 7456, no. 8. I have emended "Reeader" to "Reader." Here Astell also specifically considers Masham's *Discourse Concerning the Love of God*, treating it as if it were by Locke. See Astell's *Political Writings*, ed. Springborg, xx.

4 Paula McDowell, *The Women of Grub Street: Press, Politics, and Gender in the London Literary Marketplace, 1678–1730* (Oxford: Clarendon Press, 1998), 219.

5 Cheryl Turner, *Living by the Pen: Women Writers in the Eighteenth Century* (London: Routledge, 1992), 87, and Ruth Herman, *The Business of a Woman: The Political Writings of Delarivier Manley* (Newark: University of Delaware Press, 2003), 30. Herman prints Manley's surviving letters to Tory politicians in Appendix II, 252–61.

6 Quoted in McDowell, *Women of Grub Street*, 242.

7 Catherine Gallagher, *Nobody's Story: The Vanishing Acts of Women Writers in the Marketplace, 1670–1820* (Berkeley: University of California Press, 1994), 113–14.

8 For a fine discussion of this new discursive sphere mapped out by Addison and Steele, see Michael G. Ketcham, *Transparent Designs: Reading, Performance, and Form in the Spectator Papers* (Athens: University of Georgia Press, 1985).

9 *Letters from Orinda to Poliarchis* (London, 1705), Preface, A4–[A4v].

10 On these letters, see, John Wilson Bowyer, *The Celebrated Mrs. Centlivre* (1952; reprint, New York: Greenwood Press, 1968), 15–31; *The Works of George Farquhar*, 2 vols., ed. Shirley Strum Kenny (Oxford: Clarendon Press, 1988), II: 392, 398–9, 411, 416–20, 441, 530–3, 593–4.

11 Carol Barash, *English Women's Poetry, 1649–1714: Politics, Community, and Linguistic Authority* (Oxford: Clarendon Press, 1996), 236.

12 Alexander Pope, *The Poems of Alexander Pope*, ed. John Butt (New Haven, Conn.: Yale University Press, 1963), 288.

13 Quoted from Bowyer, *Mrs. Centlivre*, 31. From *Familiar and Courtly Letters 1701* (*Works of George Farquhar*, ed. Kenny), II. Bowyer thinks four of these Celadon letters are Farquhar's. Farquhar's editor, Kenny, thinks only the first two are. All are attributed to Farquhar in the 1718 edition of *Familiar and Courtly Letters*. Kenny suggests that the author of the other letters was Captain William Ayloffe and that "the lady of the correspondence, not the gentleman, may have been responsible for submitting the letters for

publication. If she did, she might well have mixed letters from two different suitors in the Celadon sequence, or, indeed, invented some" (II: 532).

14 H. Bunker Wright, "Matthew Prior and Elizabeth Singer," *Philological Quarterly* 24 (1943), 71–82.

15 *Ibid.*, 79.

16 *Ibid.*, 76.

17 *Ibid.*, 75.

18 30 December 1702, *The Correspondence of John Locke*, 8 vols., ed. E. S. De Beer (Oxford: Clarendon Press, 1982), VII: 730–31.

19 Bonamy Dobrée, *English Literature in the Early Eighteenth Century: 1700–1740* (New York: Oxford University Press, 1959), 123.

20 Vincent Carretta, "'Images Reflect from Art to Art': Alexander Pope's Collected *Works* of 1717," in *Poems in their Places: The Intertextuality and Order of Poetic Collections*, ed. Neil Fraistat (Chapel Hill: University of North Carolina Press, 1986), 97–98.

21 For example, the *Works* of Rowe and Trotter Cockburn were published posthumously. Rowe died in 1737; Theophilus Rowe, her nephew, published *Miscellaneous Works in Verse and Prose* in 1739. Trotter Cockburn died in 1749; she had been trying to publish her works by subscription but did not succeed. Dr. Thomas Birch published *The Works of Mrs. Catharine Cockburn: Theological, Moral, Dramatic, and Poetical* in 1751. The novelist and playwright, Mary Davys, to be discussed in the next chapter, did publish a *Works of Mrs. Davys* by subscription in 1725.

22 Dorothy Mermin, "Women Becoming Poets: Katherine Philips, Aphra Behn, Anne Finch," *ELH* 57 (1990), 349.

23 Annabel M. Patterson, *Pastoral and Ideology: Vergil to Valéry* (Berkeley: University of California Press, 1987), 199, 205.

24 Dobrée, *English Literature*, 132.

25 "The Critick and the Writer of Fables," [Anne Finch], *Miscellany Poems, On Several Occasions, By a Lady* (London, 1713), 165.

26 Lady Mary Chudleigh, *Poems on Several Occasions. Together with the Song of the Three Children Paraphras'd* (London, 1703), preface, A4.

27 *Ibid.*, 124.

28 *Ibid.*, 11, 13.

29 *Ibid.*, 21–22.

30 *Ibid.*, 37.

31 *Ibid.*, 39.

32 *Ibid.*, 50.

33 *Ibid.*, 51.

34 *Ibid.*, 57.

35 *Ibid.*, 60.

36 Lady Mary Chudleigh, *Essays upon Several Subjects in Prose and Verse* (London, 1710), 10–11.

37 Chudleigh, "A Song," *Poems*, 12. "A Song" is separately paginated.

38 *Ibid.*, 39.

39 Useful discussions of these poems include: Hilda L. Smith, *Reason's Disciples: Seventeenth-Century English Feminists* (Urbana: University of Illinois Press, 1982), 163–87; Felicity A. Nussbaum, *The Brink of All We Hate: English Satires on Women, 1660–1750* (Lexington: University Press of Kentucky, 1984), 26–34, on Gould and Egerton; and Marilyn L. Williamson, *Raising their Voices: British Women Writers, 1650–1750* (Detroit: Wayne State University Press, 1990), 90, 92–100, 161–67.

40 Mrs. S. F. [Sarah Fyge Egerton], *Poems on Several Occasions* (London, 1703), A3.

41 Egerton, *Poems*, "The Power of Love," 55.

42 *Ibid.*, 56.

43 Egerton, "The Fond Shepherdess," *Poems*, 6; this poem is separately paginated.

44 *Ibid.*, 12.

45 *Ibid.* I have emended "Flocks" to "Flock."

46 *Ibid.*, 15.

47 Egerton, *Poems*, 70.

48 *Ibid.*, 15. I have emended "Schreiks" to "Shrieks" and "Vesevius to "Vesuvius" as directed by the list of errata. The idea of cursing the Muses and verse is in Nicolas Boileau's "Satire 2." See Boileau's *Œuvres Complètes*, ed. Françoise Escal ([Paris]: Gallimard, 1966), 17–18, and Samuel Butler's translation, "Satyr on Rhyme," in Butler's *Satires and Miscellaneous Poetry and Prose*, ed. René Lamar (Cambridge: Cambridge University Press, 1928), 125–27.

49 Egerton, *Poems*, 25.

50 Manuscript letter quoted in Barash, *Women's Poetry*, 282, n. 37.

51 Barbara McGovern follows Iola Williams in noting that the title page of the first edition declared the poems were "Written by a Lady," but that subsequent title pages printed that year gave the author as "Lady Winchilsea." Barbara McGovern, *Anne Finch and Her Poetry: A Critical Biography* (Athens: University of Georgia Press, 1992), 100.

52 Finch, *Miscellany Poems*, 33, 39.

53 *Ibid.*, 43.

54 *Ibid.*, 104.

55 *Ibid.*, 291–92.

56 "A Letter to Dafnis, April 2nd 1685," *The Poems of Anne Countess of Winchilsea*, ed. Myra Reynolds (Chicago: University of Chicago Press, 1903), 19–20. Neither this nor "An Invitation to Dafnis," were included in the 1713 volume.

57 Finch, *Miscellany Poems*, 274, 276.

58 *Ibid.*, 105.

59 *Ibid.*, 107; A "tippet" was a shoulder cape; a "palatine" was a fur tippet. Mr. Doiley or Doyley was a linen draper who introduced a new, lightweight wool fabric that *Spectator* 283 called "both cheap and genteel."

60 Finch, *Miscellany Poems*, 108.

61 [Delarivière Manley], *Secret Memoirs and Manners of Several Persons of Quality, of both Sexes. From the New Atalantis, an Island in the Mediteranean [!]. Written originally in Italian* (London, 1709), I: 171. Volume I and volume II were published separately, both in 1709. Volume II adds to its title, after *Written originally in Italian, and translated from the third edition of the French. The Second Volume.* My discussion is indebted to Rosalind Ballaster's notes for her modernized edition: *New Atalantis* (London: Pickering & Chatto, 1991).

62 *The Secret History of Queen Zarah* has usually been attributed to Manley, but J. A. Downie makes a good argument suggesting that it was written by Joseph Browne rather than Manley; other scholars have discovered that significant sections of this *Secret History* were translated from French sources. See: J. A. Downie, "What if Delariviere Manley did not write *The Secret History of Queen Zarah?*," *Library: The Transactions of the Bibliographical Society*, series 7, 5 (2004), 247–64, and Rachel Carnell, "More Borrowing from Bellegarde in Delarivier Manley's *Queen Zarah and the Zarazians*," *Notes and Queries* 51 (2004), 377–79.

63 "To Mrs. Frances Hewet, 12 Nov. [1709]," *The Complete Letters of Lady Mary Wortley Montagu*, ed. Robert Halsband, 3 vols. (Oxford: Clarendon Press, 1965), I: 18.

64 Manley, *New Atalantis*, I: 1.

65 *Ibid.*, I: 108, 229.

66 François de La Rochefoucauld, *Maxims*, trans. Leonard Tancock (Harmondsworth: Penguin, 1959), 84: Maxim 368.

67 Manley, *New Atalantis*, II: 252.

68 This point is made in D. J. Culpin, *La Rochefoucauld: Maxims* (London: Grant & Culter, 1995), an excellent discussion of the *Maxims*.

69 Manley, *New Atalantis*, II: 206.

70 *Ibid.*, I: 159. Manley's animus against Egerton, whom she knew, seems to derive from Egerton's having given evidence against Manley in Doctors' Commons in 1705, when Manley was accused of participating in a fraud. See Charles Wylie, "Mrs. Manley," *Notes and Queries*, 2nd sers., no. 72 (1957), 392–30.

71 Manley, *New Atalantis*, II: 221–23.

72 B. G. MacCarthy, *The Female Pen: Women Writers and Novelists, 1621–1808* (1946–47; reprint New York University Press, 1994), 195, 200.

73 William Beatty Warner, *Licensing Entertainment: The Elevation of Novel Reading in Britain, 1684–1750* (Berkeley: University of California Press, 1998), 92–94.

74 For example, Jane Spencer, *The Rise of the Woman Novelist: From Aphra Behn to Jane Austen* (Oxford: Basil Blackwell, 1986), 113–16.

75 Gallagher, *Nobody's Story*, 137, 119, 123.

76 [Delarivière Manley], *The Adventures of Rivella; or, The History of the Author of the Atalantis . . .* (London, 1714), 16. Published with *Court Intrigues*, but separately paginated.

77 Manley, *Rivella*, 31.

78 *Ibid.*, 20.

79 *Ibid.*, 74.

80 *Ibid.*, 120.

81 *Ibid.*, 49. I have emended "naked Bed" to "Bed naked."

82 *Ibid.*, 51.

83 Catharine Trotter, *A Defence of the Essay of Human Understanding, Written by Mr. Lock. Wherein its Principles with Reference to Morality, Reveal'd Religion, and the Immortality of the Soul, [!] are Consider'd and Justify'd. In Answer to Some Remarks on that Essay* (London, 1702), 10. EC Film, Reel 5638, no. 26. For a discussion of *A Defence*, see Martha Brandt Bolton, "Some Aspects of the Philosophical Work of Catharine Trotter," *Journal of the History of Philosophy* 31 (1993), 565–88.

84 Trotter, *Defence of the Essay*, "Preface," para. 1.

85 Catharine Trotter, *The Revolution of Sweden. A Tragedy* (London, 1706), 4.

86 René Vertot, *The History of the Revolution in Sweden, Occasion'd by the Change of Religion, and Alteration of the Government in that Kingdom*, trans. J. Mitchell, MD, 6th edn. (London, 1729), 201.

87 Trotter, *Revolution*, 20.

88 *Ibid.*, 8.

89 *Ibid.*, 31.

90 Vertot, *Revolution in Sweden*, 123–24.

91 Trotter, *Revolution*, 71.

92 Valeria in Centlivre's *The Basset-Table* (London, 1706), 40.

93 Susanna Centlivre, *The Busie Body* (London, 1709), 4.

94 *Ibid.*, 30.

95 *Ibid.*, 28.

96 *Ibid.*, 8.

97 William Hazlitt, *The Complete Works of William Hazlitt*, ed. P. P. Howe, 21 vols. (London: J. M. Dent, 1930), IX: 75. This discussion comes from Hazlitt's introduction to *The Busie Body* for Oxberry's *New English Drama* (1818–25).

98 Susanna Centlivre, *The Wonder: A Woman Keeps a Secret* (London, 1714), 10. EC Film, Reel 569, no. 20.

99 George Winchester Stone, Jr. and George M. Kahrl, *David Garrick: A Critical Biography* (Carbondale: Southern Illinois University Press, 1979), 512.

100 Centlivre, *Wonder*, 25.

101 *Ibid.*, 38.

102 *Ibid.*, 39.

103 *Ibid.*, 54.

104 *Ibid.*, 58.

105 *Ibid.*, 59.

106 *Ibid.*, 65.

107 *Ibid.*, 69.

108 *Ibid.*, 79.
109 Judith Philips Stanton, "'This New-Found Path attempting': Women Dramatists in England, 1660–1800," in *Curtain Calls: British and American Women and the Theater, 1660–1800* (Athens: Ohio University Press, 1991), 333. In these terms, Centlivre considerably outdid Behn, although *The Rover* comes in fourth.
110 Paul P. Kies, "The Sources and Basic Model of Lessing's *Miss Sara Sampson*," *Modern Philology* 24 (1926–27), 65–90.
111 See *The London Stage, 1660–1800: A Calendar of Plays . . . Part 2: 1700–1729*, ed. Emmett L. Avery (Carbondale: Southern Illinois University Press, 1960) for lengths of runs of Centlivre's plays.
112 Boyer, *Centlivre*, 98–99.
113 Ralph Strauss, *The Unspeakable Curll . . .* (1927; reprint New York: Augustus M. Kelley, 1970), 227.
114 Shirley Strum Kenny, *The Plays of Richard Steele* (Oxford: Clarendon Press, 1971), 283.
115 F. P. Lock, *Susanna Centlivre* (Boston: Twayne, 1979), 18.
116 Michel Foucault, "What is an Author?," in *Textual Strategies: Perspectives in Post-Structuralist Criticism*, ed. Josué Harari (Ithaca, NY: Cornell University Press, 1979), 148.
117 For consideration of the authorship of *The Female Tatler*, see Bernard Mandeville, *By a Society of Ladies: Essays in The Female Tatler*, ed. M. M. Goldsmith (Bristol: University of Durham and Thoemmes Press, 1999), 41–48.
118 *Poetical Miscellanies: The Sixth Part. Containing a Collection of Original Poems, with several New Translations. By the Most Eminent Hands* (London, 1709), 225.

4 BATTLE JOINED, 1715–1737

1 Cheryl Turner, *Living by the Pen: Women Writers in the Eighteenth Century* (1992; reprint London: Routledge, 1994), 34.
2 Margaret J. M. Ezell, *Writing Women's Literary History* (Baltimore, Md.: Johns Hopkins University Press, 1999), 105. Calculated from Ezell's numbers; I have subtracted first editions.
3 See, e.g., Rosalind Ballaster, *Seductive Forms: Women's Amatory Fiction from 1684 to 1740* (Oxford: Clarendon Press, 1992), 187–92.
4 Benjamin Colman, *Reliquiæ Turellæ, et lachrymæ paternæ . . .* (Boston, 1735), "On Reading the Warning by Mrs. Singer," 73. A note identifies the prophetess of old as Huldah.
5 Marcia Heinemann, "Eliza Haywood's Career in the Theatre," *Notes and Queries*, n.s., 20 (1973), 9–13.
6 [Lady Mary Wortley Montagu], *The Dean's Provocation for Writing the Lady's Dressing-Room. A Poem* (London, 1734), 8. Late in her life, Montagu boasted that she had decorated her commode with false backs of books by

Pope, Swift, and Bolingbroke, so that she had "the satisfaction of shitting on them every day." Isobel Grundy, *Lady Mary Wortley Montagu: Comet of the Enlightenment* (Oxford: Oxford University Press, 1999), 566.

7 Elizabeth Thomas, *Miscellany Poems on Several Subjects* (London, 1722), 86–87.

8 *Ibid.*, 80, 81.

9 *Ibid.*, 98.

10 *Ibid.*, 177.

11 *Ibid.*, 179.

12 *Ibid.*, 184.

13 *Ibid.*, 219.

14 *Ibid.*, 147, 148. The three poems on Chudleigh are, "To the Lady Chudleigh, the Anonymous Author of the Lady's Defence," from which my quotation is taken, and "To the Lady Chudleigh, On Printing her Excellent Poems," and "On the Death of Lady Chudleigh."

15 Lady Mary Wortley Montagu, *Essays and Poems and Simplicity, A Comedy*, ed. Robert Halsband and Isobel Grundy (Oxford: Clarendon Press, 1993), 299.

16 John Gay, *Poetry and Prose*, ed. Vinton A. Dearing and Charles E. Beckwith, 2 vols. (Oxford: Clarendon Press, 1974), I: 101.

17 Versions of this poem were claimed by both Montagu and Gay. See Isobel Grundy, "Lady Mary Wortley Montagu and the Theatrical Eclogue," *Lumen: Selected Proceedings from the Canadian Society for Eighteenth-Century Studies* 17 (1998), 63–75.

18 [Lady Mary Wortley Montagu, and others], *Court Poems. Viz; I. The Basset-Table. An Eclogue. II. The Drawing-Room. III. The Toilet. Publish'd Faithfully as they were found in a Pocket-Book taken up in Westminster-Hall, the Last Day of Lord Winton's Tryal* (London, MDCCVI [for 1716]), 14.

19 Montagu, *Essays and Poems*, 187.

20 *The Works of John Wilmot, Earl of Rochester*, ed. Harold Love (Oxford: Oxford University Press, 1999), 20.

21 Montagu, *Essays and Poems*, 297.

22 *Ibid.*, 271.

23 *Ibid.*, 244, 245.

24 Gillian Beer, "'Our Unnatural No-voice': The Heroic Epistle, Pope, and Women's Gothic," in *Modern Essays on Eighteenth-Century Literature*, ed. Leopold Damrosch, Jr. (New York: Oxford University Press, 1988), 384. This fine essay on the tradition concentrates on Pope's "Eloisa to Abelard" and argues, reasonably, that the tradition is male and not "a feminist form of literature" (384).

25 In another good essay on the Ovidian tradition, Rachel Trickett notes that Drayton in *England's Heroicall Epistles* used women from English history (for example, Jane Shore) rather than mythological ones. Rachel Trickett, "The *Heroides* and the English Augustans," in *Ovid Renewed: Ovidian Influences on Literature and Art from the Middle Ages to the Twentieth Century*, ed.

Charles Martindale (Cambridge: Cambridge University Press, 1988), 191–204.

26 Isobel Grundy first printed this poem and gave an account of the contemporary events in "Ovid and Eighteenth-Century Divorce: An Unpublished Poem by Lady Mary Wortley Montagu," *Review of English Studies*, n.s., 23 (1972), 417–28.

27 Montagu, *Essays and Poems*, 228, 229.

28 *Ibid.*, 229, 230.

29 *Ibid.*, 230.

30 *Ibid.*, 231.

31 *Ibid.*, 231.

32 *Ibid.*, 231, 232.

33 Mary Davys, *Self-Rival*, in *The Works of Mrs. Davys: Consisting of Plays, Novels, Poems and Familiar Letters, several of which never before publish'd*, 2 vols. (London, 1725), I: 31.

34 *Ibid.*, 51.

35 *Ibid.*, 68.

36 *Ibid.*, 20.

37 Francisco de Quevedo, *The Choice Humorous and Satirical Works*, ed. Charles Duff (London, [1926]), 249–50.

38 Davys, *Works*, I: 38.

39 *Ibid.*

40 *Ibid.*, 55.

41 *Ibid.*, 67.

42 [Mary Davys], *The Accomplish'd Rake: or, Modern Fine Gentleman. Being an Exact Description of the Conduct and Behaviour of a Person of Distinction* (London, 1727), 73.

43 *Ibid.*, 174.

44 *Ibid.*, 99.

45 *Ibid.*, 195.

46 *Ibid.*, 78–79.

47 *Ibid.*, 124.

48 *Ibid.*, 101.

49 *Ibid.*, 21.

50 John J. Richetti, *Popular Fiction Before Richardson: Narrative Patterns, 1700–1739* (Oxford: Clarendon Press, 1969), 157.

51 Haywood, *A Certain Island*, II: 140, also cited in Richetti, *Popular Fiction*.

52 Susanna Centlivre, *The Gotham Election. A Farce* (London, 1715), 42, 44. As Centlivre explains in the preface, the government censors refused permission for this play to be acted.

53 Heinemann, "Haywood," 11; see also, Christine Blouch, "Biographical Introduction," *Selected Works of Eliza Haywood*, ed. Alexander Pettit, 6 vols. (London: Pickering & Chatto, 2000): I: xxi–lxxxii.

54 Alexander Pope, *The Dunciad*, ed. James Sutherland, 3rd edn. (London: Methuen, 1963), 119.

55 The reference is to *The Works of Mrs. Eliza Haywood: Consisting of Novels, Letters, Poems, and Plays. In four volumes* (London, 1724). Pope, *Dunciad (A)*, 120.

56 [Eliza Haywood], *Love in Excess: or, The Fatal Enquiry* (London, 1719–20), part 3, 35. Published in three separately paginated parts.

57 *Ibid.*, 155.

58 *Ibid.*, 92–93.

59 Catherine Craft-Fairchild, *Masquerade and Gender: Disguise and Female Identity in Eighteenth-Century Fictions by Women* (University Park: Pennsylvania State University Press, 1993), 70.

60 Jane Spencer, *The Rise of the Woman Novelist: From Aphra Behn to Jane Austen* (Oxford: Basil Blackwell, 1986), 117.

61 Cynthia Richards, "'The Pleasures of Complicity': Sympathetic Identification and the Female Reader in Early Eighteenth-Century Women's Amatory Fiction," *The Eighteenth Century: Theory and Interpretation* 36 (1995), 231.

62 Ballaster, *Seductive Forms*, 192, 191.

63 Penelope Aubin, *The Life of Charlotta DuPont, an English Lady; taken from her own Memoirs. Giving an account how she was Trepan'd by her Stepmother to Virginia, how the Ship was taken by Madagascar Pirates, and retaken by a Spanish Man of War . . .* (London, 1723), 13–14.

64 Joe Snader, "The Oriental Captivity Narrative and Early English Fiction," *Eighteenth-Century Fiction* 9 (1997), 292, 291.

65 Penelope Aubin, *The Noble Slaves* (London, 1722), 41–42.

66 *Ibid.*, 153. I have emended by adding the final quotation mark.

67 *Ibid.*, 107.

68 *Ibid.*, 198.

69 *Ibid.*, 134.

70 *Ibid.*, 149.

71 Peter Borsay, "The English Urban Renaissance: the Development of Provincial Urban Culture, c. 1680–1760," in Peter Borsay, *The Eighteenth-Century Town: A Reader in English Urban History, 1688–1820* (London: Longman, 1990), 176. See also, Borsay, *The English Urban Renaissance: Culture and Society in the Provincial Town, 1770–1770* (Oxford: Clarendon Press, 1989), John Feather, *The Provincial Book Trade in Eighteenth-Century England* (Cambridge: Cambridge University Press, 1985), and G. A. Cranfield, *The Development of the Provincial Newspaper, 1700–1760* (1962; reprint Westport, Conn.: Greenwood Press, 1978).

72 Mary Chandler, *The Description of Bath. A Poem . . . 4th ed. To which are added, Several Poems by the same Author* (London, Printed for James Leake, Bookseller in Bath, 1738), 10–11.

73 Chandler, *Description of Bath*, 15. This passage does not appear in the 1733 first edition of the poem, *A Description of Bath*.

74 Mary Barber, *Poems on Several Occasions* (London, 1734), 197.

75 Sarah C. Clapp, "The Beginning of Subscription Publication in the Seventeenth Century," *Modern Philology* 29 (1931), 199–224.

76 See, e.g., F. J. G. Robinson and P. J. Wallis, *Book Subscription Lists. A Revised Guide* (Newcastle upon Tyne: H. Hill for the Book Subscription List Project, 1975), and later supplements, and Pat Rogers, "Pope and his Subscribers," *Publishing History* 3 (1978), 7–36. Thomas Lockwood dissents from this view, arguing that subscription publication instead represented "an intensely nostalgic replication of personal patronage within a publishing system long since operating on market motives – a commercialization of patronage, or even a democratization of it, but in the sense only of a commercially expanded opportunity for lots of people to play cheaply at being patrons as of old." Thomas Lockwood, "Subscription Hunters and their Prey," *Studies in the Literary Imagination* 34 (2001), 132.

77 *The Correspondence of Jonathan Swift*, ed. Harold Williams, 5 vols. (Oxford: Clarendon Press, 1965), III: 44; see also III: 429; IV: 185–87; IV: 538.

78 Margaret Doody, "Swift Among the Women," *Yearbook of English Studies* 18 (1988), 78.

79 Barber, *Poems*, 151.

80 *Ibid.*, xvii–xvii.

81 *Ibid.*, xxv.

82 *Ibid.*, 36–37.

83 *Ibid.*, 183.

84 *Ibid.*, 83–84.

85 *Ibid.*, 85–86.

86 Mary Davys, *The Northern Heiress: or, the Humours of York. A Comedy* (London, 1716), 16.

87 *Ibid.*, 23.

88 *Ibid.*, 70.

89 *Eighteenth-Century Women Poets: An Oxford Anthology*, ed. Roger Lonsdale (Oxford: Oxford University Press, 1989), 84.

90 *Clio; or, a Secret History of the Life and Amours of the Late Celebrated Mrs. S–n–m. Written by Herself, in a Letter to Hillarius* (London, 1752). The book took the form of letters to Aaron Hill; the Manuscript seems to have been found among his papers and was published two years after his death.

91 See Susan Staves, "'The Abuse of Title Pages': Men Writing as Women," in *A Concise Companion to the Restoration and Eighteenth-Century*, ed. Cynthia Wall (London: Blackwell, 2005), 162–82.

92 Henry Fielding, *The Author's Farce*, ed. Charles B. Woods (Lincoln: University of Nebraska Press, 1966), 32.

93 Charles Mish, "Mme de Gomez and *La Belle Assemblée*," *Revue de Littérature Comparée* 34 (1960), 219.

94 Penelope Aubin, trans., *History of Genghizcan the Great, First Emperor of the Antient Moguls and Tartars . . .* (London, 1722), "Preface," vi.

95 *Ibid.*, v.

96 *Ibid.*, vii.

97 *Ibid.*, 2.

98 The nonjurors, believing in the divine right of kings and hereditary succession, refused to swear the oath of allegiance to William and Mary when they ascended to the throne after the Glorious Revolution; they were ejected from their ecclesiastical offices. David Douglas, *English Scholars, 1660–1730* (London: Eyre & Spottiswoode, 1951), offers a useful overview of Anglo-Saxon scholarship and an important consideration of its political context. See also, Mechthild Gretsch, "Elizabeth Elstob: A Scholar's Fight for Anglo-Saxon Studies," *Anglia: Zeitschrift fur Englishe Philologie* 117 (1999), 163–200, 481–524. Gretsch is severe on his predecessors, in some cases, I think, unduly so.

99 Elizabeth Elstob, *An Apology for the Study of Northern Antiquities*, ed. Charles Peake, Augustan Reprint Society, 61 (Los Angeles: William Andrews Clark Memorial Library, University of California, 1956), 75.

100 Shaun F. D. Hughes, "The Anglo-Saxon Grammars of George Hickman and Elizabeth Elstob," in *Anglo-Saxon Scholarship: The First Three Centuries*, ed. Carl T. Berkhout and Milton McC. Gatch (Boston: G. K. Hall, 1982), 122.

101 Elstob, *Apology*, p. x.

102 Jonathan Swift, "A Proposal for Correcting, Improving and Ascertaining the English Tongue," in *Prose Works of Jonathan Swift*, ed. Herbert Davis with Louis Landa, 14 vols. (Oxford: Blackwell, 1957), IX: 11.

103 Ruth Perry, *The Celebrated Mary Astell: An Early English Feminist* (Chicago: University of Chicago Press, 1986), 277.

104 Voltaire, *Les Œuvres complètes de Voltaire*, ed. Theodore Besterman, et al., 67 vols. (Geneva: Institut et Musée Voltaire, 1970–), XXV: 163.

105 All three quoted in Robert Halsband, *The Life of Lady Mary Wortley Montagu* (New York: Oxford University Press, 1960), 289.

106 Quoted in Robert Halsband, *Life of Montagu*, 111.

107 For an account of the resistance to Montagu's campaign and of efforts to erase it from medical history, see, Isobel Grundy, "Medical Advances and Female Fame: Inoculation and its After-Effects," *Lumen: Selected Proceedings from the Canadian Society for Eighteenth-Century Studies* 13 (1994), 13–42.

108 Lady Mary Wortley Montagu, "To Lady Bute, 22 July [1752]," *The Complete Letters of Lady Mary Wortley Montagu*, ed. Robert Halsband, 3 vols. (Oxford: Clarendon Press, 1967), III: 15.

109 "To [Anne] Thistlethwayte," 1 April [1717], *Letters of Montagu*, I: 341–42.

110 "To the Countesse of —," [May 1718], *Letters of Montagu*, I: 405–06.

111 "To the Abbé Conti," 1 April [1717], *Letters of Montagu*, I: 315–17.

112 *Ibid.*, 318.

113 "To Lady Mar," 1 April [1717], *Letters of Montagu*, I: 327–28.

114 *Ibid.*, 328–29.

115 See, e.g., Joseph W. Lew, "Lady Mary's Portable Seraglio," *Eighteenth-Century Studies* 24 (1991), 432–50; Lisa Lowe, *Critical Terrains: French and British Orientalisms* (Ithaca, NY: Cornell University Press, 1991), Elizabeth A. Bohls, "Aesthetics and Orientalism in Lady Mary Wortley Montagu's

Letters," *Studies in Eighteenth-Century Culture* 23 (1994), 179–205; Devoney Looser, "Scolding Lady Mary Wortley Montagu?: The Problematics of Sisterhood in Feminist Criticism," in *Feminist Nightmares: Women at Odds, Feminism and the Problem of Sisterhood*, ed. Susan Ostrov Weisser and Jennifer Fleishner (New York: New York University Press, 1994), 44–61; Srinivas Aravumunden, "Lady Mary Wortley Montagu in the *Hammam*: Masquerade, Womanliness, and Levantization," *ELH* 62 (1995), 69–104.

116 Mary Jo Kietzman, "Montagu's *Turkish Embassy Letters* and Cultural Dislocation," *Studies in English Literature* 38 (1998), 539, 546, 547.

117 Billie Melman, *Women's Orients – English Women and the Middle East, 1718–1918: Sexuality, Religion, and Work* (Ann Arbor: University of Michigan Press, 1992), 95.

118 Elizabeth Rowe, *The Miscellaneous Works in Prose and Verse of Mrs. Elizabeth Rowe. . .*, 2 vols. (London, 1739), I: 71.

119 *Ibid.*, 88, 89.

120 *Ibid.*, 91.

121 "Upon the Death of her Husband. By Mrs. Elizabeth Singer," in *Eloisa to Abelard. Written by Mr. Pope*, 2nd edn. (London, 1720 [for 1719]), 48.

122 *Ibid.*

123 *Ibid.*, 49.

124 *Ibid.*

125 *Song of Solomon* 2: 8, 10.

126 Rowe, *Miscellaneous Works*, I: 234.

127 *Ibid.*, 195.

128 *Ibid.*, 139.

129 *The Poetry of Elizabeth Singer Rowe (1674–1737)*, ed. Madeleine Forell Marshall (Lewiston, NY: Edwin Mellon Press, [1987]), 58.

130 [Elizabeth Rowe], *The History of Joseph. A Poem. In Eight Books. By the Author of Friendship in Death* (London, 1736), 3.

131 *Ibid.*, 6–7.

132 Alun David, "'The Story of Semiramis': an Oriental Tale in Elizabeth Rowe's *The History of Joseph*," *Women's Writing* 4 (1997), 91–101.

133 Rowe, *Joseph*, 26.

134 *Ibid.*, 54.

135 Elizabeth Rowe, *Friendship in Death. In Twenty Letters from the Dead to the Living. To which are added, Thoughts on Death. Translated from the Moral Essays of the Messieurs du Port Royal* (London, 1728), preface, [A4v]. The book is dedicated to Edward Young.

136 *Ibid.*, 58.

137 *Ibid.*, 18–19.

138 *Ibid.*, 101.

139 Richetti, *Popular Fiction*, 247.

140 Alexander Pope, "The First Satire of the Second Book of Horace," *Imitations of Horace*, ed. John Butt (London: Methuen, 1953), 17.

141 Catharine Cockburn, "Verses, occasion'd by the Busts in the Queen's Hermitage . . . and Mr Duck being appointed Keeper of the Library in Merlin's Cave," *The Gentleman's Magazine* 7 (1737), 308.

142 "On the Death of Mrs. Rowe," *The Gentleman's Magazine* 7 (1737), 247. A revised version of this poem appears in *The Gentleman's Magazine* 9 (1739), 152. Cf. "On the Death of the celebrated Mrs. Rowe, (formerly Miss Singer) by a young Lady, her Intimate," *The Gentleman's Magazine* 7 (1737), 183.

5 WOMEN AS MEMBERS OF THE LITERARY
FAMILY, 1737–1756

1 Felicity A. Nussbaum, *The Brink of All We Hate: English Satires on Women, 1660–1750* (Lexington: University Press of Kentucky, 1984).

2 Jane Spencer, *The Rise of the Woman Novelist: From Aphra Behn to Jane Austen* (Oxford: Basil Blackwell, 1986), 75.

3 *Ibid.*, 78.

4 John Duncombe, *The Feminiad. A Poem*, Augustan Reprint Society, pub. no. 207 (Los Angeles: University of California Press, 1981), 15.

5 Eric Rothstein, *Restoration and Eighteenth-Century Poetry, 1660–1780* (Boston: Routledge & Kegan Paul, 1981), 217; Roger Lonsdale, ed., *Eighteenth-Century Women Poets: An Oxford Anthology* (Oxford: Oxford University Press, 1988), 155–56; Margaret Doody, "Swift Among the Women," *Yearbook of English Studies* 18 (1988), 68–92; Claudia N. Thomas, *Alexander Pope and His Eighteenth-Century Women Readers* (Carbondale: Southern Illinois University Press, 1994), 204–9, 230–32, including useful comments on the strains of adapting the persona of the late Pope to women's poetry.

6 A number of these letters were published in *Admiral's Wife; being the Letters of the Hon. Mrs. Edward Boscawen from 1719 to 1761*, ed. Cecil Aspinall-Oglander (London: Longmans, Green, [1940]).

7 Walter Crittendon, *The Life and Writings of Mrs. Sarah Scott, Novelist (1723–97)* (Philadelphia: University of Pennsylvania Press, 1932), 73–74; Betty Rizzo, "Introduction," Sarah Scott, *The History of Sir George Ellison* (Lexington: University Press of Kentucky, 1996), xix–xx.

8 *The Letterbook of Eliza Lucas Pinckney*, ed. Elise Pinckney and Marvin R. Zahniser (Chapel Hill: University of North Carolina Press, 1972), 63.

9 *Ibid.*, 101.

10 *Ibid*, 144.

11 *Ibid.*, 35.

12 *Ibid.*, 36.

13 *Ibid.*, 35.

14 Alexander Pope, *Pastoral Poetry and An Essay on Criticism*, ed. E. Audra and Aubrey Williams (London: Methuen, 1961), 189.

15 Pinckney, *Letterbook.*, 38.

16 *Ibid.*, 185.

17 Jeremy Black, *The English Press, 1621–1861* (Thrupp, Stroud: Sutton Pub., 2000), 9.

18 *The Correspondence of Henry and Sarah Fielding*, ed. Martin C. Battestin and Clive T. Probyn (Oxford: Clarendon Press, 1993), 51.

19 Pinckney, *Letterbook*, 138–39. For the Cherokee point of view see, the editors' notes to this edition of the *Letterbook*, and David H. Corkran, *The Cherokee Frontier: Conflict and Survival, 1740–1760* (Norman: University of Oklahoma Press, 1962).

20 Pinckney, *Letterbook*, 165.

21 For a discussion of this translation and its significance, see William Harlin McBurney and Michael Francis Shugure, eds., *The Virtuous Orphan or, The Life of Marianne Countess of *****. An Eighteenth-Century English Translation. By Mrs. Mary Mitchell Collyer of Marivaux's La Vie de Marianne* (Carbondale: Southern Illinois University Press, 1965).

22 Lennox translated Vital d'Audiguier's romance, *Histoire trage-comique de nostre temps, sous le noms de Lysandre et de Caliste* (1615) and Claudine-Alexandrine Guérin de Tencin's *Mémoirs de conte de Comminges* (1735) as *The Memoirs of the Countess of Berci* (1756); Scott translated Pierre Antoine de la Place's sentimental *Le Laideur amiable* (1752), the first-person story of a good but unattractive woman who suffers her family's contempt but finally marries for love, as *Agreeable Ugliness* (1754).

23 [Mary Collyer], *Felicia to Charlotte. Being Letters from a Young Lady in the Country, to her Friend in Town . . . chiefly tending to prove, that the Seeds of Virtue are implanted in the Mind of Every reasonable being* (London, 1744), 10.

24 *Ibid.*, 13.

25 *Ibid.*, 69.

26 *Ibid.*, 100, 101.

27 *Ibid.*, 262.

28 *Ibid.*, 306.

29 *Ibid.*, 201–02.

30 [Mary Collyer], *Letters from Felicia to Charlotte: Volume Second. By the Author of the First Volume* (London, 1749), 224–25, 257.

31 *Ibid.*, 261.

32 *Ibid.*, 36.

33 *Ibid.*, 279.

34 *Ibid.*, 282.

35 *Ibid.*, 144.

36 *Ibid.*, 170.

37 *The Monthly Review* 2 (Jan. 1750), 229.

38 *The Monthly Review* 2 (Dec. 1749), 90.

39 Frank Donoghue, *The Fame Machine: Book Reviewing and Eighteenth-Century Literary Careers* (Stanford, Calif.: Stanford University Press, 1996), 161.

40 Cockburn published *Remarks upon some writers in the Controversy concerning the Foundation of Moral Obligation* in *The History of the Works of the*

Learned (1743) and *Remarks upon the Principles . . . of Dr. Rutherforth's Essay on the Nature and Obligation of Virtue . . .* (1747). Susanna Wesley published a pamphlet defense of her son John's theology in *Some Remarks on a Letter from the Reverend Mr. Whitefield. To the Reverend Mr. Wesley, In a Letter from a Gentlewoman to her Friend* (1741). Charles Wallace, Jr., discusses the attribution and occasion of this pamphlet and reprints it in *Susanna Wesley: The Complete Writings* (New York: Oxford University Press, 1997).

41 For a more sympathetic view, see Christopher D. Johnson's introduction to his edition of *The Lives of Cleopatra and Octavia* (Lewisburg, Pa.: Bucknell University Press, 1994).

42 For an account of the complex composition of this work, for which the Duchess used a series of male secretaries, see Frances Harris, *A Passion for Government: The Life of Sarah, Duchess of Marlborough* (Oxford: Clarendon Press, 1991).

43 Quaker women and some other religious women continued to write and often to publish their lives, which often involved travel, but they did not much interest themselves in the particulars of the places or peoples they visited and were not concerned to make the enquiries about them characteristic of enlightenment travelers.

44 Miriam Rossiter Small, *Charlotte Ramsay Lennox: An Eighteenth Century Lady of Letters* (New Haven: Yale University Press, 1935), 210. *The Monthly Review* devoted two major articles to Lennox's translation, 14 (1756), 561–73; 15 (1757), 206–16. Johnson wrote the favorable review in *Literary Magazine* 1 (Sept. 1756), 281–82. Small notes that the first edition of the translation was published in 1755, although the title-page date is 1756; she describes sixteen editions.

45 Quoted in Small, *Lennox*, 21. *A Series of Letters between Mrs. Elizabeth Carter and Miss Catherine Talbot* (London, 1809), II: 47.

46 See chapter 8, "The Expanding Trade," in John Feather, *A History of British Publishing* (London: Croom Helm, 1988), 93–106.

47 Paula Backsheider, "The Story of Eliza Haywood's Novels: Caveats and Questions," in *The Passionate Fictions of Eliza Haywood: Essays on Her Life and Work*, ed. Kirsten T. Saxton and Rebecca P. Bocchicchio (Lexington: University Press of Kentucky, 2000), 2.

48 Eliza Haywood, *The Wife. By Mira, one of the Authors of the Female Spectator, and Epistles for Ladies* (London, 1756), 67, 66.

49 *Ibid.*, 193.

50 *Ibid.*, 276.

51 *Ibid.*, 269, 248.

52 Eliza Haywood, *The Husband. In Answer to the Wife* (London, 1756), 7–8.

53 *Ibid.*, 32–33.

54 Henry Fielding, *Covent Garden Journal and A Plan of the Universal Register-Office*, ed. Bertrand A. Goldgar (Middletown, Conn.: Wesleyan University Press, 1988), *Covent Garden Journal*, nos. 3 and 15.

55 Henry Fielding, *The History of Tom Jones: A Foundling*, ed. Martin C. Battestin (Hanover, NH: Wesleyan University Press, 1975), I: 487–94 (book 9, ch. 1, "Of those who lawfully may, and of those who may not write such Histories as this").

56 *Ibid.*, book 10, ch. 2, 530.

57 J. F. Burrows and A. J. Hassall, "*Anna Boleyn* and the Authenticity of Fielding's Feminine Narratives," *Eighteenth-Century Studies* 21 (1988), 427–53. Martin Battestin with Ruthe R. Battestin, *Henry Fielding: A Life* (London: Routledge, 1989), 332, 379, 371, 440 (suggesting also her contribution to *The Jacobite's Journal*, no. 30).

58 Burrows and Hassall, "Authenticity," 447.

59 Quoted in Battestin and Battestin, *Henry Fielding*, 229.

60 Hester Thrale Piozzi to the Reverend Leonard Chappelow, 15 March. 1795. Quoted in Battestin and Battestin, *Henry Fielding*. It concludes, "Given Fielding's views on the subject of scholarly females, there is probably a grain of truth in this chaff. That Sarah's mastery of the classics could have spoiled her relationship with her brother to this degree is, however, unlikely" (381).

61 Janet Todd, *The Sign of Angellica: Women, Writing and Fiction, 1660–1800* (London: Virago, 1989), 162.

62 *Ibid.*

63 [Sarah Fielding], *The Adventures of David Simple: Containing an Account of his Travels Through the Cities of London and Westminster, In the Search of a Real Friend*, 2 vols. (London, 1744), I: 36. The title page only reveals "By a Lady." This is one of the passages revised by Henry in the second edition. For a discussion see, Sarah Fielding, *The Adventures of David Simple*, ed. Malcolm Kelsall (Oxford University Press, 1994), xix–xxiii.

64 Carolyn Woodward, "Sarah Fielding's Self-Destructing Utopia: *The Adventures of David Simple*," in *Living by the Pen: Early British Women Writers*, ed. Dale Spender (New York: Teachers College Press, Columbia University, 1992), 65–81.

65 Fielding, *David Simple*, I: 183.

66 *Ibid.*, 217.

67 *Ibid.*, 222. Drawcansir is the bold hero who kills all the protagonists on both sides at the end of the play-within-a-play in George Villiers, Duke of Buckingham's *Rehearsal* (1663), a burlesque on the excesses of heroic tragedy.

68 Fielding, *David Simple*, II: 39–40.

69 [Sarah Fielding], *The Adventures of David Simple. Volume the Last, In which his History is concluded* (London, 1753), 140–41.

70 Julia Briggs, "Women Writers and Writing for Children: From Sarah Fielding to E. Nesbit," in *Children and their Books: A Celebration of the Work of Iona and Peter Opie*, ed. Gillian Avery and Julia Briggs (Oxford: Clarendon Press, 1989), 224, cited in Linda Bree, *Sarah Fielding* (New York: Twayne & Prentice Hall, 1996), 59.

71 Henry Fielding's publisher, Andrew Millar published *The Governess* for Sarah. As was the case with a good number of eighteenth-century books,

the title-page bore the phrase "Printed for the Author." This indicated that the author, rather than the printer or trade publisher, had paid for the expenses of the printing; such arrangements normally meant that the author would also receive any profit that might be earned from sales. For an account of Newbery, see John Rowe Townsend, *John Newbery and his Books* (Cambridge: Colt Books, 1994). Pages 127–34 offer a tentative list of Newbery's books for children, beginning with *A Pretty Little Pocket-Book* (1744).

72 This point is made by Arlene Fish Wilner, "Education and Ideology in Sarah Fielding's *The Governess*," *Studies in Eighteenth-Century Culture* 24 (1995), 307–27.

73 Bree, *Sarah Fielding*, argues that the book makes "a strong argument for autonomous female morality" and that some of the stories implicitly suggest "more radical" alternatives to "conventional female goals" (63, 68).

74 Sarah Fielding, *The Governess; or, Little Female Academy. Being the History of Mrs. Teachum, and her Nine Girls* . . . (London, 1749), 232.

75 *The Thresher's Labour. Stephen Duck (1736) and The Woman's Labour. Mary Collier (1737)*, pub. no. 230. Augustan Reprint Society (Los Angeles: University of California, Los Angeles, 1985), 13.

76 Collier, *Woman's Labour*, 15.

77 Mary Leapor, *Poems upon Several Occasions* (London, 1748), 163.

78 Alexander Pope, *Martinus Scriblerus, Peri Bathos: or, Of the Art of Sinking in Poetry* (1728), in *The Prose Works of Alexander Pope*, II: *The Major Works, 1725–1744*, ed. Rosemary Cowler (Hamden, Conn.: Archon Books, 1986), 214.

79 Leapor, *Poems* (1748), 29.

80 *Ibid.*, 252.

81 Richard Greene, *Mary Leapor: A Study in Eighteenth-Century Women's Poetry* (Oxford: Clarendon Press, 1993), 131.

82 Mary Leapor, *Poems upon Several Occasions. By the late Mrs. Leapor, of Brackley in Northamptonshire. The Second and Last Volume* (London, 1751), 95. Russets, pearmains, and coddlings are kinds of apples; wheatens and damsons are kinds of plums; catherine pears are either a kind of pear or a kind of plum.

83 Mary Leapor, *Poems* (1751), 118.

84 Leapor, "On the Death of a justly admir'd Author," *Poems* (1751), 253–54.

85 Leapor, *Poems* (1748), 122–23.

86 Leapor, *Poems* (1751), 51.

87 James Boswell, *Boswell's Life of Johnson*, ed. George Birkbeck Hill, 6 vols. (Oxford: Clarendon Press, 1934), II: 127.

88 Betty Rizzo, "Mary Leapor: An Anxiety for Influence," *The Age of Johnson: A Quarterly for Literature and the Arts* 4 (1991), 323.

89 Leapor, *Poems* (1751), 45.

90 *Ibid.*, 46.

91 *Ibid.*, 47.

92 *Ibid.*, 181.

93 *Ibid.*, 183.

94 Duncan Isles, "The Lennox Collection," *Harvard Library Bulletin* 18 (1970), 317–44; 36–60; 165–86; 416–35.

95 John Hawkins, *The Life of Samuel Johnson, LL.D.* (London, 1787), 286.

96 Margaret Doody, "Introduction," in Charlotte Lennox, *The Female Quixote or The Adventures of Arabella*, ed. Margaret Dalziel (Oxford: Oxford University Press, 1989), xiii.

97 Boswell, *Life of Johnson*, I: 305.

98 For attribution: of *Female Quixote* review see Goldgar's note in his edition of *Covent Garden Journal*, 159; cf. Sully review, Small, *Lennox*, 213, attribution from Boswell.

99 Charlotte Lennox, *The Female Quixote; or, the Adventures of Arabella*, 2 vols. (London, 1752), I: iv.

100 Quoted in B. G. MacCarthy, *The Female Pen: Women Writers and Novelists, 1621–1818* (1946–47; reprint New York: New York University Press, 1994), 301. He added, "but, if we consider it as a picture of life and manners, we must pronounce it more absurd than any of the romances which it was designed to ridicule." From Macaulay's "Diary and Letters of Madam d'Arblay," in *Critical and Historical Essays*, see Thomas Babington Macaulay, *The Complete Works of Lord Macaulay*, 12 vols. (London: Longmans, Green, 1898), IV: 69.

101 Lennox, *Female Quixote*, I: 29.

102 Lennox, *Female Quixote*, I: 33.

103 Henry Fielding, *Covent Garden Journal*, no. 24 (1752), in *The Criticism of Henry Fielding*, ed. Ioan Williams (New York: Barnes & Noble, 1970), 194.

104 Lennox, *Female Quixote*, I: 99.

105 *Ibid.*, 110.

106 *Ibid.*, 114.

107 *Ibid.*, II: 157.

108 *Ibid.*, 308–9.

109 *Ibid.*, 161.

110 Duncombe, *Feminiad*, 15.

111 Lynda M. Thompson, *The "Scandalous Memoirist": Constantia Phillips, Laetitia Pilkington and the Shame of "Publick Fame"* (Manchester: Manchester University Press, 2000), 46–53.

112 Thompson discusses the evidence that Paul Whitehead was the male narrator, although she seems to suggest that he wrote only brief sections (*Scandalous Memorist*, 53–58). Manley invented a male narrator for *Rivella*, and it is possible that Phillips did so as well, but I am inclined to believe the text's account of her accepting a ghostwriter. Thompson, following Lawrence Stone's study of the litigation in *Uncertain Unions: Marriage in England, 1660–1753* (Oxford: Oxford University Press, 1990), argues that the facts alleged in the *Apology* generally match facts available from external sources. Nevertheless, the language of some of the letters, including those of Phillips's father, strikes me as suspicious.

113 *An Apology for the Conduct of Mrs Teresia Constantia Phillips, More Particularly that Part of it which relates to her Marriage with an Eminent Dutch Merchant*, 3 vols. (London, 1748), I: 28. I have emended "once" to "one."

114 He cites her narrative as evidence of the slowness and dysfunctional absorption in technicalities of equity procedure in *Rationale of Judicial Evidence*, book 8, ch. 14. Comments on the impact of his first encounter are in *Memoirs of Jeremy Bentham; including Autobiographical Conversation and Correspondence. By John Bowring.* In *Works of Jeremy Bentham*, ed. John Bowring, 11 vols. (Edinburgh, 1843), X: 35, 78.

115 *Apology*, I: 112.

116 *Memoirs of Laetitia Pilkington*, ed. A. C. Elias, Jr., 2 vols. (Athens: University of Georgia Press, 1997), II: 638.

117 Quoted in Tobias Smollett, *The Adventures of Peregrine Pickle, in which are included the Memoirs of a Lady of Quality*, ed. James L. Clifford (London: Oxford University Press, 1964), xvii.

118 [Frances Holles Vane, Lady Vane], "Memoirs of a Lady of Quality," in Tobias Smollett, *The Adventures of Peregrine Pickle, in which are included the Memoirs of a Lady of Quality*, 4 vols. (London, 1751), III: 86.

119 Quoted in *Peregrine Pickle*, ed. Clifford, 796.

120 Vane, "Memoirs," II: 92–93.

121 *Ibid.*, 95.

122 *Ibid.*, 100.

123 *Ibid.*, 187.

124 *Ibid.*, 113, 159, 160.

125 *Ibid.*, 150.

126 *Ibid.*, 115.

127 *Ibid.*, 151.

128 *Ibid.*, 103.

129 *Ibid.*, 152.

130 Helene Koon, *Colley Cibber: A Biography* (Lexington: University Press of Kentucky, 1986).

131 Cheryl Wanko, "The Eighteenth-Century Actress and the Construction of Gender: Lavinia Fenton and Charlotte Charke," *Eighteenth-Century Life* 18 (1994), 82.

132 *Ibid.*, 84–85.

133 Charlotte Charke, *A Narrative of the Life of Mrs Charlotte Charke: youngest daughter of Colley Cibber, Esq., Written by Herself* (Gainsville, Fla.: Scholars Facsimiles and Reprints, 1969), 67.

134 *Ibid.*, 46.

135 Alexander Pope, *The Dunciad*, ed. James Sutherland (New Haven: Yale University Press, 1965), *Dunciad (B)*, book 1, lines 221–22, 286.

136 Pilkington published two volumes in 1748. After she died in 1750, her son Jack Pilkington used her remaining papers to complete and publish a third volume in 1754.

137 Irvin Ehrenpreis, *Swift: The Man, His Works, and the Age*, 3 vols. (Cambridge: Harvard University Press, 1962–83), III: 638, 637.

138 Laetitia Pilkington, *The Memoirs of Mrs. Lætitia Pilkington, Wife to the Rev. Mr. Matth. Pilkington . . .* 2 vols. (Dublin, 1748), I: 45. The continuation of the title differs in the two volumes, the first reading, *Wherein are Occasionally interspersed, All her Poems, with Anecdotes of Several Eminent Persons, Living and Dead*, the second, *Wherein are Occasionally interspersed, Her Poems, with Variety of secret Transactions of some Eminent Persons*. A. C. Elias uses the first Dublin edition as copy text for his edition, cited above at note 116, and makes a good argument for doing so in "Editing the Minor Writers: The Case of Laetitia Pilkington and Mary Barber," in *1650–1850 Ideas, Aesthetics, and Inquiries in Early Modern England*, vol. III, ed. Kevin Cope (New York: AMS Press, 1997), 129–47.

139 *Memoirs of Pilkington*, I: 99.

140 See Elias, ed., *Memoirs of Laetitia Pilkington*, II: 514, for an argument that Pilkington wrote this poem about a year later than she claims. He notes that Cibber includes the poem in his *The Egotist: Or Colley upon Colley* (1743) as by an unnamed female author in response to reading his *Apology* and that he prints a text longer than the one in her *Memoirs*.

141 *Memoirs of Pilkington*, I: 85.

142 *Ibid.*, II: 14.

143 *Ibid.*, 16.

144 *Ibid.*, 51.

145 *Ibid.*, 239.

146 *Ibid.*, I: 193.

147 *Ibid.*, 227.

148 *Ibid.*, 161.

149 Linda M. Thompson, *Scandalous Memoirist*, 93.

150 *Memoirs of Pilkington*, II: 239.

6 BLUESTOCKINGS AND SENTIMENTAL WRITERS, 1756–1776

1 Karen O'Brien, "The History Market in Eighteenth-Century England," in *Books and their Readers in Eighteenth-Century England: New Essays*, ed. Isobel Rivers (London: Leicester University Press, 2001), 106.

2 The attribution of *Lewis XIV* to Lennox is not entirely secure, but seems highly likely. See Duncan Isles, "The Lennox Collection," *Harvard Library Bulletin* 18 (1970), 343ff, and n. 45.

3 "Introduction," Rhoda Zuk, ed., *Bluestocking Feminism: Writings of the Bluestocking Circle, 1738–1785*. III: *Catherine Talbot and Hester Chapone* (London: Pickering & Chatto, 1999), 43.

4 Martin C. Battestin and Clive T. Probyn, "General Introduction," *The Correspondence of Henry and Sarah Fielding* (Oxford: Clarendon Press, 1993), xxxix–xl.

5 Talbot to Carter, 2 Aug. 1748, 21 July 1753, *A Series of Letters between Mrs. Elizabeth Carter and Miss Catherine Talbot, From the Year 1741 to 1770*, ed. Reverend Montagu Pennington, 4 vols. (London, 1809), I: 290, II: 131.

6 *Carter-Talbot Letters*, 20 August 1751, 27 September 1751, II: 49, 52.

7 [Hester Chapone], *Letters on the Improvement of the Mind. Addressed to a Young Lady*, 2 vols. (London, 1773), II: 179.

8 *Ibid.*, 188–89.

9 *Ibid.*, 214–15.

10 *Ibid.*, 198–99.

11 Sylvia Harcstark Myers, *The Bluestocking Circle: Women, Friendship, and the Life of the Mind in Eighteenth-Century England* (Oxford: Clarendon Press, 1990), v–vi.

12 Phillis Wheatley, *Poems on Various Subjects, Religious and Moral* (London, 1773), 17.

13 Phillis Wheatley, "To Samson Occom," *Connecticut Gazette; and Universal Intelligencer* 11, 539 (11 March 1774).

14 *Elements of the History of England, from the Invasion of the Romans to the Reign of George II*, 4 vols. (London, 1771), quoted in Lorraine McMullen, *An Odd Attempt in a Woman: The Literary Life of Frances Brooke* (Vancouver: University of British Columbia Press, 1983), 128. McMullen discusses William Kenrick's competing translation, Brooke's care with her own annotations, and Brooke's hope of having her book adopted as a school text (127–35).

15 Charlotte Haldane, *Madame de Maintenon, Uncrowned Queen of France* (London: Constable, 1970).

16 Charlotte Lennox, *Memoirs for the History of Madame de Maintenon and of the Last Age, Translated from the French by the Author of the Female Quixote* (London, 1757), 5 vols., "Preface," [v].

17 *Biographie universelle, ancienne et moderne*, 85 vols. (Paris, 1811–62), s.n. Beaumelle; Haldane, *Maintenon*, 282–86; Theodore Besterman, *Voltaire* (New York: Harcourt Brace & World, 1969), 321–24.

18 Lennox, *Memoirs of Madame de Maintenon*, III: 68.

19 *Letters of Mrs. Elizabeth Montagu. With some Letters of her Correspondents*, 3 vols. (Boston, 1825), III: 55–56.

20 Unbeknownst to Lennox, or to anyone else until 1865–66, La Beaumelle, using a tactic not unknown to other eighteenth-century writers of memoirs, in addition to authentic Maintenon documents, forged some letters which he mingled with the authentic ones and published in his subsequent edition of her letters. Voltaire, to whom La Beaumelle was a rival and an enemy, suspected him of having stolen some Maintenon letters he used in the *Memoirs*, but La Beaumelle's forgeries were good enough that even Voltaire did not suspect that he had engaged in forgery.

21 Although some of the Ninon letters were part of a French historical novel rather than authentic letters of Ninon, Griffith probably thought them authentic. For an account of this complicated book, see, Susan Staves,

"French Fire, English Asbestos: Ninon de Lenclos and Elizabeth Griffith," *Studies on Voltaire and the Eighteenth Century* 314 (1993), 193–205.

22 Lennox, *The Female Quixote*, book 2, ch. v. Miss Groves appears at court and the King is said to have called her "the finest Woman at Court"; "The ladies, however, found means to explain away all that was flattering in the Distinction; They said, Miss *Groves* was clumsy; and it was her Resemblance to the *unwieldy German* Ladies that made her so much admired by his Majesty." Cf. Lennox to [Richardson], [8 or 15 November 1751], in Isles, "The Lennox Collection," 339.

23 *Monthly Review* 28 (1763), 385, cited in Katherine Turner, *British Travel Writers in Europe, 1750–1800: Authorship, Gender, and National Identity* (Aldershot: Ashgate, 2001), 160.

24 Betty Rizzo, "Introduction," Sarah Scott, *The History of Sir George Ellison* (Lexington: University Press of Kentucky, 1996), xix.

25 On the general aesthetics of letter writing, see Bruce Redford, *The Converse of the Pen: Acts of Intimacy in the Eighteenth-Century Familiar Letter* (Chicago: University of Chicago Press, 1982). The only woman whose letters he considers is Lady Mary Wortley Montagu. See also Kathleen B. Grathwol, "Lady Mary Wortley Montagu and Madame de Sévigné: Lettered Self-definition as Woman/Mother and Woman Writer," *Studies on Voltaire and the Eighteenth-Century* 332 (1995), 189–212.

26 *The Complete Tales of Voltaire*, trans. William Walton, 3 vols. (New York: Howard Fertig, 1990), II: 130.

27 *Letters of Sarah Byng Osborn, 1721–1773. From the Collection of the Hon. Mrs. McDonnel*, ed. John McClelland (Stanford, Calif.: Stanford University Press, 1930), 87–88.

28 *Ibid.*, 10 February 1767, 122.

29 *Ibid.*, 29 April 1766, 102.

30 *Ibid.*, 18 July 1766, 109.

31 *Ibid.*, 22 March 1767, 125.

32 *Ibid.*, 29 September 1767, 133.

33 *Ibid.*, 3 May 1768, 141. For a recent consideration of contemporary upper-class women's involvement in politics, see, Elaine Chalus, "'That Epidemical Madness': Women and Electoral Politics in the late Eighteenth Century," in *Gender in Eighteenth-Century England: Roles, Representations and Responsibilities*, ed. Hannah Barker and Elaine Chalus (London: Longman, 1997), 158–78; "'My Minerva at my Elbow': the Political Roles of Women in Eighteenth-Century England," in *Hanoverian Britain and Empire: Essays in Memory of Philip Lawson*, ed. Stephen Taylor, Richard Connors, and Clive Jones (Woodbridge, Suffolk: Boydell, 1998), 210–28; "'To Serve my Friends': Women and Political Patronage in Eighteenth-Century England," in *Women, Privilege and Power: British Politics 1750 to the Present*, ed. Amanda Vickery (Stanford, Calif.: Stanford University Press, 2001), 57–88.

34 Joel Gold, "'Buried Alive': Charlotte Forman in Grub Street," *Eighteenth-Century Life* 8 (1982), 28–45; Susan Staves, s.n. "Charlotte Forman," *Oxford Dictionary of National Biography*.

35 Abigail Adams to John Adams, [4 March 1776], *Adams Family Correspondence*, ed. L. H. Butterfield, et al., 6 vols. (Cambridge, Mass.: Belknap Press of Harvard University, 1963–93), I: 353.

36 *Ibid.*, 16 October 1774, [16?] June 1775, I: 172, 217.

37 *Ibid.*, 5 July 1775, I: 239.

38 Plutarch, *The Lives of the Noble Grecians and Romans*, trans. John Dryden, ed. and revised, Arthur Hugh Clough, 2 vols. (New York: Modern Library, 1992), II: 580.

39 *Adams Family Correspondence*, 21 October 1775, I: 307.

40 *Ibid.*, 18 June 1775, I: 222.

41 *Ibid.*, 22 October 1775, I: 311.

42 *Ibid.*, "Plimouth June 17 [1776] a remarkable Day," II: 14.

43 *Ibid.*, 14 September 1774, I: 151–52.

44 For a good account of the impact of Montagu's friendship on one man of talent and of the importance of his access to English and French salons presided over by women, see, George Winchester Stone and George M. Kahrl, *David Garrick: a Critical Biography* (Carbondale: Southern Illinois University Press, 1979), ch. 23, "Garrick's Friendships with Women of Distinction," 403–86.

45 Myers, *Bluestocking Circle*, 6–10.

46 Neither Montagu, Carter, nor Talbot published letters in their lifetimes. We owe the publication of their letters to Carter's nephew, Montagu Pennington (see note 5 above). He notes that Carter had in some ways prepared her letters for publication by grouping them and making some excisions; he admits to making more excisions of what he deemed appropriate. Many Montagu manuscript letters survive at the Huntington Library, but the originals of most of Carter's letters apparently do not. We thus have only a partial view of what the bluestockings had to say in the discursive sphere of the familiar letter.

47 David Williams, "Voltaire's 'War with England': The Appeal to Europe, 1760–1764," *Studies on Voltaire and the Eighteenth Century* 179 (1979), 84.

48 Voltaire to Charles Pinot Duclos, 20 January 1760, *Les Oeuvres Complètes de Voltaire / The Complete Works of Voltaire*, ed. Theodore Besterman, et al., 135 vols. (Banbury: The Voltaire Foundation, 1970–2002), D10279.

49 Williams, "Voltaire's War with England," 96.

50 On Lennox's role in this project, see, James Gray, "Dr. Johnson, Charlotte Lennox, and the Englishing of Father Brumoy," *Modern Philology* 83 (1985), 142–50.

51 Elizabeth Montagu, *An Essay on the Writings and Genius of Shakespear, Compared with the Greek and French Dramatic Poets. With some Remarks upon the Misrepresentations of Mons. de Voltaire* (London, 1769), I, 17–18.

52 *Ibid.*, 66.
53 *Ibid.*, 56.
54 *Ibid.*, 68.
55 Samuel Johnson, "Preface to Shakespeare" (1765), *Johnson on Shakespeare*, ed. Arthur Sherbo, 2 vols. (New Haven: Yale University Press, 1968), I: 65, 66.
56 Montagu, *Essay*, 248.
57 *Ibid.*, 239.
58 Turner, *Travel Writers*, 50. Turner analyzes how women writers of travel books attempted to negotiate the fact that their travels seemed to violate contemporary models of good domestic femininity. I do not find Miller as prudish as Turner does.
59 Cited in Myers, *Bluestocking Circle*, 212.
60 Talbot to Carter, 9 Feb. 1747, *Carter–Talbot Letters*, I: 190–91.
61 Elizabeth Carter, *All the Works of Epictetus, Which are Now Extant; Consisting of his Discourses, Preserved by Arrian, in Four Books, The Enchiridion, and Fragments* (London, 1758), 135, 137, 143.
62 *Ibid.*, 172, 177.
63 Carolyn D. Williams, "Poetry, Pudding, and Epictetus: The Consistency of Elizabeth Carter," in *Tradition in Transition: Women Writers, Marginal Texts, and the Eighteenth-Century Canon*, ed. Alvaro Ribeiro, SJ, and James G. Basker (Oxford: Clarendon Press, 1996), 19.
64 Carter, *Epictetus*, xxxiii.
65 *Ibid.*, 98.
66 Elizabeth Carter, *Poems on Several Occasions* (London, 1762), 87–88.
67 Carter, "To —," *Poems*, 66–67.
68 Carter, *Poems*, 36–37.
69 Montagu Pennington, *Memoirs of the Life of Mrs. Elizabeth Carter*, 2 vols., 4th edn. (London, 1825), I: 187.
70 *Ibid.*, 189.
71 *Ibid.*, 196.
72 *Ibid.*, 199.
73 *Letters of Mrs. Elizabeth Montagu, with some of the Letters of her Correspondents*, 4 vols. (London, 1809–13), III: III.
74 *Ibid.*, IV: 188–89.
75 *Letters from Mrs. Elizabeth Carter, to Mrs. Montagu, Between the Years 1755 and 1800. Chiefly upon Literary and Moral Subjects*, 3 vols. (1817; reprint, New York: AMS Press, 1973), I: 19.
76 Harriet Guest, *Small Change: Women, Learning, Patriotism, 1750–1810* (Chicago: University of Chicago Press, 2000), 117, 125, 126.
77 William Roberts, *Memoirs of the Life and Correspondence of Mrs. Hannah More*, 2 vols. (New York: Harper & Brothers, 1834), I: 39.
78 Charles Burney, *A General History of Music from the Earliest Age to the Present Period (1789)*, 2 vols. (New York: Dover, 1957), II: 753. See also Roger Fiske, *English Theatre Music in the Eighteenth Century*, 2nd edn. (Oxford: Oxford University Press, 1986).

79 Roger Parker, *The Oxford Illustrated History of Opera* (Oxford: Oxford University Press, 1994), 54.

80 Hannah More, *The Inflexible Captive: A Tragedy* (Bristol, [1774]), 31.

81 *Ibid.*, 39,

82 *Ibid.*, 27.

83 Anna Letitia Aikin, *Poems* (London, 1773 [for 1772]), 102.

84 Kirsteen McCue, "Women and Song, 1750–1850," *A History of Scottish Writing*, ed. Douglas Gifford and Dorothy McMillan (Edinburgh: Edinburgh University Press, 1997), 58–70.

85 Patricia Phillips, *The Adventurous Muse: Theories of Originality in English Poetics, 1650–1760* (Uppsala: Almquist & Wiksell, 1984).

86 Aikin, *Poems*, 48.

87 *Ibid.*, 37.

88 *Ibid.*, 31.

89 *Ibid.*, 17.

90 *Ibid.*, 36.

91 Vol. I (1763), II (1765), III (1767), IV (1768), V (1771), IV (1781), VII (1781), VIII (1783). Vol. VIII of the *History* ends with the Glorious Revolution of 1688–9, rather than with the establishment of the "Brunswick Line" by the coronation of George I, the first Hanoverian king in 1714. Macaulay's unusual but important critical interpretation of the Glorious Revolution and its aftermath is further developed in her *History of England from the Revolution to the Present Time in a Series of Letters to a Friend* (1778).

92 Natalie Zemon Davis, "Gender and Genre: Women as Historical Writers, 1400–1820," in *Beyond their Sex: Learned Women of the European Past*, ed. Patricia H. Labalme (New York: New York University Press, 1980), 155.

93 *Ibid.*, 165.

94 Catharine Macaulay, *The History of England from the Accession of James I to that of the Brunswick Line*, vol. II (London, 1765), 211–12.

95 *Ibid.*, I (London, 1763), xi.

96 *Ibid.*, viii–xi. Macaulay's first name is spelled "Catherine" on the title page of this volume.

97 *Ibid.*, xii.

98 *Ibid.*, xi.

99 *Ibid.*, II: 61.

100 *Ibid.*, 154.

101 *Ibid.*, 158–59.

102 *Ibid.*, 159.

103 *Ibid.*, 161.

104 *Ibid.*, 244.

105 A useful account of these cases may be found in Peter D. G. Thomas, *John Wilkes: A Friend to Liberty* (Oxford: Clarendon Press, 1996), 19–56.

106 Macaulay, *History* 2: 246.

107 *Ibid.*, 99.

108 *Ibid.*, 247.

109 *Ibid.*, 248.

110 *Ibid.*, 248.

111 David Hume, *The History of England*. I: *Containing the Reigns of James I and Charles I* (Edinburgh, 1754), 174.

112 David Hume, *The History of England from the Invasion of Julius Caesar to the Revolution in 1688*, 6 vols. (Indianapolis, Ind.: Liberty Classics, n.d.), VI: 533. This sentence is not in the first edition of *The History of Great Britain*. II: *Containing the Commonwealth, and the Reigns of Charles II and James II* (London, 1762), but appears in the edition of 1778.

113 Hume, *History*. I: 469–70.

114 Bridget Hill, *The Republican Virago: The Life and Times of Catharine Macaulay, Historian* (Oxford: Clarendon Press, 1992), 49–50.

115 *Critical Review* 16 (1763), 321–30, at 324, 330. Cf. *Monthly Review* 29 (1763), 372–82, 411–20.

116 *Critical Review* 16 (1763), 328, 329.

117 *Critical Review* 27 (1769), 6.

118 *Critical Review* 16 (1763), 323.

119 Duncan Forbes, "Introduction," David Hume, *History of Great Britain: The Reigns of James I and Charles I* (Harmondsworth: Penguin Books, 1970), 46.

120 *Critical Review* 55 (1783), 213, 216.

121 Mary Scott, *The Female Advocate; A Poem. Occasioned by a Reading of Mr. Duncombe's Feminead* (London, 1774), 27.

122 9 August 1770, *The Diary and Autobiography of John Adams*, ed. L. H. Butterfield, 4 vols. (Cambridge, Mass.: Belknap Press of Harvard University Press, 1961), I: 360.

123 Hill, *Macaulay*, 184–204.

124 20 April 1771, *Family Correspondence*, I: 77; Abigail Adams to Catharine Macaulay, [1774], *Family Correspondence*, I: 178.

125 Adam Smith, *The Theory of Moral Sentiments*, ed. D. D. Raphael and A. L. Macfie (Indianapolis, Ind.: Liberty Fund, 1984), I. i. 2.3.

126 [John and Anna Letitia Aikin], *Miscellaneous Pieces in Prose* (London, 1773), 194. The volume contains some essays by Anna's brother, but this one has been attributed to her.

127 Aiken, *Prose*, 211.

128 There were multiple editions of *The Discovery* published in London, Dublin, and Edinburgh in 1763. This line is not in the first London edition, but it is in the second London edition (1763), 72.

129 Frances Sheridan, *The Discovery. A Comedy* (London, 1763), 125. This is the first edition.

130 *Ibid.*, 78–79.

131 *Ibid.*, 130.

132 Chapone, *Letters*, II: 144–45.

133 Carter to Montagu, 11 Dec. 1759, *Carter–Montagu Letters*, I: 69–70.

134 Hill, *Macaulay*, 50.

135 I have calculated this figure from tables in James Raven, *British Fiction 1750–1770: A Chronological Check-List of Prose Fiction Printed in Britain and Ireland* (Newark: University of Delaware Press, 1987), table 4: "Publication of Novels by Women Writers 1750–1769," 19, and James Raven, Antonia Forster, and Stephen Bending, *The English Novel, 1770–1829: A Bibliographical Survey of Prose Fiction Published in the British Isles.* 2 vols. (Oxford: Oxford University Press, 2000), table 6, "Authorship of New Novels," I: 46–47. Numbers in these tables, although very useful, must be considered approximate. In all the available bibliographies the category "novel" is not perfectly clear, translations still masquerade as original fiction, and journalistic narratives about real people are sometimes sorted as fiction.

136 Raven, Forster, and Bending *English Novel, 1770–1829*, table 7, "Surviving Receipts for Novelists for Surrender of Copyright, 1770–1799," I: 52–53.

137 Quoted in J. M. S. Tompkins, *The Popular Novel in England* (London: Methuen, 1962), 120.

138 McMullen, *Frances Brooke*, 53. Brooke also translated from French Nicolas-Etienne Framery's novel, *Mémoires de M. le marquis de S. Forlaix* (1770) as *Memoirs of the Marquis de St. Forlaix* (1770).

139 Quoted in McMullen, *Brooke*, 65–66.

140 [Frances Brooke], *The History of Emily Montague: In Four Volumes. By the Author of Lady Julia Mandeville* (London, 1769), I: 8.

141 *Ibid.*, II: 233; III: 57.

142 *Ibid.*, I: 68–69.

143 Heinz Antor, "The International Contexts of Frances Brooke's *The History of Emily Montague* (1769)," in *English Literatures in International Contexts*, ed. Heinz Antor and Klaus Stierstrofer (Heidelberg: Carl Winter Universitätsverlag, 2000), 272.

144 Ann Messenger, *His and Hers: Essays in Restoration and Eighteenth-Century Literature* (Lexington: University Press of Kentucky, 1986), 154–55.

145 [Sarah Fielding], *The History of the Countess of Dellwyn. In two Volumes. By the Author of David Simple*, 2 vols. (London, 1759), II: 184.

146 Susan Snaider Lanser, *Fictions of Authority: Women Writers and Narrative Voice* (Ithaca, NY: Cornell University Press, 1992), 48.

147 Fielding, *Countess*, I: xxx, xxxiii.

148 *Ibid.*, 21.

149 *Ibid.*, 19.

150 *Ibid.*, 24–25.

151 *Ibid.*, 2.

152 *Ibid.*, 40.

153 *Ibid.*, 74.

154 *Ibid.*, 94, 102.

155 *Ibid.*, 118.

156 *Ibid.*, 121.

157 *Ibid.*, 145.

158 *Ibid.*, 146.

159 *Ibid.*, 150.

160 *Ibid.*, 168.

161 *Ibid.*, 207.

162 *Ibid.*, 207. The reference is to Nicholas Rowe's she tragedy.

163 Fielding, *Countess*, II: 277, 257 [for 275].

164 *Ibid.*, 283.

165 *Ibid.*, I: 186.

166 *Ibid.*, 192.

167 *Ibid.*, 206.

168 Elizabeth Griffith, *The History of Lady Barton. A Novel, In Letters*, 3 vols. (London, 1771), I: 2.

169 *Ibid.*, 109.

170 *Ibid.*, 60.

171 [Frances Sheridan], *Memoirs of Miss Sidney Bidulph. Extracted from her Own Journal, and now First Published*, 3 vols. (London, 1761), I: iii.

172 Sheridan, *Sidney Bidulph*, "The Editor's Introduction," I: 5.

173 *Ibid.*, 6.

174 Sheridan, *Sidney Bidulph*, I: 51.

175 *Ibid.*, 91.

176 *Ibid.*, 96.

177 [Elizabeth Griffith], *The School for Rakes: A Comedy* (London, 1769), 90.

178 Pennington, *Memoires of Carter*, I: 29–30.

179 Myers, *Bluestocking Circle*, 109.

180 *Sidney Bidulph*, I: 230.

181 *Ibid.*, 299.

182 *Ibid.*, II: 215.

183 *Ibid.*, 232.

184 *Ibid.*, 236.

185 Patricia Meyer Spacks, *Desire and Truth: Functions of Plot in Eighteenth-Century English Novels* (Chicago: University of Chicago Press, 1990), 136, 138, 140.

186 Elizabeth Robinson Montagu and Sarah Robinson Scott were daughters of a mother who had been educated by Bathsua Makin, who was presumably familiar with Astell's idea. Astell's work was also circulated in *The Ladies Library*.

187 [Sarah Scott], *A Description of Millenium Hall, and the Country Adjacent: Together with the Characters of the Inhabitants and such Historical Anecdotes and Reflections, as may Excite in the Reader proper Sentiments of Humanity, and lead the Mind to the Love of Virtue. By a Gentleman on his Travels* (London, 1762), 181.

188 *Ibid.*, 183, 185.

189 *Ibid.*, 184–85.

190 *Ibid.*, 186.

191 *Ibid.*, 92.

192 *Ibid.*, 93.

193 *Ibid.*, 94.

194 *Ibid.*

195 *Ibid.*, 135.

196 *Ibid.*, 255.

197 *Ibid.*, 146.

198 *Ibid.*, 140.

199 *Ibid.*, 254.

200 This point is made in Dorice Williams Elliot, "Sarah Scott's *Millenium Hall* and Female Philanthropy," *Studies in English Literature* 35 (1995), 544.

201 Scott, *Millenium Hall*, 153.

202 *Ibid.*, 154.

203 Betty Rizzo, "Introduction," Sarah Scott, *The History of Sir George Ellison* (Lexington: University Press of Kentucky, 1996), xxxi–xxxii.

204 [Lady Sarah Pennington], *An Unfortunate Mother's Advice to her Absent Daughters; in a Letter to Miss Pennington* (London, 1761), 25.

205 *Ibid.*, 32.

206 [Charlotte Lennox], *The Lady's Museum*, 2 vols. (London, 1760–61), I: 130.

207 Kathryn Shevelow, *Women and Print Culture: the Construction of Femininity in the Early Periodical* (London: Routledge, 1989). For a reading that emphasizes Lennox's concern with imposing constraints on women and argues that *The Lady's Museum* "challenges the exclusion of women from historical import by printing essays that describe their past agency in historical events," see Judith Dorn, "Reading Women Reading History: The Philosophy of Periodical Form in Charlotte Lennox's *The Lady's Museum*," *Historical Reflections / Reflexions Historiques* 18 (1992), 7–27, at 21.

208 Hannah More, *The Search After Happiness. A Pastoral*, 5th edn. (Bristol, 1774), 43, 44.

209 Cheryl Turner, *Living by the Pen: Women Writers in the Eighteenth Century* (London: Routledge, 1994), 135–36.

7 ROMANCE AND COMEDY, 1777–1789

1 Written in 1779, Murray's "Essay" was first published in the *Massachusetts Magazine* (March, April 1790), 132–35, 223–26. Her notice of the women writers appears in another series originally published in the *Massachusetts Magazine*, "Observations on Female Abilities," collected in *The Gleaner* (1798), vol. 3, nos. 88–91.

2 Elizabeth Carter, *Letters from Mrs. Elizabeth Carter, To Mrs. Montagu, Between the Years 1755 and 1800. Chiefly upon Literary and Moral Subjects*, ed. Montagu Pennington, 3 vols. (London, 1817), III: 30–31.

3 Harriet Guest, *Small Change: Women, Learning, Patriotism, 1750–1810* (Chicago: University of Chicago Press, 2000), 265.

4 Hannah Cowley, *Which is the Man? A Comedy, As Acted at the Theatre-Royal in Covent-Garden* (London, 1783), 53.

5 Frances Burney, *The Diary and Letters of Frances Burney, Madame D'Arblay*, ed. Sarah Chauncey Woolsey, 2 vols. (Boston, 1880), 1: 447.

6 These numbers are calculated from tables in James Raven, Antonia Forster, and Stephen Bending, *The English Novel, 1770–1829: A Bibliographical Survey of Prose Fiction Published in the British Isles* (Oxford: Oxford University Press, 2000), 46–47. Raven makes the point about the changing proportion of female novelists to male. This bibliography includes stories for children.

7 This number is calculated from a list in Judith Phillips Stanton, "'This New Found Path Attempting': Women Dramatists in England, 1660–1800," in *Curtain Calls: British and American Women and the Theater, 1660–1820*, ed. Mary Anne Schofield and Cecilia Macheski (Athens: Ohio University Press, 1991), 225–54.

8 Hannah More, *Sacred Dramas: Chiefly Intended for Young Persons: The Subjects Taken from the Bible. To Which is Added, Sensibility. A Poem* (London, 1782), 175.

9 Hannah Cowley, *The Scottish Village: Or, Pitcairne Green* (London, 1786), 6.

10 *Ibid.*, 9, 13.

11 See Jayne Elizabeth Lewis, "'Ev'ry Lost Relation': Historical Fictions and Sentimental Incidents in Sophia Lee's *The Recess*," *Eighteenth-Century Fiction* 7 (1995), 165–84, for an argument that Lee in this novel reflects on ways in which historical and sentimental representations are implicated in one another. Lee invents twin daughters of Mary Queen of Scots.

12 More, *Sacred Dramas*, 276, 277.

13 *Ibid.*, 277.

14 *Ibid.*, 278–80.

15 *Ibid.*, 286.

16 *Ibid.*, 281.

17 *Ibid.*, 283.

18 Hannah More, *Essays on Various Subjects, Principally Designed for Young Ladies* (London, 1777), 102. EC Film, Reel 5872.

19 *Ibid.*, 78.

20 *Ibid.*, 95.

21 Jane Spencer, *Aphra Behn's Afterlife* (Oxford: Oxford University Press, 2000), 174.

22 R. Roberts, *Albert, Edward and Laura, and the Hermit of Priestland; Three Legendary Tales* (London, 1783), 25.

23 On this impressive project, see Ralph Merritt Cox, *The Rev. John Bowle: The Genesis of Cervantean Criticism* (Chapel Hill: University of North Carolina Press, 1971).

24 David Hume, *Selected Essays* (Oxford: World's Classics, 1990), 154.

25 Susannah Dobson, *The Life of Petrarch. Collected from Memoirs pour la vie de Petrarch. By Mrs. Dobson* (Philadelphia, 1817), 46.

26 John Nott, *Sonnets and Odes Translated from the Italian of Petrarch, with the Original Texts, and Some Account of his Life* (London, 1777), vii.

27 Pierre Joseph Alary, *Discours prononcé dans l'Academie Françoise, Le Lundi 26 Juin M.DCC.LVIII. A le reception de M. de La Curne de Sainte-Palaye* (Paris, 1758), 11–12, my trans.

28 *Ibid.*, 5.

29 For an explanation of these themes see Lionel Gossman, *Medievalism and the Ideologies of the Enlightenment: The World and Work of La Curne de Sainte-Palaye* (Baltimore, Md.: Johns Hopkins University Press, 1968).

30 *Ibid.*, 278–79.

31 *Ibid.*, 330; the quotation about Hurd is from *The Dictionary of National Biography*, s.n. "Hurd, Richard, DD."

32 *Memoirs of Ancient Chivalry. To which are added, the Anecdotes of the Times, From the Romance Writers and Historians of those Ages. Translated from the French of Mr. de St. Palaye, by the Translator of the Life of Petrarch* (London, 1784), 64.

33 *Ibid.*, 136.

34 *Mémoirs sur l'ancienne chevalerie, considéré comme un établissement politique et militairie*, 3 vols. (Paris, 1759–81).

35 *Memoirs of Ancient Chivalry*, xi–xii.

36 *Ibid.*, xix.

37 [Hannah More], *Percy. A Tragedy. As it is Acted at the Theatre-Royal in Covent Garden* (London, 1778), 6.

38 *Ibid.*, 29.

39 *Ibid.*, 30.

40 William Roberts, *Memoirs of the Life and Correspondence of Mrs. Hannah More*, 2 vols. (New York, 1834), I: 79.

41 More, *Percy*, 31.

42 *Ibid.*, 59.

43 *Ibid.*, 60.

44 *Ibid.*, 75.

45 *Ibid.*, 76.

46 *Ibid.*, 12.

47 *Ibid.*, 45.

48 J. M. S. Tompkins, *The Popular Novel in England, 1770–1800* (1932; reprint, Lincoln: University of Nebraska Press, 1961), 208.

49 Clara Reeve, *The Old English Baron*, 2nd edn. (London, 1778), "Preface," A2, v.

50 Clara Reeve, *The Champion of Virtue. A Gothic Story. By the Editor of the Phœnix; A Translation of Barclay's Argenis* (Colchester, 1777), 2.

51 Tompkins, *Popular Novel*, 209.

52 Reeve, *Champion*, 17–18.

53 B. G. MacCarthy, *The Female Pen: Women Writers and Novelists, 1621–1818* (1946–47; reprint, New York: New York University Press, 1994), 378.

54 James Watt, *Contesting the Gothic: Fiction, Genre and Cultural Conflict, 1764–1832* (Cambridge: Cambridge University Press, 1999). Kate Ferguson Ellis, *The Contested Castle: Gothic Novels and the Subversion of Domestic*

Ideology (Urbana: University of Illinois Press, 1989), reads the novel as working toward a meritocratic bourgeois ideology and toward a model of a meritocratic family preparing children for life in a meritocratic bourgeois world (60–68).

55 Reeve, *Champion*, 102.
56 *Ibid.*, 102.
57 *Ibid.*, 25.
58 *Ibid.*, 26.
59 *Ibid.*, 174.
60 Clara Reeve, *The Progress of Romance, through Times, Countries, and Manners; with Remarks on the Good and Bad Effects of It, On Them Respectively; In the Course of Evening Conversations, by C. R. Author of the English Baron, the Two Mentors, &c,* 2 vols. (Colchester, 1785), preface, I: xi.
61 *Ibid.*, vi–vii.
62 *Ibid.*, 98.
63 E. J. Clery, "The Genesis of 'Gothic' Fiction," in *The Cambridge Companion to Gothic Fiction,* ed. Jerrold E. Hogle (Cambridge: Cambridge University Press, 2002), 34.
64 Reeve, *Progress,* I: 117–18.
65 *Ibid.*, 16, 21.
66 [Lady Mary Walker], *Munster Village. A Novel,* 2 vols. (London, 1778), I: 56.
67 Walker, *Munster Village,* I: 72, 77.
68 *Ibid.*, 84.
69 *Ibid.*, 68.
70 *Ibid.*, 69.
71 *Ibid.*, 92.
72 *Ibid.*, 85.
73 *Ibid.*, 91.
74 On women and the Society, see Charlotte Grant, "The Choice of Hercules: the Polite Arts and 'Female Excellence' in Eighteenth-Century London," in *Women, Writing and the Public Sphere, 1700–1830,* ed. Elizabeth Eger, Charlotte Grant, Clíona Ó Gallichoir, and Penny Warburton (Cambridge: Cambridge University Press, 2001), 75–103.
75 Walker, *Munster Village,* I: 122.
76 *Ibid.*, II: 48.
77 Isabel De Madaraga, *Catherine the Great. A Short History* (New Haven: Yale University Press, 1990).
78 Walker, *Munster Village,* I: 123.
79 Charlotte Smith, *Emmeline: The Orphan of the Castle,* 4 vols. (London, 1788), I: 61.
80 *Ibid.*, II: 217.
81 *Ibid.*, III: 96.
82 *Ibid.*, IV: 146.
83 *Ibid.*, 147.
84 *Ibid.*, 168.

85 *Ibid.*, I: 90–91.
86 *Ibid.*, III: 303.
87 Lorraine Fletcher, *Charlotte Smith: A Critical Biography* (Basingstoke: Macmillan Press, 1998), 1.
88 Tompkins, *Popular Novel*, 266.
89 Anna Seward, *Louisa. A Poetical Novel, in Four Epistles* (Lichfield, 1784), 13.
90 *Ibid.*, 34.
91 *Ibid.*, 45.
92 *Ibid.*, 76–77.
93 *Ibid.*, 2.
94 Lorraine McMullen, *An Odd Attempt in a Woman: The Literary life of Frances Brooke* (Vancouver: University of British Columbia Press, 1983), 189–90.
95 Favart is most famous for opera-comique libretti, but he did also write more sentimental libretti like *Les Moissoneurs*. See Alfred Iacuzz, *The European Vogue of Favart. The Diffusion of the Opéra-Comique* (1932; reprint, New York: Publications of the Institute of French Studies, 1978).
96 [Frances Brooke], *Rosina. A Comic Opera in Two Acts. Performed at the Theatre-Royal, Covent Garden* (London, 1783), 5. EC Film, Reel 6704, no. 14. Libretto only.
97 Brooke, *Rosina*, 9.
98 *Ibid.*, 17.
99 *Ibid.*, 41.
100 *Ibid.*, 31.
101 *Ibid.*, 30.
102 *New Grove Dictionary of Music and Musicians*, ed. Stanley Sadie, 2nd edn., 29 vols. (London: Macmillan, 2001), s.n., "Shield, William."
103 Charlotte Smith, *Elegiac Sonnets* (London, 1789), "Sonnet 30. To the River Arun."
104 *Ibid.*, 76–77.
105 *Ibid.*, "Sonnet 9."
106 *Ibid.*, "Sonnet 31, Written on Farm Wood, South Downs, in May 1784."
107 *Ibid.*, "Sonnet 2. Written at the Close of Spring."
108 *Ibid.*, "Sonnet 5. To the South Downs."
109 *Ibid.*, "Sonnet 44. Written in the Church Yard at Middleton in Sussex."
110 Caroll Fry, *Charlotte Smith* (New York: Twayne, 1996), 17.
111 Smith, *Elegiac Sonnets*, "Sonnet 36."
112 William J. Burling, *Summer Theatre in London, 1661–1820, and the Rise of the Haymarket Theatre* (Madison, NJ: Fairleigh Dickinson Press, 2000), 149.
113 *Ibid.*, 138, 149.
114 Sums are from Robert Hume and Judith Milhous, "Playwrights' Remuneration in Eighteenth-Century London," *Harvard Library Bulletin*, n.s. 10 (1999), appendices.
115 Sophia Lee, *The Chapter of Accidents: A Comedy in Five Acts, As it is performed at the Theatre-Royal in the Hay-Market* (London, 1780), vii.

116 *Ibid.*, 16.
117 *Ibid.*, 13.
118 *Ibid.*, 5.
119 *Ibid.*, 9.
120 *Ibid.*, 22–23.
121 *Ibid.*, 73.
122 *Ibid.*, 98.
123 *Westminster Magazine* 8 (August 1780), 410. This reviewer, although frequently snide, is one of the most thoughtful of the period. Part of his argument is that there is no language which could express the feelings of a woman in Cecilia's position.
124 Lee, *Chapter of Accidents*, 30.
125 Charles Beecher Hogan. *The London Stage, 1776–1800: A Critical Introduction* (Carbondale and Edwardsville: Southern Illinois University Press, 1968), clxxxi–clxxxiii.
126 Hannah Cowley, *Who's the Dupe? A Farce. As it is Acted at the Theatre-Royal in Drury Lane* (London, 1779), 3.
127 *Ibid.*, 6
128 *Ibid.*
129 *Ibid.*, 20.
130 Hannah Cowley, *A Bold Stroke for a Husband, A Comedy, As Acted at the Theatre-Royal in Covent Garden* (London, 1784), 20. This is the second edition. The first edition was a Dublin edition of 1783, but that seems unauthorized and inferior to this, although more careful textual study would be useful. A number of the best lines are not in the Dublin edition.
131 Cowley, *Who's the Dupe?*, 8.
132 *Ibid.*, 9.
133 *Ibid.*, 8.
134 Hannah Cowley, *The Belle's Stratagem. A Comedy* (London, 1782), 18. There was a previous, unauthorized, Dublin edition in 1781.
135 *Ibid.*, 38.
136 *Ibid.*, 25.
137 Samuel Richardson, *Rambler* 97, 19 February 1751, in [Samuel Johnson], *The Rambler*, 2 vols. (New York and London: Garland, 1978), I: 576.
138 Cowley, *Which is the Man?*, 30.
139 Cowley, *Bold Stroke*, 13. The Dublin edition gives "a smart oath" rather than "an empty oath," which might be an earlier reading corrected to something that seemed more decent.
140 *Ibid.*, 25.
141 *Ibid.*, 25.
142 *Ibid.*, 16.
143 Quoted in Frances Burney, *The Early Journals and Letters of Fanny Burney*, ed. Lars E. Troide, et al., 9 vols. (Oxford: Clarendon Press, 1988–2000), III: 183.
144 Cowley, *Bold Stroke*, 27.

145 *Ibid.*, 27.
146 *Ibid.*, 28–29. He may sing these lines.
147 *Ibid.*, 31.
148 *Ibid.*, 51.
149 *Ibid.*, 74.
150 *Monthly Review* 58 (1778), 316.
151 *Critical Review* 46 (1778), 202.
152 Burney, *Early Journals*, III: 144.
153 *Ibid.*, 157–58.
154 [Frances Burney], *Evelina, or, a Young Lady's Entrance into the World*, 3 vols. (London, 1778) II: 117–18.
155 Burney, *Evelina*, II: 119–20. Missing quotation marks supplied.
156 *Ibid.*, 132.
157 *Ibid.*, 133–34.
158 Ruth Bernard Yeazell, *Fictions of Modesty: Women and Courtship in the English Novel* (Chicago and London: University of Chicago Press, 1984), 139.
159 Burney, *Evelina*, III: 157.
160 *Ibid.*, 177.
161 *Ibid.*, 254.
162 *The Complete Plays of Frances Burney*, ed. Peter Sabor, Geoffrey M. Sill, and Stewart J. Cooke, 2 vols. (Montreal: McGill-Queen's University Press, 1995), I: 61.
163 *Ibid.*, 13.
164 *Ibid.*, 15.
165 *Ibid.*, 21.
166 Hester Thrale, *Thraliana: The Diary of Mrs. Hester Lynch Thrale (later Mrs. Piozzi), 1776–1809*, ed. Katherine C. Balderston, 2 vols. (Oxford: Clarendon Press, 1951), I: 381.
167 Clayton Delrey edited the play in a 1989 dissertation. Katharine Rogers published it in her *Meridian Anthology of Restoration and Eighteenth-Century Plays by Women* (New York: Meridian, 1994).
168 Catherine Gallagher, *Nobody's Story: The Vanishing Acts of Women Writers in the Marketplace, 1660–1820* (Berkeley: University of California Press, 1994), 234. See Margaret Anne Doody, *Frances Burney: The Life in the Works* (New Brunswick, NJ: Rutgers University Press, 1988), 66–98, for an important reading of the play and further speculation on Charles Burney's motives for suppressing it; and Barbara Darby, *Frances Burney Dramatist; Gender, Performance, and the Late-Eighteenth-Century Stage* (Lexington: University Press of Kentucky, 1997), 22–42, for a feminist reading that sees the play "exposing the unequal distribution of power between men and women." Darby and some others argue that Burney's satire is not directed at women wits but only at women who affect wit and learning.
169 James Boaden, *Memoirs of Mrs. Inchbald: Including her Familiar Correspondence with the Most Distinguished Persons of her Time*, 2 vols. (London, 1833), I: 18.

170 Ellen Donkin, *Getting into the Act: Women Playwrights in London, 1776–1829* (London: Routledge, 1996), 128.

171 James Raven, Antonia Forster, and Stephen Bending, *The English Novel, 1770–1829: A Bibliographical Survey of Prose Fiction Published in the British Isles*, 2 vols. (Oxford: Oxford University Press, 2000), table 7: "Surviving Receipts to Novelists for the Surrender of Copyright, 1770–1799," I: 52.

172 [Elizabeth Inchbald], *The Mogul Tale: or, The Descent of the Balloon. A Farce. As it is acted at the Theatre-Royal. Smoke-Alley* ([Dublin], 1788), 7.

173 *Ibid.*

174 *Ibid.*, 11–12.

175 *Ibid.*, 16.

176 *Ibid.*, 19.

177 *Ibid.*, 19–20.

178 *Ibid.*, 12.

179 Quoted in Annibel Jenkins, *I'll Tell You What: The Life of Elizabeth Inchbald* (Lexington: University Press of Kentucky, 2003), 159. For a different view of *The Mogul Tale*, see Mita Choudhury, "Gazing at his Seraglio: Late Eighteenth-Century Women Playwrights as Orientalists," *Theatre Journal* 47 (1995), 481–502. Choudhury finds that Inchbald offers an image of a "feminized and castrated court" that "strips the Mogul of his power and legitimacy." I would agree with her that farcical representations of Mogul power make it less threatening than it actually was to contemporaries.

180 Boaden, *Memoirs of Inchbald*, I: 240.

181 Elizabeth Inchbald, *Such Things Are; A Play in Five Acts. As Performed at the Theatre Royal, Covent Garden* (London, 1788), 27.

182 *Ibid.*, 16.

183 *Ibid.*, 36.

184 *Ibid.*, 9.

185 *Ibid.*, 56.

186 *Ibid.*, 39.

187 *Ibid.*, 22.

188 *Ibid.*, 28.

189 Boaden, *Memoirs of Inchbald*, I: 242.

190 Raven, Forster and Bending, *The English Novel 1770–1829*, I: 52.

191 Choderlos de Laclos, "Cecilia ou les 'Mémoirs d'une héritère,'" *Oeuvres complètes* (Paris: Gallimard, 1979), 469.

192 Frances Burney, *Cecilia, or Memoirs of an Heiress*, 5 vols. (London, 1782), I: 91, 92.

193 *Ibid.*, II: 414.

194 *Ibid.*, III: 244, 245.

195 *Ibid.*, 185–86.

196 *Ibid.*, II: 189.

197 *Ibid.*, 185.

198 *Ibid.*, 186.
199 *Ibid.*, III: 141.
200 *Ibid.*, 143.
201 *Ibid.*, 222–23.
202 *Ibid.* 224.
203 *Ibid.*, V: 25.
204 Jane Austen, *The Complete Novels* (Oxford: Oxford University Press, 1994), 1086. I quote the narrator in *Northanger Abbey*.
205 Hester Lynch Piozzi, *Anecdotes of the Late Samuel Johnson, LL.D. during the Last Twenty Years of his Life*, 4th edn. (London, 1786), 115. "Hester" is spelled "Hesther" on the title page.
206 *Ibid.*, 76.
207 *Ibid.*, 169.
208 *Ibid.*
209 *Ibid.*, 39.
210 *Ibid.*, 40.
211 *Ibid.*, 166.
212 *Ibid.*, 153.
213 *Ibid.*, 284.
214 *Ibid.*, 58.
215 *Ibid.*, 80.
216 *Ibid.*, 83.
217 *Ibid.*, 60.
218 *Ibid.*, 123, 74.
219 *Monthly Review* 58 (1778), 112. Macaulay's *History of England, from the Revolution to the Present Time. In a Series of Letters to the Rev. Dr. Wilson*, not part of the main eight-volume *History*, which prompted this remark, was thought to require an exceptionally long three-part review.
220 [Mary Wollstonecraft], *Analytical Review* 1 (July 1788), 333, 328, 333. This review is signed "M." See the discussion of attribution of the reviews in the *Analytical Review* in *The Works of Mary Wollstonecraft*, ed. Janet Todd and Marilyn Butler, 7 vols. (New York: New York University Press, 1989), VII: 14–18.
221 Carter, *Letters to Montagu*, III: 91.
222 Chapone to W. W. Pepys, 24 August 1784, quoted in William McCarthy, *Hester Thrale Piozzi: Portrait of a Literary Woman* (Chapel Hill: University of North Carolina Press, 1985), 59.
223 Piozzi, *Anecdotes*, 166.
224 *Ibid.*, 119.
225 For the story of how this denial came to be written and to appear as a postscript in *Anecdotes*, see James Lowry Clifford, "The Printing of Mrs. Piozzi's *Anecdotes of Dr. Johnson*," *Bulletin of the John Rylands Library* 20 (1936), 157–72.

226 Mary Wollstonecraft, *Works*, V: 174–75.

227 Bridget Hill, "The Links between Mary Wollstonecraft and Catharine Macaulay: New Evidence," *Women's History Review* 4 (1995), 177.

228 Ann Yearsley, "Addressed to Sensibility," in *Poems on Various Subjects. By Ann Yearsley, A Milkwoman of Clifton, near Bristol, Being her Second Work* (London, 1787), 6.

229 Anna Seward, *The Letters of Anna Seward written between the Years 1784 and 1807*, 6 vols. (1811; reprint New York: AMS Press, 1995), II: 287.

Recommended modern editions

We need better or more complete editions of Rowe, Aubin, Manley, Trotter Cockburn, Pix, Masham, Finch, Centlivre, Thomas, Barber, Collyer, Carter, Macaulay, Con Phillips, Cowley, and Lee. This list concentrates on texts discussed in this history and does not include facsimile reprint editions.

Adams, Abigail. *Adams Family Correspondence*. Ed. L. H. Butterfield, et al. 6 vols. Cambridge, Mass.: Belknap Press of Harvard University, 1963–93.

Astell, Mary. *Astell: Political Writings*. Ed. Patricia Springborg. Cambridge Texts in the History of Political Thought. Cambridge: Cambridge University Press, 1996.

Barbauld, Anna Letitia Aikin. *The Poems of Anna Letitia Barbauld*. Ed. William McCarthy and Elizabeth Kraft. Athens: University of Georgia Press, 1994.

Behn, Aphra. *The Works of Aphra Behn*. 7 vols. Ed. Janet Todd. Columbus: Ohio State University Press, 1992–96.

Bradstreet, Anne. *The Complete Works of Anne Bradstreet*. Ed. Joseph R. McElrath, Jr. and Allan P. Robb. Boston: Twayne Publishers, 1981.

Brooke, Frances. *Rosina*. Ambrosian Singers and the London Symphony Orchestra. Decca/London Records [1967].

The Excursion. Ed. Paula R. Backscheider and Hope D. Cotton. Lexington: University Press of Kentucky, 1997.

Brooke, Frances and William Shield. *Rosina*. Ed. John Drummond. London: Stainer & Bell, 1998. (Libretto and score. Vol. LXXII of *Musica Britannica: A National Collection of Music.*)

Burney, Frances. *Evelina, or, The History of Young Lady's Entrance into the World (1778)*. Ed. Edward A. Bloom with the assistance of Lillian D. Bloom. Oxford: Oxford University Press, 1968.

The Early Journals and Letters of Fanny Burney. 4 vols. Ed. Lars E. Troide. Kingston and Montreal: McGill-Queen's University Press, 1988.

Cecilia, or Memoirs of an Heiress. Ed. Peter Sabor and Margaret Anne Doody. Oxford: Oxford University Press, 1988.

The Complete Plays of Frances Burney. 2 vols. Ed. Peter Sabor, Geoffrey M. Sill, and Stewart J. Cooke. Kingston: McGill-Queen's University Press, 1995.

Carter, Elizabeth. *Bluestocking Feminism: Writings of the Bluestocking Circle*, vol. II. Ed. Judith Hawley. London: Pickering & Chatto, 1999.

Cavendish, Margaret. *The Life of William Cavendish, Duke of Newcastle. To which is added the True Relation of my Birth, Breeding, and Life*. Ed. C. H. Firth. 2nd edn. London: G. Routledge; New York: E. P. Dutton, 1906.

The Description of a New World Called the Blazing World and Other Writing. Ed. Kate Lilley. New York: New York University Press, 1992.

Centlivre, Susanna. *Eighteenth-Century Women Playwrights,*. vol. III. Ed. Jacqueline Pearson. London: Pickering & Chatto, 2001 (4 plays).

The Wonder: A Woman Keeps a Secret. Ed. John O'Brien. Peterborough, Ontario: Broadview Press, 2003.

Chapone, Hester. *Bluestocking Feminism: Writings of the Bluestocking Circle*, vol. III. Ed. Rhoda Zuk. London: Pickering & Chatto, 1999.

Charke, Charlotte. *A Narrative of the Life of Mrs Charlotte Charke*. Ed. Robert Rehder. Pickering & Chatto, 1999.

Chudleigh, Mary. *The Poems and Prose of Mary, Lady Chudleigh*. Ed. Margaret J. M. Ezell. New York: Oxford University Press, 1993.

Cockburn, Catherine Trotter. *Eighteenth-Century Women Playwrights*, vol. II. Ed. Anne Kelly. London: Pickering & Chatto, 2001 (2 plays).

Cowley, Hannah. *Eighteenth-Century Women Playwrights*, vol. V. Ed. Antje Blank. London: Pickering & Chatto, 2001 (4 plays).

Davys, Mary. *The Reform'd Coquet, Familiar Letters Betwixt a Gentleman and a Lady, and The Accomplish'd Rake*. Ed. Martha F. Bowden. Lexington: University Press of Kentucky, 1999.

Fielding, Sarah. *The Lives of Cleopatra and Octavia*. Ed. by Christopher D. Johnson. Lewisburg, Penn.: Bucknell University Press, 1994.

The Adventures of David Simple and Volume the Last. Ed. Peter Sabor. Lexington: University Press of Kentucky, 1998.

Finch, Anne. *The Poems of Anne Countess of Winchilsea*. Ed. Myra Reynolds. Chicago: University of Chicago Press, 1903.

The Anne Finch Wellesley Manuscript Poems: A Critical Edition. Ed. Barbara McGovern and Charles H. Hinnant. Athens: University of Georgia Press, 1998 (53 poems not published in Finch's lifetime and not included in Reynolds edition).

Griffith, Elizabeth. *The Delicate Distress*. Ed. Cynthia Booth Ricciardi and Susan Staves. Lexington: University Press of Kentucky, 1997.

Eighteenth-Century Women Playwrights, vol. IV. Ed. Betty Rizzo. London: Pickering & Chatto, 2001 (4 plays).

Haywood, Eliza. *Love in Excess*. Ed. David Oakleaf. Peterborough, Ontario: Broadview Press, 1996.

The History of Miss Betsy Thoughtless. Ed. Beth Fowkes-Tobin. Oxford: Oxford University Press, 1997.

Adventures of Eovaai, Princess of Ijavoo: A Pre-Adamitical History. Ed. Earla Wilputte. Peterborough, Ontario: Broadview Press, 1999.

The Injur'd Husband, or The Mistaken Resentment; and Lasselia, or, The Self-Abandoned. Ed. Jerry C. Beasley. Lexington: University Press of Kentucky, 1999.

Selected Works of Eliza Haywood. Ed. Alexander Petit, Margo Collins, Christine Blouch, Rebecca Sayers Hanson, and Kathryn B. King. 6 vols. London: Pickering & Chatto, 2000.

Hollis, Frances Anne, Lady Vane. "Memoirs of a Lady of Quality." In Tobias Smollett. *The Adventures of Peregrine Pickle in Which are Included Memoirs of a Lady of Quality.* Ed. James L. Clifford. London: Oxford University Press, 1964.

Hutchinson, Lucy. *The Life of Colonel Hutchinson.* Ed. James Sutherland. London: Oxford University Press, 1973.

Inchbald, Elizabeth. *Eighteenth-Century Women Playwrights*, vol. VI. Ed. Angela Smallwood. London: Pickering and Chatto, 2001 (4 plays).

Leapor, Mary. *The Works of Mary Leapor.* Ed. Richard Greene and Ann Messenger. Oxford University Press, 1999.

Lee, Sophia. *The Recess, or, A Tale of Other Times.* Ed. April Alliston. Lexington: University Press of Kentucky, 2000.

Lennox, Charlotte. *The Female Quixote, or, The Adventures of Arabella.* Ed. Margaret Dalziel. Oxford: Oxford University Press, 1989.

The Life of Harriot Stuart, Written by Herself. Ed. Susan Kubica Howard. Madison, NJ: Fairleigh Dickinson Press; London: Associated University Presses, 1995.

Manley, Delarivière. *The New Atalantis.* Ed. Rosalind Ballaster. London: Pickering and Chatto, 1991. (Valuable introduction and notes, but unsatisfactory text.)

The Adventures of Rivella. Ed. Katherine Zelinsky. Peterborough, Ontario: Broadview Press, 1999. (Useful supporting material and notes, but sporadically modernized text and inadequate textual information.)

Eighteenth-Century Women Playwrights, vol. I. Ed. Margarete Rubik and Eva Mueller-Zettelman. London: Pickering & Chatto, 2001 (2 plays).

Montagu, Mary Wortley. *The Complete Letters of Lady Mary Wortley Montagu.* Ed. Robert Halsband. 3 vols. Oxford: Clarendon Press, 1965.

Embassy to Constantinople: The Travels of Lady Mary Wortley Montagu. Ed. Christopher Pick. Introduction by Dervla Murphy. New York: New Amsterdam, 1988. (Lavish and illuminating contemporary illustrations. Text based on Robert Halsband's modernized version of his own text and notes derived from Halsband.)

Essays and Poems and Simplicity, A Comedy. Ed. Robert Halsband and Isobel Grundy. Oxford: Clarendon Press, 1993.

Romance Writings. Ed. Isobel Grundy. Oxford: Clarendon Press, 1996.

Osborn, Sarah Byng. *Letters of Sarah Byng Osborn, 1721–1773, From the Collection of the Hon. Mrs. McDonnell.* Ed. John McClelland. Stanford, Calif.: Stanford University Press, 1930.

Philips, Katherine. *The Collected Works of Katherine Philips, The Matchless Orinda*. Ed. Patrick Thomas. 3 vols. Stump Cross, Essex: Stump Cross Books, 1990.

Pilkington, Laetitia. *Memoirs of Laetitia Pilkington*. Ed. A. C. Elias, Jr. 2 vols. Athens: University of Georgia Press, 1997.

Pinckney, Eliza Lucas. *The Letterbook of Eliza Lucas Pinckney*. Ed. Elise Pinckney and Marvin R. Zahniser. Chapel Hill: University of North Carolina Press, 1972.

Piozzi, Hester [Lynch] Thrale. *Thraliana. The Diary of Mrs. Hester Lynch Thrale (Later Mrs. Piozzi), 1776–1809*. Ed. Katharine C. Balderston. 2 vols. 2nd edn. Oxford: Clarendon Press, 1951.

The Letters of Samuel Johnson: With Mrs. Thrale's Genuine Letters to Him. Ed. R. W. Chapman. 3 vols. Oxford: Oxford Clarendon Press, 1984.

The Piozzi Letters: Correspondence of Hester Lynch Piozzi, 1784–1821 (formerly Mrs. Thrale). Ed. Edward A. Bloom and Lillian D. Bloom. 6 vols. Newark: University of Delaware Press; London: Associated University Press, 1989–2000.

Pix, Mary. *Eighteenth-Century Women Playwrights*, vol. II. Ed. Anne Kelly. London: Pickering & Chatto, 2001 (2 plays).

Reeve, Clara. *The Old English Baron: a Gothic Story*. Ed. James Trainer. London: Oxford University Press, 1967.

Bluestocking Feminism: Writings of the Bluestocking Circle, vol. VI. Ed. Gary Kelly. London: Pickering & Chatto, 1999.

Rowe, Elizabeth Singer. *The Poetry of Elizabeth Singer Rowe (1674–1737)*. Ed. Madeleine Forell Marshall. Studies in Women and Religion, vol. XXV. Lewiston, NY: Edwin Mellon Press [1987]. (Useful introduction and collection, but incomplete and noncritical texts.)

Rowlandson, Mary. *The Sovereignty and Goodness of God: Together with the Faithfulness of his Promises Displayed: Being a Narrative of the Captivity and Restoration of Mrs. Mary Rowlandson and Related Documents*. Ed. Neal Salisbury. Boston: Bedford Books, 1997.

Scott, Sarah. *A Description of Millenium Hall*. Ed. Gary Kelly. Peterborough, Ontario: Broadview Press, 1995.

Bluestocking Feminism: Writings of the Bluestocking Circle, vols. V and VI. Ed. Gary Kelly. London: Pickering & Chatto, 1999.

Seward, Anna. *Bluestocking Feminism: Writings of the Bluestocking Circle*, vol. IV. Ed. Jennifer Kelly. London: Pickering & Chatto, 1999.

Sheridan, Frances. *The Plays of Frances Sheridan*. Ed. Robert Hogan and Jerry C. Beasley. Newark: University of Delaware Press, 1984.

Oriental Tales. Ed. Robert L. Mack. Oxford: Oxford University Press, 1992. ("The History of Nourjahad.")

Smith, Charlotte. *The Poems of Charlotte Smith*. Ed. Stuart Curran. New York: Oxford University Press, 1993.

The Collected Letters of Charlotte Smith. Ed. Judith Phillips Stanton. Bloomington: Indiana University Press, 2003.

Emmeline: The Orphan of the Castle. Ed. Loraine Fletcher. Peterborough, Ontario: Broadview Press, 2003.

Wollstonecraft, Mary. *The Works of Mary Wollstonecraft.* Ed. Janet Todd and Marilyn Butler. 7 vols. New York: New York University Press, 1989.

Wheatley, Phillis. *The Poems of Phillis Wheatley: Revised and Enlarged Edition.* Ed. Julian D. Mason, Jr. Chapel Hill: University of North Carolina Press, 1989.

Select bibliography

GENERAL WORKS

Items in this section deal with women's writing across several chronological periods. Many consider particular genres of writing, others are collections of essays, still others consider matters like women's relation to the book trade or the problematics of writing women's literary history. Items more tightly focused on particular texts or the literature of a shorter period are listed in the select bibliography sections for the appropriate chapters.

Adburgham, Alison. *Women in Print: Writing Women and Women's Magazines from the Restoration to the Accession of Victoria*. London: George Allen & Unwin, 1972.

Agorni, Mirella. *Translating Italy for the Eighteenth Century: Women, Translation, and Travel Writing, 1739–1797*. Manchester: St. Jerome, 2002.

Anderson, Misty G. *Female Playwrights and Eighteenth-Century Comedy: Negotiating Marriage on the London Stage*. New York: Palgrave, 2002.

Armstrong, Isobel, ed. *New Feminist Discourses: Critical Essays on Theories and Texts*. London: Routledge, 1992.

Armstrong, Isobel and Virginia Blain, eds. *Women's Poetry of the Enlightenment: The Making of a Canon, 1730–1820*. Basingstoke: Macmillan; New York: St. Martin's Press in Association with the Centre for English Studies, School of Advanced Study, University of London, 1999.

Ballaster, Rosalind. *Seductive Forms: Women's Amatory Fiction from 1684 to 1740*. Oxford: Clarendon Press, 1992.

Blodgett, Harriet. *Centuries of Female Days: Englishwomen's Private Diaries*. New Brunswick, NJ: Rutgers University Press, 1988.

Brant, Clare and Diana Purkiss, eds. *Women, Texts, and Histories, 1575–1760*. London: Routledge, 1992.

Brink, J. R. *Female Scholars: A Tradition of Learned Women before 1800*. Montreal: Eden Press Women's Publications, 1980.

Christmas, William J. *The Labr'ing Muses: Work, Writing, and the Social Order in English Plebian Poetry, 1730–1830*. Newark: University of Delaware Press, 2001.

Clarke, Norma. *The Rise and Fall of the Woman of Letters*. London: Pimlico, 2004.

Cotton, Nancy. *Women Playwrights in England, c. 1363–1750*. Lewisburg, Penn.: Bucknell University Press, 1980.

Craft-Fairchild, Catherine. *Masquerade and Gender: Disguise and Female Identity in Eighteenth-Century Fictions by Women*. University Park: Pennsylvania State University Press, 1993.

Crawford, Patricia. "Women's Published Writings, 1660–1700." In *Women in English Society, 1500–1800*. Ed. Mary Prior. London: Methuen, 1985, 211–82.

Davis, Natalie Zeman. "Gender and Genre: Women as Historical Writers, 1400–1820." In *Beyond their Sex: Learned Women of the European Past*. Ed. Patricia H. Labalme. New York: New York University Press, 1980, 153–82.

D'Monté, Rebecca and Nicole Pohl. *Female Communities, 1600–1800: Literary Visions and Cultural Realities*. New York: St. Martin's Press, 1999.

Donkin, Ellen. *Getting into the Act: Women Playwrights in London, 1776–1829*. London: Routledge, 1995.

Donovan, Josephine. *Women and the Rise of the Novel, 1405–1726*. New York: St. Martin's Press, 1999.

Ezell, Margaret. *Writing Women's Literary History*. Baltimore, Md.: Johns Hopkins University Press, 1993.

Ferguson, Moira. *Subject to Others: British Women Writers and Colonial Slavery, 1670–1834*. London: Routledge, 1992.

Gallagher, Catherine. *Nobody's Story: The Vanishing Acts of Women Writers in the Marketplace, 1670–1820*. Berkeley: University of California Press, 1994.

Greider, Josephine. *Translations of French Sentimental Prose Fiction in Late Eighteenth-Century England: The History of a Vogue*. Durham, NC: Duke University Press, 1975.

Griffin, Dustin H. *Literary Patronage in England, 1650–1800*. Cambridge: Cambridge University Press, 1996.

Grundy, Isobel and Susan Wiseman. *Women, Writing, History, 1640–1740*. Athens: University of Georgia Press, 1992.

Guest, Harriet. *Small Change: Women, Learning, Patriotism, 1750–1810*. Chicago: University of Chicago Press, 2000.

Horner, Joyce M. *The English Women Novelists and their Connection with the Feminist Movement (1688–1787)*. Smith College Studies in Modern Languages, vol. XI, nos. 1 and 2 (1929–30).

Ingrassia, Catherine. *Authorship, Commerce, and Gender in Early Eighteenth-Century England: A Culture of Paper Credit*. Cambridge: Cambridge University Press, 1998.

Johns, Alessa. *Women's Utopias of the Eighteenth Century*. Urbana: University of Illinois Press, 2003.

Justice, George L. and Nathan Tinker. *Women's Writing and the Circulation of Ideas: Manuscript Publication in England, 1550–1800*. Cambridge: Cambridge University Press, 2002.

Landry, Donna. *The Muses of Resistance: Laboring-class Women's Poetry in Britain, 1739–1796*. Cambridge: Cambridge University Press, 1990.

Looser, Devoney. *British Women Writers and the Writing of History, 1670–1820.* Baltimore, Md.: Johns Hopkins University Press, 2000.

MacCarthy, B[ridget] G. *The Female Pen: Women Writers and Novelists, 1621–1818.* 1946–47. Reprint. New York: New York University Press, 1994.

McDowell, Paula. *The Women of Grub Street: Press, Politics, and Gender in the London Literary Marketplace, 1678–1730.* Oxford: Clarendon Press, 1998.

Maison, Margaret. "'Thine, Only Thine': Women Hymn Writers in Britain, 1760–1825." In *Religion in the Lives of English Women, 1760–1930.* Ed. Gail Malmgreen. Bloomington: Indiana University Press, 1986, 11–40.

Melman, Billie. *Women's Orients – English Women and the Middle East, 1718–1918.* Ann Arbor: University of Michigan Press, 1992.

Messenger, Ann. *His and Hers: Essays in Restoration and Eighteenth-Century Literature.* Lexington: University Press of Kentucky, 1986.

Pastoral Tradition and the Female Talent: Studies in Augustan Poetry. New York: AMS Press, 2001.

Messenger, Ann, ed. *Gender at Work: Four Women Writers of the Eighteenth Century.* Detroit, Mich.: Wayne State University Press, 1990.

Myers, Sylvia Harcstack. *The Bluestocking Circle: Women, Friendship, and the Life of the Mind in Eighteenth-Century England.* Oxford: Clarendon Press, 1990.

Pearson, Jacqueline. *The Prostituted Muse: Images of Women and Women Dramatists, 1642–1737.* New York: St. Martin's Press, 1988.

Perry, Ruth. *Women, Letters, and the Novel.* New York: AMS Press, 1980.

Quinsey, Katherine M., ed. *Broken Boundaries: Women and Feminism in Restoration Drama.* Lexington: University Press of Kentucky, 1986.

Reynolds, Myra. *The Learned Lady in England, 1650–1760.* Boston: Houghton Mifflin, 1920.

Rubik, Margarete. *Early Women Dramatists, 1550–1800.* Basingstoke: Macmillan; New York: St. Martin's Press, 1998.

Schofield, Mary Anne. *Masking and Unmasking the Female Mind: Disguising Romances in Feminine Fiction, 1713–1799.* Newark: University of Delaware Press, 1990.

Schofield, Mary Anne and Cecila Macheski, eds. *Curtain Calls: British and American Women and the Theater, 1660–1800.* Athens: Ohio University Press, 1991.

Smith, Hilda. *Reason's Disciples: Seventeenth-Century English Feminists.* Urbana: University of Illinois Press, 1982.

Spacks, Patricia Meyer. *Desire and Truth: Functions of Plot in Eighteenth-Century English Novels.* Chicago: University of Chicago Press, 1990.

Spencer, Jane. *The Rise of the Woman Novelist: From Aphra Behn to Jane Austen.* Oxford: Basil Blackwell, 1986.

Stanton, Judith Phillips. "Statistical Profiles of Women's Writing in English from 1660 to 1800." In *Eighteenth-Century Women and the Arts.* Ed. Frederick M. Keener and Susan E. Lorsch. New York: Greenwood Press, 1988, 247–54.

Thompson, Lynda M. *The "Scandalous Memoirists": Constantia Phillips, Laetitia Pilkington and the Shame of "Publick Fame."* Manchester: Manchester University Press, 2000.

Turner, Cheryl. *Living by the Pen: Women Writers in the Eighteenth Century.* 1992. Reprint. London: Routledge, 1994.

Turner, Katherine. *British Travel Writers in Europe, 1750–1800: Authorship, Gender, and National Identity.* Studies in European Cultural Transition, vol. X. Aldershot: Ashgate, 2001.

Vickery, Amanda. "Golden Age to Separate Spheres? A Review of the Categories and Chronology of English Women's History." *Historical Journal* 36 (1993), 383–414.

Wanko, Cheryl. "The Player in Print from Betterton to Garrick." Unpublished dissertation. Pennsylvania State University, 1993.

Williamson, Marilyn. *Raising their Voices: British Women Writers, 1650–1750.* Detroit, Mich.: Wayne State University Press, 1990.

1 PUBLIC WOMEN: THE RESTORATION TO THE DEATH OF APHRA BEHN, 1660–1689

Adam, Michel. "Katherine Philips, traductrice du théâtre de Pierre Corneille." *Revue d'histoire littéraire de la France* 85 (1985), 841–51.

Ballaster, Rosalind "New Hystericism: Aphra Behn's *Oroonoko*: The Body, the Text and the Feminist Critic." In *New Feminist Discourses: Critical Essays on Theories and Texts.* Ed. Isobel Armstrong. London: Routledge, 1992, 283–95.

Barash, Carol. *English Women's Poetry, 1649–1714: Politics, Community, and Linguistic Authority.* Oxford: Clarendon Press, 1996.

Battigelli, Anna. *Margaret Cavendish and the Exiles of the Mind.* Lexington: University Press of Kentucky, 1998.

Chibka, Robert. "'Oh! Do not Fear a Woman's Invention': Truth, Falsehood, and Fiction in Aphra Behn's *Oroonoko*." *Texas Studies in Literature and Language* 30 (1988), 510–37.

Cook, Susan. "'The story I most particularly intend': The Narrative Style of Lucy Hutchinson." *Critical Survey* 5 (1993), 271–77.

Cotton, Nancy. "Re-Producing *The Rover*: John Barton's *Rover* at the Swan." *Essays in Theatre* 9 (1990), 45–59.

Crawford, Patricia. "Women's Published Writings, 1600–1700." In *Women in English Society, 1500–1800.* Ed. Mary Prior. London, Methuen, 1985, 211–82.

Day, Robert. "Aphra Behn and the Works of the Intellect." In *Fetter'd or Free?: British Women Novelists, 1670–1815.* Ed. Mary Anne Schofield and Cecilia Macheski. Athens: Ohio University Press, 1986, 372–82.

Diamond, Elin. "'Gestus' and Signature in Aphra Behn's *The Rover*." *ELH* 56 (1989), 519–41.

Downing, David. "'Streams of Scripture Comfort': Mary Rowlandson's Typological Use of the Bible." *Early American Literature* 15 (1980–81), 252–59.

Duyfhuizen, Bernard. "'That Which I Dare Not Name': Aphra Behn's 'The Willing Mistress.'" *ELH* 58 (1991), 63–82.

Easton, Celia. "Excusing the Breach of Nature's Laws: The Discourse of Desire and Denial in Katherine Philips's Friendship Poetry." *Restoration* 14, 1 (1990), 1–14.

Fabricant, Carole. "Rochester's World of Imperfect Enjoyment." *Journal of English and Germanic Philology* 73 (1974), 338–50.

Ferguson, Margaret W. "Juggling the Categories of Race, Class and Gender: Aphra Behn's *Oroonoko*." *Women's Studies* 19 (1991), 159–81.

Gallagher, Catherine. "Who Was that Masked Woman? The Prostitute and the Playwright in the Comedies of Aphra Behn." *Women's Studies* 15 (1988), 23–42.

Gardiner, Judith Kegan. "Liberty, Equality, Fraternity: Utopian Longings in Behn's Lyric Poetry." In *Rereading Aphra Behn: History, Theory, and Criticism*. Ed. Heidi Hutner. Charlottesville: University Press of Virginia, 1993, 273–300.

Henwood, Dawn. "Mary Rowlandson and the Psalms: The Textuality of Survival." *Early American Literature* 32 (1997), 169–86.

Hoby, Elaine. *Virtue of Necessity: English Women's Writing, 1649–1688*. London: Virago, 1988.

Hughes, Derek. *The Theatre of Aphra Behn*. Basingstoke and New York: Palgrave, 2001.

Hughes, Derek and Janet Todd, eds. *The Cambridge Companion to Aphra Behn*. Cambridge: Cambridge University Press, 2004.

Keeble, N. H. "'The Colonel's Shadow': Lucy Hutchinson, Women's Writing and the Civil War." In *Literature and the English Civil War*. Ed. Thomas F. Healy and Jonathan Sawday. Cambridge: Cambridge University Press, 1990, 227–47.

Lilley, Kate. "Blazing Worlds: Seventeenth-Century Women's Utopian Writing." In *Women, Texts and Histories*. Ed. Clare Brant and Diane Purkiss. London: Routledge, 1992, 72–92.

"True State Within: Women's Elegy, 1640–1740." In *Women, Writing, History, 1640–1740*. Ed. Isobel Grundy and Susan Wiseman. Athens: University of Georgia Press, 1992, 72–82.

Mermin, Dorothy. "Women Becoming Poets: Katherine Philips, Aphra Behn, Anne Finch." *ELH* 57 (1990), 335–55.

Oser, Lee. "Almost a Golden World: Sidney, Spenser, and Puritan Conflict in Bradstreet's 'Contemplations.'" *Renascence: Essays on Values in Literature* 52 (2000), 187–202.

Pearson, Jacqueline. "Gender and Narrative in the Fiction of Aphra Behn, I." *Review of English Studies* 42 (1991), 40–56.

"Gender and Narrative in the Fiction of Aphra Behn, II." *Review of English Studies* 42 (1991), 179–90.

Quaintance, Richard E. "French Sources of the Restoration 'Imperfect Enjoyment' Poem." *Philological Quarterly* 42 (1963), 190–99.

Sarasohn, Lisa T. "A Science Turned Upside Down: Feminism and the Natural Philosophy of Margaret Cavendish." *Huntington Library Quarterly* 47 (1984), 289–307.

Schweitzer, Ivy. "Anne Bradstreet Wrestles with the Renaissance." *Early American Literature* 23 (1988), 291–312.

Spengemann, William C. "The Earliest American Novel: Aphra Behn's *Oroonoko.*" *Nineteenth-Century Fiction* 38 (1984), 384–414.

Stiebel, Arlene. "Subversive Sexuality: Masking the Erotic in Poems by Katherine Philips and Aphra Behn." In *Renaissance Discourses of Desire.* Ed. Claude J. Summers and Ted-Larry Pebworth. Columbia: University of Missouri Press, 1993, 223–36.

Todd, Janet. *The Secret Life of Aphra Behn.* New Brunswick, NJ: Rutgers University Press, 1996.

Trubowitz, Rachel. "The Reenchantment of Utopia and the Female Monarchical Self: Margaret Cavendish's Blazing World." *Tulsa Studies in Women's Literature* 11 (1992), 229–45.

Wahl, Elizabeth Susan. *Invisible Relations: Representations of Female Intimacy in the Age of Enlightenment.* Stanford, Calif.: Stanford University Press, 1999.

White, Elizabeth Wade. *Anne Bradstreet: "The Tenth Muse."* New York: Oxford University Press, 1971.

Wiseman, S. J. *Aphra Behn.* Plymouth: Northcote House, 1996.

Young, Elizabeth. "Aphra Behn, Gender, and Pastoral." *Studies in English Literature, 1500–1900* 33 (1993), 523–43.

2 PARTISANS OF VIRTUE AND RELIGION, 1689–1702

Atherton, Margaret. "Cartesian Reason and Gendered Reason." In *A Mind of her Own.* Ed. Louise Anthony and Charlotte Will. Boulder, Colo: Westview Press, 1992, 19–34.

Backscheider, Paula. *Spectacular Politics: Theatrical Power and Mass Culture in Early Modern England.* Baltimore, Md.: Johns Hopkins University Press, 1993.

Boulton, Martha Brandt. "Some Aspects of the Philosophy of Catharine Trotter." *Journal of the History of Philosophy* 31 (1993), 565–88.

Clark, Constance. *Three Augustan Women Playwrights.* New York: Peter Lang, 1986.

Davis-Perry, Lori Ann. "Elizabeth Singer Rowe: A Literary History and Critical Analysis." Unpublished PhD dissertation, Brandeis University, 2003.

Ferguson, Moira, ed. *First Feminists: British Women Writers, 1578–1799.* Bloomington: Indiana University Press and Old Westbury, NY: Feminist Press, 1985.

Frankel, Lois. "Damaris Cudworth Masham: A Seventeenth-Century Feminist Philosopher." In *Hypathia's Daughters: Fifteen Hundred Years of Women Philosophers.* Ed. Linda Lopez McAlister. Bloomington: Indiana University Press, 1996, 128–38.

Hill, Bridget. "A Refuge from Men: The Idea of a Protestant Nunnery." *Past and Present* 117 (Nov. 1979), 107–30.

Hughes, Derek. *English Drama, 1660–1700.* Oxford: Clarendon Press, 1996.

Hutton, Sarah. "Damaris Cudworth, Lady Masham: Between Platonism and Enlightenment." *The British Journal for the History of Philosophy* 1 (1993), 29–54.

Johns, Alessa. "Mary Astell's 'Excited Needles': Theorizing Feminist Utopia in Seventeenth-Century England." In *Female Communities: Literary Visions and Cultural Realities.* Ed. Rebecca D'Monté and Nicole Pohl. New York: St. Martin's Press, in association with the Institute of English Studies, School of Advanced Study, University of London, 2000, 129–48.

Kelley, Anne. *Catharine Trotter: An Early Modern Writer in the Vanguard of Feminism.* Aldershot: Ashgate, 2002.

Lowenthal, Cynthia. "Portraits and Spectators in the Late Restoration Playhouse: Delariviere Manley's *Royal Mischief.*" *The Eighteenth Century: Theory and Interpretation* 35 (1994), 119–34.

McLaren, Juliet. "'Presumptuous Poetess, Pen-Feathered Muse": The Comedies of Mary Pix." In *Gender at Work: Four Women Writers of the Eighteenth Century.* Ed. Ann Messinger. Detroit, Mich.: Wayne State University Press, 1990, 77–113.

Merrens, Rebecca. "'Unmanned with thy Words'": Regendering Tragedy in Manley and Trotter." In *Broken Boundaries: Women and Feminism in Restoration Drama.* Ed. Katherin M. Quinsey. Lexington: University Press of Kentucky, 1996, 31–53.

O'Donnell, Sheryl. "'My Idea in your Mind'": John Locke and Damaris Cudworth Masham." In *Mothering the Mind.* Ed. Ruth Perry and Martine Watson Brownley. New York: Holmes and Meier, 1984, 26–46.

Perry, Ruth. *The Celebrated Mary Astell: An Early English Feminist.* Chicago: University of Chicago Press, 1986.

Rabb, Melinda. "Angry Beauties: (Wo)Manley Satire and the Stage." In *Cutting Edges: Postmodern Critical Essays on Eighteenth-Century Satire.* Ed. James E. Gill. Knoxville: University of Tennessee Press, 1995, 127–58.

Smith, Hilda. *Reason's Disciples: Seventeenth-Century English Feminists.* Urbana: University of Illinois Press, 1982.

Springborg, Patricia. "Mary Astell (1666–1731), Critic of Locke." *American Political Science Review* 89 (1995), 621–33.

"Astell, Masham, and Locke: Religion and Politics." In *Women Writers and the Early Modern British Political Tradition.* Ed. Hilda L. Smith. Cambridge: Cambridge University Press, 1998, 105–25.

Stecher, Henry F. *Elizabeth Singer Rowe, the Poetess of Frome: A Study in Eighteenth-Century Pietism.* Berne: Herbert Lang; Frankfurt: Peter Lang, 1973.

Sutherland, Christine Mason. "Mary Astell: 'Reclaiming Rhetorica' in the Seventeenth Century." In *Reclaiming Rhetorica: Women in the Rhetorical Tradition.* Ed. Andrea A. Lunsford. Pittsburgh, Penn.: University of Pittsburgh Press, 1995, 93–116.

Tooley, Brenda. "'Like a False Renegade': The Ends and Means of Feminist Apologetics in a *Dialogue Concerning Women* and *An Essay in Defence of the Female Sex.*" *The Eighteenth Century: Theory and Interpretation* 36 (1995), 157–77.

Waithe, Mary Ellen, ed. *A History of Women Philosophers*, vol. III: *Modern Women Philosophers, 1600–1900*. Dordrecht: Kluwer Academic Publishers, 1991.

3 POLITICS, GALLANTRY, AND LADIES IN THE REIGN OF QUEEN ANNE, 1702–1714

Adam, Michel. "L'héroïne tragique dans le théâtre de Catharine Trotter." In *Aspects du théâtre anglais, 1554–1730*. Ed. Nadia Rigaud. Aix-en-Provence: University of Provence, 1987, 97–115.

Ballaster, Rosalind. *Seductive Forms: Women's Amatory Fiction from 1684 to 1740*. Oxford: Clarendon Press, 1992.

Barash, Carol. *English Women's Poetry, 1649–1714: Politics, Community, and Linguistic Authority*. Oxford: Clarendon Press, 1996.

Bolton, Martha Brandt. "Some Aspects of the Philosophical Work of Catharine Trotter." *Journal of the History of Philosophy* 31 (1993), 565–88.

Bowyer, John Wilson. *The Celebrated Mrs. Centlivre*. Durham, NC: Duke University Press, 1952.

Clark, Constance. *Three Augustan Women Playwrights*. New York: Peter Lang, 1986.

Corman, Brian. *Genre and Generic Change in English Comedy, 1660–1710*. Toronto: University of Toronto Press, 1993.

Fowler, Patsy S. "Rejecting the Status Quo: the Attempt of Mary Pix and Susanna Centlivre to Reform Society's Patriarchal Attitudes." *Restoration and Eighteenth-Century Theatre Research* 11 (1996), 49–59.

Frushell, Richard C. "Marriage and Marrying in Susanna Centlivre's Plays." *Papers on Language and Literature* 22 (1986), 16–38.

Hinnant, Charles H. *The Poetry of Anne Finch: An Essay in Interpretation*. Newark: University of Delaware Press, 1994.

Kelley, Anne. *Catharine Trotter: An Early Modern Writer in the Vanguard of Feminism*. Aldershot: Ashgate, 2002.

Kinney, Suz-Anne. "Confinement Sharpens the Invention: Aphra Behn's *The Rover* and Susanna Centlivre's *The Busie Body.*" In *Look Who's Laughing: Gender and Comedy*. Ed. Gail Finney. Langhorne, Pa.: Gordon & Breach, 1994, 81–98.

Lewis, Jayne Elizabeth. *The English Fable: Aesop and Literary Culture, 1651–1740*. Cambridge: Cambridge University Press, 1996.

Lock, F. P. *Susanna Centlivre*. Boston: Twayne-G. K. Hall, 1979.

McGovern, Barbara. *Anne Finch and Her Poetry: A Critical Biography*. Athens: University of Georgia Press, 1992.

Medoff, Jeslyn. "New Light on Sarah Fyge (Field, Egerton)." *Tulsa Studies in Women's Literature* 1 (1982), 155–75.

"The Daughters of Behn and the Problem of Reputation." In *Women, Writing, History 1640–1740*. Ed. Isobel Grundy and Susan Wiseman. Athens: University of Georgia Press, 1992, 33–54.

Mermin, Dorothy. "Women Becoming Poets: Katherine Philips, Aphra Behn, Anne Finch." *ELH* 57 (1990), 335–55.

Morgan, Fidelis. *A Woman of No Character: An Autobiography of Mrs. Manley.* London: Faber & Faber, 1986.

Needham, Gwendolyn. "Mary de la Riviere Manley, Tory Defender." *Huntington Library Quarterly* 12 (1948–9), 255–85.

Rabb, Melinda Alliker. "Swift and the Spider-Woman: Manley and the Tory Satires." In *Locating Swift: Essays on the 250th Anniversary of the Death of Swift, 1667–1745*. Ed. Aileen Douglas, Patrick Kelly, and Ian Campbell Ross. Dublin: Four Courts Press, 1998, 60–81.

Richetti, John J. *Popular Fiction before Richardson: Narrative Patterns, 1700–39.* Oxford: Clarendon Press, 1969.

Shevelow, Kathryn. *Women and Print Culture: The Construction of Femininity in the Early Periodical.* London: Routledge, 1989.

Spencer, Jane. *The Rise of the Woman Novelist: From Aphra Behn to Jane Austen.* Oxford: Basil Blackwell, 1986.

Sutherland, James R. "The Progress of Error: Mrs. Centlivre and the Biographers." *Review of English Studies* 18 (1942), 167–82.

Todd, Janet. "Life after Sex: the Fictional Autobiography of Delariviere Manley." *Women's Studies. An Interdisciplinary Journal* 15 (1988), 43–55.

Warner, William B. *Licensing Entertainment: The Elevation of Novel Reading in Britain, 1684–1750.* Berkeley: University of California Press, 1998.

Williamson, Marilyn. *Raising their Voices: British Women Writers, 1650–1750.* Detroit, Mich.: Wayne State University Press, 1990.

4 BATTLE JOINED, 1715–1737

Aravamunden, Srinivas. "Lady Mary Wortley Montagu in the *Hammam*: Masquerade, Womanliness, and Levantization." *ELH* 62 (1995), 69–104.

Beer, Gillian. "'Our Unnatural No-voice': The Heroic Epistle, Pope, and Women's Gothic." In *Modern Essays on Eighteenth-Century Literature*. Ed. Leopold Damrosch, Jr. New York: Oxford University Press, 1988.

Bowden, Martha, ed., "Introduction." In *Mary Davys: The Reform'd Coquet; or Memoirs of Amoranda; Familiar Letters Betwixt a Gentlman and a Lady; and The Accomplish'd Rake, or Modern Fine Gentleman*. Lexington: University Press of Kentucky, 1999.

Campbell, Jill. "Lady Mary Wortley Montagu and the Historical Machinery of Female Identity." In *History, Gender, and Eighteenth-Century Literature*. Ed. Beth Fowkes Tobin. Athens: University of Georgia Press, 1994.

Collins, Sarah H. "The Elstobs and the End of the Saxon Revival." In *Anglo-Saxon Scholarship: The First Three Centuries*. Ed. C. T. Berkhout and Milton McC. Gatch. Boston, Mass.: G. K. Hall, 1982, 107–18.

David, Alun. "'The Story of Semiramis': an Oriental Tale in Elizabeth Rowe's *The History of Joseph.*" *Women's Writing* 4 (1997), 91–100.

Day, Robert Adams. *Told in Letters: Epistolary Fiction before Richardson.* Ann Arbor: University of Michigan Press, 1966.

De Bruyn, Frans. "Mary Davys." *Dictionary of Literary Biography*, vol. xxxix. Detroit, Mich.: Gale, 1985, 131–38.

Donovan, Josephine. *Women and the Rise of the Novel, 1405–1726.* New York: St. Martin's Press, 1999.

Doody, Margaret. "Swift Among the Women." *Yearbook of English Studies* 18 (1988), 68–92.

Doughty, Oswald. "A Bath Poetess of the Eighteenth Century." *Review of English Studies* 1 (1925), 404–20. (Chandler)

Elias, A. C., Jr. "Editing Minor Writers: The Case of Laetitia Pilkington and Mary Barber." In *1650–1850: Ideas, Aesthetics, and Inquiries in Early Modern England.* Vol. iii. Ed. Kevin Cope. New York: AMS Press, 1997, 129–47.

Fairchild, Hoxie Neal Fairchild. *Religious Trends in English Poetry*, vol. i: *1700–1740. Protestantism and the Cult of Sentiment.* New York: Columbia University Press, 1939.

Gretsch, Mechthild. "Elizabeth Elstob: A Scholar's Fight for Anglo-Saxon Studies." *Anglia: Zeitschrift fur Englishe Philologie* 117 (1999), 163–200, 481–524.

Grundy, Isobel. "Ovid and Eighteenth-Century Divorce: An Unpublished Poem by Lady Mary Wortley Montagu." *Review of English Studies*, n.s., 23 (1972), 417–28.

  Lady Mary Wortley Montagu: Comet of the Enlightenment. Oxford: Oxford University Press, 1999.

Halsband, Robert. "The First English Version of Marivaux's *Le Jeu de l'amour et du hasard.*" *Modern Philology* 79 (1981), 16–23. (M. Montagu's version)

Heffernan, Teresa. "Feminism Against the East/West Divide: Lady Mary's *Turkish Embassy Letters.*" *Eighteenth-Century Studies* 33 (2000), 201–15.

Hollis, Karen. "Eliza Haywood and the Gender of Print." *The Eighteenth-Century: Theory and Practice* 38 (1997), 43–62.

Hughes, Shaun F. D. "The Anglo-Saxon Grammars of George Hickman and Elizabeth Elstob." In *Anglo-Saxon Scholarship: The First Three Centuries.* Ed. Carl T. Berkhout and Milton McC. Gatch. Boston: G. K. Hall, 1982.

Kern, Jean. "Mrs. Mary Davys as Novelist of Manners." *Essays in Literature* 10 (1983), 29–38.

Kietzman, Mary Jo. "Montagu's *Turkish Embassy Letters* and Cultural Dislocation." *Studies in English Literature* 38 (1998), 537–51.

Lowenthal, Cynthia. *Lady Mary Wortley Montagu and the Eighteenth-Century Familiar Letter.* Athens: University of Georgia Press, 1994.

McBurney, William. "Penelope Aubin and the Early English Novel." *Huntington Library Quarterly* 20 (1957), 245–67.

  "Mrs. Mary Davys: Forerunner of Fielding." PMLA 74 (1959), 348–55.

Melman, Billie. *Women's Orients – English Women and the Middle East, 1718–1918.* Ann Arbor: University of Michigan Press, 1992.

Mish, Charles. "Mme de Gomez and *La Belle Assemblée.*" *Revue de Littérature Comparée*, 34 (1960), 213–25.

Morris, David B. *The Religious Sublime: Christian Poetry and Critical Tradition in Eighteenth-Century England.* Lexington: University Press of Kentucky, 1972.

Morton, Richard. "Elizabeth Elstob's Rudiments of Grammar (1715): Germanic Philology for Women." *Studies in Eighteenth-Century Culture* 20 (1990), 267–87.

Needham, Gwendolyn B. "Mary de la Rivière Manley, Tory Defender." *Huntington Library Quarterly* 12 (1948–49), 253–88.

O'Loughlin, Katrina. "'Having lived much in the world': Inhabitation, Embodiment and English Women Travellers' Representations of Russia in the Eighteenth Century." *Women's Writing* 8 (2001), 419–39.

O'Shaughnessy Bowers, Toni. "Sex, Lies, and Invisibility: Amatory Fiction from the Restoration to Mid-Century." In *The Columbia History of the British Novel.* Ed. John Richetti, et al. New York: Columbia University Press, 1994, 50–72.

Richetti, John J. *Popular Fiction Before Richardson: Narrative Patterns, 1700–1739.* Oxford: Clarendon Press, 1969.

Riely, Linda. "Mary Davys's Satiric Novel *Familiar Letters*; Refusing Patriarchal Inscription of Women." In *Cutting Edges: Postmodern Critical Essays on Eighteenth-Century Satire.* Ed. James E. Gill. Tennessee Studies in Literature, vol. XXXVII. Knoxville: University of Tennessee Press, 1995, 206–21.

Sajé, Natasha. "'The Assurance to Write, the Vanity of Expecting to be Read': Deception and Reform in Mary Davys's *The Reformed Coquette.*" *Essays in Literature* 23 (1996), 165–77.

Saxton, Kirsten T. and Rebecca P. Bocchicchio, eds. *The Passionate Fictions of Eliza Haywood: Essays on Her Life and Work.* Lexington: University of Kentucky Press, 2000.

Schofield, Mary Anne. *Eliza Haywood.* Boston: Twayne, 1985.

Schulz, Dieter. "The Coquette's Progress from Satire to Sentimental Novel." *Literatur in Wissenschaft und Unterricht* 6 (1973), 77–99.

Shaw, Jane. "Gender and the 'Nature' of Religion: Lady Mary Wortley Montagu's Embassy Letters and their Place in Enlightenment Philosophy of Religion." *Bulletin of the John Rylands University Library of Manchester* 80 (1998), 129–45.

Snader, Joe. "The Oriental Captivity Narrative and Early English Fiction." *Eighteenth-Century Fiction* 9 (1997), 267–98.

Caught Between Worlds: British Captivity Narratives in Fact and Fiction. Lexington: University Press of Kentucky, 2000.

Troost, Linda Veronika. "Geography and Gender: Mary Chandler and Alexander Pope." In *Pope, Swift, and Women Writers.* Ed. Donald C. Mell. Newark, NJ: University of Delaware, 1996.

5 WOMEN AS MEMBERS OF THE LITERARY FAMILY, 1737–1756

Baruth, Philip E., ed. *Introducing Charlotte Charke: Actress, Author, Enigma.* Urbana: University of Illinois Press, 1998.

Bree, Linda. *Sarah Fielding.* New York: Twayne & Prentice Hall, 1996.

Burrows, J. F. and A. J. Hassall. "*Anna Boleyn* and the Authenticity of Fielding's Feminine Narratives." *Eighteenth-Century Studies* 21 (1988), 427–53.

Christmas, William J. *The Labr'ing Muses: Work, Writing, and the Social Order in English Plebian Poetry.* Newark: University of Delaware Press, 2001.

Crittendon, Walter. *The Life and Writings of Mrs. Sarah Scott, Novelist (1723–97).* Philadelphia: University of Pennsylvania Press, 1932.

Doody, Margaret. "Introduction." In Charlotte Lennox, *The Female Quixote, or, The Adventures of Arabella.* Ed. Margaret Dalziel. Oxford: Oxford University Press, 1989.

Dorn, Judith. "Reading Women Reading History: The Philosophy of Periodical Form in Charlotte Lennox's *The Lady's Museum.*" *Historical Reflections/ Reflexions historiques* 18 (1992), 2–27.

Elias, A. C., Jr. "Introduction." *Memoirs of Laetitia Pilkington.* 2 vols. Athens: University of Georgia Press, 1997.

Folkenflick, Robert. "Gender, Genre, and Theatricality in the Autobiography of Charlotte Charke." In *Representations of the Self from the Renaissance to Romanticism.* Ed. Patrick Coleman, Jayne Lewis, and Jill Kowalik. Cambridge: Cambridge University Press, 2000, 97–116.

Greene, Richard. *Mary Leapor: A Study in Eighteenth-Century Women's Poetry.* Oxford: Clarendon Press, 1993.

Isles, Duncan. "The Lennox Collection." *Harvard Library Bulletin* 18 (1970), 317–44; 36–60; 165–86; 416–35.

Kelsall, Malcolm. "Introduction." Sarah Fielding, *The Adventures of David Simple.* Oxford: Oxford University Press, 1994.

Landry, Donna. *The Muses of Resistance: Laboring-class Women's Poetry in Britain, 1739–1796.* Cambridge: Cambridge University Press, 1990.

Mackie, Erin. "Desperate Measures: The Narratives of the Life of Mrs. Charlotte Charke." *ELH* 58 (1991), 641–65.

Nussbaum, Felicity A. *The Autobiographical Subject: Gender and Ideology in Eighteenth-Century England.* Baltimore, Md.: Johns Hopkins University Press, 1989. Ch. 8, "Teteroclites: The Scandalous Memoirs," 178–200.

Relke, Diana M. A. "In Search of Mrs. Pilkington." In *Gender at Work.* Ed. Ann Messenger. Detroit, Mich.: Wayne State University Press, 1990, 114–49.

Séjourné, Philippe. *The Mystery of Charlotte Lennox. First Novelist of Colonial America.* Aix-en-Provence: Publications des Annales de la Faculté des Lettres, n.s. 62, 1967.

Shevelow, Kathryn. "Rewriting the Moral Essay: Eliza Haywood's *Female Spectator.*" *Reader* 13 (1985), 19–31.

Shugrue, Michael Francis, and William Harlin McBurney. "Introduction." *The Virtuous Orphan or, The Life of Marianne Countess of ****. An Eighteenth-Century English Translation. By Mrs. Mary Mitchell Collyer of Marivaux's La Vie de Marianne.* Carbondale: Southern Illinois University Press, 1965.

Skinner, Gillian. "'The Price of a Tear': Economic Sense and Sensibility in Sarah Fielding's *David Simple.*" *Literature and History*, 3rd ser., 1 (1992), 16–28.

Small, Miriam Rossiter. *Charlotte Ramsay Lennox: An Eighteenth-Century Lady of Letters.* New Haven: Yale University Press, 1935.

Thomas, Claudia. *Alexander Pope and His Eighteenth-Century Women Readers.* Carbondale: Southern Illinois University Press, 1994.

Thompson, Lynda M. *The "Scandalous Memoirist": Constantia Phillips, Laetitia Pilkington and the Shame of "Publick Fame."* Manchester: Manchester University Press, 2000.

Wanko, Cheryl. "The Player in Print from Betterton to Garrick." Unpublished PhD dissertation, Pennsylvania State University, 1993.

"The Eighteenth-Century Actress and the Construction of Gender: Lavinia Fenton and Charlotte Charke." *Eighteenth-Century Life* 18 (1994), 75–90.

Wilner, Arlene Fish. "Education and Ideology in Sarah Fielding's *The Governess.*" *Studies in Eighteenth-Century Culture* 24 (1995), 307–27.

Woodward, Carolyn. "Sarah Fielding's Self-Destructing Utopia: *The Adventures of David Simple.*" In *Living by the Pen: Early British Women Writers.* Ed. Dale Spender. New York: Teachers College Press, Columbia University, 1992, 65–81.

6 BLUESTOCKINGS AND SENTIMENTAL WRITERS, 1756–1776

Antor, Heinz. "The International Contexts of Frances Brooke's *The History of Emily Montague* (1769)." In *English Literatures in International Contexts.* Ed. Hienz Antor and Klaus Stierstorfer. Heidelberg: Carl Winter Universitäts-verlag, 2000, 245–77.

Benedict, Barbara. "The Margins of Sentiment: Nature, Letter, and Law in Frances Brooke's Epistolary Novels." *Ariel* 23 (1992), 7–25.

Climenson, Emily J. *Elizabeth Montagu, the Queen of the Blue-Stockings.* 2 vols. London: John Murray, 1906.

Cruise, James. "A House Divided: Sarah Scott's *Millenium Hall.*" *Studies in English Literature* 35 (1995), 555–73.

Demars, Patricia. *The World of Hannah More.* Lexington: University Press of Kentucky, 1996.

Donnelley, Lucy Martin. "The Celebrated Mrs. Macaulay." *William and Mary Quarterly*, 3rd ser., 6 (1949), 173–207.

Doody, Margaret Anne. "Frances Sheridan: Morality and Annihilated Time." In *Fetter'd or Free? British Women Novelists, 1670–1815.* Ed. Mary Anne Schofield and Cecilia Macheski. Athens: Ohio University Press, 1986, 324–58.

Elliott, Dorice Williams. "Sarah Scott's *Millenium Hall* and Female Philan-thropy." *Studies in English Literature* 35 (1995), 535–53.

Ellis, Frank H. *Sentimental Comedy: Theory and Practice.* Cambridge: Cambridge University Press, 1991.

Ellison, Julie. "There and Back: Transatlantic Novels and Anglo-American Careers." In *The Past as Prologue: Essays to Celebrate the Twenty-fifth Anniversary of ASECS.* Ed. Carla H. Hay and Syndy M. Conger. New York, NY: AMS Press, 1995, 303–24.

Erkkila, Betsy. "Revolutionary Women." *Tulsa Studies in Women's Literature* 6 (1987), 189–223. (Adams and Wheatley)

Freeman, Lisa. "'A Dialogue': Elizabeth Carter's Passion for the Female Mind." In *Women's Poetry in the Enlightenment: The Making of a Canon, 1730–1820.* Ed. Isobel Armstrong and Virginia Blain. Basingstoke: Macmillan, 1999, 50–63.

Grathwol, Kathleen B. "Lady Mary Wortley Montagu and Madame de Sévigné: Lettered Self-definition as Woman/Mother and Woman Writer." *Studies on Voltaire and the Eighteenth-Century* 332 (1995), 189–212.

Guest, Harriet. *Small Change: Women, Learning, Patriotism, 1750–1810.* Chicago: University of Chicago Press, 2000.

Harris, Marla. "Strategies of Silence: Sentimental Heroinism and Narrative Authority in Novels by Frances Sheridan, Frances Burney, Elizabeth Inchbald, and Hannah More." Unpublished PhD dissertation, Brandeis University, 1993.

Hicks, Philip. "Catharine Macaulay's Civil War: Gender, History, and Republicanism in Georgian Britain." *Journal of British Studies* 41 (2002), 170–98.

Hill, Bridget. *The Republican Virago: The Life and Times of Catharine Macaulay, Historian.* Oxford: Clarendon Press, 1992.

Hill, Bridget and Christopher Hill. "Catharine Macaulay and the Seventeenth Century." *The Welsh History Review* 3 (1967), 381–402.

"Catharine's Macaulay's *History* and her Catalogue of Tracts." *The Seventeenth Century* 8 (1993), 269–85.

Keener, Frederick M. *English Dialogues of the Dead: A Critical History, An Anthology, and a Check List.* New York: Columbia University Press, 1973. (E. Montagu's dialogues)

Keller, Rosemary. *Patriotism and the Female Sex: Abigail Adams and the American Revolution.* Brooklyn, NY: Carlson, 1994.

McMullen, Lorraine. *An Odd Attempt in a Woman: The Literary Life of Frances Brooke.* Vancouver: University of British Columbia Press, 1983.

Myers, Sylvia Harcstark. *The Bluestocking Circle: Women, Friendship, and the Life of the Mind in Eighteenth-Century England.* Oxford: Clarendon Press, 1990.

Pennington, Montagu. *Memoirs of the Life of Mrs. Elizabeth Carter, with a new Edition of her Poems. To Which are Added some Miscellaneous Essays in Prose.* 2 vols. 4th edn. London, 1825.

Perry, Ruth. "Clarissa's Daughters, or the History of Innocence Betrayed: How Women Writers Rewrote Richardson." *Women's Writing* 1 (1994), 5–24.

Pohl, Nicole and Betty A. Schellenberg, eds. *Reconsidering the Bluestockings. Huntington Library Quarterly.* Special issue. 65, 1 and 2 (2002).

Ricciardi, Cynthia and Susan Staves. "Introduction." In Elizabeth Griffith, *The Delicate Distress*. Lexington: University Press of Kentucky, 1997.

Schnorrenberg, Barbara B. "The Brood-hen of Faction: Mrs. Macaulay and Radical Politics, 1765–75." *Albion* 11 (1979), 33–45.

"An Opportunity Missed: Catharine Macaulay on the Revolution of 1688." *Studies in Eighteenth-Century Culture* 20 (1990), 231–40.

Spacks, Patricia Meyer. *Desire and Truth: Functions of Plot in Eighteenth-Century English Novels*. Chicago: University of Chicago Press, 1990. Ch. 5: "The Sentimental Novel and the Challenge to Power," 114–46.

Staves, Susan. "The Liberty of a She-Subject of England": Rights Rhetoric and the Female Thucydides." *Cardozo Studies in Law and Literature* 1 (1989), 161–83. (Macaulay)

"French Fire, English Asbestos: Ninon de Lenclos and Elizabeth Griffith." *Studies on Voltaire and the Eighteenth Century* 314 (1993), 193–205.

Thomas, Claudia. "'Th'Instructive Moral, and Important Thought': Elizabeth Carter Reads Pope, Johnson, and Epictetus." *The Age of Johnson: A Scholarly Annual* 4 (1991), 137–69.

Williams, Carolyn D. "Poetry, Pudding, and Epictetus: The Consistency of Elizabeth Carter." In *Tradition in Transition; Women Writers, Marginal Texts, and the Eighteenth-Century Canon*. Ed. Alvaro Ribeiro, SJ, and James G. Basker. Oxford: Clarendon Press, 1996, 3–24.

Williamson, Marilyn L. "Who's Afraid of Mrs. Barbauld? The Blue Stockings and Feminism." *International Journal of Women's Studies* 3 (Jan./Feb. 1980), 89–102.

Withey, Lynne E. "Catharine Macaulay and the Uses of History: Ancient Rights, Perfectionism, and Propaganda." *Journal of British Studies* 16 (1976), 59–83.

7 ROMANCE AND COMEDY, 1777–1789

Ashmun, Margaret. *The Singing Swan: An Account of Anna Seward and her Acquaintance with Dr. Johnson, Boswell, and others of Their Time*. New Haven: Yale University Press, 1931.

Bilger, Audrey. "Mocking the 'Lords of Creation': Comic Male Characters in Frances Burney, Maria Edgeworth and Jane Austen." *Women's Writing* 1 (1994), 77–97.

Brewer, John. "'Queen Muse of Britain': Anna Seward of Lichfield and the Literary Provinces." In *The Pleasures of the Imagination: English Culture in the Eighteenth Century*. New York: Farrar Straus Giroux, 1997.

Carr, Diana Guiragossian. "*Le Père de famille* et sa descendance anglaise." *Enlightenment Studies in Honor of Lester G. Crocker*. Ed. Albert J. Bingham and Virgil W. Trapizio. Oxford: Voltaire Foundation at the Taylor Institute, 1979, 49–58.

Casler, Jeannie. "The Primacy of the Rougher Version: Neo-Conservative Editorial Practices and Clara Reeve's *Old English Baron*." *Papers on Language and Literature* 37 (2001), 404–37.

Clery, E. J. *Women's Gothic from Charlotte Reeve to Mary Shelly*. Plymouth: Northcote House in Association with the British Council, 2000.

"The Genesis of 'Gothic' Fiction." *The Cambridge Companion to Gothic Fiction*. Ed. Jerrold E. Hogle. Cambridge: Cambridge University Press, 2002, 21–39.

Darby, Barbara. *Frances Burney Dramatist: Gender, Performance, and the Late-Eighteenth-Century Stage*. Lexington: University Press of Kentucky, 1997.

Demars, Patricia. *The World of Hannah More*. Lexington: University Press of Kentucky, 1996.

Doody, Margaret Anne. *Frances Burney: The Life in the Works*. New Brunswick, NJ: Rutgers University Press, 1988.

Ellis, Kate Ferguson. *The Contested Castle: Gothic Novels and the Subversion of Domestic Ideology*. Urbana: University of Illinois Press, 1989.

Epstein, Julia. *The Iron Pen: Frances Burney and the Politics of Women's Writing*. Madison: University of Wisconsin Press, 1989.

Fletcher, Loraine. *Charlotte Smith: A Critical Biography*. Basingstoke: Macmillan Press, 1998.

Ford, Charles Howard. *Hannah More: A Critical Biography*. New York: Peter Lang, 1996.

Fry, Carrol. *Charlotte Smith*. New York: Twayne, 1996.

Hawley, Judith. "Charlotte Smith's *Elegiac Sonnets*: Losses and Gains." In *Women's Poetry in the Enlightenment: The Making of a Canon, 1730–1820*. Ed. Isobel Armstrong and Virginia Blain. London: Macmillan, 1999, 184–98.

Isikoff, Erin. "Masquerade, Modesty, and Comedy in Hannah Cowley's *The Belle's Strategem*." In *Look Who's Laughing: Gender and Comedy*. Ed. Gail Finney. Langhorne, Penn.: Gordon and Breach, 1994, 99–117.

Jenkins, Annibel. *I'll Tell You What: The Life of Elizabeth Inchbald*. Lexington: University Press of Kentucky, 2003.

Lewis, Jayne Elizabeth. "'Ev'ry Lost Relation': Historical Fictions and Sentimental Incidents in Sophia Lee's *The Recess*." *Eighteenth-Century Fiction* 7 (1995), 165–184.

McCarthy, William. *Hester Thrale Piozzi: Portrait of a Literary Woman*. Chapel Hill: University of North Carolina Press, 1985.

McMaster, Juliet. "The Silent Angel: Impediments to Female Expression in Frances Burney's Novels." *Studies in the Novel* 21 (1989), 235–52.

Pinch, Adela. *Strange Fits of Passion: Epistemologies of Emotion, Hume to Austen*. Stanford, Calif.: Stanford University Press, 1996.

Rhodes, R. Crompton. "The Belle's Stategem." *Review of English Studies* 5 (1929), 129–42.

Robinson, Daniel. "Forging the Political Novel: *Louisa*." *Wordsworth Circle* 27 (1996), 25–29.

Spencer, Jane. "Adapting Aphra Behn: Hannah Cowley's *A School for Greybeards* and *The Lucky Chances*." *Women's Writing* 2 (1995), 221–34.

Thaddeus, Janice Farrar. *Frances Burney: A Literary Life*. Basingstoke: Macmillan Press, 2000.

Stott, Anne. *Hannah More: The First Victorian.* New York: Oxford University Press, 2003.

Straub, Kristina. *Divided Fictions: Fanny Burney and Feminine Strategy.* Lexington: University Press of Kentucky, 1987.

Waldron, Mary. *Lactilla, Milkwoman of Clifton: the Life and Writing of Ann Yearsley, 1753–1806.* Athens: University of Georgia Press, 1996.

Watt, James. *Contesting the Gothic: Fiction, Genre and Cultural Conflict, 1764– 1832.* Cambridge: Cambridge University Press, 1999.

Zimmerman, Sarah M. *Romanticism, Lyricism, and History.* Albany: State University of New York Press, 1999.

Zomchick, John. "Satire and the Bourgeois Subject in Frances Burney's *Evelina.*" In *Cutting Edges: Postmodern Critical Essays on Eighteenth-Century Satire.* Ed. James E. Gill. Knoxville: University of Tennessee Press, 1995, 347–66.

Index